The Yankees

The Yankees
AN ILLUSTRATED HISTORY

George Sullivan and John Powers

Temple University Press • Philadelphia

In the series **Baseball in America,** edited by Rich Westcott

Temple University Press, Philadelphia 19122

Published 1997

Printed in the United States of America

⊗ The paper used in this publication meets the requirements of the American National Standard for Information Sciences—Permanence of Paper for Printed Library Materials, ANSI Z39.48-1984

Text design by Bill Donnelly

Library of Congress Cataloging-in-Publication Data
Sullivan, George, 1933–
    The Yankees : an illustrated history / George Sullivan and John Powers.
        p. cm.—(Baseball in America)
    Includes bibliographical references.
    ISBN 1-56639-553-4 (cloth)
    1. New York Yankees (Baseball team) History. 2. New York Yankees (Baseball team)—History—Pictorial works. I. Powers, John, 1948– .
II. Title. III. Series.
GV875.N4S84 1997
796.357′64′097471—dc21   97-6536

For Evan, who wore pinstripes . . .

And for six promising all-stars:
Derek and Brian, George and Daniel,
Michael and Samantha.

Contents

Foreword *by Ralph Houk* ix

Acknowledgments xi

The Yankee Way 1

All the Seasons 5

Portraits of the Greats 233

The Record 255

Reading List 327

Foreword

By Ralph Houk

Joe DiMaggio stood at home plate on his "day" at the Stadium, October 1, 1949, and told the overflow crowd, "I'd like to thank the Good Lord for making me a Yankee."

Watching with DiMag's teammates nearby, I thought, "Me too, Joe, me too." Nearly half a century later, I am still grateful. I always will be.

If the great DiMaggio felt lucky to be a Yankee, how about this Kansas farmboy who signed on for the journey of his life for $75 a month and a $200 bonus? I was blessed fourfold: as a Yankee player, coach, manager, and general manager. Twenty-four years in all, half of them climaxing in the World Series.

And every time I put on the pinstripes it was a thrill. *Every* time. That may sound corny, but it's true. I knew that a Yankee was the greatest thing that anyone in baseball could be.

The *New York Yankees*. It's a magic name known around the world, the epitome of success. The name is synonymous with winning: 34 pennants, 23 world championships. There has never been another team like it, the most storied in all of sports history. And the most respected. Fans love 'em or hate 'em, but they all admire 'em.

The Yankees are an American institution and legend, literally a storybook team. Over the decades, a library of books has been written about them, including two by me. None is better than this one. *The Yankees: An Illustrated History* is an authoritative, four-in-one grand slam of information: a detailed year-by-year chronicle, an album of almost 500 photographs, an encyclopedia of records, and a treasury of columns profiling some Yankee greats by some great media superstars.

It's the complete Yankee story crafted by veteran sportswriters George Sullivan and John Powers. Their flowing prose and easy-to-digest format make it a joy whether you have a few minutes or a few hours to share with Ruth and Gehrig, DiMaggio and Berra, Stengel and Mantle, Jackson and Mattingly.

The book is one of a kind, really, a celebration that's already provided many trips down Yankee memory lane for Bette and me. We've enjoyed it thoroughly and suspect you will too. It's all here, and as Casey would say, you can look it up.

Ralph Houk

Acknowledgments

Our boxscore has a long assist column.

Particular thanks go to the Yankees organization, which has been most cooperative—from principal owner George Steinbrenner through his entire club, on and off the field.

Special recognition goes to zealous and versatile David Szen, the onetime media relations and publications director, now the traveling secretary. He and former president Lou Saban encouraged and supported this project from the start, as did the late Bob Fishel, patron saint of baseball public relations.

The Yankees' media relations staff—notably director Rick Cerrone and senior consultant Arthur Richman—has always been obliging. So have publications manager Tim Wood, his predecessor Gregg Mazzola, and the staff at *Yankees Magazine*.

The Yankees' help in locating and providing photographs and information was above and beyond. So was that of the National Baseball Hall of Fame. Bill Guilfoile, Jeff Idelson, and the rest of the Cooperstown lineup were always accommodating while probing the archives at the baseball mecca on the shores of Lake Otsego.

Other substantial aid was provided in assorted ways by a number of people. Fellow authors Donald Honig, Ed Linn, and Tom Horton were there in the clutch, always, as were journalists Kevin Paul Dupont, Jeff Wagenheim, and Frank Dyer. *Boston Herald* librarian John Cronin and New England Sports Museum curator Dick Johnson cheerfully pitched in significantly, as did Nancy Powers, Frank O'Brien of the *Boston Globe*, and Dennis Brearley, formerly of the *Boston Herald*.

We're grateful to the gifted Andy Jurinko, whose artwork brightens the book's cover, and to the platoon of skilled photographers who have helped tell the Yankee story, including team photographer Steve Crandall, Jack Balletti, and John Reid III.

Also appreciated is the help of Rich Westcott, Dale Berra, Ed Markey, Betsy Leesman, Alan Aronson, and the brothers Cannon, Jack and Tom.

The advice, enthusiasm, and patience of Temple University Press associate director Barry Morrill are much valued. So are the cooperation and expertise of Joe Barron and the gang at P. M. Gordon Associates of Philadelphia.

Finally, we are most grateful to our partners behind the Sullivan-Powers double-play combination—Betty Sullivan and Elaine Powers—for their love and support through all the extra innings. Like the Yankees, they are champions.

To all of the above, as Charles Dillon Stengel would say, you done splendid.

George Sullivan and John Powers
Boston, Massachusetts

The Yankees

The Yankee Way

They were America's best road show when a certain Ohio schoolboy was growing up in the thirties, a collection of summer heroes who appeared just long enough in your town to re-affirm their invulnerability.

Gehrig, DiMaggio, and the rest of them would check into the Hotel Cleveland, perform flawlessly for three days at Municipal Stadium, then move on to Detroit, Chicago, and the world championship.

"When the Yankees came to town it was like Barnum and Bailey coming to town," George Steinbrenner would reminisce after he'd bought the club decades later. "The excitement."

The New York Yankees have been larger than life ever since a wealthy brewery owner named Ruppert imported a boisterous man-child named Ruth and built a stadium in the Bronx to accommodate him.

Joe McCarthy, who managed the club during Steinbrenner's childhood, deliberately had the uniforms cut half a size large and the caps squared off. The Yankees, he reasoned, would thus appear more intimidating to rivals.

The amateur psychology was unnecessary. Any baseball team that won seven pennants in eight years was likely to be imposing enough in street clothes.

When manager Miller Huggins realized that the Pirates were watching his Yankees take batting practice before the 1927 World Series, he had Babe Ruth, Lou Gehrig, and Bob Meusel casually stage a home run derby for their benefit.

"Do they do this all the time?" Pittsburgh shortstop Glenn Wright gulped as ball after ball plopped into Forbes Field's upper deck.

For most of this century, the Yankees have performed with the instincts, continuity, and success of a blue-chip corporation.

Rooting for New York, as the cliché had it, was like rooting for U.S. Steel—the players even wore pinstripes. The Yankees were crisp, dignified, and dispassionate.

And their employers, from Jacob Ruppert to George Steinbrenner, have believed that those qualities were part of a club tradition, a certain way of conducting business.

The Yankee Way was a 10-game lead by Independence Day, a clinched pennant by Labor Day, and champagne in October.

The Yankee Way was generations of players—from Gehrig to DiMaggio, from Mickey Mantle to Thurman Munson—who never wore another uniform. Many others either retired with a handful of championship rings or wept when traded away.

The Yankee Way was also a front office that took those championships as its due. "Fine, fine, McCardy," Ruppert would tell McCarthy after each Series triumph in the 1930s. "Do it again next year."

By the '50s, championship money was routinely figured into a player's salary. "Don't forget you get a World Series share," a club executive assured pitcher Jim Bouton in 1963 while offering him a $9,000 contract. "You can always count on that."

For decades, until Steinbrenner spent handsome sums to rebuild the franchise in the '70s, the New York front office was corporate America in microcosm.

It coolly looted the Red Sox roster in the early '20s once it realized that Boston owner Harry Frazee was desperate for ready cash. It used the downtrodden Kansas City Athletics as a separate farm system in the '50s, exchanging used-up veterans for promising young talent. And it paid salaries that were no higher than they had to be.

"What do you fellows think I am, a millionaire?" Ruppert, a millionaire, told his players in the '20s, thus setting the negotiating stance for decades to come.

Gehrig, a walking embodiment of Yankee virtues, never earned more than $37,000. Other employees were frequently treated as replacement parts, their service records given cursory consideration. After winning 10 pennants in a dozen years, manager Casey Stengel was shunted aside at age 70.

To baseball fans and rivals who resented their monopoly, the Yankees appeared smug, insensitive, and tightfisted. But what Yankee-haters resented most was their monotonous consistency, one Chinese-style dynasty rising from the ashes of its predecessor, producing more than 8,000 victories in all, 34 American League pennants, and 23 world championships.

By 1954, after New York had dominated baseball for six of the previous seven years, Douglass Wallop would write an enormously popular, if wistful, tale—*The Year the Yankees Lost the Pennant* (later to be a Broadway and film hit, *Damn Yankees*). Even the devil, Wallop mused, was a Yankee fan.

From 1921 until 1929, New York lost only two pennant races. From 1936 until 1944, they lost one. From 1947 until 1965, only three. "Every year is next year," New York sportswriter Roger Kahn typed moments after the final game of the 1952 World Series, "for the New York Yankees."

It was the farm system, carefully stocked and replenished since the days of general manager Ed Barrow, that produced New York's autumn monopolies.

"It's good to see some good young players coming into the league," well-traveled American League manager Jimmy Dykes would say in 1963. "But why do they always have to be wearing the Yankee uniform?"

There was always another .350 hitter ripening in Newark, a 20-game winner waiting in Kansas City. The year Ruth left, creaky with age and dissipation, a Yankee scout was scribbling notes on a San Francisco minor leaguer named DiMaggio. When DiMaggio retired, Stengel merely beckoned to "the kid," Mantle.

Thus the Yankees linked generation to generation and championship to championship. Whatever the year, there was always a Hall of Famer three cubicles away to point to as an example.

Gehrig played 2,130 straight games, shrugging off split fingers, beanings, and lumbago until his body literally gave out on him. DiMaggio performed flawlessly, spoke softly, and picked up all dinner checks. "When you eat with the dago," he informed the greenest rookie, "the dago pays."

Mantle stuffed bleeding abscesses with gauze and went out to play on rickety knees in August heat.

A team code evolved, unspoken unless it was violated. "You're with the Yankees now," McCarthy admonished newcomer Jake Powell, who'd just administered a hotfoot to a teammate in a Boston train station. "We don't do those things."

It might be a road show, but Barnum and Bailey it wasn't. The club furnished three sets of pinstripes, so the players would always be immaculately turned out. Off the field, coats and ties were the rule. From the day McCarthy had the card table broken apart with an axe in 1931, the Yankee clubhouse was considered a place of business. When former player Billy Martin arrived in August of 1975 to take over a club that had fallen 10 games behind Boston, he quickly pinpointed the clubhouse atmosphere as one reason.

"It wasn't the Yankee clubhouse the way I remembered it," he remarked. "Anyone who wanted to was running around."

When seasons went sour, as they did from

time to time, divergence from the Yankee Way was invariably listed as a reason.

"The trouble with this club," growled one veteran, as the 1930 club slipped to third, "is that there are too many fellows on it who aren't Yankees."

It meant something to play for New York. DiMaggio's own story, published in 1946, was entitled *Lucky To Be a Yankee*. After he retired, Mantle had nightmares about hearing the Stadium loudspeaker announcing his name and not being able to get there.

Rollie Sheldon wept when the front office traded him. John Blanchard, who said he'd rather sit on the bench as a third-string Yankee catcher than start anywhere else, was crestfallen when he was dealt to Kansas City. "I don't want to play every day," he said. "I want to stay here."

Even during the turbulence that marked much of the Steinbrenner era, when the franchise was dubbed the "Bronx Zoo," free agents still were drawn to the Yankees by the pinstriped mystique and the legendary promise of a pennant.

Wade Boggs, one strike away from a world championship with the Red Sox, sobbed in the visitors' dugout of a Queens ballpark in 1986 after the Mets had prevailed. A decade later, he rode a police horse in the Stadium outfield with an index finger in the air after the Yankees had brought down the Braves and returned the championship to the Bronx. "The feeling," said Boggs, "is something you can't describe."

That's the Yankee Way.

All the Seasons

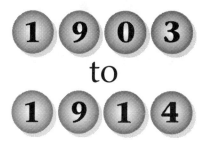

1903 to 1914

They began as one of Byron Bancroft Johnson's daydreams and grew out of his hatred for the National League and his bitterness toward New York Giants manager John McGraw.

The New York Highlanders played in a wooden ballpark on a rocky hilltop in uptown Manhattan, their record fluctuating wildly from year to year. They were known by any number of last names—the Hill Dwellers, Cliffmen, Gordon Highlanders, Porch Climbers or Burglars—but their first name would remain New York.

To Ban Johnson, whose embryonic American League was embroiled in a fierce struggle for primacy with its established National League cousins, that was the important thing. You could not be taken seriously without a New York franchise.

How Johnson finally got one there in 1903 was the product of a chain reaction that began in the previous season, after he'd indefinitely suspended McGraw, then the Baltimore Orioles' manager, for abusing umpires.

So McGraw had gotten Giant owner John T. Brush to buy the team and free half a dozen players to sign with National League clubs. And when the Orioles were unable to field a team against St. Louis one afternoon, Johnson revoked the Baltimore franchise, stretched the roster with temporary filler from other league clubs, and appointed Wilbert Robinson as manager.

Then he moved the club to New York that fall and raided National League rosters—most notably Pittsburgh's—to build a contender. The only thing Johnson lacked was land for a ballpark, and Brush and partner Andrew Freedman had vowed to make that impossible.

Bleacher crowd at Yankee Stadium during the 1962 World Series.

Left: *Frank Farrell was one of two partners who purchased the Baltimore Orioles franchise that moved to New York. He was a gambler who was betting that his Highlanders and the fledgling American League would succeed in the National League Giants' backyard.* **Right:** *"Big Bill" Devery, onetime bartender, prize fighter, and police chief with political connections, was the Highlanders' other co-owner. Purchasing the franchise for $18,000, Devery and Farrell owned the club a dozen years until early 1915, when they sold it for $460,000 to Jacob Ruppert and Tillinghast L'Hommedieu Huston.*

They had friends in Tammany Hall, the corrupt but powerful political organization that had run New York for decades. Any likely parcel of land, Johnson was told, either would be unavailable to him or would soon have streets cut through it.

But during the winter a derbied gambler named Frank Farrell turned up at Johnson's office with a certified check for $25,000 and a plot of ground in mind. He and his sidekick William Devery, an unusually wealthy retired police chief with an ample belly, would buy the Orioles for $18,000, Farrell said, and build a stadium along Broadway on Washington Heights between 165th and 168th Streets.

The $25,000 check was a token of good faith. "That's a pretty big forfeit, Mr. Farrell," Johnson reminded him. *New York Sun* sports editor Joe Vila, who'd accompanied Farrell, snickered. "He bets that much," he assured Johnson, "on a horse race."

Besides the cash, Farrell and Devery had political friends of their own. Within three months they'd bought the land (a former Revolutionary War battlefield; workers unearthed bullets, gunstocks, grapeshot, and bayonets), surrounded it with a wooden fence, leveled the hummocky ground, and erected a grandstand and bleachers that would accommodate 15,000 spectators.

"You could look from the stands," said infielder Jimmy Austin, "and see all the way down the Hudson River." Hilltop Park was neither as large nor as dignified as the Polo Grounds, where the Giants gamboled, and it was barely ready for opening day—right fielder Willie Keeler nearly fell into an unfilled ditch chasing a fly.

But it was a stadium in New York, and the club that played inside quickly became a pennant challenger under new manager Clark Griffith, a seven-time 20-game winner who doubled as a

Hilltop Park was built in the Washington Heights section of Manhattan, on the west side of Broadway between 165th and 168th streets. It was the Highlanders' home from 1903 to 1912. Since the 1920s it has been the site of the Columbia-Presbyterian Medical Center.

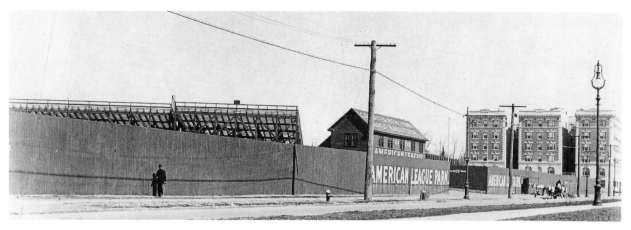

The Broadway entrance to Hilltop Park, which seated 15,000 plus standing room.

starting pitcher that year—at age 33—and won 14 games.

They were christened the Highlanders, a name recognizing both the elevation of their workplace and figurehead president Joseph W. Gordon (the Gordon Highlanders were—and are—a legendary Scottish regiment). But newspapers called them anything that fit conveniently into a headline.

Their first-year roster was a pastiche of seven rookies and refugees from 11 clubs, and injuries and poor hitting consigned them to fourth place, 17 games behind Boston. But relying on a sturdy right-handed spitballer named Happy Jack Chesbro to pitch every third day, the Highlanders fought Boston down to the season's final day in 1904.

As Keeler, whose secret was to "hit 'em where

Popular Wee Willie Keeler was the franchise's first gate attraction, earning $10,000. A classic place hitter with extraordinary bat control, the 5'4", 140-pound right fielder "hit 'em where they ain't" frequently enough to lead the Highlanders in batting their first three seasons.

they ain't," built a .343 average out of 162 singles, Chesbro started 51 games, completed 48, and won 41—a league record that still stands. Yet he blew the pennant with a single spitter that got away in his final inning as he pitched his third game in four days.

Defending champion Boston (then called the Pilgrims) had come to New York for the concluding doubleheader leading by a game and a half and were greeted by a crowd of 28,540 that clustered 15 deep around the Hilltop outfield. With the score 2–2 in the ninth inning of the opener Boston's Lou Criger beat out an infield hit, went to third on a bunt and a grounder, and lumbered home when Chesbro's 2–2 pitch to Fred Parent sailed over catcher Red Kleinow's head to the chicken-wire backstop.

Criger, hardly the fastest man in the game, scored without sliding. The Highlanders, winners of 92 games, would never again come so close to a pennant.

The 1905 season proved grim. At one point every regular was on the disabled list; the Highlanders had to borrow catcher Mike Powers from the Athletics to fill in for 11 games. Chesbro, who'd been 41–13, slumped to 19–13; his teammates followed, dropping to 71–78 and sixth place, 21½ games behind Philadelphia.

But along the way they'd found a nimble first baseman named Hal Chase (dubbed Prince Hal), one of the best fielders ever to play the position, a rollicking free spirit who lured crowds to Hilltop Park that otherwise had no reason to come.

Chase would hit .323 and steal 28 bases in 1906, and New York would contend throughout the season, winning five consecutive doubleheaders and holding first place several times. But erratic pitching—the fewest complete games (99) and fourth-highest earned run average (2.78) in

Left: *Jack Powell was 23–19 in 1904—his only full season as a Highlander—while teaming with 41–12 Jack Chesbro as the league's premier pitching duo. The pair started 100 of the team's 151 games, accounting for 64 of its 92 wins. Struggling at 9–13 the next year, Powell was traded away.* **Right:** *John Anderson became a legend of sorts while a Highlander. During a 1904 game, the veteran outfielder stole second—with bases loaded. For decades thereafter, that sort of bonehead baserunning was called "a John Anderson."*

Jack Chesbro, the Highlanders' first ace. The spitballer totalled 105 victories during the club's first four seasons, crowned by the league's best-ever 41–12 record in 1904. The team lost the pennant to Boston on the final day of the season—ironically on a Chesbro wild pitch.

Left: *Clark Griffith was the club's first manager— player-manager, actually. A onetime star pitcher, Griff still had enough at age 33 to win 14 games and post the team's best ERA at 2.70 in 1903. The first manager hired, he'd be the first fired—in 1908. He went on to own the Washington Senators.* **Right:** *Controversial Hal Chase succeeded Wee Willie Keeler as the team's superstar. "Prince Hal" was a gifted first baseman and solid hitter, but had what a New York sports editor claimed was "a corkscrew brain"—a dark side that allegedly had him throwing games and becoming an outcast.*

the league—undid them, and the Highlanders finished second, three games behind Chicago.

Thus began a period of ineptitude and confusion that would continue—except for the 1910 season—until Farrell and Devery sold the club in 1915.

The 1907 Highlanders were a second-division club almost from the start and finished fifth, eight games below .500. Farrell had taken over as club president; now he and Devery would shout from behind the dugout and proffer unwanted advice to Griffith on lineups and strategy.

Left: *Al Orth led 1906 American League pitchers at 27–17, tying the Giants' Iron Joe McGinnity for most wins in the majors. Orth and 24–16 Jack Chesbro gave the Highlanders baseball's top one-two pitching punch that powered a pennant drive that fell three games short.* **Right:** *Versatile Wid Conroy was the club's original third baseman, and later a regular shortstop and outfielder during his six seasons at Hilltop. The speedy Conroy led the team in a variety of departments over the years, including home runs in 1906—four.*

By the middle of 1908, with attendance off (it had dipped from 434,700 to 305,500 in two years), his club destined for the cellar, and the interference from Farrell and Devery unabated, Griffith quit in June, thus beginning a procession of five managers in the next six years.

The first was shortstop Norman Elberfeld, nicknamed the Tabasco Kid for his spicy tongue. He and Chase grated against each other from the start, and, as dissension mounted, Chase jumped the club and pitched for a renegade league in California, waiting for the crash he guessed lay ahead.

The Highlanders quickly fell to last place and ended up with what would be the worst record in franchise history, 51–103. Along the way Washington's Walter Johnson shut them out three times in four days, and Boston's 41-year-old Cy Young threw a 27-batter no-hitter at them.

So Elberfeld gave way to George Stallings, a Southern miracle worker who would later bring the 1914 Braves from the basement to the National League pennant in less than three months. With Chase back in the lineup and an infusion of young talent around him, the Highlanders climbed back into the first division for most of the 1909 season, finished fifth as attendance set a franchise record (501,000), and carried their momentum into 1910.

With Stallings alternating patience and harsh words, New York challenged throughout the season. "He was a fine manager," Austin would insist. "One of the best. We finished in second place, and he deserved a lot of the credit for that."

But before the season ended Stallings was gone, too. He had also had his difficulties with Chase, who had complained to the owners about him. When Farrell and Devery backed Chase, Stallings resigned, 11 games from the end of the season. So Chase, who'd never particularly cared for any kind of authority, was made manager.

"God, what a way to run a ball club," Austin

The Yankees found a unique way of getting around during 1908 training camp.

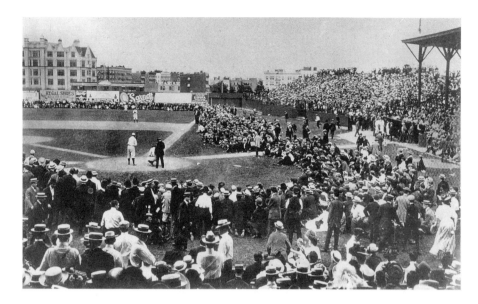

Hilltop Park, July 4, 1907, New York vs. the Philadephia Athletics.

groaned. "Well, you know how good a manager Hal Chase was." A sixth-place manager, as it turned out, sitting uneasily astride a .500 club full of former teammates who wouldn't respond to him. It was the second of six unsuccessful player-to-manager experiments that New York would try over the years (Elberfeld, Roger Peckinpaugh in 1914, Bob Shawkey in 1930, Bill Dickey in 1946, Yogi Berra in 1964); by the fall of 1911, Chase was back at first base and a minor league manager named Harry Wolverton, who was fond of sombreros and sleek cigars, was in charge.

Wolverton was given a ceremonial wreath on opening day of the 1912 season, which some

Left: *American League founder Ban Johnson arranged for the Baltimore Oriole franchise's shift to New York in 1903 to bolster his struggling circuit in its war against the established National League.* **Right:** *Norman Elberfeld—a fiery competitor nicknamed the "Tabasco Kid"—was the team's first shortstop and second manager. Fans got a kick out of the colorful Kid, and so nearly did an umpire. Elberfeld chased the ump around Hilltop Park reportedly trying to kick him—until restrained by police.*

wags later joked should have been saved for his professional funeral that autumn. The Highlanders came entirely undone under his direction, losing 102 games and reverting to eighth.

The only constant was a pack of unruly fans who hooted at visitors. One of them had singled out Detroit's Ty Cobb on May 16. "There's going to be trouble if that fellow isn't stopped," Cobb warned Wolverton. When he wasn't, Cobb jumped into the stands and beat the heckler bloody.

"He hit me in the face with his fist," recalled the fan, who was missing several fingers because of a printing-plant accident, "knocked me down, jumped on me, kicked me, spiked me, and booted me behind the ear."

Cobb responded, "I'm pleased I didn't overlook any important punitive measures."

Johnson immediately suspended Cobb, and when the Tigers threatened to go on strike to support him, Johnson vowed to suspend the entire team.

When the Tigers carried out their threat at Philadelphia, manager Hugh Jennings rounded up a bunch of sandlotters to play the next game against the Athletics, which Detroit promptly lost, 24–2. A theology student named Aloysius Travers, who would become a Catholic priest, made major league history by allowing all 24 runs and promptly retired with a lifetime 15.75 earned run average (his teammates made nine errors behind him). Finally, after Cobb's penalty was reduced to a 10-day suspension and a $50 fine, the Tigers returned—each assessed $100.

The Highlanders, meanwhile, sank to their natural level, and Farrell and Devery shucked Wolverton at the end of the season. In his place they hired Cubs first baseman–manager Frank

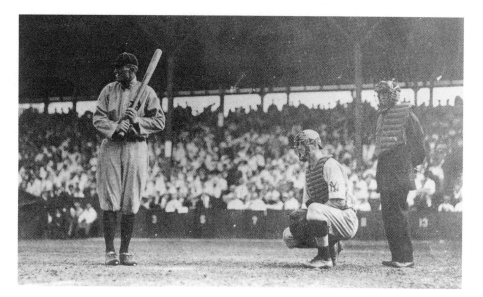

Ty Cobb was both despised and secretly admired by fans at Hilltop, where the combustible Tiger once climbed into the stands and stomped a handicapped (and loudmouthed) spectator. The attack resulted in Cobb's suspension and the first walkout by a team in baseball history.

Chance (of Tinker-to-Evers-to-Chance fame), who'd managed Chicago to four pennants and two world championships in five years and had been labeled the Peerless Leader.

If the club remained hapless, at least the field manager's name and address could be changed. In the spring of 1913, *New York Press* sports editor Jim Price, tired of trying to cram the word "Highlanders" into his headlines, began using "Yankees" instead. So the team, which figured it might smell sweeter by any other name, adopted it.

Branch Rickey was an unlikely future Hall of Famer while a 1907 Highlander utility man. He batted .182 in 52 games, the most notable a June merry-go-round at Hilltop. Filling in as catcher, he surrendered a record 13 stolen bases to Washington. Rickey would gain more fame 40 years later, when as a Brooklyn Dodger executive he broke baseball's color line by signing Jackie Robinson.

They also decided to abandon the rickety instability of Hilltop Park and share the Polo Grounds with their National League neighbors, the Giants.

In 1910, when fire had raced through the Polo Grounds and left the Giants homeless, the Highlanders had offered them squatting privileges atop Washington Heights. Now the Giants were reciprocating with roomier quarters in a tonier neighborhood—Eighth Avenue between 155th and 157th streets.

Yet the Yankees proved no more adept or successful than the Highlanders had been. "The season of 1913 opened with nothing to speak of," George Moreland wrote in *Balldom,* his "Britannica of Baseball," "except that Chance was handed about as poor a lot of ball players as any man ever undertook to mold into a ball club."

Only four men—catcher Ed Sweeney, outfielders Birdie Cree and Harry Wolter, and utility man Roy Hartzell—were left from the awful 1912 club, but even that fact proved to be no benefit. Forty-five men would wear the Yankee uniform before the summer was done, including seven catchers.

The record was better, if 57–94 and seventh place can be considered an improvement. Attendance jumped from 242,194 to 357,551, but that increase was mostly due to the change in address. The Yankees were less promising and more anonymous than the club Griffith had left in exasperation six years earlier.

When 1914 began, Chance was still in the manager's chair—but Chase was gone. Chase, who knew that Chance had gone deaf in one ear from one beaning too many, had delighted in sitting to his deaf side and mimicking Chance's orders. Finally Sweeney, who liked Chance, exploded.

The 1913 club was the first officially known as the Yankees and moved into the Polo Grounds after training in Bermuda—the first major league team to conduct spring training outside the U.S. It did little good; under Frank Chance, the club climbed from last place (55 games behind) to seventh (38 out).

Debates with umpires were not uncommon at the Polo Grounds—like this one featuring the Washington Nationals, April 1913. That's Nats manager Clark Griffith, the former Highlander skipper, remonstrating with the umps while pitcher Walter Johnson looks on above the plate umpire. Among the New Yorkers is manager Frank Chance, wearing the dark sweater.

"I'm no stool pigeon," he told Chase. "But you're not going to make fun of the big guy in front of me any more." Thus made aware, Chance took away the first-base job that Chase had held since 1905, ordered him into street clothes, and traded him to the White Sox early in the 1913 season for sore-footed third baseman Rollie Zeider and incompetent first baseman Babe Borton.

"Chance traded Chase," Mark Roth wrote in the *New York Globe,* "for a bunion and an onion." Neither pleased the owners, who eventually fired Chance two weeks before the end of the 1914 season.

And once again, as they'd done when they replaced Griffith with Elberfeld and Stallings with Chase, Farrell and Devery elevated a player, this time shortstop Roger Peckinpaugh.

The season would turn out with a slightly nicer odor—70–84 and sixth place—but little else changed. The club was still a laughingstock, followed by rowdies and peopled with journeymen who rarely looked at or cared about the standings.

"The Yankees at that time were what we used to call a 'joy club,'" Peckinpaugh admitted. "Lots of joy and lots of losing. Nobody thought we could win, and most of the time we didn't. But it didn't seem to bother the boys too much. They would start singing songs in the infield right in the middle of a game."

But Farrell, whose luck at the racetrack had fled, was singing the blues. His club hadn't had a winning season or finished better than sixth since 1910. The move to the Polo Grounds, where the Giants had won three straight National League pennants, had only served to display the Yankees as stylistic hoboes by comparison.

Worst of all, the club had been a bust at the gate. Only once since the franchise had been moved from Baltimore in 1903 had attendance surpassed 500,000 for a season; usually it was less than 350,000.

Farrell was quarreling with Devery, and Johnson, as league president, was sorely disappointed in what he had hoped would become the cornerstone of the American League.

Meanwhile, two millionaire sportsmen had been sitting in companion boxes at the Polo Grounds with some regularity. They were watching the Giants, of course, who were the city's fashionable club. Their names were Jacob Ruppert and Tillinghast L'Hommedieu Huston, and they were looking for a plaything.

1915

All Ruppert and Huston had in common was a rooting interest in the Giants, a season's box at the Polo Grounds, and enough ready cash to indulge their caprices.

Colonel Jacob Ruppert had inherited millions and added to them by shrewd management of his father's uptown brewery; Captain Tillinghast L'Hommedieu Huston had made his fortune as a civil engineer in Cuba after the Spanish-American War. Giants manager John McGraw had introduced them as mutually affluent sportsmen and they began passing summer afternoons together behind the team dugout.

Neither was a stranger to professional baseball. Huston loved ballparks and the men that haunted them. Ruppert had passed up earlier chances to buy the Giants and the Chicago Cubs. After owner John T. Brush died in 1912, both men approached McGraw about buying the club.

"No," McGraw replied. "No chance." Brush's widow and daughters wanted to retain ownership. "But if you really want to buy a ball club," McGraw continued, "I think I can get one for you. How about the Yankees? I hear Farrell and Devery are fed up and want out."

Jacob Ruppert bought the Yankees with Tillinghast L'Hommedieu Huston and began building sport's most storied dynasty.

That was hardly what Ruppert and Huston had in mind. The Yankees were haphazard and mediocre, playing before sections of empty seats at the Polo Grounds. The Giants were the city's glamour team, and Ruppert and Huston were rich enough to fancy them as a diversion.

Ruppert was a 47-year-old bachelor clubman who owned a Fifth Avenue town house and a Rhenish castle on the Hudson across from West Point, and lived meticulously well, changing clothes several times daily—assisted by a valet—from a vast wardrobe. He raced horses, raised Saint Bernards for show, maintained a yacht, and called everybody by his last name.

His colonelcy was honorary, given him at age 22 by Governor David B. Hill. The extent of Ruppert's military service was membership in the socially correct Company B of the New York National Guard's 7th Regiment.

Huston's captaincy, though, had been earned—with an engineering unit in Cuba, where he lived for a decade after the Spanish-American War, modernizing harbors and planning Havana's sewerage system. When he returned to New York, he was a man of considerable means, wealthy enough to maintain a 30,000-acre hunting preserve in Georgia with a lodge where cronies sipped aged corn whiskey by the fire and swapped stories. First names were good enough for Cap Huston, who lived from day to day with the rumpled informality of an unmade four-poster bed.

Where Ruppert was immaculately barbered and crisply turned out, Huston wore the same wrinkled suit for days and jammed a derby over his ears. A New York newspaperman dubbed him "The Man in the Iron Hat." Yet when he decided to build an estate on Butler Island in the middle of Georgia's Altamaha River, Huston used the Pe-

tit Trianon at Versailles as a model. "Marie Antoinette could sure pick houses," he mused, "even if she didn't have much luck with her boyfriends."

For all his earthiness there was a touch of the dilettante to Huston, and the Yankees hardly seemed a suitable plaything. But they were available, and, after two years of friendly persuasion by McGraw and American League president Ban Johnson, Huston and Ruppert decided to gamble. "See Farrell," they told McGraw. "Ask him if they want to sell."

A deal was quickly struck. Farrell's passion for the racetrack had left him desperately short of cash, and he and Devery were quarreling frequently. The prospect of splitting $460,000 and parting company was irresistible. Once they sold the club on January 11, 1915, Farrell and Devery never spoke again and pursued their separate paths to poverty. Devery, his real estate holdings gone sour, was dead within four years, leaving debts of $1,023; Farrell died in 1926 with assets of $1,072.

Meanwhile, Ruppert and Huston had inherited something of an urban renewal project at the foot of Coogan's Bluff. The Yankees had finished in the American League's second division for the four previous seasons and were drawing fewer than 360,000 spectators a year.

So Ruppert installed himself as president and set about reorganizing the club. He knew little about baseball; as a child he'd captained his neighborhood nine only because he'd bought them equipment and uniforms. But Jake Ruppert could run a company.

He signed on Harry Sparrow—who'd put together the White Sox–Giants world tour the winter before—as business manager and hired two road secretaries to help him. Wild Bill Don-

Fritz Maisel led Yankee hitters at .281. The fleet third baseman also stole 51 bases, down from his majors-leading 74 the previous season, which would stand as the Yankee record for nearly three-quarters of a century.

Left: *Spitballer Ray Caldwell was the Yankee ace for the second straight season—following 1914's 17–9, 1.94 ERA performance with 19–16 and 2.89 in 1915.* **Right:** *Ray Fisher, another spitballer, enjoyed his best season at 18–11 while posting a 2.11 ERA, the staff's best.*

Roy Hartzell, a versatile infielder/outfielder, batted .251 in his fifth and final full Yankee season.

ovan, a former Detroit pitcher who'd just managed Providence (and a young left-hander named George Ruth) to the International League pennant, was brought in as field manager. Players were more difficult to come by.

"I want to win," Ruppert had insisted. "Every day I want to win ten–nothing. Close games make me nervous."

Yet except for first baseman Wally Pipp, who was acquired from the Tigers for the $7,500 waiver price, and pitcher Bob Shawkey, for whom Ruppert paid the Athletics a steep $85,000, the Yankees were forced to field virtually the same lineup for the 1915 season.

And while they began the year in dignified new pinstriped uniforms, they ended it with virtually the same record, 69–83, in fifth place. Neither Ruppert nor Huston had ever finished fifth in anything.

Seven years filled with endless railroad tracks, hotel rooms, and travel bags had driven him back to the farm, and nothing manager Connie Mack could say had changed his mind. J. Franklin Baker, the best third baseman in the game, had retired at age 28 from the Philadelphia Athletics after the 1914 season and gone back to Trappe, Maryland, and the pastoral life.

A 50-game lark with the town team in nearby Upland had satisfied his competitive urges during the summer of 1915—or had it? Yankee manager Bill Donovan guessed that a spark still burned in Baker that might be fanned by the prospect of playing in New York. So during the next winter he approached Philadelphia, which still owned Baker's rights, for permission to talk to him.

Mack, convinced that Baker would still prefer Philadelphia if he ever changed his mind, agreed. And so, surprisingly enough, did Baker, provided Mack would sell his rights. The price was $35,000—and Home Run Baker was wearing pinstripes. He'd earned the nickname five years earlier by crashing two home runs off Giant aces Christy Mathewson and Rube Marquard in successive games to propel the A's to the world championship, and had become the cornerstone of Mack's "$100,000 Infield," playing alongside Jack Barry, Eddie Collins, and Stuffy McInnis.

Baker was everything the Yankees wanted—a durable, aggressive fielder who once had knocked down Ty Cobb after being spiked, a superior base stealer, and a power hitter in a dead-ball era. More important, he was a proven draw at the gate which the Yankees, having attracted only 256,035 customers in 1915, needed desperately.

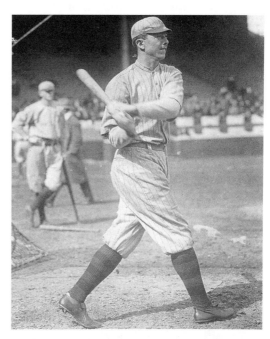

The Yankees lured Frank "Home Run" Baker out of retirement and into pinstripes in 1916. An aggressive, rifle-armed third baseman, Baker was a power hitter in a dead-ball era—and a gate attraction that helped nearly double home attendance.

Left: *Wild Bill Donovan managed the 1916 Yankees to a first-division finish for the first time since 1910.*
Right: *Bob Shawkey was the ace at 23–14.*

Once Donovan installed him at third and shifted Fritz Maisel to the outfield, Baker's impact was immediate. No Yankee since Hal Chase had lured quite as many spectators to the Polo Grounds (attendance nearly doubled overnight), and the club responded with a hustling style that quickly involved them in the pennant race for the first time in six years.

The euphoria was short-lived. In midseason Baker crashed into the grandstand chasing a pop foul and missed 50 games with broken ribs; it was one in a series of injuries that soon made hash of the starting lineup. Donovan was forced to use seven outfielders, and only center fielder Lee Magee started more than 110 games. Except for Bob Shawkey (23–14) and Nick Cullop (12–6), the pitching grew uninspired. By season's end the club had fallen to fourth, 11 games behind the Red Sox. Still, it was a landmark season. Not since 1910 had the Yankees finished in the first division, and only once, in 1909, had more paying customers filed through the turnstiles.

Captain Tillinghast L'Hommedieu Huston, a war veteran who could foresee disjointed times as well as any man, had decided that spring training and baseball bats should have a dual purpose. So while America prepared for battle and the American League for the 1917 season, the Yankees did both.

Huston brought army drill sergeants to Macon, Georgia, to teach his people how to present arms with a Louisville Slugger, then went overseas himself as an officer with the 18th Engineers.

With America about to enter World War I, the Yankees drilled in more ways than one during spring training at Macon, Georgia. Even the press corps got into the act.

Wally Pipp led the league in home runs for the second consecutive year, although his production fell from 12 to 9. The durable first baseman also led the Yankees in doubles and, for a second straight season, in RBIs, runs, and triples.

France was in turmoil, and before long the Yankees were, too.

Once again the club started aggressively—George Mogridge's no-hitter at Fenway Park on April 24 would be the only one by a Yankee left-hander until Dave Righetti's in 1983. Yet by July the best hope was another first-division finish; by August even that seemed a fantasy.

New York's team batting average—.239—was the worst in the league and the pitching dismal across the board. Only Urban Shocker (8–5) and Slim Love (6–5) posted winning seasons. Mogridge, the April hero, finished at 9–11.

And worst of all to owner Jacob Ruppert's corporate mind, attendance had fallen off dramatically, from 469,000 to 330,000. The colonel rarely attended games now or consulted with Bill Donovan, his beleaguered manager, brooding instead at his brewery at the corner of Third Avenue and 90th Street.

Finally, after the club had finished sixth, 28 ½ games behind Chicago, the manager was summoned downtown. "I like you, Donovan," Ruppert admitted. "But we have to make some changes around here."

"I know it, colonel," Donovan conceded. So after three years, 239 losses, and two second-division efforts, the Wild Bill era ended (he would die six years later, at 47, in a freakish train wreck). And Ruppert called American League president Ban Johnson, who'd urged him into this quagmire several years before, for advice.

"Get Miller Huggins," he was told.

He was born in Cincinnati to English parents who preferred cricket and wanted him to be a lawyer. Instead, Miller Huggins had turned sec-

Spitballer Ray Caldwell pitched 9⅔ frames of hitless relief in a 17-inning victory over St. Louis—one of 13 that tied him with Bob Shawkey for most wins.

Jake Ruppert hired Miller Huggins (left) as the Yankees' new manager over the objections of partner Cap Huston.

Cap Huston (right) wanted Brooklyn manager Wilbert Robinson as the Yankee skipper, but was overruled by Jake Ruppert—causing a split between the colonels that never healed.

Miller Huggins, the new Yankee manager in 1918.

ond baseman and player-manager and applied his intensity, intelligence, and quick wit to the dugout. Huggins had actually earned a law degree from the University of Cincinnati, passed the bar, and established a practice before turning to baseball. Laconic among strangers, he was humorous and digressive with intimates, read widely, favored pipe tobacco over cut plug, and followed the stock market. And he knew baseball intimately and had played it well.

His only failing, thought American League president Ban Johnson, was that Huggins was working in the wrong league. Johnson despised the National League, and when Yankee president Jacob Ruppert asked him to suggest a replacement for Wild Bill Donovan for the 1918 season Johnson immediately recommended Huggins.

Only two roadblocks loomed. Huggins, who'd just brought the St. Louis Cardinals from the cellar to third place and owned stock in the franchise, didn't want the job. And Ruppert's partner, Cap Huston, didn't want Huggins, preferring Brooklyn manager "Uncle" Wilbert Robinson.

It proved easier to change Huggins' mind, and *The Sporting News* publisher J.G. Taylor Spink began trying as soon as Huggins arrived in New York for the National League meetings in December. Why didn't Huggins go up to the brewery for a chat with the colonel, he urged. No, Huggins told Spink, I'm happy where I am.

"If you won't go willingly," Spink replied, "I'll hit you on the head and drag you there."

"All right," Huggins conceded. "To please you, I'll go."

Ruppert quickly offered Huggins the job—and the reverberations from France, where Huston was serving with the 18th Engineers, was immediate. A stream of telegrams, invective, and letters to Huston's cronies in the New York press followed, causing a split between the partners that was never repaired.

Ruppert's real offense had been the brusque treatment accorded Robinson, whom Huston hunted and drank with at his Dover Hall lodge in Georgia during the off-season. "I don't think [Ruppert] cared for me," Robinson would tell friends afterward. "And personally, I didn't care a lot for him."

Robinson, at 54, was still hearty and vigorous. The jovial onetime cornerstone of the legendary Baltimore Orioles had led the Dodgers to the pennant a year earlier, would win another in 1920, and would manage for 14 more years. Yet his interview with Ruppert was brief.

"No," the colonel had decided. "You will not do. For one thing, you are too old." Robinson had stalked out of the office and cabled Huston, who'd called Ruppert, who'd shrugged and gone off to pursue a man 16 years younger and more tautly wound.

Though Huggins stood only 5 foot 6 and weighed 140 pounds, he had played 13 seasons for Cincinnati and St. Louis as a nimble fielder (which brought the nickname "Little Everywhere") and a leadoff man with a knack for reaching base. As a manager he was inventive yet driven, pacing the foul line from his third-base coaching box with shoulders hunched. He stressed fundamentals and discipline, and the Yankees quickly bore his mark.

In a span of less than a month the club executed a league-record eight sacrifices (six of them bunts) to beat star southpaw Babe Ruth in Boston, turned a game-ending triple play to snuff out Detroit, and hung in with Cleveland for 19 innings (with Indian pitcher Stan Coveleski going the distance) before losing.

Such a combination of proficiency and spirit was a welcome novelty, and in a normal year might have produced a contender, but 1918 was anything but normal. War shortened the season by 26 games, ending it on Labor Day, and played havoc with rosters. The Yankees lost 11 men to the armed forces (Huston's training-camp drill sergeants had been worthwhile after all), including first baseman Wally Pipp and pitcher Bob Shawkey, and finished fourth, three games below .500.

Still, the season marked a return to the first division and promised future stability—so long as Huston, now a colonel himself, was laying railroad track in France.

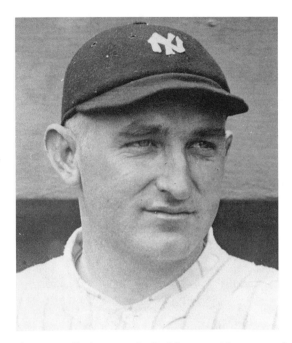

Carl Mays walked out on the Red Sox at midseason and wound up a Yankee—a matter that ended up in court and threw the American League into chaos that resulted in two sets of standings. Controversy was a constant companion for the crusty submarine pitcher, who won 62 games for the Yankees the next 2½ seasons. But Mays was never a favorite of manager Miller Huggins, who exiled him to Cincinnati.

For three months, while his record sank to 5–10, he had suspected his Boston teammates were deliberately playing carelessly behind him. Now, on a July afternoon at Comiskey Park, Carl Mays was convinced of it.

Several Chicago batters had reached base on errors, and a throw from catcher Wally Schang didn't improve the pitcher's humor; it was supposed to nail a runner at second base, but somehow bounced off Mays' head. When the inning was done he stormed off the mound and into the clubhouse.

"I'll never pitch for this club again," he growled en route to manager Ed Barrow, who had learned

Shortstop Roger Peckinpaugh hit safely in 29 consecutive games in 1919. No Yankee hit safely in more until Joe DiMaggio's 56 in 1941.

Del Pratt was among top Yankee hitters at .292 and collaborated with shortstop Roger Peckinpaugh as the Yankees' second-base combination.

to take such outbursts philosophically. Mays was a peevish loner whose temper frayed easily.

"Tell Carl to forget about it and get back in the game," Barrow told pitcher Sam Jones, but Mays had already dressed and packed his gear.

Duffy Lewis, another Red Sox star dealt to New York. He played two seasons in left field for the Yankees.

"Tell Barrow I've gone fishing," he told Jones—and disappeared.

Thus began an unprecedented dispute that ended up in New York State Supreme Court, plunged the American League (and its standings) into chaos, and precipitated the demise of the league's founder and president, Ban Johnson. It also gave the Yankees a 20-game winner.

Mays did go fishing, then returned to Boston to find that Johnson had not only ordered him suspended but forbidden the club from trading him. But Boston owner Harry Frazee soon shipped him to New York anyway, for $40,000 and two mediocre pitchers named Allan Russell and Bob McGraw. And the Yankees, who badly needed a stopper to supplement Bob Shawkey, immediately put Mays into uniform and on the mound.

So the battle lines were drawn, with Johnson instructing his umpires to keep Mays from playing and the league owners split into factions.

Yankee president Jacob Ruppert had a natural ally in Frazee, and found another in Chicago's Charles Comiskey, who'd been eager to curb Johnson's virtually unlimited powers. They ultimately slapped Johnson and the five loyalist owners with a $500,000 lawsuit and obtained an injunction that allowed Mays to pitch for the Yankees, who were battling Chicago and Cleveland for the pennant.

To nobody's surprise, Mays' impact on the club was immediate. At 27 he'd been a superior pitcher for Boston, teaming with Babe Ruth to win two pennants in three years. The right-hander's specialty was a fastball thrown submarine style that could kill—and literally did a year later when Cleveland shortstop Ray Chapman died hours after being beaned at the Polo Grounds.

Mays was both durable and prolific; in the first days of the 1918 pennant race he'd won both ends of a doubleheader and taken it as a matter of course.

Mays won his first game in pinstripes, only hours after Yankee management had served the umpiring staff with an injunction before a double-header at St. Louis on August 7, and went on to win nine of 12 games for the club—depending upon whose records you wanted to believe. Johnson had ruled that Mays' victories would not count in the standings; consequently newspapers kept two sets, with Mays and without.

So when the season ended, New York had finished either third or fourth, according to which version you preferred. Johnson preferred fourth and refused to award the third-place money the club thought it had earned, so Ruppert and partner Cap Huston paid the difference out of their own coffers. And at the winter meetings the colonels, Frazee, and Comiskey made their move against Johnson.

They forced Cincinnati owner August Herrmann, who chaired the three-man National Commission that Johnson dominated, to resign. Finally, the commission, which served as the sport's ruling body in those days, conceded New York both its third place and the cash that came with it.

A year later, in the wake of the Black Sox scandal, the commission was shelved and replaced by baseball Commissioner Kenesaw Mountain Landis—the game's first czar—as Johnson's influence dwindled. With one stroke Ruppert and Huston had improved their pitching staff decisively, quashed Johnson, and continued an exodus of players from Boston to New York that would change both franchises permanently.

Rambunctious George Ruth, playing baseball at a Baltimore school for orphans and incorrigibles.

He was born of uncertain parentage above a waterfront saloon in Baltimore, grew up speaking German, and spent his youth in a Catholic school for orphans and incorrigibles.

He had an enormous appetite for food, drink, and women, a casual disdain for training rules, and a complete inability to remember names. A Washington pitcher named Joe Engel noticed him at a schoolboy baseball game in Maryland and mentioned him to Baltimore president Jack Dunn. "I think his name," Engel said, "is Ruth."

His name was George Herman Ruth, and by 1919, at age 24, he was the cornerstone of the Red Sox franchise, a superb left-handed pitcher who'd been shifted to the outfield because Boston needed his bat—and his drawing power—in the lineup every day.

Nobody, not even the entire pennant-winning White Sox, hit as many home runs as Ruth did (29) that year, or did it with as much flair.

He was broad-shouldered and profane, carrying a blacksmith's torso atop spindly legs, which caused him to round the bases with a pigeon-toed gait. There was nobody remotely like him in a New York uniform, yet he might never have worn one had Boston owner Harry Frazee not been on the verge of bankruptcy.

He was a Broadway producer who'd bought the franchise on credit from Joseph Lannin and John I. Taylor three years earlier. When several of his shows flopped and Lannin and Taylor were pressing him for payment, Frazee walked several doors down 42nd Street to the Yankee offices and asked President Jacob Ruppert for a $500,000 loan. Ruppert asked for Ruth and a mortgage on Fenway Park.

So Frazee called his manager, Ed Barrow, on a Sunday in January 1920, and told him to drop by the bar at the fashionable Hotel Knickerbocker that evening.

"You're going to be sore as hell at me for what I'm going to tell you," Frazee began.

"You're going to sell the Big Fellow," Barrow guessed. "I expected it, Harry. But let me tell you this—you're going to ruin yourself and the Red Sox in Boston for a long time to come."

"I can't help it," Frazee shrugged. "I'm up against the wall. I need money desperately."

Ruppert would pay him about $100,000 (reports vary from $100,000 to $139,000) outright and loan him $350,000 with Boston's ballpark as security. "Gentlemen," the colonel would inform

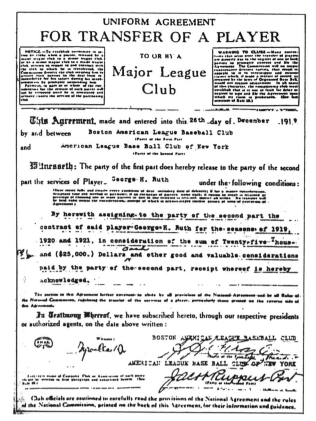

The paper that brought Babe Ruth to New York. The Red Sox agree to assign Ruth's contract to the Yankees for the 1919, 1920, and 1921 seasons in return for $25,000 cash and "other good and valuable considerations," which added up to a sale price of over $100,000 plus a $350,000 mortgage on Boston's Fenway Park.

The Yankees' new star.

a group of New York newspapermen. "We have just bought Babe Root."

The reaction was immediate—outrage in Boston, where Ruth had helped produce three pennants, delight in New York, and concern among the Yankees' landlords, the Giants, who'd monopolized both the hearts and pocketbooks of Manhattan fans for more than four decades.

The Giants felt the impact in spring training. Before the trade they'd arranged a barnstorming tour with the Red Sox, hoping to capitalize on their own natural lure and Ruth's big bat. Instead, the Yankees, preceding the Giants on the tour, were cleaning up at the gate. And so was Ruth, his salary now doubled to $20,000.

It was an omen of what was to come at the Polo Grounds during the regular season; with Ruth attracting spectators who couldn't tell a fastball from a slider, the Yankees shattered the Giants' major league attendance record, drawing 1,289,422 (more than double their 1919 figure), which still stands as a mark for daytime play.

Not that it was any surprise. Ruth was already

established as the league's most popular player. By age 23 he'd had a five-cent cigar named after him. He'd arrived in the majors at age 19, and the next season he won 18 games for Boston's world champions. "He would have been the greatest left-handed pitcher of his generation," guessed Detroit's Ty Cobb.

From the moment a Catholic clergyman discovered him catching in an intramural league at St. Mary's Industrial School, an overgrown 19-year-old in blue overalls, Ruth had seemed larger than life.

Carl Mays was the Yankees' ace at 26–11, but a submarine pitch by the right-hander killed Indians shortstop Ray Chapman at the Polo Grounds—the only fatality in major-league history.

Miller Huggins and Jacob Ruppert watch their Bambino take batting practice—always a show.

"The ball was three feet off the ground going through the box," Brother Gilbert noticed, "and three feet off the ground when it got to second base. I knew that with an arm like that he could be made into a pitcher."

Engel watched Ruth strike out 18 college freshmen one afternoon and informed Dunn, who signed Ruth to a $600 contract sight unseen and brought him to the Orioles' 1914 training camp at Fayetteville, North Carolina. Until then Ruth had never been on a train, had more than five dollars in his pocket, or been given unlimited breakfast privileges.

"You mean I can eat anything I want and it won't cost me anything?" Ruth asked Dunn.

"Sure. Anything."

After Ruth had eaten three stacks of wheatcakes and ham, his new teammates stood aghast. "I wouldn't have believed it," said sportswriter Roger Pippen, "if I hadn't seen it."

Presently Dunn led Ruth, a 6-foot-2, 220-pound man-child, out to the diamond, "Here comes Dunnie," crowed one Oriole, "with his latest babe."

After Ruth beat both of the previous year's pennant winners, the Athletics and the Giants, in exhibition games, his future seemed assured. By

Ping Bodie was a Yankee outfielder when Babe Ruth was acquired, and the colorful veteran pondered, "I suppose this means I'll be sent to China." Instead, Bodie was roomed with Ruth—or, as Ping corrected, "I don't room with the Babe, I room with his suitcase."

Harry Frazee, Broadway producer and Red Sox owner, was loved in New York, despised in Boston after he sold a parade of stars to the Yankees—most grievously, Babe Ruth.

early July, the teenager was a big-leaguer himself—sold to Boston in a package deal with Ernie Shore and Ben Egan for what amounted to $8,000—$2,900 of it for Dunn's "babe."

By the end of 1919, Ruth had won 89 games plus all three of his World Series starts and had been shifted to the outfield where he led the American League in home runs (29), runs (103), runs batted in (114), slugging average (.657), and total bases (284)—all for a sixth-place club.

With Ruth's passage from one franchise to the other, the Red Sox sank gradually into the cellar, where they finished during nine of the next 12 years. The Yankees grew into the sport's most enduring dynasty.

The 1920 season produced their first stirrings, a 95–59 record (their best ever) in a pennant race that went down to the final week. The club's success was tied directly to Ruth's, and his was prodigious that year—a .376 batting average, 137 runs batted in, and an incredible 54 home runs, more than every team in either league save the Phillies (playing in their Baker Bowl bandbox).

But the Yankees' pennant duel with Cleveland was marred by the death of Indian shortstop Ray Chapman in mid-August, beaned by a submarine ball from New York pitcher Carl Mays. Possibly it was a brush-back pitch; Chapman did like to crowd the plate.

"I've always had a horror of hitting a player," Mays said. "Poor Chapman was one of the hardest to pitch to. The ball I pitched was a straight one on the inside. I expected Chapman to be able to gauge it."

In any case Chapman never moved. The ball fractured his skull and he died at five o'clock the next morning. His teammates dedicated the remainder of the season to Chapman and went on to win the pennant by two games over Chicago. The Yankees would finish third, as they had the year before, but this was hardly the same team. The Big Fellow and Harry Frazee's theatrical woes had changed that for all time.

The ball had skimmed viciously along the grass toward right field, and Aaron Ward, a second baseman himself, simply assumed it had gone through. He'd been leading off first, had seen Home Run Baker rip Art Nehf's pitch, sensed Gi-

Waite Hoyt was acquired from the Red Sox at age 21. He won 19 before adding two of the Yankees' three World Series victories. Though he lost the 1–0 finale, he posted a 0.00 ERA for the Series. Nicknamed the "Brooklyn Schoolboy," Hoyt became the club's winningest pitcher of the '20s, building a 157–98 Yankee career record.

Ed Barrow, who had managed the Red Sox to the 1918 world championship, joined the Boston-to-New York exodus in 1921, becoming the Yankees' general manager, and shrewdly built a dynasty.

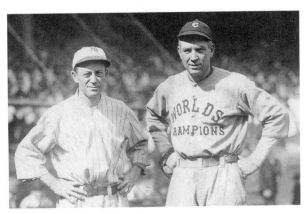

Miller Huggins and Cleveland player-manager Tris Speaker meet before a crucial late-September series at the Polo Grounds. The Yankees won three of four and dethroned the defending champions, ensuring that the Indians got new jerseys.

Versatile Aaron Ward was shifted from third to second base. The transfer agreed with him; he hit .306—his only .300 season as a regular.

ant second baseman Johnny Rawlings lunging for it, and thought instinctively of third base.

This was the bottom half of the ninth inning of the eighth game of the Yankees' first World Series appearance, and Ward represented the tying run that would keep them alive. Instead, he became the final out of the Giants' first world championship in 16 years as Rawlings, George Kelly, and Frankie Frisch combined for a 4-3-5

Wally Schang came to New York in the same deal that brought Waite Hoyt from the Red Sox in December 1920. He batted .316 in his first Yankee season and averaged .297 during his five years in pinstripes—the first in a memorable line of notable Yank catchers.

Babe Ruth challenged sports editor Joe Vila to publish this photo so the public could see the abscess that sidelined him in the last three games of the World Series. Vila chose not to run the picture.

double play that stands as one of the most bizarre and dramatic of all Series finishes. "You won't see one play like that in 10 years," moaned Babe Ruth.

It left the Yankees—who'd won the first two games and held a 4–0 lead in the third—stunned and their partisans frozen in their seats for minutes afterward, while Giant fans exulted around them.

Thus ended their most successful season to that point, a season in which the Yankees won their first American League pennant, drew 1.2 million paying customers to the Polo Grounds, and created a roistering image for themselves both on and off the diamond.

Their symbol was Ruth, whose daytime feats in the batter's box were merely a prelude to excessive nights at the dining table and behind the wheel.

Since the front office (with manager Miller Huggins' misgivings) allowed the players to drive their own cars from city to city during eastern road trips, Ruth organized a merry crew of highwaymen to share his 12-cylinder, fire-engine-red Packard roadster at 110 miles an hour.

One night after a game at Washington, Ruth tipped the car over on a curve 30 miles from Philadelphia while singing "The Trail of the Lonesome Pine." Then he shrugged and called a cab, arriving in the city to find headlines claiming "Babe Ruth Killed in Auto Accident."

An exaggeration, as Mark Twain would say. Ruth hit a home run against the Athletics the next day and went on to enjoy his best season, smashing a record 59 home runs, knocking in a league-leading 170 runs, and batting .378. "Nobody gave me a good ball to hit," he mused. "But if they were anywhere near the plate I took a cut at them."

So did his teammates, as the Yankees accounted for 134 of the American League's 477 homers that year. With Carl Mays (27–9), Waite Hoyt (19–13), and Bob Shawkey (18–12) anchoring a pitching staff that led the league in complete games, strike-outs, and earned run average, the Yankees quickly took control of the pennant race, aided by a new policy of noninterference from the front office.

Three years of fussing from Jacob Ruppert and meddling by Cap Huston had driven Huggins to distraction. But when business manager Harry Sparrow had died late in 1920, the colonels hired Boston manager Ed Barrow as general manager and gave him authority over day-to-day operations.

Barrow, who'd dealt with Ruth and Mays during their days as Red Sox, quickly moved to reassure Huggins.

"I know what you've been up against," Barrow told him. "You're the manager and you'll not be second-guessed by me. Your job is to win, mine is to see that you get the players you need to win. I'll take responsibility for every deal I make. What do you want right now?"

"Well, I could use about eight players," Huggins replied. "But I'll take what I can get."

Before the season Barrow had put together a deal with Boston—who else?—exchanging Muddy Ruel, Herb Thormahlen, Sam Vick, and Del Pratt for Hoyt, Wally Schang, Harry Harper, and Mike McNally. And Huggins molded his nine for the New Era.

The pennant race came down to a weekend series at the Polo Grounds against the world champion Indians in late September, with the Yankees leading by two percentage points. Hoyt won the opener, 4–2. Then New York battered half a dozen pitchers, 21–7, and went two games up. But Cleveland's George Uhle dazzled the Yankees, 9–0, and presented Huggins with a knotty pitching problem to think through.

He had used most of what was in his bullpen in game three. Did he go back to Hoyt? Or gamble with Jack Quinn, who'd beaten the Indians at Cleveland earlier in the month but hadn't worked since?

"Fellows, I'm up against it," Huggins told his staff shortly before game time. "I don't know who to pitch."

The players opted for Quinn, but the Indians riddled him for three runs before he could retire a man. The Yankees answered with four in the bottom of the inning and, with Hoyt relieving, managed to nurse the lead into the ninth while dusk was falling rapidly.

With two out and Mays now pitching, the Indians loaded the bases and sent catcher Steve O'Neill to the plate and a nervous Ruppert from his box seat to the New York bullpen where he joined his players—and fidgeted.

"Hofmann, you think we'll win?" he asked a reserve catcher. "Say yes, Hofmann, don't tell me no. You think Mays can get this man O'Neill, Hofmann? Is O'Neill good?"

Mays blew his first pitch past O'Neill.

"What is it, is it a strike, Hofmann?" asked the owner, unable to watch.

"Yes, one strike," Hofmann replied. "Two to go."

"Two more. Oh fellows, win this game for me. Please win this game for me. If you win it I'll give you anything. I'll give you the brewery."

The colonel fretted all the way to a full count, whereupon Mays, helped by the dying light, got O'Neill to swing at a pitch in the dirt. The Yankees went on to win the pennant by 4½ games, but Ruppert kept the brewery.

More elusive game remained in the form of Ruppert's uptown landlords, the Giants, who'd erased a 7½-game Pittsburgh lead in the final six weeks to win the National League pennant.

It was the first World Series played entirely in the same park and the last of the revived best-of-nine format. With Mays and Hoyt each hurling 3–0 shutouts the Yankees quickly swept the first two games. No club had ever done that and still lost the Series, and when they grabbed a 4–0 lead in the third inning of game three a sweep seemed conceivable.

But the Giants chased Shawkey with four runs in the bottom half of the inning, racked relievers Quinn and Rip Collins for eight more in the seventh, won 13–5, and tied the Series two days later.

Meanwhile, Ruth, who'd developed an elbow abscess, could barely swing a bat. He struck out three times as the Yankees won game five and repaired to the bench for the final three games while *New York Sun* sports editor Joe Vila questioned his resilience in print.

That produced an angry outburst from Ruth prior to game six. "You're accusing me of not having any guts," Ruth shouted at Vila. "Now if you have any, print a picture of my arm with this hole in it and let your readers see my side of it."

The Yankees never won another game. Trailing 1–0 in the bottom of the ninth in game eight, Huggins had Ruth bat for Wally Pipp, but he managed only a grounder to first. Then Ward walked, bringing Baker to the plate.

"He was a tough left-handed pull hitter," said Rawlings, "and I would have been playing him over toward first base anyway. But with a man on first I figured Baker would be trying to hit behind him and edged over even more."

Ward never saw Rawlings knock down Baker's grounder and make the play at first from the seat of his pants. So Kelly, whose arm was not to be trifled with, fired across the diamond to Frisch, who tagged Ward sliding.

"He jumped into me," Frisch said. "He tumbled me over pretty good, trying to knock the ball out of my hands. They all did in those days."

Particularly when a world championship and Manhattan bragging rights were involved.

1922

The turbulence had begun during the previous autumn, only hours after the Yankees had lost the World Series to the Giants. Commissioner Kenesaw Mountain Landis had received word that Babe Ruth and several of his teammates, most notably outfielder Bob Meusel, catcher Wally Schang, and pitcher Carl Mays, were taking the

With Grantland Rice at the microphone, 1922 marked the first World Series broadcast from a ballpark. It was heard by at least a million (some reports claimed five million) within 300 miles of the Polo Grounds. "There came even the cries of the peanut vendors," marvelled a critic.

And, the New York Times said, "the clamor of the 40,000 baseball fans inside the Polo Grounds made radio listeners feel as if they were in the grandstand. The cheers which greeted Babe Ruth when he stepped to the plate could be heard throughout the land."

Realistic or not, the Series' last two games were not broadcast.

John McGraw and Babe Ruth pose before game one of the World Series, but clearly none too happily. They were not friendly rivals.

Left: Bullet Joe Bush was another star pickpocketed from the Red Sox and immediately became the Yankees' ace. Despite a finger injury, Bush won 26 and lost only 7 for a .788 percentage that was 113 points better than that of any other pitcher in the majors. **Right:** Jumping Joe Dugan was acquired at midseason from Boston—where else?—to replace aging Home Run Baker at third base. (The July 23 deal ignited a furor that led to baseball's June 15 trading deadline.) The colorful Dugan would defend the hot corner seven seasons, contributing to five pennants and three world championships.

midnight train to Buffalo for a barnstorming tour, in defiance of Landis's edict against them.

Distressed, Landis ordered Ruth to telephone him. "Babe, you'd better not make that trip," warned Landis, who felt such tours diminished the World Series. "If you do there will be a lot of consequences."

Sorry, Ruth told him, I'm already committed. Schang and Mays backed out, but Ruth, Meusel,

Miller Huggins (right) welcomes another Red Sox refugee, Everett "Deacon" Scott, the best and most durable shortstop of the era. Continuing a consecutive-games string begun in Boston in 1918, Scott would play every Yankee game of 1922–24 before his streak ended at 1,307 in May 1925. Scott's mark ranks as the majors' third longest behind those of Cal Ripken, Jr. and Lou Gehrig.

Center fielder Whitey Witt was conked by a bottle during a decisive and riotous late-season series in St. Louis. He played the next day with a bandage around his forehead and drew cheers when he raced into the overflow crowd to snare a fly ball.

The site of the future Yankee Stadium, 1921—11.6 acres of farmland just across the Harlem River from the Polo Grounds at 161st Street and River Avenue in the Bronx.

Construction begins on the Stadium, which would be America's largest ballpark.

and two reserve pitchers went anyway. After three games, Yankee co-owner Cap Huston paid off the promoters to abort the tour, and Landis set down the punishment—Ruth and Meusel's World Series shares would be withheld, and they would be suspended for the first 39 games of the 1922 season.

Thus began a year during which the Yankees squabbled with their manager and fought among themselves, the Giants evicted them from the Polo Grounds, Huston split with partner Jacob Ruppert, and the club was swept in a World Series for the only time until 1963.

Though Ruth was banned until mid-May, he was allowed to work with the club at its new spring training headquarters in New Orleans, which meant sumptuous meals at Antoine's, evenings awash in cocktails at the Little Club across from the hotel, and a generally undisciplined atmosphere.

"Yankees Training on Scotch" read one New York headline, which so alarmed the front office that they hired a private detective to trail the team on its first western swing and report to both the club and a perturbed Landis.

Yet roistering seemed to agree with the Yankees. When Ruth and Meusel returned to a sold-out Polo Grounds on May 20, the club was in first place. The only rival that threatened was St. Louis—unless the Yankees self-destructed, which actually seemed conceivable.

As the season headed into August with the Browns still chasing them, Yankee composure unraveled on a western trip. Wally Pipp and Ruth exchanged punches in St. Louis after Ruth had criticized Pipp's fielding. In Detroit reserve catcher Al DeVormer fought with Mays one day, Fred Hofmann the next.

Finally, manager Miller Huggins threatened to fine and suspend any brawlers, and the club turned its attention to a pivotal September series in St. Louis, where brown beer barrels had been set on street corners for contributions for gifts for the Browns once they clinched the pennant.

Instead, New York took two of three in a riotous series during which center fielder Whitey Witt was beaned and gashed by a bottle. The barrels were dumped into the gutter and the money given to charity. Three weeks later the Yankees won the pennant by a single game and prepared for another, more bitter Series duel with their landlords, this time with a stronger lineup.

During another preseason raiding party on Boston's roster, general manager Ed Barrow had acquired shortstop Everett Scott, the league's best fielder, plus right-handers Joe Bush (26–7) and Sam Jones (13–13) for shortstop Roger Peckinpaugh and pitchers Rip Collins and Jack Quinn. Witt had been bought from the Athletics in April, and Joe Dugan, the league's best third baseman, was acquired from the Red Sox in July—which outraged St. Louis fans and American League president Ban Johnson, and ultimately produced a June 1 trading deadline.

Yet the Series was a disaster. The Giants grabbed the opener by wiping out a 2–0 Yankee lead in the eighth with four consecutive singles before Bush retired a man. And after the Yankees had climbed out of a three-run deficit to tie game two, umpire George Hildebrand, anticipating darkness, called the game after 10 innings, with 45 minutes of daylight remaining.

"It was crazy," Dugan would say. "The people were milling around yelling. They were mad at everybody. They could have played another inning or two anyway. It was broad daylight. Everyone was laughing. It was a joke among the players."

Not so with Landis, who was hounded across Eighth Avenue by angry spectators demanding refunds, and who decided to turn over the profits to charity.

All of which merely prolonged the inevitable. Ruth, who batted .118 for the Series without a home run, was concluding a miserable season during which he was suspended several times, chased hecklers, and wrangled frequently with Huggins.

"If you don't want to play ball, why don't you go home?" the manager would shout. "You go home!" Ruth would retort. "If you don't like the way I play ball, why don't you fire me?"

As Ruth slumped in the Series, so did the Yankees. The Giants blanked them in game three, held Ruth hitless, heckled him, and finally hooted him out of their clubhouse when he turned up to warn them about the "personal stuff" they'd been shouting.

After erasing a 2–0 deficit to take game four the Giants closed it out the following afternoon after Huggins, with the Yankees leading 3–2 in the eighth, ordered a reluctant Bush to walk Pep Youngs, thus loading the bases with two out.

George Kelly, who'd thrown out Aaron Ward to kill off the Yankees in the 1921 Series, hit Bush's next pitch into left-center field, scoring two runs and essentially ending it.

Huston, who'd disliked Huggins ever since he'd been hired instead of Brooklyn manager Wilbert Robinson in 1918, brooded all the way to the press headquarters downtown where he smashed a row of cocktail glasses. "Miller Huggins," he vowed, "has managed his last game for the Yankees."

Instead, Huston had basically watched his last game as co-owner. Barrow, fed up with the colonels' bickering, threatened to quit unless the lines of authority were more clearly drawn. On May 1, Ruppert bought out Huston for $1.5 million. By then a new stadium had been constructed on a 240,000-square-foot plot of land at 161st Street and River Avenue in the Bronx. It was The House that Ruth Built—and Ruppert paid for.

For a decade they had been fellow residents and business rivals, competing for the same spectator dollar. But the Giants were the landlords at the Polo Grounds, the Yankees their tenants, as Giant owner Charles Stoneham was quick to remind them.

As long as the tenants were no financial or artistic threat to the landlords, they'd been tolerated. But the arrival of Babe Ruth in 1920 had changed that relationship permanently. The Yankees had drawn 619,000 customers the previous year, but that number soared to 1,290,000, which was 100,000 more than the Giants attracted while finishing second in the National League.

When that trend continued in 1921, Giant manager John McGraw, who'd urged Jacob Ruppert and Cap Huston to buy the Yankees a decade earlier, approached Stoneham about an eviction notice.

"The Yankees will have to build a park in Queens or some other out-of-the-way place," McGraw told him. "Let them go away and wither on the vine."

Stoneham had served notice on Ruppert during the middle of the 1922 season—and found that the Colonel had anticipated him. During the winter of 1921, Ruppert had bought for $600,000 from the estate of William Ward Astor a 10-acre parcel across the Harlem River between 157th and 161st streets.

Now he called a Cleveland engineering company and ordered plans and specifications drawn and told White Construction Company that it had one year and $1.9 million to build him a house for Babe Ruth.

The stadium would be in the Bronx, yet it could be reached in 16 minutes by subway from the club offices downtown. The result was well worth the trip—a massive triple-tiered piece of cement-and-steel wedding cake that the *New York Times* labeled "a skyscraper among ballparks."

The contractors had needed 13,000 cubic yards of topsoil, 116,000 square feet of sod, 20,000 cubic yards of concrete, 2,200 tons of structural steel, and 950,000 board feet of Pacific Coast fir for the bleachers, which stretched from foul line to foul line. As a hallmark, Ruppert added a copper frieze 16 feet deep atop the stadium. There was no other structure like it anywhere.

Yankee Stadium would be the last privately financed ballpark in the land, and Ruppert, with his systematic raiding of the Red Sox roster, had put together a ball club worthy of it.

And it was his club, finally. After he'd bought out Huston's share for $1.5 million, Ruppert had dashed off a telegram to the team in Chicago. "I now am the sole owner of the Yankees," it read. "Miller Huggins is my manager."

The roster was a manager's dream. The pitching staff—with Herb Pennock, Joe Bush, Sam Jones, Waite Hoyt, Bob Shawkey, and Carl Mays—was so reliable that New York writers dubbed it the "Six-Star Final." Joe Dugan, at third base, was the game's best. Shortstop Everett Scott was the league's iron man. And a repentant and recharged Ruth was back in the outfield.

The Babe's worst year, ruined by bickering with his teammates and Huggins, a .315 average, and a .118 World Series, was behind him. Now there was a new stadium to fill, a $1,000-a-week contract to, live up to and a pennant to defend.

So Ruth reported to spring training at 200 pounds, his lowest weight as a Yankee, and on April 18 turned up at the Stadium for opening day eager for work.

THE NEW HOME OF THE AMERICAN LEAGUE BASEBALL CLUB OF NEW YORK
THE · OSBORN · ENGINEERING · CO · · CLEVELAND ·

Drawing of Yankee Stadium, which never would be fully double-decked as shown.

Opening day at Yankee Stadium: April 18, 1923.

So did a record major league crowd of nearly 65,000 New Yorkers (the announced figure of 74,200 was exaggerated) who nearly crushed Commissioner Kenesaw Mountain Landis in their eagerness to reach the turnstiles. As it was, the gates had to be closed half an hour early and 25,000 were turned away.

Inside, John Philip Sousa and his 7th Regiment Band led a procession to center field that included Landis, Stoneham, and Red Sox owner

Harry Frazee, who'd sold the Yankees 11 members of their roster.

The 1922 pennant was raised to an ovation that the *New York Times* said "floated across the Harlem and far beyond." Governor Al Smith threw out the first ball. And by the third inning Ruth had hit the first home run in his house, a three-run shot into the right-field bleachers that sent the Yankees on to a 4–1 victory over Boston.

It was his first of 41 home runs that summer, as Ruth enjoyed his best year for average (.393), hits (205), and doubles (45), won the American

A flag is raised over the Stadium for the first time—on the playing field in center.

Main entrance, opening day.

Left: *Sad Sam Jones was the Yankees' top pitcher at 21–8, including a no-hitter over Connie Mack's Athletics in Philadelphia.* **Right:** *Lou Gehrig made his Yankee debut at age 20, hitting .423 (and his first homer) in 13 games after being summoned from Hartford near season's end. Giants manager John McGraw refused a Yankee request to make the rookie eligible for the World Series.*

Miller Huggins and Jacob Ruppert pose before the 1923 World Series opener at the Stadium. They would have reason to smile, as their Yankees won that game over the rival Giants and captured the Series for the club's first world title.

League's MVP Award unanimously, and helped the club draw a million spectators, thus burying McGraw's prophecy that "the fans will soon forget about them over there."

The Yankees, hardly coincidentally, won the pennant by 16 games over Detroit and met the Giants for their third straight subway Series. This time it was no longer landlord versus tenant but neighbor against neighbor, and McGraw was quick to draw the boundary line. He forbade his Giants to dress in Ruppert's stadium; instead they suited up at the Polo Grounds and took taxicabs across Central Bridge.

Where upon Casey Stengel, their 33-year-old outfielder, doubled the insult, legging out an inside-the-park home run with two out in the ninth to beat the Yankees, 5–4, in the opener at the Stadium.

His shot to left-center field bounced past Bob Meusel, but the cushion popped out of one of Stengel's shoes as he was rounding second. As he hobbled toward the plate like a spavined old workhorse, Damon Runyon scribbled notes for a timeless lead:

"This is the way old Casey Stengel ran yesterday afternoon, running his home run home. His mouth wide open. His warped old legs bending beneath him at every stride. His arms flying back and forth like those of a man swimming with a crawl stroke. His flanks heaving, his breath whistling, his head far back."

Finally Stengel collapsed atop the plate, his wind done, the game won. He had one more great blow left in him, a home run that won game three, 1–0—and infuriated Ruppert, since

A veteran named Casey Stengel gave the Giants their only two victories in the World Series. He smacked two winning homers against his future team. After his second, as he rounded the Stadium bases, he thumbed his nose at the Yankee dugout.

The 1923 Yankees—the club's first world champions.

Stengel thumbed his nose at the Yankee dugout while trotting around the bases.

"When a man wins a World Series game with a home run he should be permitted some exuberance," Landis told Ruppert. "Particularly when his name is Casey Stengel."

And particularly when it was the Giants' last gasp. Ruth, who hit .368 for the Series, had bashed two of his three home runs to give the Yankees game two. "The Ruth is mighty," wrote Heywood Broun, "and shall prevail."

So did his teammates. They cleaned up their former landlords in six games for their first world championship, winning all three at the Polo Grounds. Ruppert buoyantly threw a suitably lavish party at the Commodore downtown. "This is a wonderful occasion," the colonel decreed. "I now have baseball's greatest park, baseball'sgreatest players, and baseball's greatest team."

They were two of baseball's most legendary figures, yet they disliked each other on sight with a bitterness that knew no season. Once at a winter hunting lodge in Georgia, Detroit outfielder Ty Cobb had refused to share a cabin with Babe Ruth, who he suggested had black ancestry. "I've never bedded down with a nigger," Cobb growled, "and I'm not going to start now."

In season Cobb had flung a series of epithets at Ruth whenever their paths crossed. Ruth was "an egg on stilts, a beer keg on two straws." Now, on June 13, the league-leading Yankees and second-place Tigers were matched in a critical series at Detroit and tempers were ready to flare.

A few words from Cobb to Ruth ("Do you smell something? Something around here really stinks. Like a polecat."), a 10–6 New York lead in the ninth inning, and a "duster" signal from

Herb Pennock, another gift from Boston, had a 21–9 record and 2.83 earned run average while becoming the Yankee ace and winning 60 games over 1924–26.

Women and children loved Babe Ruth—and vice versa.

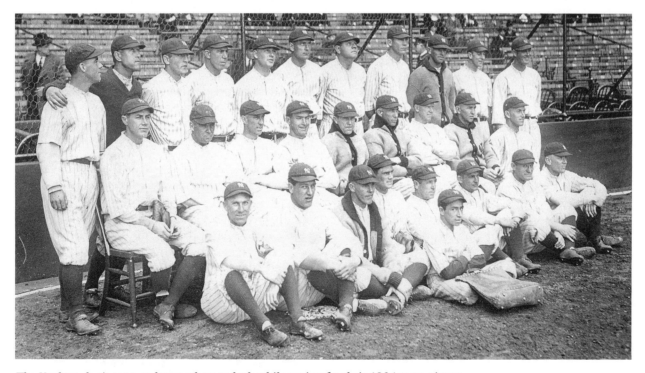

The Yankees don't seem to know where to look while posing for their 1924 team picture.

player-manager Cobb to pitcher Leonard "King" Cole provided the spark.

Cole's pitch hit Bob Meusel in the small of the back, Meusel flung his bat at Cole's head and charged the mound, and Cobb ran full-tilt from center to meet Ruth at the plate.

"I rushed at him like a football player trying to knock an opposing man out of the play," Ruth would say. What ensued was a 30-minute riot that got Cole and Meusel suspended for 10 days and lured 40,000 fans to Navin Field the next day, eager for an encore.

The game—and the series—were anticlimactic. There were no further brawls, and neither New York nor Detroit won the pennant. Instead, a Washington club with a 27-year-old manager (Bucky Harris) and a 36-year-old pitcher (Walter Johnson) came from seventh place to win its first American League pennant by two games over the Yankees.

"Washington got hot quicker than almost any club I ever saw," marveled Ruth, whose teammates had hoped to win an unprecedented fourth straight pennant.

Indeed, the Yankees led the league for eight weeks. They won five in a row at Washington in August and 18 of 22 games in September. Yet they lost a critical series at the Stadium at the end of August, and the Senators never let them back in the race.

Washington won the series opener, 11–6, despite two Ruth home runs, and went on to win three of the four games, bearing off the finale in the tenth inning.

There were still 27 games left in the season, but New York never held first place alone again, even though they forced the issue until the final four days.

When the Senators lost the opener of a series at Boston and the Yankees prevailed at Philadelphia, the deficit shrank to a single game. But Washington won the next two to the delight of Boston fans, who still carried a grudge from Ruppert's postwar talent raids. And the Yankees went on to lose two to the Athletics.

So the Senators proceeded to beat the Giants in seven games for their only world championship. And Huggins went home, filled his pipe and philosophized.

"The first pennant is the easiest to win," he told intimates, "no matter how hard the struggle may seem at the time. Then it is all new to your players. Once they have been through it, some of the shine has gone off it."

1925

The "stomachache heard 'round the world" was brought on, legend has it, by a dozen hot dogs and eight bottles of lemon soda. Nobody who knew Babe Ruth found that unusual; his idea of breakfast rarely corresponded to anybody else's. Six eggs, fried potatoes, and a porterhouse steak seemed to him a reasonable start, washed down by a pot of coffee and a pint of bourbon mixed with ginger ale.

But on this particular morning, as the Yankees were making their way from Tennessee to North Carolina on their spring barnstorming tour, Ruth was gobbling whatever happened to be available on station platforms as the train was taking on passengers.

He'd been feeling feverish in Chattanooga and slept fitfully the night before. When the club arrived in Asheville, Ruth headed for a taxicab with catcher Steve O'Neill, then pitched headlong.

"Severe grippe and nervous attack," guessed the hotel doctor, but by the next morning Ruth was being loaded onto a Pullman bound for New York with sportswriters filing bedside updates at every station stop. Amateur diagnoses ranged from acute indigestion to venereal disease.

"Every goddamn bone in my body aches," Ruth told them. "But I'll be in the opener anyway. Don't worry."

But the opener came and went with Ruth lying restlessly in St. Vincent's Hospital. London newspapers had already pronounced him dead. Instead, surgeons found an intestinal abscess. The hot dogs and soda had merely been the crowning gustatory indignity to a decade of overindulgence.

From the moment Jack Dunn had brought him to Baltimore's training camp and he'd wolfed down three stacks of wheat cakes and three orders of ham, Ruth had force-fed himself like a Strasbourg goose. His legendary breakfasts were simply preludes to days filled with huge meals, exotic snacks, and prodigious quantities of beer.

"You've never seen a man eat the way he did," marveled teammate Waite Hoyt. "If you cut that big slob in half, most of the concessions at Yankee Stadium would come pouring out."

To Ruth a midnight "snack" would include half a dozen club sandwiches, a platter of pigs' knuckles, and a pitcher of beer, topped by a fat black cigar. Pickled eels and chocolate ice cream would do between games of a double-header. And in St. Louis, his favorite road town, the usual fare would be supplemented by tubs of spare ribs and frogs' legs.

No stomach ailment existed that couldn't be relieved by a fistful of bicarbonate of soda and a loud belch. But now he was flat on his broad back in a Manhattan hospital bed, and as Ruth went, so went the Yankees. They were in fourth place at the end of the first week of the season; ironically, it was their best achievement of the year.

By the time Ruth returned to the lineup in June, pale and unsteady on his legs, the club had fallen to seventh while manager Miller Huggins despaired.

"They're through, Ed," he told Barrow after a particularly abysmal western trip. "I can't even make 'em mad any more. They've just lost the urge to win. They just don't care any more."

"Very well," the general manager replied. "We'll get rid of them and get a new team."

So shortstop Everett Scott, who'd started a major league record 1,307 games, was benched, then waived. A rookie named Lou Gehrig replaced Wally Pipp at first base, catcher Bennie Bengough took over for slumping Wally Schang, and outfielder Whitey Witt was released.

Still the Yankees remained mired in seventh, and Ruth's return only produced further dissension between the club and Huggins, who was grimly trying to restore pride and discipline, particularly on Ruth's part.

His innards healed, Ruth had quickly gone back to his old training regimen—which was no regimen at all. He rarely stayed in the three-dollar hotel rooms the club reserved, opting for $100-a-day suites instead. And he rarely returned from his evening revels before dawn. No novelty there. "Who are you rooming with?" somebody had asked outfielder Ping Bodie during Ruth's first year in New York. "A suitcase," Bodie had replied.

Now, rebukes from Huggins merely provoked a torrent of criticism of managerial strategy from Ruth, who'd labeled the 5-foot 6-inch Huggins "Little Boy" and "The Flea" and, it was said, once hung him over the platform railing of a moving train.

A showdown was inevitable, and it came, suitably, on August 29 in St. Louis, where Ruth habitually made himself invisible. After two nights of this Huggins phoned Barrow in Manhattan.

"I want to fine that big ape."

"Well, it's all right with me," Barrow responded.

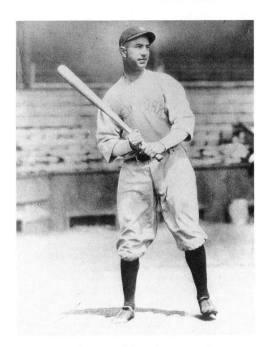

Shortstop Everett "Deacon" Scott's consecutive-game streak ended on May 6 when he was benched by Miller Huggins—a record 1,307 straight games. Less than a month later, Lou Gehrig would begin the streak that would surpass Scott's.

Bob Meusel was one of the few bright lights for the seventh-place Yankees, leading the league in home runs (33) and RBIs (138), both career highs.

Benny Bengough took over most of the catching from the aging Wally Schang, who turned 36 during the season.

Jacob Ruppert met with Babe Ruth when the superstar was suspended by Miller Huggins.

Except for starting pitcher Hoyt, the clubhouse was deserted when Ruth breezed in late for batting practice the third day.

"Sorry I'm late, Hug," he said. "Had some personal business to attend to."

"I know," Huggins told him. "Don't bother to uniform today. You're suspended."

"I'm what? Why you miserable little son of a bitch."

"What's more, you're fined five thousand dollars."

"I'm fined? I'm fined? Like hell I am. I'll see Jake about this. You think Jake will let you get away with this? You're crazy. Five thousand dollars? Why, you little bastard, I'll never play for you again. I'll see Jake. He'll throw you out on your ass."

Huggins shrugged. "That's what I want you to do. And I'd just like to be there when you burst into Ruppert's office carrying that .246 average and telling him I'm picking on you."

So Ruth boarded a train for Chicago, changed for the Twentieth Century Limited, and "got indignant for the benefit of every reporter who interviewed me at station stops."

Huggins is alibiing for his seventh-place effort, Ruth told them. He'd never wear a Yankee uniform again as long as Huggins was manager. The choice would be Ruppert's.

Ruth held court briefly at his Manhattan apartment, then led a trail of newspapermen to Ruppert's brewery where the colonel and Barrow read him out for half an hour behind closed doors.

"Gentlemen," Ruppert would tell the press, "I think maybe Root has changed his mind and

will continue playing for Mr. Huckins. That's right, isn't it, Root?"

"Yes," Ruth murmured.

"Root is sorry about the whole thing," Ruppert continued. "We are all sorry. But it had to be."

Though the fine stood until Huggins' death four years later, the suspension was lifted when the club went to Boston on September 7. Ruth brought his average from .246 to .290 over the season's final month. But the season was gone (the Yankees finished 28½ games behind Washington, in seventh place). By the following winter, so was much of the team.

He was 39 years old, and he had beaten the Yankees twice in six days and celebrated with a bottle or two. Now, all Grover Cleveland Alexander wanted was a chance to stretch his legs on the bench and rest.

"I'm going down to the bullpen," the Cardinal pitcher informed player-manager Rogers Hornsby before the seventh game of the World Series. "If you need me, I'll be there."

The call had come with two out in the bottom of the seventh inning after New York had loaded the bases and sent Tony Lazzeri to the plate. "We're in a tough spot," Hornsby would inform Alexander as the veteran trudged to the mound. "And there's no place to put this guy."

"I'll take care of that," Alexander assured him—and went out to strike out Lazzeri, one of the Yankees' most reliable clutch hitters, on four

All the Seasons ••• **39**

pitches, in one of baseball's most dramatic moments. Two innings later, after what New York general manager Ed Barrow called "the only dumb play Babe Ruth ever made," the Cardinals had won the day, 3–2, and with it their first world championship.

And Alexander, an epileptic old-timer who'd been picked up for a song from the Cubs early in the season but still had four seasons left in him, was amused by his sudden elevation to demigod.

"You know, you never want to take this hullabaloo and hero stuff too seriously," he told friends afterward. "Yes, I struck out Lazzeri. But suppose that line drive he hit foul had gone fair? Boys, Lazzeri would be the hero tonight and I—well, I'd just be a bum."

Had Lazzeri's drive one pitch earlier passed to the other side of the left-field foul pole, New York would have won its second world championship in four years and capped a remarkable season during which the Yankees submerged memories of their seventh-place finish in 1925 and laid the foundation for the greatest team the game had ever known.

Their revival had begun quietly enough amid a number of new faces, a fair amount of confusion at the club's St. Petersburg training quarters, and considerable press skepticism.

Whitey Witt, Wally Schang, Wally Pipp, and Everett Scott all had been traded or released since July 1925. One rookie, Mark Koenig, would start at shortstop. Lazzeri, a newcomer from San Francisco, was the new second baseman. And a quiet slugger named Lou Gehrig had become a fixture at first.

Gehrig had joined the lineup virtually unnoticed in June of the previous year when Pipp, a 10-year regular, had complained of a headache after being beaned in batting practice by rookie Charlie Caldwell, who would make a more enduring reputation as Princeton football coach.

"Why don't you take the day off, Wally?" manager Miller Huggins had suggested. "We'll put the kid from Columbia on first today."

Pipp never started another game as a Yankee. Now he and several of his mates were gone, and the New York lineup was a patchwork quilt of youngsters and veterans who openly doubted Huggins' competence. "The Yankees are a collection of individuals," Westbrook Pegler wrote from spring training, "who are convinced that their manager is a sap."

Only one New York sportswriter picked the Yankees to win the pennant, yet Huggins, who'd given up the 1925 season for lost after the first western trip, remained curiously optimistic.

"I believe we will win the pennant," he predicted as the club broke camp. "We'll either do that or fall apart. And I don't think we'll fall apart."

As if on cue the Yankees defeated Brooklyn 12 straight times on their barnstorming tour, won eight in a row shortly after returning north, and found themselves in first place by the end of April.

Then, after a late-season stumble, they clinched their fourth pennant in six years by sweeping a doubleheader from the Browns in St. Louis the day after expectant Cardinal fans had howled and pounded drums outside the Yankees' hotel windows.

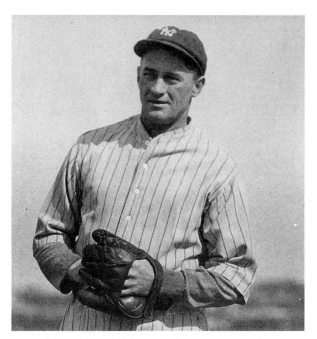

At age 36, Urban Shocker returned to the Yankees and was a solid 19–11. Proving it was no fluke, the veteran right-hander would be 18–6 in 1927 despite an ailing heart—and died late in the 1928 season.

The Yankees won the pennant with a rookie keystone combination—second baseman Tony Lazzeri (left) and shortstop Mark Koenig.

St. Louis had never played in a Series and had won the National League race with a .578 percentage, the lowest ever to that point. New York had limped in three games ahead of Cleveland. Yet the two clubs produced a classic, breaking records for attendance (328,000) and gate receipts.

Once Ruth crashed three home runs in game four at Sportsman's Park, the Yankees had taken control and returned to the Stadium leading three games to two.

But Alexander, who'd beaten them 6–2 in game two, easily evened the Series with a 10–2 triumph that barely exercised him, then stepped out for a Saturday night on the town. "If you need me tomorrow," he informed Hornsby, "I'll have a little left. This was fairly easy today."

What happened between then and Sunday morning is suspended somewhere between myth and reality. Alexander had an indisputable capacity and liking for hard liquor. With two complete-game Series victories in two starts he had ample reason to indulge.

Some accounts have him struggling in at dawn, breakfasting on a ham sandwich, falling asleep in the bullpen, and waking with a vicious hangover and no idea of the score. Others claim he drank moderately, slept well, and watched the game alertly.

"I was cold sober the night after I pitched the sixth game," Alexander insisted in later years. "There may have been plenty of times before and since when I wasn't, but I was sober that night."

What is beyond doubt is that the Cardinals brought a 3–2 lead into the bottom of the seventh and that starter Jesse Haines had developed a blood blister from throwing knucklers.

Now, New York's Earle Combs singled and Koenig sacrificed him to second. So Haines walked Ruth intentionally and got Bob Meusel to force him at second. Another walk, this time to Gehrig, loaded the bases with two out. But Haines' blister had burst and blood was dripping from his fingers.

"Can you make it, Jesse?" Hornsby asked him.

Haines grimaced.

"Well, I guess I'll have to relieve you."

So Hornsby motioned to the bullpen and Alexander emerged and began walking toward the infield, working on a chaw and unbuttoning his scarlet sweater jacket.

"We could hardly believe it," Ruth would say, "when the old fellow himself came through the gate."

Since the bullpen was wedged beneath the bleachers, Alexander had no idea of the jam that faced him. "All you know," he said, "is what you

That's Cardinal southpaw Bill Sherdel warming up in game one of the World Series at the Stadium. The Yankees beat him, 2–1, and edged him again in game five, 3–2. But they managed only one other victory, and St. Louis took the Series, 4–3, in a thriller that went down to the final out.

learn from the voices of the fans overhead. So when I came out I saw the bases filled and Lazzeri standing in the box."

From his station at second base Hornsby met Alexander halfway in, peered into his eyes and found them clear. Or clear enough. "All right, get in there," Hornsby said, slapping Alexander on the back. "You can do it, Pete."

Next to Ruth, Lazzeri was New York's most productive hitter (114 RBIs). "I guess there's nothing much to do except give Tony a lot of hell," Alexander decided.

His first pitch, a fastball, barely missed, and Alexander walked down to umpire George Hildebrand, "I've been pitching 20 years," he told him. "You might have given me that one."

The second, a low fastball, was a called strike. Then Lazzeri lashed a drive just inches to the wrong side of the foul pole. "No more of that for you, my lad," Alexander muttered.

Now, where he'd curved him 24 hours earlier, Alexander unleashed a fastball across the letters that left the swinging Lazzeri with his legs spread wide, his mouth agape.

There would be one more chance when Ruth walked with two out in the ninth and Meusel and Gehrig were due up. But Ruth, who'd only stolen 12 bases all season, inexplicably took off for second. Catcher Bob O'Farrell's throw beat him by 10 feet, ending the game and the Series.

"I'll always remember putting the ball on him," Hornsby would say. "He didn't say a word. He didn't even look around or up at me. He just picked himself off the ground and walked away."

1927

Center fielder Earle Combs, who was leadoff man for this devastating sound-and-light show, called it "five o'clock lightning." When the eighth inning rolled around and New York bats exploded in a thunderstorm of home runs and extra-base hits victory was a foregone conclusion.

The 1927 Yankees were probably the finest team in baseball history and certainly the most dramatic. With their Murderers' Row of right fielder Babe Ruth (.356), first baseman Lou Gehrig (.373), second baseman Tony Lazzeri (.309), and left fielder Bob Meusel (.337) at the heart of the lineup, the club won 110 games and led the

American League in average (.307), runs (975), home runs (158), and pyrotechnics.

The most productive, stylish, and dramatic of them all was Ruth, who chose that year to set the sport's most cherished mark—60 home runs—a record which stood for 34 years, and still stands for a 154-game season.

He was a svelter Ruth in 1927, thanks to an off-season exercise regimen supervised by Artie McGovern in a Manhattan gymnasium that replaced Babe's mostly symbolic Hot Springs boil-offs. And with a new $70,000-a-year contract in his pocket, he was a richer Ruth, too.

The stance and the swing, however, had remained unchanged since he'd set the major league record of 59 in 1921. Ruth had always dug the knob of his big bat—variously estimated between 42 and 52 ounces—into his right palm and swung from the heels. Choking up was for lesser men. "I never found out whether Babe didn't ever know he had two strikes on him," mused White Sox catcher Moe Berg, "or whether he didn't care."

For the first two weeks of 1927 Ruth's swing found mostly air; after 10 games he'd hit only one homer, that off Philadelphia's Howard Ehmke. Then he crashed one off Rube Walberg, his favorite pigeon that year, which touched off a spree of five in six games.

By the end of May the count was 16, by July 4, 26. With Gehrig matching him virtually shot

Babe Ruth had it made in the shade. He wanted $75,000 a year, but he settled for a three-year contract at $70,000 per season.

for shot, Ruth had piled up 43 at the beginning of September and finished the season with a burst, 17 in the final 26 games.

In all, Ruth would hit homers off 33 pitchers, 23 of them right-handers. Though 28 of his shots came inside Yankee Stadium, Ruth had belted one in every American League park by July 24 and eventually hit at least four in every one but Chicago's Comiskey Park.

The record breaker, a fly ball down the right-field line off a screwball that Ruth golfed from his shoetops, came off Washington left-hander Tom Zachary in the next-to-last game of the season.

For all practical purposes, the season ended on Independence Day, when the Yankees shredded the second-place Senators in a doubleheader to the incredible tune of 12–1 and 21–1.

"Those fellows not only beat you, they tear your heart out," moaned Washington first baseman Joe Judge. "I wish the season was over."

It was a team without a discernible weakness, from outfielders Combs, Ruth, and Meusel, to infielders Gehrig and Lazzeri, to a superior pitching staff that led the league in ERA (3.20) and shutouts (11). Every pitcher had a winning record, and four of them—Waite Hoyt, Herb Pennock, Urban Shocker, and reliever Wilcy Moore—won at least 18 games.

Five of their starting eight fielders had averages of .309 or better, and, on their more inspired afternoons, the Yankees strained credulity. Once, when their train into Detroit was delayed and they had to forgo both batting and fielding practice, the club simply wolfed down a pregame repast of hot dogs and soda, then went out and beat the Tigers, 19–2. The Pirates, who were struggling to win the National League race, hardly seemed a match for them.

"The Yanks will murder 'em," prophesied Brooklyn manager Wilbert Robinson. "They've got the best club that was ever in baseball." Murderers' Row, after all, had knocked in 544 runs; Ruth had hit six more homers than the entire Pittsburgh roster.

When the Yankees arrived at Forbes Field for batting practice prior to the Series, manager Miller Huggins decided to play mind games with his hosts, who had already worked out, dressed, and taken seats in the stands.

"See those upper bleachers?" he told his sluggers. "I want to see how many of these nice unblemished baseballs you can drop into those stands." Then, after instructing Hoyt to "lay it in there," Huggins sent Ruth (6-feet-2, 215 pounds), Gehrig (6 feet, 200 pounds), and Meusel (6-feet-3,

The Yankee outfield averaged .350. Earle Combs (left) and Babe Ruth each batted .356; Bob Meusel (right) batted .337.

190 pounds) into the cage and watched them smash consecutive home runs.

"You could actually hear them gulp while they watched us," Ruth would say, after belting half a dozen. Gehrig, who'd hit 47 during the season, smashed two of his five over the center-field fence, where no National League ball had

Wilcy Moore gave the Yankees an unexpected boost. The 30-year-old rookie was 19–7 with 13 hard-to-earn saves as a spot starter and ace reliever.

The 1927 Yankees—generally acclaimed baseball's greatest team ever. They won 110 games, capturing the pennant by 19 and becoming the first American League team to sweep a World Series. **Front row** (left to right): Julie Wera, Mike Gazella, Pat Collins, Eddie Bennett (mascot), Benny Bengough, Ray Morehart, Myles Thomas, Cedric Durst. **Middle row:** Urban Shocker, Joe Dugan, Earle Combs, Charlie O'Leary (coach), Miller Huggins (manager), Art Fletcher (coach), Mark Koenig, Dutch Ruether, Johnny Grabowski, George Pipgras. **Back row:** Lou Gehrig, Herb Pennock, Tony Lazzeri, Wilcy Moore, Babe Ruth, Don Miller, Bob Meusel, Bob Shawkey, Waite Hoyt, Joe Giard, Ben Paschal, unidentified, Doc Woods (trainer).

ever ventured. The ploy had its effect; the Pirates sat stunned.

"I've never seen anything like this before," said shortstop Glenn Wright. "Do they do this all the time?"

Their reconnaissance done, the Pirates filed out of the park, all but resigned to a sweep. "Boys," manager Donie Bush told them in a team meeting before the opening, "we'll now go over the Yankee lineup and check the weaknesses of each batter."

They found none. "Oh, well, what's the use?" Bush concluded. "Let's go out on the ball field and hope we all don't get killed."

If it was a killing, it was painless. New York did sweep the Pirates cleanly, but scored only 23 runs and hit only two homers, both by Ruth. Pitching and Pittsburgh errors took care of most of it.

Two walks and two errors gave the Yankees three runs in the opener. George Pipgras scattered seven hits in game two and won, 6–2. Pennock held the Pirates hitless for 7⅓ innings in game three and coasted, 8–1. Then Pittsburgh's Johnny Miljus uncorked two wild pitches in the ninth inning of game four, scoring Combs with the winner, and it was over. With barely a trace of lightning.

The play came from the same bag of tricks as the hidden ball and pinch-hitting midgets, and it was legal in the National League. A hurler would whip one pitch past a batter, keep his toe on the rubber and quickly deliver another, hoping for a cheap strike.

It would not be allowed in the 1928 World Series, Commissioner Kenesaw Mountain Landis told his umpires—but nobody remembered to inform St. Louis manager Bill McKechnie, his Yankee counterpart Miller Huggins, or their clubs.

A minor matter—until Cardinal pitcher Bill Sherdel used the "quick pitch" to strike out Babe Ruth with one out in the seventh inning of game four at Sportsman's Park, touching off one of the most emotional disputes in Series history.

"You can't do that," Ruth howled at Sherdel. Plate umpire Charlie Pfirman, a National Leaguer, agreed with him, reset the count at 0–2 and brushed aside a 10-minute argument by the Cardinals. Ruth, who'd already hit one home run in the fourth and would crash another in the eighth, proceeded to belt the next pitch onto the roof of the right-field pavilion, sending New York on to a 7–3 victory and its second consecutive Series sweep.

Thus ended another vintage season in which the Yankees won their sixth American League pennant in eight seasons, avenged their seven-game Series loss to St. Louis two years earlier, and got owner Jacob Ruppert to give them the shirt off his back—literally.

Though his club had just completed the most impressive season in baseball history, winning 110 games and ravaging Pittsburgh for the world championship, Ruppert settled in for the winter of 1928 with his wallet all but padlocked.

As the contracts came back predictably unsigned, Ruppert and general manager Ed Barrow resorted to what the players came to term the "Elevated treatment," which involved a financial stone wall at either end and a five-cent rapid-transit ride in between.

When a player turned up at the club offices on 42nd Street to negotiate face-to-face, Barrow would murmur something about soaring operating expenses and shrinking profits and suggest a trip uptown to the colonel's brewery. "It's Ruppert's money," Barrow would shrug. "Go up and see him."

While the player headed for the train Barrow would brief Ruppert by phone and the futile circle would be complete. "I can't understand what has got into you fellows," Ruppert would sigh when the player arrived. "One wants this, another wants that. Root wants $80,000. Gehrig wants more money. Dugan wants more. What do you fellows think I am, a millionaire?"

Ruth settled for the same $70,000, his teammates gradually came to terms, and the Yankees went about their customary business of making hash of the pennant race.

Shortly after Independence Day their lead over Philadelphia was 13½ games—yet the club inexplicably came apart down the stretch and was trailing by half a game in early September.

The race came down to a four-game series with the Athletics in the Stadium, and New York quickly moved to claim it by sweeping a doubleheader before 80,000 partisans on the first day. George Pipgras won the first game by shutout, Bob Meusel won the nightcap with a grand slam—and the Yankees proceeded to take three of four and eventually win the pennant by 2½ games.

On paper the Series seemed uncompetitive. The Yankees hadn't lost a Series game since Pete Alexander struck out Tony Lazzeri in the 1926 finale; the Cardinals had struggled to win the National League by two games over the Giants.

The Yankee pennant was Miller Huggins' sixth, tying him with Connie Mack (left) for most by an American League manager. Coincidentally, Mack's Philadelphia Athletics battled the Yankees for the flag until season's end.

The Yankees got even with 1926 World Series nemesis Grover Cleveland Alexander (left) in game two, when the veteran right-hander opposed George Pipgras (right). Hammered for eight runs, "Old Pete" was routed by the third inning. Pipgras's easy 7–3 victory in the opener crowned his best year—24–13. No Yankee right-hander since has had more victories in a season.

Yet the Yankees were hobbled. Left fielder Earle Combs had broken a finger; pitcher Herb Pennock was nursing a sore arm. Neither was available. Ruth (sprained ankle and a charley horse), third baseman Joe Dugan (bad knee), and Lazzeri (sore arm) were all playing hurt.

Still, New York won the opener, 4–1, and quickly came to dominate the Series. In game two the Yankees scored eight runs in 2⅓ innings off (sweet irony) Alexander. And nothing changed when the Series moved to St. Louis. New York took a 7–3 victory in game three and started talking sweep.

Meanwhile, Ruth was on his way to the finest Series of his career (.625) in stark contrast to 1926 when Cardinal pitchers had walked him 11 times. This time McKechnie told them to challenge him and Ruth merrily hit away.

His leadoff homer over the right-field pavilion was merely a warning signal in game four; still St. Louis led, 2–1, in the seventh, and Sherdel quickly got two strikes on Ruth. Now his "quick pitch" caught the Babe flat-footed and staring. But Pfirman ruled otherwise. "Ruth isn't out," he explained. "Sherdel will have to pitch over to him."

While the Cardinals argued with Pfirman, Ruth laughed as he ducked bottles from the stands, then returned to the batter's box and challenged Sherdel.

"Put one in here again," he shouted to the southpaw, "and I'll knock it out of the park for you." So Ruth did, tying the game and setting off an ovation. Gehrig followed with his fourth homer of the Series to the same spot, and the Yankees proceeded to send eight men to the plate and score four runs.

For punctuation, Ruth closed out the game and the Series in the ninth with a one-handed grab of a foul ball that he plucked from the lap of a spectator in the left-field stands. No team had ever swept consecutive World Series. "My boys don't believe in letting these things drag out," Ruppert crowed.

Whereupon the Yankees celebrated all the way back to the Bronx during one of the wildest train rides in memory. At its center was Ruth, naturally, fortified by a 50-pound basket of choice spare ribs and buckets of beer, and crying, "Is everybody happy?" to the well-wishers that crowded station platforms en route.

Even the reticent, pipe-smoking Huggins got tipsy and spent the following morning searching for his false teeth.

As the night wore on the Yankees organized a raucous parade that snaked through the railroad

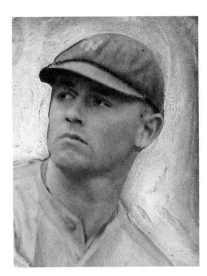

Waite Hoyt hurled a career-best 23–7 (plus a majors-leading eight saves), adding two victories and a 1.50 ERA in the Series sweep. Asked the key to his 157-win Yankee success, Hoyt replied, "Playing with Babe Ruth on my side."

cars, commandeering pajama tops from passengers on the way, and arriving finally at Ruppert's berth to find the door locked.

"This is no night for sleeping," Ruth decided.

"Go away, Root," Ruppert cried.

So Ruth and Gehrig broke down the door, found Ruppert in lavender nightclothes, and stripped him to the waist.

"Is this usual, Root?" the Colonel protested.

It wasn't—and there would be no more celebrations for four years, until after Huggins was dead and Ruth was in the twilight of his career.

He'd noticed the blotch with half a month left in the season and had shrugged it off, even after it had grown into a boil and threatened to close an eye.

"Go to a doctor because I've got a red spot on my face?" Miller Huggins scoffed. Five days later, at 50, the Yankee manager was dead from massive blood poisoning, and an era had ended. The passing of Huggins was the grim climax of a season prefaced by personal tragedies when the New York dynasty came crashing down.

The bad omens had actually begun toward the end of the 1928 season when pitcher Urban Shocker died from heart trouble at 38. Then

Near season's end, after a dozen years at the Yankee helm, Miller Huggins died suddenly at age 50. The first of the team's great managers, Hug led the club to 1,067 victories, six pennants, and three world titles, trailing only Joe McCarthy and Casey Stengel. "This is the man who cut the Yankee pennant pattern," McCarthy said when his predecessor's plaque was dedicated at the Stadium.

Tony Lazzeri, one of baseball's best power-hitting second basemen ever, drove in 106 runs in one of seven 100-RBI seasons during his 12 years with the Yankees.

Helen Ruth, Babe's estranged first wife, was killed in a fire outside Boston.

The Yankees, who'd won six pennants in eight years and swept consecutive World Series, never left the ground, winning only 88 games and finishing 18 behind Connie Mack's Philadelphia Athletics.

The 1927 and 1928 clubs had been so dominant, so flawless, that the first strains of what would become a periodic lament had been heard—"Break up the Yankees." But owner Jacob Ruppert, who'd spent 14 years and several million dollars building them, merely snorted. "I not only have no thought of breaking up the Yankees," he maintained, "but Ed Barrow, Huckins, and myself will exert our best efforts to strengthen them."

Yet there was perceptible slippage, even though the meat of the lineup—Ruth, Lou Gehrig, Tony Lazzeri, Earle Combs, Bob Meusel—remained unchanged.

Gehrig's average dropped from .374 to .300, Meusel's from .297 to .261. And a lippy .246 hitter named Leo Durocher, whom Ruth quickly dubbed the "All-American Out," was playing shortstop.

Time and changing chemistry were doing what

American League rivals could not, just as Huggins had predicted. "It won't be necessary to break up the Yankees," he'd said prior to the season. "No matter what we do, the law of averages will take care of us. We can go on trying to improve this team to the best of our abilities, but the time will come when we will crash."

Bill Dickey was the new catcher, a job he would hold game in, game out for 13 seasons until World War II. A standout receiver, he was a career .313 hitter and one of baseball's all-time great two-way catchers.

Babe Ruth disliked Lippy Leo Durocher (left), dubbing the brash and light-hitting shortstop "the All-America out." Durocher was waived after the season but would return to face the Yankees as opposing manager in the 1941 and 1951 World Series. He lost to his old team both times.

As a spot starter and reliever, Tom Zachary was 12–0 with a 2.47 ERA. It's still the most wins without a loss in one season by a Yankee. But the southpaw is best remembered for a different distinction: Two years earlier, in a Washington uniform, he served up Babe Ruth's record 60th home run.

Although the Yankees were in the 1929 pennant race until August they were never in command after mid-May and would chase the Athletics, who hadn't won a pennant in 15 years, all summer. Huggins realized that in May. His club had no spark, no hunger.

"I don't think the Yankees are going to catch the Athletics," he told a Cleveland sportswriter. "I don't think these Yankees are going to win any more pennants, certainly not this one. They're getting older, and they've become glutted with success. They're getting good salaries, and they've taken a great deal of money out of baseball. The Yankees turn to the financial page before the sports page."

Neither was a fruitful pursuit that year. The stock market crashed in October and the Yankees in August, when the fourth-place Browns shut them out three days in a row.

Exasperated, Huggins called a team meeting. "I don't want anybody to leave," he began. "I have something to say to you." What followed was a long managerial tirade that produced no reaction at all.

"They're through, Colonel," Huggins told Ruppert minutes later.

"But we still have a month . . ."

"Forget about it," Huggins said. "Start getting ready for next year. These fellows are through."

"But how do you know?"

"I just finished talking to them. I talked to them 20 minutes. I talked to them calmly, I pleaded with them. Then I abused them. No matter what I said or how I said it, it didn't make the slightest difference. I couldn't make them mad. I couldn't even make them laugh. When I realized that I might as well have been talking to that wall over there, I quit."

Ruppert was mystified. "But why? Why should they be through?"

"I guess they're just tired, Colonel. I'm tired myself. I'm tired out and can't sleep."

Huggins had been molding, teaching, cajoling this team for 11 years, transforming the Yankees from laughable Polo Grounds tenants into the sport's greatest dynasty. Along the way he had endured the derision of one owning partner (and another who never could pronounce his name), squabbled with his greatest star, and brushed aside insults from his players about his 5-foot-6-inch height, .265 lifetime batting average, and professional judgment.

Yet his teams had won 1,067 games, six pen-

To avoid crowds, Babe and Claire Ruth were married at 6 A.M. in a Manhattan church on opening day 1929. Happily, the game was rained out. The next day, the groom homered for his bride, tipping his cap and blowing kisses to her. The couple honeymooned on a Yankee road trip; the first stop was Boston, where only months earlier Babe had attended the funeral of his long-estranged first wife, Helen.

Jacob Ruppert encouraged Claire to travel with the team so she could keep an eye on Babe. That bothered other Yankee wives, who weren't allowed on the road. Claire was irritated in turn because, she said, while management wanted her to baby-sit her husband, it never picked up her travel tab.

Art Fletcher became interim manager after the death of Miller Huggins. But Fletcher turned down the permanent job, preferring to remain the Yankees' third-base coach, which he did through 1945, stealing countless signs along the way.

nants, and three world championships. Now neuritis, worry, and insomnia were chewing Huggins up. And an ugly red blemish had appeared under his left eye.

"I must have picked up some kind of infection," he told coach Art Fletcher. "I first noticed it last night. I'll have a doctor look at it after the game."

But before the game Huggins turned the team over to Fletcher and walked into the clubhouse to sit beneath a sun lamp. Five days later he was dead.

Eventually, a memorial would be erected in center field at the Stadium. For the moment, grieving players carried his casket out of the Little Church Around the Corner in Manhattan.

Even Ruth, who'd spent a decade shouting at the manager, defying his orders, and reportedly holding him over the platform railing of a moving train, wept openly. "A great little guy," he concluded, "was Hug."

He had played in this league for 16 years and worn pinstripes for 10, won 92 games as a left-handed pitcher, then became the greatest slugger in baseball history. And at 35 he was older, if not wiser.

And now that Miller Huggins was dead and coach Art Fletcher had turned down the chance to succeed him, Babe Ruth realized that Babe Ruth would be the perfect manager for the Yankees.

He'd mentioned as much to a newspaperman before Huggins' casket was even in the ground. During the off-season he put together an oral résumé and went up to owner Jacob Ruppert's brewery to apply in person.

"I told him that I knew how to handle young pitchers because I had been one myself," Ruth would say. "And I knew how to handle hitters because I was one myself. I told him everything I could think of, but when I had finished he just shook his head, kind of sadly."

"You can't manage yourself, Root," Ruppert concluded. "How do you expect to handle others?"

Only two men had managed the club since Ruppert and Cap Huston had bought it in 1915, yet Ruppert soon found that qualified candidates were scarce.

Another star was imported from the Red Sox in May—pitcher Red Ruffing, shown with Jacob Ruppert. Ruffing's success was not hindered by the absence of four toes on one foot from a mining accident as a youngster. He became the winningest righthander in Yankee history (231–124 in 15 New York seasons) and was an outstanding batter, hitting .300 six times as a Yankee.

Fletcher, who'd been Huggins' ablest lieutenant and had taken over command when blood poisoning had killed the Yankee manager 11 games from the end of the 1929 season, had managed the Phillies for four years. Long enough to know, Fletcher realized, that he'd rather remain a third-base coach. "I just turned down the best job in baseball," he told his wife. Next, general manager Ed Barrow approached former Pittsburgh manager Donie Bush—and found that he'd just signed on with the White Sox. And Eddie Collins, who'd managed the White Sox for two years, had consulted Athletics manager Connie Mack and decided that he wasn't quite ready for the most demanding job in baseball.

Finally, Barrow decided on a candidate and phoned Ruppert. "I'm bringing your new manager up to see you."

"Who is it?" Ruppert asked.

"Bob Shawkey."

At first glance it seemed a reasonable compromise. Shawkey had forged a brilliant career as a right-handed pitcher, winning 196 games and playing in five World Series. He had been a Yankee; he knew the standards, the expectations, the players. And from Ruth to the pitching staff the players knew him . . . probably too well.

After a decade of Huggins' reticence and disciplinary tendencies, the Yankees approached Shawkey's ascendancy as a time of indulgence and casually defied his training rules. The blowup came in Philadelphia after Al Simmons had belted a home run off Shawkey's old stablemate Waite Hoyt.

"What did you throw him?" Shawkey asked Hoyt.

"A fastball."

"Well, don't do it again. After this, make him hit your curveball."

"If I ever threw him my curveball," Hoyt shouted at Shawkey, "he'd hit it over the stand. Don't tell me how to pitch to Simmons. I'll go on pitching him my way."

"You'll pitch the way I tell you," Shawkey retorted, "or you won't pitch for me at all."

Two weeks later Hoyt and shortstop Mark Koenig were gone, traded to Detroit. Bob Meusel, the left fielder since 1921, had been sent to Cincinnati before the season opened.

In all, 36 men wore New York pinstripes that year. Meanwhile, the club was sliding to third, where it would finish the season 16 games behind Philadelphia.

"The trouble with this club," one veteran concluded after glancing around the clubhouse, "is

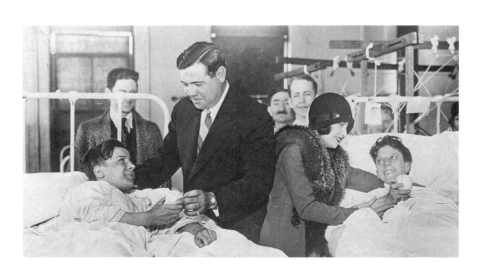

Babe Ruth really did visit ill youngsters. So did wife Claire sometimes. Here, they present autographed baseballs to two young fans injured in a stampede at the stadium.

that there are too many fellows on it who aren't Yankees."

Or that one Yankee was expected to control his former teammates. Though Ruppert and Barrow told Shawkey they were satisfied with his efforts and implied they'd rehire him, they came to realize they needed a dispassionate outsider, and prior to the World Series they approached a tough disciplinarian who'd never played a game in the majors yet had an instinctive feel for managing. His name was Joe McCarthy, and he would reestablish a dynasty in the Bronx.

Meanwhile, Shawkey, unaware, turned up at the team offices on 42nd Street hoping to talk contract. "I was heading for Barrow's office when the door opened and McCarthy came walking out," he said. "I took one look and turned around and got out of there. I knew what had happened."

Babe Ruth greets new manager Joe McCarthy, but the two would never be friendly.

The experiment had lasted for one season and one third-place finish and it had worked fitfully from the beginning. One Yankee, owner Jacob Ruppert and general manager Ed Barrow realized, could not manage his teammates. So Bob Shawkey, who'd been a compromise choice in the first place, was dismissed after the 1930 season, and this time Barrow was certain of his man.

The new manager would be well grounded in fundamentals, a gifted handler of personnel, and, most important, a stern disciplinarian. Fortunately, he would be immediately available.

Joe McCarthy, who'd brought the Cubs from the National League cellar to the World Series in four years, had just been let go. So Barrow contacted him just prior to the Series opener between the Athletics and Cardinals in Philadelphia and arranged a meeting in Ruppert's New York apartment.

But Ruppert, who was accustomed to personalizing salary negotiations with his world champions, quickly found that McCarthy drove a harder bargain.

"Those are my terms, Colonel," McCarthy insisted when Ruppert balked. "After all, you sent for me. I didn't ask to see you." And McCarthy had departed, with a stunned Ruppert pursuing him down the hallway shouting, "McCardy, McCardy, come back."

The McCarthy approach proved to be equally inflexible—and effective—with players. Though he'd never played a game in the major leagues, he'd learned a lifetime's worth of baseball during 20 years in the bushes.

Joe McCarthy had been a fine fielder and a clever tactician during his International League days and had stressed those qualities as a manager. His clubs turned textbook double plays and absorbed changing game situations instinctively. It was expected.

"I'm no second-division manager," he told the Yankees from the beginning. "And I won't stand for the second division."

McCarthy thought little of conventional psychology. "Had a pitcher with us this spring who majored in psychology," he once told writers. "Sent him to Newark last week." Yet McCarthy was an adept psychologist with a flair for dramatic symbolism.

He ordered the Yankees' uniforms a half size larger and had their caps squared off to make them appear bigger. He forbade pregame shaving in the clubhouse. And when he discovered a round table in a clubhouse corner when the team arrived for the 1931 opener he immediately summoned attendant Fred Logan.

"What's that?"

"Why, that's the card table," Logan informed him.

"Take it out of here." McCarthy paused. "Wait a minute. Get an axe. Break it up. Now take it out."

Then, turning to the players, he laid down Chapter One of McCarthy's Rules of Order. "This is a clubhouse, not a clubroom. Do your card playing in your homes. When you come in here, I want you to have your minds on baseball."

Lou Gehrig and Babe Ruth tied for the major-league home-run title with 46 each. Gehrig, whose total included three grand slams in four days, lost the outright championship on a teammate's blunder in Washington. Thinking Gehrig's drive over the fence had been caught for the third out, Lyn Lary ran off the basepath—costing Lou a 47th homer that for once would have topped Ruth.

New York might not catch the Athletics, who would make a triumphant last stand in 1931, but they would play more like the Yankees—with verve, abandon, and vigor. For the moment, Ruppert would settle for a stylistic improvement.

"I will stand for you finishing second this year because you are new in this league," the owner had told his manager in spring training. "But I warn you, McCardy. I don't like to finish second."

"Neither do I, Colonel," McCarthy had re-

Lefty Gomez led Yankee pitchers at 21–9 in the first of his four 20-victory seasons.

Fiery Ben Chapman stole 81 bases, nearly double the number by any other big leaguer in 1931. The fleet outfielder would lead the majors in thefts three straight seasons while averaging .309 at bat. Chapman hit three homers in a 1932 game—two inside the park.

Left: *Earle Combs' 29-game hitting streak tied the Yankee record that stood until Joe DiMaggio's 56 in 1941.*
Right: *Lyn Lary led the team in doubles with 35 and drove in 107 runs—the most in a season by a Yankee shortstop. Yet Lary would be out of a starting job the next year, replaced by rookie Frank Crosetti.*

plied. Ironically, McCarthy's clubs would finish second four of his first five seasons. They would also lay the foundation for the greatest dynasty in baseball history.

Half a century later, no photograph has ever been found. The only testimony beyond newspaper accounts are contradictory memories and an artist's reconstruction that freezes the moment: packed Wrigley Field stands as a backdrop, Cub catcher Gabby Hartnett squatting before impassive umpire Roy Van Graflan, and George Herman Ruth with his right index finger pointing to center field. Calling his shot.

Players and managers on both sides disagree on where Ruth pointed or whether he pointed at all. Chicago pitcher Charlie Root, who delivered the ball, swore it never happened and refused to play himself in the Hollywood version of Ruth's life. And seven persons brandished scuffed baseballs outside the park afterward, all claiming they had the genuine article.

But this much is beyond doubt: After taking two strikes from Root, Ruth crashed a prodigious

Babe Ruth crosses the plate on his 15th and final World Series home run—and his most fabled, the "called" shot against the Cubs at Chicago's Wrigley Field. He's congratulated by Lou Gehrig, who would homer on the next pitch.

Joe McCarthy and Cubs manager Charlie Grimm meet before the World Series opener at the Stadium. McCarthy would relish sweeping the team that had fired him two years earlier.

Charlie Root served up the Babe's storied "called" homer and would go to his grave denying that Ruth had pointed to the fence.

home run over the bleacher screen at the base of the center-field flagpole to break a 4–4 tie in the fifth inning of the third game to spur the Yankees to a 7–5 victory and a sweep of the 1932 World Series.

It was Ruth's 15th—and last—Series homer and, for pure dramatic impact, his most memorable. The Babe had called—and made—other shots: once at the Polo Grounds after an umpire had just ruled one home run an inch foul, another for an ailing boy named Johnny Sylvester, yet another to silence a drunk heckler at Fenway Park, and still another to break up a 13-inning game, enabling the Yankees to make a train.

Yet none of them was predicted and executed with as much flair, or before so hostile an audience. Although the two clubs had never played previously and the Yankees would prevail easily, the encounter was one of the most vitriolic in Series history, marked by bitter bench-jockeying throughout.

To begin with, the Cubs had dismissed Yankee manager Joe McCarthy two years earlier after he'd produced a second-place finish. Then, after former Yankee shortstop Mark Koenig had reemerged from the minors and hit .353 during the last 33 games to ensure the 1932 pennant, his Chicago teammates had voted him only a partial share of their winnings.

They were misers, the Yankees decided angrily. Nickel nursers. When the Cubs filed through the New York dugout on the way to their own before the Series opener at the Stadium, Ruth led a hooting serenade.

"Hey, you lousy bunch of cheapskates," he shouted. "Why do you associate with a bunch of bums like that, Mark?"

And once the Yankees had cleaned up the first two games and the Series shifted to Wrigley, the Ruthian chorus climbed an octave. "Hey, mugs," he called to the Cubs during batting practice before the third game. "You mugs aren't going to see Yankee Stadium any more this year. This is going to be over Sunday afternoon. Four straight."

As punctuation Ruth knocked nine balls into the bleacher seats. "I'd play for half my salary," he informed his hosts, "if I could hit in this dump all my life."

The Cubs responded in kind. Their female fans had jeered and spat on Babe and his wife Claire as they'd arrived at their hotel. Now, as Ruth came to bat in the first inning, they waved a white towel from the dugout steps. "If I had you on my team," trainer Andy Lotshaw hollered, "I'd hitch you to a wagon, you big balloon-belly."

Ruth answered with a three-run shot into the right-center-field bleachers. In the fifth, more abuse emanated from the Chicago dugout, augmented by aged fruit and vegetables from the grandstand. Ruth, delighted, flashed the choke sign to the Cub bench and peered out at Root on the mound. "If that bum throws one in here," he advised Hartnett, "I'll hit it over the fence again."

Root's first pitch split the plate. "I raised my hand," Ruth would say, "stuck out one finger and yelled strike one." Root sent another fastball toward the same spot, which Ruth treated the same way. Two fingers. Two strikes.

Kneeling in the on-deck circle, Lou Gehrig heard Ruth shout to Root: "I'm going to knock the next pitch down your goddamn throat."

Then, the Babe pointed to deepest center field. Or did he?

"If Ruth had pointed to the center-field stands I'd have knocked him on his fanny with the next pitch, believe me," Root insisted. "He just held up two fingers to show there were only two strikes and he still had one coming."

Other witnesses, including McCarthy and Hartnett, claim Ruth first pointed to off-duty Cub pitcher Guy Bush, who was heckling him from the dugout, and then to the mound, reminding Bush he'd be the next day's victim.

"What happened was this," insisted Zack Taylor, one of the Cubs' substitute catchers. "Our bench was yelling just awful things about Babe's personal life. Anyway, he turned to us. He put up two fingers. Two strikes. Then he put up one finger saying, 'I got one left.' And then he pointed to direct center field. He hit that pitch right into what must have been a 60-mile-an-hour wind coming off that lake, and I don't know how he did it."

As Ruth trotted around the bases on his 37-year-old legs, the Chicago dugout was dumbstruck. "There they were, all out on the top step and yelling their brains out," center fielder Earle Combs told Ruth afterward. "And then you connected and they watched it and then fell back as if they were being machine-gunned."

Ruth roared with laughter as he rounded the bases. "You lucky bum," he told himself. "Lucky, lucky." He stopped long enough at third to exe-

George Weiss joined the Yankees in 1932 and built a farm system that would yield great dividends. He would become general manager in 1948 and hire Casey Stengel as manager that fall. Together, they would direct the Yankees to 10 pennants and seven world titles during the next 10 seasons.

Left: *Newcomer Frank Crosetti was a key ingredient as the Bombers regained their crown—the first of four rookies ever to shortstop the Yankees to a world championship.* **Right:** *Red Ruffing led the league with 190 strikeouts, won 18 games, and added another victory in the World Series opener.*

A memorial to Miller Huggins was unveiled at the Stadium, the first of the monuments in center field.

cute a mock-formal bow to his tormentors, then headed home. "That's the first time I ever got the players and the fans going at the same time," he would boast. "I never had so much fun in all my life."

Gehrig, whose brilliant Series (.529 with three home runs) was overshadowed by Ruth's theatrics, followed with another homer to right field, and the Cubs were finished. The Yankees buried them, 13–6, the next afternoon for their third consecutive Series sweep.

It was the Babe's last hurrah, and he willingly let fans and sportswriters embroider it with mythic exaggeration. "I didn't exactly point to any spot like the flagpole," he would confess when pressed. "Anyway, I didn't mean to. I just sorta waved at the whole fence. All I wanted to do was give that thing a ride. Outa the park. Anywhere."

Before April was even played out they suspected that the odds had come back on them, that the Senators were grimly serious this time, that the summer would be long, turbulent, and ultimately empty.

In 1933 the Yankees fielded the same lineup that had won the 1932 pennant by 13 games and swept the Cubs for the world championship, but every important hitter had a less inspired season. Lou Gehrig's average dropped from .349 to .334, Babe Ruth's from .341 to .301, Tony Lazzeri's from .300 to .294, Earle Combs' from .321 to .298.

The pitching staff, which had led the American League in complete games and earned run average, fell off visibly. From the beginning, Washington, rallying around new 26-year-old player-manager Joe Cronin, literally fought them for the pennant.

The bad blood went back to the previous season when New York catcher Bill Dickey had broken Carl Reynolds' jaw with a punch after a collision at the plate. In their first 1933 series at Griffith Stadium, Senator second baseman Buddy Myer set the tone by sliding into first and spiking Gehrig, and Ruth by crashing into shortstop Cronin. Three days later New York outfielder Ben Chapman spiked Myer, who kicked Chapman, sparking a brawl that emptied both benches and several rows of the grandstand.

And after outfielder Dixie Walker had jumped

Lefty Gomez (right) opposed Boston's Ivy Andrews in the 1933 season opener. Gomez would lead the league in strikeouts and remained the Yankee ace with a 3.18 ERA and most wins, but his record slipped from 24–7 to 16–10, mirroring the Yankees' slide in fortunes.

Lou and Eleanor Gehrig were married on the season's final weekend, and—just like the movie—got a motorcycle escort from New Rochelle to the Stadium as the Iron Horse continued his consecutive-games streak. But—unlike the movie—Gehrig didn't homer for his bride; he went 0-for-4 as the Yankees lost.

With the dethroned Yankees playing out the string in the 1933 finale at the Stadium, Babe Ruth took the mound one last time. At 38, he defeated his old team, the Red Sox, 6–5, with the help of a homer from—of course—himself. Babe pitched five shutout innings before tiring, but went the distance, giving up a dozen hits. The effort exhausted him; he took an hour to dress afterward, and his left arm was so sore he had to wave with his right hand to the estimated crowd of 5,000 waiting outside. But his performance also wrapped up remarkable 94–46, 2.28–ERA pitching career, and a perfect 5–0 in five mound performances for the Yankees.

Myer from behind, Yankee pitcher Lefty Gomez had knocked down a plainclothes policeman with a bat, five spectators had been arrested, and Chapman, Myer, and Walker had been ejected, the battle flared anew. Washington pitcher Earl Whitehill challenged Chapman as he headed for the showers, Chapman punched Whitehill, and a dozen Senators pursued Chapman and Walker down the dugout stairs.

New York prevailed that day, 16–0, but when hostilities shifted to the Bronx a week later the Yankees stumbled into a bizarre double play that left them mumbling to themselves and convinced the Senators that pinstripes were not necessarily synonymous with infallibility.

With New York trailing 6–4 in the ninth inning, Gehrig and Walker on base and none out, Lazzeri lashed a line drive over Goose Goslin's head in right-center field. Gehrig cautiously hugged second, and Walker, head down, sprinted from first. As Goslin played the ball off the wall both men rounded third only a few feet apart and Washington catcher Luke Sewell braced for a stampede.

"I could see the ball coming in, and out of the corner of my eye caught sight of Gehrig running down the third base line," Sewell remembered years later. "Maybe Lou didn't think the play was going to be close as he didn't slide, and half broke his stride before he reached the plate."

But Cronin's relay was dead on, and Sewell tagged Gehrig standing up. "He hit me hard at the plate and spun me completely around," said Sewell. "But as I spun I caught sight of Walker

coming down. I dove down the line, blocking him off from the plate and also tagged him." Dickey grounded to second a moment later, and 35,000 New Yorkers sat mystified. "We went downhill from there," Ruth decided.

The Yankees managed to play at a .700 clip until June, then dropped 30 percentage points in eight days as the pitching soured and Ruth slumped. On June 23, Washington took over first place, then swept a symbolic July Fourth doubleheader (a year to the day after Reynolds' broken jaw) and stayed in command. In all the Senators won 14 of their 22 games with the Yankees, built a nine-game lead by September 10, and went on to win the pennant by seven.

Meanwhile, back at 161st Street, memories of 1932 had vanished. With home attendance off by nearly a quarter of a million, the Yankees had Ruth, at 38, pitch the season finale with Boston. He won 6–5 and hit a home run. It had come to that.

The box score still included his name, as it had daily for more than two decades. He made the All-Star team and by conventional standards his statistics—batting .288, with 22 home runs and 84 RBIs—were impressive enough. But they were no longer Ruthian—and the Babe knew it.

He was 39 years old now, and after 2,349 games and nights filled with overindulgence, his body had come apart from the ground up. "It was becoming more and more difficult for me to drive my legs over the outfield grass," Ruth conceded. He would play in only 125 games in 1934, frequently giving way to pinch runners Sammy Byrd (a.k.a. Babe Ruth's Legs) and Myril Hoag in the late innings, and he would play for less money.

As a concession to Depression economics and his own dropping productivity, Ruth had agreed to still another pay cut, this time to $35,000, which was $45,000 less than he'd commanded three years earlier.

On a Yankee roster that included Lou Gehrig and Bill Dickey, both of whom were hitting for better averages and playing every day, Ruth had become a nostalgic period piece, frequently at odds with manager Joe McCarthy, whose job he wanted.

"McCarthy and Ruth barely spoke to one an-

They don't pose for pictures like this anymore. Clowning around in Boston, former Yankee Billy Werber (right) catches Ben Chapman picking the pocket of Al Schacht, the Red Sox coach. Opponents kept a wary eye on Chapman, who led the majors in stolen bases for a third straight year.

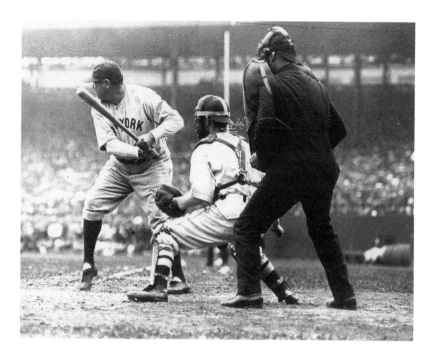

Although he could still pull the trigger, (racking up his 700th homer), Babe Ruth suffered through a wretched season as his batting average dwindled to .288 and his home run production to 22. At season's end, he was gone, chasing a managing dream that never materialized.

other," said reserve pitcher Burleigh Grimes. "Babe wanted to manage, and he didn't particularly care for Joe. There wasn't a hell of a lot Joe could do about Ruth. Christ, the man was an institution."

Yet when a New York columnist polled the team anonymously in June, they unanimously felt that Ruth should be removed from the lineup. It never happened; still, Ruth fretted that he'd blown a golden chance at a new career.

Detroit owner Frank Navin had called about a manager's job the previous fall, and Ruth, about to embark on a barnstorming tour of Hawaii, had brushed him off.

"Can't it wait until I get back?"

"No," Navin had replied. "It can't wait. I would like to get this matter settled."

So while Ruth clouted baseballs into the Pacific, Navin bought Athletics catcher Mickey Cochrane and made him player-manager. Late in 1934, Cochrane was managing the Tigers to the first of two consecutive pennants. "One of the great boners of my career," Ruth concluded, and resolved to see owner Jacob Ruppert about the Yankee job, just as he had done in 1929 and 1930.

"Well, Root, this is a surprise," Ruppert said when Ruth turned up at the brewery later in the season. "What's on your mind?"

"Are you satisfied with McCarthy as your manager?"

"Why, yes."

"Well, I'm not."

"Root, I know you would like to manage this ball club. Don't think I haven't considered the matter. I have. But this is a big business, Root, and you are unproven as a manager. No one has a greater admiration for you as a player than I have. As a manager . . . I don't know."

Ruppert paused. Perhaps Ruth would consider managing the Yankees' top farm club.

"Would you go to Newark, Root?"

"No. I won't go to Newark or any other minor league club. Why should I? I'm a big leaguer. Why should I go to the minors?"

"I think you're being foolish," Ruppert told him.

"Maybe," Ruth replied, "but that's the way I feel about it."

"Then I can do nothing."

The Yankees went on to finish seven games behind the Tigers, and Ruth, disgusted, went off to watch the World Series. As he boarded the train leaving St. Louis for Detroit and the final two games, an engineer poked his head out.

"How many home runs you going to hit for the Yankees next year?"

"The hell with the Yankees," Ruth told him. "I wouldn't play with them again if they gave me the club. I'm quitting."

A newspaperman overheard the conversation and printed Ruth's comments; Ruppert and general manager Ed Barrow read them in New York the next morning. While Ruth was in Japan on another barnstorming tour, they decided to unload him.

"They had an interesting contract waiting for me when I returned," Ruth would say. One dol-

Lefty Gomez (left) and Red Ruffing once again were the Yankees' potent one-two lefty-righty pitching punch, accounting for nearly half the team's 94 victories—45 wins, 20 more than the previous year. Gomez led the league with 26 wins, a 2.33 ERA, 25 complete games, and 158 strikeouts. Ruffing won 19 with 19 complete games and 149 K's.

lar, Ruppert decreed, unless Ruth proved worthy of more in spring training. So after Ruth had the Boston Braves owner, Judge Emil Fuchs, over for dinner on a Sunday night in February he dropped by Ruppert's office the next morning.

"You're still satisfied with McCarthy as your manager?"

"Yes."

"And there is no chance that you will change your mind?"

Red Rolfe backed up third base and shortstop as a rookie before becoming a hot-corner fixture. An All-Star fielder, the Dartmouth product was a solid .289 hitter during his 10 Yankee seasons and a backbone of four straight world-champion teams, 1936–39.

"Fordham Johnny" Murphy was 14–10 as a rookie. The next season he'd move to the bullpen and become the league's premier relief pitcher. In 1969, he was general manager of the Miracle Mets.

"No."

Ruth retreated to the anteroom to fetch Fuchs, who informed Ruppert that he was willing to purchase Ruth and bring him back to Boston, where he'd begun his career in 1914. Whereupon the Colonel handed Ruth a paper containing his unconditional release. Barrow had called every American League club, and Ruth had cleared waivers. He was free to go. "I think this is what you want, isn't it, Root?" Ruppert asked him.

"But the price?" Fuchs asked. "What do you want for him?"

"Nothing," Ruppert decided. "Ruth has been a great ballplayer for this club. I am sorry we could not satisfy him now. But I do not wish to stand

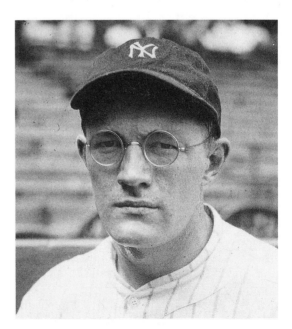

Yale's Johnny Broaca, another in the Yankees' bumper rookie crop, was 12–9 including a one-hit shutout.

Lou Gehrig's consecutive-games streak nearly came to a crashing halt during a midseason exhibition game at Norfolk, Virginia. He was struck on the head by a pitch from a Yankee farmhand who didn't like him. He was unconscious over three minutes, but X-rays revealed a concussion and not the feared skull fracture. Gehrig played game 1,415 the next day in Washington after squeezing his swollen head into a cap by cutting the seams.

in his way now to make any profit from his opportunity to better himself."

So Ruth, at 40, returned to Boston and a club that would tumble from fourth to the National League cellar and lose 115 games in 1935. He was to earn $35,000 and a percentage of profits as club vice president, assistant to manager Bill McKechnie, and sometime right fielder. "More titles than an incurable lodge joiner," joked Ruth, but the adventure quickly soured.

There would be no profits. McKechnie hadn't been consulted about an assistant. And Ruth, who'd had trouble in the field for several seasons ("My old dogs just couldn't take it any longer"), could barely make contact at the plate.

"The kids were striking me out or making me pop up on balls I could have hit out of the lot a few years before," Ruth admitted. "It was a rotten feeling."

After 28 games his average had shrunk to .181 and his value as a drawing card—the real reason Fuchs had sought him—had dwindled. "People wouldn't have come out," Ruth said, "to see Saint Peter himself hit .181."

There was one last hurrah in Pittsburgh, where Ruth hit three home runs in a game for the fourth time in his career. It would, he thought, have been a fine note to retire on, but

Fuchs, with one eye on the box office, begged him to stay on at least through a Decoration Day doubleheader at Philadelphia.

"They had advertised me," Ruth shrugged. "But I never should have listened." The Babe played the first inning of the opener, striking out in his only at bat before limping off with a charley horse. It was the last time, after 2,503 games and 714 home runs, that the name George Herman Ruth ever appeared in a box score. *New York Post* beat man Jerry Mitchell added the epitaph as his lead paragraph the next morning: "He's nobody's Baby now."

The left foot had gone numb one summer night in 1934 while he was crammed into the back of a San Francisco jitney cab, but Joe DiMaggio hadn't realized it.

"I jumped out and my left knee popped like a pistol," he would recall. "I'm sure you could have heard it down the block. I went down as though I'd been shot. The pain was terrific, like a whole set of aching teeth in my knee, and I don't know why I didn't pass out."

Hospital doctors diagnosed sprained tendons and prescribed hot towels and Epsom salts, but those proved useless. DiMaggio's leg gave way again the next morning, and after he was forced to walk around the bases following a home run one day later, he was encased from ankle to thigh in an aluminum splint. Word was quickly relayed from the West Coast to every major league club: The best minor league player in the country was damaged goods.

Within days, as DiMaggio's market value (which had spiraled to $70,000) diminished, so did scout attendance at San Francisco Seals' games. But the Yankees' Bill Essick was not a man to jump to conclusions. When DiMaggio returned to the lineup three weeks later, Essick carefully inspected his running stride and batting pivot for evidence of strain and found none.

"Don't give up on DiMaggio," he advised New York general manager Ed Barrow by telephone. "Everybody out here thinks I'm crazy, but I'm not. I still think he's all right. Let me watch him for a couple of weeks more, and I'll have the final answer on him."

When Essick's hunch had hardened into conviction, he called Barrow again. "Buy DiMaggio.

While the Ruth-less Yankees were finishing second again, 20-year-old Joe DiMaggio blossomed with the San Francisco Seals.

Lou Gehrig wasn't always smiling as he is here with manager Joe McCarthy. Although he was finally out of Babe Ruth's shadow, his batting average fell 34 points from 1934, and he had 46 fewer RBIs and 19 fewer home runs. But the captain still led Yankee offense with a .329 average, 30 homers, 119 RBIs.

I think you can get him cheap. They're all laughing at me, but I know I'm right."

"What's the name of the best orthopedic man in San Francisco?" Barrow asked.

"Dr. Richard Spencer," Essick replied.

"Have him check the kid's knee," Barrow said. "And tell [Seals' owner Charley] Graham if the doc okays it, we'll talk business with him."

Spencer's prognosis was optimistic, and a deal was struck. The Yankees would give Graham $25,000 and five anonymities (outfielder Ted Norbert, first baseman Les Powers, third baseman Ed Farrell, and pitchers Jim Densmore and Floyd Newkirk). DiMaggio would stay with the Seals through 1935, take therapy, and report to New York's training camp for the 1936 season. If the purchase of Babe Ruth from Boston for $100,000 or so had been a bargain 15 years earlier, this was a steal.

DiMaggio would wear pinstripes for 13 seasons, bat .325, and serve as cornerstone for 10 pennant winners and nine world championship clubs. For now, he was merely a 19-year-old son of a fisherman with a landlubber's stomach and a natural swing.

Joseph Paul DiMaggio was the eighth of nine children of Sicilian immigrants who felt that base-

George Selkirk was Babe Ruth's replacement in right field—even wearing the Babe's number 3, which wouldn't be retired for another decade. Though booed at first, he proved the team's second most potent hitter, batting .312 with 94 RBIs.

Red Ruffing led in victories with 16 and batted .339, including 8-for-18 .444 as a pinch hitter. No other Yankee regular pitcher has ever hit that high in a season.

Earle Combs retired at mid-season at age 36, not fully recovered from multiple injuries (including a fractured skull) suffered when he crashed into a wall in St. Louis the previous season.

ball was a Sunday thing, hardly secure enough as a profession. While two older brothers had joined their father aboard the family fishing boat, the *Rosalie D,* Joe had dropped out of Galileo High School, worked odd jobs, and played shortstop for local sandlot teams.

"*Lagnuso* [lazy]," his father had muttered, but young Joe was entranced. A third brother, Vince, had signed with the Seals. Before long the San Francisco Missions, the Seals' Pacific Coast League rivals, were offering Joe $150 a month. Instead, the Seals grabbed him. He hit safely in 61 straight games during his first full season in 1933, ended up batting .340 with 169 RBIs, and became the league's top drawing card.

And once the knee healed, DiMaggio dominated, just as Essick had predicted—.398, 34 home runs, and 154 RBI's in 1935.

Meanwhile, the Yankees were finishing three games behind Detroit in the American League race, with a transitional outfield of Jesse Hill,

Lou Gehrig was kayoed again, this time at Boston's Fenway Park. But he kept his iron-man streak alive, passing the 1,600-game milestone in August.

Johnny Broaca (left) was the second-winningest pitcher at 15–7. He is joined here by rookie Vito Tamulis, who was 10–5.

Ben Chapman, and George Selkirk. Babe Ruth was gone. Earle Combs, never the same after having fractured his skull in 1934, was playing out his last season as a reserve.

So a job was waiting, along with limousine service, provided by a couple of fellow San Francisco Italians—second baseman Tony Lazzeri and shortstop Frank Crosetti. They delivered DiMaggio to the Yankees' training base at St. Petersburg where pitcher Red Ruffing stared at him and growled.

"So you're the great DiMaggio."

Giants traveling secretary Eddie Brannick, who worked across the Harlem River from the Yankees but within their range, had dubbed them the Window Breakers—with due respect, of course. For offensive power and balance, not even the 1927 Yankees with their Murderers' Row were a match.

Where Babe Ruth and Lou Gehrig had carried that club, hitting 107 of its 158 home runs, every 1936 regular except center fielder Jake Powell belted at least 10. They led the majors in homers (182), runs (1,065), and slugging average (.483) and the American League in defense and pitching.

They controlled the American League pennant race by June, clinching it earlier (September 9) and winning it more easily (by 19½ games) than any other club in history.

Now Brannick's Giants were seeing the Yankees close-up, in a subway Series for the first time since 1923, and also baffling them—for at least one game. Carl Hubbell, who'd won his last 16 games of the regular season, had uncorked his screwball in the murk and rain of the Polo Grounds and beaten the Yankees 6–1 while allowing only one fly ball, a home run by George Selkirk.

The breakout came in game two, then the longest nine-inning Series game ever played (2 hours, 49 minutes), and it quickly dashed any illusions as the Yankees drummed out a record 18 runs, tattooing five Giant pitchers for 17 hits and setting or equaling six Series records. With President Franklin D. Roosevelt looking on from a box seat, every Yankee starter hit safely and scored a run. And catcher Bill Dickey and second baseman Tony Lazzeri each knocked in five.

By the third inning, when Lazzeri hit the second grand slam in Series history, the Yankees, who had already chased Giant starter Hal Schumacher and reliever Al Smith, were working on Dick Coffman and were leading, 9–1. By the ninth,

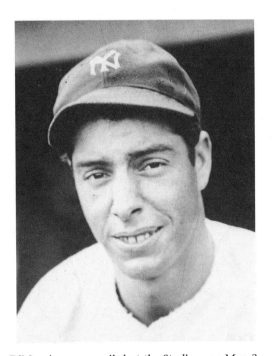

Joe DiMaggio was unveiled at the Stadium on May 3. (The heralded 21-year-old had missed the first 16 games after a training-room heat lamp burned his left foot.) Batting third, ahead of Lou Gehrig, he tripled and singled twice in his debut, added three more hits the next day, and soon had an 18-game hitting streak. He went on to bat .323 and slug .576, collecting 206 hits (including 44 doubles, 15 triples, and 29 homers, two of them in one inning), scoring 132 runs, and driving in 125.

Rookie Joe DiMaggio is welcomed by manager Joe McCarthy and captain Lou Gehrig.

they were laughing in the dugout as Harry Gumbert, who'd been 11–3 during the season, was being strafed for six more runs, including a three-run shot by Dickey.

"Does he ever get anybody out in the National League?" Gehrig asked a teammate. The final was 18–4—"I let 'em score a couple runs to make it close," cracked Yankee starter Lefty Gomez—and the Giants never recovered.

They lost game three in the eighth, 2–1, when a bouncer by Frank Crosetti caromed off pitcher Fred Fitzsimmons' glove. Then Gehrig busted Hubbell with a two-run homer in game four and it was all but over. The Yankees cleaned up the Series back at the Polo Grounds in game six with a seven-run ninth inning, scoring five before the Giants could retire a man, and in the 13–5 after-

They were called the "Window Breakers," baseball's most powerful lineup ever, as the Yankees led the majors in homers (a record 182), slugging, and runs. While the Yankees batted an even .300 as a team, the starting lineup hit a collective .318 (from left): Joe DiMaggio (.323), Frank Crosetti (.288), Tony Lazzeri (.287), Bill Dickey (.362), Lou Gehrig (.354), Jake Powell (.306) and George Selkirk (.308). Only third baseman Red Rolfe (.319) missed the photo.

The Window Breakers powered the Yankees to a runaway pennant, their first without Babe Ruth. The 19½-game margin over the defending world champion Tigers is the largest in Yankee history—and the September 9 clinch the club's earliest ever.

Tony Lazzeri went on a batting rampage at Philadelphia in May, launching three homers (two of them grand slams) and narrowly missing a fourth that went for a two-run triple. In a 25–2 runaway, he drove in 11 runs, still a league record. That put the power-hitting second baseman on his way to five homers and a still-majors-record 15 RBIs in two games (as the Yankees outscored the Athletics, 40–2) and seven homers in four games. In the fall, Lazzeri would crunch only the second grand slam in World Series history, the first by a Yankee, during an 18–4 rout of the Giants at the Polo Grounds.

Joe McCarthy retreaded Pat Malone, a two-time 20-game winner under him with the Cubs, as a Yankee reliever. The 33-year-old right-hander became the league's top fireman with eight wins and nine saves out of the bullpen, and was 12–4 overall.

glow the Yankees were swilling championship champagne.

It was their first in four years, their first ever without Babe Ruth, and it marked the birth of the greatest dynasty any professional sport had ever known. Under McCarthy, who'd finally shed the "Second Place Joe" label, New York would win the next three world championships with

the loss of one game, and six of the next seven American League pennants.

By 1964 the string would stretch to 22 pennants and 16 championships in 29 years. And they would do it with the distinctly crisp and businesslike style that McCarthy had instilled.

The roistering, profane behavior of the Ruth era, with its midnight revels and clubhouse brawls, was taboo. McCarthy, a laconic, jut-jawed disciplinarian, had made that clear. In June, with the

Jacob Ruppert leads the locker-room celebration at the Polo Grounds after the Yankees beat the Giants, four games to two, for the first of four straight world championships.

Bill Dickey batted a career-best .362 in 112 games, 107 as a catcher–the highest batting average ever by a major-leaguer catching 100 or more games. He hit 22 homers, contributing to a career-high .617 slugging average.

club crashing its way to the pennant, he'd shipped fielder Ben Chapman, a .302 lifetime hitter, to Washington for Powell because he felt Chapman was temperamental and divisive. Then, when Powell administered a hotfoot to a teammate at a Boston train station during his first road trip, McCarthy led him aside. "You're with the Yan-

kees now," he told Powell. "We don't do those things."

The Yankee way would be three sets of immaculate pinstripes worn half a size large, to make them appear more imposing, and a jacket and necktie off the field at all times. And, as McCarthy had made it plain from the very first, there would be no card playing or pregame shaving in the clubhouse—the clubhouse was the office, after all, and baseball was a business. No public scenes, no late nights.

The symbols would be Gehrig, the modest workhorse who was named MVP at 33, and rookie Joe DiMaggio, who walked into spring training at age 21, walked out with the left fielder's job, and hit .323 with 29 home runs despite missing the first 16 games with a burned foot. He called the manager Mr. McCarthy and said he'd happily play the sun field in Yankee Stadium.

"Ruth would never play it," he was told.

"I'll play it," DiMaggio decided, "if Mr. McCarthy wants me to."

That was the Yankee way.

With the count 3-and-1 in the fifth inning, a man on first, and Black Mike himself crowding

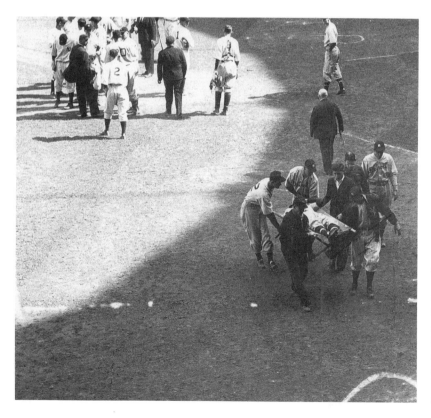

A near-fatal beaning occurred at Yankee Stadium in May, when a pitch by Bump Hadley struck Detroit catcher-manager Mickey Cochrane. Cochrane suffered a triple skull fracture. He recovered, and though he never played again, his name would live on at the Stadium—the Mickey that a future Yankee named Mantle was named after.

the plate, Yankee pitcher Bump Hadley wanted something low on the inside corner. He never thought of a duster. Not at 3-and-1. But somehow his next pitch screeched toward Detroit star catcher Mickey Cochrane's head. "The ball sailed," Hadley would say, horrified. "I don't know why. It just did."

And Cochrane, the Tigers' marvelously combative player-manager, lost sight of it six feet from the plate, threw up his hands, and tried to duck.

The ball struck with a dull thud just above the right temple and Cochrane fell on his face in the Yankee Stadium dirt. "Good God Almighty," he groaned—and passed out.

For three days Cochrane lay unconscious and near death at New York's St. Elizabeth's Hospital, his skull fractured in three places. "The only time I came to," he would say, "was when they were tapping my spine."

When the danger passed, doctors told Cochrane that at 34 his playing days were over. He could manage if he liked, but not for another several weeks. And so, on May 25, the 1937 American League pennant race between New York and Detroit came to a symbolic end.

The Yankees had actually taken the lead two days earlier, and with Cochrane, the Tigers' spiritual heart, out of action, Detroit would never seriously challenge again. New York retained the pennant, this time by 13 games, and prepared to meet the Giants in the World Series for the second straight year, this time as 3–1 favorites.

The duel was that predictable. In fact, Hearst newspaper columnist Bill Corum said that Giant manager Bill Terry refused to bet him on the outcome. "I'm no sucker," he claimed Terry told him.

From the beginning the Yankees hammered their former landlords and did it ironically for good measure. They pounced on Giant ace Carl Hubbell, who'd dazed them in the 1936 opener, racking him for seven runs in the sixth inning of the first game, and won 8–1 at the Stadium.

The next afternoon the Yankees pummeled three Giant pitchers and posted the same score. "Change your signals," a fan wired Terry, but it was useless. No National League club, no club anywhere, was a match for Joe McCarthy's Yankees that year.

He'd named five of them—first baseman Lou Gehrig, third baseman Red Rolfe, center fielder Joe DiMaggio, catcher Bill Dickey, and pitcher Lefty Gomez—to the starting All-Star team that July and they'd beaten the National League, 8–3, by themselves. Gehrig had knocked in four runs, Rolfe had tripled home the winner, and Gomez wound up with the victory.

So deep was their roster and so confident were they of the talent ripening on their minor league vines that the Yankees would willingly let second baseman Tony Lazzeri go to the Cubs after the season for the waiver price after hitting .400 in the 1937 Series, capping a dozen years in pinstripes. He was 34, after all, and they had "a kid in Newark" named Joe Gordon who seemed ready. Gordon would play seven years in a New York uniform before the Yankees traded him to Cleveland for Allie Reynolds, who'd pitch in six Series for them. There would always be "a kid in Newark," thanks to the farming instincts of general managers Ed Barrow and George Weiss.

"I read the papers every day to see how Tommy Henrich and Red Rolfe were doing down in Triple-A ball," outfielder George Selkirk had admitted several years before. "If they had gone four for four, you'd better believe it made me try harder."

Meanwhile, New York still had five Hall of Famers in Gehrig, DiMaggio, Dickey, Gomez, and Red Ruffing, and when they went back across the Harlem River for game three there were thou-

To the delight of Joe McCarthy, Lefty Gomez bounced back from two mediocre seasons. After leading the league in wins (21) and the majors in ERA (2.33) and shutouts (6), he won twice and posted a 1.50 ERA in the World Series. It was the fourth time Gomez won 21 or more— and the last.

After spring training workouts with John Jr., Johnny Murphy went on to his best season—13–4. Twelve of those victories came in relief, along with 10 hard-to-get saves.

sands of empty seats in the unreserved sections of the Polo Grounds.

Only 37,385 people watched the Yankees rub out the Giants, 5–1, on a Saturday afternoon. It was a Series virtually devoid of suspense, and the Yankees closed it out in five games with Gomez, a .147 lifetime hitter, driving in the winning run of the 4–2 finale.

The only Giant outburst had come in the second inning of game four when they scored six runs on seven singles and an error. It proved to be their swan song; after three National League pennants in five years, the Giants wouldn't win another until Bobby Thomson's "shot heard 'round the world" sank the Dodgers in the 1951 playoff. There was no longer any question as to who owned New York.

Jacob Ruppert, sick in bed, heard the news from McCarthy.

"Colonel, you're the champion again," his manager told him.

"Fine, fine, McCardy," Ruppert nodded. "Do it again next year."

The mandate was that simple, that inflexible. "Those were the only orders I ever got from him after each World Series," McCarthy would muse. "Do it again next year. And generally we did. You've got to follow orders, right?"

Rival managers Joe McCarthy of the Yankees and Bill Terry of the Giants meet again before yet another subway Series.

For seven years he'd fed them nothing but haze from his seamless three-quarter overhand delivery. "I just rare back and fog 'er through," Dizzy Dean would say.

But the fastball had fled after a freakish afternoon at the 1937 All-Star Game when Cleveland outfielder Earl Averill had smashed the big toe of Dean's planted left foot with a line drive through the box. "Fractured, hell," Dean groaned to teammates. "It's broke."

Doctors told him it was foolish to hurry back into action—the Cardinals were a fourth-place club that year—but Dean had shrugged. He would favor the toe, develop a jerky unbalanced delivery, and throw sidearm.

"Don't, Jerome, don't," advised Braves manager Bill McKechnie when St. Louis came to Boston. "You'll hurt your arm." As predicted, Dean felt something snap in his right arm late in the game and watched it fall limp. "You've done it, Jerome," moaned McKechnie, who was coaching third base. "You've done it."

Jay Hanna Dean (a.k.a. Jerome), who'd won 102 games in four years and led the Cardinals' Gashouse Gang to the 1934 world championship, won only one more game in 1937. When doctors found a frightening assortment of inflamed muscles in his back and shoulder during the off-season, they told him he'd never again throw normally. No more fastballs. No more fog.

Still the Cubs gave the Cardinals a club-record $185,000 and three players for Dean in the spring of 1938. "We got Dizzy's spirit, courage, and enthusiasm in addition to his arm," reasoned owner Philip Wrigley.

Chicago also wrung seven critical victories from Dean's new repertoire of soft junk, curves, and "nuthin' balls," and came from the middle of the National League pack to overtake Pittsburgh for the pennant in the final week.

While the Yankees had won the American League race by 9½ games over Boston, the Cubs had struggled, firing manager Charlie Grimm in midseason. They needed a 10-game winning streak and player-manager Gabby Hartnett's miracle home run "in the gloamin'" to beat Pittsburgh, which had already ordered Series press badges and built a new press box atop the Forbes Field roof.

Still, National League President Ford Frick had told the players that the Yankees could be taken.

Joe DiMaggio returned to California, where he trained with his hometown San Francisco Seals while holding out for more money. During the stalemate, the Yankee Clipper missed the season opener. Finally, he signed for the $25,000 originally offered instead of the $40,000 he sought. When he showed up at the Stadium, fans booed him for the first time. But DiMaggio turned the jeers to cheers by leading the team in batting (.324), hits (194), homers (32), and RBIs (140).

They'd had a slow start (probably because of Joe DiMaggio, who'd held out for $40,000, signed for $25,000, and missed nine games), hadn't taken over first place until July 12, and lost 11 of their final 15 after clinching the pennant.

"They've let down," Frick insisted, "and it'll be difficult for them to get back." Yet only one of the Cubs, former Yankee second baseman Tony Lazzeri, seemed to believe it. "We're as good as they are," he growled. "We'll beat their brains out."

Most of his teammates weren't as certain. "How do you figure this Series?" they asked New York sportswriters. "Do you think we can win?"

Now the Cubs were down a game to the Yankees in the World Series, and Hartnett had decided to go with Dean, a 27-year-old with a 65-year-old arm. For seven innings Dean had New York batters—"DiMaggio, Dickey, all those fellas"—popping up his goofballs and grinding them into the dirt of Wrigley Field.

"My arm was about to kill me," he'd admit. "At times it felt as if the bone was sticking out of the flesh. I had nothing on the ball. I was making a big motion, a big windmill motion, and then throwing off-speed balls."

Monte Pearson pitched the first no-hitter at Yankee Stadium, breezing to a 13–0 victory over his former Cleveland teammates on August 27. Only two Indians reached, on walks, and both were erased on double plays; so Pearson faced only the minimum 27 batters. Pearson ended up at 16–7, third on the Yankee staff behind Red Ruffing (21–7), and Lefty Gomez (18–12), and added one more victory in the World Series sweep of the Cubs.

But for a crazy second-inning pratfall, when third baseman Stan Hack and shortstop Billy Jurges had cracked heads chasing Joe Gordon's dribbler through the hole, Dean would have been leading 3–0. Instead it was 3–2 and Dean was hanging in gamely.

He got Gordon and Myril Hoag to hit into force plays in the eighth, then watched shortstop Frank Crosetti, New York's weakest bat, step into the box. Dean worked him to 2–2, then slipped a curve past for a third strike—but the umpire disagreed

Joe Gordon enjoyed a notable rookie season, a stylish power-hitting second baseman who delivered 25 homers and 97 RBIs.

Thus reprieved, Crosetti whacked the next pitch into the left-field bleachers, scoring Hoag ahead of him. "That was the lowest moment of my life," Dean would say. "I knowed my arm was gone. l couldn't break a pane of glass. But Crosetti never was a powerful hitter, so I figured I had a chance."

Instead Dean, scowling and cursing, watched Crosetti circle the bases, a .245 lifetime hitter celebrating his only Series homer. "You couldn't a done that five years ago," Dean shouted at him. "I know, Diz," Crosetti admitted. "I know."

End of game, end of Dean, end of Series—for practical purposes, at least. Not that the Cubs had expected much more. New York had swept them six years earlier when Babe Ruth had called his shot.

Now Crosetti had them down two games to none, and the Series was shifting to Yankee Stadium, where the Cubs had never won. The result was predictable—5–2 and 8–3 victories for New York, who worked over nine Cub pitchers—and a grim train ride back to Chicago, with Hartnett muttering that he'd be happy to unload the entire roster during the off-season.

Hartnett was half as good as his word—four starters and two regular pitchers were shipped out—and the Cubs didn't contend again until 1945. Dean, his arm consigned to the grave, won only nine more games, thus rewriting a basic rule of anatomy. The toebone was connected to the armbone.

Dizzy Dean's already sore arm ached even more after he lost to the Yankees in game two of the World Series, but not too much to prevent the Cub veteran from shaking hands with Claire and Babe Ruth before the next game.

The extroverted Dean would return to the Stadium as a broadcaster on 1950–51 Yankee telecasts, teaming with Mel Allen in a unique mix of accents. New York never warmed up to Ol' Diz's unsophisticated, folksy style of diction-fracturing and name-mangling—in which Stengel was "Stingle" and Rizzuto became "Rizooti," Henrich "Hendricks" or "Henry," and Berra "Barry" or "Barrow."

Lou Gehrig's iron-man streak of 2,130 consecutive games ended in Detroit on a day in May, and he would watch from the dugout for the remainder of the season. The dying captain had played his last game.

Nobody wanted to leave the dressing room. Nobody wanted to talk. The Yankees pulled on their uniforms silently that afternoon, stalling for time at their lockers. Then coach Art Fletcher walked slowly over to Ellsworth Dahlgren and whispered a sentence no Yankee but Lou Gehrig had heard in 14 years—"Babe," Fletcher said, "you're playing first base today."

Dahlgren, stunned, felt his teammates patting his back and wishing him good luck as he headed down the ramp to the dugout at Detroit's Briggs Stadium and came face to face with Gehrig.

"There were tears in our eyes as we looked at each other," Dahlgren said. "Then I heard myself saying: 'Come on, Lou, you better get out there. You've put me in a terrible spot.'"

"Go on, get out there," Gehrig urged him, "and knock in some runs." Then Henry Louis Gehrig shuffled out to home plate as New York's captain and handed over the lineup card to um-

pire Steve Basil without a word. Basil glanced at it casually—Crosetti, Rolfe, DiMaggio, Yankee names never seemed to change—then looked up abruptly.

"Dahlgren, first base?" he noticed. "Hey, what's this, Lou?" Then he realized that Gehrig was weeping. After 2,130 consecutive games, all of them in Yankee pinstripes, the Iron Horse was benching himself.

His legs had turned to lead. His arms had lost their power, his hands their deftness. Gehrig had slogged through 1938—his worst season since his rookie days—hitting .295 with only 29 home runs and managing just four singles in a World Series where his teammates had feasted on Cub pitching.

The malaise had continued during spring training, where he was slow afield and powerless at the plate, even though he was making contact. "He tried to go from first to third on a single in a game at Clearwater," teammate Tommy Henrich noticed. "And when he went around second it looked like he was trying to run uphill at a 45-degree angle."

Maybe it was his age, his peers guessed. Gehrig was 36 and never had been a gifted athlete; his strength, determination, and hard work had

Babe Dahlgren was Lou Gehrig's successor at first base. "Go out there, Babe, and knock in some runs," Gehrig ordered the day he sat down. Dahlgren did, slamming a homer and double during a 22–2 rout of the Tigers. He also contributed "two fielding gems," according to the New York Times. He went on to hit 15 homers and drive in 89 runs while leading league first basemen in double plays. Dahlgren played the position capably if not spectacularly for two seasons despite the pressure of following a legend.

made him a Hall of Famer. "These big guys, they go fast," Detroit's Ty Cobb had remarked. "When they fall apart it's like the one-hoss shay."

Gehrig had voluntarily taken a $5,000 salary cut. But the job, manager Joe McCarthy said, was his. "The kid stays in," McCarthy told all inquisitors, "until he takes himself out."

Now, on May 2, eight games into the 1939 season, his batting average had tumbled to .143 with one run batted in.

In the last game, a 3–2 loss to the second-division Senators, Gehrig, according to John Kieran of the *Times*, resembled "a man trying to lift heavy trunks into a truck." And when pitcher Johnny Murphy congratulated him for making an easy ninth-inning putout, Gehrig made up his mind.

"That's when I decided to quit," he said. "It was an ordinary routine play, and I should have been on the bag waiting for the throw. When they start feeling sorry for you, it's time to hang up your glove."

So when McCarthy arrived at the Book-Cad-

illac hotel in Detroit for the next series, Gehrig was waiting for him.

"I'm benching myself, Joe."

"Why?"

"For the good of the team. I just can't seem to get going, and nobody has to tell me how bad I've been and how much of a drawback I've been to the team. I've been thinking—the time has come for me to quit."

McCarthy sighed. "All right, Lou. Take a rest. I'll put Babe Dahlgren on first base today. But remember, that's your position, and whenever you want it back just walk out and take it."

But Lou Gehrig never played another game. Seven weeks later the Mayo Clinic informed him he was suffering from amyotrophic lateral sclerosis, a form of infantile paralysis. As his spine was hardening, his central nervous system was deteriorating. There was no known cure, doctors told him, and no chance of playing again. At best, he had a 50–50 chance to live.

Still, Gehrig was the captain and as long as he could put on a uniform and walk he would carry out his duties. So while his teammates cruised to a record fourth straight American League pennant that summer, leaving Boston 17 games behind, Gehrig limped out to deliver the lineup card that included Dahlgren's name and watched the games from the dugout.

He was, after all, "The Pride of the Yankees," the club's most enduring symbol, repository of all the virtues—class, dignity, confidence, discipline—that McCarthy and Jacob Ruppert had tried to drill into the franchise.

Yet his most dominant quality had been his durability. From the moment he pinch-hit for shortstop Pee Wee Wanninger on June 1, 1925, Gehrig hadn't missed a game. Manager Miller Huggins had given him a starting assignment the next afternoon when regular Wally Pipp complained of a headache after having been beaned in batting practice.

"Why don't you take the day off?" Huggins had suggested. "We'll put the kid from Columbia on first today." The kid from Columbia was actually a dropout, the only child of German immigrants, who'd grown up in upper Manhattan, rode the trolley to high school, and waited tables at a fraternity house.

Yankee scout Paul Krichell had spotted him at a Columbia-Rutgers game in New Brunswick and immediately phoned general manager Ed Barrow.

"I've just seen the next Babe Ruth," Krichell announced.

"Go home and sleep it off," Barrow advised him, "and tell me about it in the morning."

The Pride of the Yankees wipes away a tear as 61,808 chant "We love you, Lou!" during Gehrig Appreciation Day at Yankee Stadium on July 4.

Babe Ruth embraces Lou Gehrig during ceremonies, the first time the onetime close friends had really spoken since 1933. In the stillness that punctuated Gehrig's moving speech, Babe walked over to Lou and draped his arms around him. "I wanted to laugh and cheer him up," Ruth would say. "I wound up crying like a baby."

Gehrig was a powerfully built sophomore with thick legs who was studying to be an accountant. But his father needed surgery, and the Yankees were offering a $1,500 bonus. So Gehrig signed and set about mastering his craft. "Lou didn't learn quickly, but he learned thoroughly,"

Pipp noticed. "He sweated out each detail, step by step, until he had mastered it."

Gehrig came to the plate 8,001 times, batted .340 lifetime with 1,990 runs batted in and 493 home runs, and easily made the Hall of Fame that very December in a special election, when the usual five-year waiting period was waived.

Yet he never earned more than $37,000 in a season and was overshadowed for a decade by a roistering, profane teammate with an affinity for late nights, home brew, and camel's-hair caps.

"I'm not a headline guy," Gehrig shrugged. "I'm just the guy who follows Babe Ruth in the batting order." He'd followed Ruth's "called shot" blast in the 1932 Series with a home run of his own—yet nobody seemed to remember. And when he'd crashed four home runs in Philadelphia that year ("Keed, that was the greatest I ever seen," Ruth told him), the feat was given secondary play in the next morning's newspapers. Giants manager John McGraw had chosen that day to resign.

Yet Gehrig was the sole constant through three generations of Yankees. He'd played on the 1927 club, perhaps the most dominant in baseball history, as one of its Murderer's Row. He had been the cornerstone for three second-place teams in the mid-1930s when McCarthy was retooling the franchise, then earned three more Series rings as the dynasty was reborn. And his 2,130 consecu-

Gehrig appeared "near collapse," the New York Times *reported, when manager Joe McCarthy presented a trophy from teammates. Their names were inscribed on one side, this verse composed by* Times *columnist John Kieran on the other:*
  We've been to the wars together,
    We took our foes as they came;
  And always you were the leader
    And ever you played the game.

  Idol of cheering millions,
    Records are yours by the sheaves;
  Iron of frame they hailed you,
    Decked you with laurel leaves.

  But higher than that we hold you,
    We who have known you best;
  Knowing the way you came through
    Every human test.

  Let this be a silent token
    Of lasting friendship's gleam,
  And all that we've left unspoken,
    Your pals of the Yankee team.

Red Rolfe led the majors in hits with 213, and his .329 batting average still ranks as the highest by a Yankee third baseman playing 100 or more games in a season.

As a spot starter and reliever, Steve Sundra was 11–1 with a 2.76 ERA. His .917 winning percentage is the second best by a Yankee with 10 or more decisions.

tive games had set a standard that seemed unapproachable.

Gehrig had played through bumps, fractured fingers, lumbago, illness, assorted aches and wounds, and a 1934 beaning that produced a concussion. The next day Gehrig had merely borrowed one of Ruth's oversized caps, sliced it open to accommodate his swollen skull, and rapped out three triples.

Now, married for only five years, he was dying,

and the Yankees quickly made arrangements for a July Fourth tribute at the Stadium, summoning back Gehrig's 1927 teammates.

"For the past two weeks you have been reading about the bad break I got," Gehrig told a capacity crowd that was blinking back tears along with him. "Yet today I consider myself the luckiest man on the face of the earth."

He had worked for Ruppert and Barrow, Huggins and McCarthy, and played alongside nine Hall of Famers, from Ruth to Joe DiMaggio. He

Yankee hitters, leading the majors with a .451 slugging average, lined up to tee off on Cincinnati pitching in the World Series (from left): Frank Crosetti, Red Rolfe, Tom Henrich, Bill Dickey, Charlie Keller, George Selkirk, Joe Gordon, and Babe Dahlgren. Joe DiMaggio missed the picture, but not the Series, hitting .313, second to Keller's .438.

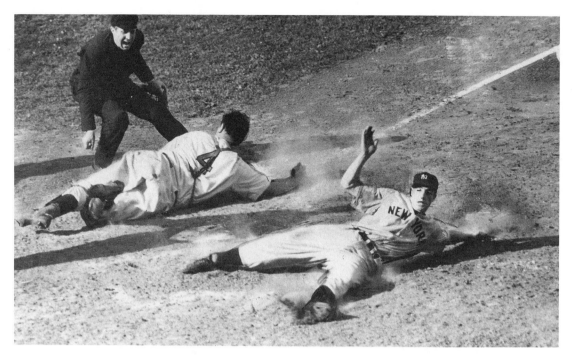

Joe DiMaggio slides past dazed Reds catcher Ernie Lombardi, who took his storied "snooze" in the 10th inning of game four at Cincinnati. In one of the most bizarre plays in World Series history, DiMaggio singled, two runs scored, and Joe alertly sprinted around the bases after Charlie Keller crashed into Lombardi, stunning the big catcher. DiMag circled while Lombardi lay sprawled, the ball only a few feet away—a twilight-zone climax that wrapped up the Yankees' fourth straight world title.

had worn one uniform and had a hand in seven pennants and six world championships, with another of each to come at season's end. "I may have had a tough break," he concluded, "but I have an awful lot to live for."

His name would never appear in another box score, but Gehrig was in uniform when the Yankees met Cincinnati in the World Series. As expected it was another foregone conclusion.

New York won the first three games (as right-hander Monte Pearson pitched a no-hitter for 7⅓ innings in game two) then closed out the Redlegs, 7–4, in the 10th inning of game four at Crosley Field as Cincinnati catcher Ernie Lombardi "swooned" when a throw from right fielder Ival Goodman struck him in the protective cup. New York's Charlie Keller knocked Lombardi down coming in from third and three Yankees scored.

On the train ride back to Manhattan, which McCarthy wanted kept subdued, Gehrig played an agonizing game of bridge, his shaking hands unable to deal, his fingers mangling the cards. The signs, his teammates now realized, had been visible in spring training.

Gehrig, pitcher Wes Ferrell remembered, had inexplicably fallen to the clubhouse floor. "He

lay there for a second, frowning," Ferrell noticed. "Like he couldn't understand what was happening."

In two years, Gehrig would be dead, and an era would die with him.

After four unprecedented championship seasons in a row they had struck bottom after one month and had stayed there for two weeks. It had taken the Yankees three more months to inch as high as fifth place in the American League and a .500 record.

Now, after winning 16 of 19 games during the last three weeks of August, New York was only half a game behind first-place Detroit and had two rested pitchers ready for a September 11 doubleheader with dissension-torn Cleveland in Municipal Stadium.

These were the fabled "Crybaby Indians," so dubbed because they'd tried to persuade club president Alva Bradley to fire manager Oscar Vitt

Charlie "King Kong" Keller muscled three homers in a game, a feared hitter who led the league in walks. But his average slipped to .286 from his .334 as a 1939 rookie.

(whom they found excessively critical), then went public with their complaints.

In three weeks, during late August and early September, the Indians had blown a 5½-game lead and surrendered first place to the Tigers. They seemed ripe for a sweep, and after the Yankees knocked 27-game winner Bob Feller out of the box in the fourth inning to take the opener, it seemed inevitable.

Word had come from Detroit that Boston had beaten the Tigers in their first game; New York had taken over the league lead. And Yankee ace Red Ruffing would pitch the second game.

Tommy Henrich, a regular irregular who played 99 games in the outfield and as a pinch hitter, batted .307—the only Yankee besides Joe DiMaggio (.352) to top .300.

But storm clouds settled in over Lake Erie, literally and figuratively, before the nightcap. The Yankees lost their early lead after first baseman Babe Dahlgren muffed a routine throw from shortstop Frank Crosetti in the sixth inning. Then, as the heavens opened over the stadium, the Bossard brothers, who'd been the Indians' groundskeepers for years, realized they'd "mislaid" the infield tarpaulin.

Rain quickly turned the dirt to muck, play was called, and Cleveland declared the victor. Meanwhile, Detroit defeated the Red Sox in the second game, and New York never saw first place again.

A miserable western swing—Detroit, St. Louis, and Chicago passed for the West in those days— finished the Yankees off, and they ended up third, two games behind the pennant-winning Tigers.

It was a forgettable end to New York's worst season (88–66) since 1930—pockmarked by gloomy individual performances throughout. Crosetti (.194), catcher Bill Dickey (.247), and third baseman Red Rolfe (.250) all had their poorest years simultaneously. Lefty Gomez's sore arm limited him to nine appearances. And Ruffing, with four straight 20-victory seasons behind him, ended up 15–12.

The only .300 hitter was the likely one, center fielder Joe DiMaggio, who'd inherited the slugger's mantle from retired Lou Gehrig. After an unremarkable start he put together a 23-game hitting streak in July that led to a final .352 average and DiMaggio's second straight American League batting title (following his career-high .381 of 1939). The streak was merely an appetizer for another more than twice as long in 1941 that would make him a baseball immortal.

The way it started, with a first-inning single off a mediocre Chicago pitcher named Edgar Smith in a game the Yankees would lose 3–1, was eminently forgettable.

Joe DiMaggio didn't realize what he was up to for another three weeks, when a few New York newspapermen rummaged in the record books and informed him that his 24-game hitting streak was only five short of the club record.

"That's when I became conscious of the streak," DiMaggio would say. "When the writers started talking about the records I could break. But at that stage I didn't think too much about it."

Hitting streaks were no novelty to him, after all. He'd strung 61 games together as a minor leaguer in 1933 and 23 games as a Yankee in 1940. Yet this one seemed touched by magic.

His teammates had been stumbling along in fourth place on May 15, 5½ games behind Cleveland, their bats sound asleep. They'd lost four in a row and seven of nine. "Yank Attack Weakest in Years," groaned the *New York Journal-American* after a 13–1 collapse to the White Sox, and manager Joe McCarthy had immediately reshuffled his lineup.

And DiMaggio had slipped to .306, 46 points lower than his previous year's batting title figure. But as he stacked one game atop another the Yankees rose out of the slough and became contenders. By early June, when DiMaggio's streak reached 24 games, New York had won eight straight.

When it ended, 32 games later in Cleveland, DiMaggio had crafted baseball's most enduring record, and New York was on its way to an absurdly easy pennant.

It took two superb fielding plays by Indian third baseman Ken Keltner to snap DiMaggio's spell at 56 games; otherwise the streak would have run on to an astounding 73 games, nearly half a season.

As it was, the feat consumed more than a third of the 154-game schedule and overshadowed Ted Williams' .406 season for the Red Sox, the last .400 year by a major leaguer.

When the streak ended with DiMaggio grounding into a ninth-inning double play, he had

rapped out 91 hits (including 16 doubles, four triples, and 15 home runs) in 223 at bats for a .408 average, had knocked in 55 runs, and had struck out only seven times.

More impressively he had maintained his grace and composure throughout. "I never saw a guy so calm," marveled roommate Lefty Gomez. "I wound up with the upset stomachs."

Indeed, the streak was halfway along before DiMaggio realized that he might be making history. At 30 games he broke the club record shared by Roger Peckinpaugh and Earle Combs; still ahead loomed the 41-game American League mark set by St. Louis's George Sisler two decades earlier.

Meanwhile, the task grew progressively more difficult—official scorers, conscious of their critical role, scrutinized each ground ball like Talmudic scholars. And pitchers bore down even harder.

Yet everyone seemed imbued with a sense of history and propriety. In the 36th game, with Yankees on second and third, two out, and DiMaggio hitting in the ninth, St. Louis manager Luke Sewell forbade pitcher Bob Muncrief to deliver the obvious intentional walk. "He means too much to baseball to be cheated out of his chance at a record through a technicality," Sewell declared.

So Muncrief, who agreed with Sewell, pitched to DiMaggio—and watched him single. "It wouldn't have been fair to walk him," Muncrief realized. "Not to him or to me. Hell, he's the greatest player I ever saw."

Others—specifically Athletics pitcher Johnny Babich—weren't quite as altruistic. Babich, a cer-

Yankee pitching was balanced and stingy, allowing the fewest runs in the league though only Lefty Gomez and Red Ruffing won more than 15. With Joe McCarthy (from left) are Spud Chandler, Atley Donald, Marv Breuer, Gomez, Ruffing, Steve Peek, Tiny Bonham, and Johnny Murphy. Missing is Marius Russo, who won 14.

tified Yankee killer who'd beaten them five times in 1940, had vowed that DiMaggio wouldn't get a hit.

So Babich walked him the first time, then threw him three wide pitches the next. DiMaggio, desperate, glanced at third-base coach Art Fletcher, was delighted to see his flashing the "hit" sign, and lashed the next pitch through Babich's legs for a double and his 40th straight.

"After I took my turn at first I looked at him," DiMaggio would recall with pleasure. "His face was white as a sheet."

By now the pressure had built to a peak. "In those last 20 days," DiMaggio admitted, "I went to bat with my palms wet." With one good week he could pass not only Sisler but Wee Willie Keeler, who'd set the major league record of 44 in 1897. A herd of newspapermen followed the Yankees everywhere, and fans mobbed DiMaggio any time he appeared in public. He had to turn over his fan mail to the front office to answer. The world had closed in.

"I was able to control myself," he would say. "But that doesn't mean I wasn't dying inside. I had no tomorrows. It was either do it today or fail."

He tied Sisler's record with a two-base hit at Washington in the first game of a doubleheader, then went to the bat rack between games and found that someone had stolen his lucky bat, which he had sanded and oiled and heated until it had turned black.

But momentum overcame superstition. DiMaggio borrowed a bat from Tommy Henrich and ripped a single into left field in the seventh inning of the nightcap.

So Sisler was behind him. Three days later he took Keeler by crashing a high inside fastball off Boston's Dick Newsome into the left-field stands at Yankee Stadium. Only 8,682 spectators saw it; the temperature that day was 100 degrees on the field.

With the pressure eased, the Bat returned. An anonymous caller from Newark said that a friend had filched it as a prank; it would be returned to the Stadium for game 45 of what was now a national obsession. Newspapers held their late afternoon editions for word.

Les Brown and His Band of Renown memorialized him with a song ("Joltin' Joe DiMaggio, we want you on our side"). Opposing clubs ran three-column advertisements announcing his presence. The streak reached 50; the All-Star break came and went. DiMaggio was chasing DiMaggio, nobody else. "I did want to keep on going," he mused. "I wanted it to go on forever."

Then, on the evening of July 17, he and Gomez walked out of the Hotel Cleveland and climbed into a taxi for Municipal Stadium, where 67,468 spectators—the largest crowd ever to watch a night game to that time—were waiting.

"I got a feeling if you don't get a hit the first time up," the driver told DiMaggio, "they're going to stop you tonight."

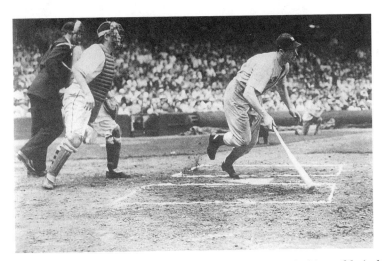 

Joltin' Joe's streak ended in Cleveland. At left, DiMaggio hits safely in his 56th game at old League Park on July 16 while going 3-for-4. But the next night (right), across town at Municipal Stadium, hitless Joe awaits his last at-bat in the eighth inning, when 67,468 (then the biggest night crowd ever) would see him ground into a double play. The next day, DiMaggio had two hits against Bob Feller, baseball's best pitcher, to launch a new 16-game streak. Thus, Joe hit safely in 72 of 73 games while the Yankees vaulted from fourth place to a commanding lead en route to the pennant.

Gomez exploded. "What the hell is this? What are you trying to do, jinx him?" DiMaggio shrugged and tipped the driver anyway. "Well," he philosophized, "if it is, it is."

Al Smith, who'd end up 12–13 that year, was on the mound for the Indians, and in the first inning DiMaggio ripped one of his pitches on the ground just inside the bag at third. But Keltner, backhanding the ball neatly, made the play from foul territory. In the New York dugout Gomez cursed. "That lousy cabdriver."

Smith walked DiMaggio in the fourth, then got him to bounce another ball to Keltner in the seventh. "Keltner's two plays down the line," DiMaggio would reminisce years later. "I remember that like it was yesterday."

Keltner was a gifted fielder and had the further advantage of playing deep because he knew the proud DiMaggio would not try to bunt his way on base—not because he couldn't, but because he *wouldn't.*

There would be one more chance in the ninth, but by then Jim Bagby had relieved Smith. DiMaggio had faced Bagby once during the streak and had homered in game 28.

This time DiMaggio waited out two balls and a strike, then lashed a fastball "as hard as I ever hit any ground ball" at shortstop Lou Boudreau. The ball bounced off Boudreau's shoulder, but he managed to pluck it out of the air and turn a double play. DiMaggio rounded first, retrieved his glove, and jogged to center field without a trace of emotion.

"Well, that's over," DiMaggio said softly, reaching for a cigarette in the clubhouse. But the Yankees swept on. They'd won 41 games during DiMaggio's streak and would take 14 of their next 16 (as Joe added a 16-game mini-streak) and leave the Red Sox 17 games behind, clinching the pennant on September 4. Along the way they found time to have a silver cigar humidor engraved at Tiffany's for the man who spurred them on.

Meanwhile, across the East River, the Dodgers were pulling off a feat of their own, winning their first National League pennant in 21 years. When they arrived home after clinching the pennant, hundreds of fans jammed Grand Central Station to greet them. The Yankees were forgotten conquerors, their achievement old news.

"It ain't fair," cracked former (and future) Dodger utility man Frenchy Bordagaray, now a Yankee reserve. "There wasn't anybody there to meet us when we came back with the pennant. I couldn't even find a redcap to carry my bag."

The idea of the Yankees in a World Series was

no novelty. They'd won four of the previous five and were riding a streak of nine straight victories in Series games.

But where the Giants, Cubs, and Redlegs had been compliant, the Yankees' Brooklyn neighbors proved stubborn. After stranding the lead runs in the ninth inning of the opener, the Dodgers rubbed out a 2–0 deficit and won game two. Then, with 40-year-old Fred Fitzsimmons (the oldest pitcher ever to start a Series game) performing heroically, Brooklyn held the Yankees scoreless through the seventh inning of the third game. Then they watched New York pitcher Marius Russo chip Fitzsimmons' kneecap with a line drive. That knocked out Fitzsimmons, and the Dodgers followed in the eighth.

But in the ninth inning of game four at Ebbets Field they finally had the Yankees in a hammerlock, one strike away from a 4–3 victory that would tie the Series.

Reliever Hugh Casey had gotten first baseman Johnny Sturm and third baseman Red Rolfe to hit easy grounders. Now he had a full count on right fielder Tommy Henrich, who'd been hitless all afternoon, and decided to go for the spitter. Or did he? "Everybody says it was a spitter, but I don't buy that," Henrich insisted. "Casey didn't have a great curve, but that ball exploded. It was

Dodger star Whitlow Wyatt dueled Spud Chandler in game two and stopped the Yankees, 3–2. But Wyatt would be outpitched by Tiny Bonham in the game five finale, 3–1, as the Yankees regained the world championship after a year in exile.

A classic moment in World Series history occurred when Tommy Henrich fanned for what appeared to be the final out of game four at Brooklyn. But as umpire Larry Goetz signaled the out, Hugh Casey's pitch eluded catcher Mickey Owen, who chased the ball as Henrich sprinted for first base. Trailing 4–3, the Yankees rallied for four runs. The loss devastated the Dodgers, who instead of being tied 2–2 in the Series, now trailed 3–1. They were eliminated the next afternoon.

Babe Ruth says goodbye to Lou Gehrig, who passed away in June at age 37 and was waked at his church in Riverdale.

the best one he threw all afternoon, and it had me fooled completely. I'll admit that."

Henrich lunged—and missed. Unfortunately for the Dodgers, catcher Mickey Owen missed it as well. The ball dropped abruptly and skidded past Owen. "Even as I was trying to hold up I was thinking that the ball had broken so fast that Owen might have trouble with it too," Henrich figured. "When I saw that little white jackrabbit bouncing I said, 'Let's go.' It rolled all the way to the fence. I could have walked to first."

With umpire Larry Goetz's right arm still raised, Owen, one of the finest defensive catchers in the game, chased the ball all the way to the backstop. "It was all my fault," he said. "It was a great breaking curve and I should have had it. It got away from me, and by the time I got hold of it near the corner of the dugout I couldn't have thrown anyone out at first."

So the Yankees, resigned to defeat, found themselves reborn. "When Henrich swung and missed we all got up and started toward the runway that led out of the dugout," shortstop Phil Rizzuto said. "Some of us were already in it. I know I was."

The Dodgers merely sat stunned—particularly manager Leo Durocher. "For the first time in my life I was shell-shocked," he conceded. "I should have gotten off the bench and gone out to the mound to talk to my pitcher. Instead, I just sat on my ass."

And let a badly shaken Casey (who would shoot himself 10 years later) face six more batters as the Yankees staged the most dramatic uprising since the Athletics' 10-run seventh inning against the Cubs in the 1929 Series.

"All hell broke loose after that," said Yankee pitcher Spud Chandler. "Base hits like thunder." DiMaggio ripped an 0–2 slider into left field for a single. Left fielder Charlie Keller fouled off half a dozen balls at 0–2, then blasted a fastball off the right-field wall that scored Henrich and DiMaggio. Then catcher Bill Dickey walked, second baseman Joe Gordon doubled him home behind Keller, and it was 7–4. "Well," DiMaggio laughed, "they say everything happens in Brooklyn."

After the Dodgers went down in order in their half, Owen and club president Larry MacPhail wept in the clubhouse. Why did fate always favor pinstripes? "They haven't beaten you a blasted game yet," MacPhail told his men. But it was over. You never gave the Yankees a second life.

Brooklyn fans gave Owen a sympathetic ovation the next afternoon—"they stood and cheered," said Rizzuto, "and it rocked old Ebbets Field." But New York buried the Dodgers, 3–1, as pitcher Tiny Bonham retired 20 of the last 22 batters he faced.

"Wait 'til Next Year," groused an eight-column headline in the next day's *Brooklyn Eagle*. It was the first chorus of what would be a 14-year refrain.

World War II had players thinking about matters besides baseball, including Joe DiMaggio and brother Dom of the Red Sox. Both would enlist after the season and wear different uniforms the next three years.

Joltin' Joe had another distraction—a bitter salary dispute. After his '41 super-season, he expected a raise from $37,500, but was offered a $5,000 cut. After ordering DiMag not to discuss the matter with the media, GM Ed Barrow cheap-shotted his superstar by telling newsmen, "Soldiers are making $21 a month, but DiMaggio wants a big raise."

The humiliated Yankee Clipper signed for $43,750 and was left riled—and booed around the league, including at the Stadium. It all may have contributed to an off season by DiMaggio standards; his batting average sagged 52 points to .305, his home-run output from 30 to 21.

For more than a decade St. Louis had been a pleasant oasis for them, offering a fine view of the Mississippi, delicious spare ribs, yeasty beer, and easy victories over the Browns, who'd managed one first–division finish since 1929.

"Somehow I can't seem to get it through my head that we're going out there to play the Series," catcher Bill Dickey mused as the train headed west. "It seemed just like any other trip to St. Louis."

Yankee clubs rarely played for world championships there and rarely lost them anywhere. Since 1927, when they'd swept Pittsburgh, New York had won all eight of their Series appearances with the loss of only four games. This time they'd cruised to another American League pen-

Joe Gordon was the American League's Most Valuable Player, batting a career-high .322 and hitting safely in 29 straight games. The star second baseman also drove in 103 runs while sparking the Yankees to their 13th pennant.

Phil Rizzuto, 5'6" sophomore shortstop, looks up to Johnny Lindell, the 6'4½" rookie pitcher who would be moved to the outfield the next year to get his bat into the daily lineup.

Veteran Rollie Hemsley was acquired during the season at age 35 and proved a valuable addition, effectively sharing Yankee catching for two and a half seasons.

Red Ruffing (left) outpitched Johnny Beasley (right) in the World Series opener, flirting with immortality by holding the Cardinals hitless until two were out in the eighth inning. It proved the Yankees' lone victory as St. Louis swept the next four games—the Yanks' first loss of a World Series after winning eight in a row dating back to 1926.

nant by nine games over Boston and twiddled their thumbs while the Cardinals edged Brooklyn for the National League title on the final day. Even in St. Louis, fans wanted odds on Series bets with New York partisans.

No St. Louis club had won a pennant since the 1934 Gashouse Gang, and this one had to erase a 10-game Dodger lead on August 6. They were young (no starters over 30) and unproven, the fruit of Branch Rickey's farm system.

And now, as predicted, the Yankees were murdering them in their own park in the opener. Pitcher Red Ruffing, who'd had a no-hitter brewing until the eighth inning, was breezing behind a 7–0 lead with two outs and one man on base in the ninth. All that remained was rookie Ray Sanders pinch-hitting for rookie Whitey Kurowski.

But Ruffing walked him—and never got another out. Marty Marion tripled, scoring Walker Cooper and Sanders. Four singles produced two more runs, chased Ruffing, and brought up rookie Stan Musial. The Cardinals had batted around.

Yankee reliever Spud Chandler put an end to it by getting Musial to ground out to first, but the point had been made. The Cardinals could score on these people. "We went into the clubhouse and said, well, we gave them one hell of a scare," said right fielder Enos Slaughter.

The Yankees *were* vulnerable, even seven runs ahead and one out from victory. "That was just the shot in the arm our boys needed," crowed former St. Louis pitcher Dizzy Dean. "We'll never stop now."

The grinding pennant race with the Dodgers

they now regarded as a boon. "We'll go out and beat the Yankees the same way," insisted manager Billy Southworth. "One thing this young club isn't afraid of is reputations."

The Cardinals had performed beautifully down the stretch, winning 43 of their last 52 games, and 106 in all, the most by a National League champion since 1909. Since most of them had come up hungry from Southern mill towns or dirt farms, a $6,000 winner's share seemed like a fortune.

They were confident, enthusiastic, and aggressive on the base paths. "They might not be so hot at the plate," Braves manager Casey Stengel conceded. "But they sure got a lot of strength in their ankles."

Once New York showed signs of uncertainty, the Cardinals were convinced they could win it. In the most dramatic reversal of Series form since the 1915 Red Sox, St. Louis lost the opener and then swept the Yankees, leaving them disbelieving, arguing with umpires, and on the defensive. Very un-Yankeelike.

The Cardinals, Dickey and his mates learned, were not at all like the Browns. They relished tight squeezes in late innings and seemed to enjoy squandering leads because it was so much fun regaining them.

Game two was typical. After the Yankees had climbed out of a three-run hole to tie the score in the eighth inning, Slaughter doubled and Musial singled him home to put St. Louis ahead, 4–3. Then with one out in the ninth Slaughter threw out pinch runner Tucker Stainback at third base from right field.

"Some fellows like to say that throw of mine cut the hearts out of the Yankees," Slaughter said. Possibly. Whatever, New York was never the same. The Cardinals saved their masterpiece for the Stadium and game three. Everything that had distinguished their play during the season—inspired pitching, fundamental offense, timely defense—was put on display.

St. Louis scored one run on a walk, a bunt, a sacrifice and an infield out, the other on two singles and an error. In the late innings, center fielder Terry Moore robbed Joe DiMaggio of a triple, Musial dove into the left-field boxes to filch a home run from Joe Gordon, and Slaughter scaled the right-field wall to haul down a Charlie Keller drive. And Cardinal pitcher Ernie White scattered six hits to shut out New York in a Series game for the first time in 16 years.

The Yankees, barely pressed during the season, were now unraveling like a nickel baseball. Losing 6–1 in game four, they groused to the um-

pires, came back to score five runs in the sixth, then lost it 9–6, after a walk and a wild and unnecessary throw to second by Dickey had opened the floodgates.

Now it was a matter of pride, of not becoming the first American League team to lose all three games at home. As incentive, club officials posted a notice on the clubhouse blackboard: "Train for St. Louis Leaves 8 P.M. Tonight. Grand Central Terminal. Bring Your Hand Luggage with You."

The fifth game went down to the ninth inning tied at 2–2. Then Kurowski, who would never hit another Series homer, belted a two-run blast to left field just inside the foul pole. "There it goes," shouted Moore as ball met bat. "There it goes."

And so went the Yankees, amid a flurry of second-guessing, as the Cardinals sang "Pass the Biscuits, Mirandy," their theme song down the stretch.

"What's the matter?" growled Yankee manager Joe McCarthy. "Have they forgotten that this ball club had won eight World Series in a row? What do you have to do, win all the time?"

It was a suitable year for a Last Hurrah. With Europe and the South Pacific in flames, half of their lineup in the armed forces, and the game itself more of a home-front diversion than the national pastime, the Yankees chose 1943 to tack one final championship onto the Joe McCarthy era and settle a World Series score with St. Louis.

The Yankees' regular first baseman, shortstop, and two outfielders were gone. Catcher Bill Dickey, at 36, was the only starter who would hit .300. Yet New York won the American League pennant by 13½ games over Washington and cleaned up the Cardinals in five.

After seven pennants in eight years it would be the Yankees' last summer atop the league until 1947, when their roster would have undergone a transformation. It was also the last year that major league baseball would be truly major until 1946; by the spring of 1944 most of its regulars would belong to military rosters.

As it was, war had already engulfed the world, and baseball seemed frivolous by comparison. In fact, before the 1942 season, Commissioner Kenesaw Mountain Landis had offered to "close down for the duration of the war" if the president deemed it necessary.

Franklin D. Roosevelt hadn't. In a "Green Light Letter," he told Landis that while individual players would be expected to serve just like any American of draft age, the game was a "definite recreational asset" to the country and thus was worthwhile.

Even so, baseball made practical concessions to a wartime economy. Bowing to travel restrictions most clubs conducted spring training close to home under sandlot conditions. The Yankees forsook St. Petersburg for Asbury Park, a seaside resort on the Jersey shore where saltwater taffy was provided them gratis and temperatures hovered around 45 degrees. They worked out, shivering, on the local high school diamond, then retreated to the clubhouse where scout Paul Krichell kept a potbellied stove burning wood all day.

Meanwhile, McCarthy tried to fill in his lineup card. First baseman Buddy Hassett, shortstop Phil Rizzuto, center fielder Joe DiMaggio, right fielder Tommy Henrich, and pitcher Red Ruffing had all been called to active duty. So McCarthy put Nick Etten, who'd been acquired from the Phillies for two minor leaguers and $10,000 during the winter, at first base. Frank Crosetti was shifted to short and replaced at third base by rookie Billy Johnson. Rookie Bud Metheny filled in for Henrich. A converted pitcher, Johnny Lindell, took up for DiMaggio.

Yet there were enough old and proven faces for McCarthy to mold a contender. Joe Gordon still turned crisp double plays at second. Crosetti was a 12-year veteran, Charlie Keller a fixture in left, Dickey a Hall of Famer. And the nucleus of the league's best pitching staff—Spud Chandler,

Among the parade of players entering the military, Red Ruffing kissed baseball goodbye—inducted despite the absence of four toes on one foot.

Tiny Bonham, Hank Borowy, and Atley Donald—was still on hand.

The Yankees coalesced into an easy pennant winner as Chandler (20–4, 1.64) was named league MVP, Etten knocked in 107 runs, and Keller muscled 31 home runs. Now the Yankees wanted to correct history.

They'd stumbled badly before the Cardinals in the 1942 Series, losing four straight games after winning the opener. As destiny would have it, St. Louis won the National League race by 18 games

First baseman Nick Etten (second from left) was acquired from the Phillies and led the Yankees in RBIs with 107, second most in the league, and in doubles with 35. Etten earned a spot in the heart of the lineup with veteran Bombers (from left) Joe Gordon, Bill Dickey, and Charlie Keller.

Fireman Johnny Murphy again led the league in relief victories while going 12–4 with eight saves and 2.51 ERA.

pled between left and center, clearing the bases and sparking a five-run rally. The Cardinals, who committed four errors (and 10 in all during the Series), were never the same.

After a two-day break and a train ride west, McCarthy sent out Marius Russo, a sore-armed left-hander who'd been 5–10 during the season, to face Max Lanier. Russo would never win another game, but he limited the Cardinals to seven hits, doubled twice, and scored the deciding run in the eighth for a 2–1 victory.

The next day Chandler, capping the finest year of his career, went out to face Mort Cooper and end it. So confident were the Yankees that they wouldn't have to stay for a sixth game that they'd packed their bags and checked out of the hotel. "I wasn't what you'd call brilliant even though I shut them out," Chandler admitted. "I gave up 10 base hits and a couple of walks, but they left 11 men on base."

The turning point came in the fourth inning after Chandler yielded a single to Kurowski, walked Ray Sanders on four pitches, then went 3–0 to Johnny Hopp. That brought Dickey out to the mound.

over Cincinnati, yet the war had played havoc with the Cardinal roster, too.

Enos Slaughter and Terry Moore, two thirds of St. Louis' fine defensive outfield, had been snapped up. So had pitcher Johnny Beazley, who'd beaten New York twice in 1942.

But thanks to deep farm systems—and New York and St. Louis boasted the best—the rosters were still of Series caliber. And after the Yankees won the opener, 4–2, at the Stadium, the Cardinals took it as a positive omen.

They'd lost the 1942 opener and it had galvanized them. Again they came back to win the second game, 4–3, as battery mates Mort and Walker Cooper dedicated the victory to their father, who'd died the night before.

The similarity ended there. As another concession to travel restrictions, Landis had ordered that the first three games be played in New York; the Yankees would have the advantage of an extra home game before the Series shifted parks. The Yankees used a giddy eighth-inning burst to rub out a 2–1 Cardinal lead in game three and break the pattern.

It began with a bobbled ball by St. Louis center fielder Harry Walker and a dropped tag by third baseman Whitey Kurowski. That put Yankees on first and third with none out. After Crosetti was intentionally walked, Johnson tri-

Spud Chandler was selected the American League's Most Valuable Player by the baseball writers and the Major League Player of the Year by The Sporting News. *He was 20–4 with a tops-in-majors 1.64 ERA, the best ever by a Yankee pitcher. Chandler added two more wins in the World Series while allowing just one earned run for a 0.50 ERA as the Yanks reclaimed the world title from the Cardinals.*

"What's the matter?" the catcher asked Chandler.

"Nothing."

"Then get the ball over the plate."

Chandler proceeded to strike out Hopp on three pitches, the last an outside fastball, and escaped from the inning.

"Fellows," Chandler informed his mates, "there's no way I can lose today."

It was left to Dickey, the last link to the club's Glory Era of the twenties, to apply the crusher in the sixth. With two out Keller had singled. Now Dickey, who'd been one of the five batters Cooper had struck out consecutively to begin the game, stepped into the box hoping for a fastball.

"Well, I got it," he said, "and hit it good, but not hard. At least I didn't think so. But when I was running to first I saw the ball heading for the roof, and [coach] Earle Combs yelled at me: 'You got one, Bill!' Then I saw Art Fletcher at third waving his cap, and I knew it was a home run."

It was Dickey's 37th—and final—Series hit and it clinched New York's 10th world championship, the seventh and last for McCarthy. Less than an hour later the Yankees were singing "The Sidewalks of New York" under the showers.

They would accept 10 percent of their $6,100 winner's share in war bonds, and their caps—along with those of their rivals—would be shipped to the South Pacific, where they'd be awarded to American pilots who shot down Japanese Zeroes. There was, after all, a war on.

The question seemed traditional enough. Spring training had just begun, the Yankees were coming off their seventh American League pennant in eight years, and manager Joe McCarthy was being asked to speculate on his opening-day lineup. But these were not traditional times.

"How could I possibly do that?" McCarthy replied. "Why, I couldn't tell you who will be here next Tuesday." He paused, and riffled through his mental file. "Well, I could give you an infield," McCarthy allowed. "Neun could play first. I could cover second. Schulte on short, Fletcher on third, Krichell catching, and Schreiber pitching. And some of you writers could fill in, too."

Johnny Neun, John Schulte, and Art Fletcher were McCarthy's coaches, Paul Krichell a scout. And Paul Schreiber was a batting-practice pitcher who eventually *would* be activated in 1945, at age 42, and pitch four innings after a 22-year layoff. This was wartime baseball; the caliber, *Time* magazine guessed, was "between AA and A, but still baseball."

Just barely. Most of what happened in 1944 had never been seen before or since in the major leagues. With rubber needed for military use, Spalding developed a ball with a core of cork and balata (from South American tree sap) that was deader than Jacob Marley. Yankee first baseman Nick Etten managed to muscle 22 of them for

Sluggers Charlie Keller and Stan Musial posed at the World Series opener—before the Yankees reversed 1942's outcome and dethroned the Cardinals in five games for their 10th world title, the last of the Joe McCarthy era.

Manager Joe McCarthy fashioned a contender despite the daily challenge of patching together a lineup card with so many Yankees serving in the military—including Bill Dickey in the navy.

Rookie Walt "Monk" Dubiel (left) and veteran Atley Donald each won 13 games, trailing only ace Hank Borowy's 17.

George "Snuffy" Stirnweiss pilfers one of his majors-leading 55 stolen bases. In his first season as a regular, he made good in his hometown, batting .319, fourth in the league. He also led the majors in hits (205) and runs (125). And he and teammate Johnny Lindell topped the league in triples (16 apiece) and total bases (Lindell with 297, Stirnweiss with 296).

Johnny Lindell, a converted pitcher, blossomed as a hitter during his second season as Joe DiMaggio's replacement in center field. Batting an even .300, Lindell led the league in total bases (297). He was third in slugging (.500) and RBIs (103) and tied for third in homers (18).

home runs and led the league with the lowest total in 26 years.

And the St. Louis Browns, who'd seen the first division only once since 1929, won their first and only pennant—without a 20-game winner and with only one hitter above .295. Their secret? Eighteen 4-F specimens with creaky ankles, bad backs, and missing fingers—unfit for military duty but sound enough to flesh out a roster.

With 470 major leaguers on active military service by the end of the season, the Browns represented the best of the worst. The Yankees, who'd won the 1943 pennant by 13½ games and beaten the Cardinals in five, had been decimated.

Buddy Hassett, Phil Rizzuto, Joe DiMaggio, Tommy Henrich, and Red Ruffing had been called up before the 1943 season; now second baseman Joe Gordon, third baseman Billy Johnson, left fielder Charlie Keller, catcher Bill Dickey, and their best pitcher, Spud Chandler, had been claimed. Not one of the eight regulars from the 1942 club remained; anonymous faces appeared at most positions.

"McCarthy will really have to go to work this season," mused White Sox manager Jimmy Dykes. "He won't be able to sit back the way he did in other years and simply push buttons."

This time the buttons were named Snuffy Stirnweiss, Mollie Milosevich, Oscar Grimes, Hersh Martin, and Mike Garbark. Yet McCarthy managed to mold a contender out of them. The Yankees held first place as late as mid-September and had a mathematical chance at the pennant until the final weekend, when the Browns swept four games from them and edged Detroit by a game.

Oscar Grimes, the Yankees' 1944–45 third baseman, looked as though he was guarding the hot corner with his life—and perhaps he was, considering the harsh infield surface at spring training in Atlantic City.

New York would finish third, its 83 victories the fewest since 1925.

It was a year when anyone might have worn pinstripes—even 41-year-old Paul Waner, who'd played for the Pirates against Ruth, Gehrig, & Co. in 1927. "How come you're in the outfield with the Yankees?" called a voice from the bleachers one afternoon.

"Because Joe DiMaggio's in the army," Waner replied.

Paul Waner, former Pirates star and future Hall of Famer, was picked up on waivers near season's end and batted .143 in nine games. He'd go to bat once the following spring, draw a walk, and retire at age 42.

1945

The Colonel had been dead for six years, yet his franchise and its tradition had continued to flourish. Jacob Ruppert, who'd signed the paycheck of every Yankee from Home Run Baker to Joe DiMaggio, had passed away during the winter of 1939 while the club was still in mid-Renaissance.

New York had won a fourth straight pennant that fall and would claim three more before the war siphoned off the entire lineup. Some things—the farm system, the pinstripes, general manager Ed Barrow, field manager Joe McCarthy—remained constant.

Yet, as the turmoil in Europe and the Pacific built to a climax in the winter of 1945, the Yankees were heading for a crossroads. Their worst finish in 20 years lay ahead. The Stadium, scouting system, and minor-league structure were showing signs of decline. And an imaginative promoter named Larry MacPhail was pondering getting up a syndicate to buy all of it.

He was a colonel, too, a staff officer for the undersecretary of war, but MacPhail had nothing in common with Ruppert, certainly not a Rhenish castle on the Hudson and several million dollars. MacPhail was audacious and flamboyant—he'd tried to capture Kaiser Wilhelm II shortly after the World War I armistice was signed, and ended up with a House of Hohenzollern ashtray.

Larry MacPhail (right) was one of the Yankees' three new co-owners. The flammable and flamboyant veteran executive didn't get along with his new general manager George Weiss (left) and manager Joe McCarthy. McCarthy would be gone by next mid-season and MacPhail by late 1947, bought out by partners Del Webb and Dan Topping.

Where Ruppert had been a patrician sportsman who regarded a baseball franchise as a diversion, MacPhail was a natural general manager with a flair for marketing. He'd introduced night baseball to the major leagues a decade earlier when he was at Cincinnati, and laid the foundation for two pennants there. Then he'd revived a flagging Brooklyn team in a bandbox of a ballpark and watched it win its first pennant in two decades.

Now MacPhail approached millionaire Dan Topping and construction magnate Del Webb with a plan to buy the Yankees from the Ruppert estate, which had been willed to Ruppert's two nieces and a lady friend. The price was $2.8 million and it included everything—the club, the Stadium, minor-league parks in Newark and Kansas City, and the whole farm system. The deal was cut in January over the objections of Barrow, who'd been general manager since 1920 and who viewed MacPhail as something between a hustler and a charlatan.

"Only over my dead body will MacPhail buy the Yankees," Barrow had vowed, but now MacPhail was president and Barrow was working for him. Barrow's role—chairman of the board—was

largely ceremonial. MacPhail was running the enterprise and things changed quickly. He set about retooling the scouting and farm systems, devised a Stadium Club, and moved the Yankee offices from 42nd Street to the more fashionable Fifth Avenue and 57th.

For the time being, though, the lineup remained relatively unchanged and relentlessly mediocre. The war was still on and the heart of the club—Joe DiMaggio, Joe Gordon, Phil Rizzuto, Tommy Henrich, Charlie Keller, Spud Chandler—was still involved in it. The Yankees were Nick Etten, Snuffy Stirnweiss, Oscar Grimes, Mike Garbark, Tucker Stainback—and they were destined for a fourth-place finish and an 81–71 record in 1945, their worst since 1925.

In July an exasperated MacPhail told a New York sportswriter that a number of the players were going through the motions, that Etten (despite a league-leading 111 RBIs) wasn't earning his salary, that two of the pitchers were useless. Then he dropped a bomb—Hank Borowy, the best pitcher on New York's marginal staff, had been waived and then shipped to the Cubs for $97,000. Borowy, explained MacPhail, aware of his ace's 10–5 record, rarely pitched well during the second half of the season; but Borowy went 11–2 from there, and the Cubs won the pennant.

The deal ran counter to Yankee tradition; the club rarely sold its stars. Besides, New York was only four games out of first place.

McCarthy, saying his nerves were acting up,

Left: *Joe Page blossomed to 6–3 with a 2.82 ERA in his second season—more as a starter. The southpaw soon would be a building block in a new Yankee dynasty as an ace reliever.* **Right:** *Paul Schreiber, the Yankees' veteran batting-practice hurler, pitched in two games, a testimony to the wartime manpower crunch. Going on 43, he hadn't pitched in a big-league game in 22 years.*

The Yankees signed pledges supporting a war fund as WW II wound down to a conclusion.

went back to his Buffalo farm, stayed there for three weeks, and offered to resign. Thirty-five games into the 1946 season he would do so. Barrow was already gone by then—"No ship can have two captains," he said.

The Ruppert era had vanished.

The warning flag had been hoisted midway through the 1945 season when president Larry MacPhail had sold his best pitcher to the Cubs and Joe McCarthy responded with his three-week sabbatical. When he returned, McCarthy had offered his resignation, which MacPhail had refused.

Now it was late May of 1946 and McCarthy, his gallbladder acting up again, was packing his bags in a Detroit hotel and planning to board a plane for Buffalo—and retirement. He had been feeling poorly as the club had departed for its first western swing and had missed three games. "He was in bad shape," Joe DiMaggio had noticed. "He was drinking too much and he wasn't eating right and he was worried about the team because it was playing so lousy." After 15 years as

New York's manager and 20 in the majors total, McCarthy believed the pressures were damaging his health. This time he would go home to Buffalo and stay there.

The next morning when the Yankees arrived in Boston, MacPhail was waiting for them with a telegram. "My doctor advised me that my health will be seriously jeopardized if I continue," McCarthy had cabled. "This is the sole reason for my decision which, as you know, is entirely voluntary on my part. I have enjoyed our pleasant relations . . ."

Yet it was clear to most observers that McCarthy had enjoyed it less since the arrival of Mac-Phail, an impetuous promoter with an active hand. McCarthy was used to a passive owner in Jacob Ruppert, and to a general manager, in Ed Barrow, who backed him. Since MacPhail had taken over the club presidency in the winter of 1945 McCarthy had neither.

Though the heart of New York's prewar championship lineup had returned from military service, the atmosphere was hardly the same. Mac-Phail had established two training camps, in St. Petersburg and Bradenton, which irked McCarthy, who wanted his people in one place. Press conferences were being called to announce anything MacPhail found promotable. McCarthy's declining health was a factor in his leaving, but so was front-office interference.

Joe McCarthy retired to his farm outside Buffalo in late May during his 16th season in the Bronx. He won the most games of any Yankee manager ever, 1,460, while collecting eight pennants and seven world championships. Marse Joe's .627 winning percentage is the best of any Yank manager with 100 victories, and that doesn't include his .763 (29–9) in the World Series. His career percentage .615 (2,125–1,333), over 24 seasons directing the Yankees, Red Sox, and Cubs, makes him the most successful manager in big-league history.

Phil Rizzuto was welcomed home by a new second-base partner, Snuffy Stirnweiss. Both were New York City products: Rizzuto from Brooklyn, Stirnweiss from the Bronx. Besides their double-play combination, the pair provided speed; Stirnweiss was second in the league in stolen bases with 18, Rizzuto tied for fourth with 14.

So, 35 games into the season with the club 22–13, McCarthy walked away from it, and the era of Marse Joe, which had produced eight pennants and seven world championships, came to an end. And while the majority of the championship 1943 regulars were back in pinstripes—second baseman Joe Gordon, shortstop Phil Rizzuto, outfielders Tommy Henrich, Charlie Keller, and Joe DiMaggio, pitchers Spud Chandler and Johnny Murphy—what they returned to was unlike anything they'd known.

The team offices had been moved from 42nd Street to 57th and Fifth Avenue. Arc lights had

Night baseball came to Yankee Stadium on May 28, when 49,917 turned out on a raw, windy evening and saw the home team lose to Washington, 2–1. Each of New York's three teams hosted seven night games that summer.

The Yankee outfield was reunited (from left): Charlie Keller, Joe DiMaggio, and Tommy Henrich. They were the heart of the lineup's power: 1-2-3 in homers and RBIs—Keller at 30/101, DiMaggio at 25/95, and Henrich at 19/83. Keller led the team in most offensive categories. It was his last productive season; the next year, he suffered a slipped disk that reduced him to part-time duty.

been rigged for night games (the first would be played four days after McCarthy's resignation). And MacPhail, ever the huckster, would stage promotion after promotion to fill the Stadium. He held archery contests and footraces. He ar-

Bill Dickey, in his final season as a player, was a popular choice as the new manager after Joe McCarthy retired. But Dickey wouldn't last the season, quitting in mid-September when Larry MacPhail stalled in committing on Bill's future at the helm.

ranged fashion shows to lure female customers and passed out nylons. Attendance, coincidentally or not, soared from 880,000 to nearly 2.3 million, nearly double the franchise's best previous year.

Yet the on-field mediocrity that had marked their wartime clubs dogged the Yankees still. New York held first place for one day (in April) and finished third, 17 games behind a Red Sox club that hadn't won a pennant in 28 years. By the end of the season a New York club that hadn't changed managers in midseason since 1914 (except when Miller Huggins died in 1929) had had three—McCarthy, former catcher Bill Dickey (who lasted 105 games, then resigned when MacPhail wouldn't make a longer commitment), and coach Johnny Neun.

"It grows more and more un-Yankeelike," Will Wedge wrote in the *New York Sun*.

He was an unspectacular right-handed pitcher who'd lost twice as many games as he'd won during the season and would pitch only 2⅔ more innings in the major leagues. Yet, for one afternoon Floyd (Bill) Bevens had found magic amid his wildness and now was only one out from immortality in Cooperstown.

This was the ninth inning of the fourth game of the 1947 World Series, and no Dodger player had hit safely. Nine of them had walked, though, and now Carl Furillo stood on first with pitcher Hugh Casey due up. Instead, Dodger manager Burt Shotton made two strategic moves. Al Gionfriddo, a rarely used outfielder with sprinter's speed, would run for Furillo. And Pete Reiser would bat for Casey.

One stolen base, an intentional walk, a pinch runner, and a pinch double later, Bevens was trudging through a jubilant mob to the Ebbets Field showers, the only man ever to pitch a Series one-hitter and lose.

It was the crowning oddity to probably the most emotional and dramatic October to that time, whose two most memorable games were won by the Series loser and whose most memorable participants—Bevens, Gionfriddo, and Dodger veteran Cookie Lavagetto—never played another major league season.

This was the year when the Yankee dynasty was revived for the second time under a new manager, when Joe DiMaggio returned to his prewar form, when a new pitching staff signed on, and when president Larry MacPhail tearfully announced his farewell at the end.

Most of all it was the season when the Yankees rediscovered the stability and confidence that had brought them seven pennants in eight years prior to the wartime manpower drain.

After three managers—Joe McCarthy, Bill Dickey, and Johnny Neun—had held the reins in 1946, MacPhail had hired Bucky Harris, whose Washington clubs had beaten New York out of pennants in 1924 and 1925. Harris hadn't managed since an abortive stint with the seventh-place Phillies in 1943, yet he quickly restored a calm, professional ambience to the Yankee clubhouse.

And although the club had nobody among the league's top five in batting average or home runs, New York won 19 straight in midseason and left Detroit a dozen games behind. The ingredients were basic—a .315 season by DiMaggio, who'd undergone heel surgery, fine defense, and the league's best pitching, served up by a superb new rotation.

Only Spud Chandler remained from the prewar staff. Allie Reynolds, obtained from Cleveland for second baseman Joe Gordon the previous fall, was the new Yankee ace—he'd win 19 games. Rookie Spec Shea won 14. And light-hearted Joe Page, DiMaggio's roommate, had de-

Bucky Harris was the Yankees' new manager.

veloped into the league's best reliever with 14 victories and 17 saves.

Yet after two Series games with their borough rivals, observers wondered whether the Yankees needed any staff at all. They landed on Brooklyn's Ralph Branca for five runs in the fifth inning of the Stadium opener and coasted, 5–3. Then they riddled four Dodger pitchers for 15 hits in game two and won, 10–3. During the entire Series no Brooklyn starter would survive the

Hard-throwing Allie Reynolds became the Yankees' new ace at 19–8 after being obtained from Cleveland for Joe Gordon.

Joe Page was the majors' top reliever with 14 wins, 17 saves and 2.15 earned run average while going 14–8. The southpaw also picked up an All-Star Game save and pitched in four World Series games, including a five-inning one-hit gem closing out the Yankees' deciding victory in game seven.

fifth inning. This was a world championship worth televising for the first time?

"The worst we've ever seen," decided *New York Daily News* columnist Jimmy Powers. "It took exactly four minutes short of five dismal hours to play the first two alleged games."

But once the clubs crossed the Brooklyn Bridge

for game three the roles switched and the clock ran on. The Dodgers pounced on Bobo Newsom and Vic Raschi for six runs in the second inning and kept five New York pitchers busy for three hours and five minutes of a 9–8 Brooklyn triumph, the longest Series game to that point.

Yet the next day Bevens, who'd been 7–13 during the season, either baffled or walked every Dodger he faced. Control was his only problem; in the fifth inning, two walks, a sacrifice, and a fielder's choice cost Bevens a shutout. His mates had already dug up two runs for him. The victory—and the no-hitter—were still within his grasp.

When left fielder Johnny Lindell went back against the wall to haul down Bruce Edwards' leadoff drive in the ninth, it seemed possible. After Furillo walked, Bevens got Spider Jorgensen to foul out to first baseman George McQuinn, and the Dodgers were down to their last out and the bottom of their batting order.

So Shotton sent in Gionfriddo to run for Furillo. And Reiser, who'd busted an ankle breaking up a double play the day before but had sworn the team doctor to secrecy, limped out to hit for Casey.

Harris let Bevens throw Reiser two balls and a strike. Then Gionfriddo stole second base on his belly, and with the count 3–1 Harris ordered Bevens to walk Reiser. Second baseman Eddie Stanky, a singles hitter, was on deck; the percentages seemed better.

"Reiser had power and could hit a home run," Harris would explain to second-guessers who chided him for putting the winning run on base.

Aaron Robinson (left) had catching help from newcomers Ralph "Major" Houk and Larry "Yogi" Berra, both of whom would leave imprints on Yankee history.

The Yankee infield had a new first baseman: George McQuinn (right), who teamed with shortstop Phil Rizzuto (front), third baseman Billy Johnson (left) and second baseman Snuffy Stirnweiss (top). McQuinn was a key addition, salvaged from waivers at age 38. The 10-season veteran, a onetime Yankee farmhand traded away because he was buried behind Lou Gehrig, played a solid first base and batted .304, second only to Joe DiMaggio's .315.

"I knew that Stanky would be easier to pitch to and that they were out of left-handed hitters. I'd do it again tomorrow."

Reiser, who could not have run out a ground ball, shrugged and hobbled to first, where he was replaced by pinch runner Eddie Miksis. "DiMaggio told me years later that Harris knew I had a broken ankle," Reiser would say, "but that he still didn't want to pitch to me. 'He'll still swing, ankle or no ankle,' Harris said. That was a nice tribute, but it cost him."

Instead of Stanky, Shotton chose Lavagetto, a 34-year-old journeyman infielder who'd played in only 41 games that season and was one-for-12 lifetime in Series play. "The scouting sheets said to throw hard to Lavagetto and away from him," Bevens remembered. But the sheets were wrong. Inside fastballs were problems for Lavagetto, but he could handle something outside.

Bevens' first pitch, a fastball high and away, got Lavagetto to fan. But Lavagetto ripped the second, in the same spot, to the opposite field

and presented right fielder Tommy Henrich with a tough judgment.

"I knew it was creamed," Henrich said. "At least to the wall. But 15 feet high or seven? That was the dilemma. If I get away from the wall to play the carom and it's only six feet high I've given away a no-hitter. If I go to the wall and it's too high, I've given away the game. Those are five seconds I could have lived without."

As it was the ball cleared Henrich's head by six feet and bounced off the wall. Lavagetto, rounding first on his way to a double, glanced at the third-base line. "I turned and saw the two runs scoring and that's all there was to it," he said. "You can throw everything else out. That's the top thrill of my life. Nothing else can happen."

Gionfriddo scored easily. Then Bevens, backing up the plate, watched Miksis slide across, grinning. Umpire Larry Goetz bent over to dust off the plate, then caught himself. "What am I doing?" he murmured. "The game is over."

It was Brooklyn 3, New York 2, and the Series was tied. Casey, who'd thrown one pitch in the eighth inning, was the winner. As Dodger fans celebrated, Bevens walked unnoticed to the clubhouse. Behind him, a movie advertisement loomed large on the wall for *The Secret Life of Walter Mitty*.

The next afternoon with the score again 2–1 in New York's favor, a Dodger on base and two out in the ninth, Lavagetto emerged from the Dodger dugout once more, this time batting for Casey with a chance to force the Yankees to the brink. In the outfield, DiMaggio and Henrich stared at each other. "For Christ's sake," DiMaggio told Henrich, "say a prayer."

This time Lavagetto struck out. Now Brooklyn, down three games to two, had been cornered, with the Series shifting back to the Stadium. The Dodgers piled up a 4–0 lead in the third inning of game six, chasing Reynolds, but New York tied it on a double, a wild pitch, an error, and five straight singles, then took the lead in the fourth.

But the Dodgers pounded Page for four runs in the sixth and went ahead, 8–5. Whereupon the Yankees put two men on in the bottom of the inning and got DiMaggio to the plate with two out. Gionfriddo, meanwhile, had replaced Miksis in left for defensive purposes. "Shotton said play DiMaggio to pull," Gionfriddo said. "Keep him from getting an extra-base hit."

So DiMaggio, whose homer had won game five, crashed one toward the left-field bullpen, just to the left of the 415-foot marker and just above the waist-high fence.

Although the World Series was being televised for the first time, the largest crowd in Series history up to that time—73,365—jammed the Stadium for the opener and saw Spec Shea and the Yankees beat Ralph Branca and the Dodgers, 5–3.

Johnny Lindell didn't need much batting advice from manager Bucky Harris during the Series. The pitcher-turned-outfielder hit a record 9-for-18 .500. He also led both teams in slugging (.778), RBIs (7), and doubles (3). "After that Series," the career .273 hitter cracked later, "the Dodgers asked me to take a saliva test."

Gionfriddo turned, chased, lost his cap, and, just as reserve Dodger catcher Bobby Bragan was about to catch the ball inside the bullpen, grabbed it after it had cleared the rail. "My butt hit the bullpen fence," the 5-foot-6 outfielder said.

As Yankee partisans gasped, Gionfriddo's teammates whooped. "I have seen many, many greater plays," said Brooklyn shortstop Pee Wee Reese, "but I did not expect that one to be made."

Neither did DiMaggio. Six years earlier he had watched Cleveland third baseman Ken Keltner snap his 56-game hitting streak and hadn't shown a trace of emotion. Now, he was furious.

"In all the years I played with Joe, I think I only saw him get mad once," said New York shortstop Phil Rizzuto. "Joe was at second when Gionfriddo caught it and Joe knocked the base loose from its hinges and kicked some dirt free. He was really steamed."

The Yankees would load the bases with one out in the ninth, but Casey got out of it with only one run's damage, and Brooklyn prevailed, 8–6.

The Dodgers would make one last charge in the final game the next afternoon, knocking out Shea in the second and taking a 2–0 lead. But they'd used a dozen pitchers in three days. The

Larry MacPhail stunned baseball by resigning as Yankee president during the locker-room celebration of the championship. He was bought out by partners Del Webb (center) and Dan Topping (right).

He had been gone since 1934, but they had never gotten around to retiring his number. George Herman Ruth had finished his career as a Boston Brave and limped off into the shadows, finished at 40. The Yankees had seen him occasionally since, as a raspy-voiced spectator. And in 1947 they'd held a day for him at the Stadium, yet didn't retire his number.

Now it was 1948 and there might not be another chance. Ruth was 53, and cancer had ravaged his throat. He'd realized it during the winter and told friends that he was not going to waste away in a hospital bed.

So Ruth turned up at spring training for a last look at his game, and on June 13 the Yankees said goodbye with the formality and dignity the man deserved. Twenty-five years had passed since the Stadium, the House That Ruth Built, had opened. So the front office brought back Babe's teammates for a retirement ceremony, staged a brief exhibition with the current club, and installed Ruth as the old-timers' manager for a day.

He did not—could not—play. His old pin-striped uniform, with its number 3, hung loosely on shoulders and a torso that had once perched atop spindly legs like a beer barrel on stilts, as Ty Cobb had said.

So Ruth sat in the dugout in uniform, a camel's-

Yankees got rid of Hal Gregg in the fourth, took a 3–2 lead, added two more for good measure and let Page (who appeared in four games) clean up. He allowed only one Dodger to reach base in five innings (and that runner was promptly erased in a Series-ending double play). The Yankees had won their first championship since 1943.

In a raucous Stadium clubhouse MacPhail waved a beer bottle and announced his resignation. "I'm through, I'm through," he cried. "My heart won't stand it."

Little Al Gionfriddo makes an epic catch in game six at the Stadium, a twisting game-saver that deprives Joe DiMaggio of a three run-homer. The 5'6" outfielder grabbed the ball at the 415-foot mark just before it went over the bullpen fence. On seeing the catch, DiMaggio kicked the infield dirt in a rare show of emotion. This was hero Gionfriddo's last big-league game.

On June 13, a dying icon said farewell at the House That Ruth Built. Once again, the Stadium echoed with thundering cheers for the Bambino. His body was wasting away, and using a bat for a cane, the shrunken Babe stood before the crowd of 49,641, amid, as W. C. Heinz wrote, "a cauldron of sound he must know better than any other man."

Afterward, Ruth shed his pinstripes—the final time number 3 was worn by a Yankee. It was the last of the ninth for Babe, and he knew it, telling longtime teammate and pal Joe Dugan, "I'm gone, Joe." And two months later he was.

Babe Ruth's body was brought to Yankee Stadium for one final appearance. Crowds—estimates ranged from 77,000 to 200,000—ringed the ballpark before passing Ruth's open coffin inside the main entrance. Street vendors sold hot dogs, soda, and souvenir pictures. And Babe's funeral packed St. Patrick's Cathedral while tens of thousands stood outside in the rain and humidity.

The Yankees stood in silent tribute when Babe Ruth's passing was announced during an August 16 exhibition game with the Giants at the Polo Grounds, where Babe had cracked his first homer as a Red Sox sophomore in 1915 and where he starred in his first three seasons in New York with the 1920–22 Yankees.

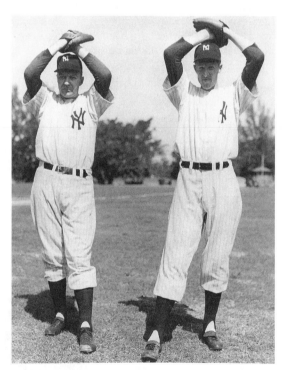

It was the Stadium's 25th anniversary, and Joe McCarthy returned as new manager of the archrival Red Sox on opening day. He and Yankee manager Bucky Harris look on as Governor Thomas Dewey tosses out the first ball. All three men would be frustrated in 1948. Harris lost his job when the Yanks were dethroned, finishing third, 2½ games out. McCarthy's Red Sox lost a one-game pennant playoff to Cleveland. And Dewey was upset by Harry Truman for the Presidency.

hair coat buttoned around his tender throat to keep out the damp air, and his teammates approached him for his autograph.

"They took a good many years to retire your number, Babe," joked pitcher Waite Hoyt. "They retired mine in 1930—damn quick, too. And without notice."

Ruth had had 14 years' notice. When he walked out to make a final appearance as a Yankee, nearly 50,000 spectators blinked back tears. His voice a hoarse whisper now, Ruth told them how

Veterans Ed Lopat (left) and Red Embree were acquired to bolster the pitching staff—Lopat from the White Sox, Embree the Indians. Embree was only 5–3 before moving on, but Lopat went 17–11 and proved a key to the 1949–53 world championships. The southpaw's assorted off-speed "junk" was a sharp contrast to the speed of colleagues Allie Reynolds and Vic Raschi, and Steady Eddie was 113–59 during eight Yankee seasons, plus 4–1 in World Series play. The native New Yorker later was a Yankee pitching coach and scout.

Left: *Tommy Henrich rapped four grand slams during the season, the equal of Lou Gehrig's 1934 feat and still the Yankee record. In all, Henrich hit 25 homers, his second most in a season, while batting .308, his highest as a regular.* **Right:** *Bobby Brown hit an even .300 again in his first full season. The sweet-swinging medical student would quit baseball before age 30 to pursue a career as a cardiologist. He served as American League president in 1984–94.*

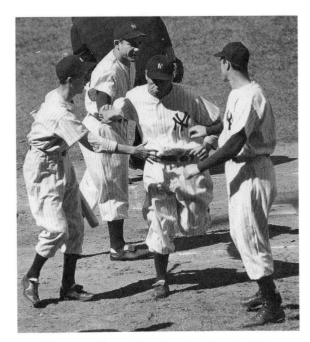

Ailing Charlie Keller walloped consecutive pinch homers in three days, only the third American Leaguer ever to do it. He was sidelined much of the season by a broken hand along with his aching back.

wonderful it was to be back and how proud he was to have hit the first homer in the Stadium. Then he was gone, and the Yankees of 1948 came out to defeat the Indians, 5–3, and stay in a pennant race that Cleveland and Boston had been threatening to decide between themselves.

The Yankees would remain in contention until the final two days of the season, when the Red Sox would eliminate them and go on to play—and lose—a one-game playoff with the Indians for the pennant.

But Ruth would not be there to see it. On August 16 the cancer had taken him, stilling the voice that had guffawed through railroad dining cars and ballpark clubhouses for two decades.

"Game called by darkness—let the curtain fall," Grantland Rice wrote. "No more remembered thunder sweeps the field. No more the ancient echoes hear the call to one who wore so well both sword and shield. The Big Guy's left us with the night to face, and there is no one who can take his place."

There had never been another like Ruth. Tens of thousands of fans passed his remains lying in state at the Stadium and jammed the streets outside St. Patrick's Cathedral for his funeral. They buried him on a brutally hot day as his former teammates sweltered by his casket.

"Lord, I'd give my right arm for an ice-cold beer right now," Joe Dugan whispered as he helped carry the heavy coffin out of the cathedral and into the sweltering humidity. Fellow pallbearer Waite Hoyt grunted. "So would the Babe," he said.

He was a clown. Always had been. Charles Dillon Stengel had played for five National League clubs in 14 years and rarely had a serious moment. As a Giant, he won a World Series game with a home run and thumbed his nose at the Yankees as he rounded the bases. He lifted his cap to greet his old friends in Brooklyn as he stepped into the batter's box at Ebbets Field, and a sparrow flew out. He spoke in a roundabout version of English called Stengelese that contained a thread of indisputable logic—somewhere.

Stengel had managed one winning major league club in nine years. The seventh-place Dodgers actually paid him not to manage in 1937; six years later, when a Boston taxi knocked Stengel down and broke his leg and he missed two months as Braves manager, a Boston sports columnist voted the cabbie "the man who did the most for Boston baseball in 1943."

Casey Stengel receives a spray of flowers on opening day in his Stadium debut as Yankee manager. Babe Ruth's widow Claire and Governor Thomas Dewey join the ceremony.

Stengel hadn't held a major league job since, but now Yankee management had chosen him, at age 58, to run a club that had just won 94 games and lost the pennant on the next-to-last day of the season.

Observers who were stunned when general manager George Weiss dismissed Bucky Harris the day after the 1948 season ended ("It was like being socked in the head with a steel pipe," admitted Harris, 1947 Manager of the Year) were equally surprised when Stengel was plucked from the minor league Oakland Oaks, where he'd just won the Pacific Coast League pennant.

"They don't hand out jobs like this just because they like your company," Stengel reasoned. "I got this job because these people think I can produce for them."

Weiss had liked what Stengel had done with the Yankees' farm club in Kansas City in 1945. At Oakland, the pennant was its first in 27 years.

Beneath the verbal haze of his Stengelese whirred a mind that believed firmly in fundamentals and had a shrewd command of tactics. If Stengel's teams at Brooklyn and Boston had been relentlessly mediocre, Weiss reasoned, it was only because his material was, too. With a lineup stocked with DiMaggios, Henrichs, and fine pitchers, Stengel would produce contenders.

Skeptical sportswriters picked the Yankees for third—which delighted Stengel, who was accustomed to trudging wearily through the second division. "Third ain't so bad," he figured. "I never finished third before. That's pretty high up."

So he set to work in spring training and drilled basics into a club that was thought to be beyond them. "It will look new and baffling," Stengel conceded, but the approach paid off immediately. The Yankees won 16 of their first 21 games and grabbed first place in a hammerlock, even without Joe DiMaggio. Winter surgery on his aching right heel hadn't eased the pain that had bothered him since the end of the war. "Fellas," Stengel told his club in spring training, "Joe won't be with us for a while."

Meaning three months. When DiMaggio finally returned at the end of June after missing the season's first 65 games, he joined a sagging New York team that was facing a three-game series with the Red Sox in Fenway Park and clinging gamely to the league lead.

He was hardly in playing shape and hadn't seen a ball thrown by a rival in an official game in nine months, but DiMaggio was no longer in pain. That was enough to make him buoyantly optimistic in the clubhouse before what he would afterward label "the greatest series of my career."

The heel had held up nicely in an exhibition with the Giants the day before. "I might be ready for the series with Boston," DiMaggio had informed Stengel. "You're the boss," Stengel told him.

DiMaggio had lunched with Manhattan restaurateur Toots Shor that afternoon, still uncertain. "Night game tonight, eh?" Shor said. "Who's going for the Sox?"

"McDermott," DiMaggio replied. "Tough boy under the lights." Thus the challenge, and Joe took an afternoon flight to Boston to meet it. Eagerly. And before 36,000 spectators, the largest night crowd in Fenway history to that time, the limping, 34-year-old DiMaggio made a classic re-entry, his tender heel encased in a cushioned spiked shoe. DiMaggio's two-run homer in the third provided the winning runs, and his catch of Ted Williams' long fly ball with two out in the ninth insured them.

The next afternoon, with the Yankees trailing 7–1 in the fifth, DiMaggio belted a three-run homer to drag them back into the game, then won it with a blast over the left-field wall with two out in the eighth.

During batting practice the next day, a biplane circled packed Fenway trailing a banner: *The Great DiMaggio!* And he delivered the coup de grâce in that finale, a mammoth three-run shot off Red Sox ace Mel Parnell that hit the light tower in left, about 80 feet above the field. Boston fans, who'd never borne any love for anybody in pinstripes except the great Ruth, instinctively stood and applauded what amounted to a sweep of their home team by one man.

The gaunt and drained DiMaggio was mobbed by the media seeking to analyze his nine-RBI, five-runs-scored, .455 splurge. Asked how he could muster such an outburst after only eight workouts, DiMag shrugged, "You swing the bat and hit the ball."

The sweep cooled off the Red Sox (now 8½ games behind) while revitalizing the Yankees—for awhile. But as the season progressed, so did New York's casualty list. As the Yankees lost DiMaggio (viral infection), Johnny Mize (sprained shoulder), and Yogi Berra (broken thumb), and harnessed Tommy Henrich's cracked ribs, Boston won 59 and lost 19 over the second half and claimed first place with five games to play.

With two games left and a one-game lead the Red Sox came to the Stadium, and Stengel spent a sleepless night scribbling down lineups, tossing them away and scribbling more. Could DiMaggio play, having lost 15 pounds? Could Berra, his fractured thumb still sore, catch Allie Reynolds' fastballs?

The most controversial play of the season occurred at the Stadium early in the final week when Boston's Johnny Pesky was called safe at home on Bobby Doerr's squeeze bunt. Umpire Bill Grieve ruled Pesky had slid under catcher Ralph Houk's tag for the winning run that gave the Red Sox a one-game lead.

The real question, it turned out, was whether Reynolds could find the plate. After he'd walked three straight batters, thrown a wild pitch, and allowed three singles and two runs in three innings, Stengel yanked him and sent in reliever Joe Page. But Page immediately walked in two more runs as Stengel, distraught, paced and cursed in the dugout.

Furious at himself, Page yielded only one single the rest of the way, and his mates tied the game, 4–4, by the bottom of the fifth. When outfielder Johnny Lindell, who hadn't hit a homer since July and only five all season, poled one down the left-field line with two out in the eighth for a 5–4 victory, Stengel winked. "I think we've got 'em," he said. "I can feel it in my bones."

So, once again, a season had come down to one game, but this time the Yankees were playing in it. With Williams blinded by the sun in left field, shortstop Phil Rizzuto dumped a triple 20 feet from him and scored on an infield out by Henrich in the first inning. A Henrich homer

and a bloop double by rookie second baseman Jerry Coleman with the bases loaded and two out added four more runs in the eighth for a 5–0 lead.

But New York right-hander Vic Raschi, three outs from the pennant, relaxed perceptibly, and a triple by Bobby Doerr past a stumbling DiMaggio led to three quick Boston runs. So not to jeopardize a Yankee team on the threshold of a pennant, the exhausted, hurting DiMaggio limped in from center field, removing himself in favor of younger and healthier legs. And soon there were two outs. With the tying run at the plate in Birdie Tebbetts, Berra walked out to calm Raschi down—or fire him up.

"Give me the goddamn ball," Raschi growled, "and get the hell out of here." Moments later Henrich would settle under a pop foul, squeezing it near the first-base stands, and New York celebrated its second pennant in three years—its first under a clown.

For purposes of poetic justice, the World Series opponent would be the Dodgers, who'd traded

Rookie Jerry Coleman was the new second baseman and combined smoothly with shortstop Phil Rizzuto. Rizzuto has flipped the ball to Coleman, who turns the double play over sliding Jim Hegan of Cleveland.

Stengel in 1917 and fired him in 1936. Brooklyn, too, had won its pennant on the final day of the season, beating Philadelphia in extra innings to finish a game ahead of St. Louis.

Emotionally drained, the two clubs sleep-walked through the first eight innings of the Stadium opener scoreless, blinded by Reynolds on one side and Don Newcombe on the other. Finally, Henrich, who'd carried the Yankees in the early season when their entire outfield was side-lined, poked a home run into the lower right-field stands to end it.

Brooklyn returned the favor the next afternoon as Preacher Roe shut out New York on six hits and bore off a victory by the same 1–0 score. So the duel shifted to Ebbets Field, and the Series turned on a two-out, bases-loaded single in the ninth by Yankee Johnny Mize, who would make a habit of October pinch hits. This one gave the Yankees a 4–3 victory that survived homers by Luis Olmo and Roy Campanella in the bottom of the inning and put New York in command.

Newcombe, who would never be able to beat New York in a Series game despite a brilliant career, came back the next day and was chased with three runs in the fourth. Then replacement Joe Hatten loaded the bases in the fifth and let Bobby Brown clear them with a triple.

Four Dodger runs off Ed Lopat in the sixth merely brought out Reynolds and inspired him to throw shutout stuff the rest of the way. Its

pitching exhausted, Brooklyn died peacefully the following afternoon before loved ones. New York rattled three pitchers for 10 runs in six innings, forced Dodger manager Burt Shotton to trot out three more, and prevailed, 10–6. The Yankees would not lose another Series until 1955, when Stengel had already established himself alongside Miller Huggins and Joe McCarthy.

"I am the same kind of manager I always was," he would say, drinking his first official champagne since 1923. "But nowadays I seem to get a little more assistance from my help."

He was born on East 66th Street and grew up in Queens, a cocky blond city kid who was always throwing a Spalding rubber ball against the wall of a trolley garage and saw no reason why he couldn't pitch for the Yankees. Eddie Ford had telephoned scout Paul Krichell after Binghamton, his minor league team, finished its 1949 season and asked him to have manager Casey Stengel bring him up for the Yankees' pennant drive.

"You may think I'm cocky," Ford had conceded, "but I can win for you. I've learned everything I can learn in the minor leagues."

Ed "Whitey" Ford proved the Yankees' prize rookie. Called up in July, he won nine straight as a starter before losing one in relief. Ford was 9–1 with a 2.81 ERA, and added the clinching victory in the World Series. Despite spending only half that summer in pinstripes, the cocky, 21-year-old southpaw from Queens was the Sporting News' *Rookie of the Year.*

The offer had been politely refused, but now it was July of 1950. Ford was pitching well for a hopeless Kansas City affiliate in the American Association, and the Yankees were embroiled in a four-way pennant race. So one morning at six o'clock Ford was aroused by a call from Kansas City manager Joe Kuhel. "The Yankees want you to get up to Boston," Kuhel told him. "As soon as you can."

Ford's debut, relieving in an 11–2 lost cause at Fenway, was eminently forgettable. Five runs, seven hits, six walks, and a wild pitch—all the while tipping off his pitches. "I think we ended up losing 17–4," Ford would recall. "Something tidy like that."

But Stengel liked Ford's deceptive fastball, his breaking pitch, and his attitude, and began starting him against second-division clubs. By the end of the season he'd gone 9–1, with the only earned run average under 3.00 on the New York staff, and the Yankees had won the pennant by three games over Detroit.

Now it was the fourth game of the World Se-

ries and the Yankees were looking for a sweep from a young Philadelphia Phillies club that was playing for a championship for the first time since 1915.

So Stengel looked to a 21-year-old city kid who wouldn't mind walking out to the Yankee Stadium mound and facing a desperate opponent before 68,000 people. "Hell," Ford figured, "half of them were my relatives anyway."

For 8⅔ innings he baffled the Phillies, scattering six hits. Now with two men on base and one out from a Series shutout, Ford got Andy Seminick to lift a fly toward Gene Woodling in left field, deep but catchable.

But sun and haze from cigarette smoke obscured Woodling's vision as he drifted back; the ball glanced off his glove, allowing Puddinhead Jones and Ken Johnson to score. When Mike Goliat followed with a single Stengel came out, concerned about a lead that had suddenly shrunk to 5–2, replaced Ford with Allie Reynolds, and listened to Ford's relatives—about 34,000 of them—boo.

"I'll never forget Reynolds coming in," Ford would say. "He was the meanest-looking pitcher I ever saw. Allie just came in and blew three fastballs [in four pitches] past [pinch hitter] Stan Lopata, and that was the Series."

It was the first of a Series-record 10 victories for Ford, the Yankees' third championship in four years, and their sixth sweep, which they achieved by scoring a grand total of 11 runs. The reason was pitching, a solid rotation that was the backbone of a club that didn't overwhelm anybody yet managed to win every vital series.

All season long they'd been scuffling with Detroit, Cleveland, and Boston, losing their grip on first place in mid-June and not regaining it until September. But when the crunch came, New York had taken two of three from the Tigers at Detroit (with Ford winning the decisive game) and two from the Red Sox at Yankee Stadium.

They'd clinched the pennant on the next-to-last day of the season, but instead of the defending National League champion Dodgers, the Yankees found themselves facing Philadelphia's "Whiz Kids," who'd beaten Brooklyn on Dick Sisler's 10th-inning home run in the season finale.

Phillies manager Eddie Sawyer found himself in a quandary. His number-two starter, Curt Simmons, had been claimed by the military late in the season. His ace, Robin Roberts, had pitched in three of the Phils' final five games. Stengel was opening with 20-game winner Vic Raschi.

So Sawyer tapped Jim Konstanty, who was the

Yogi Berra holds the pitching arm of the unbeaten Whitey Ford following the rookie's ninth straight victory.

best reliever in either league (16–7, 22 saves in 74 appearances) but hadn't started a game in four years. Thus began three of the best consecutive pitcher's duels in Series annals.

Konstanty, who would pitch in all but one

Vic Raschi was 21–8 for a league-leading .724 winning percentage in the second of three straight 20-victory seasons.

game, yielded only four hits and one run. But Raschi, a hulking right-hander who always took the mound unshaven, and who uncorked rising fastballs as a substitute for conversation, allowed only two hits, no runs and nothing at all after the fifth inning.

A double by Bobby Brown and two fly balls provided the only run Raschi needed. When Sawyer came up with Roberts the next afternoon, Stengel countered with Reynolds, who was riding a streak of 12 consecutive scoreless Series innings, and the string of zeroes continued.

The Yankees nicked Roberts for a run in the second on a walk and two singles; the Phillies retaliated in the fifth inning with their own on two singles and a sacrifice fly. So it went until the top of the tenth.

Reynolds, who'd just gotten out of a jam when Phil Rizzuto and Jerry Coleman had turned a double play behind him, had ducked into the clubhouse for a quick cigarette. Suddenly he heard a muffled roar from the stands. Roberts had tried to slip a fastball past Joe DiMaggio, who'd deposited it in Shibe Park's upper left-field stands. New York 2, Philadelphia 1. "If it was a speck off," marveled Seminick, the Phillies catcher, "DiMaggio could put it in the seats for you."

So the Series shifted to Yankee Stadium—and little changed. Sawyer was down to left-hander Ken Heintzelman, who'd been 3–9 during the season. Stengel still had a horse in reserve in Ed Lopat, who'd won 18 games with a deft assortment of junk.

The Phillies led 2–1 with two out in the eighth, but Heintzelman, tiring, grew wild. He walked Coleman, Yogi Berra, and DiMaggio in a row and was yanked for Konstanty, who got

Veteran first baseman, outfielder, and pinch hitter Johnny Hopp (.333) was acquired during the season. Hopp is on the right, shown with Johnny Mize, another National League retread.

Opposing managers Casey Stengel and Eddie Sawyer of the Phillies meet before the World Series opener. By Series end, Sawyer may have wanted to really strangle Stengel. The Yankees posted three one-run victories en route to a sweep of Philadelphia's "Whiz Kids."

Jerry Coleman was the Series MVP after driving home the winning run in two of the three one-run victories. In all, Coleman had a Series-most 3 RBIs—equal to the Phillies' total.

Brown to ground to Granny Hamner at short. "I can still see it," Seminick would say. "Granny took his eyes off the ball for an instant and that's all you have to do. If he had made the play, we would have been alive."

Instead, Coleman came home with the tying run, and with two out in the ninth Woodling, Rizzuto, and Coleman all singled to end it. The

Phil Rizzuto steals second base in game three. He took third as catcher Andy Seminick's throw bounced into center field, and scored the game's first run on Jerry Coleman's single. The Yankees went on to win, 3–2.

Far from the Bronx in Joplin, Missouri, an 18-year-old shortstop named Mickey Charles Mantle was batting .383 in a Class C league. Few in New York knew the name, but would the following Spring upon his arrival at the Stadium as Casey Stengel's "my phee-nom."

For more than a month Brooklyn scout Andy High had followed the Yankees during their stretch drive, scribbling down his impressions of everything, particularly their aging center fielder. His report was blunt and dead on, but when the Dodgers blew a 13½-game lead and lost a play-off to the Giants it was useless—at least to Brooklyn.

So in the spirit of National League fraternity, High had turned over his notes to the Giants, and now, after they'd stunned the Yankees in the 1951 World Series opener, Giant manager Leo Durocher was exultant. "It's great," he told reporters. "I never saw a report like it."

Neither had the Yankee center fielder. "He can't stop quickly or throw hard," High had written about Joe DiMaggio. "You can take the extra base on him. . . . He can't run and won't

Phillies had allowed New York six runs and were trailing three games to none; taken with their four losses in 1915 they had now lost seven straight Series games by one run.

So Stengel sent out his youngest, brashest pitcher to finish them off the next day. As Ford shut down Philadelphia inning after inning, his teammates chased Bob Miller in the first and piled up a 5–0 lead after six.

The only question was whether a hometown rookie from Astoria could nail down a shutout in his Series debut and limit the Phillies to three runs total, the lowest since that made by the 1905 Athletics. Seminick's fly ball was the crowning touch—or so it seemed.

"It wasn't an easy fly ball," Ford said. "It was sort of a line drive, and I could see it was trouble the way Gene was going after it, trying to flip his sunglasses down so he could see it."

Woodling never did. So it ended 5–2, and Ford shrugged and consoled Woodling afterward. "I went over to let him know I wasn't mad," Ford said. "Especially a guy like Woodling, the way he used to put out."

No harm done. The Yankees were still world champions, the dynasty well on its way. "In another five years," decided general manager George Weiss, "they'll appreciate how good this club really is."

Billy Martin (right), a 22-year-old "veteran" with 36 at bats for the 1950 Yankees, instructs infield candidates Mickey Mantle (left) and Gil McDougald during a pre-camp instruction school at Phoenix. Both aspirants made the varsity. At 23, McDougald, led Yankee batters at .306 while playing third and second bases. He was voted the league's Rookie of the Year over 19-year-old Mantle, who was moved from shortstop to the outfield and hit .267.

bunt . . . His reflexes are very slow, and he can't pull a good fastball."

DiMaggio had known it before anybody. He'd told sportswriters during spring training that the upcoming season would be his last. He was not yet 37, but his legs hurt every day. He'd had surgery on both heels, his right knee had bothered him for several years, his throwing shoulder was arthritic. "It was agony for him just getting in and out of a taxicab," shortstop Phil Rizzuto noticed.

Most of all it was agony for DiMaggio to play below his own demanding standards. As 1951 wore on, it was obvious he was headed for his worst season at the plate—.263 with only 71 RBIs and 12 homers. He simply couldn't get around on pitches any more. "Certain pitchers were getting Joe out with the slider," teammate Ed Lopat would say, "and he felt bad about it. He knew he just couldn't handle the pitch."

Young Mick was also a spectacular ballhawk in his first season playing the outfield.

Mickey Mantle had a storybook spring, batting .402 with nine homers and 32 RBIs. The 19-year-old Wunderkind became the first ever to jump from Class C to the Yankees. A speedy switch-hitter, Mantle powered the ball from both sides of the plate.

"That kid can hit balls over buildings," Casey Stengel marveled. "There's never been anyone like this kid. He has more speed than any slugger and more slug than any speedster—and nobody has ever had more of both of them together."

As the summer continued DiMaggio drew more and more within himself. He became moody, spoke rarely, brooded. In July manager Casey Stengel yanked him after he'd misplayed a ball in the first inning. Yet when the Series began Di-Maggio was still in center field—but hitting miserably. And the Yankees, who'd swept the Phillies for their third world championship in four years in 1950, were suddenly in trouble.

The Giants hadn't won a pennant since 1937. Now, after Bobby Thomson's "shot heard 'round the world" had given them a dramatic last-pitch playoff victory over the Dodgers, they'd used that momentum to take two of the first three games from their crosstown rivals.

His pitching staff exhausted, Durocher had gone with journeyman left-hander Dave Koslo in the opener at the Stadium—and Koslo had mastered the Yankees, 5–1, on seven hits, their first loss in a Series opener since 1936.

The Yankees had won the second game, 3–1, but lost rookie Mickey Mantle with torn knee ligaments. Then second baseman Eddie Stanky had kicked the ball out of Rizzuto's glove on an aborted hit-and-run attempt, and the Giants had scored five runs in an inning to grab game three.

Alarmed, Stengel had held a team meeting before the fourth game. "Fellas, I just want to mention one thing to you," he said. "You are not playing these guys 22 games. You only have four or five to play. What the hell are you going to do, let them run you out of the ball park? Let's go."

Duly chastened, the Yankees rubbed out the Giants in three straight and closed out the Series.

DiMaggio hit a two-run homer, the last of his career, to help even it. Then a grand slam by rookie Gil McDougald touched off a 13–1 cakewalk. Finally, Hank Bauer tripled home three runs in the sixth inning of game six and speared a Sal Yvars liner on his knees in the ninth to end it.

Afterward, in a jammed Yankee clubhouse, Stengel sought out DiMaggio, who'd doubled in the eighth and trotted out to center field to a five-minute Stadium ovation before his final inning. "If it wasn't for you, we wouldn't have done it," Stengel told him. "Joe, this is your title. Yours alone. You did it."

It was one to quit on, and DiMaggio vowed he would. "I have played my final game," he murmured, popping open a beer at his locker. Babe

Shy rookie Mickey Mantle blushed when asked to pose with idols Joe DiMaggio and Ted Williams on opening day at the Stadium. DiMaggio was beginning his final season as the Yankee Clipper. In an autobiography, Mantle would call Joltin' Joe "the hitter I most admired" and Williams "the best batter I ever saw." Mickey later wrote, "Ted was in a class by himself—an Einstein at the bat." Soon after this photo was taken, Mantle made his first big-league putout—a lunging catch of a dizzying fly ball by Williams. It was "a real cloudbreaker," Mick would recall. "I circled beneath, searching, searching, and finally jumped sideways, barely grabbing the damn thing."

Mickey Mantle and Jackie Jensen flanked Joe DiMaggio in the Yankee outfield on opening day. Jensen, a former Rose Bowl star, hit .298 but would be traded the next season, a deal Stengel would say was his worst. Jensen went on to be league MVP for Boston, where he batted cleanup behind Ted Williams, thus having played alongside two legends: Williams and DiMaggio.

Ruth had been a pathetic figure at the end, playing out his final year as a Boston Brave after the Yankees had offered him a one-dollar contract. Lou Gehrig had slowed to a limp, his arms powerless when he retired, just two years before a

Vic Raschi pitched the pennant clincher, topping off his record at 21–10 for his third-in-a-row 20-victory season—and his last.

nerve disease killed him. DiMaggio would not hang on past his time.

He'd told a *New York Times* photographer that the retirement was imminent: "Because I don't want them to remember me struggling." The entire season had been a struggle. There were flashes of brilliance, but they were largely obscured by pain that engendered mediocrity. "I don't want your pity," DiMaggio told writers who crowded around him after he'd beaten seventh-place Washington with a triple and a home run. "I have not asked anything from anybody."

Above all the man would not be patronized. As the pennant race built to a climax, league-leading Cleveland came to the Stadium for their final meeting of the season. After he tripled home two runs to chase pitcher Bob Feller and insure a victory, DiMaggio arrived at his locker to find a stack of congratulatory cables. "Now when I get a hit," he winced, "they send me telegrams."

He would knock in five runs in the Series and win one game, but nothing would change DiMaggio's mind. Shortly after the Series, *Life* magazine printed excerpts from High's scouting report; if there were any doubts lingering, that probably ended them. Before long DiMaggio met with club owners Dan Topping and Del Webb.

Like old times, the Yankees and Giants collided in the World Series and the battle was waged on opposite banks of the Harlem River. Yankee Stadium is in the foreground, the Polo Grounds in the background. It was the first Series televised coast to coast.

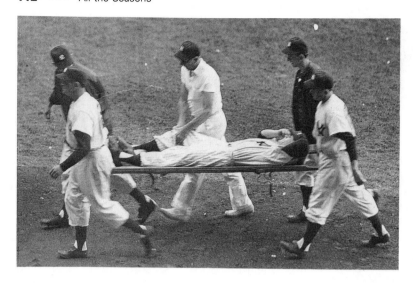

Mickey Mantle's right knee buckled when his spikes caught in a Stadium outfield drain as he and Joe DiMaggio converged on Willie Mays' flyball during game two. "Don't move," DiMaggio advised him, and Mantle remained motionless, leading some to guess he'd been shot.

"I'm never going to put that goddamn uniform on again," he told them. "Nobody knows how much pain I've been in. I'm finished. I can't play any more."

"Take some time to think about it," Topping advised. Webb nodded. "Don't worry about the money. You can have the same $100,000 next year. We'll get the contact drawn up and send it to you."

DiMaggio shook his head. "It's not the money,"

he replied. "It's me. I don't want to play baseball like this."

Later he called Topping and Webb again and told them to set a date for a press conference. And on December 12 he walked into the club office where Yankee publicist Red Patterson was handing a printed release to a roomful of reporters. "Joe DiMaggio," it announced, "today announced his retirement as an active player."

The Clipper had worn pinstripes for 13 years,

Rookie Gil McDougald tagged veteran Larry Jansen for only the third grand slam in Series history, breaking open game five at the Polo Grounds. The Yankees went on to pummel the Giants in a 13–1 laugher that gave them the Series lead for good.

had batted .325 lifetime, knocked in 1,537 runs, hit 361 homers. He had played in 1,736 games (despite missing three war years) and 10 Series, and the Yankees had won nine of them. He had been to the Yankees of his generation what Gehrig had been to the previous one, the embodiment of endurance, productivity, and class. Now it was time to go.

"Why?" he was asked.

"Because I no longer have it," DiMaggio said simply. "I once made a solemn promise to myself that I wouldn't try to hang on once the end is in sight. I've seen too many beat-up players struggle to stay up there and it was always a sad spectacle.

"You all know that I've had more than my share of injuries and setbacks during my career. Lately they've been too frequent and too serious to laugh off. And when baseball is no longer fun, it is no longer a game. So I've played my last game of ball."

In another corner of the room Stengel was asked about 1952 and his new center fielder. "The kid," he said, nodding. "Mickey Mantle."

1952

Joe Collins, the Yankee first baseman, never saw the ball. It was late afternoon in Ebbets Field, the sun had flooded the right side of the infield and now Dodger second baseman Jackie Robinson skied a pop fly between the mound and first base. Catcher Yogi Berra called for Collins to take the ball, but Collins, blinded, never moved.

This was the seventh inning of the seventh game of the 1952 World Series, and Brooklyn had loaded the bases with two out. If the ball fell in, the Yankees' 4–2 lead—and possibly the game and the championship—were gone. So, with Dodger runners galloping around the bases, New York second baseman Billy Martin, stationed almost on the outfield grass, glanced over at Collins and decided to take matters into his own bare hand.

"I could see that he didn't know where the ball was," Martin would say, "and I knew if he didn't get it the ball would drop and two, probably three runs would score. I took off."

Three Yankees—Collins, Berra, and pitcher Bob Kuzava—had formed a loose triangle around the ball. Into the vortex rushed Martin as the Dodgers were racing around the bases.

"I could tell the wind was taking it toward home plate," Martin said. "And I was thinking about Yogi. I was afraid he'd be coming out for the ball, and sometimes when he did he kept his mask on. I heard nothing, no one yelling, no one calling me off the ball. But I knew I might knock into somebody. I didn't realize how long a run I had to make until I watched the play on the motion pictures."

Martin was past the mound and heading toward the plate when he gloved the ball two feet from the ground. Carl Furillo had already crossed the plate, and Billy Cox was on his way home with the tying run. Martin, still worried about a collision, pulled the ball out of his glove and squeezed it in his bare hand. If he was knocked cold, he thought, he'd subconsciously grip the ball better that way.

"But I didn't run into anybody," Martin said, "and I didn't think the play was so much until I got to the dugout and they were all slapping me on the back and saying, great play."

It was the play of the Series. Kuzava shut out Brooklyn in the final two innings, and the Yankees had won their fifth world championship in six years. And the hero was a fiery 24-year-old named Alfred Manuel Martin, who had a knack for pulling out tough games, particularly in October.

Billy Martin broke an ankle in two places while sliding during spring training. He would return and prove a Yankee life-saver.

He'd grown up poor and combative in West Berkeley, California, and while he claimed he never started a fight, he never backed away from one. Yankee general manager George Weiss and most opponents considered him brassy and obnoxious—"that fresh kid" was the usual description. But Casey Stengel, who'd managed Martin at Oakland in the Pacific Coast League, loved him.

"It should wake my other tigers up," Stengel mused after Martin had bloodied the face of Red Sox rookie Jimmy Piersall in a pregame fistfight at Fenway Park. "It's about time they realize they gotta fight harder this year. I just hope that some of the kid's fire spreads to some of the others."

This was a new era, and Stengel wasn't quite sure how to approach it. Joe DiMaggio had retired during the winter. "Who's gonna hit the fence this year?" Stengel wondered aloud in spring training. "Who's gonna make home runs now that DiMaggio is gone?"

He had candidates—Bob Cerv, Jackie Jensen, and a fresh-faced, 20-year-old miner's son from Commerce, Oklahoma, named Mickey Charles Mantle. Just two years earlier Mantle had been a promising shortstop in Class C ball. By the middle of 1952 Stengel was calling him the best switch-hitter he'd ever seen.

In between Stengel had noticed him at his 1951 "instructual" camp in Phoenix. "Kiddo, I

Johnny Sain was 11–6 as a spot starter and reliever, three of his wins and a team-high seven saves coming out of the bullpen.

think we'll try you in the outfield," Stengel suggested. "What do you think of it?"

On opening day Mantle was in right field playing alongside DiMaggio. At mid-year he would go to the Yankees' Kansas City farm club for 40 games of seasoning (hitting .361 there) and never spend another day in the minors. When the Yankees met the Giants in the 1951 Series, Mantle was starting again—for two games. Chasing a Willie Mays fly ball with DiMaggio, Mantle caught a cleat in a Stadium outfield drain and damaged his right knee.

It was the first of what would be a series of serious leg ailments that bothered Mantle daily and that he later felt cut short his career. But, by May 1952, he was in center field as DiMaggio's permanent replacement. The team that Stengel had inherited in 1949 was undergoing a metamorphosis.

Tommy Henrich, along with DiMaggio the last link to the '30s, had given way to Collins at first base. Martin had taken over for service-bound Jerry Coleman at second. Gil McDougald, the 1951 Rookie of the Year, had inherited third. Yet the core of three championship clubs was still there—Phil Rizzuto at short, Gene Woodling and Hank Bauer in the outfield, and Berra catching a pitching staff anchored by Vic Raschi, Allie Reynolds, and Ed Lopat. (Whitey Ford was still the army.)

Again the main contender was Cleveland. The

The Yankees' top pitcher at 20–8 with a 2.06 ERA, Allie Reynolds enjoyed his best season at age 37. He added two victories, a save, and a 1.77 ERA in the World Series.

Mickey Mantle moved over to Joe DiMaggio's center-field post and blossomed as the Yankees' top hitter at .311, followed by outfield mates Gene Woodling (right) at .309, Hank Bauer (left) at .293.

pennant race came down to the last game of the two teams' season series, at Municipal Stadium, on September 14, with New York leading by 1½ games. Indian manager Al Lopez, who'd decided he'd use 20-game winners Mike Garcia, Early Wynn, and Bob Lemon exclusively down the stretch, chose Garcia, since he was 4–0 against New York that summer.

"What do you think of Lopez's plan?" Stengel was asked.

"I always heard it couldn't be done," he replied, "but sometimes it don't always work."

Whatever—the Yankees pounced on Garcia, who'd pitched 30 scoreless innings, for four runs in the third inning and ended up with seven. Lopat and Reynolds, in their turn, held the In-

The Yankee artillery faced by Brooklyn's storied "Boys of Summer" Dodgers in the World Series (from left): Johnny Mize, Joe Collins, Gene Woodling, Gil McDougald, Hank Bauer, Phil Rizzuto, Billy Martin, Irv Noren, Yogi Berra and Mickey Mantle.

One of the most infamous miscalls in World Series history blemished the Yankees' 11-inning 6–5 loss in game five when umpire Art Passarella ruled Johnny Sain out, even though his foot was sinking into the bag before the ball reached Dodger first baseman Gil Hodges.

dians to one run. That was the turning point; the New York lead was now 2½ games with 11 to play. Though Cleveland won nine of its next 10, New York took eight of nine and won the pennant by two games.

"They said we couldn't win in 1949," said Berra. "They said we weren't good enough in 1950. They gave us a chance in 1951. In 1952 all the experts said Cleveland was going to win. We won again. And we will keep winning."

Meanwhile, the Dodgers, who'd blown a 13½-game lead and a playoff to the Giants in 1951, had won the National League pennant by 4½ games this time and smelled destiny.

As Philadelphia manager Eddie Sawyer had done two years before, Brooklyn's Chuck Dressen gave the opening assignment to his best reliever, Joe Black, and watched him scatter six hits. Pee Wee Reese, Duke Snider, and Robinson, who loved the intimate dimensions of their Ebbets bandbox, poked home runs, and the Dodgers prevailed, 4–2.

Behind Raschi's three-hitter and a three-run homer by Martin, the Yankees grabbed the second game and confidently crossed the bridges to the Bronx. Three days later they returned to Brooklyn, shaken. A double steal and a passed ball by Berra had given the Dodgers game three in the ninth inning; Snider had won game five with an 11th-inning double.

Now, trailing three games to two and facing extinction before a Brooklyn crowd that thoroughly despised them, the Yankees fell behind in the sixth, 1–0. It took homers by Berra and Mantle to force a seventh game.

Mantle put New York ahead 3–2 with a sixth-

inning homer in the finale and added another run with a single in the seventh. Then Stengel, who'd replaced Lopat with Reynolds and Reynolds with Raschi, sent for Kuzava, who'd locked up the 1951 championship with some ninth-inning relief. Yankee fans gulped.

Brooklyn had loaded the bases on Raschi. Kuzava, a left-hander, was pitching in a park with a 10-foot left-field barrier. But Kuzava got Snider to pop to third. Two out. Now Robinson approached the plate, and "he hit the lousiest pop-up I ever seen in a World Series," Stengel would say. Except that nobody was moving to catch it except Martin, who'd broken his ankle in two places in spring training while making a film on sliding techniques for DiMaggio's television show.

"I got it just as it reached knee level," Martin said. "Kuzava held them the rest of the way, and we were champs again."

And all of Brooklyn sighed. Six straight Series lost, four in a row to New York. As the Yankees uncorked champagne, Dodger organist Gladys Gooding played "This Nearly Was Mine," and *New York Herald Tribune* writer Roger Kahn typed a Brooklyn lament in the press box. "Every year," he began, "is next year for the New York Yankees."

Why should this year, this World Series have been any different? "The Dodgers are the Dodgers," Yankee second baseman Billy Martin crowed after the final out at the Stadium. "If they had eight Babe Ruths they couldn't beat us."

Another October had come and gone, and the tableau was unchanged. Jubilant men in pinstripes were rubbing champagne into each other's hair, celebrating an unprecedented fifth straight world championship. And their Brooklyn counterparts, heads in hands, were staring into their lockers. Series losers for the seventh straight time.

Once again it had been Martin, the brashest Yankee of them all, who had delivered the crushing blow. In 1952 he'd come racing in from the edge of the outfield to grab a Jackie Robinson pop fly that first baseman Joe Collins had lost in the sun, saving a 4–2 New York victory with the bases full in the seventh inning of the seventh game.

This time his grinning face had poked through virtually every game, right from the Series opener at the Stadium. With the bases full in the first inning Martin had hit Carl Erskine's breaking ball over Robinson's head in left field for a triple and a 4–0 New York lead that led to a 9–5 victory. In the second game, with the Yankees trailing 2–1 in the seventh, he'd deposited a Preacher Roe screwball into the left-field seats to tie the score and set up a 4–2 triumph.

He'd tried to save a lost cause in game four by sprinting from second on Mickey Mantle's single to left with two out in the ninth, but Dodger catcher Roy Campanella had tagged him between the eyes and knocked him sprawling, providing a lovely photograph of Martin airborne for the next day's tabloids.

He'd hit a two-run homer in the seventh inning of game five to put a 6–2 New York lead beyond question and force the Dodgers to the brink. And now he'd broken their hearts again, knocking in one run in the first inning of game six and the winner with one out in the ninth, lashing a single to center that scored Hank Bauer from second.

In all, Martin had gone 12 for 24, with a double, two triples, two home runs, and eight runs batted in. His 12 hits had tied a Series record. Only Ruth in 1928 had enjoyed a more prolific October; fittingly, Martin walked off with the Babe Ruth Award as the Series MVP. "That's the worst thing that coulda happened to Martin," manager Casey Stengel would sigh. "I ain't gonna be able to live with that little sonovabitch next year."

Actually, Stengel loved Martin's intensity and scrap, which had a way of sparking a Yankee club that might otherwise have become complacent. They'd dominated the American League every year but one since 1947, winning the Series each time. In 1953 they'd assumed the pennant almost by divine right, winning 11 of 14 in April and picking up 18 straight victories in late May and early June for a 10½-game lead over Cleveland.

Then they'd gone into a puzzling and dramatic tailspin, losing nine straight at home at the end of June. Stengel, who'd been patient throughout, grew annoyed at persistent probing by newspapermen and closed his clubhouse to them. After New York finally beat Boston in the

Hank Bauer, Yogi Berra, Billy Martin, and Joe Collins were the Yankee hitting heroes in the 9–5 victory in the Series opener. Martin had three hits, the others two apiece, including homers by Berra and Collins, triples by Bauer and Martin.

Joe Collins crosses the plate (greeted by Irv Noren) after one of his 35 home runs during 1952–53. He hit career-highs of 18 in 1952 and 17 in 1953.

ninth inning, he held a team meeting and chewed out his players. The result was a breakout that kept the Yankees in control of the race until the end.

Only two barriers might have stopped them. One was a low railroad trestle in Philadelphia that ripped off the roof of their bus and sent glass and Yankees flying after a night game with the Athletics. Yet only pitcher Allie Reynolds, who arose the next morning with back pains, was injured; he never pitched as effectively again.

The other roadblock was a four-game Stadium series in August with Chicago, which had joined Cleveland as the primary challenger. The Yankees and White Sox thoroughly disliked each other, and Stengel took particular delight in deflating counterpart Paul Richards, who'd said he'd discovered a hidden flaw in the New York machine.

"If he's so smart," Stengel cracked, "why can't he beat Philadelphia?"

Whatever the flaw might have been, the White Sox never came close to unveiling it; Stengel buried them with left-handers. Ed Lopat stifled them 6–1 in the opener as Martin, Mantle, and Yogi Berra crashed home runs. Then Stengel sent out Whitey Ford and Bob Kuzava for a doubleheader and chuckled as Ford won 1–0 and Kuzava spun a no-hitter for 8⅓ innings of a 3–0 victory.

Chicago won the finale but left the Bronx seven games out. The race was over; the Yankees would finish 8½ games ahead of Cleveland. They were truly in mid-dynasty now, as Stengel had

predicted in spring training. "They better catch us this year," he'd warned, "because with the rookies we have coming up it may be difficult for quite some time."

Not even the best Dodger team in history, the Boys of Summer in full flower, could stop them. Brooklyn had won 105 games, the most in either league since the 1944 Cardinals, and had finished 13 games ahead of Milwaukee. There would never, they thought, be a better chance to bring down the Yankees.

Instead, the Dodgers found themselves gasping for air throughout the Series. After losing the first two games in the Bronx ("Egad, Men, Wake Up," the *Brooklyn Eagle* urged them), they needed a Series record 14 strikeouts from Erskine and an eighth-inning homer from Campanella to save game three and Campanella's tag of Martin to choke off a New York rally in game four.

There was a final chance in game six once Carl Furillo ripped a two-run homer into the Stadium stands in right field in the ninth to tie the game at 3–3. But Bauer walked and Mantle singled him to second. With one out Martin walked to the plate. "This fella," Stengel told shortstop Phil Rizzuto in the dugout, "is gonna break up the game."

With the count 1–1, Brooklyn pitcher Clem Labine fired a fastball, Martin laced it on a line into center field and Bauer came pounding home. Fielding the ball hopelessly, Duke Snider merely stuffed the ball into his pocket and jogged in; Bauer was only a few feet from home. Why bother? "I should have thrown," Snider realized much later. "Suppose Bauer had fallen down?"

No chance. The Yankees were the Yankees, just as the Dodgers always seemed to remain the Dodgers. And Martin was Martin, whipping himself to glory in the Series. "My career average may only have been .257," he later looked back, "but my one-for-four would kill you. In October, my one-for-three would kill you."

It was the Year the Yankees Lost the Pennant after a five-year reign—or more precisely the year Cleveland tore it away. The Yankees, after all, won 103 games in 1954, their best record since 1942. Yet they still finished eight games behind the Indians, whom Casey Stengel had been regarding with alarm for two years.

"I better watch that fella," he said of Cleveland manager Al Lopez, who had been a Brooklyn Dodger and a Boston Brave under Stengel. "He was a pretty good catcher for me, and he knows what it's all about."

Lopez also knew he had one of the finest pitching staffs in baseball history, built around right-handed starters Early Wynn (23–11), Bob Lemon (23–7), and Mike Garcia (19–8) and a bullpen of Don Mossi, Ray Narleski, and Hal Newhouser. His fourth and fifth starters, Art Houtteman and 35-year-old Bob Feller, won 28 games between them. And his starting lineup, including a Jew (Al Rosen), a Latin (Bobby Avila), and two blacks (Larry Doby and Al Smith), was a true melting pot of ambition and drive.

They held first place for all but a few hours of the season and cut the heart out of the Yankees in a September doubleheader at Municipal Stadium before the largest crowd (86,563) ever to witness a non-Series game. When the Indians blew the World Series in four straight to a Giant club that would have finished 14 games behind them in the American League, people found it inconceivable.

Particularly the Yankees, who'd been having

Bill "Moose" Skowron was another headline rookie, adding his big bat and .340 average to the powerful Yankee arsenal, and impressing coach Bill Dickey (left) among others. Veteran Joe Collins was still the regular at first base, but Skowron played 61 games there. He was also a pinch hitter with a grand slam in August.

trouble with Cleveland since 1948, when the Indians had dethroned them as league champions.

Cleveland had been second for three years now, and when August became September the Indians arrived in New York 4½ games in front for a three-game series. The Indians had thumped the Yankees there in July, irking Stengel, who respected Lopez but considered his players a "bunch of plumbers."

"They ain't gonna beat me, neither," he vowed.

Pitcher Bob Grim was American League Rookie of the Year, his 20–6 record third best in the league and the top Yankee mark, ahead of Whitey Ford's 16–8. Grim was the club's first rookie to win 20 since Russ Ford in 1910 and the only Yankee to win 20 from 1953 to 1957. Arm trouble dogged him in 1955, and he became essentially a reliever, winning 12 and saving 19 in 1957, his last notable season in pinstripes.

Enos Slaughter cried when traded to the Yankees after 13 seasons with the Cardinals. But at age 38, he found a second career in New York, dividing his energy between the outfield and pinch-hitting through parts of six seasons and three World Series.

Wynn managed to win the opener, but Ed Lopat limited Cleveland to one run in the second game. And Whitey Ford's pitching, a homer by Mickey Mantle, and a lovely catch by leftfielder Irv Noren that cost Hank Majeski a two-run homer won the third. The gap was now 3½ games. "We're back in business," Stengel proclaimed afterward, putting his feet up on his clubhouse desk.

But 10 days later the Cleveland lead had ballooned to 6½ games; losing a doubleheader by Lake Erie would virtually put New York out of the race. The Yankees had to have both, and Stengel knew it. "We're six behind," he calculated, "and we go in there tomorra and we win two and we're only four behind and we go from there."

Instead, New York took a double-dunking, their first since the middle of 1953. Lopez had rested Lemon and Wynn, his two aces. Stengel had Ford for the opener but in the nightcap had to use Tommy Byrne, a 34-year-old left-hander who'd been reacquired from the minors. It might not have made a shred of difference. Lemon threw a six-hitter to smother the Yankees, 4–1. Then Wynn shrugged off a two-run Yogi Berra homer in the first inning, gave New York only a bunt single by Hank Bauer the rest of the way, and won 3–2. The Cleveland lead was now 8½ games, the magic number three.

"Until after the last two games I didn't expect to lose it," Stengel would admit. "The fault was carelessness in all parts including myself. I kept saying, 'We'll catch 'em next week.'"

Instead, the dynasty burped; a fledgling magazine called *Sports Illustrated* dubbed it "The Twilight of the Gods." Yet the twilight was brief. Between 1955 and 1964 New York would only lose one pennant. It took the Indians 41 years to win another.

![1955]

They danced all night in the streets, from Flatbush to Bay Ridge. Church bells tolled, motorcades snaked along, strangers embraced, confetti rained everywhere.

"There was one guy who kept telling me he'd been waiting for this since 1916," said Dodger pitcher Johnny Podres, the Series MVP. "Can you imagine waiting 39 years for something? I don't know how late the party went on or if it ended at all."

After half a century and seven straight losses in World Series, five of them to the Yankees, *this* was the long-awaited "next year" in Brooklyn. When shortstop Pee Wee Reese scooped up Elston Howard's grounder and flipped the ball to Gil Hodges at first base, the Dodgers had come from two games down to shut out the Yankees in the finale, 2–0, and there was a championship to celebrate.

The hero was a happy-go-lucky Cuban named Sandy Amoros, whom manager Walter Alston had installed in left field for defensive purposes in the sixth inning. Within moments, with two Yankees on and none out, Amoros had raced to the left-field corner, speared Yogi Berra's slicing fly ball, and doubled Gil McDougald off first.

But it was really a victory for the aging Boys of Summer—Jackie Robinson, Carl Furillo, and Reese—who'd been losing Octobers to the Yankees since 1947. And it was a galling defeat for New York, which had retooled its pitching staff, regained the American League pennant, and taken a victory over the Dodgers for granted.

There'd never been any reason to do otherwise; the Yankees had snuffed out Brooklyn in 1941, 1947, 1949, 1952, and 1953. "Don't worry," Casey Stengel assured inquisitors. "The Yankees always take care of the Series."

Elston Howard became the Yankees' first black player, batting .290 in 97 games. He played mostly in the outfield but sometimes behind the plate; he would become baseball's best catcher.

Whitey Ford pitched back-to-back one-hitters during the September stretch en route to an 18–7 record, and was named the league's Pitcher of the Year by the Sporting News.

They hadn't lost one since 1942, when the Cardinals had come from a game down to win four straight. And after losing the 1954 pennant to Cleveland in the final two weeks, New York had rebuilt an aging pitching staff largely through one 17-player trade with Baltimore in November.

Bullet Bob Turley was acquired from the Orioles in an 18-player deal, the largest in big-league history. Working with coach Jim Turner (right), Turley used his blazing fastball to strike out 210 while going 17–13 with a 3.05 ERA. Don Larsen was another front-line pitcher harvested in the mega-deal with Baltimore. He was 9–2 with a pair of saves, but would pay a more spectacular and historic dividend the next season.

Essentially, for the price of 32-year-old outfielder Gene Woodling, the Yankees picked up right-handers Bob Turley and Don Larsen and infielder Billy Hunter. Turley would win 17 games, Larsen nine, and Hunter would play regularly at shortstop.

When Billy Martin returned from the army on September 2, the Yankees trailed the Indians by half a game. That day, in celebration of their friend's return, Whitey Ford pitched a one-hitter, and Mickey Mantle hit a game-winning three-run homer. Martin, the Yankees felt, would provide the same prod he always had to their autumnal ambitions. "The fresh little bastard," Stengel would say fondly. "How I love him."

But with 11 games remaining, Cleveland still led by half a game when the fourth-place Red Sox arrived at Yankee Stadium for a three-game series. "I had three cars when I went into the army," Martin told his mates, "and now I don't even have one. I'm broke, and you're playing as though you're trying to lose. We gotta get into the Series. We gotta."

Yet by the ninth inning of the opener prospects looked bleak. Mantle had torn a thigh muscle running out a bunt in the second inning. Moose Skowron, furious at having struck out, kicked a dugout water cooler and broke a toe. With two of his top hitters gone and Boston's top reliever, Ellis Kinder, on the mound, Stengel looked to Hank Bauer, who crashed the tying home run. Berra followed with another. New York 5, Boston 4.

The Yankees never lost the league lead again and took their seventh pennant in nine years by three games over Cleveland. The Indians' management, which had already sold $3 million worth of Series tickets, mailed back refunds with the words "We're Sorry" on the envelope.

Meanwhile, the Dodgers had won the National League in a breeze over Milwaukee. After setting a major league record by sweeping their first 10 games, Brooklyn had dropped two to the Giants, then won 11 more. The Dodgers went on to win 25 of their first 29 and had a 9½-game lead by mid-May, a 15½-game advantage by August 4. The final margin was 13½ games, and the stage was set. The Yankees were still missing Mantle. Perhaps it was an omen.

Yet when the Series began in the Bronx (it was no longer a nickel series; the fare was now 15 cents) all the ghosts came flooding back. The Yankees rocked Don Newcombe, Brooklyn's only 20-game winner, for three home runs in the first six innings, two by first baseman Joe Collins, and won 6–5.

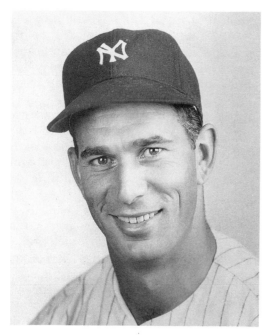

Tommy Byrne was 16–5 after being recycled from the minors at age 35. The southpaw's .762 winning percentage led the league. Byrne added a World Series victory before losing a 2–0 heartbeaker in deciding game seven. He was generally viewed as baseball's comeback player of the year.

The Yankees' one-two bullpen punch: Jim Konstanty (left) and Tom Morgan. Konstanty was 7–2 with 11 saves in 45 appearances, Morgan 7–3 with 10 saves in 40 games.

Then Tommy Byrne, a former Yankee who'd bounced from the Browns to the White Sox to the Senators to the minors before the Yankees had brought him back, twirled a five-hitter in game two. New York scored all four runs (two driven in by Byrne) after two were out in the fourth, on four singles, a walk, and a hit batsman. Was destiny always to be so for New York?

"We gotta win this one," Robinson told the Dodgers before game three. "If we lose again they'll be calling us choke-up guys for the rest of our lives. Do we want that?"

No club had ever won a Series after losing the first two games, but Brooklyn took the first step the next afternoon by relying on an unlikely source, 23-year-old left-hander Johnny Podres, who'd won nine and lost 10 during the season.

Podres had failed to finish his previous 13 starts, but this time—as the Dodgers got him two runs in the first, second, fourth, and seventh innings—he went the distance. Then, in game four, homers by Roy Campanella, Duke Snider, and Hodges turned a 3–1 New York lead into what became an 8–5 Dodger victory and the Series was tied.

One gamble—with Podres—had paid off, so Alston now tried another. Where custom dictated he come back with Newcombe, Alston se-

lected rookie Roger Craig, and Brooklyn bats made it work at Ebbets Field. Amoros hit a two-run shot in the second inning, Snider added two more homers (he had four in the Series), and the Yankees had not only been beaten, 5–3, but, incredibly, nudged to the brink. "I'll be glad to get out of this rat trap," muttered Bauer.

The Dodgers, surprisingly enough, now had breathing room, so Alston gambled again and started 24-year-old Karl Spooner. He lasted one third of an inning and never pitched another game in the majors; New York pounded him for five runs, including a three-run homer by Skowron, cruised 5–1, and forced a seventh game.

Not since 1926 had the Yankees lost a Series that had gone the distance. Newcombe, who'd lost three of his last five outings after boasting an 18–2 record, had never beaten the Yankees in three Series attempts. So Alston went back to Podres and watched him go the route again scattering eight hits. Suddenly a Series that had produced a record 17 home runs in six games lost its thunder.

Brooklyn scratched for one run in the fourth on a Campanella double and a Hodges single. A Reese single, two sacrifice bunts, and a sacrifice fly squeezed out another in the sixth. But Alston, trying to capitalize on loaded bases, had batted George Shuba for light-hitting second baseman Don Zimmer and watched him ground out.

So Junior Gilliam, a gifted utility man, was moved to second and Amoros trotted out to left. Martin and McDougald, the tying runs, were on base with none out when Berra, a left-handed batter who hit with power, banged a long fly to the opposite field with the Dodgers shifted toward right.

"The ball seemed to hang up in the air forever," said Podres, "and Amoros is still running. I started to think: Is he going to get it? I'll tell you, that's a helpless goddamned feeling, standing on the mound at a moment like that."

Amoros ran full tilt toward the left-field line and with his right arm fully extended gloved the ball, spun, and caught McDougald too. In the dugout, Yankees cursed. Amoros had cheated on the shift and had actually been out of position, playing closer to the left-field line than he should have. "We couldn't believe it," said Ford. "Only a left-handed fielder could have made that catch at all. No fielder should have made it, period."

New York would threaten once more, placing men on first and third with one out in the eighth. But Berra flied to right, and Bauer struck out. Podres got the Yankees in order in the ninth, and Brooklyn released three generations' worth of bottled emotion in one all-night whoosh.

Amoros, who spoke almost no English, grinned broadly at sportswriters who literally couldn't interview him. In the Yankee clubhouse Martin, who'd saved the 1952 Series with a running catch and won the 1953 championship with a ninth-inning single, sobbed and pounded his hands bloody against the wall. "I still thought we were going to win," he said.

But that night belonged to the people on the other side of the bridge.

"The champagne was really pouring," said Podres, recalling the victory party at Brooklyn's Hotel Bossert. "All you had to do was hold out your glass and somebody would fill it up. The streets were filled with people and every so often I had to go out and wave to them, then go back inside again to the handshakes, the pats on the back, the champagne. Boy, the champagne."

This year, finally, a championship tree had grown in Brooklyn that no Yankee was going to chop down. None would ever grow again.

He'd had the worst record in the American League just two years earlier, a 21-game loser who tipped off his pitches and never did have much respect for a convention called spring training. Three days earlier he'd walked four

Dodgers in less than two innings and had been removed.

Now Don Larsen was one out from a kind of flawlessness no pitcher had ever known, a World Series perfect game. He had thrown 92 pitches and retired 26 Brooklyn batters. Only Dale Mitchell, pinch-hitting for pitcher Sal Maglie, remained.

"I was so weak in the knees I thought I was going to faint," Larsen would say. "When Mitchell came up I was so nervous I almost fell down. My legs were rubbery, and my fingers didn't feel like they were on my hand. I said to myself, 'Please help me, somebody.'"

Umpire Babe Pinelli, calling his last game, would not. If Larsen was going to Cooperstown, he would have to make it on his own. "Refusing Larsen anything he didn't earn 100 percent was the hardest thing I've ever done in baseball," Pinelli admitted.

Five pitches later Larsen had carved himself out a piece of immortality with a rising fastball that caught Mitchell looking as the Stadium shook. Since then reality and myth have blurred together.

It was neither the Series opener nor clincher as some believe. Larsen's 2–0 victory gave the Yankees a 3–2 edge in the 1956 Series, but it didn't turn the tide; the next afternoon Brooklyn's Clem Labine shut out New York in 10 innings and forced a suspenseless finale at Ebbets Field that the Yankees won 9–0 to regain the world championship the Dodgers had filched the year before.

One moment remains frozen in a timeless photograph—Larsen's right arm in midaction, second baseman Billy Martin behind him, hands on knees, and a string of zeroes behind Martin on the scoreboard. Perfection.

"People have asked me what I did in the game," catcher Yogi Berra said much later. "I had to look it up because I couldn't remember. I don't remember what any of us did. I just remember Larsen."

Yet few knew him then as anything beyond another face in the New York rotation. Larsen was a tall 27-year-old who'd spent only four years in the majors. The St. Louis Browns, for whom he'd won seven and lost 12 in 1953, had wanted to make an outfielder of him. He'd come to New York in the fall of 1954 as one body in a 17-man trade with Baltimore that Yankee general manager George Weiss hoped would rebuild his aging pitching staff.

With a contending team behind him and Casey Stengel tutoring him, Larsen had been 9–2 in 1955 and seemed promising, providing he would take the game seriously.

Larsen liked parties and late hours. "Let the good times roll, baby doll," was his credo. "The only thing Don fears," quipped Oriole manager Jimmy Dykes, "is sleep." Teammates dubbed him "Gooneybird," and after Larsen wrapped a car around a St. Petersburg light pole in the spring of 1956, Stengel had shrugged, "He went out to mail a letter." At four in the morning.

Yet there was a gift there somewhere ("He should be good, but he ain't," Stengel would sigh before trading Larsen three years later). Larsen had a deceptive curve that he could throw at varying speeds. After Stengel urged him to deliver the ball without a windup early that season—the better to disguise his pitches—Larsen won 11 and lost five.

Still, he labored unnoticed through the summer, obscured by three stablemates with better records in Whitey Ford, Johnny Kucks, and Tom Sturdivant, by a club that was running away with the pennant, and by center fielder Mickey Mantle, who had burst into full flower at 24.

Mantle had crashed two long home runs at Washington on opening day. By the end of May he'd hit 20 and despite a gimpy knee was in pursuit of Babe Ruth's season record of 60. By Au-

gust 25 the total had reached 44. On September 18 he slammed number 50 so decisively into the upper deck at Chicago's Comiskey Park that Stengel swore "seats were flyin' around for five minutes."

Mantle finished the season with 52, added a .353 average and 130 runs batted in for the Triple Crown, and walked off with the American League MVP Award. The pennant, New York's eighth in 10 years, was a foregone conclusion; the Yankees led by 10½ games in July and eventually won the race by nine games over Cleveland.

Again, for the sixth time since 1947, the Series opponent was Brooklyn, which had clinched the pennant on the season's final day. But where the Dodgers had lost the first two games in 1955 they swept both at home this time and dumped the Yankees into an early ditch.

Johnny Podres, who'd won two of the 1955 Series games for Brooklyn, including the seventh, had been claimed by the navy. Yet the Dodgers had found another Yankee-killer in 39-year-old Sal "The Barber" Maglie, whose unshaven scowl and right arm they'd purchased from the Indians in May.

Maglie yielded a two-run homer to Mantle in the first inning of the opener but recovered to go

The Yankees led the league with 190 home runs, and this fearsome foursome accounted for 131 of them (from left): Bill Skowron (23), Mickey Mantle (52), Yogi Berra (30) and Hank Bauer (26). Mantle and Berra added three homers apiece in the World Series, Bauer and Skowron one each as the Yankees outhomered the Dodgers, 12–3.

the distance, and homers by Jackie Robinson and Gil Hodges did the rest.

Spurred by a Berra grand slam, the Yankees unloaded on their favorite Series pigeon, Dodger pitcher Don Newcombe, for five runs in the second inning of the second game, took a 6–0 lead and sent him, furious, to the showers.

"You never can win the big ones," a parking lot attendant taunted Newcombe outside. "You're a choke." Newcombe, who'd won 27 games that season plus the Cy Young Award, bristled and punched his tormentor in the face. Back inside Ebbets Field, though, his teammates were rallying manfully. Two singles, two walks, an error, a sacrifice, and a three-run homer by Duke Snider produced six runs in the bottom half of the inning, and the Dodgers went on to a 13–8 triumph. "Yankees Moidered," crowed a Brooklyn newspaper headline the next morning.

Once the Series crossed over to the Bronx, though, the momentum reversed. Enos Slaughter, hero of the 1946 Series, had been disgusted when the Cardinals traded him at age 38 to New York two years earlier. "I feel sick all over," he'd cried. Now he clouted a three-run homer in the sixth inning of game three, and the Yankees had finally drawn blood.

The next day Sturdivant went the distance. Hank Bauer boomed a two-run shot in the seventh to assure a 6–2 breeze, tie the Series, and clear the decks for Larsen. A New York loss would force the Yankees to the edge of the pit when the Series returned to Brooklyn, yet Larsen was unruffled.

He ate pizza and drank beer the night before,

Tom Morgan was the top reliever with 11 saves and six wins, including a five-inning-plus gem on May 16 in which he retired all 17 Cleveland batters he faced as the Yankees vaulted into first place to stay. After the season, Morgan would be traded away to the Athletics.

telling New York sportswriter Arthur Richman, "I might even pitch a no-hitter."

From the first batter he faced, the control that had deserted Larsen three days earlier was back in force. "Oh-oh, Larsen's got it today," Pinelli realized as Dodger leadoff batter Junior Gilliam struck out on a breaking ball.

But for six innings neither Larsen nor anybody else thought much about what was happening. As it was he'd needed a combination of luck and circumstance to keep Dodgers off base and runs off the board.

A Robinson bouncer in the second inning had skipped off third baseman Andy Carey's glove, but the ball had caromed to shortstop Gil McDougald, who'd thrown out Robinson, 37 and heavy-legged, by half a step. In the fourth a long drive down the right-field line by Snider just veered foul; in the fifth Mantle tracked down a smash to left-center field by Hodges, and a Sandy Amoros drive turned foul by inches.

Meanwhile, Mantle had poled a homer in the fourth, and the Yankees had pushed across a second run off Maglie with two singles and a sacrifice in the sixth. After Larsen had retired the side in the seventh he stepped into the dugout runway for a cigarette. "Do you think I'll make it?" he murmured to Mantle. But Mantle passed by, stone-faced and horrified; you did not mention a no-hitter in progress for fear of jinxing it.

As Larsen took the mound for the eighth to face the middle of the Brooklyn order, the enormity of it all struck him. Four men had pitched one-hitters in Series games. One of them, Yankee Bill Bevens, had lost his no-hitter and the game on a pinch double with two outs in the ninth in 1947. "I hope what happened to him doesn't happen to me," Larsen thought.

He got Robinson to ground back to him, Hodges to line to third, and Amoros to fly to center, then returned to the dugout to a standing ovation. When Larsen emerged to lead off the New York half he received another.

Now only Carl Furillo, Roy Campanella, and Maglie stood between Larsen and immortality. Voices shouted advice from the Yankee dugout. "Everybody suddenly got scared we weren't playing the outfield right," Stengel said. "I never seen so many managers." Martin had already called Carey, McDougald, and first baseman Joe Collins together. "Nothing gets through," he told them.

Furillo fouled off four pitches, then flied to Bauer in right. Campanella grounded limply to Martin, who gave the ball an extra squeeze before firing it to Collins. So manager Walter Alston sent Mitchell, a 35-year-old left-handed hitter, to bat for Maglie.

The Dodgers had bought Mitchell at midseason from Cleveland, where he'd spent a decade as an outfielder, and he had gone six-for-14 as a pinch hitter for them down the stretch. "I was afraid he might get one of those nice big hoppers or a line drive somewhere," fretted Larsen, familiar with the batter he'd faced during four seasons in the American league.

Which was Mitchell's only goal—to reach base. He watched Larsen's first offering break high for a ball. The second caught him looking the third swinging. Then Mitchell fouled off the fourth. Still, one ball and two strikes. Berra signaled for the fastball and it came in rising. Mitchell moved to it—then let it go by. "We all stood frozen," Pinelli said. Then the umpire's right hand went up. "The third strike," he proclaimed. "And out!"

Perfect bedlam. Larsen came woodenly off the mound, dazed. Berra dashed out to meet him and leaped into his arms. In the press box sportswriter Shirley Povich of the *Washington Post* tapped out a suitable lead: "The million-to-one shot came in. Hell froze over. A month of Sundays hit the calendar."

It would be nice to report that Larsen turned one flawless day into a magnificent career and that the Yankees proceeded to sweep the Dodgers away the next afternoon at Ebbets Field and claimed the championship. Neither happened.

Larsen turned in essentially the same record in 1957. By 1959 he was a losing pitcher again; in 1960 he would be 1–10 for Kansas City. By the time Larsen retired in 1967 he would have labored for the Athletics, White Sox, Giants, Astros, Orioles, and Cubs and finished with a lifetime record of 81–91—plus 4–2 in Series play, including his one-of-a-kind masterpiece.

Don Larsen made baseball history in game five when he pitched the first World Series no-hitter and the major leagues' first perfect game in 34 years. The Stadium scoreboard tells the story as Larsen throws the final pitch. An instant later, Dodger pinch-hitter Dale Mitchell was called out on strikes for the final out.

Larsen was the center of attention in the locker room afterward. The mob included co-owners Dan Topping (left) and Del Webb (right).

That perfect day brought lasting fame and a standing invitation to Yankee old-timers' days, but hardly riches; ironically, while Larsen was on the mound that day his estranged wife was in court trying to attach his $8,715 Series share.

And the Yankees found themselves shut out by Clem Labine in 10 innings in game six, 1–0, despite a four-hitter by Bob Turley, Larsen's former stablemate in Baltimore. "Kid, just hold 'em for seven innings and you got it made," advised Collins, the veteran of six Series. "Because the shadows will come in and you'll win."

Through the ninth Turley had conceded Brooklyn no runs; but in the tenth a walk, a sacrifice, and Robinson's game-ending single beat him. "Hey, Joe, the damn shadows are out in right field," Turley had yelled to Collins in exasperation. "Where are my runs?"

Being held in reserve for Newcombe in game seven, of course. Alston had avoided using him since his game two shelling; now he had no option. Stengel spent a sleepless night in deliberation, then chose Kucks, whose sinker was more likely to be grounded into the Ebbets Field dirt than popped over the fence.

Kucks responded by tossing a three-hit shutout, and Berra, who'd chased Newcombe with a slam in the second game, tagged him for a two-run homer right away.

Then, after Campanella couldn't hold a foul tip that would have ended the third inning, Berra crashed another. "It was a good pitch, Newk," Berra called in consolation as he rounded the bases, and Newcombe nodded in frustration. "I couldn't be any more ready than I am now," Newcombe had said before the game. "I want to beat them more than anything else in my life. I won't rest until I do."

Now it was 4–0 and Brooklyn fans, always quick to label Newcombe "gutless" in the Big One, hooted. "I feel sorry for him," Yankee pitcher Whitey Ford would say. "It was awful the way the fans booed him." Then Elston Howard led off the fourth with another homer, and Alston came out to replace Newcombe with Don Bessent.

Humiliated, Newcombe showered, dressed, and drove home weeping. He would be 149–90 lifetime but 0–4 against the Yankees. There was no greater sin in Flatbush. "I'm sorry, Ma," Newcombe told his mother half an hour later. "What's to be sorry?" she shrugged.

Back at Ebbets, Moose Skowron had bashed a

The scorebook told the story.

slam off Roger Craig in the seventh; the Yankees would win 9–0 and collect their seventh championship in 10 years. No Brooklyn team would ever see another one. "Aargh," grumbled Dodger fans, "wait till *last* year." ·

For the price of a shine a Series was lost. The Yankees had a two-to-one edge in games and a 5–4 lead in the tenth inning of game four. Milwaukee pinch hitter Nippy Jones had one pair of highly polished shoes and wits enough to demand that plate umpire Augie Donatelli examine the ball after Yankee reliever Tommy Byrne had hit him on the foot with a low pitch.

When the ball showed a telltale black smudge, Jones was awarded first base and the gears reversed in the Braves' direction. Jones was replaced by pinch runner Felix Mantilla, who was sacrificed to second. Then shortstop Johnny Logan doubled Mantilla home to tie the score, and third baseman Eddie Mathews deposited a home run over the right-field fence for a 7–5 victory.

Thus turned what was dubbed the Shinola Series. Reprieved, the Braves turned to ex-Yankee pitcher Lew Burdette twice in the final three games for his wicked assortment of screwballs,

sinkers, sliders, and alleged spitters, and came out of it with their first world championship since 1914.

For the Braves, who'd changed from a seventh-place club into a contender as soon as owner Lou Perini moved them from Boston in 1953, it was a stunning achievement. For the Yankees, a baffling setback. They had been odds-on favorites to win their ninth pennant in 11 years and had done so, by eight games over Chicago. Yet in some ways it had been an ill-starred season from the first, pocked by bad omens.

"I don't think it's gonna be a runaway," Casey Stengel told reporters at spring training. "Because that fella in center field can get hurt." He meant Mickey Mantle, who'd been bothered by a series of knee and leg injuries since he'd broken in six years earlier. Before training camp was done Stengel had been proven prophetic.

While playing demolition derby with electric carts at a golf course, teammate Billy Martin knocked over Mantle's cart, pinning the Mick's foot underneath and spraining ligaments. Mantle, consigned to crutches, missed the first month of the season and later developed shin splints (after gashing his leg with a golf putter) that hampered him throughout the Series.

Then Martin hurt his own foot, came down with tonsilitis, was beaned, and wound up losing his position to 22-year-old Bobby Richardson. And the Third Musketeer, Whitey Ford, hurt his arm in the opening-day cold and missed two months.

So it went. On May 7, Gil McDougald caught Cleveland fireballer Herb Score full in the face

Casey Stengel welcomed two veteran pitchers arriving on the Kansas City shuttle. Bobby Shantz (right) would go 11–5 while leading the majors with a 2.45 ERA and becoming the Yankees' first Gold Glove winner. And Art Ditmar (left) was 8–3 overall, 6–1 in relief with six saves.

Tom Sturdivant was the top Yankee winner at 16–6 with a 2.54 ERA. It was Sturdivant's second consecutive 16-victory season before he hurt his pitching arm.

with a line drive, shattering his nose and damaging his right eye. "If anything happens to his eye," McDougald vowed, "I will quit baseball."

As it turned out neither was the same player again. Score, who'd won 20 games the year before and had drawn a $1 million offer from Boston, never had another winning season. McDougald, the league's best shortstop, was out of baseball by the end of 1960.

A week later, in the wake of an incident at New York's Copacabana nightclub, where Hank Bauer was accused of breaking a drunken bowler's nose, general manager George Weiss fined Mantle, Martin, Bauer, Ford, and Yogi Berra $1,000 apiece, and traded Martin, whom he had never liked, to Kansas City a month later.

All of which had begun turning up in the American League standings, where the Yankees trailed the White Sox by six games in early June. It took a full-tilt brawl at Comiskey Park that same week to turn the season around.

A duster thrown by New York's Art Ditmar at Larry Doby touched it off; giant White Sox first baseman Walt Dropo finished it by shredding Enos Slaughter's jersey and undershirt. Enlivened, the Yankees won their next nine games and assumed the league lead. Before long they were brandishing the kind of late-inning threat that revived memories of the 1927 club and its "5 o'clock lightning."

Whitey Ford spun a four-hitter for a 3–1 Yankee victory in the World Series opener. Ford had missed the season's first two months after hurting his pitching arm in opening-day cold.

Sal Maglie, age 40, was acquired from the Dodgers for the September pennant push. The previous October, Maglie lost a five-hitter, 2–0, at the Stadium, the victim of Don Larsen's perfect game in the 1956 World Series. Maglie bore no grudge and won two games for the '57 Yanks during the final month.

"Please warn the fans that they are not to leave until the last man is out," Stengel advised reporters after Mantle's bases-loaded triple in the ninth had beaten Chicago one day. "Not to sit there worryin' about the traffic."

The White Sox were dispatched during the final week in August with a three-game sweep at Comiskey that inflated New York's lead to 6½ games. Meanwhile, the Braves, whom New York had never played in a World Series, were winning their first National League pennant since 1948 by eight games over St. Louis.

Though the Yankees had two regulars hurt—Mantle with his shin splints and first baseman Moose Skowron with a bad back—they were still solid favorites to retain the world championship, and Ford disposed of Milwaukee with a crisp four-hitter in the opener.

Then the Braves unveiled Burdette, a tall 30-year-old right-hander whom the Yankees had last seen when they traded him plus $50,000 for Johnny Sain in 1951, when they'd needed a proven pitcher for the stretch run. Along with Warren Spahn, the last link from the 1948 pennant winners, Burdette had developed into a certified ace with a spitter that was widely respected yet never detected.

He shut out New York for the final six innings of the second game as the Braves won, 4–2, and brought the Series back to a Milwaukee populace that had never witnessed one.

Lew Burdette, pictured in pinstripes which he wore briefly in 1950, returned to haunt his old team as a Milwaukee Brave, and beat the Yankees three times in the '57 Series.

What they saw was a third game that slipped totally away from the Braves after Stengel summoned Don Larsen in relief to retire Henry Aaron with two outs and the bases loaded in the second. The Yankees, who'd grabbed a three-run lead in the first, went on to score two more in the third, two in the fourth, and five in the seventh on Tony Kubek's second home run for a jarring 12–3 final score with a three-run homer by Elston Howard.

New York erased a 4–1 deficit that was greeted with total silence with two out in the ninth inning of game four. When the Yankees took the lead in the tenth, the Braves were staring at a 3–1 gap in games and the prospect of extinction at home the next day.

So Milwaukee manager Fred Haney sent up Jones, a 32-year-old journeyman playing his last year in the majors who was 12–for–52 lifetime as a pinch hitter, to bat for Spahn. A Byrne curve glanced off his right foot, skipped to the grandstand barrier, rebounded, and rolled back to the plate.

Donatelli, assuming the ball had just gotten away from Berra, called Jones back. While the Braves argued that Jones had been struck, Byrne tried to signal Berra to retrieve the ball for alterations. Too late. Milwaukee third base coach Connie Ryan brought it back to Donatelli and Jones pointed out the evidence: "Polish from my shoe."

So Donatelli waved him on and moments later the Series was tied. The next afternoon Burdette spun a seven-hitter, allowing no Yankee past second base. Three singles in the sixth got him the only run he needed, and left fielder Wes Covington, spearing McDougald's drive in the fourth as it was going over the fence, stifled New York's best chance.

Now it was the Yankees who were teetering on the edge, and Stengel looked for Bob Turley's fastball to even the Series.

Bullet Bob yielded homers to Aaron and Frank Torre, but Berra, playing in a record-breaking 53rd Series game, had already poked a two-run shot in the third, and Bauer would win it, 3–2, with a blast into the left-field stands.

So for the third straight year the world championship would be decided in a seventh game. Stengel chose Larsen, who'd yielded up perfection a year earlier. Haney looked again to Burdette, who had shut out the Yankees for 15 straight innings. With the help of bad Yankee baserunning (Bauer and Enos Slaughter both ended up on second in the first inning) Burdette extended his string to 24. Only Giant pitcher Christy Mathewson, tossing three shutouts at Philadelphia in 1905, had ever done more to win a Series.

The Yankees, who'd always peaked in October, found themselves bereft of heroes. Skowron, whose grand slam had buried Brooklyn in the

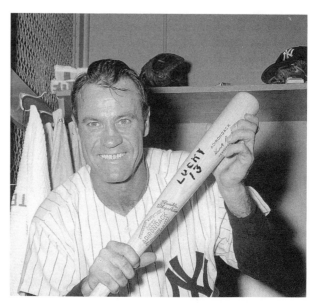

Hank Bauer slammed his "lucky" 13th World Series home run off the Stadium's left-field foul pole, breaking a 2–2 tie and giving the Yankees a 3–2 victory in game six that evened the Series and set up a winner-take-all showdown the next day.

1956 Series, had hobbled to the sidelines with a bad back in the opener. Mantle, whose shin splints had cost him a second straight Triple Crown, had torn shoulder ligaments in game four during a base-path tumble and was clearly sub-par. And Martin, who'd saved the 1952 Series and won it in 1953, had been traded.

Now Milwaukee jumped on Larsen for three of their four runs in the third, helped by one of three Yankee errors, and forced Stengel to go to his bullpen four times. When it was done the Braves had taken the game, 5–0, and the championship—and were eager for a rematch.

"We'd like to play them again next year," Burdette said. "I'm sure we're going to win the pennant. But I'm not sure about them." The Yankees read that remark—and burned silently all winter.

Warren Spahn's remark had been made in the hilarity of the champions' dressing room after the 1957 World Series, but the Yankees had remembered it all winter.

"The Yankees couldn't finish fifth in the National League," proclaimed the Milwaukee ace. His pitching stablemate, Lew Burdette, said he wasn't sure New York would qualify for a rematch the following year. The Yankees set out to prove both of them wrong.

The American League pennant was a foregone conclusion, a 10-game cakewalk over Chicago that was all but decided by Memorial Day. What New York wanted was revenge for a squandered championship the year before—and for the salt that had been rubbed in afterward. No revenge ever came tougher, yet few tasted sweeter.

Trailing the Braves three games to one and playing their last game in the Stadium, the Yankees rose from the grave to beat down Milwaukee in seven, sending the Braves fans they despised silently into the Wisconsin twilight.

The man most responsible was a burly right-hander named Bob Turley who, after being shelled in the second game, came back to win the fifth, save the sixth, and win the seventh in relief. He was the only 20-game winner on a staff where only one other pitcher, left-hander Whitey Ford, won more than nine—yet it was the best staff for earned run average (3.22) in the league.

And though the lineup included only one man with a batting average over .300 (Mickey Mantle at .304), New York so dominated the league that their rivals essentially gave up the chase before midseason.

"In this league there are no pennant contenders," sighed Cleveland manager Joe Gordon, a former Yankee himself. "There is just the Yankees and no one to challenge them."

Late in May their record was 25–6, their lead on pursuers a full nine games. By the end of July New York had lengthened it to 15 games, by August 2 to 17, the largest ever crafted that early in the season. The Yankees were young, deep, and confident. The rest of the league was collapsing under them.

While rival fans hooted and sporting columnists condemned their monopoly, Stengel chafed. "Why is everyone mad at us?" he growled. "What do they expect us to do, roll over and play dead?"

As it happened, injuries would level the Yankees out. Ford won 14 games by early August, strained his arm, and didn't win another the rest of the season. Bobby Shantz's spikes pierced Tom Sturdivant's heel while the two pitchers were fooling in the outfield before a game, Sturdivant ended up on the disabled list. Johnny Kucks

Left: *Bob Turley won the Cy Young Award as baseball's best pitcher, the first Yankee to receive the trophy after its inauguration in 1956 as one selection for both leagues. Turley led the league with a 21–7 record, and would be even more sensational in the World Series. With the Yankees down three games to one, Bullet Bob pitched a five-hit shutout in game five, added a save in game six, and won game seven with 6⅔ innings of two-hit, one-run relief to be Series MVP.* **Right:** *Relief pitcher Ryne Duren was the* Sporting News' *Rookie of the Year, sharing the majors' lead in saves with 20 along with six victories out of the bullpen—then added a win and a save in the World Series. The hard-throwing, 6'2", 195-pounder with thick eyeglasses intimidated hitters even before they stepped into the batter's box, often firing his first warm-up pitch high against the backstop.*

went 1–5 during the last two months, Art Ditmar 2–6.

The miseries spread into the field as well. Second baseman Gil McDougald's back went into spasms; he batted .207 down the stretch. Shortstop Tony Kubek lost 20 pounds with an impacted tooth, then pulled a thigh muscle. First baseman Moose Skowron's back had been bad to begin with.

Hardly coincidentally, the club skidded through August and September, losing 28 of their last 51 games and limping home like a lame miler who'd already lapped the field.

When they finally clinched the pennant in Kansas City on September 14, the Yankees let loose with a whoosh of relief and swilled champagne on the train to Detroit. While the steam was being blown off, pitcher Ryne Duren, well into his cups, challenged coach Ralph Houk to a fist-fight, tried to shove Houk's lighted cigar down his throat, and ended up kicking pitcher Don Larsen in the mouth.

When the club arrived in Detroit, George Weiss hired private detectives to tail a number of his players. It was an old Yankee tradition—Jacob Ruppert had done it to Babe Ruth & Co. in the '20s; Larry MacPhail had done the same to Joe Page and friends in the '40s.

So one pair of detectives shadowed Mantle, Ford, and catcher Darrell Johnson—and lost them in a Catholic church. Others followed Bobby Richardson, Kubek, Shantz, and Kucks to a YMCA and watched them play Ping-Pong. Maybe the Yankees really were "milk drinkers," to use Stengel's terminology.

At any rate they had retentive memories, and once the Braves had retained the National League pennant (with the same 92–62 record as New York's) the rematch was joined. Yet from the start Spahn and Burdette—a classic lefty-righty tandem—seemed bent on proving their prophecies.

As Spahn went the distance at County Stadium, Milwaukee came from behind to tie the opener in the eighth inning and win it in the tenth. Center fielder Billy Bruton, who'd missed the entire 1957 Series with a bad knee, ripped a single between center and right to score Joe Adcock from second as Mantle and Bauer, disgusted, let the ball roll all the way to the fence.

Then, after the Yankees managed only one run with the bases loaded in the first inning of the second game, the Braves mauled Turley for four of their seven runs in the bottom half. Bruton led off with a homer into the right-field bleachers; by the time his teammates had batted

Hank Bauer out-slugged Hank Aaron (right) when the Yankees and Braves were rematched in the World Series. Bauer led both teams with four homers and eight RBIs while Aaron, although hitting .333, was homerless with two RBIs in his second and last Series. Hammering Hank had led both teams with three homers in the 1957 Series.

around, Milwaukee had chased both Turley and reliever Duke Maas, lashed out a double and two singles, and watched Burdette, a lifetime .183 hitter, crunch a three-run homer.

The final was 13–5, and New York needed two home runs in the ninth to make it even that respectable. Back in the comparative sanity of Yankee Stadium, Larsen pitched shutout ball for seven innings of game three, Bauer knocked in all four runs with a single and a 400-foot homer, and Duren wrapped up a 4–0 victory that got New York breathing again. For one day.

Spahn came back the following afternoon with a two-hitter, yielding only a triple in the fourth to Mantle (who withered on third with one out) and a single to Skowron in the seventh. Yankee left fielder Norm Siebern lost two balls in the sun, the Braves exploited them for two runs, and New York was suddenly faced with the prospect of losing successive Series at home.

It wouldn't be necessary, Spahn predicted, to return to County Stadium. After all, Burdette, who'd beaten the Yankees four straight times, would be on the mound the next day. No club since the 1925 Pirates had ever come back from a 3–1 deficit to win a championship, and for five innings of game five it seemed unlikely that the Yankees would do the same.

McDougald had poled a homer in the third, but Bruton had singled over Kubek's head to lead off the sixth. Now Braves second baseman Red Schoendienst looped a fly toward Elston Howard in left field that seemed certain to advance

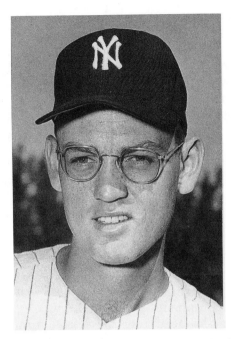

Left fielder Norm Siebern lost two fly balls in the late-afternoon haze in the sixth and seventh innings of game four, as the Braves cracked open a scoreless tie and beat Whitey Ford 3–0. Casey Stengel had reason to worry when his Yankees faced elimination, trailing the defending champion Braves three games to one.

Bruton to third. Instead, Howard dived, saved the ball just before it touched the grass, and doubled up Bruton. Eddie Mathews proceeded to single, giving birth to a number of what-ifs.

"To tell you the truth I thought it was going to fall in," Howard admitted, "and so did Bruton. He was already around second when I caught it."

Thus reprieved, the Yankees batted around in the bottom half of the seventh and hung six runs on Burdette, who would never win another Series game. Turley went on to shut out the Braves, 7–0, on five hits, and the Yankees packed their bags with a vengeance.

Milwaukee would come back with Spahn at home; New York would send out Ford. But Ford loaded the bases with one out in the second and the Yankees behind 2–1 and was yanked for Ditmar, who eventually gave way to Duren.

Two singles, a Bruton error, and a sacrifice enabled the Yankees to tie it in the sixth. With Spahn, at 37, still working, the game went into extra innings.

McDougald immediately tagged Spahn for a homer, and three New York singles—the third off reliever Don McMahon—shook down another run. If Duren could hold the top of the Milwaukee order, there would be a seventh game.

But a walk and two singles later it was 4–3 and Stengel was motioning for Turley. He got Frank Torre to line sharply to McDougald on the fringe of the outfield and it was over. For the fourth consecutive year the Series would go to the limit.

The Braves would ride with Burdette. Stengel kept his choice secret until an hour before the game, then chose Larsen. Milwaukee touched him for a run within minutes and put two men on base with one out in the third. With New York leading 2–1 (two errors by Torre on routine 3–1 grounders in the second led to both runs) Stengel was taking no chances. Turley strolled in from the bullpen.

He was Bullet Bob, a fastball addict in the Allie Reynolds tradition. He'd come from Baltimore with Larsen four years earlier when Weiss had re-tooled an aging pitching staff and had developed, over time, into the Yankees' right-handed ace.

Turley drank milk, read real estate books, and did not appear to need a private detective to chronicle his comings and goings. He would give the Braves one run, a homer by Del Crandall, to tie the score in the sixth but nothing else until two were out in the ninth. By then the Yankees had pummeled Burdette for four more runs in the eighth, three of them from the bat of Skowron, who'd missed virtually the entire 1957 Series.

As Skowron rounded the bases, a 6–2 victory on ice, County Stadium emptied quickly. A few minutes later the Yankees were champions again, the way they'd wanted to be. They'd beaten Spahn and Burdette in their own yard to complete the best Series comeback in 33 years. On

Elston Howard turned the Series around with a crucial diving catch that saved the Yankees in game five. He'd be chosen Series MVP.

the flight back to LaGuardia they drained champagne bottles, burned the corks, and arrived in blackface.

"I guess," Stengel decided, a large dollar sign scribbled onto his face, "that we could play in the National League after all."

1959

Nothing like this had happened in 19 years. The Yankees, long accustomed to being booed on the road, were hearing catcalls every day in Yankee Stadium. Everybody from the White Sox to their favorite farm team, the Athletics, were teeing off on them.

There were injuries on the field, sore arms in the bullpen, and doubt in the front office. On May 20 they all came together in a stark headline over a photograph showing a disconsolate Mickey Mantle, his head down. "The Day the Yankees Hit the Bottom," it read.

The standings told the tale—for the first time since May 1940, New York could be found in last place, 8½ games behind Cleveland. Detroit righthander Frank Lary, the foremost Yankee-killer of his day, had beaten them 13–6 in the Stadium that day, and Mantle, who would struggle through his most painful and dismal year yet, had been hooted even while circling the bases after a two-run homer.

When it was done and the Yankees were filing silently into the clubhouse, the front office set a restraining line for photographers 50 feet from the players' path. "The Yankee players," decreed a club official, "are not to be humiliated."

They had been world champions just seven months before and technically still were. They could pull themselves back into the pennant race and did, within two weeks. But this was destined to be New York's leanest season since 1925. The Yankees would finish with a 79–75 record, in third place 15 games behind a Chicago club that hadn't won a pennant in 40 years.

It was the beginning of the end for manager Casey Stengel, who'd won nine pennants and seven championships but would eventually be cashiered for one he didn't win. "This bad season was an emergency to our owners," Stengel said wryly. "They thought the manager was slipping. They thought the coaches were slipping. They thought the players were slipping. But

maybe the people in the front office didn't have such a good year themselves."

The problems had begun during the off-season when co-owner Dan Topping did away with Stengel's beloved "instructual" schools (where he'd discovered Mantle) and ordered general manager George Weiss to take a hard line on contracts even though the club had staged the greatest Series resurrection in 33 years by coming from a 3–1 deficit to beat Milwaukee in 1958.

Not that it was any novelty. The New York front office traditionally managed to turn a championship season into a disadvantage at signing time, explaining that since pennants were automatic in the Bronx, Series shares should be considered part of the salary.

So Mantle and pitcher Whitey Ford were both unsigned when spring training began and many of their teammates were grumbling.

From the beginning the season turned sour. Bob Turley, who'd won two Series games and saved a third the previous autumn, went blah, his fastball gone, his record sliding from 21–7 to 8–11. Two starting pitchers, Don Larsen and Tom Sturdivant, turned up with sore arms. Third baseman Andy Carey developed an infected hand. Utility infielder Gil McDougald was hit on the

Bobby Richardson batted .301, the Yankees' only .300 hitter.

Ralph Terry (right) was reacquired from Kansas City in a May deal that also brought third baseman-outfielder Hector Lopez to the Yankees. Lopez stepped in, hit a solid .283, and finished among team leaders in a variety of categories. Terry would begin paying dividends the next season. He won 66 regular-season games from 1960 to 1963, including 23 in 1962, plus two World Series victories that year.

hands by Boston pitcher Bill Monbouquette and missed two weeks. Hank Bauer slipped from .268 to .238 with only 39 runs batted in. Mantle strained his throwing shoulder, broke an index finger in the batting cage, then, along with four teammates, was leveled by the flu.

In less than two months the league had turned upside down on the Yankees. Then they mounted an offensive, led by a red-hot Mantle (who raised his average 50 points in 11 days), a briefly healthy Moose Skowron, Kansas City refugee Hector Lopez, and Ryne Duren, who pitched 36 consecutive shutout innings over 18 games.

Within two weeks New York had closed to within 2½ games of the Indians. Then they went to Chicago, where new owner Bill Veeck was putting his promotional genius to work. Amid skyrockets from an exploding scoreboard and Handel's *Messiah,* the Yankees lost three of four in 100-degree heat to a crew of White Sox that couldn't hit but never stopped running. Their battle song, Veeck said, was "Bobbles, Bingles, and Bunts."

A few days later Mantle hurt an ankle and hobbled through the balance of the season. The summer came undone permanently during the second week of July, when the Yankees lost five of six at Boston to the delight of long-suffering Fenway patrons and fell to fifth, 7½ games out.

From there it was a Midsummer's Nightmare. McDougald and Tony Kubek collided chasing a pop-up and ended up dazed. Skowron, whose

back hadn't been right for two years, broke an arm in a base-path collision with Detroit's Coot Veal. Lopez banged an elbow, and Carey, his replacement, contracted hepatitis. Finally, Duren, running from the bullpen to the dugout after a game at Boston, tripped over two fans and broke a wrist.

"We're having a lot of trouble with everything," Stengel concluded. "You got nine guys not hitting and the pitching not so hot either and what are you going to do?"

Bill Virdon cursed the moment he watched the ball leave his bat and bounce toward Yankee shortstop Tony Kubek. Routine grounder, classic double-play ball, he thought. Kubek would get Gino Cimoli at second, Virdon would be nipped at first, and the Pirates' eighth-inning rally would die aborning. And New York, leading 7–4 in the seventh game at Pittsburgh, would go on to claim the world championship.

But the ball was never gloved, the throw never made. Instead, Virdon arrived at first base and discovered Kubek on the ground near second, his hand clutching his Adam's apple. The grounder had ricocheted off a pebble, a clot of dirt, a rut . . . something . . . and angled up sharply. Everybody was safe and Kubek, breathless and hurt, was on his way to a hospital.

From there unraveled a championship the Yankees had won, lost, and won again—depending upon the day of the week—and finally would lose. The double play that wasn't led to five Pirate runs, and after the Yankees had scored twice in their half of the ninth to tie the score, a miner's son named Bill Mazeroski hit the most dramatic home run in Series history to push Pittsburgh to a 10–9 triumph and its first world championship since 1925.

The Yankees had set Series records for runs (55), hits (91), extra-base hits (27), and batting average (.338). They had drubbed the Pirates 16–3, 10–0, and 12–0. They did everything possible in a Series—except win it.

"I can't believe it," moaned left fielder Yogi Berra.

"I'll never believe it," decided Yankee pinch hitter Dale Long, a former Pirate.

Neither would the Yankee front office, which had fidgeted through the club's worst season in

Roger Maris became a Yankee via the Kansas City shuttle and won the first of two consecutive American League Most Valuable Player Awards.

34 years in 1959, and had expected nothing less than a return to championship form in 1960. So, two days after the cheering had died down in Pittsburgh, president Dan Topping identified the scapegoat, 70-year-old manager Casey Stengel, and dismissed him. The term Topping used was resignation, but it was a euphemism.

Art Ditmar was the Yankees' winningest pitcher at 15–9, but would be shelled in two World Series starts.

"You're goddamn right I was fired," Stengel growled at his farewell press conference. Thus ended the most successful span in franchise history, a 12-season stretch during which Stengel managed the Yankees to 10 pennants and seven championships and built a dynasty that would win four more American League flags before the talent ran out in 1965.

"Competence has ceased to be the measuring rod in the Yankee scheme of things," wrote *New York Times* columnist Arthur Daley. "It can be overruled and negated by the date on a man's birth certificate."

Stengel had seen the end coming well before. He'd squabbled with the front office for much of the disappointing 1959 season. "They would have liked to get rid of a lot of people, including the manager and most of the coaches," he realized. If management hadn't been reluctant to swallow a full year of Stengel's salary, they might have released him then. As it was, Topping had offered the job to Al Lopez, who'd just managed the White Sox to their first pennant in 40 years. Lopez had refused, but the front office's intentions were obvious.

Meanwhile, Weiss cleaned as much of his personnel house as he could. Pitcher Don Larsen (he of the 1956 Series perfect game), outfielders Norm Siebern and Hank Bauer, and reserve first baseman Marv Throneberry were shipped to Kansas City, the Yankees' favorite junkyard. In return they received shortstop Joe DeMaestri, first baseman Kent Hadley, and a promising outfielder named Roger Maris.

Still, the Yankees slogged through spring training, and, after Stengel was hospitalized with a virus, the club fell six games behind Baltimore by the end of May. Both team and manager recovered nicely.

"They examined all my organs," Stengel said proudly. "Some of them are quite remarkable, and others are not so good. A lot of museums are bidding for them." Upon his return the Yankees won 14 of 15, sweeping four from the White Sox at Chicago, and took over first place.

Yet poor pitching kept New York from pulling away. When the staff returned to form, thanks to the infusion of rookie Bill Stafford and recycled National Leaguer Luis Arroyo, the Yankees won their final 15 games and finished eight ahead of the Orioles. Waiting for the Yankees this time was not the Milwaukee club they'd struggled with in 1957 and 1958 but the Pirates, who hadn't won the National League pennant since Babe Ruth and his colleagues had swept them in 1927.

This fearsome foursome in the middle of the Yankee lineup accounted for 120 of the team's majors-leading 193 homers (from left): Roger Maris (39), Yogi Berra (15), Mickey Mantle (40), and Bill Skowron (26).

Stengel wanted to use Stafford, whom the Yankees considered their best pitching prospect since Whitey Ford, in the first game. Coaches Ralph Houk and Frank Crosetti disagreed; a rookie, they believed, shouldn't start a World Series opener. So right-hander Art Ditmar, a seven-year veteran who'd pitched in three previous Series games in relief, was chosen, and the Pirates evicted him with three runs in the first inning en route to a 6–4 victory.

Then, on the verge of erasing a 3–1 Yankee lead in the fourth inning of the second game, Pittsburgh manager Danny Murtaugh gambled, pinch-hit for pitcher Bob Friend, and watched New York blow the game apart.

The Yankees easily retired pinch hitter Gene Baker and Virdon to snuff out the embryonic rally, then cannonaded five Pirate relievers (including old Dodger acquaintance Clem Labine) for 13 runs and a 16–3 victory, the most one-sided Series game since 1936. Seven of the runs came in the sixth when New York sent a dozen batters to the plate. And only two came on home runs, both by Mickey Mantle. The second, a 475-foot, three-run blast, cleared the center-field wall. No right-handed hitter had ever done that at Forbes Field.

The Pirates, with ghosts of 1927 and Murderers' Row dancing in their heads, were easy prey at Yankee Stadium two days later. Yankee second baseman Bobby Richardson, who'd hit only one home run during the season but would set a Series record with 12 runs batted in, smashed

Gil McDougald stabs a line drive during his final campaign; he retired after the season at age 32 to enter business and coach at Fordham. During his 10 seasons, the versatile McDougald was variously the Yankees' regular shortstop and second and third baseman, an All-Star Game starter at each position. A solid fielder and hitter, he played for eight Yank pennant-winners and five world champions.

a two-strike grand slam off Labine to complete a six-run first inning that ended the afternoon early. New York added four more in the fourth on a two-run single by Richardson and a homer by Mantle, and it was 10–0; Ford's sparkling four-hitter was delightfully unnecessary.

Yet Pittsburgh, which should have been put to rout by now, fought back in game four and tied the Series with a 3–2 victory. Then the Pirates shelled Ditmar again, scoring three runs in the second, and grabbed game five, 5–2, turning the Series completely around. Masters of their fate just two days earlier, the Yankees now needed to win the final two games at Forbes Field and beat Pittsburgh's two aces, Friend and Vernon Law, in the process.

As Ford held the Pirates at bay, the Yankees tattooed Friend for two runs with a double and two singles before a man was out in the third and nicked reliever Tom Cheney for three more. So it was 6–0, and the Yankees added half a dozen more before the day was done to garland Ford's seven-hit shutout, 12–0, and even the Series and set the stage for a classic game seven showdown.

Law loomed as a tougher proposition; he'd won 20 games during the season, plus Series games one and four. Now, through four innings, he'd allowed only two singles. And Bob Turley, whom Stengel had chosen just before the game after originally awarding the assignment to Stafford and changing his mind, had lasted just 20 pitches. With two out in the first inning Pirate first baseman Rocky Nelson swung at a bad pitch for a two-run homer.

"It was cap-high and a foot wide," Turley said. "Yet he pulled it over the fence in right field." But logic had long since fled from this Series. So Stengel went back to Stafford, whom he'd bypassed as a starter in two games, and watched the Pirates extract two more runs from him with two out in the second inning.

Now it was 4–0 for Pittsburgh and slipping away rapidly. But Moose Skowron greeted Law with a home run into the lower right-field stands in the fifth, and the momentum shifted abruptly toward New York. When Richardson led off the sixth with a single and Kubek walked, Murtaugh replaced Law with ace reliever Elroy Face—exactly what the Yankees had been hoping for.

Face had saved all three Pittsburgh victories and had popped off about it (to New York minds, anyway) in the newspaper. "If we can get Law out and Face in," Berra had predicted, "we'll win."

After Mantle had singled home Richardson,

Bobby Richardson was Series MVP with a record 12 runs batted in, four of them on his grand slam in game three.

Berra poked a three-run homer into the upper right-field stands and it was 5–4. When Murtaugh let Face continue, New York rattled him for two more in the eighth after two were out. So it was 7–4, and Stengel was six outs from his eighth championship. Cimoli, pinch-hitting for Face, led off with a single. But Bobby Shantz, who'd held the Pirates scoreless since relieving in the third, got Virdon to hit the ball on the ground.

Moments later Kubek was sprawling, choking, and Stengel was running out of the dugout rasping, "Give him room, give him room. He'll be all right."

But Kubek wasn't all right, and couldn't play. And as the shortstop was bundled off in an ambulance, the Yankees began coming unstuck. Dick Groat, hitless all day and 5-for-27 in the Series, lashed a single into left to score Cimoli. So Shantz left for reliever Jim Coates, who nailed two quick outs and got Roberto Clemente to chop a grounder toward Skowron at first. It seemed an easy 3–1 play but Coates, assuming Skowron would make it alone, held up. So Clemente reached base and Virdon scored. New York 7, Pittsburgh 6.

Still Coates needed only to retire reserve catcher Hal Smith, a former Yankee farmhand who had played five years for the Orioles and Athletics. Coates worked Smith to 3–2 then watched, disgusted, as Smith put the next pitch over the left-field wall for a three-run homer and a 9–7 Pirate lead. Coates threw his glove high into the air;

before it came down Stengel had replaced him with Ralph Terry, his fourth reliever of the day.

Terry got Don Hoak to fly to Berra in left, so the Series had come down to one inning and the top of the Yankee order was waiting to unload on Friend, whom Murtaugh was using for the second day in a row.

When Richardson and Long dinged Friend for singles, Murtaugh summoned Harvey Haddix. But Mantle singled Richardson home, and Gil McDougald, running for Long, came home on an infield out.

New York 9, Pittsburgh 9 now, but the Pirates had made a season out of ninth-inning resurrections. They'd won 23 games in the final time at bat, 12 of them with two out. Did it matter that Mazeroski, the number-eight hitter, was at bat?

"One to go home," Murtaugh yelled to him. Terry's first pitch, a slider, sailed high. The second—"the wrong one," Terry would say glumly—was a high fastball. "I came to bat intending to go for the long ball," Mazeroski said, and it was unlikely he'd see a better offering. "I caught it on the fat of my bat. I knew immediately it was a well-hit ball. I watched it sail over the fence as I rounded the bases. I touched every one."

Berra, in left field, never moved. No need to. As joyous Pirate fans leaped from the stands and escorted Mazeroski home, and Mantle wept in the clubhouse, Terry cursed. "Casey," he told his manager, "I hate to have it end this way."

"How were you operatin'?" Stengel asked him. "What were you tryin' to throw him?"

"I was trying to keep it low," Terry replied.

"As long as you were trying to pitch him the right way, I'm gonna sleep easy at night," Stengel assured him. Not so the Yankee front office. When the club returned to New York Topping called a press conference and had his lawyer prepare a statement for Stengel to read.

Stengel was retiring because of age and the Yankees, grateful for more than a decade of championship baseball, were going to give him $160,000. It was something less than true. Stengel was being dismissed, and he'd earned the $160,000 as part of a profit-sharing program. The prepared statement came apart under questioning moments after it was read.

"I couldn't be a yes-man," Stengel said. "I never was, and I never will be." He could have continued, Stengel believed, and would have liked to. "But they have a program which should run into an old-age program," Stengel said, "and I am positive they are the owners of the ball club. Mr. Webb is of the same opinion as Mr. Topping as regarding the age limit and Mr. Top-

ping runs the ball club. I was told my services were no longer desired."

Ralph Houk, who'd coached under Stengel for five years and had taken over when Stengel had been hospitalized early in the season, would be the new manager. Stengel, who didn't need the money anyway, would be hired two seasons later to preside over the birth of the Mets, New York's new National League franchise. He was young enough to work in the Polo Grounds, a battered relic of a ballyard, but not in Yankee Stadium. "I'll never make the mistake," Casey grumbled, "of being 70 again."

He was 26 years old, and he was losing his crew cut in clumps. "Look at this," Roger Maris showed manager Ralph Houk. "My goddamn hair is coming out. Did your hair ever fall out from playing baseball?"

No, Houk conceded, it hadn't. But then, Houk had played eight years with the Yankees and never hit a home run. In one season Maris was already somewhere between 50 and 61, chasing a dead man and being haunted by him.

It had been 34 years since George Herman Ruth had set the major league record of 60 in one season. Now Maris, New York's right fielder, was on the verge and realizing that neither the commissioner of baseball, nor Yankee management, nor a fair number of sportswriters, nor most rival fans, nor the grandstand spectators behind him at Yankee Stadium wanted him to.

"Do you really want to break Babe Ruth's record?" one reporter asked in Chicago.

"Damn right."

"What I mean is, Ruth was a great man."

"Maybe I'm not a great man," Maris replied. "But I damn well want to break the record."

Commissioner Ford Frick, who'd been friendly with Ruth as a New York sportswriter, wanted that record kept intact. In July, when it was apparent that Maris had a chance at 61, Frick announced that he would have to hit them in 154 games, the length of the season in Ruth's day. If the record had to fall, the New York front office preferred that Mickey Mantle, who had hit 52 in 1956 and was matching Maris almost blast for blast, would be the man.

"They favored Mickey to break it," Maris said years later. "I was never the fair-haired boy over

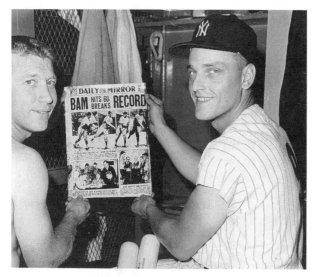

Mickey Mantle and Roger Maris engaged in their own long-ball derby while chasing Babe Ruth's home-run record. The ailing Mantle stalled at 54 as Maris hit 61.

Besides exceeding Ruth/Gehrig's 107 homers in 1927, the roommates' 115 topped the team totals of four clubs—the Angels' 60, Cardinals' and Phillies' 103 apiece, and the Red Sox' 112. "Roger's achievement was the greatest of my time," Mantle wrote in an autobiography.

there." To begin with, he had not been bred to be a Yankee. Maris had been discovered and signed by the Cleveland organization and had played one year as a regular before being traded to the Kansas City A's for Vic Power.

When the Yankees made another in a series of raids on the Athletics roster in 1959 (between 1953 and 1961 New York and Kansas City would deal with each other 17 times), Maris arrived unheralded in a seven-player deal designed to rejuvenate the New York outfield.

Though he was hardly a power hitter in the Ruth or Mantle mold, Maris was a fine fielder with a reliable arm who had a knack for pulling any ball within the strike zone. Manager Casey Stengel loved him, and Maris made an immediate impact, winning the American League MVP Award as the Yankees regained the pennant in 1960.

He had hit only 39 homers that year and batted an unspectacular .283 (his career best, as it turned out), yet in camp prior to the 1961 season Stengel conceded that Maris could eclipse Ruth's mark. "Why shouldn't he break it?" Stengel mused. "He's got more power than Staleen."

Or at least more productive power. "If I hit a ball just right," Maris figured, "it goes about 450 feet. But they don't give you two home runs for hitting one 800 feet, do they?"

For the first 10 games Maris didn't hit any. By May 2, 16 games into the season, he'd hit only one. His fourth, in the 29th game, didn't come until May 17. Ruth had already hit nine by that date.

But, as May turned into June, the shots came in bunches—two on Memorial Day at Boston, then nearly one a day for the next two weeks. By June 22, Maris had piled up 27, found himself 12 games ahead of the Babe's pace, and began hearing the Question for the first time. "Do you think you can break Ruth's record?" a New York writer asked. "How the hell do I know?" Maris shrugged.

But pushed by Mantle, who was rarely more than one or two behind, Maris continued in his rhythm through July. He hit four off four different Chicago pitchers (including ex-Yankee Don Larsen) on July 25 to reach 40, with Mantle still only two behind him. By now, reporters were laying siege to him daily, and Frick had cranked the pressure a few notches higher by announcing a week earlier that Maris had to break the record by the 154th game. Beyond that, an asterisk would accompany his achievement in the record book.

Maris bristled. "Frick should have said that all records made during the new schedule would have an asterisk," he would reflect years later. "And he should have said it before the season, if he said it at all. But he decided on the asterisk when it looked like I'd break the record."

Gradually it struck Maris that despite the crowds that jammed ballparks to watch him and the publicity that threatened to engulf him, a great number of people did not want him to break the record. "I guess I came along and did something that evidently was sacred," he mused. "Something that nobody was supposed to do, especially me."

Comparisons to Ruth, in which Maris invariably suffered, were inevitable. He was not the gregarious man Ruth was, had nowhere near the capacity for food, drink, women, and late hours, and neither sought adulation nor relished it. "It would have been a hell of a lot more fun to play the game under one mask and then leave the park wearing another," Maris said. "Some guys loved the life of a celebrity. Some of them would have walked down Fifth Avenue in their Yankee uniforms if they could have. But all it brought me was headaches. You can't eat glamour."

By August, Maris found he could barely eat at all, at least not in public. His favorite breakfast was bologna and eggs at the Stage Delicatessen. He had to avoid the place after fans began de-

Co-owner Dan Topping (left) and new manager Ralph Houk weren't smiling here during spring training but would be by season's end, when the Yankees regained the world championship. The Sporting News *named Houk the Major League Manager of the Year and Topping the Major League Executive of the Year. Sitting behind Houk is Roy Hamey, who also hit the jackpot in his first season as Yankee general manager.*

scending on him. The only place where he retained a shred of privacy, Maris concluded gloomily, was in the bathroom. "They even ask for autographs at Mass," he sighed.

And the clubhouse provided no escape. Maris began arriving earlier and earlier before games, then realized that he couldn't duck the crush of inquisitors or the multitude or grinding sameness of their questions.

Some were irrelevant. "Who's your favorite female singer?"

"I don't have a favorite female singer," Maris replied.

"Well, is it all right if I wrote down Doris Day?"

Others were outrageously personal. "Do you play around on the road?"

"I'm a married man," Maris said.

"I'm married myself," the questioner continued, "but I play around on the road."

"That's your business."

The rest were either ludicrous (Would you rather bat .300 or hit 60 home runs?) or simply the same. Are you excited? . . . Can you? . . . Will you? A Japanese sports editor wired a list of 18 questions he wanted answered to the Associated Press. After half a dozen Maris threw up his hands. "This is driving me nuts," he said. "That's my next question," the AP man nodded. "They want to know how you're reacting to all this."

Directly, often bluntly. That was Maris's way. "You've got to be an idiot," he told a man who asked him what a .260 hitter was doing hitting all those home runs. As the summer wore on Maris began to be described as surly, uncooperative, unworthy. How dare he?

"Throw the first two inside and make him foul them," Hall of Famer Rogers Hornsby advised prospective pitchers. "Then come outside so he can't pull. It would be a shame if Ruth's record got beaten by a .270 hitter."

Yet Maris stayed well ahead of Ruth's pace. By August 22, 125 games into the season, he had reached 50, 13 games before the Babe had. The horde of camp followers increased, finally reaching six dozen reporters, grilling him every day.

"Mick, it's driving me nuts, I'm telling you," he confessed to Mantle.

"And I'm telling you," Mantle responded, "you've got to get used to it."

Maris never did—no more than he could comprehend the chorus of boos cascading down on him, particularly at the Stadium. For years Mantle had been the target of boo-birds there, but now they had taken sides in the long-ball derby and were zeroing in on newcomer Maris instead. "Rog," the Mick needled his roommate, "you have stolen my fans."

Meanwhile, the flood of homers slowed to a trickle. After hitting his 51st, Maris went a week without belting another. After his 56th, on September 9, he went another week without one. While pitchers were throwing him balls and marginal strikes, Maris was going 6-for-50.

With four games left before Frick's deadline and his total at 56, Maris now stood alone. Mantle had been knocked out of the race by an infection that developed after a penicillin shot. He would finish with 54, happy to play Lou Gehrig to Maris's Ruth. In 1927, Gehrig, batting behind Ruth, had hit 47 and pushed the Babe toward immortality. Mantle hit behind Maris forcing most pitchers to deal with Maris. "Well, I got my man," Mantle told Maris, joking, after he'd passed Gehrig's total. "The pressure's off me."

It would never leave Maris, not even after the 154th game came and went. He was stuck at 58 as the Yankees arrived in Baltimore. Oriole manager Paul Richards was pitching fastballer Milt Pappas with a strong wind, the residue of Hurricane Esther, blowing from right field. Maris, distraught, went to Houk's office before the deadline game, the opener of a doubleheader.

"I need help," he told the manager, weeping. "I can't handle this. They keep asking the same questions. It never lets up."

"You've got to handle this all by yourself," Houk told him. "Just get your hits, and everything will take care of itself."

Maris had never asked for the comparison. Beating Ruth's record did not tarnish the Babe's memory. "Why can't they understand?" Maris would repeat. "I don't want to be Babe Ruth. He was a great ballplayer. I'm not trying to replace him. The record is there, and damn right I want to break it. But that isn't replacing him."

Maris left Houk's office and went out to chase a ghost in Ruth's hometown. Pappas got him to fly to right field in the first inning, but Maris dumped a rising ball into the bleachers in the third for number 59. He had passed Jimmie Foxx and Hank Greenberg. Only Ruth remained.

But there would be no record—not according to Frick, anyway. In the ninth Hoyt Wilhelm, arguably the finest reliever in baseball history, got Maris to ground harmlessly down the first-base line. "If you throw him anything but knuckleballs," Richards had warned Wilhelm, "it will cost you five thousand dollars."

The Yankees had clinched the pennant that day but their celebration was overlooked. Reporters surrounded Maris. "I tried," he said. "I tried." Yet the pressure only slightly abated. A season was still a season. Nine games remained, the last five at home.

In game 158, with Baltimore pitcher Jack Fisher on the Stadium mound and fewer than 22,000 spectators in the stands, Maris equaled the record. One of Fisher's curves landed in the upper deck in right field. "The minute I threw it I said to myself, that does it," Fisher said. "That's number sixty."

Maris leaned on his bat at the plate, watched the ball disappear, then trotted around the bases. He would take the next day off. Then the sixth-place Red Sox shut him down two days in a row. Now game 162, the season finale, loomed at the Stadium. Boston rookie Tracy Stallard could make history either way. He got Maris to fly out in the first. Then in the fourth, after he let an outside fastball and an inside curve go by for balls, Maris clubbed a waist-high fastball over Lu Clinton's head into the lower right-field stands for the game's only run.

A young Coney Island truck driver named Sal Durante came up with the ball, thus earning a $5,000 reward and a free trip to the Seattle World's Fair. Maris was forced to make four curtain calls for the Sunday crowd of 23,154, none of them booing now. "If I never hit another home run," he said, "this is one they can never take away from me."

Maris would win the MVP Award again, and the Yankees would nearly double his salary to $72,000. Meanwhile, a championship season had been somewhat obscured. Houk, replacing Casey Stengel, had led the Yankees to the pennant by eight games over Detroit in his first season. Pitcher Whitey Ford had enjoyed his best season (25–4), backed by one of the finest staffs in club history.

The World Series, against a Cincinnati team that had won its first pennant in 21 years, was anticlimactic. The Yankees grabbed it in five games, relying on reserves. Ford shut out the Reds, 2–0, in the opener at the Stadium and went on to wipe out Ruth's Series pitching record of 29⅔ consecutive scoreless innings until an ankle injury in the fifth inning of game four stopped him.

Mantle, with blood from a thigh abscess soaking through his uniform, had been yanked an inning earlier. Yogi Berra, who'd played in 65 Series games, sat down with a bad shoulder for the finale, but it barely mattered.

John Blanchard crashed a two-run homer in the first inning that led to a 5–0 lead. Hector Lopez, filling in in left field, proceeded to knock in five more runs, and the Yankees laughed their way to a 13–5 clincher. "The Reds," someone joked, "didn't even look good throwing the ball back to the pitcher."

As for Maris, he punctuated his season of seasons with a Series homer that was a fitting icing

Johnny Blanchard smacks his second homer of the World Series to launch the Yankees' 13–5 rout of the Reds in the game five finale.

Roger Maris connects on record-smashing home run number 61, crushing a fastball from Boston's Tracy Stallard into the Stadium's right-field stands near the Yankee bullpen.

Clete Boyer, becoming established at 24 as one of the best-fielding third basemen ever, was a Series defensive acrobat, spectacularly frustrating one Cincinnati hitter after another, including Frank Robinson in game two at the Stadium.

but something of an anticlimax—bringing down the curtain on his storybook year that embraced both agony and ecstasy.

Maris would play five more seasons in pinstripes and strike 103 more home runs for the Yankees. And he'd play in five more World Series, the last two for St. Louis. But, he'd say years later looking back, "The game was never really fun after hitting those sixty-one homers."

He had begun to wonder if this was his destiny, always to be undone by October. Ralph Terry had served up the waist-high fastball that Pittsburgh's Bill Mazeroski powdered in the ninth inning of the seventh game of the 1960 World Series and stole a championship away from the Yankees. The next fall New York lost one game in a giggler of a Series with Cincinnati. Ralph Terry was the losing pitcher.

Now in the 1962 Series the Giants had beaten him in game two and forced him to the brink in game five before teammate Tom Tresh had saved the day with a three-run homer in the eighth inning. Now, again, it was the ninth inning of a seventh game, with the Yankees leading by one run at San Francisco. Thoughts of Mazeroski and a fastball vanishing above an ivy-covered wall came flashing back.

The Giants' Matty Alou, batting for pitcher Billy O'Dell, had led off by beating out a bunt. Terry, bearing down, had struck out Alou's brother Felipe and Chuck Hiller. But Willie Mays had doubled and only a perfect throw from right fielder Roger Maris and a crisp relay from second baseman Bobby Richardson had held Alou at third.

Which brought up Willie McCovey, the 6-foot-4, 200-pound slugger who'd lashed a towering homer off Terry in the second game. One bloop single, with both Alou and Mays running, would give the Giants their first championship over the Yankees since 1922.

Instead, seconds later Richardson had snared McCovey's line smash, and Terry was being borne off the Candlestick Park diamond on his teammates' shoulders. Later, as Terry was guzzling champagne at his locker, Joe DiMaggio spotted him. "You can forget that Pittsburgh thing now, Ralph," he shouted. Terry nodded.

"I want to thank God for a second opportunity," he would say. "You don't often get a second chance to prove yourself, in baseball or in life."

For the pitcher and his teammates the championship was a reaffirmation that Terry, who'd won 39 games in two years, was one of the finest right-handers in the game. And that the Yankees dynasty, interrupted by Chicago in 1959 and by Pittsburgh in 1960, had been fully restored.

The lineup was strong and deep again, the pitching flexible and well-stocked. And in Ralph Houk, the only manager to win world championships in his first two years on the job, New York had discovered a worthy replacement for Casey Stengel.

Where Stengel had been the master manipulator, platooning regulars, juggling staffs, cajoling, growling, pushing, Houk was a combative optimist. He picked one lineup and one rotation and stayed with it, praised his players daily, and always thought the pennant was not only possible but likely.

After all, Houk had survived the Battle of the Bulge at Bastogne, winning the Silver and Bronze Stars as well as a Purple Heart, emerging from World War II as a major. He'd played eight years in a Yankee uniform (most as a rarely used catcher) and earned six Series rings. He'd managed the Yankees' farm club in Denver and coached under Stengel. Now the job was his, and even as the 1962 season showed signs of coming apart early, Houk saw silver linings everywhere.

Within four days in mid-May, Mickey Mantle tore a thigh muscle (he missed 40 games), top reliever Luis Arroyo blew out his arm and wound up on the disabled list, and left-hander Whitey Ford, who'd won 25 games in 1961, strained his arm.

With Mantle unavailable enemy hurlers gleefully pitched around Maris, who went 21-for-110 during Mantle's absence. As spectators hooted and press criticism grew in intensity, Maris fretted. "Sometimes," he brooded, "I wish I never hit those 60 home runs." Meanwhile, as the Yankees went 15–15 during the next month, they slipped to fourth place, four games behind leader Cleveland. Through it all, Houk displayed his what-me-worry? grin. "When Whitey and Mickey return," he told all doubters, "we will win."

And so they did. In early July, Mantle and Maris each hit six homers in four games, and Mantle went on to bat .321. Ford came back to win 17 games with a 2.90 earned run average.

Former catcher Mike Tresh (left) was a proud father when son Tom won the Dawson Award as the Yankees' outstanding rookie in spring training and then became American League Rookie of the Year. With Tony Kubek in the Army, young Tresh stepped in and hit .286 with 20 homers while playing 111 games at shortstop and 43 in the outfield after Kubek returned.

Roger Maris and Luis Arroyo (right) collected their 1961 hardware as MVP and Fireman of the Year, respectively. But their production dropped sharply in 1962—Maris from 61 to 33 home runs, Arroyo from 15–5 and 29 saves to 1–3 and seven saves. Arroyo was sidelined most of the year with a sore arm that would end his career.

The Yankees won 10 straight games almost immediately, took a three-game lead over the Angels, and proceeded to win the pennant by five games over the Twins.

Meanwhile, the Yankees watched with a mounting sense of déjà vu as the Dodgers lost 10 of their final 13 games, blew a four-game lead in the final week, and ended up losing a playoff to the Giants in the last inning of the final game by walking home the winning run.

This was 1951 all over again . . . except that only Mays remained from that roster and that the Giants and Yankees were no longer a subway ride away from each other.

The IRT didn't reach San Francisco, where owner Horace Stoneham had moved his club four years earlier. And the Polo Grounds had never seen the kind of clouds that seemed permanently suspended above Candlestick Park.

Baseball's first coast-to-coast World Series also proved the longest to date. It consumed 13 days and was split by four days of rain between games five and six as the Yankees, leading three games to two, waited anxiously to close it out.

They'd alternated victories throughout—the Yankees winning the odd-numbered games, the Giants the evens. Now, as the clubs warmed up before game seven, clubhouse attendants placed a bottle of Mumm's extra dry champagne in every Giant locker. But Terry, gratified that Houk was entrusting him with the finale, was feeling buoyant. He'd won $300 from Mr. Berra, the team's lucky charm, the night before on one poker hand. "I beat Yogi, I beat Yogi," he crowed. "It's an omen."

Perhaps it was. For nearly six innings, until Giant pitcher Jack Sanford singled, Terry spun a perfect game. Until the eighth inning, he never threw two called balls in a row. A 40-mile-an-hour wind, a souvenir of Typhoon Frieda, whistled in from the Candlestick outfield.

Finally, in the seventh, the Giants began hitting Terry. Mays lashed a line drive to the left-field corner that Tresh just managed to run down and take backhanded, out of sight of the New York dugout. Then McCovey tripled over Mantle's head to the center-field fence. On another day, in another park, it might have gone out. "I can't say what would have happened if the wind wasn't blowing," McCovey shrugged. "Because the wind was blowing, and it's always blowing."

So Terry struck out Orlando Cepeda, and finally it came down to the ninth. New York had pushed one run across in the fifth when Tony

Ralph Terry's 23–12 topped the American League, and he added two complete-game victories in the World Series, including a crucial 1–0 four-hitter in game seven.

Kubek hit into a double play with the bases loaded. Now, once Matty Alou had bunted his way on, the top of the San Francisco order loomed.

But Terry got Felipe Alou and Hiller. Only Mays remained, and Mays was looking for the fences. "I was going for the bomb," he admitted. "We needed a home run. I was going for it. But I was a little behind the pitch."

Instead of a soaring shot, he skidded a sizzler across the grass to the corner in right. As Alou rounded second and raced for third Maris simultaneously came up with the ball and pegged it to Richardson, who relayed it to Elston Howard at the plate. Third-base coach Whitey Lockman, computing angles and player placement, had held Alou on third as Mays pulled up with a double. Later, second-guessers would castigate Lockman, but no Giant did.

"Wouldn't that have been a hell of a way to end the season?" mused reserve catcher Ed Bailey. "McCovey coming up and the tying run thrown out at the plate by 15 feet."

As McCovey approached the plate Houk went out to chat with Terry. "I really don't know what the hell I'm doing out here," Houk admitted. "But I thought I'd better come out and talk with you anyway. What I'm getting at is, do you want to pitch to this guy or walk him?"

Terry glanced at Cepeda on deck and decided, all things considered, he'd rather pitch to McCovey. "Let's give him good stuff just outside the strike zone and hope he'll fish for it," he told Houk. Houk returned to the dugout and motioned to Richardson to move over, but Richardson decided to stay where he was.

"Some strange sense told me to play him more toward the first-base side," Richardson said. "I guess I was really out of position. A yard to one side or the other and I couldn't have had a chance at that ball."

Terry's first pitch was a slow curve outside. McCovey pushed it down the right-field line and

The cannons in the World Series figured to be (from left) Roger Maris, the Giants' Willie Mays, and Mickey Mantle. The trio played all seven games, but managed just one homer—by Maris. Mays batted .250 (one RBI), Maris .174 (five RBIs), and Mantle .120 (no RBIs).

the wind blew it foul. The second pitch was an inside fastball that McCovey ripped chest-high right at Richardson. It was, McCovey would tell Richardson a decade later, the hardest ball he ever hit. Richardson gloved the rocket without moving, then dropped to one knee to make sure.

"I was running toward third when I looked and saw Richardson catch the ball," said Mays. "And I thought, oh geez, there goes three, four thousand dollars."

Terry threw his glove, then his cap in the air before being carried off by his joyous teammates. The Giants' champagne remained unopened.

The devastation was so quick, so complete, so unquestionable that they had to laugh. Four games, four runs scored—and out. After Los Angeles pitcher Sandy Koufax got Hector Lopez to ground harmlessly to shortstop Maury Wills and put an end to a five-day World Series, the Yankees sat stunned in their clubhouse at Dodger Stadium.

First baseman Joe Pepitone, who'd missed a routine throw from third baseman Clete Boyer that had led to the winning run in the seventh inning, was in tears. Then pitcher Whitey Ford, who'd lost a two-hitter, walked over to Pepitone. "You really blew that sonovabitch," he cracked, "didn't you, kid?" Pepitone, Ford, and Mickey Mantle broke up, and the gloom lifted. "Okay," shouted manager Ralph Houk. "Let's get the hell out of here."

There was nothing else to do, and despite the humor of the moment, the loss burned. No Yankee club since 1922 had been swept in a Series. And by the Dodgers, yet, who had been one-for-seven lifetime against New York in October.

"There are only two ways you can come out of a Series," Mantle would say. "You can come out of it feeling great or feeling like we are. That was the worst beating I'd ever seen the Yankees take."

They had batted .171 as a team, the lowest in Series history. They had scored only two runs in the final three games. They had never led in any game.

Was this the same club that was gunning for a third consecutive world championship? That had suffered injuries to so many regulars that it

Elston Howard was the American League's Most Valuable Player after leading the Yankees in batting (.287), homers (28), and slugging (.528), and collecting a Gold Glove as the league's best catcher. The 34-year-old veteran was the league's first black MVP, and it marked the fourth straight year a Yankee won the award; Howard followed Roger Maris (1960, 1961) and Mickey Mantle (1962).

didn't have its normal lineup together once from June until the final week of September and still won the American League pennant by 10½ games over the White Sox?

"We're better than we were last year," Houk had decided in spring training. Deeper, younger where it counted, with an impeccable pitching staff. In June the Yankees lost shortstop Tony Kubek for two weeks with leg and neck injuries, replacement Phil Linz with torn knee ligaments, right fielder Roger Maris with a bruised ankle—and Mantle with a fractured foot and torn ankle tendons. He had enmeshed his spikes in a chain-link fence chasing a Brooks Robinson fly at Baltimore. "It's broke," he told teammates. "I know it's broke."

Yet New York went on to win 10 of its next 11 without Mantle, passed the Orioles and White Sox, and took over first place by the middle of the month.

Between the first of July and the first of August the Yankees increased their lead from 2½ games over the White Sox to eight games. Then Mantle returned, after missing 61 games, crashed a pinch-hit home run in his first at bat, and Yankee pitching took it from there. The rotation of Ford (24–7), Jim Bouton (21–7), Ralph Terry

The Yankee infield had a new member as Joe Pepitone (far right) replaced traded Bill Skowron as first baseman and joined (from left) third baseman Clete Boyer, shortstop Tony Kubek, and second baseman Bobby Richardson. The 22-year-old Brooklyn native homered twice on opening day, hit 23 homers in all, played the entire All-Star Game, and went on to be a Yankee regular for seven seasons.

(17–15), and rookie Al Downing (13–5) was unsurpassed: in early August they completed 11 of 13 starts and at one point allowed only three earned runs in 60 innings.

"It's good to see some good young players coming into the league," said former well-traveled manager Jimmy Dykes. "But why do they always have to be wearing the Yankee uniform?"

By September the lead was 11 games, then 14. The Series was assumed; it would open in Yankee Stadium against the same Dodger club that had blown the National League pennant to the Giants in the last inning of the final game of a playoff the year before. New York was a clear 8–5 favorite and its ace, Ford, would be starting the

opener in his favorite ball park, dueling a left-hander in Koufax, who'd won 25 games, 11 by shutout, and struck out 306 batters.

Rested and emotionally pumped, Koufax took the mound in the ballpark he'd considered a baseball cathedral as a youngster—a "monument of a ballpark, big and green and aristocratic," he described it. The flame-throwing southpaw cooly blew away the first five Yankees he faced, fanning the cream of the New York order—Kubek, Bobby Richardson, Tresh, Mantle, and Maris. Koufax had grown up in Brooklyn when the Yankees were ruining Dodger seasons every autumn. This was symbolic for him.

"I felt I had to show myself and my team and

Rookie Al Downing (right) contributed 13–5 success to a pitching staff headed by 21–7 Jim Bouton (left) and 24–7 Whitey Ford. Ford led the league in victories, and Bouton (2.53) and Downing (2.56) were among ERA leaders. Downing averaged nearly one strikeout per inning to lead the league in that category.

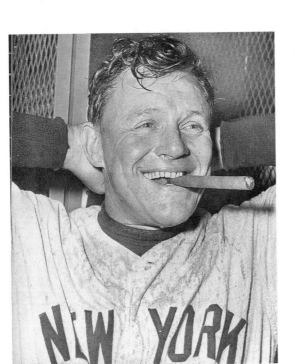

Ralph Houk lit his third pennant cigar in as many seasons as manager. The Yanks would capture other flags, but Houk would never manage another pennant-winner.

the Yankees, too, that the Yankees were just a team of baseball players and not a pride of supermen," he figured.

Nobody since the Cardinals' Mort Cooper in 1943 had fanned the first five batters in a Series game; the key was getting Richardson, who'd struck out only 22 times in 630 at bats during the season. "One of the Yankees told me that when he saw Richardson go down swinging on a high fastball he had a feeling they were in trouble," Koufax said.

The procession of K's continued. Six of seven, 10 of 13. Until two were out in the fifth Koufax was working on a perfect game. By then, thanks to catcher John Roseboro's three-run homer into the upper right-field deck, he also had a 5–0 lead as a base.

"I threw nice and easy," Koufax said, "and I knew I had great stuff. Not good stuff. Great stuff." In the fifth, with the bases full, he struck out pinch hitter Lopez to end the inning.

Koufax would only waver twice. In the sixth, tiring slightly, he walked Richardson and Tresh in succession and got a visit from Roseboro.

"What's the matter?" his catcher wondered.

"My elbow's a little tight," Koufax replied. "I'm having trouble throwing the curve."

"Just throw the fastball," Roseboro said. So he did—and Mantle and Maris popped two of them up to end the inning.

Then with two out in the eighth Tresh nicked Koufax for a two-run homer into the left-field stands. But that was all. Moments before that, Koufax had struck out Richardson for the third time. "There's no use me even going up there," Richardson muttered to Mantle while passing the on-deck circle en route back to the dugout.

As Los Angeles carried its 5–2 lead into the ninth inning, the only question was whether Koufax could break the Series record of 14 strikeouts set by Dodger Carl Erskine against the Yankees—10 years earlier to the day. Koufax had already tied the mark; setting a new one wouldn't be easy.

Elston Howard, whom Koufax had struck out in the seventh, lined to Dick Tracewski at second. Then Pepitone singled, and Boyer, the only Yankee starter who hadn't whiffed, flied to center—the only outfield flyout by New York all day. Now Harry Bright, pinch-hitting for reliever Steve Hamilton, stepped up—in the curious po-

Bill Skowron (right) haunted the Yankees in the World Series, batting .385 despite the boos of Dodger fans after his poor regular-season performance. "I'm hitting like a Yankee again," Moose said as his three RBIs nearly equaled the Yanks' total of four and his homer was half as many as his old team's two. At left is the pitcher the Yankees got for Skowron, Stan Williams; he struck out five Dodgers in three innings of one-hit relief in his only appearance in the Series.

sition of having hometown fans root for him to strike out. Koufax got him swinging and went into the clubhouse to accept Erskine's congratulations along with all the others.

It was the kind of Series performance that comes along once a decade. The Yankees shrugged and planned to unload on Johnny Podres, who'd beaten them twice in 1955, the only time New York had ever lost a championship to the Dodgers. Instead, Podres hummed a six-hitter and his teammates extracted two runs from Downing before a man was out.

Leadoff man Wills had singled, then had been trapped off first. But Pepitone's throw to Richardson at second was high, and Wills made it safely on his belly. "The team that didn't beat itself," Koufax realized, "had handed us another opening."

So Junior Gilliam singled, and a double by Willie Davis scored two runs. Then Moose Skowron, whom the Yankees had unloaded over the winter for pitcher Stan Williams, homered in the fourth, and the Yankees were finished. The final score was 4–1, New York's only run coming with one out in the ninth, and the Dodgers gleefully boarded a plane for the West Coast.

This time they would use right-hander Don Drysdale, who felt compelled to live up to his colleagues' newly established standard.

Don Drysdale (left) and Jim Bouton dueled in game three at Los Angeles. Bouton allowed only four hits but lost 1–0 as Drysdale gave up just three. New York bats were feeble throughout the Series. The Yankees hit .171, with only two homers and four runs, struck out 37 times, and were swept in four games.

After Los Angeles scratched Bouton for a run in the first on a walk, a wild pitch, and a grounder that bounced off the mound and Richardson's shin, Drysdale blanked New York on three hits, striking out Bouton with the bases full in the second, and fanning Mantle to strand Kubek on third base in the sixth.

"We're not hitting," sighed Houk, but denied that a sweep was likely. "They still got twenty-seven more men to get out," he growled. "It's not the end."

It might as well have been. Koufax continued where he'd left off. He struck out Kubek and Tresh in the first, Pepitone and Boyer in the third. He had a no-hitter boiling until center-fielder Willie Davis lost a Richardson double in the sun in the fourth inning.

But this time Ford was also pitching beautifully. Except for Frank Howard's booming home run into the second deck of the left-field stands in the fifth, he didn't make a mistake. "Later they even painted the seat that Howard hit a different color," Ford marveled. "As though it was some kind of landmark."

Mantle made up for it with a 380-foot blast into the left-center-field seats in the seventh, and it was tied. Ford, realizing that a cheap run would probably mean a sweep, bore down. "I threw mostly mud balls or cut balls the whole game," he admitted years later. "I used enough mud that day to build a dam but not enough to hold back the Dodgers."

Ford's fragile dam came apart in the bottom half of the inning. Gilliam hit a routine grounder to Boyer, but Pepitone lost his throw in a sea of white shirts behind third base. Then Gilliam, who ended up on third as the ball bounced to the grandstand, came home on Willie Davis' sacrifice.

So it was 2–1 going into the ninth, and when Richardson led off with a single with Tresh on deck and Mantle following, the Yankees still breathed. But Koufax caught Tresh looking. Then, with two strikes on Mantle, Koufax looked in and saw Roseboro wiggling two fingers. Change-up curve. It caught Mantle looking, too, and the Dodgers were one out from their first championship since 1955 and their first sweep ever.

But Tracewski, the second baseman, boggled a force that would have nailed Richardson at second. One last chance now, with Lopez at bat. This time Koufax got him to ground to short, and it was over. Five days, four games. "It worked out just about the way I thought," chuckled Dodger manager Walter Alston. "Although maybe a little faster."

1964

It was their last hurrah before the darkest hours the modern franchise had ever known: 11 years without a pennant, three straight seasons in the second division, fewer fans than the National League's last-place Mets.

The Yankees limped through a tortured summer, retained the American League pennant by a single game over Chicago, then lost the World Series in the seventh game to a St. Louis club that won its pennant only because Philadelphia squandered a 6½-game lead with two weeks to play.

Then, the day after the Series finale, the front office fired manager Yogi Berra.

That was the final curious scene in a complicated backstage drama during which Berra was "fired" in July and "replaced" by Cardinal manager Johnny Keane, who'd secretly agreed to take the New York job even before he'd beaten the Yankees in the Series.

Lame-duck managers were no novelty around the Stadium by now. Even before the 1963 season, Yankee manager Ralph Houk, who'd already agreed to move into the front office as general manager after the season, had summoned Berra, who was finishing an 18-year Hall of Fame stint as a Yankee.

Houk said he would manage out the year, but after that the job was Berra's. The agreement was kept quiet all season, and after the Dodgers had swept New York in the Series the shift took place, with Houk replacing retiring general manager Roy Hamey. "It was the best-kept secret I ever heard," said ex-Yankee and team broadcaster Phil Rizzuto, a close companion of Berra.

Yet it seemed a reasonable move. Berra had been a Yankee ever since the 1946 season, had established a major league record for home runs by a catcher (313), and set Series records for appearances (14), hits (71), games played (75), and championship rings (10). He was earthy, humorous, and well liked, a welcome change from the Yankees' chilly corporate image and hopefully an antidote for the charm that Casey Stengel and his Mets were working on New York's paying customers.

Only two problems loomed. Berra had never managed, and he would be supervising players who knew him as a peer, not an authority figure. "You?" son Larry puzzled when Yogi broke the news at home. "The Yankee manager?"

"What will be your biggest problem next season, Yogi?" he'd been asked at the ritual press conference.

"If I can manage," he'd replied.

From the beginning the experiment was rocky. Houk had won three pennants in three years. "The players had liked Ralph so much that they weren't able to accept anybody else," pitcher Jim

Whitey Ford became the pitching coach, chosen by longtime batterymate-turned-manager Yogi Berra and approved by another of his onetime catchers, new general manager Ralph Houk. Ford remained an active pitcher, going 17–6 with eight shutouts and a team-leading 2.13 ERA.

Al Downing led the league in strikeouts with 217 while going 13–8. It was the seventh time a Yankee pitcher was tops in strikeouts, and Downing's total eclipsed them all.

Bouton said. "And we were never able to accept Yogi."

With a sympathetic Houk sitting in the front office, players quickly found a willing shoulder to cry on. Yogi's in over his head, they told him. He can't handle pitchers. We wish we had you back.

The club lost its first three games in extra innings. Early on Mickey Mantle, Roger Maris, and Tom Tresh all pulled hamstring muscles; the New York outfield now featured ex–third baseman Hector Lopez, rookie Pedro Gonzalez, and ex-catcher John Blanchard. Then starters Al Downing and Bouton came up hurt, and before mid-June the Yankees were lodged behind Chicago and Baltimore, 6½ games off the pace.

When the injuries cleared up, though, the club went on a tear, swept five from the White Sox, then skunked them again and took over first place. Then they blew a game to the Orioles (after leading 7–2 in the seventh) and had to chase Baltimore through the dog days while criticism of Berra mounted.

Finally, after the team lost 10 of 15 games and four straight at Chicago, the tension swelled and burst on August 20. An amateurish harmonica rendition of "Mary Had a Little Lamb" by shortstop Phil Linz had irked Berra as the team bus was stuck in steamy traffic en route to O'Hare Airport. Berra told Linz to "shove that thing." "Do it yourself," Linz said and flipped the harmonica to Berra, who angrily slapped it away—the flying object nicking the leg of fun-loving Joe Pepitone, who howled in mock pain, "Ow, ow—my knee, my knee!"

While Berra and Linz argued, Mantle, reaching for the instrument, called over to pitcher Whitey Ford. "It looks like I'm going to be managing this ball club pretty soon," Mantle told him. "You can be my third-base coach and this is what we'll do. One toot—that's a bunt. Two toots—that's hit and run."

Phil Linz got into an argument with manager Yogi Berra about a harmonica in August, a sour note that was perceived by management as a lack of leadership by Berra.

Though the club went on to lose its next two in Boston, the incident broke the malaise, and the Yankees came from six games back to regain first place on September 17 as Chicago and Baltimore both reverted to .500 baseball.

The Yankees went on to win 11 in a row and 31 of their final 40, and clinched their ninth pennant in 10 years with three games to play. But Berra's fate was already sealed. Dan Topping, Del Webb, and Houk had met in July and determined that no matter what the outcome of the season, Berra would be dismissed.

Meanwhile Keane, whose Cardinals had beaten the Mets on the final day to win their first pennant since 1946, had already tendered his resignation to owner Augie Busch, annoyed by repeated rumors during the season that Leo Durocher was being considered to replace him. The resignation had not been accepted, but Keane had already arranged through an intermediary to take the New York job after the Series.

For the better part of four games the Yankees made their front office's judgment look awful. After losing a 4–2 lead and the opener, 9–5, at St. Louis, New York grabbed the second (8–3) and third (2–1) games and chased Cardinal starter Ray Sadecki with three runs in the first inning of game four.

But with one blow, a grand slam off Downing in the sixth by Ken Boyer, Clete's older brother, St. Louis turned the Series around. Bob Gibson struck out 13 Yankees the next afternoon, catcher Tim McCarver delivering a three-run homer in the tenth to win it, 5–2, and New York was perched on the brink as the Series headed back to St. Louis.

The Cardinals led the sixth game, 1–0, for four innings. Then Maris and Mantle brought back a taste of 1961 by poking back-to-back homers to right field in the sixth to give New York the lead. Pepitone applied the coup de grâce with two out in the eighth, greeting reliever Gordie Richardson with a grand slam that iced it, 8–3.

That was the dynasty's last gasp, the Yankees' final Series victory until October 11, 1977. The next day in the finale Gibson picked up the thread he'd spun two games earlier, striking out nine more for a Series total of 31. And his teammates pounced on New York for a 6–0 lead after five innings.

The unraveling began subtly in the fourth—a single, a walk, a blown double play, another single, a double steal, and a third single scored three runs. A leadoff homer by Lou Brock paved the way for three more in the fifth. Gibson conceded

Rookie Mel Stottlemyre pitched a seven-hitter as the Yankees evened the Series in game two, 8–3.

Mantle's 18th and final Series homer in the sixth, a three-run shot, and two more to Linz and Boyer in the ninth. But it wasn't nearly enough. The Cardinals prevailed, 7–5, and another era in New York had ended.

"We'll get 'em next year," Berra promised in the clubhouse. But on the flight back to New York Houk gave a message to Berra. "Mr. Topping wants to see you in his office," Yogi was told. "Tomorrow morning at 10."

Berra naturally assumed he'd be rehired; his only question was whether the new contract would be for one year or two. In anticipation, he'd already asked Ford to stay on as player-coach. Instead, Yogi was dismissed. No reason given. The press conference was set for that afternoon.

"Who's going to replace him?" a reporter asked Houk.

"We have two or three men under consideration."

"Is Keane one of them?"

He was—Keane had resigned from the Cards an hour earlier. And he and Houk had already reached an agreement. The announcement was made four days later, when Keane was introduced to the New York media wearing a Yankee cap. As Berra took a coaching job under Stengel with the Mets, so ended an 18-year reign that produced 15 pennants and 10 world championships.

He was a religious man who'd been born in St. Louis and had once considered becoming a priest. And what Johnny Keane saw in his 1965 spring training camp appalled him.

The Yankees—his Yankees now—were spending their nights at Fort Lauderdale watering holes and their days losing exhibition games. They had been doing both and then proceeding to win pennants for years, but Keane had been in St. Louis then.

He had seen the Yankees up close once, the the previous October, and his Cardinals had beaten them in seven games for the world championship. He was managing them now and their "careless habits" bothered him.

Keane began calling team meetings and lecturing his players, and each time his list of transgressors grew larger. "By the last meeting the number of guys who had gotten careless had increased to 23," said pitcher Jim Bouton. "Bobby Richardson and Tony Kubek were the only ones on the club who weren't careless."

So the Yankees began snickering at Keane, and before long they were complaining to general manager Ralph Houk about him, just as they had complained about Berra during the previous season. They nicknamed Keane "Squeaky" and compared stories about him, which Keane eventually realized. "Good afternoon," Keane would greet a cluster of his men in a hotel lobby, "gentlemen of the jury."

This was the new era, and its first year was

New manager Johnny Keane didn't like what he saw at spring training.

New York's grimmest since 1925. The dynasty had come crashing down in the seventh game of the 1964 Series after the Yankees had blown a 2–1 edge in games and a 3–0 lead in game four. The final pennant, the 15th in 18 years, hadn't saved Berra. The Yankee hierarchy had decided in July that Yogi would be dismissed at the end of the season.

Now mediocrity was in full flower around the Stadium, and the championship roster, both regulars and reserves, was beginning to come apart. Kubek, the starting shortstop for nine seasons, would struggle through his worst year (.218) with an aching back and would retire at 29. Right fielder Roger Maris broke his hand and hurt his hamstring during the season, and catcher Elston Howard injured his arm. Left-hander Whitey Ford, the staff ace since the early '50s, had felt his arm go dead in the sixth inning of the 1964 Series opener.

"It just went limp," Ford said. "No blood was getting down from the shoulder. The artery was blocked. The blood was just coming down through the little capillaries and I didn't have a pulse for a year." Winter surgery had repaired his circulation, and Ford would win 16 games in 1965, but he would also lose 13, his most ever, and post his highest earned-run average—3.24.

And Mickey Mantle, his legs gone at 33, was suffering through a frightful year. "I began to feel that I was truly headed downhill," he said. "My shoulder, which I thought had pretty well healed, began to bother me more and more, and

Manager Johnny Keane had to use the bullpen frequently, and the reliever he pointed to most was Pedro Ramos—65 times, equaling Luis Arroyo's 1961 club record. Acquired from Cleveland the previous September, the veteran right-hander was 5–5 with 19 saves and a 2.93 ERA.

no amount of treatment seemed to ease it. I just couldn't uncork those long throws any more."

Then in June, Mantle tore a hamstring trying to score on a passed ball. His final statistics—a .255 average (down from .303), 46 RBIs (down from 111), and 19 home runs (down from 35)—represented his worst full year yet in the majors. With the scouting system in disrepair and the farm teams barren there were few replacements.

"About twelve guys got old one day," Bouton realized. Suddenly the team that had made only two trades in two years made four before May. Pitcher Stan Williams, who'd been obtained for Moose Skowron two years earlier, was sold to Cleveland. Reserve catcher John Blanchard, the ultimate Yankee who'd once said he'd rather rot on the bench as a Yankee than play regularly elsewhere, was dealt to the Athletics with pitcher Rollie Sheldon.

Blanchard wept. "I'm going to Kansas City," he told Richardson. "Great," Richardson said. "You'll get a chance to play every day."

Blanchard shook his head. "I don't want to play every day. I want to stay here."

As a Yankee. But Blanchard's Yankees were vanishing. By the end of the season New York had plunged to sixth place with a 77–85 record, 10 games out of fifth and 25 behind champion Minnesota. It was their worst effort in 40 years—yet one season later it would seem decent by comparison.

It wasn't a good season for Yankee catchers. An aching elbow limited Elston Howard to 110 games, usually playing in pain as his batting average fell 80 points to .233. Backup Johnny Blanchard (right) sympathized—until early May, when he was traded to Kansas City.

Bobby Murcer, brought up in September and just turned 19, is duked by Bobby Richardson after cracking his first homer at Washington. Murcer would hit 174 more during 13 Yankee seasons, totaling 252 overall during a 17-year major-league career.

It was the Year They Fired the Messenger, the season the franchise fell totally apart, the summer the Yankees owned the cellar. It began with 16 losses in their first 20 games and ended in 10th place, the first time New York had viewed the American League from the bottom since 1912, when they were called the Highlanders.

In between, the front office fired manager Johnny Keane and radio announcer Red Barber and resolved to trade virtually every regular who wasn't going to retire. It was a season with few victories (70) and less laughter. "It was an extremely unhappy clubhouse that year," pitcher Jim Bouton would say. "Everybody was in a bad mood. I can't remember laughing and smiling and joking like we used to. Everybody was rubbing each other the wrong way."

Yet the lineup, in name at least, had changed little from that of the 1964 championship club. Joe Pepitone, Bobby Richardson, and Clete Boyer still patrolled the infield, Tom Tresh, Mickey Mantle, and Roger Maris the outfield. Elston Howard still caught much of the same pitching staff—Whitey Ford, Al Downing, Mel Stottle-

Veteran Ruben Amaro (left) was acquired from the Phillies to replace retired Tony Kubek at shortstop in tandem with second baseman Bobby Richardson. But Amaro tore knee ligaments in an April collision with teammate Tom Tresh.

myre, Hal Reniff, Steve Hamilton, Bouton. Only shortstop Tony Kubek was missing, replaced by Horace Clarke.

But the chemistry had gone bad. "These were very powerful people—Whitey, Mickey, Maris, Boyer, myself—used to having control of destinies, controlling all situations," Bouton theorized. "But when you put us all together in a losing situation, it's like taking rats and putting them in a tight situation where they can't get out and turning up the electricity. You can imag-

Horace Clarke became the shortstop after Amaro's injury.

Left: *In his first full season, 22-year-old Roy White batted .225 as a frequently used reserve outfielder and pinch-hitter. The switch-hitting White would average a career .271 during 1,881 games, the fifth highest number of games in Yankee history.* **Right:** *Rookie southpaw Fritz Peterson was 12–11, the only Yankee starting pitcher who won more than he lost.*

On Michael Burke's first day as Yankee president, broadcaster Red Barber reported the smallest crowd in Stadium history and soon was fired after 13 seasons at the Yankee microphone.

ine what they would do to each other. And that was what was happening to us at the end."

Keane, who'd presided over a sixth-place finish in 1965, had been dismissed well before that. When the record reached, 4–16, general manager Ralph Houk, who'd won pennants in 1961, 1962, and 1963, fired Keane and assumed both jobs.

"It surely was not the fault of Johnny Keane that we hit the chutes when we did," Mantle felt. "We may have subconsciously felt that Ralph was the real boss and that anybody else was an interloper. But after Ralph came back we kept

The bullpen was busy (from left): Hal Reniff appeared in 56 games (3–7, 9 saves), Jack Hamilton in 41 (7–2, 3 saves), and Pedro Ramos 51 (3–9, 13 saves). Dooley Womack (not shown) was summoned 41 times (7–2, 4 saves).

right on sliding downhill until we could go no further."

The statistics told it all. Only one starter, Fritz Peterson, won more games than he lost. Stottlemyre, the club's only 20-game winner in 1965, now lost 20 games. Just one regular, Mantle, hit above .270. Meanwhile, attendance sagged to fewer than 1.2 million for the first time since World War II.

It was the bitter fruit of age, injury, and a minor-league system that had long since stopped sending up championship-caliber prospects. The institution of the draft and the Yankees' unwillingness to pay large bonuses had taken their toll.

George Weiss, as he was being shooed from the general manager's office after the 1960 season, had predicted the decline with dismal accuracy. "The Yankees have five more years at the most under the new management," the architect of the Yankee dynasty had said while following Casey Stengel out the door and joining him at the Mets' birth. "Five more years at the most."

Unable to confront reality, management finally decided to avoid it. They had dumped one announcer, Mel Allen, after the 1964 season. Now Barber, who'd spent 13 years at a Yankee microphone after two decades at Cincinnati and Brooklyn, was marked for extinction. Two weeks from the end of 1965 his unwavering honesty sealed his fate.

It had rained for two days. The field was sticky with mud, the seats wet, the air foggy. On Michael Burke's first day as club president, Barber was supposed to do a telecast that would inevitably show the most empty seats since the Stadium had opened in 1923. Burke was sitting alone in the stands among 412 other diehards.

The pennant race was over. The story was the more than 60,000 empty seats. Barber asked for a camera shot of the empty grandstands and bleachers. "No shot," he was told. Perry Smith, the club's vice president for radio and television, had refused. So no cameras followed foul balls, none panned the sidelines. But Barber, an old radio man, would not lie.

"I don't know what the paid attendance is today," he told his audience, "but whatever it is, it is the smallest crowd in the history of the stadium. And that smallest crowd is the story, not the ball game."

The Boston Red Sox, aboard a bus en route from LaGuardia Airport for the next day's game, laughed when they heard the simulcast on the radio. "Old Red will catch hell for saying that," they agreed. Four days later Burke informed Barber that his contract would not be renewed.

And so the Yankee front office, standing amid the ruins of an empire, had reverted to ancient days. They had disposed of the messenger who brought bad news. CBS, which had bought the club two years earlier because it was "compatible with the entertainment and information business," was now providing neither.

They'd waited until the summer's leaves had fallen, and then the front office had begun its purge. A championship season in 1964 had been followed by the worst since 1925, which had been followed by the worst—10th place—since the team had been known as the Yankees. Management had fired Johnny Keane 20 games into the 1966 season (he died of heart failure eight months later) and broadcaster Red Barber at the end of it. Now, they put their hand to the roster.

On October 19, Hector Lopez, who'd played in five World Series as the game's foremost utility man, was released. A month later third baseman Clete Boyer, an eight-year Yankee, was shipped to Atlanta for outfielder Bill Robinson, whom management labeled as its next Mickey Mantle. (He proved to be something less.)

Then Roger Maris, who'd broken Babe Ruth's season home run record only five years earlier, was ferried to St. Louis for third baseman Charlie Smith. Second baseman Bobby Richardson had

Ralph Houk welcomes Bill Robinson, acquired from Atlanta for Clete Boyer. The 23-year-old outfielder was touted as the "next Mickey Mantle," and didn't waste time hitting a home run in his first major-league game on opening day at Washington.

retired at 31 after a dozen years in pinstripes. The leave-takings, in Boyer's and Maris' case, left scars.

"I loved the organization so much," Boyer would say. "I had tried to put out for them and play all the time. Richardson and Kubek quit, and I was the best infielder they had. I was really

Dooley Womack's 65 appearances—winning five, saving 17—tied those of Luis Arroyo (1961) and Pedro Ramos (1965) for most Yankee pitching appearances in a season.

the only one. And then they trade me. I didn't deserve to be traded."

Maris had helped the Yankees to their final pennant in 1964 with a brilliant burst of late-season hitting. In the summer of 1965, playing with a pulled hamstring, he dislocated two fingers on an umpire's cleat sliding into home, then broke the hand a few days later. In 1966, as his average slid to .233, his runs batted in to 43, he was booed steadily.

Maris planned to retire at season's end, but management asked that he hold off announcing it until spring, hoping he'd change his mind—then traded him even though assuring him they wouldn't, according to Roger. And not only had the Yankees traded him, they swapped him even up to the Cardinals for Smith, a journeyman who'd played for five clubs in six years. Maris responded by immediately helping St. Louis to two pennants. Smith faded into oblivion.

Old Yankees like John Blanchard were disgusted. "CBS shouldn't have bought the Yankees," he said. "How the hell can you go from first place to tenth place? Only Jackie Gleason could have made some of those trades. Or Imogene Coca. Art Carney maybe was in on some of those trades."

The 1967 lineup, not to be confused with a CBS situation comedy, was a patchwork quilt of hacks, youngsters, and great names playing out the final year or two of their careers.

Mantle, his throwing shoulder and legs already in the grave, had been shifted from the outfield to first base, where his lack of mobility was less obvious. Shortstop Horace Clarke, who'd played only 23 games at second base in his two-year career, was now the regular there, and Smith was at third.

Ruben Amaro, an ex-Phillie with a bum knee, was the shortstop. Tom Tresh, whose career would be cut short by injury two years later, was still in left, but Joe Pepitone, a natural first baseman, had to fill in for Mantle in center field as they swapped positions. Steve Whitaker, with 31 games of major league experience, was installed in right. Elston Howard who'd played in nine Series, most of them as catcher, would be traded to Boston in August and replaced by a former Mississippi quarterback named Jake Gibbs.

Ironically, it was an improvement, if moving from 10th to ninth can be considered an improvement. The Red Sox, who'd been ninth in 1966, actually won the pennant. New York was the same .400 team. Only the Stadium exterior, painted blue and white during the winter, had changed.

His father had died at 39, eaten up with Hodgkin's disease after a life spent in an Oklahoma mine, and Mickey Mantle was convinced that he was marked for the same fate. "When we were roommates I was into player relations and pensions," former Yankee second baseman Jerry Coleman would say. "But he'd say, 'I'll never get one. I won't live long enough.'"

As it was Mantle was visited with a different curse, which snuffed out his professional life several years early—a pair of legs that came apart on him piece by piece across two decades.

After he was kicked in the shin during a high school football game he'd developed osteomyelitis, a degenerative bone disease that was serious enough to keep Mantle out of the military. Everything else was done to him by baseball, beginning with a Yankee Stadium water drain that hooked a cleat during the 1951 World Series.

"I twisted my knee and got torn ligaments," Mantle would reminisce. "That was the start of my knee operations. I had four. You start out with two sets of cartilage in each knee; now I've got only one set left. Once they operated on my shoulder and tied the tendons together. I had a cyst cut out of my right knee another time."

He also broke a foot, tore hamstrings, and

Mel Stottlemyre was 21–12, the Yankees' first 20-game winner since 1965, when Stottlemyre was 20–9.

Left: *Roy White led hitters at .267 as the Yankees slipped to the lowest team batting average in club history: a feeble .214. White also had most hits (154), doubles (20), triples (7), stolen bases (20), RBIs (62), and runs scored (89).* **Right:** *Bronx native Rocky Colavito donned pinstripes in mid-June. Closing out a notable career at age 35, the rifle-armed slugger hit only .220 and five home runs, but gained some attention by pitching in a late-season game, beating the Tigers on three innings of one-hit relief, ensuring his victory with a homer. It's the last time a position player has been the winning pitcher in a major league game.*

suffered through abscesses that would turn his uniform pants scarlet with blood. Finally, after 2,400 games, almost 250 more than club iron man Lou Gehrig, the body would not accept any more. So, when the 1968 season came to an end, Mantle decided to retire at 36, reluctantly and with teeth clenched.

He had been the last link to the '50s, when world championships were assumed, the fourth figure—with Gehrig, Babe Ruth, and Joe DiMaggio—in the Yankees' Mount Rushmore.

Later he would have nightmares. "I'm in a cab trying to get to Yankee Stadium," he'd say. "Casey is calling my name, and I hear it announced on the public address. But I can't get out of the cab. Something's holding me back."

Mantle had landed in New York in 1951 as a teenage innocent from Oklahoma—the Commerce Comet—with only two years of low-minor-league experience behind him. "He was a real country boy, all shy and embarrassed," remembered Whitey Ford, his running mate throughout his career. "He arrived with a straw suitcase, two pairs of slacks, and one blue sports jacket that probably cost about eight dollars."

Yet Casey Stengel installed him in right field next to DiMaggio. When the Yankees sent him down for a while that summer for seasoning and his confidence wilted, Mantle's father chewed him out ("Hell, you ain't got no guts. I thought I

raised a man. You're nothing but a goddamned baby.") and turned him around.

That fall Mantle started in the World Series before being injured in the Stadium outfield. When he went back to Oklahoma for the off-season, a con man representing the "Will Rogers Insurance Company" fleeced him out of his World Series check. Mantle was no financier; he was a ballplayer. "He was fairly amazin'," Stengel would testify, "in several respects."

Though his legs were never the same after he tore up his right knee that first year, he was probably the best all-around player the franchise had seen. He could field, throw, run, and hit with power from either side of the plate.

Mantle hit .298 lifetime with 1,509 runs batted in and 536 home runs. He even joked about his bases on balls and strikeouts, a combined total of 3,400. "I mustn't have been so hot," Mantle would wink. "I spent seven years without even hitting the ball."

Injuries cost him the better part of the 1963 season and at least 25 games in four others. But unless the muscles were torn or bones broken it was impossible to keep him out of the lineup. "Well, I guess I gotta keep you out today," Stengel would growl, watching Mantle hobble into the clubhouse. "Goddammit, Case," Mantle would protest. "Put me in."

He would bind screaming muscles and tendons in tape, stuff open abscesses with bandages, and head out for a doubleheader in August heat. Once Cleveland third baseman Al Rosen, trying to shame a sore-limbed teammate into playing the Yankees, used Mantle as a standard. "Look at Mantle," Rosen chided him. "He plays on a worse leg than yours every day."

Mantle's legs, both of them, had been ground into mincemeat. "Sometimes we'd be sitting and talking or having dinner and he'd be there sort of rubbing his knees with his hand," Ford remembered. "Then when it came time to get up and leave he'd take a long, long while just lifting up out of his chair, like it was killing him to put all that weight on those bad knees. I think he was in pain all the time I knew him."

By 1965 it had all but ruined Mantle. First baseman Joe Pepitone, who'd replace him in center field, remembered how he found a slumping Mantle weeping in the dugout bathroom because the club was destined for sixth place and he couldn't help them.

His throwing shoulder hurt so badly that Mantle could no longer fire a ball from the outfield; he would flip it to left fielder Tom Tresh. The legs that once covered the distance from home to first in 3.1 seconds (3.0 as a lefty) could no longer move.

The Yankees shifted him to first base for his final two seasons, but by 1968, Mantle's average had slumped to .237. As DiMaggio had decided in 1951 and Gehrig in 1939 (both of them also at 36), Mantle realized it was time to go.

The players he'd won championships with— Billy Martin, Yogi Berra, Tony Kubek, Bobby Richardson—had all retired. Ford, his arm gone, had called it quits the year before at 39. Mantle's teammates now were named Bobby Cox, Roy White, Jake Gibbs, Bill Robinson.

As a final tribute, Denny McLain grooved one for Mantle in the waning days of the season as the Detroit pitcher was recording his 31st victory. It was a harmless gesture—the Tigers had clinched their first pennant in 23 years the night before, the Yankees were consigned to fifth. As Mantle crushed it for home run number 535 to pass Jimmie Foxx, McLain saluted him. "He was my idol," McLain explained. The next June they would retire Mantle's number, 7, at the Stadium, then bear him along the baselines in a golf cart. It was the only game left to him.

They had pulled him up from Richmond for the last few months of the 1964 season and the final pennant drive a dynasty could muster. Mel Stottlemyre had been 22 that summer, and after

he won nine games in seven weeks he found himself a permanent member of the best pitching rotation in baseball, starting regularly with Whitey Ford, Jim Bouton, and Al Downing.

When the World Series began, manager Yogi Berra twice paired him against St. Louis ace Bob Gibson, and Stottlemyre came in with one 8–3 victory and a seven-inning nondecision that a reliever lost in the tenth.

Finally, Berra had had to start him in the seventh game on two days' rest, and after the Cardinals whacked him for three runs in the fourth inning, Stottlemyre blamed himself for losing the Series. Elston Howard wouldn't hear it. "You did a hell of a job," the veteran catcher assured him.

Stottlemyre was going to be the cornerstone of a staff that would have to carry the Yankees through the '60s while the rest of the lineup was rejuvenated. After he won 20 games in 1965, there was no doubt.

"I figured with Stottlemyre, myself, and Downing, that we were never going to get beat," Bouton mused. "That we were going to go on forever."

Instead, the club had collapsed around Stottlemyre. In 1966, when New York finished last, he lost 20 games yet still equalled Fritz Peterson for most victories on the staff with 12. Then maverick Bouton was dispatched to Seattle. Downing, with only 10 victories in two years, would be shipped to Oakland at the end of 1969.

By then all that remained was Stottlemyre and the Kids. Attendance had slipped to barely more than a million, the lowest total since 1945. The club was still slogging along in fifth place while

Mickey Mantle said an emotional farewell to fans at "Mantle Day" on June 8th. "Playing 18 years in Yankee Stadium for you folks," he told the crowd of 60,096, "was the best thing that could ever happen to a ballplayer."

Jack Aker was acquired from Seattle in May and became the club's top reliever with eight wins, 11 saves, and a team-best 2.05 ERA.

Just past his 22nd birthday, prospect Thurman Munson was brought up in August and caught most Yankee games in September. In his second day in pinstripes, Munson received an award from Gene Woodling (right), the former Yankee who had signed him. Munson would be the team backbone until his death 10 seasons later.

manager Ralph Houk tried to nurture young talent. The roster had become a revolving door. In 1969 the front office would make a dozen trades and all but complete the housecleaning that had begun in 1966.

Tom Tresh, Joe Pepitone, and Downing were unloaded before the year was out. At its start, the

Returning from two years in the army, Bobby Murcer was converted to the outfield, and played well there. He batted .259 while leading the team in extra-base hits with 54, including 26 homers, one less than team-leader Joe Pepitone's 27.

Yankee lineup featured an infield of Pepitone, Horace Clarke, Gene Michael, and Jerry Kenney, an outfield of Roy White, Bill Robinson, and Bobby Murcer, and a promising young catcher named Thurman Munson who'd be named Rookie of the Year.

The only constant since 1964 had been Stottlemyre. He'd won 21 games for a fifth-place club in 1968. Now, as the Yankees trod water, he won 20.

When the guard changed in 1974 and new owner George Steinbrenner was installing a championship foundation, Stottlemyre was the last relic of the mid-'60s. Only Ford and Red Ruffing had pitched more innings than his 2,662 or had more starts than his 356, only Ford more shutouts than Stottlemyre's 40. His 164 victories still rank him sixth in club history, his 1,257 strikeouts fifth.

But when his right arm gave out, it happened quickly, irrevocably. A shoulder rotator cuff gave way against the Angels on a June evening; except for one August relief appearance, Stottlemyre never pitched again. In the spring of 1975, after he was told to prepare at his own pace, the Yankees released him.

"In all the years I knew him I never knew Mel to speak a bad word against anybody," Munson would say. "But this time he was furious. He felt he had been lied to. So the incident left a bad taste with everyone."

1970

He had been a Yankee ever since he returned from World War II with a chestful of medals for valor. For eight years Ralph Houk buckled on shin guards whenever Yogi Berra or Charlie Silvera couldn't make it. For six more he'd labored in the system, managing New York's minor league affiliate in Denver and serving as a Yankee coach under manager Casey Stengel.

When Stengel came down with a virus in the middle of the 1960 pennant race, it was Houk that management chose to mind the store for a few weeks. And when Stengel was dismissed after the World Series that year, it was Houk who was named to preside over the dynasty.

It wasn't that they loved Stengel less, owner Del Webb explained, but that the front office had decided that they either had to promote Houk or risk losing him. What had made Houk a model combat officer and earned him a major's oak leaf also made him a desirable manager—loyalty to the troops, a drive to win, and boundless optimism. All of those qualities were designed to inspire devotion from a club that had listened to Stengel's raspy growl for over a decade. "I thought Ralph Houk was the greatest sonovabitch ever to wear spikes," third baseman Clete Boyer would say, and most of his colleagues agreed.

Houk invariably began and ended each day with a huge grin that was impervious to slumps, injuries, summer heat, or the shadow of an opponent a few games behind and gaining. The pennant was never out of reach, the championship just a matter of faith. More important, Houk got his players believing it.

"They enjoy playing for Houk because he tells them where they stand, he alibis for their mistakes, he's continually building confidence by blowing that smoke, and he doesn't have a curfew," said pitcher Jim Bouton. "That's why he was the best manager I ever had."

And that's why the Yankee front office reinstalled Houk in the dugout in 1966 during his third year as general manager and stuck with him there through the darkest days in franchise history.

Tutored by ex-catcher Ralph Houk, Thurman Munson was named American League Rookie of the Year and led Yankee regulars in hitting at .302. Munson also gunned down 23 of 38 would-be base thieves.

Houk had been part of the dynasty ever since it was revived in 1947. He won three pennants in his first three years as manager and was the first ever to win world championships in his first two seasons. Like the military man he was (his baseball nickname, naturally, was the Major), he never lost sight of his objective. "You take the hill, you smash the gun emplacement, you win

Fritz Peterson led Yankee starters with a 20–11 record, the only 20-win season of his career.

Versatile Danny Cater, obtained from Oakland, batted .301 while playing first base, third base and the outfield.

the pennant, there's solid accomplishment," said White Sox owner Bill Veeck. "There's something you can plan and blueprint and come to grips with."

Houk was the perfect man for a tunnel that had only the merest flicker of light at its end. The Yankees' fall from grace had been immediate and final; in two years they plunged from the top of the American League to the bottom in a stunning freefall. Their climb upward would take 12 years, and Houk would be in Detroit when it was complete.

But by 1970, the fifth year of his resurrection ("The Horace Clarke Era," as some New York sportswriters dubbed it), Houk could finally smell a pennant chase.

He had a Rookie of the Year in catcher Thurman Munson, three reliable starting pitchers in Mel Stottlemyre, Stan Bahnsen, and 20-game winner Fritz Peterson, and a bullpen anchored by 34-year-old Lindy McDaniel, a religious sort who mailed out a newsletter called "Pitching for the Master."

After losing 12 of their first 21 games, the Yankees won seven of their first eight in May, were 46–39 by the All-Star break and finished second in their division with their best record since 1964. The title had been out of reach for most of the season; Baltimore would win it by 15 games, capturing its third pennant and second world championship in five years.

But after two years of fifth-place finishes, runner-up money was an achievement for the Yankees. When his people clinched it Houk ordered

a champagne party in the clubhouse. "We were whooping it up as though we'd won the pennant," Munson said. "I know old Yankee purists must have been thinking that celebrating second place was really bush, but we enjoyed it."

After all, the record was 93–69; only Baltimore, Cincinnati, and Minnesota had posted better ones. Only five Yankee clubs had ever surpassed it without winning the pennant. Miller Huggins might not have been popping corks over it, but Ralph Houk would. He would also be named American League Manager of the Year. For his tunnel vision.

They had gone so long without a pennant—seven years, by far the longest drought since 1920—that they'd taken to celebrating even marginally significant milestones. Now, as the franchise's gray days continued, they were willing to accept charity from a 63–96 team to finish above .500, an achievement that their predecessors had once taken for granted.

The 1971 Yankees struggled to keep their heads above water all summer; the end of every month found them with a losing record, despite interim bursts of good fortune. When the final day arrived, they'd lost six of their last eight games and had slipped to 81–80, with only a night date against the Senators at Robert F. Kennedy Stadium remaining.

But Washington owner Robert Short had inadvertently done them a favor. Claiming mounting pools of red ink and eyeing greener pastures in Texas, Short had announced he'd be moving the club to the Dallas area. Ten days earlier, his fellow owners had voted to let him do so.

Senators fans, who had lost one team in 1960 but had never gone without a major league franchise in seven decades, were furious. As the season wound down they draped "Short Stinks" banners from the upper deck. Now, with their club leading its final game, 7–5, with two out in the top of the ninth inning, much of the crowd of nearly 20,000 (including an estimated 4,000 gate crashers) poured onto the diamond to bear off souvenirs. Home plate was ripped from its moorings; letters were stripped from the scoreboard. Unable to clear the field and restore order, the umpires simply declared a forfeit—the first in the major leagues since 1954—and awarded the game (9–0) and a winning season to the Yankees.

Yet it was simply one more incomplete achievement in a season that had been filled with them. Outfielder Bobby Murcer hit .331, the best average of his career, yet lost the batting title by six percentage points to Minnesota's Tony Oliva.

The starting rotation of Mel Stottlemyre, Fritz

Coach Dick Howser congratulates Ron Blomberg as the 22-year-old rookie rounds the bases after hitting his first major-league home run in his first game since being recalled from Syracuse in June. Blomberg went on to hit six more homers while batting .322 in 64 games.

Veteran Felipe Alou, shown with Ralph Houk, was acquired from Oakland shortly before his 36th birthday and contributed a .289 batting average and eight home runs while dividing his time between first base and the outfield.

Curt Blefary crash-lands on Washington's Jim French, completing an inside-the-park homer that gave the Yankees a 1–0 victory.

Peterson, Stan Bahnsen, Steve Kline, and Mike Kekich completed 67 games, the best effort by a New York staff since 1952. The reason? A dismal bullpen that produced only a dozen saves, by far the league's poorest effort.

And catcher Thurman Munson was named to the American League All-Star team—then proceeded to hit .251 for the season, a drop of 51 points from his rookie year. His fielding, however, was impeccable—or nearly so. He handled 614 chances perfectly, but was charged with an error when Oriole Andy Etchebarren knocked him cold at the plate in June. All it cost him was the Yankee record for a catcher and the chance to become the only man besides Athletic Buddy Rosar in 1946 to field a perfect season behind the plate.

So it went. In a season that was every bit as unspectacular as the several that had preceded it, the Yankees sought their consolation prizes where they could. Even if it meant taking a gift from the deathbed of a franchise.

The television people had bought the club as a way of "broadening the base" in the autumn of 1964, seduced by another pennant freshly won and the great names—Mantle, Maris, Ford, Howard, Kubek, Richardson—still on the roster.

CBS was merely a cab ride away from the Stadium, and the Yankees seemed like a fine corporate acquisition—a proud tradition, worldwide visibility, a dash of chic, a touch of class. Both employer and employee even wore pinstriped suits. It was a business, network executive Michael Burke said, "that we would enjoy being in."

Instead, there had been seven Bad Years at Black Rock (the media nickname for the network's ebony granite headquarters on West 52nd Street). The farm clubs and scouting system that had nurtured Yankee success for decades had gone to seed. The names were aging and injury-prone, playing out the string. When the championship feeling evaporated with a sixth-place finish the following season, so did the fans.

Attendance had dipped by 100,000 immediately, then sagged by another 100,000 when New York sank to the American League cellar in 1966. Now, in 1972, it had slid to 966,328, the first time it had been under a million since 1945, even though the product had improved.

Sparky Lyle, acquired from the Red Sox in one of the more larcenous deals in Yankee history, emerged as baseball's top reliever. Ralph Houk used him often—59 times. The rubber-armed southpaw led the staff in ERA with 1.92 while gathering nine victories and a league-leading 35 saves to be named Fireman of the Year by the Sporting News.

The Yankees had finished second to Baltimore in 1970 and also had a winning season the following year. In 1972, studded with promising young talent, they would contend for the divisional championship until the final few weeks. Yet the Mets, their once laughable National League neighbors from Queens, would draw more

Steve Kline enjoyed his best season at 16–9, topping Yankee starters in earned run average (2.40) and winning percentage (.640).

Veteran slugger Johnny Callison joined the Yankees for his 15th big-league season. He hit .258 and nine homers (including a Stadium grand slam) as an outfield regular.

than twice as many paying customers. The difference was stylistic, the difference between pistachio and vanilla ice cream.

The Yankees, to put it bluntly, were boring. "Yankees like nothing in nature," *The New Yorker*'s

Celerino Sanchez was summoned during the season from Syracuse and played well, plugging the third-base gap until Graig Nettles arrived the next year.

Roger Angell scribbled in his notebook. "Most sedative BB team in memory, so uninspired as to suggest bestowal of new sobriquet: Bronx Sashweights? CBS Plastercasts?"

As the season wore on and New York remained in the thick of the race, the club struck sparks. In a span of three days the Yankees banged out 60 hits in doubleheaders against Kansas City and Texas. By the end of August they found themselves only a game and a half behind divisional leader Baltimore and watching the out-of-town scoreboard nightly.

They'd also developed a late-inning ritual, based on the appearance of flamboyant Sparky Lyle who'd been obtained from Boston during spring training for first baseman Danny Cater and shortstop Mario Guerrero. With men on base and New York clinging to a slender lead, manager Ralph Houk would raise his left arm and a pinstriped white automobile would bear Lyle and his hard left-handed slider to the mound while the Stadium organist played "Pomp and Circumstance." Lyle would toss his jacket to a batboy, chomp down on a wad of tobacco, and nail down a save frequently enough to keep the Yankees in the race.

When they came apart it happened all at once, in late September; New York lost its final five games and finished fourth again, three games above .500. During the winter the CBS brass decided they'd seen one summer rerun too many and opted to cancel.

They would sell the club for $10 million, a loss of more than $3 million, to a group headed by a man from Cleveland who built ships and had borne nostalgic memories of the Yankees since childhood. "When the Yankees came to town it was like Barnum and Bailey coming to town," George Steinbrenner would say. "The excitement."

For eight years, that feeling had been sorely missing in the Bronx.

He was a millionaire shipbuilder from Cleveland who knew little about baseball or the Bronx, and he promised to keep a respectable distance from his new pinstriped plaything. "I won't be active in the day-to-day operations of the club at all," announced George Steinbrenner III the day he bought the Yankees during the winter of 1973. "I can't spread myself so thin.

I've got enough headaches with my shipping company."

Yet on opening day, as the National Anthem was playing, here was Steinbrenner jotting down the numbers of several of his players. "He was developing his famous Yankee haircut policy," catcher Thurman Munson realized, "about ten years behind the times."

Afterward, manager Ralph Houk relayed the message to his team: "I want numbers 19, 47, and 28 to cut their hair." The reign of George the Third had begun, and its first year was as unpredictable and unstructured as any in franchise history.

The goofiness began in spring training when pitchers Fritz Peterson and Mike Kekich announced that they were exchanging families, a "life swap" that included wives, children, and household pets. Six feet beneath a tasteful headstone, late owner Jacob Ruppert presumably whirled.

Then the Yankees proceeded to lose their first four games, three of them in Boston. By mid-May they would be involved in the thick of the division race—but so would everybody else. All six teams in the American League East were separated by one game—and none had winning records.

But, by the end of June, spurred by trades that fetched starting pitchers Sam McDowell from San Francisco and Pat Dobson from Atlanta, the

Claire Ruth attended opening day, the 50th anniversary of the stadium's birth when her husband had christened the House That Ruth Built with a home run. The 1973 season was the Yankees' last in the "old" Stadium; the ballpark closed at year's end for a two-year rebuilding, but not before Mrs. Ruth was presented home plate, Mrs. Lou Gehrig first base.

George Steinbrenner headed a group that bought the Yankees from CBS for about $10 million in January. Michael Burke (left) remained as team president—for a while. He bowed out in late April, although he retained his small interest in the club.

The team had a new one-two power punch, Bobby Murcer joined by third baseman Graig Nettles (right), acquired from Cleveland. They shared the team's home-run leadership with 22 each, with Nettles homering in his debut off Luis Tiant at Boston. Murcer hit .304, Nettles .234.

Ron Blomberg made history on April 8 at Boston when he stepped up as the majors' first designated hitter under the new and debated American League rule. Blomberg walked with the bases full for an RBI (if not a hit) in that first DH at bat; he drove in another run while going 1-for-3 in a 15–5 New York loss. Blomberg went on to hit .329 for the season in 100 games, including 55 as DH. More often, Jim Ray Hart filled that role 106 times after being acquired from the Giants in late April.

Yankees had taken over first place for the first time since 1964. They had already acquired a solid shortstop in Fred Stanley and a superb third baseman in Graig Nettles. Molded around a nucleus of Horace Clarke, Gene Michael, Bobby Murcer, Roy White, Munson, and the Alou brothers (Felipe and Matty), it made for a contender.

From May 20 until July 4, New York won 30 of 45 games, including a stretch of 14 in 15 at home, yet attendance was slow to catch up. The Mets, managed by Yogi Berra and on their way to the National League pennant, were still moving more bodies through turnstiles. *The New Yorker*'s Roger Angell, who'd described the club as "sedative" a year earlier, was puzzled. "I think," he wrote, "the problem is ghosts."

The Yankees of Decades Past still haunted. Steinbrenner, who'd been fascinated by the Yankees when he watched them play the Indians at Municipal Stadium as a child, was determined to recreate the past.

Journeyman Duke Sims joined the team for the season's final week, just in time to go to bat nine times and earn the distinction of hitting the last home run in "old" Yankee Stadium.

The hair policy, his locker inspections, his grooming tips, were not all that different from manager Joe McCarthy's attitude in the '30s and '40s. "I want to develop pride in the players as Yankees," Steinbrenner explained. "The Yankee system isn't what it used to be, and we've got to get it back to what it was."

And the American League standings back to what *they* were. New York held the divisional lead until August. Then the club broke apart with astonishing speed, losing 18 of its next 27 games and dropping into fourth. The Yankees would finish two games below .500 and 17 behind the Orioles.

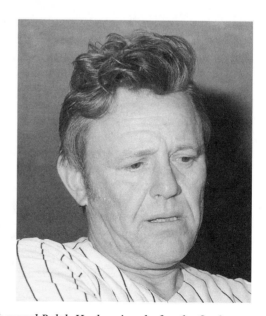

A haggard Ralph Houk resigned after the final game.

"The final month was one of the worst I've lived through," Munson would say. "The fans were on us every day, especially on Ralph. They were never worse than they were during the last game. It pained me when Ralph was forced to come out and make a pitching change late in the game. He got a terrible booing and walked back to the dugout like a beaten man."

Houk, who'd won three pennants in his first three seasons, then came back to preside over the club's long reconstruction, resigned after the finale. That night, as the club began the transition to sharing Shea Stadium with the Mets, they closed up Yankee Stadium for a two-year renovation.

To exorcise ghosts, among other things.

The players called it the Friday Night Massacre, and eventually they grew to accept it as merely another facet of Life with George. It was the 26th of April, the Yankees were only half a game out of first place in the American League East, and they'd just beaten the Rangers in Texas.

When they emerged from the showers they learned that four of the club's eight pitchers— Fritz Peterson, Fred Beene, Steve Kline, and Tom Buskey—had been traded to the Indians for first baseman Chris Chambliss and pitchers Dick Tidrow and Cecil Upshaw.

"Half the pitching staff was gone," marveled catcher Thurman Munson. "Just like that. And here came [general manager] Gabe Paul, a big smile on his face, right into the clubhouse."

The players were both furious and suspicious. Half a dozen Yankees were former Indians as it was. Both Paul and owner George Steinbrenner were from Cleveland. "The connection bothered us," admitted Munson, an Ohioan himself. "It seems as though they were bringing the whole Indian team here."

Coincidentally or not, New York toppled from first to last place within two months. Chaos had become routine—the confusion had rarely abated since Steinbrenner bought the club from CBS the year before.

It was the spring of 1974, and the Yankees were playing in a borrowed ball park in Queens with a manager they hadn't really wanted and an owner under indictment. Stability was not in their vocabulary.

They'd known about the shift in stadia; Yankee Stadium was undergoing a two-year remodeling, so the club was prepared to share Shea Stadium with their National League brethren, the Mets. And Ralph Houk had resigned after the final game of the 1973 season, so the players were prepared for a change. But not for Bill Virdon.

Steinbrenner had wanted to hire Dick Williams, who'd just managed Oakland to its second straight world championship. When A's owner Charles Finley refused to release Williams from his contract without two minor leaguers as compensation, the dispute was appealed to outgoing American League president Joe Cronin, who ruled in Finley's favor.

So the Yankees had hired Virdon, who'd been dismissed in midseason by Pittsburgh; ironically, it had been Virdon's grounder that had caught New York shortstop Tony Kubek in the throat in the final game of the 1960 World Series and led to Bill Mazeroski's home run and the championship.

But where Houk had been a rump slapper and a communicator, Virdon was a quiet man who was used to power hitting at Pittsburgh. "I don't know squat about pitching," he admitted. He had a bad stomach (Yankee players quickly dubbed him Mr. Milkshake) and an aversion to lengthy or frequent conversations. He often sent

Dick Williams was introduced as the new manager in December and donned pinstripes. But the laugh was on Williams when Athletics owner Charlie Finley refused to release him from his Oakland contract without compensation. So Bill Virdon was hired instead.

Left: *Outfielder Lou Piniella was obtained from Kansas City for Linda McDaniel and hit .305 to lead regulars in batting. He would leave an imprint on Yankee history in a number of roles.* **Right:** *Chris Chambliss was the new first baseman, acquired from Cleveland. Chambliss's bat came alive during the stretch drive and his 18-game hitting streak was the longest by a Yankee since Tony Kubek's 19 in 1961.*

Sparky Lyle's 66 appearances were the most in a season by a Yankee pitcher—until he eclipsed his own record with 72 in 1977. And Lyle finished 59 of those 66 while compiling a team-best 1.88 ERA along with a 9–3 record and 15 saves.

Doc Medich enjoyed his best Yankee season with a 19–15 record, tying Pat Dobson as the team's top starter.

coach Dick Howser to home plate with the starting lineup.

"He could go weeks without speaking to you," Munson realized, "for no other reason than he had nothing to say."

Then Steinbrenner had been informed on opening day that he was under indictment for having made illegal contributions to the Nixon campaign during the 1972 presidential election.

Meanwhile, the Yankee roster had become a revolving door; before the season was done 44 players, including 19 pitchers, would wear pinstripes. The Friday Night Massacre was only one of 12 trades or acquisitions the front office would make by New Year's Eve, yet it proved to be the turning point. "That was the start of everything," Paul would say much later. "It broke up the country club. There was great camaraderie on those losing ball clubs."

By September 5, New York had claimed first place by winning 12 of 14 games to overtake slumping Boston. Then Baltimore won 10 straight, sweeping the Yankees on consecutive complete games by Jim Palmer, Mike Cuellar, and Dave McNally, and grabbed the lead back.

The Yankees would repossess it briefly, but when the Red Sox cleaned out New York in a twi-night doubleheader at Shea on the 24th, pennant prospects looked dim. Luis Tiant, Boston's 33-year-old right-hander, had rhumbaed his way to a six-hit shutout in the first game; two New York errors and a Bobby Murcer spill on the base paths botched the nightcap.

A furious crowd of 46,000 littered the diamond

Walt "No-Neck" Williams was obtained from Cleveland, and the 5'6" outfielder quickly proved a popular Yankee, although he hit only .113 in 43 games.

with firecrackers and tennis balls and brawled among themselves. "I don't blame 'em," said a frustrated Murcer. "Tonight I wanted to get up there and whale with 'em."

So the gap was one game with five to play, but the Yankees made a final stand in Cleveland, sweeping three while Steinbrenner celebrated in the stands. The Orioles, though, were also winning. New York flew to Milwaukee for the final two games, still one game out.

Whereupon the dizziness that had pursued the club all year continued. Murcer, trying to break up a fistfight in the hotel lobby between reserve catchers Rick Dempsey and Bill Sudakis, was injured and missed the game. Possibly, he might have caught the fly ball that Elliott Maddox and Lou Piniella misplayed in the eighth, enabling the Brewers to tie the score, win in extra innings and eliminate the Yankees from their best chance at a pennant in a decade.

"Tomorrow is one of the biggest games of the year," Steinbrenner told his players at a party held that night. "You go out and show 'em that you can win tomorrow, and that way you'll get your minds off losing the pennant. Go out there and kick their asses."

The players raised their eyebrows, puzzled. "Everyone kinda said, The season's over and he

wants us to kick their ass tomorrow," said reliever Sparky Lyle.

But orders were orders in Steinbrenner's shop, so Lyle's teammates went out, beat Milwaukee by a run and finished two games behind Baltimore. By the time spring training convened in 1975, Steinbrenner would be communicating with his club by tape recorders and third parties. He was convicted in August and fined $15,000 in lieu of a six-year jail sentence on the illegal campaign contribution charges.

After the 1974 season, commissioner Bowie Kuhn, invoking the game's good name, banned Steinbrenner from operating the franchise for two years. After less than that long in power, George the Third had involuntarily abdicated.

They had packed him off into exile in 1957. Kansas City was a synonym for exile in those days, and Billy Martin had been singled out, fairly or not, as the instigator of a fistfight with a drunken bowler at New York's Copacabana nightclub. So the Yankees—specifically general manager George Weiss, who'd never liked Martin from his first days with the club—had traded him in a seven-player package in June, and Martin had gone on to play for the Tigers, Indians, Reds, Braves, and Twins before retiring four years later.

He'd been a frequent visitor to the Stadium since, managing three American League clubs with the same street-smart aggressiveness that had marked his playing days. Alfred Manuel Martin had taken unsettled teams, won divisional titles with them, squabbled with management, been fired, and moved on to do the same thing elsewhere.

He'd gone through that cycle at Minnesota and Detroit, and now, despite an unexpected second-place effort, he had been dismissed at Texas in the middle of the 1975 season and had gone off to Colorado to fish, his 1976 salary already guaranteed.

Back in the Bronx as July turned into August, Yankee owner George Steinbrenner was fidgeting in exile. His Yankees had lost their grip on first place in the American League East and had fallen 10 games behind Boston.

Bill Virdon had been named 1974 Manager of the Year for maneuvering New York to a second-

Left: *Catfish Hunter joined the Yankees as their first modern-era free agent. His five-year contract for a reported $3.2 million made him the highest-paid player in baseball history. The reigning Cy Young Award holder had won 20 or more games the past four seasons at Oakland, and would scale that plateau again in his first year in New York.* **Right:** *Bobby Bonds became a Yankee in a stunning trade that sent Bobby Murcer to San Francisco. A Gold Glove outfielder who combined speed and power, Bonds was the National League's 1973 Player of the Year.*

place finish, but Steinbrenner thought he lacked panache. His own players called him Mr. Milkshake. Billy Martin hadn't frequented a soda fountain in years.

"Your temperaments aren't compatible," president Gabe Paul told Steinbrenner. "There are going to be problems." Steinbrenner shrugged and sent Paul and scout Birdie Tebbetts to find Martin and get him interested. The deal was no better than what he'd had with the Rangers—$72,000 a year. But it was the Yankee job. Once a Yankee . . .

Yet the terms of the contract bothered Martin. He had to "personally conduct yourself at all times so as to represent the best interest of the New York Yankees and to adhere to all club policies." He could not criticize management. He had to be available to consult with the front office. Breach any of the above, and management could fire him with no liability for his salary.

"They hadn't even hired me and here the people were talking about firing me," Martin would say. "I had to be out of my mind to sign that contract."

But he did and suddenly found himself being introduced as the new manager at the Yankees Old-Timers' Day, a celebration to which he hadn't even been invited originally. Virdon had quietly cleaned out his desk several hours earlier.

Martin had fretted about working for Steinbrenner, particularly under those terms. "I was putting myself in a position where he could handcuff me, and I didn't know him very well," Martin would say. "I had heard he was wild and erratic."

And this year Steinbrenner was at a distance. After Steinbrenner's conviction for illegal contributions to the 1972 Nixon presidential campaign, baseball commissioner Bowie Kuhn had suspended him for two years. He could not frequent the team offices or the clubhouse, yet Steinbrenner was not a man to sit idle.

"Gather round here and listen," Virdon had instructed his club one day, then flicked on a tape recorder.

"I'll be a sonovabitch if I'm going to sit up here and sign these paychecks and watch us get our asses kicked by a bunch of rummies," barked a recorded voice.

"It was George," reliever Sparky Lyle realized.

George would always be there, at least figuratively, cajoling, ordering, overseeing. But until Kuhn's suspension was lifted in March 1976, Martin was running the club, at least from the

Billy Martin donned pinstripes again, this time as the new manager. George Steinbrenner introduced him on August 2, first to the media, then to an Old-Timers' Day crowd, who cheered the return of Billy the Kid.

dugout, and the players responded to him immediately.

Like them, Martin had been a Yankee. He had won two World Series personally, one with his glove, one with his bat. He had seen the inside of a cocktail lounge. "He remembers what it was like to be a player," Lyle said. "Everybody on the team really loved him. We were excited about having Billy as a manager because he'd make a move, pinch-hit or steal or bunt, and he'd walk up and down the dugout and explain why he did what he did."

Energized, the Yankees won six of their next eight before leveling off and finishing third, 12 games behind the Red Sox. But Martin had already begun planning for 1976, pruning the roster in his mind and molding a nucleus.

He had watched the club closely from the day he'd arrived, but kept his own counsel. "I wanted to see who were the clubhouse lawyers, alibiers, and complainers and get rid of them," Martin reasoned. "You can't keep those types and still have a winning team."

Pitcher Pat Dobson had mentioned to a reporter that the players probably wouldn't heed Martin. "I made a little note to myself that he'd

be the first guy we'd get rid of at the end of the season," Martin decided. Another pitcher, Doc Medich, blamed the outfielders for his losses. Medich was shipped out in December to Pittsburgh. Outfielder Bobby Bonds wanted to stay out of the lineup near the end of the season and tend to a sore leg while Martin was trying to pile up victories for psychological purposes. Bonds went to the Angels the same day Medich was jettisoned.

Finally, thanks to Steinbrenner's munificence, there was enough talent on hand to rebuild to Martin's liking. Pitcher Catfish Hunter had already been scooped up from the free-agent table for more than $3 million in salary, bonuses, and extras during the winter of 1975, and had won 23 games. Now the Dobson, Bonds, and Medich trades brought three proven pitchers (Ed Figueroa, Dock Ellis, and Ken Brett) and three everyday starters in designated hitter Oscar Gamble, second baseman Willie Randolph, and center fielder Mickey Rivers.

"I felt we were going to win," Martin said. "I couldn't wait to get to camp."

1976

He couldn't find home plate. Or third base for that matter. Yankee fans, pennant-starved after a dozen years of mediocrity or worse, had swarmed onto the Stadium diamond as soon as they saw the ball drop into the right-field stands.

They met first baseman Chris Chambliss midway between second and third and buried him with delight. Chambliss's home run off Kansas City reliever Mark Littell had just given the Yankees a 7–6 victory over the Royals and the American League pennant in the ninth inning of the final game of their playoff series.

For the first time since 1964, when the Yankees had won their last pennant by a single game over Chicago, there was something to celebrate in the Bronx.

The franchise had come full cycle since then— a different owner, a new manager, a remodeled Stadium, and a club stocked with young talent that had largely been obtained elsewhere.

For decades the Yankees had rebuilt their roster by dipping into a teeming farm system; now president Gabe Paul's horse-trading instincts and owner George Steinbrenner's cash had forged a more direct path to success. Only four men on

Despite playing with only one good leg much of the season, Bobby Bonds could beat opponents with power or speed, equally familiar crossing the plate on a home-run trot in a cloud of dust. The veteran hit 32 homers and stole 30 bases—the Yankees' only 30/30 man ever. Bonds also fanned a club-record 137 times, and after the season was traded to California in a deal for Mickey Rivers and Ed Figueroa.

the 25-player roster had come up through the system; only catcher Thurman Munson and outfielder Roy White remained from the 1970 season, when the Yankees, resigned to runner-up status, had popped champagne corks to celebrate second place.

The Yankees were an amalgam of capable refugees from Cleveland, from Pittsburgh, from California. Three of their regulars—Chambliss, third baseman Graig Nettles, and outfielder Oscar Gamble—had been Indians. Center fielder Mickey Rivers and pitchers Rudy May and Ed Figueroa were former Angels. Second baseman Willie Randolph and pitcher Dock Ellis were ex-Pirates.

The only similarities between the 1964 club and this one were the name, the pinstripes, and former catchers Yogi Berra and Elston Howard, both now Yankee coaches. When the Yankees arrived at spring training they were introduced to new ground rules and a new workout philosophy. What manager Billy Martin had found, taking over from Bill Virdon in August of 1975, had annoyed him.

"It wasn't the Yankee clubhouse the way I remembered it," Martin said. "Anyone who wanted to was running around the clubhouse. It wasn't a professional way of doing things, and the lack of professionalism was reflected in the way the team was playing. The execution was weak, the players were not doing the basic things on the field like hitting the cutoff man or advancing the runner, and too many of the players weren't being aggressive enough on the field."

Left: *Mickey Rivers also came from the Angels in the exchange for Bonds. A potent leadoff batter who drove in 67 runs, Rivers led Yankee hitters at .312, seventh in the league. He also stole 43 bases, most by a Yankee since 1944, and covered center field the best since Mickey Mantle.* **Right:** *Willie Randolph was another key addition, obtained with Dock Ellis from Pittsburgh for Doc Medich. Randolph hit a solid .267, stole 37 bases, and played a far-ranging second base.*

All of that would change. Martin abolished the traditionally leisurely double sessions at Fort Lauderdale and instituted one three-hour workout on two diamonds that kept everyone in perpetual motion, working on fundamentals.

But Steinbrenner was troubled by the shorter, if more productive working day. "You burn them up down here," Martin countered, "and by the end of the season they have nothing left."

When Martin took his people north for opening day inside a totally refurbished Yankee Stadium, they were crisp, confident, and well conditioned.

They came from four runs down to drub Minnesota in the opener with Joe DiMaggio, Mickey Mantle, and the widows of Babe Ruth and Lou Gehrig looking on, and went on to win 15 of their first 20 games. The race in the American League East, as in all four divisions that season, was over by the first week in June. "It was the happiest ball club I think I ever managed," Martin would say. "The guys were just having fun playing hard, aggressive baseball."

On May 20 the aggression had spilled over into a bench-clearing brawl at the Stadium, where New York was entertaining defending league champion Boston in a three-game series. Red Sox right fielder Dwight Evans had gunned down Yankee counterpart Lou Piniella at the plate, but Piniella had bowled over catcher Carlton Fisk, knees into chest, in an effort to jar the ball loose.

What ensued was a free-for-all between two

Ed Figueroa came from the Angels in exchange for Bobby Bonds. He became the ace with most victories (19 against 10 losses) and lowest ERA (3.01).

old archrivals that cost Boston its only left-handed starter. Bill Lee was pummeled, in succession, by Rivers and Nettles, and was assisted from the premises with a dislocated pitching shoulder.

Though the Red Sox, infuriated, scored eight runs in the next three innings and trounced New York, they were never again the same club. They dropped the final two games of the series, ended up firing 1975 Manager of the Year Darrell Johnson in July, and finished third. When owner Tom Yawkey died that summer, it marked the beginning of the dissolution of a ball club.

For several years the Red Sox, loaded with homegrown talent, had been shaping up as the club of the late '70s and early '80s; now the Yankees were replacing them with an imported lineup that was pennant caliber.

Chambliss, Randolph, Nettles, and former Indian shortstop Fred Stanley formed their infield, White, Rivers, and Gamble the outfield. Piniella, a former Royal, was designated hitter. Munson was catching an entire pitching staff that had been raised on other farms.

And Steinbrenner wasn't done yet. Hours before the trading deadline on June 15 he put together a 10-player deal with Baltimore that involved seven pitchers and two catchers and reaped him southpaw Ken Holtzman, a 20-game winner.

"This trade just won you a pennant," Martin recalls Steinbrenner saying. "You now have the best team on paper and now you're a push-button manager." But Martin was appalled. "It was one of the most ridiculous trades I had ever seen or heard of," he decided.

Three of the departed Yankees were left-handers, a must in the Stadium. Steinbrenner had given up a promising young catcher in Rick Dempsey for a lesser one in Elrod Hendricks. Still, New York immediately won eight straight games and opened a 15-game lead in July.

When the inevitable slippage occurred—six out of seven in August—Steinbrenner was shocked. Martin had turned down his request to have a recorded Steinbrenner fight talk played to his club in spring training. Now the owner wanted to pep up his pitchers and dropped by before a game to give them a speech. Martin would recall the scene vividly.

"You guys don't want it bad enough," Steinbrenner told them. "You're not giving one hundred percent. You guys are Yankees, and you have to play like Yankees." The pitchers listened, straight-faced, then laughed at Steinbrenner after he left, according to the manager. "They didn't

Carlos May hit .278 in 87 games after being acquired in mid-May from the White Sox. He performed well, mostly as a designated hitter, despite missing a thumb lost in a Marine Corps training accident.

pay any attention," Martin said. "He thought they did, but they didn't."

The slump ended in due time, and by the end of August New York's lead had swollen to 11½ games. Even a blown four-game Stadium series to the Orioles, the only challenger left, proved harmless. The Yankees clinched the divisional title in a Detroit restaurant while listening to Baltimore lose by phone, then squirted champagne on each other.

A best-of-five playoff (another novelty since 1964) still loomed with the Royals, though, and it began with bad feeling between Martin and two Kansas City players.

The Yankees had traded George Brett's brother Ken to Chicago and pitcher Larry Gura to the Royals two days apart that spring. "Brett told reporters I had lied to his brother, and Gura said I had lied to him," Martin said. "He said I had promised him a starting job."

As Martin watched, delighted, Brett threw wildly to first trying to complete a bases-loaded double play, giving the Yankees two first-inning runs, and New York went on to drill Gura (while Martin heckled him) for 12 hits and win the opener, 4–1, at Kansas City.

But the ease of the victory was deceptive. The Yankees made five errors in the second game, failed to hold a 3–2 lead in the sixth, and lost, 7–3. In game three they had to rally from a 3–0 first inning deficit to win, 5–3. And in game four, Nettles homered twice, but the Royals roughed up Catfish Hunter for five runs on five hits in three innings, won 7–4, and forced the issue to the limit at the Stadium.

When John Mayberry rocked a two-run homer off Figueroa in the first inning, the Yankees found themselves in deep trouble. By the eighth inning, though, New York had chased not only starter Dennis Leonard but relievers Paul Splittorff, Marty Pattin, and Andy Hassler and established a 6–3 lead.

But Figueroa, tiring, put two Royals on base in the eighth, with Brett due up, and Martin replaced him with Grant Jackson, one of the more anonymous journeymen in the league until he'd gone 8–0 for the Orioles in 1973 after six years of mediocrity. Moments later it was tied, 6–6, after Brett had pounded a ball over the right-field fence.

"The whole scene," Martin said, "came down to who could score one run first." So it went to the bottom of the ninth with Chambliss leading off and the clock showing after 11 P.M.

Littell, Kansas City's fifth pitcher, served up a fastball that Chambliss, after blasting it on a line to right field, paused and watched rise. He saw Royals outfielders Al Cowens and Hal McRae stare at the ball, then watched McRae leap for it and come down with glove empty.

"By the time Chris rounded third all hope of reaching the plate was gone," said Munson, who'd still been in full catching gear when Chambliss swung and had jumped, ecstatic, from the dugout. "He never did make it."

At least not until much later. Accompanied by

Excited fans mob Chris Chambliss, blocking his path around the bases after his pennant-deciding homer. He would not touch home plate until long after the game.

two policemen, Chambliss finally emerged from the clubhouse and touched home plate, just to make it official. Inside, his teammates partied until 2 A.M., then returned seven hours later to board a bus for LaGuardia Airport and a flight to Cincinnati—and both a World Series and a group

Chris Chambliss goes into orbit (as does Thurman Munson at left) at seeing his home run disappear over the Stadium's right-field fence. Chambliss led off the ninth inning of the league championship finale against Kansas City and gave the Yankees their first pennant since 1964. He led all series hitters at .524, but none of his other 10 hits compared with this sudden series-ender off Mark Littell.

of Reds that were unlike any the Yankees had ever seen.

To begin with, the Series was mostly at night, the air so cold that portable heaters had to be rigged in the dugouts. "When are we going to stop letting TV tell us when we are going to play?" griped Martin, who'd once saved a Series with a clutch catch of a ball his first baseman had lost in the sun. "This is asinine, playing night games in October. It's damn near freezing out there."

And the Reds were hardly the compliant chumps that the Yankees had dispatched in four straight in 1939 and five games in 1961. This was the Big Red Machine of Pete Rose, Johnny Bench, Tony Perez, and Joe Morgan that had beaten the Red Sox in a dramatic 1975 Series, retained their divisional title by 10 games, and swept Eastern leader Philadelphia for the pennant.

The Reds were rested, had a 20-game winner ready in left-hander Don Gullett (whom the Yankees would sign as a free agent in November), and were playing at home. The Yankees, with only one day between the playoff and Series games, were down to their number-five starter, Doyle Alexander, whom Martin considered marginal.

Morgan blasted a two-out homer off Alexander in the first inning, Gullett held New York to five hits, and the Reds ruled, 5–1. The second game, which New York had struggled gamely to tie after Cincinnati had jumped on Hunter for three runs in the second inning, came unglued with two outs in the ninth after Reds outfielder Ken Griffey had hit what appeared to be an inning-ending grounder to Stanley at shortstop. But Stanley threw the ball into the Reds' dugout, Griffey wound up on second, and scored on Perez's line-drive single. Steinbrenner, irate, forbade Martin to ever start Stanley again. "I'll get rid of him, Billy," Martin would recall Steinbrenner warning, "if you play him."

Back in the Bronx, nothing changed. Cincinnati ripped Ellis for three runs in the second inning of game three, banged out 13 hits, and won, 6–2. For the second time in three Series, the Yankees were facing a sweep and seemed helpless to prevent one.

They would take the lead for the only time in the first inning of game four, when Munson singled with two out. But Bench hit one three-run homer in the fourth and another in the ninth to rout New York, 7–2. While Martin wept in the trainer's room, Cincinnati manager Sparky Anderson was insulting the Yankee MVP at the postgame press conference. "Munson is an out-standing player, and he would hit .300 in the National League," Anderson said. "But don't ever embarrass nobody by comparing them to Johnny Bench."

Meanwhile, Steinbrenner sought out Martin in the clubhouse. "If daggers could have come out of the man's eyes they would have," Martin said. "He was looking at me like, 'How can you do this to me?'—as if I had lost the Series in four straight on purpose, like he was embarrassed. Who the hell wasn't embarrassed?

"The Reds outplayed us. It was then that George decided he was going to make some changes, that he was really going to get into things, because he wasn't going to be embarrassed like that again."

It was a feat that was Ruthian in its dimensions, but Babe Ruth had never done it. No baseball player had. Three home runs on three consecutive swings of the bat were unlikely enough, but to produce them in the final game of the World Series was stuff for Cooperstown.

"Nothing can top this," Reggie Jackson concluded after his three homers had brought the Yankees an 8–4 victory over Los Angeles and their first world championship since 1962. "Who in hell's ever going to hit three home runs in a deciding World Series game? I won't. Babe Ruth, Hank Aaron, Joe DiMaggio . . . at least I was with them for one night."

In statistical fact Jackson had surpassed them. He not only hit the first pitch into the Yankee Stadium seats in his final three at bats, but also set a Series record for most homers (five), all of them coming in his last nine at bats, the last four on consecutive swings in the final two games.

Even the Dodgers, realizing that each blow was sealing their fate more irrevocably, were moved. "I must admit when he hit the third one, and I was sure nobody was looking, I applauded into my glove," said first baseman Steve Garvey.

It was a stunning climax to one of the most turbulent seasons in Yankee history, during which the owner argued with his manager, the manager with Jackson, and Jackson with virtually all of his teammates.

New York had won 100 games, retained the

Ron Guidry, going on 27, posted his first victory as a Yankee and added 15 more for a 16–7 record, tying him with 16–11 Ed Figueroa for most wins. And Guidry's 2.82 ERA was best among starters.

pennant, and won a Series for the first time in 15 years, yet the consuming issue from November through October had been Reggie.

He had played on two world championship clubs at Oakland and built a career out of the long ball (no American Leaguer hit more during the 1970s) and clutch hitting in October, when it counted most. After A's owner Charles Finley had traded him to Baltimore after the 1975 sea-

Bucky Dent was the new shortstop, acquired just before opening day from the White Sox for three players including Oscar Gamble.

son, Jackson had played out his option and declared himself a free agent.

Owner George Steinbrenner wooed Jackson personally during the month following the 1976 Series, dining with him at the "21" Club and flying to Chicago to meet him for Thanksgiving breakfast. Four clubs sought Reggie after he'd announced his displeasure with the Orioles, but Jackson had gone with the Yankees.

"Steinbrenner took it on his own to hunt me down," Jackson said. "He's like me. He's a little crazy, but he's a hustler. It was like trying to hustle a girl in a bar. Some clubs offered several hundred thousand dollars more, possibly seven figures more, but the reason I'm a Yankee is that George Steinbrenner outhustled everybody else."

The terms of the contract were staggering—a $2.6 million package over five years. Only pitcher Catfish Hunter had ever reaped more from Yankee management, but Hunter hadn't arrived in the Bronx brimming with Jackson's confident oratory. Both the money and the oratory were resented by a number of Jackson's new teammates—particularly captain Thurman Munson, who'd been assured by Steinbrenner, when he'd foresworn free agency and signed a four-year contract the previous March, that only Hunter would draw a higher wage.

Munson was one of the few Yankees who'd come up through the club's farm system and had endured the fourth- and fifth-place finishes of the late '60s and early '70s. He was the constant, the gruff team leader holding the club together from behind the plate as its first captain since Lou Gehrig. Now came Jackson, more highly paid (if you counted the deferred money and bonuses) and taking on the role of franchise savior. Their relationship, marginally cordial to begin with, was ruptured when *Sport* magazine's May issue hit the stands with comments Jackson had reportedly made during spring training.

"It all flows from me," Jackson was quoted as saying. "I've got to keep it all going. I'm the straw that stirs the drink. . . . Munson thinks he can be the straw that stirs the drink, but he can only stir it bad."

Munson, who'd led the Yankees to their first pennant in a dozen years in 1976, fumed. "He made it clear he would never forgive Reggie for it," said Billy Martin, "and I don't think he ever did. It always stuck in his craw."

Meanwhile, relations between Jackson and Martin were decidedly cool. Jackson had been pursued, won, and signed by Steinbrenner, and it was to Steinbrenner he felt he owed his allegiance.

"He said there would be no problems: 'George and I see eye to eye on everything,'" Martin would say, irritated. "He forgot one guy—Billy Martin."

Martin had managed a club that won the pennant by 10½ games without Jackson; Jackson would be only one man among 25 in the Bronx.

So Martin ignored Steinbrenner's suggestions to bat Jackson in the cleanup spot in the order, preferring first baseman Chris Chambliss. "Who was it who hit the home run off Mark Littell to win the pennant?" Martin said. "George didn't remember that."

Jackson would bat fifth, and occasionally, when Martin figured the percentages weren't good, he benched Jackson against certain pitchers. A confrontation was inevitable and it came on national television in Boston during a weekend series in June.

The Yankees had lost Friday's game and were trailing 7–4 in the sixth on Saturday afternoon, thanks to five Red Sox home runs. Then Boston's Jim Rice lofted a long fly ball toward Jackson in right.

"He jogged toward the ball," Martin fumed, "fielded it on about the fiftieth hop, took his sweet time throwing it in, and made a weak throw in the general direction of the pitcher's mound."

So Rice wound up on second, and Martin sent out Paul Blair to replace Jackson. Moments later a network audience that included Steinbrenner watched Martin and Jackson shout at each other in the dugout.

"You showed me up," Jackson yelled. "You showed me up. How could you do it to me on television?" Curses followed. "I tried to get him," Martin said. "I went right after him, and Elston Howard tried to stop me, and I threw him out of the way."

Finally, coach Yogi Berra restrained Martin, and Jackson showered and left the park. The next day president Gabe Paul got Martin and Jackson together in his room for breakfast and an armistice. Instead, the dispute flared anew.

"Nobody's restraining me now," Martin told Jackson. "You wanted to fight me yesterday. How about now? Right now." Tempers cooled, but when the club arrived in Detroit, Steinbrenner was waiting for Martin.

"How could you have done a thing like that?" Steinbrenner asked. If it were up to him, Stein-

Reggie Jackson and Billy Martin collide in an angry confrontation in the dugout during a mid-June nationally televised Game of the Week in Boston. Jackson was irate when the manager pulled him during an inning and accused him of loafing in right field. The debate flared before coach Elston Howard held off Jackson while coach Yogi Berra restrained Martin.

brenner said, Martin would be fired, but he would leave the decision to Paul. Steinbrenner had already talked with Jackson and reserve catcher/peacemaker Fran Healy, who'd persuaded him not to dismiss Martin over one incident.

Still, Martin walked a tightrope. He'd signed a contract that allowed management to fire him if they felt his conduct was unworthy, if he criticized the front office, or if he wasn't available daily at the ball park for consultation.

Steinbrenner had already fined Martin $2,500 in May for ripping management decisions. By July, with the club in first place, the owner-manager relationship reached a crisis point. Finally, Munson and outfielder Lou Piniella went to Steinbrenner's hotel room in Milwaukee.

"You've got to get off Billy's back," Munson would recall they told him. "You're driving him crazy. If you're going to fire him, fire him. If you're not, leave him alone and let him manage."

Steinbrenner agreed to remove the irksome provisos from Martin's contract, but he wanted some answers. For his manager's benefit he scribbled the batting averages of the New York, Boston, and Baltimore lineups on a blackboard and compared them. "Well, what's wrong with the team?" he asked Martin.

"You, George, you're what's wrong with the team," Martin says he told him. "You're meddling all the time, you're creating problems leaking out stories to the newspapers. You're the problem. That isn't like the New York Yankees. We don't leak stories or do things like that. That's unlike any Yankee I ever saw in my life."

The stability and consistency that had always been a franchise hallmark had vanished. Within two weeks word filtered back to Martin that Steinbrenner had been asking around about Los Angeles manager Walter Alston, that he had offered Yankee coach Dick Howser Martin's job. Several days later Steinbrenner released his "Seven Commandments" by which Martin would henceforth be judged.

- Does he win?
- Does he work hard enough?
- Is he emotionally equipped to lead the men under him?
- Is he organized?
- Is he prepared?
- Does he understand human nature?
- Is he honorable?

Then, shortly thereafter, Steinbrenner told Martin he was doing a "great job," raised his salary to $90,000, and gave him a two-year contract. So it went.

Reggie Jackson rocketed home runs on three consecutive pitches in the World Series' deciding game six at the Stadium, an 8–4 triumph over the Dodgers that gave the Yankees their first world championship in 15 years.

"Mr. October" felt "completely vindicated" after being benched in the finale of the league championships at Kansas City (after going 1-for-14), and an emotional season full of controversy with manager, teammates and the press.

"God, it was a great moment," the Series MVP would say of the third homer, a Charlie Hough knuckleball he crushed nearly 500 feet into the center-field bleachers and the crowd rocked the Stadium with the chant Reg-gie! Reg-gie! Reg-gie! "A hundred million people had seen that Reggie Jackson was okay, no matter what they'd read, no matter what they'd heard. . . .

"I had been the villain. Couldn't do this. Couldn't do that. And now suddenly I didn't care what the manager or my teammates had said or what the media had written. . . .

"It was the happiest moment of my career," Jackson wrote in his autobiography with Mike Lupica.

"Don Larsen had his perfect game in 1956. I had mine in '77. Three swings. Three dingers. . . .

"It was called the greatest game a hitter ever had in a World Series. I can live with that."

The Yankees overhauled Boston down the stretch, Jackson hit a grand slam in the clinching game, and New York prepared to meet Kansas City again for the pennant playoff.

Once again it would go to the full five games, and in the finale Martin would take a gamble—

knowing his job was on the line by doing so—and bench Jackson against Royals left-hander Paul Splittorff, who'd always given him problems.

Once Splittorff had been replaced by right-hander Doug Bird in the eighth, Jackson singled home a run as a pinch hitter that helped New York erase a 3–1 deficit and win the game, 5–3, and the pennant. Afterward, Martin doused Steinbrenner with champagne. "That's for trying to fire me," Martin crowed. Steinbrenner was not amused. "What do you mean 'try'?" he replied. "If I want to fire you, I'll fire you."

So it continued, as New York met Los Angeles in the World Series. "After Kansas City," Martin felt, "the Dodgers were a piece of cake." New York won three of the first four games to take control. Even after the Dodgers siphoned off game five, the championship seemed secure enough for Steinbrenner to give Martin a large bonus that included a Lincoln Continental, say he'd pay for Martin's apartment, and agree to keep him on for 1978.

That night, as the Series returned to New York in game six, Jackson made it secure. With the Yankees trailing 3–2 in the fourth he ripped a low inside fastball on a line 370 feet into the right-field seats for two runs.

That disposed of starter Burt Hooten. In the fifth Jackson hit the same pitch to the same spot, again with a man on, to make it 7–3 and chase reliever Elias Sosa. Then in the eighth inning he demolished a Charlie Hough knuckler, propelling the ball 500 feet into the bleachers in dead center. Three swings, three homers.

"Twenty or thirty years ago you might have made a movie like this," third baseman Graig Nettles said. "Today people would never believe it."

Dick Tidrow enjoyed his best Yankee season: 11–4 and five saves in 49 games, mostly in relief.

For the first time since 1962, when second baseman Bobby Richardson gloved a Willie Mc-Covey line drive in Candlestick Park, the Yankees were world champions. Martin's job was guaranteed, Jackson's salary justified (a candy bar would even be named after him, just as he'd wanted). And Steinbrenner, who'd once lost a quarter of a million dollars on a forgettable basketball team called the Cleveland Pipers, was standing atop his world.

"I was happy for George," Martin would admit. "Because George wanted it so bad. I said to myself, 'Now he can really have fun at the "21" Club. He'll go around and give rings out to his friends, and he'll be able to talk about this one as long as he lives.'"

Mike Torrez pitched two complete-game victories over the Dodgers, including the game six clincher.

1978

Boston pitcher Mike Torrez had already left the mound, certain that the fly ball to left field was routine, that the seventh inning was over and he still had his 2–0 lead and his four-hitter and his former teammates well under control.

"Then I looked over my shoulder on the way to the dugout, and couldn't believe it," Torrez

Bucky Dent stomps on home plate after popping a three-run homer over Fenway Park's chummy left-field wall, erasing Boston's 2–0 lead in the one-game playoff. Dent was an unlikely offensive hero, a .243-hitting shortstop who had four homers all season.

said. "Yaz is back to the wall, popping his glove, looking up. I said, 'What's this? What the . . . '"

The routine fly, lofted by a Yankee shortstop named Bucky Dent who'd hit only .140 in his last 20 games and had just fouled a ball off his ankle, had dropped weakly into the netting above the Green Monster, Fenway Park's tantalizingly close wall.

"'Goddam,' I was saying to myself," Torrez remembered later. "'Goddam, how could that happen?' It's still hard to believe. I've seen the replays on television, Carlton Fisk calling for the fastball inside. It wasn't exactly where I wanted it, but Bucky hit it just hard enough to get out of the park with that breeze."

And Chris Chambliss, Roy White, and Dent had all trotted joyously around the bases, wiping out Boston's lead and setting the stage for a Reggie Jackson homer in the eighth that would cap the most stirring comeback in league history.

The Yankees, trailing the Red Sox by 14 games on July 19, had come back from the dead to grab first place on September 13, had lost sole possession on the final day of the season, and had won only the second playoff in American League history to get it back.

From there the Yankees would wipe out Kansas City for their third straight pennant and make World Series history by losing the first two games to the Dodgers then sweeping the next four.

Along the way they'd accepted manager Billy Martin's tearful resignation, five days later re-

hired him for the 1980 season, and finished out the summer with Bob Lemon, who'd been dismissed by the White Sox in June. Given all that, Dent's flukish homer moments after changing bats merely fit into the grand pattern.

From the beginning it had been an unsettled season, reflected in the standings, the clubhouse, and newspaper headlines. Five players, including captain Thurman Munson, were fined for missing the welcome-home luncheon on opening day. "After six games and one week of false serenity," Jack Wilkinson wrote in the *New York Daily News*, "life is back to normal with the Yankees."

They were defending world champions, thought Graig Nettles, not a Rotary group. "If they're looking for somebody to play 160 games at third base," he said, "I'm their man. If they're looking for somebody to attend luncheons, let them hire Georgie Jessel."

The club didn't rise above the .500 mark until April 28, lost seven out of eight on the West Coast in early June, and fell eight games behind Boston on June 18. By July 8 the gap had grown to 11½ games, then 14. Four pitchers (Catfish Hunter, Don Gullett, Dick Tidrow, and Andy Messersmith) were all hurting, and injuries had knocked regulars Willie Randolph, Mickey Rivers, Thurman Munson, and Dent out of the lineup at various times.

With pennant hopes glimmering and tensions running high, one incident was likely to ignite a firestorm. When Jackson defiantly ignored Martin's change of signals and fouled out bunting

Bob Lemon was the new manager and rallied the team to the greatest comeback in league history—winning 52 of the last 73 games as the Yankees and archrival Red Sox ended the schedule tied atop the AL East.

after being ordered to hit away in the 10th inning of a 7–7 game against Kansas City that the Yankees lost at home in mid-July, the fuse was there.

Martin had Jackson suspended for five games. When he rejoined the club in Chicago, Jackson told reporters, "I don't know why he suspended me." Then Martin learned from White Sox owner Bill Veeck that Yankee owner George Steinbren-

Rich Gossage signed as a free agent and was named the American League's Fireman of the Year by the Sporting News. *The Goose led the league in saves with 27 and won 10 in 63 appearances.*

ner, who'd given Martin a public vote of confidence less than a month earlier, had wanted to swap Martin for Lemon.

When the club reached O'Hare Airport, Martin's head was filled with thoughts of Jackson, Steinbrenner, and what he believed to be their deceptions. "The two of them deserve each other," Martin told two New York sportswriters. "One's a born liar; the other's convicted," the latter an allusion to Steinbrenner's contributions to the 1972 presidential election. It was a tender subject with Steinbrenner, and Martin knew it. "I didn't mean it about George," he would say. "How he came into it I don't know. I meant it about the other guy. I was mad at the other guy."

When his players read those comments the next morning, they realized the consequences. "He's gone," predicted pitcher Ken Clay. Steinbrenner, informed of Martin's quotes by telephone, had hinted at dismissal. "I've got to believe that no boss in his right mind would take that," he'd said.

Instead, Martin made the move. Tearfully. He called a press conference the next day in the lobby of the club's Kansas City hotel. Appearing haggard, Billy started by saying he would answer no questions. "That means now and forever, because I am a Yankee and Yankees do not talk or throw rocks.

"I don't want to hurt this team's chances for the pennant with this undue publicity," he began reading. "The team has a shot at the pennant and I hope they win it. I owe it to my health and my mental well-being to resign. At this time I'm also sorry about those things that were written about George Steinbrenner. He does not deserve them, nor did I say them. I've had my differences with George but we've been able to resolve them. I would like to thank the Yankee management . . . the press, the news media, my coaches, my players and most of all . . . the fans."

The final sentence had been disrupted by his own sobs. Martin left abruptly with Phil Rizzuto's arm around him, spent the afternoon in a small country-and-western bar nearby, then flew to Florida to see Mickey Mantle.

That night Steinbrenner called Martin's agent, Doug Newton. He didn't feel right, Steinbrenner said, about not having Martin as manager. So two days later Martin was sitting down with Steinbrenner in his suite at New York's Carlyle Hotel, sipping iced tea, and talking about coming back for the 1979 season.

They both liked each other, they admitted. Maybe they hadn't talked enough. After both men promised to reform their idiosyncrasies and stay in better touch, they agreed that Martin would reclaim his job for the 1980 season. Lemon, whom Steinbrenner had hired after all, would be given the chance to manage for a full year more, then would become general manager.

The announcement would be made three days later at the Stadium just prior to Old-Timers' Day. Management smuggled Martin, wearing dark glasses and a hat, into the Stadium through a side entrance.

"It was high drama, like a CIA maneuver," he said. "They took me to a little closet underneath the Stadium where I put on my uniform. I could hear the loudspeaker announcing the names of the old-timers as I dressed. Then they sneaked me into a boiler room near the dugout."

When Martin sprinted from the dugout in pinstripes, waving his cap, the crowd cheered him for 10 minutes; meanwhile, Lemon, an affable man with the unruffled nature of an Ohio town mayor, would direct a Yankee club that had already begun to come back together.

While the Red Sox, missing shortstop Rick Burleson and captain Carl Yastrzemski, lost 11 of 14 games in the second half of July, New York won 12 of 16 and whittled Boston's lead to 6½ games. When they met at Fenway Park on September 7 for a four-game series, the result turned an entire season around. The opener, before a capacity crowd that began pouring out into Yawkey Way, disgusted, after four innings, set the tone.

"It didn't matter who Boston put in there," Sparky Lyle said, "whether it was Torrez, Hassler, Drago, or Campbell. Whoever was in there got pounded. To be down for so long and to have to

hear about the unbeatable Red Sox all year and how they're better than the 1927 Yankees and all that crap, well, we beat them 15–3 and it was just terrific."

The next night New York led 8–0 after two innings, won 13–2, and cut the deficit to two games. The rest, played in broad weekend daylight, was easy. Ron Guidry, on his way to the best season (25–3) of any Yankee pitcher since Whitey Ford in 1961, shut out Boston, 7–0, on Saturday. No left-hander had done that to the Red Sox in four years. "I can't believe what I've been seeing," said New York pitching coach Clyde King. "I could understand if an expansion team fell apart like that, but Boston's got the best record in baseball. It can't go on."

Yet it did. New York rubbed out the Red Sox, 7–4, on Sunday and pulled into a tie for first place. It was the first time since 1968 that the Red Sox had lost a four-game series at home, and manager Don Zimmer was humiliated. "I don't know what happened," he muttered. "For four days I looked at the scoreboard in the third or fourth inning and we're trailing by five or six runs and they have 12 or 15 hits."

A week later, New York took two of three from Boston at the Stadium, consolidated the Yankee lead at 2½ games and began printing playoff tickets. The Red Sox, who'd been 51–19 at one point, were floundering and confused. "Every day you sit in front of your locker and ask God what the hell is going on," said the feisty Burleson.

Yet the Red Sox, stung by comparison to the classic "choke" teams in baseball history—the 1951 and 1962 Dodgers and the 1964 Phillies— regrouped to win 12 of their final 14 games and their last eight straight. When the Yankees stubbed their toes, 9–2, on the sixth-place Indians in the season finale, the Red Sox had pulled even. "This is the way it should be," Lyle realized. A playoff at Fenway Park, Guidry versus Torrez.

For six innings the Red Sox owned it. Yastrzemski had belted a homer in the second, and Jim Rice had knocked in Burleson from third in the sixth. And Torrez, who'd come to Boston from the Yankees as a free agent over the winter, had clamped down tight. In the first, fourth, and fifth innings he put the leadoff man on base and then retired the side.

Then Chambliss and White nicked him for singles in the seventh, and Dent hit his pop fly toward Yastrzemski. "I didn't know it cleared the wall," Dent admitted, "until I was past first base."

So it was New York 3, Boston 2, and the Yankees quickly added another run on a walk, a stolen base, and a double by Munson off reliever Bob Stanley. When Jackson answered a crude "Reggie sucks!" chant by dumping a fastball into the center-field bleachers in the eighth, it appeared mere frosting. Instead, it proved the winning run as the Red Sox pushed until the final out.

A double by second baseman Jerry Remy in the eighth had been followed by three singles that produced two runs. Now, with the late afternoon sun covering right field with a blinding glare, Yankee outfielder Lou Piniella became a central figure.

He'd snared a drive down the line by Fred Lynn with two out in the sixth that might have scored two runs. Now with Burleson on first and one out in the ninth, Remy lashed a ball that Piniella couldn't find in the sun—but pretended to. "If you start pounding your glove like you have it," he reasoned, "then the runner can't go." The ball hit the ground near Piniella, whose quick reflexes kept it from bounding past—holding Burleson on second on the single.

Then Rice rapped a long fly that Piniella again couldn't find initially before locating the ball and making the catch. Had Burleson been on third, it was a tied game. Instead, Burleson now advanced there with two out, not one. Now Yastrzemski needed a base hit with the tying run 90 feet away.

Goose Gossage, who'd relieved Guidry in the seventh, was determined to make Yastrzemski hit his best pitch—a fastball tailing inside—to do it. What resulted was a high pop fly barely foul behind third base that Nettles (Georgie Jessel could not have made the play) settled under as everybody inside Fenway froze and the old ballpark fell silent. Moments later Yastrzemski was weeping, the Yankees were pounding each other in celebration, and Jackson was marveling at the hair's breadth by which a season had been decided. "The 163rd game, 5–4 with a man on third and two out in the ninth," he said.

After that the pennant playoff was an anticlimax. The Yankees split the first two games in Kansas City, which was their goal, then polished the Royals off in the Bronx in four.

Was the dynasty back in full flower? "A dynasty doesn't fall fourteen games behind," Lemon figured. Or lose the first two games in the Series as New York did at Dodger Stadium by counts of 11–5 and 4–3. As dramatic punctuation Los Angeles rookie Bob Welch had struck out Jackson with two out and two on and a full count in the ninth inning of game two.

Third baseman Graig Nettles leaps into the arms of reliever Rich Gossage, still clutching Carl Yastrzemski's playoff-ending foul popup that gave the Yankees the division title and a ticket into the league championship series against Kansas City.

"It's a shame this wasn't a seven-game series and that it wasn't the World Series," George Steinbrenner said while visiting the Red Sox clubhouse. "We are the best two teams in baseball. We proved that on the field today. We won, but you didn't lose."

Graig Nettles made several spectacular stops around third base as the Yankees won another World Series.

Reggie Jackson powers a Bob Welch pitch for his second homer of the Series, this one a two-run smash to ice game six—and another world championship. For Jackson it evened a score with Welch, the 21-year-old rookie who had fanned "Mr. October" to dramatically end game two.

"Aviation fuel all the way," admitted Jackson, who had fouled off four straight pitches before fanning. "High octane. The kid came right at me."

Back in New York with a pulsating crowd behind them, the Yankees tore the Series away. "We've got 'em overconfident and tired," Nettles joked. "Tired of running around those bases." Three games and three New York victories later (5–1, 4–3, and 12–2), the Dodgers boarded a westbound jet, shattered. "I don't like this town, I don't like this park, I don't understand these people, I don't understand their existence," said center fielder Rick Monday.

The end came quickly in game six—New York 7, Los Angeles 2, an avenging two-run Jackson homer off Welch icing it—and the resurrection was complete.

"What we've done," proclaimed Dent, the Series MVP, who would become a folk hero over the winter, "will give a lot of teams years from now incentive. They'll say, 'Hey, look at the '78 Yankees. They didn't quit.'"

He had decided that the commuting probably wasn't a wise idea, that a job in the Bronx and a family in Canton, Ohio, linked by a private jet was impractical, probably unfair to teammates who had to travel with the club, and possibly dangerous.

"Why are you flying this thing?" Yankee manager Billy Martin had asked catcher Thurman Munson. "Does George know you're flying?"

Yes, Munson replied, the owner knew. The Cessna Citation, Munson's $1.3 million half-shuttle, half-toy, had even been written into his contract; if Munson died while piloting it, the Yankees had to pay the rest of his salary.

Still, Martin was worried. He'd flown from Albuquerque to Kansas City with Munson in an ice storm and had noticed a flash coming from an engine.

"Maybe that was when I switched on the de-icer," Munson mused.

"No way," Martin had told him. "I've never seen flames come out of an engine like that. You better check it out."

So mechanics had inspected the engine in Kansas City, found that the rotors were mashed and bent, and replaced it. Now George Steinbrenner, who'd originally given Munson permission to fly, wanted him to change his mind. He did, Martin would report; Munson and his wife would take an apartment in New Jersey. Two weeks later he was dead in a flaming wreckage after a training run had gone awry. Team publicist Mickey Morabito called Martin.

"I was standing there, holding the phone, and I started crying," Martin would say. "For five minutes all I did was cry. I couldn't say a thing."

There was nothing left to say, and with two months left in the 1979 season, no reason left to play. Munson's death was the final punctuation mark to a season that had been doomed from the beginning and laced through with sour incidents.

The Yankees had entered the season brimming with confidence after a 1978 campaign that had produced the most dramatic comeback in American League history (from 14 games out on July 19 to the pennant) and a world championship over the Dodgers after the loss of the first two games.

For the first time in five years there was harmony between the front office and the manager's chair, where placid Bob Lemon sat. The lineup was stable, the pitching staff even stronger since Steinbrenner had spent more than $2 million in the free-agent bazaar on Dodger left-hander Tommy John (who'd win 21) and Red Sox right-hander Luis Tiant (who'd win 13).

But this time New York fell 14 games behind the division leader (Baltimore this season) and stayed there. This time Lemon, who'd replaced Martin in midseason the year before, was replaced by Martin in midseason. This time reliever Goose Gossage, who'd saved 27 games including the playoff victory over Boston, tore thumb ligaments during a clubhouse scuffle with backup catcher Cliff Johnson and missed three months. Stability seemed a dozen years ago.

The Yankees would share first place for one day—April 20—then come apart during their first West Coast swing, losing seven of nine. By June 18, New York had slipped to fourth place, 8½ games behind the Orioles, and Steinbrenner was calling Martin.

"Billy, Lemon is doing a terrible job, just terrible," Martin heard Steinbrenner say. "He has no control over the players; he's not doing anything; the poor guy can't do it."

Left: *Luis Tiant, another veteran pitcher signed as a free agent, was lured from the Red Sox, for whom he'd rung up three 20-win seasons. Now 38, Tiant won 13 games for the fourth-place Yankees, establishing himself as a folk hero of sorts in New York, as he'd been in Boston. The colorful Cuban would fall to 8–9 in 1980 and was gone after only two seasons in the Bronx.* **Right:** *Reserve catcher/DH Cliff Johnson, who was banished to Cleveland in June after a clubhouse joust with Goose Gossage that sidelined the ace reliever for three months with a torn thumb ligament.*

Tommy John joined the Yankees as a free agent and led the staff with a 21–9 record. The 36-year-old southpaw's 21 victories tied for second-most in the majors, his 17 complete games tied for second-most in the league. And John's 2.97 ERA trailed only teammate Ron Guidry's league-leading 2.78.

The fact that one of Lemon's sons had recently been killed in an automobile accident no doubt played a part in Lemon's ineffectiveness. Still, Steinbrenner wanted a change and he was willing to overlook the facts that Martin wasn't due back until the 1980 season (having resigned and been rehired during July of 1978 with that understanding), that Martin had scuffled with a reporter in Reno during the off-season, and that Steinbrenner had wanted him to clear himself of charges there before Billy got the job.

Nothing mattered. Martin was back in pinstripes less than a year after he'd resigned. Turmoil accompanied him. That night Jackson, who'd squabbled with Martin extensively in the past, went to Steinbrenner and asked, unsuccessfully, to be traded. Then president Al Rosen, who'd been a Cleveland teammate and close friend of Lemon, quit in July.

Meanwhile, the club plummeted further behind Baltimore each week. On August 2 the Yankees were 14 games out of first place and had been written off. As they arrived home after a midwestern road trip Munson was in Canton, practicing takeoffs and landings. He failed to clear an embankment at the end of the runway, sheared off the wings on a clump of treetops, and fell short of the runway by 1,000 feet.

The flight instructor and another pilot, a friend of Munson, pulled themselves clear, but

Billy Martin replaced Bob Lemon as manager in mid-June, brought back by George Steinbrenner less than a year after resigning. The day Martin returned, Reggie Jackson asked to be traded, but Jackson stuck around and enjoyed a solid season, topping the team in homers (29) and RBIs (89), and sharing the batting lead with Lou Piniella at .297.

reserve fuel ignited and consumed Munson, still strapped in his harness. A witness called the Stadium and asked for Steinbrenner. "It's a matter of life and death," the caller said.

"Oh my God," Steinbrenner gasped, hearing the news. "Oh, no."

Munson was only 32, yet he'd been the linchpin of the franchise, its captain, its symbol, since 1970. He'd played for five managers, toasted three pennants, and seen the pitching staff transformed, then transformed again.

They held a service for him at the Stadium the next night, leaving the spot behind the plate symbolically empty as a crowd of 51,150 saluted Munson's memory with an eight-minute standing ovation, and the club announced that neither his number nor his locker would ever be

used again. And three days later the entire team flew to Canton for its captain's burial.

"I still can't believe it," right fielder Lou Piniella murmured. "I still can't believe I'm not going to walk into the locker room and see him standing there, and it's all going to be a nightmare."

Any chance for a Yankee comeback duplicating that of 1978 died with Munson. Numbed, the club lost five of its next eight games and went on to finish fourth, 13½ games behind the Orioles.

"The whole bottom fell out of the team," Martin would say. "It was difficult from then on. Wins didn't matter quite so much, and the losses became tougher. Thurman's death took everything out of the club."

Over in a corner of the Kansas City clubhouse, Royals owner Ewing Kauffman was mimicking his Yankee counterpart, George Steinbrenner, leaping to his feet and cursing as his third baseman grounded into a game-ending double play. And at his locker, starter and victor Dennis Leonard was explaining why his teammates were

Reggie Jackson and Billy Martin sob at Thurman Munson's funeral at his Canton, Ohio hometown.

Dick Howser (left) was the new manager, Gene Michael the new general manager—onetime Yankee double-play partners and coaches. They led the team to the AL East title as the Yankees set a league attendance record of 2,627,417.

in the process of burying the Second Revival of the New York dynasty.

"The Yankees are good," he conceded, "but they're not the same team we played in '78. They don't have Chambliss swinging the bat, they don't have Rivers slapping the ball, and they don't have Munson getting the clutch hit. They're just not the same."

Which was an undeniable fact. Only four New York players remained from the club that two years earlier had beaten the Red Sox in the divisional playoff, the Royals for the pennant, and the Dodgers in the Series for its first world championship in 16 years. Thurman Munson had been killed in a plane crash in August of 1979. Then Chris Chambliss, whose ninth-inning home run had won the 1976 pennant, had been traded to Toronto. Mickey Rivers had been shipped to Texas. Roy White, the last link to the dark days of the mid-'60s, had gone off reluctantly—at 36—to Japan.

Meanwhile, Kansas City had retained eight men who remembered the bitter playoff losses to the Yankees in 1976, 1977, and 1978 (two of them in the final inning of the fifth game)—but did not feel haunted by them.

"Past history doesn't mean a thing," Royals third baseman George Brett repeated for newspapermen. "Doesn't mean a thing, doesn't mean a thing."

And it didn't. After wiping out New York in the first two games of the 1980 playoff series at Kansas City, the Royals interred their tormentors at the Stadium in game three, and completed a sweep that left the Yankees speechless. It was that swift, that total, and all the more unexpected because New York had just completed a rousing regular season during which they'd dethroned defending American League champion Baltimore by winning 28 of their final 37 games.

By recent Yankee standards it had been a mellow summer. Billy Martin, who'd resigned, been rehired, and fired all within 15 months, had been replaced by coach Dick Howser, whose dealings with Steinbrenner were far less spiky.

Diplomatic relations between Steinbrenner and Martin had been severed irrevocably several weeks after the 1979 World Series over, of all things, a fight between Martin and a marshmallow salesman in a hotel bar near the Minneapolis airport.

Martin claimed the salesman goaded him into a fight; in any case the Marshmallow King, as he called himself, ended up with a split lip. "I stood there looking down at him and it was an old story," Billy the Kid would say. "I was saying to myself, 'How in the hell did I get into this?'"

Five days later Martin was out of a job. "How much can we take and still command any respect?" Steinbrenner wondered. "How can the Yankees, as an organization, keep putting their head in the sand?"

So Howser, who'd replaced Martin for a day when he'd resigned in 1978 and had turned down opportunities to replace him permanently the year before, was given the reins.

The only undue excitement during the 1980 season occurred in mid-August when the Yankees were about to blow a 9½-game lead over the Orioles and lose the grip on first place in the American League East they'd held alone since May 14.

Mired in fourth place, 11 games behind New York on July 14, Baltimore had won 25 of 34 including six of eight from the Yankees on consecutive weekends, and eventually reduced the gap to half a game.

"This is fun," Howser decided. "It's demanding and draining and nerve-racking, but it's what baseball is all about."

Yet the schedule maker, who would not put the two clubs head-to-head during the final 45 games, robbed the stretch run of most of its suspense. The Yankees cleaned up in September—rebuilding their lead back to six games by the

Tommy John again led Yankee pitchers, this time with a 22–9 record, including six shutouts, equal to the most in the majors.

17th—and won the divisional title by three games.

When catcher Rick Cerone and right fielder Lou Piniella crunched back-to-back homers off ex-Yankee Larry Gura in the second inning of the playoff opener, nothing seemed to have changed in five years. "Here we go again," Brett thought.

But New York shortstop Bucky Dent, the hero of the 1978 playoff game with Boston, lost a two-out blooper by Series MVP Frank White with two men on base and let the Royals tie it in the bottom half of the inning. Then Willie Aikens knocked in two more with a two-out, bases-loaded single off Ron Guidry in the fourth, and Brett added a 400-foot homer in the seventh, as Kansas City pulled away. The final was 7–2, and the Royals would pile it on early the next day, too. Two singles, a triple by Willie Wilson, and a double by U. L. Washington got them three runs in the third inning off New York starter Rudy May.

Then, after Graig Nettles had legged out one run on an inside-the-park homer and Willie Randolph had doubled home another to cut Kansas City's lead to 3–2, came the play that would force the Yankees to the brink. With two out in the eighth inning and Randolph on first, Bob Watson bashed a ball off the left-field wall. When Wilson's throw soared over the head of shortstop and cutoff man Washington, New York third base coach Mike Ferraro waved Randolph, who'd stumbled between first and second, on to home.

But Brett, backing up Washington as a trailer, caught the ball and nailed Randolph at the plate. "You've got to take a chance with two outs," Ferraro reasoned, "especially since we haven't been scoring. Brett had his back turned and he has to turn around and make a perfect throw."

Howser agreed. "The throw was so high I thought Brett was going to call for a fair catch," he said. "I coached third base for ten years, and I would have done the same thing."

But Steinbrenner was furious. He criticized Ferraro's judgment to the national press in the clubhouse afterward, then stalked around the room trying to revive his troops. For six innings of game three, New York stayed alive and nursed a 2–1 lead. But with two out in the seventh and nobody on base, Wilson doubled and Washington singled, chasing 22-game winner Tommy John, and Brett greeted reliever Goose Gossage—a classic confrontation that pitted "power versus power," as the pitcher described it—with a 450-foot home run that blew it apart.

"Our fans think we've already won the World

Rick Cerone responded to the pressure of succeeding Thurman Munson with his best season, placing seventh in league MVP voting. After a slow start, Cerone hit .277 (.315 with runners in scoring position), and his 85 RBIs were second to Reggie Jackson's 111 among Yankee batters. The Newark native and Seton Hall grad gunned down 47% of runners attempting to steal, leading league catchers.

Series by beating the Yankees," said Brett, whose towering three-run smash into the Stadium's third tier erased Kansas City's 2–1 deficit and finally provided the winning touch after those 1976–77–78 post-season frustations with the Yankees.

"I still think we're the better team," Howser said.

His employer expressed his disappointment more bitterly. "When Cincinnati swept us in the Series in '76, I vowed to myself that that would never happen again," Steinbrenner would say. "Now this. I was never so disappointed. It's embarrassing as hell to me. It was even more embarrassing than Cincinnati."

Before the fall was done Ferraro would be made coach at first base, where there would be few opportunities to send men home. And Howser would quit. Gene Michael, a former Yankee shortstop now general manager at age 42, would be Steinbrenner's seventh manager in eight years.

①⑨⑧①

Moments after Bob Watson hit into the final out, a typewritten statement was distributed in the Yankee Stadium press box.

"I want to sincerely apologize to the people of New York and to fans of the New York Yankees everywhere for the performance of the Yankee team in the World Series," owner George Steinbrenner had dictated. "I also want to assure you that we will be at work immediately to prepare for 1982."

This was Plan B, one of several options Steinbrenner had toyed with as New York worked its way through the American League miniseries, pennant playoff, and its 33rd World Series. Had the Yankees beaten the Dodgers for their 23rd world championship, their owner presumably would have invoked Plan A and kept the team intact.

But now that New York had squandered a 2–0 Series lead and lost in six games to a Los Angeles club that hadn't won a world championship in 16 years, Steinbrenner was embarrassed, and speculation ran rampant that a bunch of veterans would be gone by spring training.

It was an unsettling climax to the most unsettled season in baseball history, a season broken apart by a 59-day players' strike and crowned with an unprecedented playoff system that matched first- and second-half winners in a miniseries to determine each divisional champion.

Since the overall season's record meant nothing, Cincinnati, whose 66–42 mark was the best in the majors, didn't qualify for a thing. The Yankees, who otherwise would have finished third in the AL East, earned a miniseries date with Milwaukee by winning 34 of 56 first-half games.

What followed was an uninspired second-half effort that led to the dismissal of manager Gene Michael and the rehiring of Bob Lemon, who'd managed the 1978 Yankees to a world championship after taking over from Billy Martin in July.

What Michael had inherited was a wealthy but aging (eight regulars over 30) team with a $20 million left fielder in Dave Winfield, a .284 lifetime hitter whom Steinbrenner had lured from San Diego as a free agent.

What Steinbrenner expected from Winfield and his mates were performances worthy of their

Free-agent Dave Winfield signed a record $20 million long-term contract, making him baseball's highest-paid player. The outfielder would hit .294, leading the team in hits, doubles, total bases, RBIs, and game-winning RBIs, but slumped to a feeble single-for-22 .045 in the World Series.

paychecks. When the club was pounded at home by Cleveland before a near-capacity Jacket Day crowd in late May, Steinbrenner exploded.

Injuries to Watson, catcher Rick Cerone, center fielder Jerry Mumphrey, and pitchers Tommy John, Goose Gossage, and Ron Guidry might have crippled the Yankees physically, but errors and mental mistakes the owner could not excuse.

"I'm embarrassed and disgusted," he fumed. "When 55,000 people come out here and pay their hard-earned dough to see this fiasco, I'm embarrassed. But I can tell you this, these guys are the highest-paid players in baseball, and if they embarrass New York in Baltimore there's gonna be hell to pay."

But once the Yankees lost three straight to the Orioles and dropped into fifth place, Steinbrenner's focus shifted to Michael.

"Right now Gene's been snakebit," Steinbrenner mused. "The decisions he has made have not been the right ones. I'm not saying the decisions are right or wrong, but they have turned out wrong."

While Michael's fate was being pondered by the owner and "his people," and debated in the tabloids, the Yankees came alive and won 11 of their next 12 games. When the strike came on June 12, New York found itself two games ahead of Baltimore in first place.

"No other manager has sewed it up this early for George before, have they?" Michael joked when his club was awarded its miniseries berth as the season resumed in August. But the guarantee was also a liability—New York had no incentive to win the second half.

When the club lost nine of its next 15 and fell into the division cellar, Steinbrenner leveled his gaze once again upon Michael.

"I'll always do what he wants," Michael had said of his boss in May. "He knows that." But now Michael was chafing at what he considered front-office interference, including an off-day practice ordered by Steinbrenner.

"If you're ordering me to do it, I'll do it," Michael told him. "But I'm going to tell the players it's your practice."

"Tell them anything you want," Steinbrenner replied. "I think it has to be done, and I'm signing the paychecks."

Privately, Steinbrenner stewed about what he perceived as Michael's failure to be "a good soldier." Michael had hung up on the owner's intermediaries when they called. He'd told newspapermen that Steinbrenner had called him at the start of a midwestern trip and threatened to dismiss him. "George, if you're going to fire me, do it," Michael had told him. "Tonight before the game. Do it and stop threatening me about it."

Steinbrenner, who felt such conversations should be private, didn't appreciate reading about them. "You can't say those things about your boss and expect to get away with them," Steinbrenner decided. So on September 6, Michael was dismissed. "If George ever manages a team," he would say bitterly, "I hope I own it."

The new manager would be an old manager in Lemon, who'd made up a 14-game deficit on Boston the last time he'd replaced anybody.

"How are you going to turn this thing around?" reporters wondered.

"If I turn things around," Lemon replied, "we'll be losing. I want to keep things going the way they were, and they will if I don't get in the way. This is the first time I've ever been in the playoffs before managing one game."

Which turned out to be his club's main problem down the stretch. The sole reward for winning both halves of the season was an extra home game in the best-of-five miniseries. Whenever the Yankees played Milwaukee or Boston, the inequality of emotion was obvious.

"They're playing pressure baseball," outfielder Lou Piniella sighed after the Red Sox had scored seven runs in the eighth to win, 8–5, at Fenway Park in mid-September. "They're counting down. Fourteen games, thirteen. If we win or lose it doesn't make any difference. Here we are just waiting to play somebody."

That somebody was Milwaukee, which had edged Detroit and Boston by 1½ games in the second half. The Yankees had finished fifth at 25–26 (11–14 under Lemon), but their record was quickly forgotten as the club headed west for the miniseries opener.

If nothing else the guaranteed spot had given the Yankees a chance to get healthy and put their pitching rotation in order. With Cerone, Mumphrey, Watson, and Gossage all back in form the Yankees were ready to play their kind of baseball—which meant blinding pitching, taut defense, and timely hitting.

But the key was the one-two relief work of Gossage and Ron Davis, who routinely mopped up the final four innings of most games. In the opener, after New York had climbed out of a 2–0 hole with four runs in the fourth, Davis and Gossage took over for Guidry and shut out the Brewers the rest of the way with untouchable fastballs.

The next afternoon, after rookie Dave Righetti had struck out 10 Brewers and allowed only four hits in six scoreless innings, Lemon again summoned Davis and Gossage to nail down a 3–0 victory and push Milwaukee to the edge.

"There aren't five guys in the rest of the

Rich Gossage (left) and Ron Davis were a lethal one-two punch out of the bullpen with their all-but-untouchable fastballs. Gossage had three victories, 20 saves, and a 0.77 ERA in 32 appearances, Davis four wins, six saves, and a 2.71 ERA in 43 games, mostly setting up Gossage.

league who throw as hard as those four guys on the Yankees," moaned Brewer outfielder Paul Molitor. "And those four guys have been out there firing at us for 18 innings in 18 hours."

With ace Pete Vuckovich down with the flu and the series shifting to the Bronx, Milwaukee appeared doomed. But another flu-ridden mate, Randy Lerch, forgot his 7–9 record, allowed only three hits in six innings, and watched Rollie Fingers mop up a 5–3 triumph that kept the Brewers breathing.

On came Vuckovich for game four to hold the Yankees scoreless for five innings and throw up in the dugout in between. "I'd made up my mind there'd be no way that I wouldn't pitch this," he said, after four relievers finished up a 2–1 triumph.

Meanwhile, in the other clubhouse, Steinbrenner was holding kangaroo court with Cerone, who'd angered the owner by going to salary arbitration during the previous winter, as his primary target. Cerone's baserunning blunder in the seventh had killed a Yankee rally that might have won both game and series.

When Steinbrenner was done, Cerone, humiliated and in tears, had told the owner to "go —— yourself." The catcher, Steinbrenner had warned, was "on trial." So were his teammates, who were now one loss from an embarrassing elimination. Plan B, too, was a loss away.

"Today," Steinbrenner said, "we find out which guys deserve to be Yankees and which ones don't." Cerone's fate hung in the balance. So did that of Reggie Jackson, who'd squabbled all year with Steinbrenner and was headed for free agency.

"I'm interested in finding how much of this Reggie Jackson crap is true," Jackson said before game five. "Everybody's always saying I come through in the big games. Well, if I'm ever gonna do anything, it'll be tonight."

After the Brewers had touched Guidry for two runs, Jackson tied the game in the fourth inning with a towering home run to right field off Moose Haas. "I just wanted to do something dramatic," Reggie said.

When Gamble followed with another homer, it made for a four-run inning. And after the Brewers had cut the lead back to a run, Cerone belted one of his own in the seventh off Jim Slaton (one of six Milwaukee relievers).

Once Winfield tracked down a Don Money blast to the leftfield wall with two men on in the eighth ("How scared was I?" quipped Lemon. "Only my laundryman knows for sure."), the Brewers were dead.

Later, in a jubilant (and relieved) Yankee club-

house, Steinbrenner shook hands all around, even with Cerone, to whom he'd sent an explanatory "Dear Rick" letter before the game.

Thus aroused—and reprieved—the Yankees found the pennant playoff with Oakland something of an afterthought. "George's Gall vs. Billyball," announced the *New York Daily News*.

Martin had worked for Steinbrenner twice, resigning in 1978 and being fired in 1979. Now, back in the Bay Area where he'd grown up, he'd drilled his Billyball (speed, aggressiveness, defense, and complete games) into the once-pathetic A's. They'd responded by winning a record 17 of their first 18 and sweeping Kansas City in their miniseries.

"We'll beat his [Steinbrenner's] tail like a drum," Martin boasted, but Oakland vanished in three straight without ever leading once. Yankee third baseman Graig Nettles ripped a full-count, two-out, bases-loaded double in the first inning of the opener at the Stadium and John, Davis, and Gossage did the rest, 3–1.

The next day it was 13–3 as Piniella and Nettles each crashed three-run homers and New York fans sang "Goodbye Billy" in the ninth inning.

So the clubs boarded jets and flew 3,000 miles for one game, which Yankee second baseman Willie Randolph (who'd hit only two home runs all season) won with a two-run blast to left field in the sixth.

Once Davis and Gossage came out to relieve Righetti, three more New York runs in the ninth were unnecessary. "Maybe there'll be something called Bobbyball," Lemon cracked.

The only excitement came afterward at the team's victory party in an Oakland restaurant when Nettles knocked Jackson down after a dispute over several of Jackson's uninvited guests displacing Nettles' wife Ginger. "That's Yankee baseball," shrugged Oriole pitcher Jim Palmer.

While the Yankees waited for the Dodgers to beat Montreal in the final inning of the final game of the National League playoffs, Nettles and Jackson patched up their differences. "It's all in the past," Nettles said. "It's forgotten." When the Series opened in New York, the Yankees were still in form.

This time Watson, in his first Series at bat, gave the Yankees a 3–0 lead with a first-inning homer, Guidry and Gossage kept the Dodgers at bay, and Nettles, who'd frustrated Los Angeles with his glove in the 1978 Series, robbed Davey Lopes and Steve Garvey this time. "You would think by now they would have learned," Lemon said, "you don't hit the ball down there."

"Don't the Dodgers Ever Learn?" wondered a fan's hand-lettered sign the next night as John set them down in order for four innings. The Dodgers had let him get away as a free agent after the 1978 Series. When he left after seven innings, New York had a 1–0 lead, and Los Angeles had managed only one hit.

Now came the glaring, mustachioed Gossage to strike out three of the Dodgers' last six batters, the final two looking at his 90-plus-mile-per-hour fastball.

"Everyone in the ballpark," Gossage shrugged, "knows what I'm gonna throw." Groaned Dodger manager Tommy Lasorda: "Don't show me Fu Manchu no more."

And his players had had a bellyful of the Bronx, where they'd now lost six straight over three Series. "We're going home with Fernando Valenzuela pitching in Dodger Stadium," reasoned Garvey. "That's the symbol of better times. You'll see a different team Friday night."

Indeed, game three was worlds away from the first two. To begin with, Nettles had jammed a thumb and was sidelined. And what had been billed as a classic duel between two brilliant rookies came apart in the first inning, when Los Angeles third baseman Ron Cey dumped a Righetti fastball over the left-center-field fence.

Then the Yankees rocked Valenzuela with home runs in the second and third to take a 4–3 lead. George Frazier had relieved Righetti in the first, but Lasorda stuck with Valenzuela, his Cy Young Award winner. Valenzuela threw 146 pitches and let 17 Yankees reach base, but at the end, after the Dodgers had scrapped for two more runs, he stood on the mound with left fist high.

Thus the Series turned. The Yankees would knock out Dodger starter Bob Welch in the first inning of game four and run up leads of 4–0 and 6–3. But bad baserunning, shabby defensive work in the outfield, and questionable strategy (Lemon benched Mumphrey, used John in relief instead of Gossage, and pinch-hit catcher Barry Foote for third baseman Aurelio Rodriguez) brought New York to ruin, 8–7.

The next day Dodgers Pedro Guerrero and Steve Yeager clouted back-to-back home runs off Guidry in the seventh, pitcher Jerry Reuss held New York to a run, and the Yankees, who'd never lost a Series in six games after winning the first two, were facing an empty winter.

"We'll win it in New York," growled Steinbrenner, who said he'd been assaulted by two Los Angeles fans in a hotel elevator and had broken a hand in retaliation. That was a prelude to a more humiliating mugging at home, where the Dodgers rapped out eight runs in the middle three innings and bore off the championship, 9–2.

It was a collapse worthy of a formal apology, and it began when Lemon decided to yank John for pinch hitter Bobby Murcer with the score 1–1 in the fourth inning.

"We had to get runs," Lemon explained. "All I wanted was a run. I figured our bullpen could get us to the seventh and Gossage. I guess I'm not so smart."

John, for his part, was incredulous. "I hope you have someone who can hold them," he told the manager in disgust. Lemon's choice was Frazier, who'd begun the year in the Cardinals' farm system and had lost both games three and four in relief.

Los Angeles hopped on him for three runs in the fifth and racked Davis and Rick Reuschel for four more in the sixth. "I couldn't get the voodoo lady off my back," moaned Frazier, who set a Series record for most losses. "She kept sticking the needle in me."

And Frazier wasn't the only one. Winfield, the $20 million man, went 1-for-22 for the Series

With an 8–4 record and 2.06 ERA in 15 starts, Dave Righetti was the league's Rookie of the Year. The 22-year-old southpaw added three postseason victories, including the pennant-clincher at Oakland.

and uncorked a throw in the finale that bounced on the infield dirt and reached the plate on three hops. Davis, the superb middle reliever, had watched his ERA balloon to 23.14.

Nettles had been hurt, and Jackson (who'd injured a calf muscle in the Oakland series) had missed the first three games.

Meanwhile the Dodgers, who'd only beaten New York twice in 10 previous Series, returned to the West Coast as heroes to the vast relief of Lasorda, who knew what would have happened had his people lost another.

"The people would have cut off my head," he'd guessed, "and kicked it down Wilshire Boulevard."

What Steinbrenner would do with his Yankees was an open question as autumn turned into winter.

Dave Winfield did a big job offensively and defensively. He won a Gold Glove and led the team in RBIs (106), and his 37 home runs fell only two shy of Reggie Jackson's majors-leading 39.

The big black bat came whipping around as it always had, and the crisp sound of connection resounded with familiarity throughout the ballpark. The batter, corkscrewed into the dirt from that all-or-nothing-at-all swing of his, righted himself, discarded his bat, and clapped his hands in delight. As the ball took flight through the misty spring rain, he stood still at home plate, admiring his work as if he'd never seen anything quite so satisfying.

The fans at Yankee Stadium had seen this scene played out many times before, but this time, as they leaped from their seats, there was no immediate roar, just shocked silence. Then, as the baseball disappeared into the right-center-field stands and the slugger began his home-run trot, the 35,458 who had sat huddled under umbrellas for seven soggy innings—waiting for this moment—broke into thunderous applause that slowly and sweetly transformed into a familiar chant of adulation: *"Reg-gie! Reg-gie! Reg-gie!"*

But watching Reggie Jackson's triumphant trip around the bases was a bittersweet experience for the New York crowd, since his number 44 was adorning a red-and-blue-trimmed California Angels uniform, not the navy pinstripes he'd worn just six months before in the World Series.

After five thrilling if turbulent seasons in New York, Jackson had become a free agent following the defeat by the Dodgers, and Yankee owner

George Steinbrenner had chosen not to re-sign him—an unpopular decision.

As the Yankees struggled through the young season, the *"Reg-gie!"* chant would swirl around the Stadium whenever the home team fell behind. One fan was coming to games and carry-

Ken Griffey, acquired from Cincinnati, was awarded a six-year contract, but his stats—.277, 12 homers, and 10 stolen bases—didn't make New Yorkers forget the departed Reggie Jackson.

Roy Smalley was obtained from the Twins for Ron Davis and replaced Bucky Dent, who was shipped to Texas in August. Smalley hit 20 homers, including a club-record 16 as a shortstop.

Southpaw Shane Rawley, obtained from Seattle on April Fool's Day as a reliever, became a starter and in that role was a welcome surprise. He was 11–10 and would add a 14–14 record the following season before moving on in 1984.

ing around a white bedsheet inscribed with the number 44—the ghost of Reggie.

Never mind that Jackson had arrived in the Bronx for this series with a .173 batting average and no extra-base hits. Mr. October was clearly Mr. April around the Stadium. Never before had such a Yankee hero returned in a starring role for another team.

The fans recognized this fact—earlier in the night, one guy had jumped from the stands and run out into right field to present Jackson with a yellow bouquet—and they weren't about to let the team owner, who was in attendance, forget it.

So, as Jackson stood at the top of the visiting-dugout steps waving to his adoring public after his dramatic and personally satisfying homer, the *"Reg-gie! Reg-gie!"* was gradually drowned out by a chilling, swelling *"Steinbrenner sucks! Steinbrenner sucks!"*

"Some people have a way of saying the right thing at the right time," Jackson would say after the game. "I've never been a guy to directly knock somebody, but every dog has his day."

Jackson's emotional return was not the only trigger for the fans' boorish objection to Steinbrenner. Two days earlier the owner had played musical manager's chair once again, firing manager Bob Lemon and replacing him with Gene Michael, the same man Lemon had succeeded midway through the previous season.

Lemon himself was in his second go-round, taking over for Billy Martin in 1978, leading the Yankees to a World Series victory, then being ousted in favor of—who else?—Billy Martin the following season. This latest move was the Yankees' eighth managerial change in 10 seasons, the sixth in four years. And it may have been the most puzzling for fans.

Though the Yankees were off to slow start, the key word was start—the season was just 14 games old. And the Yankee faithful had been promised more stability. "There will be no change this year," Steinbrenner had vowed during the off-season. "I wouldn't care how the team is doing."

Apparently, the Boss did care. After the Yankees began the season by losing both ends of an Easter doubleheader to the White Sox—the original opening day had been wiped out by a blizzard—and didn't win a home game until April 25, Lemon was squeezed out. But the team didn't do any better under Michael. Neither Ken Griffey nor Dave Collins, the high-profile free agents signed by Steinbrenner as replacements for Jackson, made a significant contribution.

The production of new captain Graig Nettles

(.232, 18 home runs, 55 runs batted in) slipped. Tommy John (10–10, 3.66 ERA) was demoted to the bullpen, then dealt away at midseason, as was shortstop Bucky Dent. And promising Dave Righetti (11–10, 3.79) slipped into a sophomore slump and was demoted to Columbus.

A 9–16 June was the worst stretch, but when New York was swept in an August 3 home doubleheader that lasted long into the night, the Yankees were 50–50 and Steinbrenner had seen enough. The short-fused owner of the Bronx Bombers, disgusted by their performance, announced that all in attendance could have free tickets to another game—and that Michael was out as manager and Clyde King was in. By mid-September, the Yankees would lose nine straight under King on their way to a fifth-place finish, 16 games out of first place and only one out of last.

The brightest star of this dismal season was Dave Winfield, who hit 37 home runs, the most by a Yankee right-hander other than Joe DiMaggio. (Another bright spot involved Winfield as well: On September 8 he took a day off and was replaced in left field by a 21-year-old rookie called up the previous day from Columbus, a kid with a future named Don Mattingly.) Winfield's homer total left him two behind the league leader, a fellow whose power production sparked his team into the league playoffs—a formerly pinstriped Angel named Reggie Jackson.

The 41,077 fans who had come to Yankee Stadium for the Independence Day game were on their feet, clapping and cheering wildly. In the home dugout, Billy Martin was sitting quietly, praying for a no-hitter. "I've never said a prayer for myself to get a hit or a prayer for our team to win," the Yankee manager would say later. "I thought it was that important."

Standing on the mound in the eye of this hurricane of history-perhaps-in-the-making, Dave Righetti was "enjoying the fans and enjoying being a Yankee." But the left-hander was unaware of Martin's sudden shift toward piety, as he hadn't been looking toward his teammates and manager in the dugout for innings. "Everybody was nervous; they were making me nervous," explained Righetti. "I didn't look in the dugout because I didn't want to get more nervous."

Dave Righetti celebrated July 4th by pitching a no-hitter against the Red Sox at the Stadium, the Yankees' first since Don Larsen's perfect game in the 1956 World Series. "For an instant, everything seemed to stop," the southpaw said of fanning .356 hitter Wade Boggs for the final out. "I just wanted to cry."

Righetti had reason to be rattled. He was facing a Red Sox lineup that had amassed 25 runs and 38 hits, including nine home runs, over this four-game series. All of that offense, however, had come in the holiday weekend's first three games. On this day Boston had no runs—and no hits.

Now, with the Yankees ahead, 4–0, there were two outs in the ninth inning. All Righetti needed to do was retire one more Red Sox hitter, and he'd have the first Yankee no-hitter since Don Larsen's perfect game in the 1956 World Series. But it wouldn't be easy. At bat was Wade Boggs, the toughest out not only in this powerful Boston lineup but arguably in all of baseball.

The crowd was standing and cheering. Martin was reciting a Hail Mary. And then Boggs, a .357 hitter who rarely struck out, was waving weakly at a 2–2 slider. "For an instant, everything seemed to stop," said Righetti. "Then I just wanted to cry."

Emotion found its ways into Yankee hearts on more than one occasion during the 1983 season, though the feeling accompanying the urge to tears was not always joy. It was Martin's third term as New York manager, and once again he

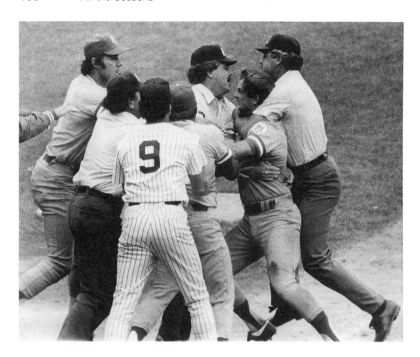

Kansas City's George Brett begs to differ with umpires who voided his "pine tar" homer at the Stadium. In a controversial ruling, the hit was restored by league president Lee MacPhail, a former Yankee general manager.

lived up to his reputation as a guy who makes things happen.

For one thing, the Yankees were an improved team, finishing at 91–71, remaining in contention into September before finishing in third place in the American League East (though with the fourth-best record in the majors). Once again, Dave Winfield was the offensive star, with 32 home runs and 116 runs batted in. Newly ac-

Don Baylor donned pinstripes as a free agent, and his powerful bat injected muscle into the lineup. The 34-year-old veteran won a Silver Bat as the league's most potent designated hitter, led the team in doubles (33) and stolen bases (17), and contributed 21 homers and 85 RBIs. His .303 average trailed only Ken Griffey's .306, marking Baylor's only .300 season of his 17-year career.

Ron Guidry confers with batterymate Butch Wynegar. The southpaw enjoyed his best season since 1978, topping the staff with a 21–9 record and a 3.42 ERA.

Turning 22, Don Mattingly won the Dawson Award as training camp's top rookie. He went on to hit .283 in 91 games, dividing his time between the outfield and first base.

quired Don Baylor belted 21 homers, Graig Nettles 20. And Don Mattingly emerged as the first baseman of the future, hitting a solid .283.

On the mound, Righetti's Fourth of July fireworks were the season's most splendid showing, but Ron Guidry was the ace, going 21–9 with 21 complete games.

But what made this a true Billy Martin season was the carnival atmosphere that followed the Yankees all season.

The most dramatic example came on July 24, during a Yankees-Royals game at the Stadium. With the home side leading, 4–3, in the ninth inning, George Brett pounded a two-run homer off Goose Gossage to give Kansas City the lead.

No sooner had Brett rounded the bases than Martin was standing at home plate protesting to the umpires that Brett's bat was illegal, that pine tar had been applied too far up the handle. The umpires agreed, the home run was wiped out, and after a Brett tirade the game ended as a Yankee victory—temporarily.

Four days later, American League president Lee MacPhail, the former Yankee general manager, overturned the ruling, saying Brett had not violated the "spirit of the rules." He declared the game suspended with the score 5–4, Kansas City. Twenty-one days and two court decisions later, the game was completed in 10 minutes before only 1,245 at the Stadium.

An outraged Martin treated the four-out completion as a joke, using Guidry in center field and Mattingly at second. After the Yankees went down meekly, Martin refused to meet the press. "If the Yankees lose the pennant by one game, I wouldn't want to be Lee MacPhail living in New York," said disgusted Yankee owner George Steinbrenner. "Maybe he should go house hunting in Kansas City."

That would be more likely than Dave Winfield house hunting in Toronto. Two weeks before the completion of the "pine tar" game, the Yankee slugger was responsible for a ball game against the Blue Jays becoming forever known as the "seagull game." Winfield was finishing up his between-innings warmup tosses in Toronto when he tried to bounce a ball near a seagull to shoo the bird off the field. Instead, his throw hit the gull in the head, killing it.

The crowd reacted with boos, and after the game Canadian authorities arrested the outfielder, charging him with cruelty to animals—a charge that was eventually dropped.

A more tragic incident occurred just hours before the completion of the "pine tar" game, August 18, when promising shortstop Andre Robertson suffered an essentially career-ending—and nearly fatal—broken neck in a Manhattan auto accident.

Despite all the turmoil—which included season-long sparring between Martin and Steinbrenner—the Yankees were still in contention when the first-place Orioles came to the Bronx for a weekend series beginning September 9. After New York won the opener to pull within four games of first, spirits were high around the ballpark.

But they plummeted quickly, along with the team, as the Yankees dropped both ends of a doubleheader, then the series finale, to fall seven games out. That would be the final margin in a season that had high hopes but, through twists and turns that sometimes were bizarre, ended in disappointment.

It came down to the second-to-last inning of the final game of the season, a ball game with no drama on the scoreboard (Yankees 9, Tigers 2) but plenty in the batter's box. Don Mattingly stepped to the plate for what was likely to be his final at bat of his first full major league season, the Yankee Stadium crowd urging him on with gusto.

When the first baseman slapped a bouncer toward the right side of the infield, the crowd turned quiet—until a bad hop sent the ball past Tigers second baseman Scott Earl and into right field. The fans were lifted into a frenzy, a mood that quieted a bit when Dave Winfield began making his way from the on-deck circle.

With the fans wide-eyed and on the edges of their seats, Winfield rapped a sharp bouncer to third base for the final out. As Mattingly and Winfield headed toward the dugout, they met near first base, clasped hands, and headed off the field together, the fans roaring in a season-ending salute.

The race was over. No, not the pennant race; that had been finished, at least as far as New York was concerned, for weeks, if not months. The Yankees had been out of serious contention in the division since June. But Mattingly and Winfield had been in contention.

Their bats had been dueling down the stretch in a bid for the league batting championship. Winfield had been well in front around the All-Star break, but as the second half of the season wore on, he had slumped as Mattingly was cranking up the pace.

By mid-September they were running neck

Phil Niekro topped Yankee pitchers with a 16–8 record and a 3.09 ERA. The 45-year-old knuckleballer was resurrected after his release by the Braves.

A familiar face reappeared in the Yankee dugout: Yogi Berra returned for a second term in the managing hotseat.

Don Baylor hit and was hit. He cracked a team-high 27 homers, drove in 89 RBIs, and was struck by a club-record 23 pitches en route to a numbing career total and a major-league mark of 267.

Toby Harrah (left) came from Cleveland to replace departed Graig Nettles at third base. But the 13-season veteran hit only .217 and one homer before being hurt at midseason; rookie Mike Pagliarulo (right) was rushed up from the minors and hit .239 and seven homers the last half of the season.

and neck, and Yankee PR folks got into the spirit by issuing daily updates that figured the respective batting averages down to nine decimal points. In the end, it came down to the final at bat of the season.

With his hit, Mattingly had raised his final batting average to .343. With his groundout, Winfield had finished at .340. The batting title belonged to the 23-year-old, the first Yankee batting champ since Mickey Mantle in 1956.

Mattingly had come into the final game trailing his veteran teammate by 1.57 points but had proceeded to rap out four hits to Winfield's one. (Had Mattingly made an out in that final inning and Winfield had a hit, Mattingly would have finished at .34163 to Winfield's .34215.)

Winfield later recalled the scene in his autobiography: "So I shower, congratulate Donnie, and leave the clubhouse, knowing that if I talk to the press I'll say something I'll regret."

Winfield was deeply disappointed, not just because he lost the batting race, but also because of the way the drama had unfolded on this final day. "Every time Donnie steps up to bat cheers fill the stadium," he wrote, "standing O's in fact. Every time I step up to bat there are boos. Stuff like that hurts, believe me. It stays with you."

Winfield did get a vote of confidence from Yogi Berra. "Winfield," said the manager, "was my most valuable player." But, no question, New York was now Mattingly's town.

Asked if Mattingly had exceeded his expectations, manager Berra offered the comment you might expect from him: "Not only that, he's done better."

Berra could have said the same about his 1984 Yankees in general, especially if he formed an assessment of his team based upon the first half of the season. Returning to the helm at the Stadium after 20 years, Berra found his "It ain't over 'til it's over" philosophy challenged as the Yankees fell 20 games behind the roaring Tigers (and their record-setting 35–5 start) by the All-Star break.

Ron Guidry was off to his worst season (10–11, 4.51 ERA). Dave Righetti was adjusting to a new role as closer—not to mention the controversy in New York over his being moved out of the starting rotation. Winfield and his .371 average over the first half were a highlight, as was the fast start—11–4 record, 1.84 ERA—of knuckleballer Phil Niekro.

Things turned around for the Yankees in the second half of the season. As the 45-year-old Niekro was fading (5–4, 5.06 over the second half), a younger breed was emerging. Third baseman Mike Pagliarulo, shortstop Bobby Meacham, outfielders Brian Dayett and Vic Mata, and pitchers Joe Cowley and Dennis Rasmussen all were promoted from Triple-A Columbus, and they helped the Yankees amass the majors' best record (51–29) over the second half.

Pagliarulo, in particular, was a steadying force at third base and at the plate, where he produced seven homers and 34 RBIs in only 201 at bats. The Yankees had a youthful enthusiasm, and Yogi Berra hated to see the season end. "I wish," said the manager, "that we could start next season right now."

George Steinbrenner strolled into the Yankee Stadium press box late in the third game of a crucial mid-September series against the Blue Jays and began asking around: "Where's Reggie Jackson?"

The owner wasn't really searching for his departed slugger; he was looking for a few sportswriter envoys to convey a message to his players via newspaper headlines. "I need Mr. October," Steinbrenner declared. "All I have is Mr. May, Dave Winfield."

The Boss was upset that his team, which had gone on a 30-of-36 tear to pull within 1½ games of first-place Toronto, was about to lose a second straight key contest and all its momentum.

Don Mattingly was the American League's Most Valuable Player, the Yankees' first since Thurman Munson in 1976. Mattingly hit .324 with 35 homers and 145 RBIs. He was the first pinstriper to lead the majors in RBIs since Roger Maris's 142 in 1961, and he topped league first basemen with a .995 fielding average for another Gold Glove.

Ron Guidry led league pitchers with a 22–6 record and a .786 winning percentage while posting a 3.27 ERA and earning a third Gold Glove.

In the end, New York would drop eight straight to fall from contention, and the owner was there every stumbling step along the way, venting on his tumbling team and singling out veterans like Winfield, who was mired in a late-season slump.

"It's hard to figure out what happened," said first baseman Don Mattingly, who finished with a .324 batting average, 35 home runs, 145 runs batted in, and the league's Most Valuable Player trophy—the first Yankee to win it since Thurman Munson in 1976. "Sometimes things just happen around here, and nobody can figure out why."

Mattingly was referring to the season's disappointing end, but he just as well could have been

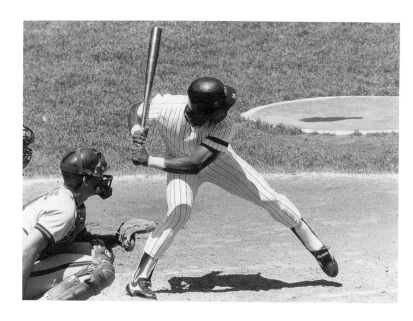

Rickey Henderson, acquired from the A's, gave the Yankees their most exciting leadoff man since Wee Willie Keeler. Combining speed and power, Henderson led the majors with 146 runs and the league with a team-record 80 stolen bases. He hit .314 with 24 homers and 72 RBIs.

speaking of its beginning. Back in April, just 16 games into the schedule, Steinbrenner had fired Yogi Berra and replaced the popular manager with Billy Martin, in his fourth go-round as Yankee skipper. This after saying during spring training, "Yogi will be the manager the entire season, win or lose. A bad start will not affect Yogi's status."

The firing after a 6–10 start had triggered an angry outburst in the Yankee clubhouse—Don Baylor kicking over a trash can, Mattingly throwing a bottle of shampoo against a wall, tears all around the room. Mattingly, after all, was like a son to Berra. And backup infielder Dale Berra literally *was* Yogi's son.

The Yankees didn't exactly snap to attention under Martin, though by the All-Star break they had crept within 2½ games of first place. They fell back to 9½ out by August, then surged into September with 11 straight triumphs, looking like a team that was about to overtake Toronto.

Aside from Mattingly, key contributors in the Yankee uprising included new arrival Rickey Henderson, who hit .314, clouted 24 homers, and led the league with a club-record 80 stolen bases and 146 runs scored, the most in the major leagues since Ted Williams' 150 in 1949; 35-year-old Ron Guidry, who returned to 1978 form with a 22–6 record and 3.27 ERA; and "Mr. May" himself, Winfield, who by season's end had 26 home runs, a Gold Glove, and his second straight 100-RBI/100-run season (114 RBIs, 105 runs). Overall, New York led the league in runs (839), RBIs (793), and stolen bases (155).

But the Yankees finally succumbed to a season of strife—the manager grating on the players, who were feuding with the owner, who was sparring with the manager. Martin had once again brought volatility to the Bronx. And his contentious way took center stage—over the pennant race, even—in mid-September when, on consecutive nights during a visit to Baltimore, Martin ended up in altercations in the hotel bar.

His first dispute was with a man who thought Martin had insulted his wife; it amounted only to shoving and shouting. The next night, however, Martin got into a serious tangle with frustrated pitcher Ed Whitson, and the manager ended up with a broken arm and cracked ribs.

Despite his league-best .628 winning percentage in his near-full season, that embarrassing incident—along with some questionable managerial decisions he had made during the September slide—sealed Martin's fate.

But first the demoralized Yankees played out the string, ending the season without a pennant but with twin milestones: In the final game of 1985, 46-year-old Phil Niekro recorded his 300th career victory, capping a 16–12 season, and became the oldest major leaguer to pitch a shutout. Shortly afterward, the reign of Billy IV also ended.

"**G**et your peanuts, hot dogs, subway tokens . . ."

All winter, this was the dream ballpark banter that had warmed the hearts of New York baseball fans—a Fall Classic played entirely in the Bronx and Queens, dividing Brooklyn families and Manhattan offices along fan-support lines. And there was good reason for such hometown hopes.

The previous summer both New York ball clubs had come close in the pennant races, the Yankees falling just two games short of first place in the American League East, the Mets barely beaten in the National League East. The crosstown rivals had won 97 and 98 games, respectively. So which train do you take to get from Yankee Stadium to Shea?

In truth, realistic hopes for the first Subway Series since 1956 vanished during spring training. That's when the Yankees discovered that Britt Burns, the 1985 18-game winner they had signed as a free agent in the off-season to solidify their starting rotation, had a degenerative hip condition and would miss the season.

"My starting rotation when spring training opened was supposed to be Ron Guidry, Britt Burns, Joe Niekro, Ed Whitson, and Phil Niekro," rookie manager Lou Piniella, who'd replaced Billy Martin, would say at season's end. "How many total wins did we get out of them?"

The Yankees got only 23, including none from Phil Niekro, a 16-game winner from 1985 who was released during spring training, and four relief victories by Whitson before he was traded at midseason. Joe Niekro had shoulder problems and did not finish the season. And Guidry missed most of July after being hit on the pitching hand by a line drive and finished with a 8–12 record, the worst of his career.

The ace of the starting rotation turned out to be left-hander Dennis Rasmussen, with an 18–6 record and 3.88 earned run average. But the heroic pitching performance was turned in by Dave Righetti, who was settling into the closer role.

Despite the season-long shakiness of the rota-

Lou Piniella was the new manager, directing the Yankees to a second-place finish, five games out. Oddly, the team was more potent away from the Stadium—a best-in-league 49–33 on the road, 41–39 at home.

Rickey Henderson dashed his way to 87 stolen bases and 130 runs, leading the league in both departments for the second consecutive year and eclipsing his own club record for thefts. He also hit 28 homers with 74 RBIs, lofty totals for a leadoff man.

tion, Righetti was given enough late-game leads to post a major-league-record 46 saves—tying and then breaking the old mark by saving both ends of a doubleheader on the final day of the season.

That was all the suspense that was left by the season finale, as the Yankees were out of contention by early September. They had started well,

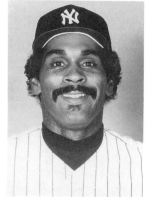

Left: Dennis Rasmussen was the pitching staff's only double-digit winner, going 18–6 with a 3.88 ERA in by far the best of his four Yankee seasons. **Right:** "Hit Man" Mike Easler batted .302 after coming from Boston in a swap for Don Baylor.

running neck and neck with the Red Sox through April and May. By the All-Star break, New York was seven games behind Boston, but pulled within 3½ games by August 13. Then an 8–13 stretch dropped the Yankees 10½ games back by September 7, and they never fully recovered.

Piniella did regroup the troops, calling a clubhouse meeting and announcing to the press, "This club will not quit on me." But even a finishing flurry (18 victories in their last 25 games) couldn't bring the Yankees any closer than second place.

It could have been worse. The Yankees compensated for their pitching woes with a powerful offense. They led the league with a .430 slugging percentage and .347 on-base percentage, tied for second in batting (.271), were third in homers (188), and finished fourth in runs (797).

Leadoff man Rickey Henderson had 28 homers and 74 runs batted in and led the league with 130 runs and a Yankee-record 87 stolen bases. Dave Winfield, though sidelined with a hamstring injury and often platooned even when he was healthy, hit 24 homers and drove in 104 runs—his fifth straight 100-RBI performance.

Dave Righetti preserved both victories in a final-day double-header at Boston, boosting his save total to a majors-record 46. With a 2.45 ERA, eight wins, and his saves, Righetti contributed to 60 percent of the Yankees' 90 victories.

Mike Easler, acquired from Boston for Don Baylor as designated hitter, batted .302 with 78 RBIs. Third baseman Mike Pagliarulo had 28 homers and 71 RBIs.

But the star of the lineup, once again, was Don Mattingly. The Gold Glove first baseman hit .352 with 31 homers and 113 RBIs, and led the league with 238 hits, 53 doubles, 388 total bases, and a .573 slugging percentage.

The figures for hits and doubles were Yankee records established by Hall of Famers Lou Gehrig and Earle Combs. At one point, Mattingly hit safely in 24 straight games. And in the final days of the season he almost caught Boston's Wade Boggs in the batting race, going 8-for-19 in a season-ending four-game series against the Red Sox. Mattingly fell short—just like his team. "It's been a season of a lot of heartbreak," said Righetti, "the biggest being the day the Red Sox clinched the division title."

Actually, the biggest heartbreak for Yankee fans didn't come until a few weeks later, when those Red Sox opened the World Series in New York—against the Mets. You could take the subway to the 1986 Series, all right. But the trains weren't going to the Bronx.

A missed phone call was the symbol of the season. George Steinbrenner had ordered Lou Piniella to be in his Cleveland hotel room when he called at 2 o'clock. Instead, Piniella was in a Pewter Mug across the street. The Yankee owner and manager had been on different wavelengths for months as the ball club drifted downward.

Piniella figured that Steinbrenner was merely blustering and wouldn't call. Steinbrenner decided Piniella was being insubordinate. It wasn't until late October that Piniella was booted upstairs to make room for Billy Martin, but he effectively lost the job on the August afternoon when his phone rang off the hook.

The Steinbrenner-Piniella relationship had begun unraveling at the end of the 1986 season when New York finished second behind the hated Red Sox, who ended up winning the pennant and coming within one strike of beating the Mets in the World Series.

Howard Cosell, the acerbic sportscaster who was close to Steinbrenner, ripped Piniella for mismanaging at least 10 games. And the owner said publicly that his manager could have used minor league seasoning before taking the helm.

When the Yankees won 10 straight games in April 1987 and went on to post a 55–34 record for a three-game lead at the All-Star break, Steinbrenner could already see banners flying. His

Left: *Rick Rhoden was acquired from Pittsburgh and topped Yankee pitchers with a 16–10 record and 3.86 ERA—the best of his two New York seasons.* **Right:** *At 44, Tommy John was the pitching staff's workhorse, hurling a team-high 188 innings and going 13–6 in his second Bronx tour.*

Third baseman Mike Pagliarulo led the team in home runs with 32 and drove in 87 runs—both career highs—despite going homerless during his last 20 games while hampered by a throwing-elbow injury that required post-season surgery.

club had already driven a psychological stake through the Blue Jays at the end of June with a wild 15–14 victory in Toronto, rallying behind grand slams from Don Mattingly and Dave Winfield.

Then Steinbrenner made a move that he felt put his club beyond challenge. "Lou, I just won you the pennant," he told Piniella. "I got you Steve Trout." Steinbrenner had dealt three pitchers (including Bob Tewksbury, who ended up an All-Star pitcher for the Cardinals) for the Cubs' million-dollar lefty.

Trout, who gave up 10 runs in his first 11 innings, never won a game for New York and was gone before Christmas. Yet he was only one in a procession of 15 starters Piniella sent to the mound that summer as the Yankees came unglued and tumbled to fourth place.

By season's end, a record 48 players had worn the pinstripes, and a dozen players—including Rickey Henderson for 55 games—had been on the disabled list. Though Piniella's club sported the best defense in franchise history (a .983 fielding average with only 102 errors), his pitching staff had a grim 4.36 earned run average, worst since 1933, and his batting order lost its punch.

The storm clouds began gathering in early August when Steinbrenner and Piniella had squabbled about a roster change before the club went on the road to play the Indians. The owner wanted to send southpaw reliever Pat Clements down to Columbus and bring up Al Holland.

Willie Randolph was the only Yankee besides Mattingly to crack .300, hitting a career-best .305 despite a month-long, mid-season knee injury. Randolph was named to the All-Star Game for the fifth time in his 12th (and penultimate) Yankee season. He'd return in 1994 as the team's third-base coach.

The manager disagreed. The owner, as usual, prevailed.

After the Yankees were blanked in the opener at Municipal Stadium, Steinbrenner got word to Piniella to await his phone call the next afternoon. Piniella, who was lunching with Bobby Murcer and two of the club's limited partners, never made it back to his room, and the Boss fumed. That night, New York was embarrassed 15–4 at Cleveland and ended up going 2–8 on the trip, dropping a doubleheader in Detroit and losing 10–1 in Kansas City.

Along the way, Steinbrenner issued a sulfurous statement charging that Piniella thought the injured Henderson had been "jaking it" and wanted him traded. "Why is he doing this to me?" Piniella asked *Daily News* beat man Bill Madden. "Doesn't he want to win? This is a mess now. He's killed whatever chances we had of winning."

The Yankees had been in first place when they began their nightmarish late-summer travels. By season's end, they'd fallen to fourth, nine games behind Detroit, and Piniella knew he wouldn't be back. He and Steinbrenner had met at the Stadium and hashed out the matter of the missed phone call, but the owner was dropping hints that there'd be a change in the dugout. "He's not a great manager," Steinbrenner said. "How many great managers are there? But I never said he was a bad manager."

Piniella, who could sense the scimitar dangling above his neck and knew that Billy Martin—yet again—was waiting in the wings, told friends he'd never work for the Boss again after he was fired. He was tired of the daily Bronx soap opera and the midgame phone calls from the owner's box ripping his tactics.

"Don't you see what [Don] Sutton's doing out there?" Steinbrenner had barked when he suspected that the Angels pitcher was doctoring the ball. "You can see him plain as day. Why aren't you doing something? Get him thrown out."

Two years of front-office meddling and second-guessing had pushed Piniella to the edge. And Steinbrenner, whose club hadn't won the division since the strike-split 1981 season, had lost patience with his manager, much as he liked Piniella personally.

The solution was classic George—provoke Woody Woodward into resigning as general manager, boot Piniella upstairs and give him a three-year contract. And put Martin, whom Steinbrenner had hired four times and fired three, back in pinstripes. The fact that the announcement was made on October 19 should have been seen as a harbinger of disaster. That day, the stock market had its worst crash since 1929.

1988

For a few days they had fantasies of replaying their 1978 resurrection, when the Yankees charged from 14 games behind the Red Sox to win the division title in a playoff. This time, despite managerial turmoil, dismal pitching, and an August implosion, New York was still in the chase in mid-September after sweeping four games from Detroit at the Stadium.

"We have reestablished ourselves," said Lou Piniella, who had come back to manage after Billy Martin had been fired—again—in June. "Now we have our task. We have to beat Boston."

Piniella was the right fielder when the Yankees made their improbable 1978 run, and he made two clutch defensive plays that killed the Red Sox in the playoff at Fenway Park. Now, he and his club were poised for a reprise. "We have the chance to redeem ourselves," said cocaptain Willie Randolph after the club had lost 20 of 29 in August after starting 20–8.

The season had begun to sour in early May

Left: *Signing on as a free agent, Jack Clark hit a team-high 27 homers and knocked in 93 runs, mostly as a designated hitter. But he batted only .242 and struck out a club-record 141 times in his only Yankee season.*
Right: *Center fielder Claudell Washington hit .308. All three Yankee outfielders made the .300 circle—Winfield at .322, Henderson at .305.*

Dave Winfield assembled a memorable last hurrah, topping the team in hitting (.322) and RBIs (107). He also hit 25 homers in his final full season in pinstripes. Disk surgery sidelined him all the next year, and he was traded to the Angels early in the 1990 season, concluding nine starry and stormy seasons in New York.

John Candelaria was another free-agent addition, and despite a knee injury, he was the team's winningest pitcher at 13–7. His 3.38 ERA topped Yankee starters.

after Martin had been beaten up in a topless bar following a loss at Texas. After drinking heavily and scuffling with another customer in the men's room, Martin ended up in the parking lot—ejected, bloodied, and needing 80 stitches. "I'm in trouble," he told a friend, after the incident made page 1 back in New York.

Though George Steinbrenner defended his manager publicly, he'd privately decided to fire Martin for a fifth time. If the Yankees hadn't been leading the division, the owner might have dismissed Martin then. But the ax didn't fall until June 23, after the club had lost seven of eight and fallen out of first place and Martin had been suspended and fined for throwing and kicking dirt on umpire Dale Scott.

Steinbrenner had sent Clyde King from the front office to Cleveland and Detroit to observe Martin and report back to him. After the Yankees lost two of three to the Indians and were swept by the Tigers, dropping two in the 10th inning and the third on a ninth-inning grand slam, King recommended that Martin be fired immediately. "It's not too late to save the season, but it's getting close to it," he told Steinbrenner.

"The pitching is a mess, and team morale is slipping fast."

So Martin was dumped. "He wasn't the same Billy Martin this time," Steinbrenner said. And Piniella, who'd resigned as general manager at the end of May and was serving as franchise factotum, was given back the manager's job. "Lou II" the New York tabloids dubbed it—but it took less than a fortnight for Piniella to decide that he'd made a dreadful error.

Though Steinbrenner had given him a new three-year contract totaling more than a million dollars and promised him "full control," Piniella quickly realized that nothing had changed. "It's right back to where it was last year," he said, after Steinbrenner complained to him about not using Dave Righetti in an extra-inning loss at Chicago. "I had to be crazy to come back to this."

Besides the owner's meddling, Piniella had to deal with injuries that played havoc with his lineup and with a weak pitching rotation that managed just 16 complete games. John Candelaria, the club's only effective starter, tore knee cartilage in August and went down for the season.

Yet even after the Yankees had lost 10 of 13, they were still only five games out of first on

September 8. Neither the Red Sox nor the Tigers had been able to pull away. "No matter what's been said, there'll still a lot of pride and talent in this clubhouse," said third baseman Mike Pagliarulo. "We all know we've got seven games left with Boston."

Sweeping fading Detroit at the Stadium provided the jump start to a moribund campaign. New York won the opener in 10 innings on a three-run homer by Gary Ward with two outs. The Yankees won the second game on Claudell Washington's ninth-inning shot after breaking up Walt Terrell's no-hitter. They came from behind to win the third by five runs. And they claimed the finale with Washington's two-run homer in the bottom of the 18th.

After winning two of three in Cleveland, New York went to Boston hoping for a reprise of the 1978 Boston Massacre, when they'd humiliated the Red Sox 15–3, 13–2, 7–0, and 7–4 at Fenway Park and claimed a share of first place. This time, New York arrived at the Fens 4½ games behind and promptly won the opener, knocking out Boston ace Roger Clemens, who was coming off a one-hitter.

The next night, the Yankees were on the verge of wiping out a five-run deficit in the eighth. But Sox right fielder Dwight Evans one-handed Pagliarulo's blast at the fence that would have tied the score. This time, there would be no massacre. "There'll be no 1978 now," Boston third baseman Wade Boggs proclaimed to sportswriters afterward. "Sorry, fellas."

Sox southpaw Bruce Hurst blinded the Yankees on Saturday, and Boston pummeled Ron Guidry and successors 9–4 on Sunday. "Our bullpen is worn out," admitted King, who'd been named pitching coach when Martin was canned. "We're using three, four, five guys a game. That's because we have to approach every game as if it were the last of the season."

The Yankees left Boston in fourth place, 6½ games out, yet still breathing. They swept three games from Baltimore in New York while the Red Sox were losing two of three at Toronto, and then braced for a final showdown with Boston, this time at the Stadium.

The Yankees banged Hurst around in the opener, took a 9–5 lead, and watched it vanish in the ninth on a string of cheap Boston hits. "This was the best win of them all," Sox manager Joe Morgan crowed after his troops had prevailed 10–9. Clemens starved New York 6–0 on Sunday, and Boston went on to win the division by one game over Detroit despite losing six of their final seven.

"There were a lot of things that hurt us," conceded Piniella, who was fired five days after New York finished fifth. "Injuries, pitching. But we were still in it when we played those seven games with Boston in September and lost five of them. That was the pennant right there."

He'd never liked Christmas, not since he was a kid, and he'd had a fight with his wife that morning. So Billy Martin went drinking with pal Bill Reedy at Morey's Tavern near his home just outside Binghamton, New York. Reedy had beer. Martin had vodka.

Coming home in the dark at suppertime, Martin skidded down a snowy hill in his Ford pickup truck, plowed into a four-foot deep culvert, and slammed into a concrete pipe next to his house. Martin, who was not wearing a seat belt, catapulted through the windshield and broke his neck. "Casey's boy," who'd been immortalized

Dallas Green was the new manager, but lasted only until August, when he was replaced by Bucky Dent. Green had been openly feuding for weeks with George Steinbrenner as the team struggled through its worst season since 1967. Mired at 56–65, Green was let go. Under Dent the team had a 15–10 September, but still finished in fifth place, 14½ games out.

Left: *Free agent Steve Sax was the new second baseman and leadoff hitter. The former Dodger led the Yankees in batting average (.315), hits (205), runs (88), and stolen bases (43).* **Right:** *Andy Hawkins, the former Padre, signed on as a free agent and became the Yankees' winningest pitcher at 15–15, the only one with double-digit victories. He also led the staff in innings (208) and strikeouts (98).*

with a center-field plaque ("A Yankee Forever") at the Stadium three years earlier, was dead at 61.

Martin's death was the tragic climax to a grim year for the franchise. After staying in the 1988 race until the final week, the Yankees finished 1989 with their worst record (74–87) since 1967. Dallas Green, hired to replace Lou Piniella as manager, was fired in August. And the front office turned the roster into a revolving door by shuttling a club-record 50 players through, most

Left: *In his first season as a regular, Roberto Kelly hit .302 with 18 homers, stole 35 bases, and aggressively patrolled center field. It was Kelly's only .300 season during his six years as a Yankee.* **Right:** *Luis Polonia batted .313 in 66 games after coming to New York (along with pitchers Greg Cadaret and Eric Plunk) in a 3-for-1 deal that sent unhappy Rickey Henderson back to Oakland.*

by a major league team since the expansion Seattle Pilots in 1969.

From the beginning of spring training, when Rickey Henderson reported late, then claimed that drinking and carousing had cost the club the 1988 pennant, it was a season of tension and turmoil. That was hardly what owner George Steinbrenner had in mind when he'd brought in Green, who'd directed the Phillies to the 1980 world title.

Green might have had no pinstriped pedigree, but he was a no-nonsense disciplinarian who figured to bring stability to the Yankee clubhouse. "I bring some new ideas to the party," Green had said when he replaced Piniella the previous October.

What Green hadn't figured was that the party would be broken up well before the All-Star break. Jack Clark had been dealt away during the autumn. Rick Rhoden, who'd logged the most innings on the staff in 1988, was shipped to Houston in January for three minor leaguers. Then outfielder Dave Winfield and shortstop Rafael Santana went down for the year during spring training.

The first week of the season, predictably, was a disaster. The Yankees lost seven of their first eight games, including a 12–2 demolition at Minnesota, an 11–1 loss to Cleveland, and an 8–0 flogging from Toronto, the last two at the Stadium. Though they had climbed back to the .500 mark by the end of April and even claimed a piece of first place for a day, the mood in the clubhouse was strained.

The players had chafed under Green's drill-sergeant leadership since their first meeting in spring training, when he told them that he was "the toughest SOB you guys will ever play for." Green had spared few feelings while prodding the Phillies to a World Series crown, and he spared few in New York.

"We stink and I told them so," Green said while the Yankees were dropping three of four to the Angels on their first West Coast trip. "Some of them must have had their heads in Disneyland or somewhere."

For a while, the owner was firmly in Green's corner. "Dallas says we stink? He's right. We stink," Steinbrenner said. "Dallas is the only reason we're still in the hunt. He's trying to turn babies into men. They don't like him saying things about them in public? Well, they play in public."

But before long, as the club drifted below .500 and sank into fourth place, Steinbrenner was second-guessing Green about team discipline (following a riotous charter flight) and his handling of pitching. By August, when New York was buried in sixth place and Steinbrenner was interfering almost daily, Green dubbed him "Manager George."

"Let's face it, there is absolutely no hope that their organization will be a winning organization as long as Steinbrenner runs the show," Green told *Philadelphia Daily News* columnist Bill Conlin. "It's sad. He has no organization there now. He has absolutely no pride. The ballplayers there now have no feeling of being a Yankee."

Once he said that, Green was gone and knew it. "George doesn't know a f—— thing about the game of baseball," Green said after he was dismissed. "That's the bottom line." Meanwhile, Steinbrenner cast about for his 17th manager in 17 seasons.

Five of them had been Martin, who was still in the organization as a roving scout, but the owner wasn't interested in Billy VI. And Piniella, who'd already been through two unpleasant terms as manager, had no stomach for a third. "I just don't like being fired," he told Steinbrenner.

So the owner tapped Bucky Dent, hero of the 1978 playoff against Boston, who was managing the Triple-A team in Columbus. But Dent fared no better. The Yankees immediately dropped three straight to the Tigers, the worst club in baseball, then went on to lose 11 of 13 to slide 14 games off the pace.

Even a nine-game winning streak at the beginning of September couldn't bring New York anywhere near contention or change the mood of the Stadium fans, who for weeks had been chanting, *"George must go! George must go!"*

Steinbrenner was virtually the only Yankee who hadn't gone. One by one, most of the old heroes and familiar faces had been traded or released or had retired—Henderson, Ron Guidry, Tommy John, Richard Dotson, Mike Pagliarulo.

There was upheaval in the front office, too. Syd Thrift, whom Steinbrenner had brought in as senior vice president of baseball operations above general manager Bob Quinn, had quit at the end of August, and Quinn left two weeks later. Piniella, whom the owner had kept on in a "special services" role, ended up leaving to become manager in Cincinnati under Quinn.

Only Dave Winfield remained from the club's last pennant winner, but he'd been on the disabled list all season and would only play 20 more games in pinstripes. Once Martin was killed (he was buried in the same cemetery as Babe Ruth), the last link to the glory days was snapped. Just ahead was the darkest season in franchise history.

The chant began spreading through Yankee Stadium during the seventh-inning stretch of a night game with the Tigers on July 30: *"No more George! No more George!"* George Steinbrenner, who'd owned the franchise through more than 17 of its most turbulent seasons, was indeed gone, banished that morning by commissioner Fay Vincent for violating the game's catchall Rule 21—"conduct not in the best interests of baseball."

Vincent, who'd been investigating the owner most of the season, had concluded that Steinbrenner had had a three-year "undisclosed working relationship" with known gambler Howard Spira, who was facing federal extortion charges, and allegedly had paid him $40,000 for negative information about outfielder Dave Winfield.

So Vincent effectively banned Steinbrenner from running the franchise again. "He does not have to sell," the commissioner said. "I did not order him to sell." But Steinbrenner was told to reduce his stake to less than 50 percent and become a limited partner, and he was banned from day-to-day operations.

Robert Nederlander, a Broadway theater owner and one of the club's limited partners, eventually was elevated to managing general partner. "Mr. Steinbrenner is to be treated as if he had been placed on the permanently ineligible list," Vincent declared.

Steinbrenner could still participate in the Yankees' major financial and business decisions in his role as limited partner. And if he asked the commissioner in writing, he would be allowed to attend a limited number of games during the 1991 season. But Steinbrenner was no longer the Boss.

It was the sixth time that an owner had been thumbed out of the game and the second time for Steinbrenner, who in 1974 had been suspended by Bowie Kuhn for 16 months for making illegal contributions to Richard Nixon's presidential re-election campaign. His forced departure in 1990 was the crowning blow to the club's worst season in 78 years.

Along the way, Winfield was traded to the Angels, manager Bucky Dent was fired and replaced by Stump Merrill, and general manager Pete Peterson was dumped for Gene Michael. And the ball club was a study in ineptness on the field, finishing last in the division and at the bottom

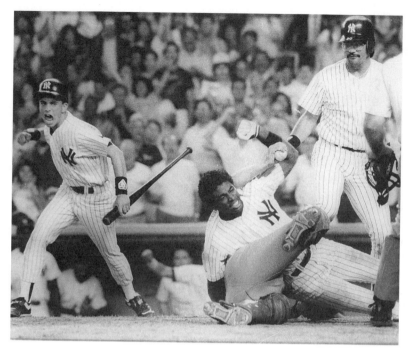

Bat boy John Blundell roots home "Neon Deion" Sanders for one of the Yankees' infrequent runs during a dismal season. A football star, flashy "Prime Time" was something less in pinstripes, hitting .178 in 71 Yankee games over parts of two seasons divided between New York and Columbus. His Yank career ended on July 29 when he left to rejoin the NFL's Atlanta Falcons. Released by the Yankees, he joined the Braves in 1991.

of the league in virtually every category. "The Yankees are only interested in one thing," outfielder Luis Polonia said. "And I don't know what it is."

The season's nadir came on July 1 in Chicago. Andy Hawkins pitched a no-hitter and still lost 4–0 when his mates made three errors in the eighth inning. That sent the Yankees into a hapless tailspin—a sweep in Kansas City by scores of 11–5, 6–1, and 13–6, and, ultimately, 10 losses in 12 games.

By then Dent, who'd replaced Dallas Green

Dave Righetti's 36 saves figured in more than half the Yankees' 67 victories in his 11th and final New York season. He departed as by far the club's all-time save leader with a total of 224 along with a 74–61 record.

Left: *Stump Merrill became the manager in early June, replacing Bucky Dent, as the Yankees struggled through their third-worst season ever: 67–95, the league's poorest record.* **Right:** *Lee Guetterman became the first pure reliever ever to lead the Yankees in victories; the 6'8" southpaw was 11–7 with two saves in 62 appearances.*

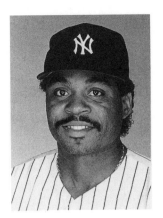

Left: *Jesse Barfield led the team in homers (25) and RBIs (78), the latter despite a scarcity of Yankee base runners. He also struck out 150 times, a club record. A rifle-armed right fielder, he led the majors in assists with 16.* **Right:** *First baseman turned designated hitter Steve "Bye Bye" Balboni hit 17 homers in his second Yankee tour. But his batting average dropped to .192, and at season's end it was bye-bye Steve. His 10-season career was over.*

near the end of the 1989 season, was long gone. He'd been dismissed in early June in Boston while the Yankees were in the process of losing 13 of 14 games. Merrill, who'd spent more than a decade paying his dues in the bushes, inherited a club that was scarcely better than the Yankees' farm team in Columbus.

The hitting—a team average .241—was the worst in the league and the club's lowest since 1969. The pitching—a staff ERA of 4.21—was third-highest in the league. The starting rotation of Hawkins, Tim Leary, Dave LaPoint, and Chuck Cary lost 53 games among them, and Michael ordered that Leary not start after September 19 to keep him from losing 20. The best record on the staff belonged to Lee Guetterman, who won 11 games without starting one.

Merrill, who was used to managing with unstable lineups in the minors, felt right at home. The Yankees went through five third basemen, three catchers, and a passel of outfielders including Deion Sanders, who hit .158 then bailed out to join his football playmates on the Atlanta Falcons.

For the fans—more than 2 million of whom still made the trek to the Bronx to watch a last-place club—the season was reminiscent of the tapped-out days of the mid-'60s. Yet even those clubs never lost 95 games, as the 1990 version did. No Yankee team since 1912 (50–102) had done that.

Such was the apparent end of the Steinbrenner era, a continuum of turmoil and turnover that had now produced two straight losing sea-

sons. "The players degraded, the rosters deforested by wrongheaded or impulsive trades, the fans depressed and driven away," Roger Angell summed up in the *New Yorker.* "And the franchise, once the proudest in the sports world, humiliated."

To those who believed that Steinbrenner was at the root of the Yankees' miseries, his exile was a welcome shaft of daylight. And it was not unexpected. Vincent had been conducting his investigation for months.

Finally, on the morning of July 30, the commissioner summoned Steinbrenner to his Park Avenue office and handed him an 11-page document that listed the terms of his banishment, effective in three weeks. It was clear to Vincent that Steinbrenner knew Spira was a gambler and should have realized he had no business paying him for dirt on a ballplayer. "In essence he [Steinbrenner] heard no internal warnings," the commissioner wrote, "because none went off."

Vincent originally had planned to give Steinbrenner only a two-year suspension, but the owner was worried that a suspension might cost him his vice presidency of the U.S. Olympic Committee. So Steinbrenner pushed for an "agreement" that he leave, which Vincent decided to make permanent.

Though Steinbrenner had hinted he might challenge the ban in court, he did not. But his lawyers wrangled with the commissioner's people for 11 hours that day over the fine points. When they were finished, Steinbrenner wasn't "suspended," but he was gone. When word filtered up to the Bronx that night with the Yankees leading the Tigers 6–2, the fans reacted with the sort of amazement and glee usually reserved for the downfall of tyrants and wicked witches.

But the players, some of whom remembered the heady pennant chases of the '80s, had mixed feelings about Steinbrenner's departure. "Put it this way," said Dave Righetti, who'd pitched against the Dodgers in the 1981 World Series. "When it happened, I wasn't cheering. I was sad."

The Yankees had lost 19 of 25 games and were buried in fifth place in the middle of August— and general manager Gene Michael was worried about hairstyles. Mel Hall's ponytail was "borderline." Pascual Perez, curls poking from beneath his cap, looked like Shirley Temple. Matt Nokes was shaggy. And Don Mattingly, the $19-million man, had hair that brushed the back of his collar.

So Michael told manager Stump Merrill to order Mattingly to get shorn. When Mattingly refused, Merrill benched him. Never mind that Mattingly was the team's captain and best player. A dress code was a dress code, Michael said. "I'm overwhelmed by the pettiness of it all," said Mattingly.

The benching might have been merely symbolic—and coincidentally or not, the Yankees won five of their next six—but it proved Merrill's undoing. Most players, who'd privately considered him a minor leaguer out of his depth, now regarded Merrill as a front-office marionette and tuned him out. "He was never in control of the ball club," said outfielder Mel Hall. "He was always a puppet."

Left: *Scott Sanderson, purchased from Oakland, was the Yankees' ace at 16–10, their only pitcher with more than eight victories. He was the team's only representative to the All-Star Game, but didn't see action.* **Right:** *Matt Nokes led the team in home runs with 24—most by a Yankee catcher since Elston Howard's 28 in 1963—tying him for tops in the majors among backstops. Acquired from Detroit during 1990, he drove in 77 runs and hit .268 in his first full pinstripe season.*

As August turned into September, the club imploded, losing 18 of 23 and falling 23 games under .500. Not that anyone had expected New York to be a contender. The roster was peopled either with past-prime veterans like Steve Sax and Alvaro Espinoza or kids up from Columbus.

At one point in June, three Yankee starting

Don Mattingly was named captain in February and benched in August for not getting a haircut. His aching back improved enough so that "Donnie Baseball" was able to play in 152 games (50 more than in 1990), hike his batting average to .288, and earn another Gold Glove, his fifth in six years.

Former Dodger Steve Howe joined the Yankees in May and contributed a 3–1 record, with 3 saves and a 1.62 ERA, despite missing most of the last two months with a tender pitching elbow.

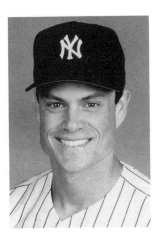

Left: *Mel Hall had a career season. Dividing his time mostly between left and right fields, with a little designated hitting, he had a team-high 80 RBIs with a third-best .285 average and fourth-best 19 homers.*
Right: *Kevin Maas was the first Yankee since Tom Tresh in the early '60s to hit 20-plus home runs in each of his first two seasons—21 in 1990 and 23 in 1991. He played mostly as a designated hitter, but also backed up Don Mattingly at first base.*

pitchers—Jeff Johnson, Wade Taylor, and Scott Kamieniecki—were fresh off the farm. "You look across our room," said Merrill. "They may not be the best, but they're the best we've got. So it's up to me to find something to like about them."

For a while, Merrill liked his club's hustle and scrap. The Yankees came from behind in 15 of their first 28 victories, but that was a telling point. Most nights, they simply were over-matched. "Frankly, it's a little depressing," Mattingly mused, "because we're so inconsistent and so far away."

The lineup varied wildly—Merrill used eight third basemen, nine outfielders, and 11 designated hitters. The pitching, except for Scott Sanderson (16–10), was dismal. The hitting was anemic. At one point, the Yankees went 32 innings without scoring, their worst drought in 22 years.

Even though the franchise was in mid-reconstruction, they'd hoped for better. "We'd rather lie in the weeds and let everybody think we can't play," Mattingly had said during spring training. "Meanwhile, we just win two of three and have everybody say, 'How did they beat us?'"

Instead, New York lost 16 of its first 23 games and tumbled into last place. For banished owner George Steinbrenner, brooding in exile in Tampa, it was slow torture. "It's bothering me not to be with my players," Steinbrenner told Steve Fainaru of the *Boston Globe*. "I feel for them when they're losing, and they've been losing a lot."

After sweeping the Red Sox in Boston, New York caught fire at the end of June, winning 13 of 16, and was in third place with a .500 record on July 24. That was the season's high-water mark. The Yankees dropped six of their next seven and began a downward drift that never stopped. There simply wasn't enough talent to withstand the grind of a pennant chase. The club sent only one player—Sanderson—to the All-Star Game, and he didn't play. That had never happened to the Yankees—except in 1943, when six pinstripers had been selected, but manager Joe McCarthy refused to play any of them in response to the criticism that he'd used too many Yankees in the past. This season, however, there was no chance of too many Bronx All-Stars.

Michael apparently saw the losing more as a matter of discipline—and unruly locks. So he singled out Mattingly, who was mystified—then annoyed. "I don't consider my hair long," he said. "To me, long hair is down my back. I feel I'm a neat, not a sloppy type of person."

Yet Michael was unmoved, and Mattingly sat out for three days before he agreed to a trim—and auctioned off the clippings for $3,000, which he gave to charity. Though Michael later admitted that he'd overreacted, the damage to Mattingly's pride, to team morale, and to Merrill's authority was palpable. The Yankees lost seven of their final 10 games in August and 19 of 28 in September.

The fault, the players concluded, was Merrill's, and they picked him apart with anonymous quotes in the New York newspapers. He didn't have the stature of Billy Martin or Lou Piniella or even Bucky Dent, who'd all worn the pinstripes as players.

Merrill had managed 11 years in the minors, and proudly proclaimed himself an organization man. "I don't think they respected him from day one," said Hall. "It was like, Stump Merrill is the new Yankee manager? So what?"

As the club sleepwalked to a fifth-place finish, 20 games below .500 and as many games out of first, Michael concluded that Merrill was the main reason. "I didn't feel the ball club was responding quite well enough," the general manager would say. "They did not lay down exactly, but they were not exactly motivated."

Three and a half weeks before the season's end, Michael decided that Merrill had to go. The day after the final game, as Merrill was about to drive home to Maine, Michael fired him with a year to go on his contract.

Merrill might have posted a 120–155 record

during his tenure, but he was still the first Yankee manager since 1987 to last a full season. "They said they wanted stability," Merrill said wryly after he'd been let go. "So they fired the manager and five coaches."

1992

The day Buck Showalter signed on as manager in October 1991, he felt a sense of urgency. "I'm on a one-year contract," said Showalter, at 35 the youngest Yankee skipper since 23-year-old Roger Peckinpaugh took charge of the club in 1914. "That means we're on a one-year plan."

Without a World Series visit since 1981, the Yankees put together a plan to spend in hopes of buying back championship riches. Their biggest deal prior to spring training was the addition of free-agent outfielder Danny Tartabull, wooed from the Royals for an astonishing five-year, $25.5-million deal. It was hailed as "a remarkable acquisition" by owner George Steinbrenner.

"I want to bring something back that hasn't been there in a while," said Tartabull, who signed on almost a month prior to the opening of spring training in Fort Lauderdale. "I want to bring a championship back to New York."

In the end, though, what was delivered on the field fell far short of the dollars spent and the expectations raised. For a fourth straight season, New York finished below .500 (76–86), tied with Cleveland for fourth, 20 games behind first-place Toronto.

Of little solace was the fact that, in another borough across town, the Mets finished 72–90—the first time since 1983 that the Yankees had a better mark than their National League neighbors.

They weren't exactly the return of the Bronx Bombers, but the Yankees had some impressive power, leading the league in homers (182) and runs batted in (791). Tartabull delivered a team-high 25 homers and 85 RBIs (one less than leader Don Mattingly), but his batting average was only .266, 50 points off his final year in Kansas City. Matt Nokes' 22 homers and Mel Hall's 81 RBIs rivaled the run production of Tartabull and Mattingly.

The soft spot was pitching, never more evident than in the record of the staff's ace, Melido Perez (a lackluster 13–16 despite a respectable 2.87 earned run average). His brother Pascual

Free agent Danny Tartabull holds up his new pinstripes after signing a five-year, $25.5-million contract. Dividing his time between right field and the designated hitter spot, the 29-year-old former Royal led the Yankees in home runs (25) and RBIs (85). Nine of those RBIs came in a game at Baltimore when Tartabull went 5-for-5, including two homers and a double—the second-most RBIs in a game ever by a Yankee. But his batting average plunged 50 points to .266, and his 3½ seasons in the Bronx proved a disappointment. He was traded to Oakland for Ruben Sierra in 1995.

Buck Showalter was the new manager, hired less than a month after being fired as a coach when Stump Merrill was let go.

Newcomer Mike Stanley was signed as a backup catcher behind Matt Nokes. The following season, he would take over the starting job and become the Yankees' best-hitting backstop since Thurman Munson. As a regular, the former Ranger averaged .290, 20 homers, and 75 RBIs a season before moving on to Boston in 1996 as a free agent again.

would have been a teammate and perhaps helped a needy pitching corps, but he ran afoul of baseball's drug policy and was suspended for the season.

"I'm the only one who enjoys himself," Pascual Perez said in spring training, prior to the suspension, crowing over his recent acquisition of a $57,000 black limousine. "You only have one life. You have to enjoy it."

Left: *Pat Kelly hit .226 in his first full season, playing second base while free-agent signee Mike Gallego was sidelined much of the year with a bruised heel and broken wrist.* **Right:** *Rookie righthander Bob Wickman was 6–1 in just eight starts after being promoted from Columbus in late August.*

Drugs became an issue again for long-troubled reliever Steve Howe, who was pitching well (3–0, 2.45 ERA, 6 saves) when he was suspended for the season on June 8—his seventh suspension for drug abuse.

It was these kinds of issues and abuses that, in part, perturbed Mattingly when looking back over the season in late September. The 10-season Yankee first baseman was the center of a ridiculous squabble the year before when then-manager Stump Merrill ordered him to get a haircut.

"We've had guys come off rehab, guys who did coke two or three times, and look what they got," recalled Mattingly, called "Donnie Baseball" by Yankee loyalists. "They want me to get a haircut, and I catch flak for that. That hurt me. Why me? You want me to get a haircut, fine. But to embarrass me across the country, that hurt."

The years of the Yankees going nowhere—out of contention and drifting well below .500 the last four—were adding up on Mattingly, who was 31 when the season ended and still without a postseason appearance.

"I want to get to the point where the last two weeks mean something," he said. "I'm not going to be choosy and ask for a World Series. I just want to be in a pennant race where every game and every at bat in September means something."

So did Steinbrenner. Amid another subpar season, the suspended 62-year-old owner received a much-wanted reprieve. On July 24 commissioner Fay Vincent announced that Steinbrenner could go back to running the team on March 1, 1993.

"I don't expect him to say he's delighted," Vincent said the day of his decision, "because he wanted to come back now." Attending the Olympic Games in Barcelona when Vincent rescinded the lifetime ban, Steinbrenner issued only a terse "My only concern now is with the Olympic team."

When the season came to a close, the Yankees continued their spending spree, reminiscent of the days when Steinbrenner had revitalized the club and brought back the glory days with his big-dollar signings of such star players as Catfish Hunter, Reggie Jackson, Rich Gossage, Tommy John, Don Baylor, and Dave Winfield.

On November 3, acknowledging the inherent "gamble" of such a move, general manager Gene Michael sent outfielder Roberto Kelly, considered by many to be an untouchable, to Cincinnati for Paul O'Neill, a lifetime .259 hitter.

"We were looking for left-handed bats because I didn't think we had enough," said Michael. "I always said we were too right-handed. I feel

[O'Neill] is a quality hitter and Yankee Stadium should be conducive to his hitting."

O'Neill, who would turn 30 before taking right field at the Stadium, never hit better than .276 in six years with the Reds and had a career 96 homers and 411 RBIs. "Hopefully, they have big plans for me," he said. "I want to go out and play and put up big numbers."

Slightly more than a month later, Michael struck again, with the first of three big acquisitions that he would make across nine days in early December.

He first dealt three prospects to the Angels for 25-year-old left-hander Jim Abbott. Born without a right hand, the ace of the 1988 U.S. Olympic baseball team had been a combined 25–26 his previous two years with California, with miserly year-end earned run averages of 2.89 and 2.77.

Next, Michael signed free-agent southpaw Jimmy Key away from the Blue Jays for $17 million over four years. Key, who was vacationing aboard a cruise ship when he agreed to the deal, arrived with an impressive 116–81 lifetime mark, including an 8–1 record against New York.

Then Michael signed free-agent third baseman Wade Boggs away from Boston, Babe Ruth's old club, for $11 million over three years. A lifetime .338 hitter, Boggs had fallen to a career-low .259 in his final season with the Sox. His swing and mobility were badly hindered by a chronic back problem.

Steinbrenner was back, and the bucks were flowing. Abbott and Key brought promise to the pitching. O'Neill stood ready to assault the right-field porch, and Boggs, if he could regain his touch, could spray his endless stream of singles and doubles all over the Bronx.

"I just got a hunch," said Steinbrenner, "that maybe [Boggs] is the best buy we've had in a long time. I think he'll hit .300 next year. I'm not prepared to believe that Wade Boggs isn't still Wade Boggs."

There were so many new faces in place. Wade Boggs at third base. Paul O'Neill in right field. Jim Abbott and Jimmy Key on the mound. All with high-price contracts. In the Yankee dugout in Fort Lauderdale, spring training just begun, former pitching great Whitey Ford mused over how much the game's finances had changed.

"My first year with the Yankees in 1950 I was paid $5,000," he said. "I never made more than $78,000 in a year. And for most of my career, I worked in the off-season. I started with the Marx Toy Company in New York, greeting their salesmen. Now, guys make millions a year . . ."

Players now came to camp prepared, in prime condition, noted Ford. It was a stark difference from his day, when spring training returned muscles to shape and dissolved a winter's fat with the aid of wind sprints and rubber suit.

Back then, manager Casey Stengel wasn't accustomed to everyone reporting so game-ready. "He told us, 'Stay out of the Copacabana,'" recalled Ford. "That was our rule for the winter."

All the new blood, combined with a far more optimistic and upbeat attitude, led to the Yankees' first winning record (88–74) since 1988. New York didn't make it to the playoffs, but some of the excitement was rekindled. A bit of the familiar baseball buzz was back in the Bronx.

For 18 days, the Yankees shared at least a piece of first place, usually with the Blue Jays, and it was still very much a pennant race into September—a month that included a Jim Abbott no-hitter.

Key (18–6) and Abbott (11–14) brought the stability to the mound that general manager Gene Michael was hoping for when he acquired them after the '92 season. When Abbott fired his no-hitter at the Stadium on September 4, a 4–0 masterpiece over the Indians, the Yankees followed the next day with a 7–2 victory over the Tribe that pulled New York back into a first-place tie with Toronto.

"I did not know how to act out there," said Abbott, cheered to the conclusion of his no-hitter by a delirious crowd of 27,225. He was the first Yankee pitcher to throw a no-hitter in the Bronx since another lefty, Dave Righetti, blanked the Red Sox on July 4, 1983. "I did not know whether to be supremely confident or supremely thankful. I guess it's a little bit of both."

Riding the high of Abbott's no-hitter and buoyed by the first-place tie with the Blue Jays, the Yankees next pulled into Arlington, Texas, and suffered a disastrous three-game sweep by the Rangers. Though they lost the series by a collective 17–10 score, they left town relatively unscathed, only a half-game behind Toronto.

"We're not happy about these three games," said skipper Buck Showalter. "We're not particularly proud. But it happened." Yankee bats, so hot for much of the year, were growing silent at the worst time. When the Texas series was over, Danny Tartabull had only six hits in his last 36

Jimmy Key signed on as a free agent and became the Yankees' ace, leading the staff in victories (18–6), ERA (3.00), innings (237), and strikeouts (173). The southpaw was fourth in Cy Young Award voting after topping the league with a .750 winning percentage.

Paul O'Neill paced Yankee hitters at .311, with 20 home runs and 75 runs batted in, after being acquired for Roberto Kelly in a swap with Cincinnati.

at bats. Worse, Don Mattingly, hindered by a right-wrist injury, was mired in a 13-for-71 slump.

Nothing, however, could stop Toronto. While the Yankees finished up a mediocre September at 11–15, their worst month all year, the Blue Jays went 17–4 over the final three weeks, an .810 winning percentage that had them seven games ahead of the second-place Yankees when the season ended.

For the first time since 1937, the Yankees finished with no fewer than six .300 hitters in their lineup. Dion James led at .332, followed by O'Neill (.311), Jim Leyritz (.309), Mike Stanley (.305), Boggs (.302), and Randy Velarde (.301).

James and Stanley were the biggest surprises

Wade Boggs donned pinstripes as a free agent and regained his batting touch, hitting .302, 43 points higher than his previous season with the Red Sox. The veteran also led league third basemen with a .970 fielding percentage and was the Yanks' only All-Star Game starter.

Jim Abbott, born without a right hand, no-hit the Indians at the Stadium during the Yankees' September pennant chase. In his first New York season after being obtained from the Angels, the 25-year-old southpaw got off to a 1–5 start en route to a disappointing 11–14, 4.37 season. The former U-Michigan and Olympic star's no-hitter was only the eighth by a Yankee pitcher.

Reggie Jackson was inducted into the Hall of Fame, choosing a Yankee cap for his Cooperstown plaque. And his number 44 was retired on Reggie Jackson Day at the Stadium.

of the bunch. James came to camp in 1992 as a 29-year-old nonroster player, having spent the previous season on the disabled list after elbow surgery.

After hitting .262 in 145 at bats in Showalter's rookie year as manager, James blossomed into a consistent-hitting regular, although he didn't officially place among the league's top three hitting leaders because his plate appearances fell short of the minimum needed to qualify. So dramatic was his turnaround that he bolted the Yankees on December 7—Pearl Harbor Day—signed to a two-year, $4-million deal by the Chunichi Dragons of the Japanese League.

"You're talking to a man who was unemployed three years ago and whose career was over," said James, whose achievements were unremarkable during stops in Milwaukee, Atlanta, and Cleveland before his breakthrough season in New York. "Then Gene Michael gave me an opportunity, and I got back on my feet. I made a business decision. I got two years of security. This was the chance of a lifetime."

Stanley, considered Matt Nokes' backup when the season opened, evolved as Showalter's favorite behind the plate. Not only did some Yankee pitchers prefer his signal calling, but Stanley also was tranformed into a big-time slugger, the club's best-hitting receiver since Thurman Munson.

He added 26 homers and 84 runs batted in to his .305 average, the 10th catcher in big league history to parlay a .300 average with 25 round-trippers. On July 20, he clubbed his third grand slam in 21 days, making him the first American League catcher to hit three in a season.

Early in spring training, Nokes was asked if he felt Stanley could pressure him for the job as catcher. "Think about the chances," responded Nokes, in the second year of a three-year pact worth $7.5 million. "That question shouldn't even be answered."

But by the end of May, Nokes' bat gone dormant, Stanley moved in as the everyday catcher. By the start of July, Stanley had gone 27-for-53 (.509) in 16 day games, also clouting four homers and driving in 19 runs.

"When you're not a superstar . . . you feel fortunate to be in the majors," said Stanley. "I think you sit back and appreciate it more when you've been the 25th man. I know I do."

Stanley wasn't the only one happy to be at the Stadium. Suspended owner George Steinbrenner made his long-awaited return to unconditional control of the club's day-to-day operations. His lifetime ban rescinded by commissioner Fay Vincent the previous season, effective March 1, the Boss was back, right on time, with some 300 media members greeting him the first day on the job.

Prior to his return, Steinbrenner fulfilled a *Sports Illustrated* request, dressing up as Napoleon and mounting a white horse for the magazine's cover, the year's most controversial pose.

"This got serious—my God, it shouldn't command this kind of attention," said Steinbrenner. "I got on that damned horse because I was poking fun at myself. Napoleon stayed at Elba a lot longer than I did, and I'm not going to have Waterloo."

For the most part, the waters remained calm in the Stadium all season. There wasn't a pennant to run up the flagpole, but a winning way was restored, and a somewhat calmer Steinbrenner was back sitting comfortably in his office.

The closest thing to a controversy arose when Steinbrenner made clear his dissatifaction with the Bronx as a suitable home for his team. Rising crime and limited parking, he said, were making it difficult to do business. Reports had the Yankees possibly moving to Manhattan's West Side or New Jersey.

"The bottom line," Vincent Tese, director of development under Governor Mario Cuomo, said in mid-June, "is that the Yankees have drawn about 40,000 less than the Mets—and the Mets are in last place."

There they were, all dressed up, first in their division, with no place to go. Led by superlative pitching from Jimmy Key (17–4) and the heavy hitting of Paul O'Neill (a league-leading .359 with 21 homers and 83 runs batted in), the Yankees were rolling to their first divisional title since 1981.

They were headed toward the playoffs at a .619 clip (70–43), 6½ games in front in the AL East, until the players' strike ended the season on August 12. For the first time since 1904, when John McGraw's Giants refused to play the American League in the World Series, there would be no postseason.

Baseball struck out, and there was no joy in Mudville, especially for the Yankees. "The whole thing is sort of sad," said left-hander Jim Abbott. Spiraling salaries, partly a result of contracts such as the $25.5 million the Yankees gave Danny Tartabull prior to the 1992 season, helped pave the way to yet another baseball work stoppage.

Owners were pushing the Players' Association to buy into a salary cap, similar to that in the National Basketball Association, but the rank and file dismissed the idea. Owners said they needed across-the-board relief from escalating

Jimmy Key was the Yankee ace, leading the majors both in victories at 17–4 (10–0 on the road) and in winning percentage at .810. The southpaw also became the first Yankee pitcher to start the All-Star Game in 15 years, since Mel Stottlemyre in 1969.

Left: *Buck Showalter was the league's Manager of the Year as the Yankees topped the AL East by 6½ games, only to be denied a shot at the championship by the season-ending strike in August.* **Right:** *Luis Polonia returned as a free agent. He batted .311 (with a team-high 20 stolen bases) and played on the left side of a solid-hitting outfield that included blossoming Bernie Williams (.289) in center and Paul O'Neill (.359) in right.*

salaries, concerned that small-market clubs such as Montreal and Pittsburgh couldn't compete with teams in bigger cities like New York, Los Angeles, and Chicago.

"Maybe they just don't support baseball in Montreal," said owner George Steinbrenner. "In that context, it's like any good business. Year after year, if your store doesn't get the customers, you move it or you close it."

The business end of it aside, said Steinbrenner, he felt particularly badly for Don Mattingly, a Yankee regular since 1983 who once again wouldn't get to play in the postseason. "My heart bleeds for the guy," Steinbrenner said of his first baseman. "Here he is after all these years and now this."

"For Yankees," read a headline in the August 12 edition of the *New York Times*, "the Field of Dreams Has a Lock on It." The end of New York's season had come the day before with an 8–7, 13-inning loss to the Blue Jays at the Stadium.

Over the public address system, a stream of songs played through the innings, their titles punctuating the inevitable: "Please Don't Go" by the KWS's, "Should I Stay or Should I Go?" by the Clash, "The End of the World as We Know

Outfielder Paul O'Neill led league hitters at .359 (.409 at the Stadium). He also led Yankee batters in RBIs with 83 and in homers with 21 in the strike-shortened season.

Holy cow, it's the Scooter—honored at Phil Rizzuto Night at the Stadium in celebration of his selection to baseball's Hall of Fame. The occasion also marked the shortstop-turned-broadcaster's 54th year in the Yankee family.

It" by R.E.M., "We Can Work It Out" by the Beatles, and "Don't Go Breakin' My Heart" by Elton John.

In the Yankee clubhouse players made plans for an unexpected midsummer vacation. Mattingly said he was taking his family to a state park, but wouldn't reveal where. "I don't want ESPN to be up there," he said.

Jim Leyritz, eager to get back to Florida to finalize divorce proceedings, figured the strike was "perfect timing for me." Buck Showalter, ready to trade in his manager's cap for a chauffeur's hat, planned to take his daughter to her first day of second grade the following Monday.

"It felt like the last day of the season," said Tartabull, who hit .339 against left-handers and totaled 19 homers and 83 RBIs. "It's not a real good feeling at all."

The Yankees had gone into the season with their fewest changes in years. In the off-season, they bolstered the pitching rotation by trading for Terry Mulholland and brought back ex-Yank Luis Polonia as a genuine leadoff hitter. Other role players were acquired (Xavier Hernandez, Bob Ojeda, Daryl Boston, and Donn Pall), but for the most part, the returnees made the Yankees into contenders.

The key series came early when the Red Sox rolled into town in May owning baseball's best record (20–7) and riding a seven-game undefeated streak. The Yankees derailed them with a three-game sweep, their first over the Sox at the Stadium since 1985.

"A reality check, but it's still May," cautioned Boston slugger Mo Vaughn. "The Yankees can't take us lightly, and we can't get down for getting swept here."

It was Showalter's third season in command, the only manager to work three straight full seasons in the Bronx during Steinbrenner's 22 years of ownership. Gene Michael, who became general manager in 1990, began the season with two more years on his contract. It was the longest anyone had remained boss while working for the Boss.

Mattingly returned to form, hitting .304. Boggs looked like the precision hitter he was in Boston, clicking at a .342 pace. And Mike Stanley continued his surprising hitting, finishing at an even .300 with 17 homers and 57 RBIs. O'Neill constructed his .359 batting title by chewing up right-handers at a .380 clip, hitting .409 in the Bronx.

Key's pitching once more made him the master of the Yankee mound. He led the league in both wins (17) and winning percentage (.810) and was 8–0 on the road. As impressive as the numbers were, the southpaw had to settle for runner-up in the Cy Young voting, edged out by former Toronto teammate David Cone.

"I'm not disappointed," Key said when the voting results were announced. "I don't put that much value in this sort of thing. It would have been nice, but it's never been a goal of mine. Who knows, I may have another chance next year."

Impressive, too, was the relief work of Steve Howe, at 36 still able to fire 90-mile-an-hour fastballs. The left-handed flamethrower collected 15 saves and had a 1.80 earned run average, with batters combining for only a .194 average against him.

"Look around the rest of the league," Showalter said after the season, "and tell me how many left-handers can get the Palmeiros, Clarks, and Griffeys out. Not that many. Howe is one of those guys. There are probably five in the league who can do it three out of four times. With the other guys, you just hope they hit it at somebody."

Howe was a staunch union supporter, having grown up in Michigan, where both his mother and father were members of the United Auto Workers. If the Players' Association said go, he was gone, with no regrets.

"It is an unwritten rule in our family to support unions," said Howe, who realized that the Players' Association helped structure language that enabled him to keep his job despite seven drug-related suspensions. "If you didn't want to live like an American, go to Russia."

Showalter returned to the Bronx in October for a news conference at the Stadium after being named manager of the year, wondering what it would have been like to have managed in the playoffs or World Series.

"When I walked out on the field this afternoon," he said, "I couldn't help but feel that I should have been doing something else."

It took them until the last day of the regular season—and a newly created wild-card ticket—but the Yankees finally made it back to the postseason for first time in 14 years.

"A great feeling . . . 13 years for me," said Don Mattingly, whose path to the playoffs led him across 1,785 games in pinstripes. "That's a long time."

Mattingly, one of the best-fielding first basemen in franchise history, hit .417 in the Yankees' five-game playoff series with the Seattle Mariners. But despite his fine hitting and the added punch of Bernie Williams (.429) and power of Paul O'Neill (3 homers, 6 runs batted in), New York couldn't get to the League Championship Series.

Like much of the year, which included a brief visit to the division basement in mid-June, the problem in the playoffs was pitching. The Yankees won the first two games at the Stadium, but needed 13 hits in the opener to stop Seattle 9–6, then required 11 hits and 15 innings for a 7–5 triumph in game two.

Game two, which turned out to be the Yankees' final victory of the season, ended dramatically at 1:22 A.M. on October 5, setting a league postseason record for innings and time played (5 hours, 13 minutes). Jim Leyritz finished it, losing a Tim Belcher pitch for a two-run homer and leaving a loyal and soggy crowd of 57,126 bellowing toward dawn. Their Bronx heroes were born again.

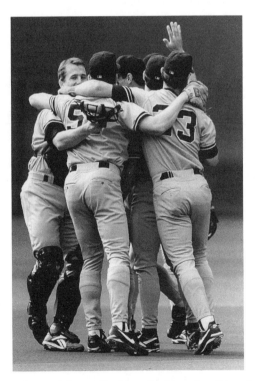

The Yankees celebrate clinching the league's wildcard berth on the schedule's last day, advancing to the playoffs for the first time in 14 years. Of all the celebrants, it was sweetest for Don Mattingly (number 23), who had never played in the postseason. Now, after 1,785 career games, he was finally going to the playoff party.

Wade Boggs led the team in hitting with a .324 average, fourth-best in the league. He won a second straight Gold Glove with a .981 fielding average, highest ever by a Yankee third baseman, joining Red Rolfe and Jumping Joe Dugan as the only Yanks to lead league third sackers in fielding. Boggs was also the only Yankee third baseman to start three straight All-Star Games.

The Yankees won 22 of their final 28 (.786) games to get into the playoffs, and the two playoff victories gave them 13 in their last 14 games. How long could the good times roll? As long as the hitting could prop up the pitching.

Yet despite their two-game lead, the end was near. "We're down," conceded former Yankee skipper Lou Piniella turned Mariners' manager, surveying the damage after game two, "but not out."

Over the next three games in Seattle, the Yankees banged out 26 hits, including 14 in game four, but the Mariners feasted upon the succulent offerings of New York's pitchers. Seattle combined for 24 runs and 38 hits over those three games, clinching the series with a 6–5, 11-inning triumph in the fifth game.

The Yankees had scraped together a 5–4 lead in the top of the 11th on Randy Velarde's run-scoring single, but it began unraveling when Joey Cora beat out a bunt. Ken Griffey then singled, and Edgar Martinez lined a Jack McDowell splitter into the left-field corner. Around came Cora with the tying run and Griffey for the winner.

Left: *David Cone was the league's second winningest pitcher at 18–8. He went 9–2 for the Yankees after being acquired in a late-July trade with Toronto. His 3.57 ERA was the league's second best. He won his last three starts (with a 1.50 ERA) as the Yanks surged for the wildcard with a 22–6 September. Cone won the playoff opener over Seattle, 9–6.* **Right:** *Veteran and four-time Gold Glover Tony Fernandez was the new Yankee shortstop after signing on as a free agent at age 33.*

"For the fans and for baseball it was one hell of a series," said Yankee pitcher David Cone, who couldn't protect the 4–2 lead he had in the eighth inning of game five. "Both teams laid their guts out on the line."

"Everything about it was great," said Mattingly, who had 10 of his club's 50 hits in the series, "except that we lost." But McDowell couldn't see a trace of a silver lining in such a black-cloud ending. "There's not really any solace to be taken from this," he said. "There's only one team left standing and that's all that matters. When you put on the uniform in spring training, that's what you play for. The rest is a waste."

Had it not been for the wild-card format, the Yankees would not have had their postseason fling, disappointingly as it might have ended. After their impressive showing during the strike-shortened 1994 season, the Yankees finished 79–65, seven games behind the division-champion Red Sox.

The schedule was trimmed from 162 games to 144 because of the early-season continuation of the player strike. Owners opened training camps with replacement players, and it wasn't until the courts forced management to reinstate portions of the expired collective bargaining agreement

Jim Leyritz circles the bases after his two-run homer in the 15th inning won game two of the division series. His only playoff hit, the blast dramatically ended the record five-hour, 13-minute marathon at 1:22 A.M., sending Stadium fans home weary but happy. It was the highlight of the Yankees' season, and their final victory of the year.

Don Mattingly said goodbye after 13 memorable seasons that transported the sweet-swinging, slick-fielding first baseman from 19th-round draftee to Yankee icon. Batting .288 in his final season for a career .307 mark, 34-year-old "Donnie Baseball" concluded a storybook career by hitting .417 in the playoffs.

that the players came back to camp during the first week of April.

Labor peace was not at hand with the return of the players, however. The two sides did not meet at the bargaining table for seven and a half months, and America's national pastime exacted an emotional toll from its fans. Average attendance at the Stadium was around 24,000, nearly a 20 percent drop from the strike-free 1993 season.

The season, delayed until April 26, also included many more roster changes than in 1994. McDowell was the key off-season addition, acquired in trade from Chicago to add to what the Yankees believed would be a sensational starting corps, despite losing Jim Abbott to the White Sox as a free agent. New York also obtained Cone from Toronto in July for three minor league pitchers. "This is large," said Wade Boggs. "He was the guy on top of everyone's Christmas list."

Cone was effective, winning nine of his 11 decisions after the trade. The pitching also received a significant boost from rookie Andy Pettitte, who went 12–9 with a 4.17 earned run average.

The biggest setback for the club—and the driving force behind acquiring Cone—was the midseason loss of ace Jimmy Key, the club's best left-hander since Ron Guidry, to rotator cuff surgery. Key, 35–10 over his two seasons with the Yankees, was 17–5 following losses.

Danny Tartabull also left, but both player and team were eager to make a change. Tartabull, the most highly paid player in team history, asked to be dealt in June. Soon after, owner George Steinbrenner charged that Tartabull refused to play hurt and was afraid to perform in front of the Bronx boo-birds.

Unlike Yankee stars Reggie Jackson and Dave Winfield, whose level of play rose as the heat grew higher in the front office and in the stands, Tartabull's game wilted next to the flame.

"I'm just kind of glad it's over," Tartabull said upon exiting, his batting average an anemic .224 and his production limited to six homers and 28 RBIs. "I just want to go the ballpark and think about baseball and play baseball."

Following the season, far-reaching changes shook up what had been a tranquil, successful management regime. Buck Showalter's days as manager ended after four seasons during which he helped shape the club into a contender. Steinbrenner offered him a contract, but Showalter balked at some of the nonfinancial conditions—believed to be differences over the makeup of the coaching staff. The owner quickly issued a news release stating that the skipper had chosen not to return. "I got to believe that he didn't want to come back," said Steinbrenner, sounding miffed when the end came on Halloween. "I can't figure it."

Nor could Showalter make sense of the abrupt end. "Turning down any offer from the Yankees is very heart-wrenching," said the stunned ex-skipper. "But it was done with the hope of getting something worked out." Never, said Showalter, did he understand that his initial contract refusal would lead him to the unemployment line.

Two days later, Brooklyn native Joe Torre took over as the club's 31st manager. Steinbrenner also named former Yankee first baseman Bob Watson as general manager and made Gene Michael director of major league scouting. In the clubhouse, though, the biggest news was that Mattingly would not return. Maybe. Sort of. Wait and see.

Steinbrenner reportedly offered the slick-fielding first baseman an open-ended contract, but the 34-year-old Mattingly opted to try retirement. He didn't exactly say he was retiring, but he felt he would like to try it. "He'll always be a Yankee," Steinbrenner said.

The Yankees also bought out Darryl Strawberry's contract for $175,000, with room for a possible later renegotiation. Strawberry, the former Met whose drug and income-tax woes led to his dramatic decline, was salvaged from the baseball scrap heap by Steinbrenner during the season and assigned to the minors. He came to the plate 87 times for New York and hit .276, but Showalter hadn't trusted his defense enough to put him in the field.

During the season, Yankee fans also had a lost record to ponder: Baltimore's Cal Ripken, Jr., eclipsed Lou Gehrig's mark of 2,130 consecutive games played, a mark many had felt would last forever. Fans also mourned the death of Mickey Mantle. The famed slugger, whose muscles once bulged out of his number 7 shirt, was 63 when he succumbed to cancer on August 13.

Mantle's final weeks were controversial. A recovered alcoholic whose drinking left him with a ravaged liver, he received a transplant on June 8. Mantle's age and his drinking history drew criticism around the country. Yet the controversy did some good, focusing awareness of the importance of organ donations.

"Don't be like me," Mantle told the public during a July 11 news conference, repentant over his self-destructive behavior. "God gave me a body and the ability to play baseball. I had everything, and I just . . ."

After the Yankees failed to make the 1995 playoffs, everyone in the Bronx and elsewhere figured that impatient owner George Steinbrenner would shake things up. They weren't disappointed. After 34 years in Fort Lauderdale, New York switched its spring training site to Tampa, Steinbrenner's hometown, and opened its 1996 camp in a new $20 million facility and with a player payroll of nearly $55 million.

There was also a new general manager (Bob Watson) in the front office, a new manager (Joe Torre) in the dugout, and a revamped roster. But the same old Boss.

"Like Sinatra said, 'I did it my way,'" Steinbrenner said during spring training, surveying

Newcomer Cecil Fielder and his joyous teammates tell the baseball universe who's number one as the Yankees celebrate their record 23rd world championship and the Stadium erupts in jubilation.

the team's new surroundings and new faces. "If it doesn't work, I'll take the heat. If we did everything right, we'll never get the praise anyway. That's okay. I feel very good about this team."

Even though the 1995 club had made the playoffs for the first time in 14 years, it had fallen short of the perennial franchise goal—the world championship. "The mission statement," said Watson, "is to return the Yankees to their rightful and proper place. We don't want to just win the division. George wants to win the whole shooting match. That's the way I am, too. I don't want to be just a contender. I want to win it all."

And so the Yankees did. They finished the season with a 92–70 mark, their most victories since 1985, and captured the divisional flag. They went on to dismiss the Rangers, 3–1, in the best-of-five-game opening round of the playoffs and then erased the Orioles, 4–1, in the best-of-seven League Championship Series to collect the club's 34th pennant.

Then, after dropping the opening two games of the World Series to the defending champion Atlanta Braves, the Yankees came storming back to win four straight and become baseball's champions for the 23rd time in their storied history.

The Yankees' first world title since 1978 ended with closer John Wetteland, arms raised above his head, jumping for joy into the arms of catcher Joe Girardi before a delirious Stadium crowd of 56,375. "It's almost like there was an angel up there orchestrating this," pitcher David Cone told *Sports Illustrated*'s Tom Verducci, "some intangible force."

It was only the 11th time in Series history that a club rebounded to win the title after dropping the first two games. The Mets, the crosstown rivals, had been the last to do it, in 1986 against the Red Sox. The Yankees themselves had done it three times—in 1978 against the Los Angeles Dodgers, in 1958 against the Milwaukee Braves, and in 1956 against the Brooklyn Dodgers.

For third baseman Wade Boggs, who'd wept in the Shea Stadium dugout after the Red Sox blew the 1986 Series to the Mets after coming within one strike of winning it, the comeback was particularly sweet. This time, he rode across the outfield atop a police horse, his right arm holding on to one of New York's finest, his left index finger aloft.

"[The memory of '86] is finally buried," said the elated Boggs, who had given way in the late innings to backup Charlie Hayes, who caught Mark Lemke's pop-up for the final out. "The joy of [celebrating] on that mound will always be a part of me. . . . People had doubts. I had doubts

Wade Boggs circles the Stadium on horseback as baseball's Paul Revere, spreading the word Stadium fans had been awaiting 18 years: The Yankees are world champions again. "That was something new for me," Boggs admitted afterward, "because I'm deathly afraid of horses."

myself. But we hung in and won, and the feeling is something you can't describe."

The clinching victory capped an astounding comeback that included an emotional off-field chapter centered on the Torre family of Marine Park in Brooklyn. In game four, with his club behind 2–1 in the Series, Joe Torre deftly directed his Yankees from a 6–0 deficit in the sixth inning to an 8–6 triumph in 10 innings. Meanwhile, the manager's brother Frank was clinging to life, desperately in need of a heart transplant.

The next day, with ex-Brave Frank Torre still in critical condition and without a heart donor, the Yankees eked out a 1–0 victory in Atlanta as left-hander Andy Pettitte outdueled John Smoltz. After deplaning from the club's charter flight home, his anxious brother Joe went to bed, only to have the phone ring half an hour later with news that a perfect donor match had been found.

Frank received his new heart the next day, with Sister Marguerite Torre praying in the chapel of the Blessed Virgin Mary School in Ozone Park. Barely a day later, Frank was on the rebound, and the Yankees were champions once more.

"This is like an out-of-body experience," Joe Torre said moments after the 3–2 victory in game six. "Everything about this World Series, what my brother is going through, the reaction of the

Joe Torre embraces baseball's holy grail, savoring his first world championship in his 32nd major-league season. "I've never been more happy," said the 56-year-old Brooklyn product, the first New York City native to manage the team. "I never thought this would happen to me." In his first season at the Yankee helm, Torre was voted the American League's Co-Manager of the Year and named baseball's Sportsman of the Year by the Sporting News.

city, it's everything and more than I hoped it would be. . . . Yesterday and today are the greatest days I've ever had in my life."

The Yankees had been on a mission all season as seven regulars hit .290 or better—including Mariano Duncan (.340), rookie of the year Derek Jeter (.314), Boggs (.311), Bernie Williams (.305), Paul O'Neill (.302), Girardi (.294), and Tino Martinez (.292).

On July 31, the Yankees dealt Ruben Sierra to Detroit for Cecil Fielder, and the longtime longball specialist hit .260 in 53 games, clouting 13 homers and driving in 37 runs. Fielder finished with 117 RBIs for the season, equaling Martinez's figure, as Williams chipped in 102.

Another key late-season pickup was the 31-year-old Hayes, a 1992 Yankee reacquired from Pittsburgh for a minor league pitcher. He hit .284 in 20 games, spelling the 38-year-old Boggs.

The ace of the pitching staff was Pettitte (21–8, 3.87 earned run average), who stole the spotlight from the aging Jimmy Key (12–11) and Cone (7–2), who both spent time on the disabled list while Pettitte emerged as the staff stopper. The 6-foot-5 left-hander, who was 13–3 fol-

lowing New York losses, became the first Yankee to win 20 games since Ron Guidry went 22–6 in 1985.

Wetteland, the Series MVP with four saves, provided the cork for 43 of the Yankees' 92 victories, giving him a major-league-leading 179 saves since 1992. Only Wetteland and Dave Righetti ever have combined consecutive 30-save seasons for New York.

The one-game Picasso of the pitching staff, however, was created by former Met Dwight Gooden, who'd been acquired as a free agent in October 1995. On May 14, he fired a no-hitter, his first, a 2–0 masterpiece over the Mariners at the Stadium that included six walks, five strikeouts, and 135 pitches. Gooden's was the 10th no-hitter thrown by a Yankee, the first since Jim Abbott's 4–0 victory over the Indians in 1993.

Cooperstown called immediately after the game, requesting that Gooden sign three balls for the Hall of Fame. "They'll want your jersey and cap, too," said Rick Cerrone, the club's director of media relations. "But I'm going to wear them until I lose," said Gooden, who immediately flew to Tampa, where his father underwent heart surgery the next day.

Though the season seemed to be graced with

Dwight Gooden's storybook comeback included a May 14 no-hitter over Seattle. The 31-year-old former Mets star went 11–7 in his first Yankee season.

magic throughout, the Yankees considered themselves fortunate to be playing in the Series at all after having to rally in three straight games to beat Texas in the postseason's first round.

The Rangers, in the playoffs for the first time in their 25-year history, belted out a 6–2 triumph in the opener as Juan Gonzalez and Dean Palmer each homered off Cone in the fourth inning, producing five runs.

For the remainder of the series, the Yankees were forced to play catch-up. They needed 12 innings to capture a 5–4 victory in game two after trailing by three runs in the fourth. In game three, they rubbed out a 2–1 deficit in the ninth to win 3–2. And in game four, buried in a 4–0 hole, they rebounded on a two-out single by Fielder in the seventh and a pair of towering homers by Williams to clinch the series 6–4.

"I've never seen the likes of this club," Torre said. "They look flat and then something happens, as if they were hit with a wet towel. They get shocked back into reality."

It was the Orioles who were shocked in the opener of the League Championship Series at the Stadium by an unlikely angel in the outfield, a 12-year-old from Old Tappan, New Jersey, named Jeff Maier. Maier reached over the right-field wall and helped usher Jeter's fly ball over the fence for an eighth-inning homer that tied the game 4–4.

But for Maier's sleight of hand, the ball might have been caught by Orioles outfielder Tony Tarasco. "It was like a magic trick," said Tarasco. "I was getting ready to catch it, and suddenly a glove appeared and the ball disappeared. When the kid reached over the wall, his glove was very close to mine. We almost touched gloves."

Befuddled umpire Rich Garcia, who signaled a home run, admitted after watching the replay that the ball would not have left the park. "At the time I saw it," said Garcia, "I never saw anybody touch the ball, and I thought the ball was out of the ballpark."

After the Yankees went on to win 5–4 on Williams' 11th-inning homer, the Orioles complained about being robbed. "Ain't nothing tainted about this as far as I'm concerned," shrugged Pettitte, who pitched the first seven innings. "We're up 1–0. Nothing else matters."

The Orioles owned one night of the series, erasing a 2–0 deficit in game two with Rafael Palmeiro's two-run homer in the seventh and winning 5–3. But the Yankees then ripped off three consecutive victories—5–2, 8–4, and 6–4—and

A 12-year-old New Jersey fan named Jeffrey Maier became the center of a controversial play when he reached down from the Stadium's right-field stands and gloved Derek Jeter's fly ball in the eighth inning of the league championship opener. "It was like magic," said Oriole right fielder Tony Tarasco. "I was about to catch the ball, and it disappeared." The ball also disappeared from the sight of umpire Rich Garcia, who ruled it a homer, which tied the score and set up Bernie Williams' game-winning homer in the 11th. It also made an instant celebrity of seventh grader Maier, who read all about it in the next day's New York Post—*and most everywhere else.*

Bernie Williams hit .305 with career-highs of 29 home runs, 102 RBIs, 108 runs scored, and 17 stolen bases. He hit seven postseason homers and was MVP of the league championships.

Mariano Rivera's 2.09 ERA led the staff. The 26-year-old right-hander went 8–3 with five saves in 61 relief appearances, usually setting up closer John Wetteland. Rivera's 130 strikeouts were the most ever by a Yankee reliever.

earned a Series berth for the first time in 15 years.

It was the long ball, ironically the hallmark of the Orioles (257 total), that brought the Yankees their final victory. Fielder, Jim Leyritz, and Darryl Strawberry all drove Scott Erickson offerings out of Camden Yards in New York's six-run third inning. "This park," declared Leyritz, "is very homer friendly."

The Yankees' turnaround in the Series bordered on the miraculous. After blowing the home-field advantage with embarrassing 12–1 and 4–0 losses in the first two games, New York seemed destined to be swept as it headed for Atlanta to face more of baseball's most heralded rotation.

But the reliable Cone settled the Yankees down in game three, pitching six gutsy innings (four hits, one run) as Williams contributed two hits, two runs, and three RBIs in a 5–2 triumph.

"The mindset of the team," said Cone, who won a Cy Young Award with Kansas City in 1994, "was that we were a little bit embarrassed. We never really got into either game in New York. So we came to Atlanta and decided to let it all hang out."

Yet after only two innings of game four, it appeared time for the Yankees to hang it up. The Braves scored four runs in the second, one in the third, and another in the fifth for a daunting 6–0 lead.

But the Yankees scratched away for three runs in the sixth, then tied it in the eighth when Leyritz socked a three-run homer off Mark Wohlers, Atlanta's ace closer. "This," said Leyritz, "is probably the biggest moment of my career."

On came relievers Mariano Rivera and Graeme Lloyd to hold the Braves scoreless in the eighth and ninth. Then Wetteland took over with one out in the 10th, after the Yankees had moved ahead by two runs.

Boggs, pinch-hitting for Andy Fox, drew a bases-loaded walk from left-hander Steve Avery for the lead tally. "It was the biggest walk I've ever had," Boggs said. Then first baseman Ryan Klesko misplayed Hayes' soft liner for another run.

Pettitte, the game one loser, allowed only five hits over 8⅓ innings in game five before giving way to Wetteland in the ninth. Smoltz allowed only four hits in eight innings, but one was a double to Fielder that scored Hayes from second.

Hayes had gotten there courtesy of a two-base error by Braves center fielder Marquis Grissom, a four-time Gold Glover, who was thrown off when rookie right fielder Jermaine Dye crossed his path and caused Grissom to muff Hayes' fly ball.

Jim Leyritz is duked by third-base coach Willie Randolph as he circles the bases after his clutch three-run, eighth-inning homer tied game four and set up an 8–6, 10-inning victory that evened the World Series at 2–2. The win stunned the Braves, who had led 6–0, and ranks as the second greatest comeback in Series history.

The 1996 New York Yankees. **Back row** *(left to right): Andy Pettitte, Andy Fox, Paul O'Neill, Graeme Lloyd, Darryl Strawberry, Dave Pavlas, Jeff Nelson, Derek Jeter, John Wetteland, Kenny Rogers, Jim Leyritz.* **Third row:** *Cecil Fielder, Tim Raines, Dale Polley, Mariano Rivera, Mariano Duncan, Bernie Williams, Dwight Gooden, Luis Sojo, Tino Martinez, Wade Boggs, Jimmy Key, Rob Cucuzza (assistant equipment manager).* **Second row:** *Gene Monahan (head trainer), Dr. Stuart Hershon (team physician), Paul Mastropasqua (strength and conditioning coach), Mike Borzello (bullpen catcher), Mike Aldrete, Pat Kelly, Wally Whitehurst, Pat Listach, Brian Boehringer, David Cone, Joe Girardi, Nick Testa (batting practice pitcher), Steve Donohue (trainer), David Szen (traveling secretary).* **Front row:** *Tony Cloninger (Coach), Mel Stottlemyre (coach), Jose Cardenal (coach), Don Zimmer (coach), Joe Torre (manager), Willie Randolph (coach), Chris Chambliss (coach), Carl Taylor (video coordinator), Charlie Wonsowicz (batting practice pitcher), Rudy Arias (bullpen catcher).* **Seated:** *Joe Lee, Chris Soto, Roy Emlet (batboys).*

"Neither of us called for it right away," said Dye. "Both of us were at full speed. He called for it at the last minute. I tried to veer away, but I'm pretty tall and I blocked his vision."

So the Series was headed back to New York, where the House That Ruth Built was charged once more with the expectancy of a world title. "The bottom line is," said Girardi, a key off-season acquisition from Colorado, "we beat [the Braves] at their own game. We have an offense that is pretty potent. You make a couple of mistakes and we're going to hurt you."

The Yankees, who batted only .216 for the Series, got all their runs in the third inning of the finale. An O'Neill double and a Girardi triple produced the first one. Then came singles by Jeter and Williams, with a stolen base mixed in, to make it 3–0. The Braves cut their deficit to 3–1 going into the ninth, and they would tighten matters further. Wetteland came on for the final time and allowed one run, but the Yankees, once more, were sitting on top of the world.

"We're not going to rate up there as far as power," said co-manager of the year Torre, whose 31 previous major league seasons had never included a World Series title. "But we will be known as a team that did whatever we needed to do to win."

Portraits of the Greats

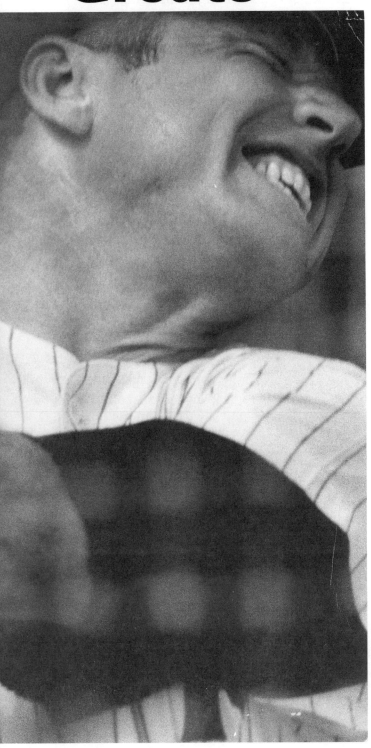

"Owning the Yankees," George Steinbrenner has said, "is like owning the Mona Lisa."

A museum full of them, really. No other baseball team has boasted so many masterpieces—a gallery of meganames over the decades, each passing the Yankee legacy from one pinstriped generation to the next.

Ruth, Gehrig, DiMaggio . . .

All have contributed to an extraordinary continuity that has built an institution known around the world—sport's most successful franchise, and the greatest team in baseball history.

Stengel, Berra, Mantle . . .

Yankee Stadium has been home to baseball's brightest collection of talent this side of Cooperstown.

Martin, Jackson, Mattingly . . .

All these and so many more—an unmatched diamond galaxy.

On the following pages, nine Yankee giants are portrayed in the reprinted words of nine press box headliners. Both lineups are incomplete, of course. Many more Yankees could be profiled by as many media stars. There isn't room for them all. So, symbolically, the number *nine* was chosen for this celebration of Yankee heroes—nine among all those individuals who have contributed notably to the world's most storied team.

Grantland Rice on Babe Ruth ....

The Bambino

There was only one Babe Ruth and only one Grantland Rice. Both were giants who altered their professions and left their imprints on sports forever. They were royalty in the golden age of the '20s and '30s, when sports was woven into the fabric of American life.

Ruth and Rice were two of a kind, each a star in his own way. Ruth was the nation's number one personality, and Rice was sport's most influential voice—the premier chronicler of the era. In an age without television, the public depended on sportswriters and radio broadcasters to be their eyes and ears. And most often they relied on Rice, whose syndicated column commanded a massive readership around the country.

"Granny wrote of men he loved and deeds he admired and never knew how much better he was than his finest hero," Red Smith wrote of the man he succeeded as the nation's most widely read sportswriter.

So who better to profile George Herman Ruth than Henry Grantland Rice, who was there for every pigeon-toed step of the Bambino's career in pinstripes, right up until the day in August 1948 when Ruth died (six summers ahead of Rice himself). On that day, Granny wrote: "The greatest figure the world of sport has ever known has passed from the field. Game called on account of darkness."

The first time I saw Babe Ruth was in April 1919. Ruth was taking his turn in batting practice at Tampa, Florida, the spring training camp of the champion Red Sox. Since covering my first World Series in 1905, I'd seen a lot of swingers. But never a swinger like this!

Years ago I stopped talking about the Babe for the simple reason that I realized that those who had never seen him didn't believe me.

—Tommy Holmes, New York sportswriter

Babe blasted one pitch clear out of the park into a ploughed field. I gauged that trip as about 500 feet—not bad, even without a publicity man around to check the distance with a tape measure. While Ruth hit, I watched, and Ed Barrow, the Red Sox manager, talked.

"At twenty-four, this fellow can become the greatest thing that's happened to baseball. He's a fine southpaw pitcher—he can become a great one. But the day I can use him in the outfield and take advantage of his bat every day—well, they'll have to build the parks bigger, just for Ruth."

After bombing about 10 shots, Ruth circled the bases, mincing along with short, pigeon-toed steps—a base-circling trot destined to become as celebrated as Man O'War's gallop.

When Ruth came over to mop his face in a towel, Barrow introduced us.

"You sound like you got a cold," said Ruth.

"I have, sort of," I replied.

Taking an enormous red onion out of his hip pocket, Ruth thrust it into my hand. "Here, gnaw on this," he said. "Raw onions are cold-killers." While Ruth talked I gnawed, with tears streaming from my eyes.

"Babe," I said, "I was watching your swing. You swing like no pitcher I ever saw."

"I may be a pitcher, but first off I'm a hitter," said Babe. "I copied my swing after Joe Jackson's. His is the perfectest. Joe aims his right shoulder square at the pitcher, with his feet about twenty inches apart. But I close my stance to about eight and a half inches or less. I find I pivot better with it closed. Once committed

Condensed from Grantland Rice's *The Tumult and the Shouting*, published in 1954 by A. S. Barnes and Company, Inc.

. . . once my swing starts, though, I can't change it or pull up. It's all or nothing at all."

Throughout a career that spanned 20 years, Ruth never changed the basic fundamentals of that gorgeous, gargantuan arc—a swing that captured the imagination of the crowd nearly as much as the man behind it. To watch Ruth go down, swinging from the heels, often sprawling from the sheer violence of his cut, was almost as exciting as seeing him blast one out of the park.

Of all the sluggers that the advent of the lively ball has spawned, Babe was the only one I ever knew who never shortened or choked his grip when the count reached two strikes.

He gripped his bat with the knob of the handle "palmed" in his right hand. So perfect was his wrist snap—and the other reflexes that go into the perfectly timed swing—that he could wait on the pitch until the last split second and "pick" the ball practically out of the catcher's mitt.

Born? Hell, Babe Ruth wasn't born. The son of a bitch fell from a tree.
—Jumping Joe Dugan, longtime teammate and one of Ruth's pallbearers

The Babe liked plenty of lumber in his war clubs. Many of his bludgeons weighed 42 ounces—about a half pound more than the average bat.

That spring the Red Sox and McGraw's Giants played a four-out-of-seven exhibition series at Tampa. I hung around for several games to watch Ruth hit and play left field. The New York writers were pop-eyed; the Boston boys had already oiled up their best adjectives for him. In the first game he hit the longest ball I ever saw—some six miles over the right-center-field fence and into the infield of an adjacent race track.

Bill McGeehan, of the *New York Tribune,* who didn't impress easily, wrote: *The ball sailed so high that when it came down it was coated with ice . . . a drive that would have rattled off the clubhouse roof at the Polo Grounds.*

That Giants series put the exclamation mark on Ruth, the home-run hitter, and practically wrote his finis as a pitcher.

Boston finished in sixth place as Chicago's brilliant team roared in, despite the fact that Ruth hit 29 homers. In January 1920, when owner Harry Frazee of the Red Sox was heavily in debt, he sold Ruth to Jake Ruppert's third-place Yankees for 125,000 dollars outright, plus a 350,000 dollar loan. The transaction remains baseball's all-time bargain.

In 1920, the year following the Black Sox scandal, baseball needed a Superman, a man who could capture the imagination of the public—who could restore America's faith in baseball. Babe fit the bill. The public wanted to see the ball smashed out of the park—where there couldn't be any question of inside baseball—and the game's leaders moved to help. The ball was given a shot of rabbit juice, and in '20 Babe's big bat boomed for 54 homers. He alone realigned the game on the order of the long hit—the big inning. Lifting the Yankees aboard his shoulders, Ruth immediately became the heartwood of what was to become "Murderers' Row." In '20 the Yanks, again third, outdrew the Giants—in the Polo Grounds, to McGraw's chagrin. In '21, '22, and '23 the Giants and Yanks tangled in the World Series—'23 being the year Ruppert's team moved from the Polo Grounds into their own million-dollar home across the Harlem River, "The House That Ruth Built."

Babe's love of kids was sincere. In many ways he was a big kid himself. I was in his room for dinner on the eve of the World Series in Chicago in 1932. (He always ate in his room before games because he would have been mobbed by fans and autograph hustlers in the hotel dining room.)

"I've got to go for a short trip, Grant," he said.

"Where are you going on the night before a World Series?" I asked.

"I'll tell you, but if you print it I'll shoot you. I'm going to take a baseball to a sick kid on the other side of town. I promised his mother and father I'd come. He's pretty sick."

The place was 20 or 30 miles away—over an hour to get there and another to get back. No publicity.

Babe was known by more motorcycle cops than any athlete who ever lived. They enjoyed giving Ruth an escort to the Stadium or helping him to get away after a game. They were usually there, like the Travelers' Aid, whenever the Babe needed a lift home to Riverside Drive after a late party.

One morning Babe asked me to pick him up for our golf game at Leewood, in Tuckahoe. "Sure," I replied, "but what happened to your car?"

"I lost it," said Babe.

"Lost it?" I said. "You had it last night."

"That was last night," replied Babe. "I wrecked it somewhere in Westchester and left it."

So he had. The cops had driven him home.

Pick a good one and sock it.
—Babe Ruth

Another time, when Babe was roaring along by dawn's early light, the law stopped him, checked on his condition, and suggested he be driven home.

"Why you (censored)!" roared Babe, and punched the cop on the nose.

"Now I *know* you're drunk," said the cop. "Move over! I'm drivin' you home."

I was with Babe one evening when he turned down a one-way street—the wrong way. "This is a one-way street," said the cop.

"I'm only drivin' one way!" yelled Ruth.

"Oh, hello, Babe! I didn't know it was you," replied the cop. "Go anywhere you please—but take it easy!"

And so it went.

Moe Berg, the eminent linguist, Princetonian and major league catcher, once said: "Ruth isn't a man; he's an institution." Ruth was a man who loved crowds. And the crowds always swarmed to see Babe hit. The Yankees from 1926 to '34 were a terrific aggregation, each man big in his own right. But it was Babe the crowds came to see.

I've seen the great ones, from Cobb through Williams, but Ruth was the only ballplayer I have known who could turn out capacity crowds every time. He did this in every city the Yankees played. When the Yankee Stadium was dedicated in April 1923, more than 74,000 people turned up—to see the Yankees, sure, but more important, to see Ruth cavort around "The House That Babe Built."

He was the greatest single magnet sport has ever known. He lured packed stands in the big cities and he drew them out in the bush. I know, for I followed him from 1919 to his final game in 1935. Big league, bush league, the great cities, small hamlets—at the ballpark or train depot—always capacity.

I've ridden in cars with Babe in cities all over the map. Everywhere, the mobs would wave or call his name, and Babe would answer, "How're you, Mom!" . . . "Hello, Pop!" "How can they miss this silly mug?" he used to ask.

Whether it was playing baseball or golf, hunting, fishing or sitting around a room drinking and punching the bag, I can recall no one who got as much joy out of sheer living as the Babe. Ruth, the man–boy, was the complete embodiment of everything uninhibited.

Paul Gallico on Lou Gehrig ·················

Pride of the Yankees

Of all the images of Lou Gehrig, one is frozen in time for the ages. There is the Ironman, now suddenly fragile, standing by home plate at hushed Yankee Stadium, head bowed and eyes wet while others eulogize him before he steps to the microphone and declares to the world that he is the luckiest man on earth.

It is one of the most poignant images in all of sports, and surely baseball's most dramatic nonaction moment. Six decades later, it is still what is seen in the mind's eye when Gehrig's name is mentioned. His iron-man streak may register, but triggers no image. The mental picture is of a dying hero in his defining moment, transcending his sport.

Photographers captured that image, and Hollywood helped immortalize the spirit of the moment in a flawed but acclaimed motion picture. But when it came to the written word, nobody told the story better than Paul Gallico.

Gallico, like Gehrig a New York City nativer and onetime Columbia athlete, was the New York Daily News' *sports editor and star columnist during sports' golden age of the '20s and '30s. In 1936 he moved on to write best-selling fiction, but he returned to the sports world briefly to tackle a story no fiction writer could have invented. This is what he wrote.*

On July 4th, 1939, there took place the most tragic and touching scene ever enacted on a baseball diamond—the funeral services for Henry Louis Gehrig.

Lou Gehrig attended them in person.

Gehrig Day, as it was called, was a gesture of love and appreciation on the part of everyone concerned, a spontaneous reaching out to a man who had been good and kind and decent, to thank him for having been so.

It was a day of sparkling sunshine and cheers, bunting and bands, a great and warmhearted crowd, fine gifts and fine speeches.

But only much, much later, seen in complete and true perspective, do we feel the full and bitter impact of its tragic implications.

The suggestion that there be a Gehrig Appreciation Day began in the sports column of Bill Corum, who credits the idea to the telephone call of one Bill Hirsch. The *Journal* took up the idea. Other columnists concurred.

It was suggested that the All-Star Game be the occasion. But the Yankee management—or rather, Ed Barrow, a burly bear of a man with the kindest of hearts—did not want to share Gehrig's due with any other event. Gehrig Appreciation Day was set to take place between games of a Fourth of July doubleheader.

The most touching conception of the day was the coming from the ends of the country of Gehrig's former teammates, the famous Murderers' Row, the powerful Yankees of 1927.

Bob Meusel, balding Benny Bengough, Gehrig's first pal, gray-eyed Mark Koenig, and dead-panned Poosh-'em-op Tony Lazzeri, the clown of the team, tall skinny Joe Dugan, and even skinnier and taller Pipp the Pickler, the Yankee first baseman whose place Gehrig had taken so many years ago, all came.

He was a symbol of indestructibility—a Gibralter in cleats.

—Jim Murray, columnist

Little Everett Scott turned up, the man whose endurance record Gehrig had conquered so decisively, and the great pitching staff of yesterdays, Herb Pennock from his Pennsylvania fox farm, Waite Hoyt from the broadcasting booths. George

Reprinted from Paul Gallico's *Lou Gehrig: Pride of the Yankees*, published in 1942 by Grosset & Dunlap, Inc.

Pipgras was there too, but wearing the blue uniform of an umpire. Earle Combs and Art Fletcher still were in Yankee uniforms as coaches.

And finally there was George Herman Ruth. The Babe and Lou hadn't got along very well the last years they played together. Baseball writers knew that they weren't speaking. And after Babe had retired he had criticized Lou's long playing record in a newspaper interview. The original feud was a childish affair which began before Lou's marriage, women instigated, and which gains nothing in dignity or sense in retelling. Suffice it to say that the Babe was there on that Requiem Day, with an arm around Lou and a whispered pleasantry that came at a time when Gehrig was very near to collapse from the emotions that turmoiled within him. It needed Babe's Rabelasian nonsense to make him smile.

Present too were Lou's more recent teammates, the Bronx Bombers under Joe McCarthy, and the Washington Senators, who were the opponents of the Yankees for the Fourth of July doubleheader.

Sid Mercer, president of the Baseball Writers Association, was the master of ceremonies. The principal speakers were Jim Farley, Postmaster General, and Mayor Fiorello LaGuardia. Sixty-one thousand, eight hundred and eight were in the stands. It was what was known as a Great Day.

To Lou Gehrig, it was goodbye to everything that he had known and loved.

It was goodbye to baseball, to the big steel-and-concrete stadium where he had served so long, to the neat green diamond with the smooth dirt paths cut by the sharp steel baseball cleats, to the towering stands with the waving pennons, the crowds, their roar and their color.

Goodbye too, to his colleagues, the friends and the men with whom he had played for fourteen years, the happy, friendly men who had been his shipmates through life.

We constituted the greatest one-two punch in baseball history.
—Babe Ruth

Lou Gehrig was a man who came through in the clutch above all others.
—Joe McCarthy, manager

In the stands was all that he held dear, his family, mother and father seated in a box, unaware of his doom, his wife seated in another. Lifelong friends were in the boxes, cheering and applauding. And as Lou looked out over them gathered there in his honor, he knew he was seeing them thus for the last time.

For he was the living dead, and this was his funeral.

Gifts piled up for him, a silver service, smoking sets, writing sets, fishing tackle. They were from the Yankees, from his great rivals, the Giants, from the baseball writers and even from the ushers in the stadium and the peanut boys. The objects were a mockery, because he could no longer possess them. But the warmth of the feeling that prompted their purchase and presentation melted the iron reserve in him and broke him down.

It was so human, so great, so heroic that he should have wept there in public before the sixty-one-odd thousand, not for pity of his situation, or for the beauty and sweetness of the world he would soon depart, but because the boy who all his life had convinced himself that he had no worth, that he did not matter and never would, understood on this day, for the first time perhaps, how much people loved him.

Not only his immediate family and his adored wife, his personal friends and acquaintances, but huge masses of plain, simple people, ordinary human beings with whom he felt a deep kinship, were broadcasting their warmth to him, sending it out through the air to the figure on the field below them. He was the lone receiving station. To tune in suddenly upon so much love was nearly too much for him.

238

The speeches were ended at last, the gifts given, and the stadium rocked as wave after wave of cheers rolled down from the stands, huge combers of sound, and broke over him. For a little while as he stood at the microphones of the sound cameras and broadcasting companies, it seemed as though they might engulf him. He stood with his head bowed to the tumult—the tumult within and without, and pressed a handkerchief to his eyes to hold back the tears.

But when at last, encouraged by his friend Ed Barrow, he faced the instruments and the people behind them, the noise stopped abruptly. The echo barked once and was silent too. Everyone waited for what he would say. With a curled finger he dashed the tears that would not stay back from his eyes, lifted his head and brought his obsequies to the heart-breaking, never-to-be-forgotten finish, when he spoke his epitaph. . . .

"For the past two weeks you have been reading about a bad break I got. Yet today I consider myself the luckiest man on the face of the earth. . . ."

The clangy, iron echo of the Yankee stadium picked up the sentence that poured from the loudspeakers and hurled it forth into the world . . . "The luckiest man on the face of the earth . . . luckiest man on the face of the earth . . . luckiest man . . ."

> *I'm the fellow who follows the Babe in the batting order. If I stood on my head, nobody would pay any attention.*
> —Lou Gehrig

Fans, for the past two weeks you have been reading about a bad break I got. Yet today I consider myself the luckiest man on the face of the earth.

I have been in ballparks for seventeen years, and have never received anything but kindness and encouragement from you fans. Look at these grand men. Which of you wouldn't consider it the highlight of his career just to associate with them for even one day?

Sure I'm lucky. Who wouldn't consider it an honor to have known Jacob Ruppert? Also, the builder of baseball's greatest empire, Ed Barrow? To have spent six years with that wonderful little fellow, Miller Huggins? Then to have spent the next nine years with that outstanding leader, that smart student of psychology, the best manager in baseball today, Joe McCarthy?

Sure I'm lucky. When the New York Giants, a team you would give your right arm to beat, and vice versa, sends you a gift—that's something. When everybody down to the groundskeepers and those boys in white coats remember you with trophies—that's something. When you have a wonderful mother-in-law who takes sides with you in squabbles with her own daughter—that's something. When you have a father and a mother who work all their lives so you can have an education and build your body—it's a blessing. When you have a wife who has been a tower of strength and shown more courage than you dreamed existed—that's the finest I know.

So I close in saying that I may have had a tough break, but I have an awful lot to live for.
    —Lou Gehrig,
        July 4, 1939

Jimmy Cannon on Joe DiMaggio ....

The Yankee Clipper

"There has been only one truly great baseball player in this generation," Jimmy Cannon wrote in the early '50s. "The man's name is Joe DiMaggio, who could do it all. . . . He was running toward Cooperstown the first day he chased a baseball."

Cannon knew DiMaggio better than any other writer. The Yankee Clipper got along with the media in general, but was closest to the New York Post *columnist.*

They were often in each other's company, particularly during Joe's bachelor days, when they both resided at the Hotel Edison. They were a classic mismatch, a case of opposites attracting, the original odd couple: DiMaggio quiet and dignified with a stately reserve, Cannon brash and gruff with native Lower West Side street-smarts. Where DiMaggio was by nature aloof, the gabby Cannon was usually in the middle of any conversation.

Their friendship might have provoked a concern that the writer was too close to his subject, that his objectivity was compromised and his opinions were flavored, but Cannon was too much of a professional to let that happen.

"DiMaggio has been my friend since he broke in with the Yankees in 1936," he wrote in 1951, the year Joe retired. "It has been more than the relationship of a reporter covering a famous athlete. We are as close as our business will allow. We have gone on vacation together, sat around the same restaurants, killed a lot of time together and know the same Broadway people. It hasn't impaired my job of writing about him."

Years later, Cannon admitted to having rooted for DiMaggio inwardly. "I always considered myself a fair and neutral man," he told Jerome Holtzman in his classic No Cheering in the Press Box, *"and yet how could I not be for Joe DiMaggio? We were great friends."*

Fortunately for Cannon, DiMaggio was DiMaggio. There was little to criticize. So when Jimmy wrote about Joe, he wasn't writing about a pal. He was writing the greatest Yankee of his time and the best all-around player in baseball, a gifted athlete whose grace and purity of style made all his accomplishments look easy.

Anyone who ever saw Joe DiMaggio play ball should remember him always. Only a few men have what Joe had and he brought it with him to the big leagues. There was nothing they could teach him when he came up. It was there, big and clear. There never was any doubt about it. The record books will not substantiate the claim that he has been the greatest of his age. Other guys hit for higher averages, struck more home runs. But this is the whole ballplayer, complete and great. There are no defects to discuss.

> *Sometimes a fellow gets a little tired of writing about DiMaggio. A fellow thinks, "There must be some other ballplayer in the world worth mentioning." But there isn't really, not worth mentioning in the same breath as DiMaggio.*
>
> —Red Smith, columnist

The ballplayers, trying to be what he is, know how superior he is. On the field Joe performs without passion, but he has a stately grace. Only Joe Louis matched his pure athlete's dignity. Many times, watching him from the press box, I wondered what this man would have been if he hadn't come into baseball. But there seems no other trade for him.

It may sound sentimental and foolishly romantic, but this was a guy who was born to be a ballplayer. I can't imagine him doing anything else. Joe is a man who was meant to play ball on hot afternoons on the grass of big cities. He doesn't belong in the rain.

Reprinted from Jimmy Cannon's *Who Struck John?*, published in 1956 by The Dial Press.

You, who pay your way into ballparks, will probably never forget him coming up with the bases full and hitting a home run off Bob Feller in the Stadium . . . Drifting back after a fly ball with that slow and marvelous certainty . . . Going from first to third on a single, his long neck arched, and running round-shouldered . . . Occasionally being called out on a three-two pitch and going back to the dugout without a protest . . . Hobbling, crippled and in pain, around the outfield with the chipped bones in his foot making it seem like he was walking on slivers of glass . . . Playing in a World Series, weak from pneumonia . . . Doing what he had to do when the time came . . . Standing up and proving his greatness every time there was a crisis . . . Making a speech at home plate and apologizing to the people in the bleachers because the microphones made him turn his back to them . . . Three times the league's Most Valuable Player . . . A lifetime average of .329 . . . Nine World Series . . . The All-Star team every year . . . Hitting in 56 consecutive games in 1941 . . . Doing it every day and making it easier than it is . . . Being the leader of the Yankees no matter who the manager was . . . Winning sometimes with his presence alone because the other people knew how good he was and choked up a little.

Joe wasn't happy when he wasn't perfect.
—Jerry Coleman, teammate turned broadcaster

On the road trip, the first time around the league, he was a quiet kid but friendly. There were some who insisted he was inaccessible then and suspicious. But I found him easy to be with, and his constant companions were Lefty Gomez and Pat Malone. We had a lot of laughs that first season. There was a banquet for him in every town he played. Old men of Italian descent, who never saw a ballgame before, turned out in big crowds. They liked it better in the bleachers because they were nearer to him.

There was the time in Detroit when he asked me if I liked Italian food and I said I did. The season was '36.

"Meet me in the lobby after the game," Joe said. "They're giving me a dinner in a spaghetti joint. It's great food."

I came down into the lobby and asked one of the Yankees where Joe was. They told me he was in the dining room. He was eating a steak, a mixed green salad and french fried potatoes.

"If the Italian food's so good," I asked him, "why are you ducking it?"

"I'm just having a little snack," Joe explained.

He went to the Italian restaurant and never passed up a course and asked for seconds on the spaghetti. He led the league with the knife and fork then.

No matter what Mickey Mantle does I'll always remember . . . Fishing for sail with him in the Gulf . . . Walking down Broadway and the delight he caused when they recognized him . . . Sitting with him in his apartment at the Edison Hotel when his leg was in a cast and listening to the ballgames at the Stadium . . . Drinking Coke

There is always some kid who may be seeing me for the first or last time. I owe him my best.
—Joe DiMaggio

with him after the ballgames in front of his locker at the Stadium . . . Nights at the dog track in St. Pete . . . The late Eddie Duchin, who was his friend, playing a special concert for Joe in the private room upstairs in Shor's . . . Listening to him explain why his brother Dom was the best ballplayer in the family . . . Telling stories to his son . . . Remembering DiMaggio never lied to me . . . Or broke his word . . . or hurt anyone to make himself a bigger man.

You don't forget a guy like this.

Red Smith on Casey Stengel ....

The Ol' Perfesser

Charles Dillon Stengel and Walter Wellesley Smith were the best at what they did, masters of their crafts who became legends in their own time. And both surely had a way with words.

No manager will duplicate the 10 pennants and seven world championships achieved during Stengel's 12 Yankee seasons. And no sportswriter will assemble words with the same graceful touch as the artist that Jerome Holtzman hailed as "most likely the best sports columnist-reporter in the history of American journalism." Or be more faithfully and widely read, from sports pages coast to coast to anthologies of baseball literature. Or more decorated with honorary degrees and prizes including a 1977 Pulitzer. Smith's smooth literary elegance—light and witty and laced with wry humor—was as distinctive as Casey's convoluted (but similarly insightful) "Stengelese."

Like most everyone else, Red was confounded, amused, and intrigued by the Ol' Perfesser's way of talking. He once wrote, "Students of Stengelese, which is a live language only superficially resembling Sanskrit, have endeavored for years to capture in print the special quality, the pure body and flavor, the rich, crunchy goodness of Mr. Stengel's speech.

"They have not succeeded. The human ear is a wonderful instrument, but not so wonderful as the Stengel larynx. The mother tongue of the Yankees' manager is an oil that rolls over the consciousness but is not retained. The pencil of a stenographer may catch a phrase and hold it, quivering in beauty like a butterfly on the entomologist's pin, but something escapes in translation from notebook to type."

Stengel and Smith shared a perspective not common anymore. "Casey had a terrible hangup," Jim Murray wrote of the man he called a "genuine American heirloom." "He thought baseball should be fun."

So did Smith, who said, "I've always tried to remember that sports isn't Armageddon. These are just games that little boys can play, and [the result] isn't important to the future of civilization."

For all his talent, the gracious Smith was always self-effacing, poking fun at himself as quickly as he punctured the pomposity of others. "I'd dearly love to write a good piece today," he told a colleague in the Yankee Stadium press box before the opening pitch of the 1977 World Series. "Gee, I was lousy yesterday. I had nothing to say and, by God, I said it."

Red was entitled to his own opinion, but his columns were never lousy. As successor to Grantland Rice as dean of American sportswriters, he continued to elevate the profession and gave it respect and dignity. "I went on newspapers," Smith explained, "because I disliked lifting." But Red made a career of lifting things after all—his readers' spirits.

As he did readers of the New York Times *the morning after Stengel's funeral in October 1975.*

When Casey Stengel was still playing ball, his friend, Ring Lardner, gave him a piece of advice. "Just keep talking," the writer said. "When you're with a newspaper guy, don't try to feed him a story because you don't really know what makes a story that he can use. Just keep talking, and he'll get his story." Casey did more than merely follow that advice. He worked at it. Naturally loquacious with a genius for digression, he polished and refined those talents until they approached the level of art. It is a pity he couldn't deliver the eulogy at his funeral yesterday, for only he had the gift of tongues to suit the occasion.

> *Mr. Stengel can talk all day and all night on any kind of track, wet or dry.*
> —John Lardner, writer

The special language called Stengelese with its mangled syntax and fugitive non sequiturs was not created by accident. Though Casey was never a slave to the rules of rhetoric, it was not until he became manager of the Yankees that he learned to use the spoken word to spread confusion and bewilderment. Wherever he went on that job, there were always a dozen or more newspaper and magazine writers, radio and television men around him asking questions and frequently there were questions he didn't want to answer. He was too wise in the way of public relations, however, to use "no comment" as a way out.

You couldn't fool Casey because he'd pulled every stunt there was ever thought up, and he did it fifty years before we even got there.
—Mickey Mantle

"That's a very good question," he would say. "I'm glad you asked it." For the next 10 minutes he would discourse on what John McGraw had done in 1921 and what Wilbert Robinson had said to Zack Wheat in 1917, and it might be half an hour later before the man who had asked the question would realize it had not been answered.

The man wouldn't mind. He hadn't got the information he sought but he had been richly entertained.

It is an old story that when the Yankees were seeking a successor to Bucky Harris, George Weiss proposed Casey and Dan Topping said: "That clown! You couldn't bring him into New York." After that tale had been written half a dozen times, Weiss was asked why he had been so sure of the man's ability that he argued away the owner's objections.

He said his respect for Casey as a student of baseball had been born many years earlier when he operated the New Haven team in the Eastern League and Casey was manager and part-owner of the Worcester club. More than once they had started talking baseball at dinner and were still at it when the sun rose. George felt he had never known anyone with Casey's grasp of the niceties of the game.

"He went on to manage in the majors and minors," George said, "and I followed his career

Well, God is getting an earful today. I hope He understands the infield-fly rule, the hit-and-run, how to pitch to Hornsby with men on, when to platoon, when it would do you some good to bunt, and what really happened in the 1913 World Series. He will get an illustrated lecture on the hook slide, the best place to play Babe Ruth, when to order the infield in, and how to steal on left-handers.

—Jim Murray, columnist, on Stengel's death

and never saw anything to change my mind. Then when the Yankees owned the Kansas City club in the American Association, he managed for us there. Time and again he'd do something unusual and when you'd ask him about it he always had a good reason, often a reason you wouldn't think of yourself."

So, putting his judgment on the line as general manager, George Weiss convinced Topping and his partner, Del Webb, that they could bring that clown to New York. And in 12 seasons the clown delivered 10 pennants and eight world championships, five of them in a row.

Perhaps it is incorrect to say he "delivered" all those championships because Casey himself

Sometimes I get a little hard-of-speaking.
—Casey Stengel

conceded: "I couldn't'a done it without the players." That statement has often been quoted as evidence of a monumental conceit but actually it was 24 carat Stengelese. He was disclaiming credit, saying in his own special way, "Don't applaud me; the players did it."

Arthur Daley on Yogi Berra ....

Yogi

Lawrence Peter Berra is unique in Yankee history. There is not another like him—from his distinctive appearance to his unique way with words to his marvelous nickname. When somebody says "Yogi," no one asks "Yogi who?"

It might seem odd to include a column on Berra written at the start of his storied career. Arthur Daley's handiwork appeared in the New York Times *on March 20, 1949. Yogi had played just 215 games during little more than two seasons in pinstripes, 221 if you count the 1947 World Series. Who would have dreamed he'd play in 1,905 more as a Yankee? And that total doesn't include 69 more appearances in the World Series.*

All that was impossible to foresee during 1949 spring training. That's when new manager Casey Stengel brought back catching great Bill Dickey to tutor the awkward youngster, who had divided his time in pinstripes between catching and the outfield, neither spectacularly.

Dickey did his job, and so did Berra, and the rest, of course, is legend. So it's interesting to look back and see how this Hall of Fame career began—as captured in the graceful style of Daley, the New York Times *columnist who in 1956 became only the second sports scribe to be awarded the Pulitzer Prize, the first for general sportswriting.*

And to see that from the start, Yogi was always Yogi.

Just about the time the war was ending, Larry MacPhail, then the president of the Yankees, conferred with Master Melvin Ott, then the manager of the Giants—which should show you what ancient history all this is. The Rambunctious Redhead had under contract four catchers of various degrees of ability and experience.

"I'd like to buy one of your catchers, Larry," said Master Melvin. "In fact, the Giants are willing to pay $50,000 for one of them."

"Which one?" asked MacPhail, suddenly cautious.

"I'd like a guy you probably don't even know you've got," continued Ottie. "He's a kid named Berra."

MacPhail thought a while and slowly shook his head. "Not Berra," he said. "He's not for sale."

Perhaps there are some fans who promptly would think that the astute MacPhail merely was showing the prescience which bespeaks genius. Stop jumping at conclusions, please. Laughing Larry was telling the story on himself in Havana a couple of seasons ago.

"If the truth must be told," he chuckled, "I'd never even heard of Berra, but I figured that if he was worth fifty grand to Ottie he must be worth fifty grand to me. That's why I turned him down. But one day I'm in my office and the girl comes in to announce that Mr. Berra is outside to see me. 'Berra?' I say to myself. 'That must be the kid Ottie was trying to buy.' So I tell her to show him in.

He's my lucky fella. I allus win whenever I have him in the lineup.

—Casey Stengel

"So I waited for my first look at the prize package which was worth $50,000. The instant I saw him my heart sank and I wondered why I had been so foolish as to refuse to sell him. In bustled a stocky little guy in a sailor suit. He had no neck and his muscles were virtually busting the buttons off his uniform. He was one of the most unprepossessing fellows I ever set eyes on in my life. And the sailor suit accentuated every defect." MacPhail sighed and continued, "Since then, though, I've never regretted the move."

Berra is just as unique a character as he looked the first time that Laughing

Larry saw him. His honest moniker is Lawrence. But everyone calls him Yogi—as well as other less kindly names. However, Yogi is one of nature's noblemen, the honest heart that beats beneath that rough exterior. No ballplayer is ridden as cruelly or as unmercifully as he. But he accepts it all with a homely grin. He hasn't the quick wit to retort in kind. So he laughs it all off and has won the deep affection—sometimes it almost amounts to admiration—of his teammates and the rival players.

The perfect description of him was supplied by Milton Gross, who called him "The Kid Ring Lardner Missed." Yogi is a pure throwback to the ballplayers of the "You Know Me, Al" Lardner era. The writers go around from day to day asking each other: "Did you hear the latest Berraism?" They even have coined a word, Berraism, to set him aside in a separate category.

Perhaps the most wonderful one he ever pulled came the night in St. Louis, Yogi's hometown, when the fans set aside a separate night in his honor. They showered him with gifts, and then came one of the most terrifying moments in Berra's life. He had to approach a microphone and make a speech. They hauled him up there. Yogi shuffled up in a daze. Even his vocal chords were paralyzed. He spoke only one sentence. It was a classic.

> *Talking to Yogi Berra about baseball is like talking to Homer about the gods.*
> —A. Bartlett Giamatti

"I want to thank all you fans," he blurted, "for making this night *necessary*."

Yogi hits a tremendously long ball—when he hits it. But he has a pernicious habit of swinging at bad balls. No one tried harder to cure him of that habit than Bucky Harris. One day Bucky sent him in as a pinch hitter, but first he cautioned him.

"Don't swing at a bad ball, Yogi," he warned. "Wait for it to be in there. When you get up to the plate think. Think, Yogi, think."

Yogi struck out and came back to the bench muttering.

Harris bent an ear in his direction and started laughing uproariously. What Yogi was saying was this: "How can a guy be expected to think and bat at the same time?"

> *So I'm ugly. So what? I never saw anyone hit with his face.*
> —Yogi Berra

Bucky was deeply enamored with him. Before the 1947 World Series someone asked him if Yogi would be nervous. He howled. "Yogi nervous?" he chortled. "He has about as much emotion as a fire hydrant."

But Berra was nervous. The Dodgers stole everything from him except his chest protector.

"A guy doesn't get into a World Series every day," he protested. "After all, I'm human, ain't I?" No one ever had thought of it before.

However, Berra is a whale of a ballplayer. The Yanks won a pennant with him as a catcher, even though his stubby fingers were so short that he had to paint them so that the pitchers could distinguish the signs. Then he was an outfielder last season (a presentable one, too), and now he is a catcher again.

Bill Dickey, one of the greatest catchers of all time, is busy instructing him in the rudiments of the position. As Yogi describes it: "Dickey is learning me all his experience."

Yogi grew up across the street from Joe Garagiola of the Cardinals in St. Louis. In the sandlots Berra was a pitcher, Garagiola a catcher. They have been inseparable companions ever since, with Joe serving as Yogi's best man at his wedding two months ago. Perhaps we had better move in the Card catcher as spokesman for the defense. "Yogi married a beautiful and wonderful girl," he said with earnest simplicity. "But she couldn't have married a nicer, more gentle, or finer man in this world than Yogi Berra." The defense rests.

Bob Costas on Mickey Mantle ....

The Mick

Few Americans under 40, and none under 30, ever saw Mickey Mantle play ball. Their lasting image of him will be that of an imperfect icon courageously baring his soul in an indelible interview with NBC's gifted Bob Costas in March 1994. Mantle died 17 months later. Costas delivered the eulogy in Dallas to family, teammates, and more than a thousand mourners—a farewell joined here in progress:

. . . I guess I'm here, not so much to speak for myself as to simply represent the millions of baseball-loving kids who grew up in the '50s and '60s and for whom Mickey Mantle was baseball.

And more than that, he was a presence in our lives—a fragile hero to whom we had an emotional attachment so strong and lasting that it defied logic. Mickey often said he didn't understand it, this enduring connection and affection—the men now in their 40s and 50s, otherwise perfectly sensible, who went dry in the mouth and stammered like schoolboys in the presence of Mickey Mantle.

Maybe Mick was uncomfortable with it, not just because of his basic shyness, but because he was always too honest to regard himself as some kind of deity.

But that was never really the point. In a very different time than today, the first baseball commissioner, Kenesaw Mountain Landis, said every boy builds a shrine to some baseball hero, and before that shrine, a candle always burns.

For a huge portion of my generation, Mickey Mantle was that baseball hero. And for reasons that no statistics, no dry recitation of facts can possibly capture, he was the most compelling baseball hero of our lifetime. And he was our symbol of baseball at a time when the game meant something to us that perhaps it no longer does.

Mickey Mantle had those dual qualities so seldom seen, exuding dynamism and excitement but at the same time touching your heart—flawed, wounded. We knew there was something poignant about Mickey Mantle before we knew what poignant meant.

We didn't just root for him, we felt for him.

Long before many of us ever cracked a serious book, we knew something about mythology as we watched Mickey Mantle run out a home run through the lengthening shadows of a late Sunday afternoon at Yankee Stadium.

There was greatness in him, but vulnerability too.

He was our guy. When he was hot, we felt great. When he slumped or got hurt, we sagged a bit too. We tried to crease our caps like him; kneel in an imaginary on-deck circle like him; run like him—heads down, elbows up. . . .

It's been said that the truth is never pure and rarely simple.

Mickey Mantle was too humble and honest to believe that the whole truth about him could be found on a Wheaties box or a baseball card. But the emotional truths of childhood have a power that transcends objective fact. They stay with us through all the years, withstanding the ambivalence that so often accompanies the experiences of adults.

That's why we can still recall the immediate tingle in that instant of recognition when a Mickey Mantle popped up in a pack of Topps bubble gum cards—a treasure lodged between an Eli Grba and a Pumpsie Green.

That's why we smile today, recalling those October afternoons when we'd sneak a transistor radio into school to follow Mickey and the Yankees in the World Series. . . .

My phone's been ringing the past few weeks as Mickey fought for his life. I've

Reprinted with the permission of Bob Costas, condensed from his eulogy.

heard from people I hadn't seen or talked to in years—guys I played stickball with, even some guys who took Willie's side in those endless Mantle-Mays arguments. They're grown up now. They have their families. They're not even necessarily big baseball fans anymore. But they *felt* something hearing about Mickey, and they figured I did too.

In the last year, Mickey Mantle, always so hard on himself, finally came to accept and appreciate that distinction between a role model and a hero. The first he often was not, the second he always will be.

> *Hitting the ball was easy. Running around the bases was the tough part.*
> —Mickey Mantle

And in the end, people got it. And Mickey Mantle got from America something other than misplaced and mindless celebrity worship. He got something far more meaningful. He got love—love for what he had been; love for what he made us feel; love for the humanity and sweetness that was *always* there mixed in with the flaws, and all the pain that wracked his body and his soul.

We wanted to tell him that it was OK, that what he had been was enough. We hoped he felt that Mutt Mantle would have understood and that Merlyn and the boys loved him.

And then in the end, something remarkable happened—the way it does for champions. Mickey Mantle rallied. His heart took over, and he had some innings as fine as any in 1956 or with his buddy, Roger, in 1961.

But this time, he did it in the harsh and trying summer of '95. And what he did was stunning. The sheer grace of that ninth inning—the humility, the sense of humor, the total absence of self-pity, the simple eloquence and honesty of his pleas to others to take heed of his mistakes.

All of America watched in admiration. His doctors said he was, in many ways, the most remarkable patient they'd ever seen. His bravery, so stark and real, that even those used to seeing people in dire circumstances were moved by his example.

Because of that example, organ donations are up dramatically all across America. A cautionary tale has been honestly told and perhaps will affect some lives for the better.

And our last memories of Mickey Mantle are as heroic as the first.

None of us, Mickey included, would want to be held to account for every moment of our lives. But how many of us could say that our best moments were as magnificent as his?

This is the cartoon from this morning's *Dallas Morning News*. . . . There's a figure here, St. Peter I take it to be, with his arm around Mickey, that broad back and the number 7. He's holding his book of admissions. He says, "Kid, that was the most courageous ninth inning I've ever seen."

It brings to mind a story Mickey liked to tell on himself, and maybe some of you have heard it. He pictured himself at the pearly gates, met by St. Peter, who shook his head and said, "Mick, we checked the record. We know some of what went on. Sorry, we can't let you in. But before you go, God wants to know if you'd sign these six dozen baseballs."

Well, there were days when Mickey Mantle was so darn good that we kids would bet that even God would want his autograph. . . .

I just hope God has a place for him where he can run again. Where he can play practical jokes on his teammates and smile that boyish smile, 'cause God knows, no one's perfect. And God knows there's something special about heroes.

So long, Mick. And thanks.

George Vecsey on Billy Martin . . . .

Billy the Kid

He was a clutch player and, when focused, one of baseball's better managers during a total of six tours in his beloved pinstripes. All ended in exile, but it always seemed appropriate that he wore the number 1, which eventually was retired in his honor.

Billy Martin was baseball's bad boy, frequently in the middle of a swirling hurricane of controversy and turmoil.

He had a split personality. One side could be a volatile troublemaker: hostile, mean-spirited, petty, vengeful, profane, a bully and a brawler. He also could be congenial, considerate, forthright, loyal, and even charming.

One thing Billy the Kid was not was dull. Never. That was one constant. So was his vulnerable nature, troubled and self-destructive; he was his own worst enemy.

"He had his faults," longtime New York sportswriter Leonard Koppett wrote after Martin's death in 1989, "but he was ultimately more victim than culprit."

It was not surprising that Martin died relatively young and violently—ironically on Christmas, a day of peace and renewal.

The next day, New York Times *columnist George Vecsey sat at his keyboard and wrote deftly and poignantly (as usual) of the contradiction that was Alfred Manuel Martin.*

This was in the summer of 1961, while Billy Martin was serving what would turn out to be the first of many sentences of exile from New York. He was finishing up as a player with the Minnesota Twins, wearing a gray road uniform in his old ball park, Yankee Stadium.

"I always thought I'd come back to the Yankees," he said that day. "I loved being a Yankee. I loved playing for the old man with the ball in his sock."

He was talking about Casey Stengel, his mentor. The reference to the ball in his sock was to a gnarled lump of bone on Casey's ankle, the souvenir of being hit by a taxi in Boston many years earlier. The old man part was a tacit acceptance of Casey as the only male authority figure Martin would every permit himself in his career.

Most of the time it was rage, rage against opponents, rage against critics, rage against strangers he had just met in a drinking place, rage against George Weiss for sending him away from New York, even rage against Stengel for not protecting him, and later rage against George Steinbrenner for alternately coddling and cashiering him.

It is a matter of record that Billy Martin's father left when Martin was a year old.

He always said he wanted to die a Yankee.
—Bucky Dent

The headlines added up. Just going through an inch-thick manila folder labeled "Martin, Billy," one finds headlines that say: Billy Needs Help. How Healthy Is Billy Martin? Police: Martin Lied. Martin Jokes After Brawl. The capital letters seem to tick like time bombs.

On Monday the 61-year-old Martin died as a passenger in a crash in a pickup truck being driven by a friend who has been charged with driving while intoxicated. Oh, yes, and Martin was not wearing a seat belt.

There were seldom safety nets around Billy Martin. To be around him was to constantly suck in one's breath, fearful that he might start something.

A few years ago, there was an elevator ride that seemed to take an hour. Martin was enclosed with a columnist from another paper who had needled him in print.

The major vessels in his neck pulsing, Martin now taunted the columnist while all the other passengers watched the elevator needle dip slowly from press level to street level. The target did not shoot from the lip. He knew this was a man who had once coldcocked a pitcher named Jim Brewer on the mound, and had fought with athletes and civilians for whatever the provocation. When the elevator reached street level, we breathed again.

That was life around Billy Martin, who always seem to resent the injustice of 1957 when Weiss banished him for being the most expendable Yankee in the fight at the night club called the Copacabana. Martin was not a fool. He occasionally admitted that his life had been spent trying to get back to square one.

The fresh little bastard. How I love him.
—Casey Stengel

He was not without charm and intelligence. During the years he was a scout and a coach in Minnesota, he could smoke his pipe and sip a drink in a stadium press room and talk baseball or military history with equal knowledge. He would say, quite evenly, that he never expected to receive a managing job because of his reputation.

Martin would eventually manage parts of 16 seasons, winning five division titles, two pennants and one World Series. He was one of the best managers ever to pace the dugout. He could steal a game as explicitly as he could teach Rod Carew and Rickey Henderson how to steal home.

The day I become a good loser, I'm quitting baseball.
—Billy Martin

But his hours were chaotic away from the games. One weekend in 1981, during the exile in his hometown of Oakland, Martin made an 11 A.M. appointment with a New York columnist, before a Sunday doubleheader. By game time, Martin had still not showed. Clete Boyer made out the lineup card and muttered something about Martin being caught in traffic. Later, it was learned Martin had driven the brother of his girlfriend to the airport.

And yet fans still wonder why he was exiled, time and again. The Yankees had a 40–28 record when Martin was sacked in 1988, but the pitching staff was chewed up because of erratic managing, and the clubhouse was in chaos. The spasms of responsibility were growing shorter and shorter.

Some fans blame Steinbrenner for undermining Martin in each of the five regimes. The real problem was rehiring a man of whom Steinbrenner has said, "I know Billy has a problem, but you can't do anything about it." So who really had the problem?

The problem, bluntly, was drinking to hide the pain. Managing made it worse. Steinbrenner said he had finally learned the lesson, that Martin was now to be a valued friend and counsel, never a manager. He kept Martin away from the stadium, and the man looked healthy, as he usually did when he wasn't managing. Earlier this year, Martin's mother, a feisty and stabilizing presence, passed away. On Monday, her son died, violently. Rarely is the sentiment "Rest in Peace" more applicable.

Dave Anderson on Reggie Jackson ....

Mr. October

When he took up a bat in a big game, Reggie Jackson had a flair for the dramatic unsurpassed by any Yankee except Babe Ruth.

Jackson relished the spotlight. In the clutch, he yearned to be in the batter's box. That's where Yankee fans wanted him, too, their chants of Reg-gie, Reg-gie, Reg-gie! *rocking the Stadium. And Jackson would respond, thrilling them even when he struck out mightily, just as the Babe had their grandparents.*

Reggie's signature overswing was matched only by a massive ego. "His ego, like his swing, took your breath away," Roger Angell wrote in the New Yorker—*also noting a dedication in one of Jackson's autobiographies to "my biggest supporter of all . . . God."*

Of all Jackson's great moments, the crowning achievement was his three homers on three pitches in the 1977 World Series finale, an achievement that forever stamped Reggie Jackson as "Mr. October."

Pulitzer Prize–winner Dave Anderson was there and took New York Times *readers into the locker room afterward.*

Nearly three hours after his three home runs had won the World Series for the Yankees and redemption for himself, Reggie Jackson, like almost everyone else, appeared in awe of what he had accomplished. "There's a part of me I don't know," he was saying softly at his locker. "There's the ballplayer in me who responds to all that pressure. I'm not sure I hit three home runs but the ballplayer in me did."

And above all his complex parts, Reggie Jackson is a ballplayer. When he took nearly $3 million from the Yankees, most people scoffed that he wasn't worth it. He even agreed he wasn't worth it. But he's worth it now. No matter what he does from now on is a bonus. What he did Tuesday night put Reggie Jackson up there with Muhammad Ali winning back the heavyweight title in Zaire, up there with Joe Namath and the Jets winning Super Bowl III, up there with Tom Seaver and the Mets winning the 1969 World Series, but to appreciate how the "part of me I don't know" put Reggie Jackson up there, it is necessary to remember how another part, his sensitive ego, put Reggie Jackson down so that he might ascend.

"I got to get dressed," he was saying now. "I told some people I'd meet them at Seventy-sixth and Third."

> He'd give you the shirt off his back. Of course, he'd call a press conference to announce it.
> —Catfish Hunter, teammate

In that same East Side area, at a sidewalk table at Arthur's Court in July, he was sipping white wine and saying, "I'm still the straw that stirs the drink. Not Munson, not nobody else on this club."

All the other Yankees had dressed and departed Tuesday night except for Thurman Munson, who was on his way out now.

"Hey, coon," called the catcher, grinning. "Nice goin', coon."

Reggie Jackson laughed and hurried over and hugged the captain.

"I'm goin' down to that party here in the ballpark," Thurman Munson said, grinning again. "Just white people but they'll let you in. Come on down."

"I'll be there," Reggie Jackson said. "Wait for me."

"I got to make myself go to the ballpark," he said in July. "I don't want to go."

"You'll change your mind," somebody told him.

"I don't want to change. I've closed my mind. Remember the thing in Boston," he said, referring to his dugout confrontation with Billy Martin in Fenway Park. "The next day we had a meeting in Gabe Paul's suite and Billy challenged me. He stood over me and said,

'I'll make you fight me, boy.' But there was no way I was going to fight him. I'm two hundred and fifteen pounds, he's almost fifty years old. I win the fight, but I lose."

In the manager's office half an hour earlier, Reggie Jackson and Billy Martin had finished a TV interview together when the slugger overheard the manager talking about punching somebody.

> *There isn't enough mustard in the whole world to cover that hot dog.*
> —Darold Knowles, opposing pitcher

"Anybody fights you, Skip," Reggie Jackson said, "he's got to fight both of us."

"And anybody who fights you," Billy Martin said, "got to fight the both of us."

"We can't win this way," he said in July. "The Red Sox can hammer. We got nobody who can hammer except me. I should be batting third or cleanup, not sixth. I always hit third or cleanup."

"How far did that last homer go?" the cleanup hitter asked.

"I figured it to be about four hundred and fifty feet," a sportswriter said.

"Make it four hundred and seventy-five, it sounds better," the cleanup hitter said, laughing. "I hit that one off a knuckler, the first two off fastballs. The general consensus on how to pitch to me is hard and in.

"On the first one, I knew [Burt] Hooton would pitch me there, but I had an inkling I'd hit one. As soon as they brought in [Elias] Sosa, I got on the phone to Stick [Gene Michael, the Yankee scout] upstairs and asked him about Sosa, be-

> *Fans don't boo nobodies.*
> —Reggie Jackson

cause Sosa popped me up with a fastball in spring training. Stick told me he throws hard stuff—fastball, slider, good curve. I hit another fastball. I hit the second one even better than I hit the third, the one off [Charlie] Hough's knuckler. Brooks Robinson taught me how to hit a knuckler. Just time the ball."

"Hough said that knuckler didn't move much," somebody said.

"It didn't," Reggie Jackson said, "until I got hold of it."

"I should've signed with the Padres," he said in July. "I'd be happy there. Or with the Dodgers."

"Did you hear," Reggie Jackson was told, "what Steve Garvey said—that after your third homer, he applauded in his glove?"

"What a great player Steve Garvey is, what a great man," Reggie Jackson said. "He's the best all-around human being in baseball. My one regret about not playing with the Dodgers is not being around Steve Garvey, but I got a security blanket here, Fran Healy [the Yankees' bullpen catcher]. Before the game he told me I was swinging the bat good."

"I don't need baseball," he said in July, "I'm a businessman. That means as much to me as baseball. I don't need cheers."

"When you hit the third one," a visitor was saying now, "George Steinbrenner had tears in his eyes."

"Get my bat, Nick, please," Reggie Jackson told a clubhouse man. "I started using this bat Saturday after I broke one in Friday's game. Look at the wide grain. The older the tree, the wider the grain, the harder the wood. I think I'll give this bat to George, he'll appreciate it."

"George," somebody said, "ought to put a marker out there halfway up the bleachers where that third homer landed."

"That'd be something. Babe Ruth, Lou Gehrig, Joe DiMaggio, Mickey Mantle and Reggie Jackson. Somehow I don't fit."

Thomas Boswell on Don Mattingly ....

"Donnie Baseball"

He was dubbed "Donnie Baseball" by the Twins' Kirby Puckett. A throwback to an earlier diamond era, Don Mattingly exuded a passion for the game undiminished by a bitter distinction: He was the only Yankee great never to play in a World Series. Nonetheless, Mattingly was anything but a loser—as baseball's Boswell, Tom, informed readers early on in his celebrated column in the Washington Post.

It's tough to win a batting title your first full season, follow that with a Most Valuable Player Award and still remain somewhat unknown. To do so while playing for the New York Yankees ought to be impossible. But then, Don Mattingly's a tough guy. Tough to know, tough to predict, tough to evaluate. Toughest to get out.

Most 24-year-olds would recall the winter night when they received the MVP plaque as one of glory. Mattingly says, "I don't remember much about it, except our son Taylor lost his pacifier and we were up all night with him. That'll bring you back to earth."

Just when you think you have the Don of the Bronx pegged as a phlegmatic stoic, he comes to a banquet after the Super Bowl wearing punk sunglasses and a headband with "Steinbrenner" on it. "Did it because Pete Rozelle was there," he says. That argument with George III over his new $1.37 million contract—close to a million-buck raise in a year—couldn't have anything to do with it?

If you guess along with Mattingly, you'll be the one who gets burned. That's the pitchers' book on the compact five-foot-eleven, 185-pound first baseman—little good it does them. . . .

Ask what pitcher and what pitch are hardest for him and he pulls a perfect Mattingly. "John Candelaria. Haven't got a clue to him yet. And high fastballs on the inner half. Write that down." True, Candy Man owns him. But the pitch Mattingly hits best is the fastball in his wheelhouse. If he tells this white lie often enough, some dumb pitcher somewhere is going to believe it.

Nobody has figured out Mattingly yet, that's true. Two years ago, he was just a prospect who'd hit .283 as a rookie but with no power (4 homers in 279 at bats). Then the Yankees hoped he might be a perennial .300 hitter. Now that estimate's radically revised.

"Who do you compare him to?" says former Yankees star Roy White. "Compare him to anybody you want. Stan Musial, Ted Williams, Joe DiMaggio."

For historical reference, the Musial analogy works. Left-handed hitter. Eccentric closed and coiled stance. Sprays the ball. Tons of doubles. Not too many walks. Hard to strike out. . . .

The difference between Stan the Man and Mattingly is that, at similar ages, Mattingly is undeniably ahead. Sure, Musial averaged 209 hits, 79 extra-base hits and a .352 average in his first two big years. But Mattingly has been in that stratospheric range, too, for the last two years: 209 hits, 77 extra-base hits and a .333 average.

Plus, Mattingly hit 23, then 35 homers and drove in 110, then 145 runs. When Musial was 23, 24 years old, he was a comparative stripling, hitting about a dozen homers and driving in 80 or 90 runs. . . .

The last Yankee to drive in more runs than Mattingly was DiMaggio in '48. Nobody in the American League has led the majors in doubles back to back since Tris Speaker. Special players do special things. Immediately.

Another Mattingly distinction is a Gold Glove. "Day game after a night game, Mattingly's still out there taking his hundred ground balls," says coach Jeff Torborg. When Mattingly botched one last July, it ended a streak of 1,371 plays without error. Try that playing catch.

Sometimes he sneaks out to shortstop during the . . . Yankees' batting practice to take grounders and fire clean, accurate, right-handed pegs to first base. Usually nobody notices him because he's built like a shortstop, moves nimbly like a shortstop and wears an inconspicuous infielder's number—23.

Because Don Mattingly throws left-handed, very few people realize he is out at shortstop—learning, polishing, plotting, dreaming. . . .

Encircling Mattingly in comparisons only highlights his glow. He's Wade Boggs with power. Eddie Murray with hustle. George Brett but younger and in a home run park with Rickey Henderson on base and Dave Winfield on deck.

None of these parallels charm Mattingly much. "I appreciate it . . . but it doesn't help me on the field. So let it go. I'd compare myself more to Bill Buckner. He's consistent, hard-nosed, good in the clutch. I love the way he plays. . . ."

Why Buckner? When Mattingly was a teenager in Evansville, Indiana, Buckner was hitting .300 for the Cubs, the Midwest's darlings. Why the passion for consistency—the neither-rain-nor-sleet approach to performance? Well, (okay, laugh) his dad was a postman.

> I love playing the game. That's what I'm here for.
> —Don Mattingly

Mattingly's the easiest sort of player to praise—the quiet gamer with eye black like a punt returner and low, unstylish stirrups below his pants. . . .

"What I do on the field, that's me," says Mattingly. "If I take care of my game, everything falls in place. The game is the thing you can control. Especially in New York, where so much stuff can clutter you up."

Like Ron Guidry, who clings to the bayou, Mattingly is defiantly anti-style. Just by existing, Mattingly is a standing critique of Henderson. A Yankees prankster has tacked a sign above Henderson's locker . . . : "O Lord, help my words to be gracious and tender today, for tomorrow I may have to eat them." No one ever snipes at Mattingly.

As they say, no brag, just fact. "I feel like I earned the MVP. I've worked hard," says Mattingly, "I kind of expected it. If I didn't win it last year, I didn't know when I ever would. I don't know if I'll ever do that again."

Don't bet against him. He adjusts. Mattingly abandoned a written "book" on pitchers. "Too monotonous . . . Actually, they're all tough, or none of them are. I get everybody or everybody gets me." What he really discovered was that a chronicle on catchers helped more. When lefties troubled him, he found a way to trouble them back: though he hits 60 points less against them, he slugs more homers in far fewer at bats.

If Mattingly has a flaw, it's probably ineradicable because it runs to the core. Will he, like Buckner, be too tough to stay in one piece? Last spring, arthroscopic knee surgery. This spring, a bone bruise to the thumb that has him benched. So far, not much. But will it add up?

Come back in 2001 for that. Then we'll really see how well he stacks up with Musial. For now, let Scott McGregor speak for a multitude of pained pitchers who have gotten to know Don Mattingly far too well, far too quickly. "How does he strike me?" says the Oriole. "All over the place. He just waxes you and goes home."

The Record

ALL-TIME ROSTER *(Alphabetical Order)*

MANAGERS (31)

Yogi Berra 1964, 1984–85
Frank Chance 1913–14
Hal Chase 1910–11
Bucky Dent 1989–90
Bill Dickey 1946
Bill Donovan 1915–17
Kid Elberfeld 1908
Art Fletcher 1929
Dallas Green 1989
Clark Griffith 1903–08
Bucky Harris 1947–48
Ralph Houk 1961–63, 1966–73
Dick Howser 1980
Miller Huggins 1918–29
Johnny Keane 1965–66
Clyde King 1982

Bob Lemon 1978–79, 1981–82
Billy Martin 1975–78, 1979, 1983, 1985, 1988
Joe McCarthy 1931–46
Stump Merrill 1990–91
Gene Michael 1981, 1982
Johnny Neun 1946
Roger Peckinpaugh 1914
Lou Piniella 1986–87, 1988
Bob Shawkey 1930
Buck Showalter 1992–95
George Stallings 1909–10
Casey Stengel 1949–60
Joe Torre 1996
Bill Virdon 1974–75
Harry Wolverton 1912

COACHES (89)

Joe Altobelli 1981–82, 1986
Loren Babe 1967
Vern Benson 1965–66
*Yogi Berra 1963, 1976–83
Clete Boyer 1988, 1992–94
Cloyd Boyer 1975, 1977
Jimmy Burke 1931–33
Brian Butterfield 1994–95
Jose Cardenal 1996
Chris Chambliss 1988, 1996
Tony Cloninger 1992–96
Earle Combs 1936–44
Mark Connor 1984–85, 1986–87, 1990–93
Billy Connors 1989–90, 1994–95
Pat Corrales 1989
Red Corriden 1947–48
Bobby Cox 1977
Frank Crosetti 1947–68
Cot Deal 1965
*Bill Dickey 1949–57, 1960
Rick Down 1993–95
Chuck Dressen 1947–48
Lee Elia 1989
Sammy Ellis 1982, 1983–84, 1986
Darrell Evans 1990
Mike Ferraro 1979–82, 1987–88, 1989–91
*Art Fletcher 1927–45
Whitey Ford 1964, 1968, 1974–75
Art Fowler 1977–79, 1983, 1988
Charlie Fox 1989
Jim Gleason 1964
Jim Hegan 1960–73, 1979–80
Tommy Henrich 1951
Marc Hill 1991

Doug Holmquist 1984, 1985
Willie Horton 1985
*Ralph Houk 1954, 1958–60
Elston Howard 1969–79
Frank Howard 1989, 1991–92
*Dick Howser 1969–78
Charlie Keller 1957, 1959
*Clyde King 1978, 1981, 1988
Charlie Lau 1979–81
*Bob Lemon 1976
Dale Long 1963
Ed Lopat 1960
Mickey Mantle 1970
Harry Mathews 1929
Fred Merkle 1925–26
*Stump Merrill 1985, 1986–87
Russ Meyer 1992
*Gene Michael 1976–77, 1978, 1984–86, 1988, 1989
George Mitterwald 1988
Bill Monbouquette 1985
Tom Morgan 1979
Wally Moses 1961–62, 1966
Ed Napoleon 1992–93
Graig Nettles 1991
*Johnny Neun 1944–46
Paddy O'Connor 1918–21
Charlie O'Leary 1921–30
Joe Pepitone 1982
Cy Perkins 1932–33
*Lou Piniella 1984–85
Willie Randolph 1994–96
Red Rolfe 1946
Frank Roth 1921–22
Johnny Sain 1961–63
Paul Schreiber 1942

Player/coach Yogi Berra, number 8, talks shop in the clubhouse with Bobby Richardson, 1963.

Johnny Schulte 1934–48
Joe Sewell 1934–35
*Bob Shawkey 1929
*Buck Showalter 1990–91
Joe Sparks 1990
John Stearns 1989
Mel Stottlemyre 1996
Champ Summers 1989–90
Jeff Torborg 1979–88
Earl Torgeson 1961

Jim Turner 1949–59, 1966–73
Mickey Vernon 1982
Jerry Walker 1981–82
Lee Walls 1983
Jay Ward 1987
Roy White 1983–84, 1986
Stan Williams 1980–81, 1982, 1987
Hooks Wiltse 1925
Mel Wright 1974–75
Don Zimmer 1983, 1986, 1996

*Also managed Yankees.

NOTE: Some coaches may be missed in early decades, when coaches were few and their listing in baseball records was often incomplete.

PLAYERS (1,210)

A (33)

Jim Abbott 1993–94
Harry Ables 1911
Spencer Adams 1926
Doc Adkins 1903
Steve Adkins 1990
Luis Aguayo 1988
Jack Aker 1969–72
Mike Aldrete 1996
Doyle Alexander 1976, 1982–83
Walt Alexander 1915–17
Bernie Allen 1972–73
Johnny Allen 1932–35
Neil Allen 1985, 1987–88
Sandy Alomar 1974–76
Felipe Alou 1971–73
Matty Alou 1973
Dell Alston 1977–78
Ruben Amaro 1966–68
John Anderson 1904–05
Rick Anderson 1979
Ivy Andrews 1931–32, 1937–38
Pete Appleton 1933
Angel Aragon 1914, 1916–17
Rugger Ardizola 1947
Mike Armstrong 1984–86
Brad Arnsberg 1986–87
Luis Arroyo 1960–63
Tucker Ashford 1981
Paul Assenmacher 1993
Joe Ausanio 1994–95
Jimmy Austin 1909–10
Martin Autry 1924
Oscar Azocar 1990

B (114)

Loren Babe 1952–53
Stan Bahnsen 1966, 1968–71
Bill Bailey 1911
Frank Baker 1916–19, 1921–22
Frank Baker 1970–71
Steve Balboni 1981–83, 1989–90
Neal Ball 1907–09
Scott Bankhead 1995
Steve Barber 1967–68
Jesse Barfield 1989–92
Cy Barger 1906–07
Ray Barker 1965–67
Frank Barnes 1930
Honey Barnes 1926
Ed Barney 1915
George Batten 1912
Hank Bauer 1948–59
Paddy Baumann 1915–17
Don Baylor 1983–85
Walter Beall 1924–27

Jim Beattie 1978–79
Rich Beck 1965
Zinn Beck 1918
Fred Beene 1972–74
Joe Beggs 1938
John Bell 1907
Zeke Bella 1957
Benny Bengough 1923–30
Juan Beniquez 1979
Lou Berberet 1954–55
Dave Bergman 1975, 1977
Juan Bernhardt 1976
Walter Bernhardt 1918
Dale Berra 1985–86
Yogi Berra 1946–63
Bill Bevens 1944–47
Monte Beville 1903–04
Harry Billiard 1908
Doug Bird 1980–81
Ewell Blackwell 1952–53
Rick Bladt 1975
Paul Blair 1977–80
Walter Blair 1907–11
Johnny Blanchard 1955, 1959–65
Gil Blanco 1965
Wade Blasingame 1972
Steve Blateric 1972
Gary Blaylock 1959
Curt Blefary 1970–71
Elmer Bliss 1903–04
Ron Blomberg 1969, 1971–76
Mike Blowers 1989–91
Eddie Bockman 1946
Ping Bodie 1918–21
Len Boehmer 1969, 1971
Brian Boehringer 1995–96
Wade Boggs 1993–96
Don Bollweg 1953
Bobby Bonds 1975
Ricky Bones 1996
Ernie Bonham 1940–46
Juan Bonilla 1985, 1987
Luke Boone 1913–16
Frenchy Bordagaray 1941
Rich Bordi 1985, 1987
Hank Borowy 1942–45
Babe Borton 1913
Daryl Boston 1994
Jim Bouton 1962–68
Clete Boyer 1959–66
Scott Bradley 1984–85
Neal Brady 1915, 1917
Ralph Branca 1954
Norm Branch 1941–42
Marshall Brant 1980
Garland Braxton 1925–26

Don Brennan 1933
Jim Brenneman 1965
Ken Brett 1976
Marv Breuer 1939–43
Billy Brewer 1996
Fritz Brickell 1958–59
Jim Brideweser 1951–53
Marshall Bridges 1962–63
Harry Bright 1963–64
Ed Brinkman 1975
Johnny Broaca 1934–37
Lew Brockett 1907, 1909, 1911
Jim Bronstad 1959
Tom Brookens 1989
Bob Brower 1989
Boardwalk Brown 1914–15
Bobby Brown 1946–52, 1954
Bobby Brown 1979–81
Curt Brown 1984
Hal Brown 1962
Jumbo Brown 1932–33, 1935–36
Billy Bryan 1966–67
Jess Buckles 1916
Jay Buhner 1987–88
Bill Burbach 1969–71
Lew Burdette 1950
Tim Burke 1992
George Burns 1928–29
Alex Burr 1914
Ray Burris 1979
Joe Bush 1922–24
Tom Buskey 1973–74
Ralph Buxton 1949
Joe Buzas 1945
Harry Byrd 1954
Sammy Byrd 1929–34
Tommy Byrne 1943, 1946–51, 1954–57
Marty Bystrom 1984–85

C (94)

Greg Cadaret 1989–92
Charlie Caldwell 1925
Ray Caldwell 1910–18
Johnny Callison 1972–73
Howie Camp 1917
Bert Campaneris 1983
Archie Campbell 1928
John Candelaria 1988–89
Mike Cantwell 1916
Andy Carey 1952–60
Roy Carlyle 1926
Duke Carmel 1965
Dick Carroll 1909
Ownie Carroll 1930
Tommy Carroll 1955–56
Chuck Cary 1989–91
Hugh Casey 1949
Roy Castleton 1907
Bill Castro 1981
Danny Cater 1970–71
Rick Cerone 1980–84, 1987, 1990
Bob Cerv 1951–56, 1960–62
Chris Chambliss 1974–79, 1988
Frank Chance 1913–14
Spud Chandler 1937–47
Les Channell 1910, 1914
Darrin Chapin 1991
Ben Chapman 1930–36
Mike Chartak 1940, 1942
Hal Chase 1905–13
Jack Chesbro 1903–09
Clay Christiansen 1984
Al Cicotte 1957

Allie Clark 1947
George Clark 1913
Jack Clark 1988
Horace Clarke 1965–74
Walter Clarkson 1904–07
Ken Clay 1977–79
Pat Clements 1987–88
Tex Clevenger 1961–62
Lu Clinton 1966–67
Al Closter 1971–72
Andy Coakley 1911
Jim Coates 1956, 1959–62
Jim Cockman 1905
Rich Coggins 1975–76
Rocky Colavito 1968
King Cole 1914–15
Curt Coleman 1912
Jerry Coleman 1949–57
Rip Coleman 1955–56
Bob Collins 1944
Dave Collins 1982
Joe Collins 1948–57
Orth Collins 1904
Pat Collins 1926–28
Rip Collins 1920–21
Frank Colman 1946–47
Lloyd Colson 1970
Earle Combs 1924–35
David Cone 1995–96
Tom Connelly 1920–21
Joe Connor 1905
Wid Conroy 1903–08
Andy Cook 1993
Doc Cook 1913–16
Dusty Cooke 1930–32
Johnny Cooney 1944
Phil Cooney 1905
Don Cooper 1985
Guy Cooper 1914
Dan Costello 1913
Henry Cotto 1985–87
Ensign Cottrell 1915
Clint Courtney 1951
Ernie Courtney 1903
Stan Coveleski 1928
Billy Cowan 1969
Joe Cowley 1984–85
Bobby Cox 1968–69
Casey Cox 1972–73
Birdie Cree 1908–15
Lou Criger 1910
Herb Crompton 1945
Frank Crosetti 1932–48
Jose Cruz 1988
Jack Cullen 1962, 1965–66
Roy Cullenbine 1942
Nick Cullop (LHP) 1916–17
Nick Cullop (OF) 1926
John Cumberland 1968–70
Jim Curry 1911
Fred Curtis 1905

D (56)

Babe Dahlgren 1937–40
Bud Daley 1961–64
Tom Daley 1914–15
Bert Daniels 1910–13
Bobby Davidson 1989
George Davis 1912
Kiddo Davis 1926
Lefty Davis 1903
Ron Davis 1978–81
Russ Davis 1994–95
Brian Dayett 1983–84

John Deering 1903
Jim Deidel 1974
Ivan DeJesus 1986
Frank Delahanty 1905–06, 1908
Bobby Del Greco 1957–58
Jim Delsing 1949–50
Joe DeMaestri 1960–61
Ray Demmitt 1909
Rick Dempsey 1973–76
Bucky Dent 1977–82
Claud Derrick 1913
Russ Derry 1944–45
Jim Deshaies 1984
Jimmie DeShong 1934–35
Orestes Destrade 1987
Charlie Devens 1932–34
Al DeVormer 1921–22
Bill Dickey 1928–43, 1946
Murry Dickson 1958
Joe DiMaggio 1936–42, 1946–51
Kerry Dineen 1975–76
Art Ditmar 1957–61
Sonny Dixon 1956
Pat Dobson 1973–75
Cozy Dolan 1911–12
Atley Donald 1938–45
Mike Donovan 1908
Wild Bill Donovan 1915–16
Brian Dorsett 1989–90
Richard Dotson 1988–89
Patsy Dougherty 1904–06
John Dowd 1912
Al Downing 1961–69
Brian Doyle 1978–80
Jack Doyle 1905
Slow Joe Doyle 1906–10
Doug Drabek 1986
Bill Drescher 1944–46
Karl Drews 1946–48
Monk Dubiel 1944–45
Joe Dugan 1922–28
Mariano Duncan 1996
Ryne Duren 1958–61
Leo Durocher 1925, 1928–29
Cedric Durst 1927–30

E (19)

Mike Easler 1986–87
Rawly Eastwick 1978
Doc Edwards 1965
Foster Edwards 1930
Robert Eenhoorn 1994–96
Dave Eiland 1988–91, 1995
Kid Elberfeld 1903–09
Gene Elliott 1911
Dock Ellis 1976–77
John Ellis 1969–72
Kevin Elster 1994–95
Red Embree 1948
Clyde Engle 1909–10
John Enright 1917
Roger Erickson 1982–83
Juan Espino 1982–83, 1985–86
Alvaro Espinoza 1988–91
Nick Etten 1943–46
Barry Evans 1982

F (37)

Charles Fallon 1905
Steve Farr 1991–93
Doc Farrell 1932–33
Alex Ferguson 1918, 1921, 1925
Frank Fernandez 1967–69
Tony Fernandez 1995–96

Mike Ferraro 1966, 1968
Wes Ferrell 1938–39
Tom Ferrick 1950–51
Chick Fewster 1917–22
Cecil Fielder 1996
Ed Figueroa 1976–80
Pete Filson 1987
Happy Finneran 1918
Mike Fischlin 1986
Brian Fisher 1985–86
Gus Fisher 1912
Ray Fisher 1910–17
Mike Fitzgerald 1911
Tim Foli 1984
Ray Fontenot 1983–84
Barry Foote 1981–82
Russ Ford 1909–13
Whitey Ford 1950, 1953–67
Eddie Foster 1910
Jack Fournier 1918
Andy Fox 1995–96
Ray Francis 1925
George Frazier 1981–83
Mark Freeman 1959
Ray French 1920
Lonny Frey 1947–48
Bob Friend 1966
John Frill 1910
Bill Fulton 1987
Dave Fultz 1903–05
Liz Funk 1929

G (58)

John Gabler 1959–60
Joe Gallagher 1939
Mike Gallego 1992–94
Oscar Gamble 1976, 1979–81
John Ganzel 1903–04
Mike Garbark 1944–45
Damaso Garcia 1978–79
Billy Gardner 1961–62
Earl Gardner 1908–12
Rob Gardner 1970–72
Ned Garvin 1904
Milt Gaston 1924
Mike Gazella 1923, 1926–28
Joe Gedeon 1916–17
Lou Gehrig 1923–39
Bob Geren 1988–91
Al Gettel 1945–46
Joe Giard 1927
Jake Gibbs 1962–71
Paul Gibson 1993–94, 1996
Sam Gibson 1930
Frank Gilhooley 1913–18
Joe Girardi 1996
Fred Glade 1908
Fran Gleich 1919–20
Joe Glenn 1932–33, 1935–38
Lefty Gomez 1930–42
Jesse Gonder 1960–61
Fernando Gonzalez 1974
Pedro Gonzalez 1963–65
Wilbur Good 1905
Dwight Gooden 1996
Art Goodwin 1905
Joe Gordon 1938–43, 1946
Tom Gorman 1952–54
Rich Gossage 1978–83, 1989
Dick Gossett 1913–14
Larry Gowell 1972
Johnny Grabowski 1927–29
Wayne Granger 1973
Ted Gray 1955

Eli Grba 1959–60
Willie Greene 1903
Ken Griffey 1982–86
Mike Griffin 1979–81
Clark Griffith 1903–07
Bob Grim 1954–58
Burleigh Grimes 1934
Oscar Grimes 1943–46
Lee Grissom 1940
Cecilio Guante 1987–88
Lee Guetteman 1988–92
Ron Guidry 1975–88
Brad Gulden 1979–80
Don Gullett 1977–80
Bill Gullickson 1987
Randy Gumpert 1946–48
Larry Gura 1974–75

H (97)

John Habyan 1990–93
Bump Hadley 1936–40
Kent Hadley 1960
Ed Hahn 1905–06
Noodles Hahn 1906
Hinkey Haines 1923
George Halas 1919
Bob Hale 1961
Jimmie Hall 1969
Mel Hall 1989–92
Roger Hambright 1971
Steve Hamilton 1963–70
Mike Handiboe 1911
Jim Hanley 1913
Truck Hannah 1918–20
Ron Hansen 1970–71
Joe Hanson 1913
Jim Hardin 1971
Bubbles Hargrave 1930
Harry Harper 1921
Toby Harrah 1984
Greg Harris 1994
Joe Harris 1914
Jim Hart 1973–74
Roy Hartzell 1911–16
Buddy Hassett 1942
Ron Hassey 1985–86
Andy Hawkins 1989–91
Chicken Hawks 1921
Charlie Hayes 1992, 1996
Fran Healy 1976–78
Mike Heath 1978
Neal Heaton 1993
Don Heffner 1934–37
Mike Hegan 1964, 1966–67, 1973–74
Fred Heimach 1928–29
Woodie Held 1954
Charlie Hemphill 1908–11
Rollie Hemsley 1942–44
Bill Henderson 1930
Rickey Henderson 1985–89
Harvey Hendrick 1923–24
Elrod Hendricks 1976–77
Tim Hendryx 1915–17
Tommy Henrich 1937–42, 1946–50
Billy Henry 1966
Leo Hernandez 1986
Xavier Hernandez 1994
Ed Herrmann 1975
Hugh High 1915–18
Oral Hildebrand 1939–40
Jesse Hill 1935
Shawn Hillegas 1992

Frank Hiller 1946, 1948–49
Mack Hillis 1924
Rich Hinton 1972
Sterling Hitchcock 1992–95
Myril Hoag 1931–32, 1934–38
Butch Hobson 1982
Red Hoff 1911–13
Danny Hoffman 1906–07
Solly Hofman 1916
Fred Hofmann 1919–25
Bill Hogg 1905–08
Bobby Hogue 1951–52
Ken Holcombe 1945
Bill Holden 1913–14
Al Holland 1986–87
Ken Holloway 1930
Fred Holmes 1903
Roger Holt 1980
Ken Holtzman 1976–78
Rick Honeycutt 1995
Don Hood 1979
Wally Hood 1949
Johnny Hopp 1950–52
Shags Horan 1924
Ralph Houk 1947–54
Elston Howard 1955–67
Matt Howard 1996
Steve Howe 1991–96
Harry Howell 1903
Jay Howell 1982–84
Dick Howser 1967–68
Waite Hoyt 1921–30
Rex Hudler 1984–85
Charles Hudson 1987–88
Keith Hughes 1987
Long Tom Hughes 1904
Tom Hughes 1906–07, 1909–10
John Hummel 1918
Mike Humphreys 1991–93
Ken Hunt 1959–60
Billy Hunter 1955–56
Catfish Hunter 1975–79
Mark Hutton 1993–94, 1996
Ham Hyatt 1918

J (34)

Fred Jacklitsch 1905
Grant Jackson 1976
Reggie Jackson 1977–81
Dion James 1992–93, 1995–96
Johnny James 1958, 1960–61
Stan Javier 1984
Domingo Jean 1993
Stan Jefferson 1989
Jackie Jensen 1950–52
Derek Jeter 1995–96
Elvio Jimenez 1964
Tommy John 1979–82, 1986–89
Alex Johnson 1974–75
Billy Johnson 1943, 1946–51
Cliff Johnson 1977–79
Darrell Johnson 1957–58
Deron Johnson 1960–61
Don Johnson 1947, 1950
Ernie Johnson 1923–25
Hank Johnson 1925–26, 1928–32
Jeff Johnson 1991–93
Johnny Johnson 1944
Ken Johnson 1969
Otis Johnson 1911
Roy Johnson 1936–37
Jay Johnstone 1978–79
Gary Jones 1970–71
Darryl Jones 1979

Jimmy Jones 1989–90
Ruppert Jones 1980
Sam Jones 1922–26
Tim Jordan 1903
Art Jorgens 1929–39
Mike Jurewicz 1965

K (46)

Jim Kaat 1979–80
Scott Kamieniecki 1991–96
Bob Kammeyer 1978–79
Frank Kane 1919
Bill Karlon 1930
Herb Karpel 1946
Benny Kauff 1912
Curt Kaufman 1982–83
Eddie Kearse 1942
Ray Keating 1912–16, 1918
Bob Keefe 1907
Willie Keeler 1903–09
Mike Kekich 1969–73
Charlie Keller 1939–43, 1945–49, 1952
Pat Kelly 1991–96
Roberto Kelly 1987–92
Steve Kemp 1983–84
John Kennedy 1967
Jerry Kenney 1967, 1969–72
Matt Keough 1983
Jimmy Key 1993–96
Steve Kiefer 1989
Dave Kingman 1977
Harry Kingman 1914
Fred Kipp 1960
Frank Kitson 1907
Ron Kittle 1986–87
Ted Kleinhans 1936
Red Kleinow 1904–10
Ed Klepfer 1911, 1913
Ron Klimkowski 1969–70, 1972
Steve Kline 1970–74
Mickey Klutts 1976–78
Bill Knickerbocker 1938–40
John Knight 1909–11, 1913
Mark Koenig 1925–30
Jim Konstanty 1954–56
Andy Kosco 1968
Steve Kraly 1953
Jack Kramer 1951
Ernie Krueger 1915
Dick Kryhoski 1949
Tony Kubek 1957–65
Johnny Kucks 1955–59
Bill Kunkel 1963
Bob Kuzava 1951–54

L (52)

Joe Lake 1908–09
Bill Lamar 1917–19
Hal Lanier 1972–73
Dave LaPoint 1989–90
Frank LaPorte 1905–10
Dave LaRoche 1981–83
Don Larsen 1955–59
Lyn Lary 1929–34
Marcus Lawton 1989
Gene Layden 1915
Tony Lazzeri 1926–37
Tim Leary 1990–92
Joe Lefebvre 1980
Al Leiter 1987–89
Mark Leiter 1990
Frank Leja 1954–55
Jack Lelivelt 1912–13

Eddie Leon 1975
Louis LeRoy 1905–06
Ed Levy 1942–44
Duffy Lewis 1919–20
Jim Lewis 1982
Terry Ley 1971
Jim Leyritz 1990–96
Paul Lindblad 1978
Johnny Lindell 1941–50
Phil Linz 1962–65
Bryan Little 1986
Jack Little 1912
Clem Llewellyn 1922
Graeme Lloyd 1996
Gene Locklear 1976–77
Sherm Lollar 1947–48
Tim Lollar 1980
Phil Lombardi 1985–87
Dale Long 1960, 1962–63
Herman Long 1903
Ed Lopat 1948–55
Art Lopez 1965
Hector Lopez 1959–66
Baldy Louden 1907
Slim Love 1916–18
Torey Lovullo 1991
Johnny Lucadello 1947
Joe Lucey 1920
Ray Luebbe 1925
Matt Luke 1996
Jerry Lumpe 1956–59
Scott Lusader 1991
Sparky Lyle 1972–78
Al Lyons 1944, 1946–47
Jim Lyttle 1969–71

M (135)

Duke Maas 1958–61
Kevin Maas 1990–93
Bob MacDonald 1995
Danny MacFayden 1932–34
Ray Mack 1947
Bunny Madden 1910
Elliot Maddox 1974–76
Dave Madison 1950
Lee Magee 1916–17
Sal Maglie 1957–58
Stubby Magner 1911
Jim Magnuson 1973
Fritz Maisel 1913–17
Hank Majeski 1946
Frank Makosky 1937
Pat Malone 1935–37
Pat Maloney 1912
Al Mamaux 1924
Rube Manning 1907–10
Mickey Mantle 1951–68
Josias Manzanillo 1995
Cliff Mapes 1948–51
Roger Maris 1960–66
Cliff Markle 1915–16, 1924
Jim Marquis 1925
Armando Marsans 1917–18
Cuddles Marshall 1946, 1948–49
Billy Martin 1950–53, 1955–57
Hersh Martin 1944–45
Jack Martin 1912
Tino Martinez 1996
Tippy Martinez 1974–76
Jim Mason 1974–76
Vic Mata 1984–85
Don Mattingly 1982–95
Carlos May 1976–77
Rudy May 1974–76, 1980–83

John Mayberry 1982
Carl Mays 1919–23
Lee Mazzilli 1982
Larry McCall 1977–78
Joe McCarthy 1905
Pat McCauley 1903
Larry McClure 1910
George McConnell 1909, 1912–13
Mike McCormick 1970
Lance McCullers 1989–90
Lindy McDaniel 1968–73
Mickey McDermott 1956
Danny McDevitt 1961
Dave McDonald 1969
Jim McDonald 1952–54
Gil McDougald 1951–60
Jack McDowell 1995
Sam McDowell 1973–74
Lou McEvoy 1930–31
Herm McFarland 1903
Andy McGaffigan 1981
Lynn McGlothen 1982
Bob McGraw 1917–20
Deacon McGuire 1904–07
Marty McHale 1913–15
Irish McIlveen 1908–09
Tim McIntosh 1996
Bill McKechnie 1913
Rich McKinney 1972
Frank McManus 1904
Norm McMillan 1922
Tommy McMillan 1912
Mike McNally 1921–24
Herb McQuaid 1926
George McQuinn 1947–48
Bobby Meacham 1983–88
Charlie Meara 1914
Jim Mecir 1996
George Medich 1972–75
Bob Melvin 1994
Ramiro Mendoza 1996
Fred Merkle 1925–26
Andy Messersmith 1978
Tom Metcalf 1963
Bud Metheny 1943–46
Hensley Meulens 1989–93
Bob Meusel 1920–29
Bob Meyer 1964
Gene Michael 1968–74
Ezra Midkiff 1912–13
Pete Mikkelsen 1964–65
Larry Milbourne 1981–82, 1983
Sam Militello 1992–93
Bill Miller 1952–54
Elmer Miller 1915–18, 1921–22
John Miller 1966
Alan Mills 1990–91
Buster Mills 1940
Mike Milosevich 1944–45
Paul Mirabella 1979
Willie Miranda 1953–54
Bobby Mitchell 1970
Fred Mitchell 1910
Johnny Mitchell 1921–22
Johnny Mize 1949–53
Kevin Mmahat 1989
George Mogridge 1915–20
Dale Mohorcic 1988–89
Fenton Mole 1949
Bill Monbouquette 1967–68
Ed Monroe 1917–18
Zack Monroe 1958–59
John Montefusco 1983–86

Rich Monteleone 1990–93
Archie Moore 1964–65
Earl Moore 1907
Wilcy Moore 1927–29, 1932–33
Ray Morehart 1927
Omar Moreno 1983–85
Mike Morgan 1982
Tom Morgan 1951–52, 1954–56
George Moriarty 1906–08
Jeff Moronko 1987
Hal Morris 1988–89
Ross Moschitto 1965, 1967
Gerry Moses 1973
Terry Mulholland 1994
Charlie Mullen 1914–16
Jerry Mumphrey 1981–83
Bob Muncrief 1951
Bobby Munoz 1993
Thurman Munson 1969–79
Bobby Murcer 1965–66, 1969–74, 1979–83
Johnny Murphy 1932, 1934–43, 1946
Rob Murphy 1994
Dale Murray 1983–85
George Murray 1922
Larry Murray 1974–76

N (22)

Jerry Narron 1979
Bots Nekola 1929
Gene Nelson 1981
Jeff Nelson 1996
Luke Nelson 1919
Graig Nettles 1973–83
Tex Neuer 1907
Ernie Nevel 1950–51
Floyd Newkirk 1934
Bobo Newsom 1947
Doc Newton 1905–09
Gus Niarhos 1946, 1948–50
Joe Niekro 1985–87
Phil Niekro 1984–85
Jerry Nielsen 1992
Scott Nielsen 1986, 1988–89
Harry Niles 1908
Otis Nixon 1983
Matt Nokes 1990–94
Irv Noren 1952–56
Don Nottebart 1969
Les Nunamaker 1914–17

O (21)

Johnny Oates 1980–81
Mike O'Berry 1984
Andy O'Connor 1908
Jack O'Connor 1903
Paddy O'Connor 1918
Heinie Odom 1925
Lefty O'Doul 1919–20, 1922
Rowland Office 1983
Bob Ojeda 1994
Rube Oldring 1905, 1916
Bob Oliver 1975
Nate Oliver 1969
Paul O'Neill 1993–96
Steve O'Neill 1925
Queenie O'Rourke 1908
Al Orth 1904–09
Champ Osteen 1904
Joe Ostrowski 1950–52
Bill Otis 1912
Stubby Overmire 1951
Spike Owen 1993

P (50)

John Pacella 1982
Del Paddock 1912
Dave Pagan 1973–76
Joe Page 1944–50
Mike Pagliarulo 1984–89
Donn Pall 1994
Clay Parker 1989–90
Ben Paschal 1924–29
Dan Pasqua 1985–87
Gil Patterson 1977
Jeff Patterson 1995
Mike Patterson 1981–82
Dave Pavlas 1995–96
Monte Pearson 1936–40
Roger Peckinpaugh 1913–21
Steve Peek 1941
Hipolito Pena 1988
Herb Pennock 1923–33
Joe Pepitone 1962–69
Marty Perez 1977
Melido Perez 1992–95
Pascual Perez 1990–91
Cecil Perkins 1967
Cy Perkins 1931
Gaylord Perry 1980
Fritz Peterson 1966–74
Andy Pettitte 1995–96
Ken Phelps 1988–89
Eddie Phillips 1932
Jack Phillips 1947–49
Cy Pieh 1913–15
Bill Piercy 1917, 1921
Duane Pillette 1949–50
Lou Piniella 1974–84
George Pipgras 1923–24, 1927–33
Wally Pipp 1915–25
Jim Pisoni 1959–60
Eric Plunk 1989–91
Dale Polley 1996
Luis Polonia 1989–90, 1994–95
Bob Porterfield 1948–51
Jorge Posada 1995–96
Jack Powell 1904–05
Jake Powell 1936–40
Mike Powers 1905
Del Pratt 1918–20
Gerry Priddy 1941–42
Johnnie Priest 1911–12
Alfonso Pulido 1986
Ambrose Puttman 1903–05

Q (4)

Mel Queen 1942, 1944, 1946–47
Ed Quick 1903
Jack Quinn 1909–12, 1919–21
Jamie Quirk 1989

R (68)

Tim Raines 1996
Dave Rajsich 1978
Bobby Ramos 1982
Domingo Ramos 1978
John Ramos 1991
Pedro Ramos 1964–66
Lenny Randle 1979
Willie Randolph 1976–88
Vic Raschi 1946–53
Dennis Rasmussen 1984–87
Shane Rawley 1982–84
Jeff Reardon 1994
Jack Reed 1961–63
Jimmy Reese 1930–31
Hal Reniff 1961–67

Bill Renna 1953
Tony Rensa 1933
Roger Repoz 1964–66
Rick Reuschel 1981–82
Dave Revering 1981–82
Allie Reynolds 1947–54
Bill Reynolds 1913–14
Rick Rhoden 1987–88
Gordon Rhodes 1929–32
Harry Rice 1930
Bobby Richardson 1955–66
Nolan Richardson 1935
Branch Rickey 1907
Dave Righetti 1979, 1981–90
Jose Rijo 1984
Mariano Rivera 1995–96
Ruben Rivera 1995–96
Mickey Rivers 1976–79
Phil Rizzuto 1941–42, 1946–56
Roxy Roach 1910–11
Dale Roberts 1967
Andre Robertson 1981–85
Gene Robertson 1928–29
Aaron Robinson 1943, 1945–47
Bill Robinson 1967–69
Bruce Robinson 1979–80
Eddie Robinson 1954–56
Hank Robinson 1918
Jeff Robinson 1990
Aurelio Rodriguez 1980–81
Carlos Rodriguez 1991
Edwin Rodriguez 1982
Ellie Rodriguez 1968
Gary Roenicke 1986
Oscar Roettger 1923–24
Jay Rogers 1914
Kenny Rogers 1996
Tom Rogers 1921
Jim Roland 1972
Red Rolfe 1931, 1934–42
Buddy Rosar 1939–42
Larry Rosenthal 1944
Steve Roser 1944–46
Braggo Roth 1921
Jerry Royster 1987
Muddy Ruel 1917–20
Dutch Ruether 1926–27
Red Ruffing 1930–42, 1945–46
Allen Russell 1915–19
Marius Russo 1939–43, 1946
Babe Ruth 1920–34
Blondy Ryan 1935
Rosy Ryan 1928

S (125)

Johnny Sain 1951–55
Lenn Sakata 1987
Mark Salas 1987
Jack Saltzgaver 1932, 1934–37
Billy Sample 1985
Celerino Sanchez 1972–73
Deion Sanders 1989–90
Roy Sanders 1918
Scott Sanderson 1991–92
Charlie Sands 1967
Fred Sanford 1949–51
Rafael Santana 1988
Don Savage 1944–45
Rick Sawyer 1974–75
Steve Sax 1989–91
Ray Scarborough 1952–53
Germany Schaefer 1916
Harry Schaeffer 1952
Roy Schalk 1932

Art Schallock 1951–55
Wally Schang 1921–25
Bob Schmidt 1965
Butch Schmidt 1909
Johnny Schmitz 1952–53
Pete Schneider 1919
Dick Schofield 1966
Paul Schreiber 1945
Art Schult 1953
Al Schulz 1912–14
Don Schulze 1989
Bill Schwartz 1914
Pius Schwert 1914–15
Everett Scott 1922–25
George Scott 1979
Rodney Scott 1982
Rod Scurry 1985–86
Ken Sears 1943
Bob Seeds 1936
Kal Segrist 1952
George Selkirk 1934–42
Ted Sepkowski 1947
Hank Severeid 1926
Joe Sewell 1931–33
Howard Shanks 1925
Billy Shantz 1960
Bobby Shantz 1957–60
Bob Shawkey 1915–27
Spec Shea 1947–49, 1951
Al Shealy 1928
George Shears 1912
Tom Sheehan 1921
Rollie Sheldon 1961–62, 1964–65
Skeeter Shelton 1915
Roy Sherid 1929–31
Pat Sheridan 1991
Dennis Sherrill 1978, 1980
Ben Shields 1924–25
Steve Shields 1988
Bob Shirley 1983–87
Urban Shocker 1916–17, 1925–28
Tom Shopay 1967, 1969
Ernie Shore 1919–20
Bill Short 1960
Norm Siebern 1956, 1958–59
Ruben Sierra 1995–96
Charlie Silvera 1948–56
Dave Silvestri 1992–95
Ken Silvestri 1941, 1946–47
Hack Simmons 1912
Dick Simpson 1969
Harry Simpson 1957–58
Duke Sims 1973–74
Bill Skiff 1926
Camp Skinner 1922
Joel Skinner 1986–88
Lou Skizas 1956
Bill Skowron 1954–62
Roger Slagle 1979
Don Slaught 1988–89
Enos Slaughter 1954–59
Roy Smalley 1982–84
Walt Smallwood 1917, 1919
Charlie Smith 1967–68
Elmer Smith 1922–23
Joe Smith 1913
Keith Smith 1984–85
Klondike Smith 1912
Lee Smith 1993
Harry Smythe 1934
J. T. Snow 1992
Eric Soderholm 1980
Luis Sojo 1996
Tony Solaita 1968

Steve Souchock 1946, 1948
Jim Spencer 1978–81
Charlie Spikes 1972
Russ Springer 1992
Bill Stafford 1960–65
Jake Stahl 1908
Roy Staiger 1979
Tuck Stainback 1942–45
Gerry Staley 1955–56
Charley Stanceu 1941
Andy Stankiewicz 1992–93
Fred Stanley 1973–80
Mike Stanley 1992–95
Dick Starr 1947–48
Dave Stegman 1982
Dutch Sterrett 1912–13
Bud Stewart 1948
Lee Stine 1938
Snuffy Stirnweiss 1943–50
Tim Stoddard 1986–88
Mel Stottlemyre 1964–74
Hal Stowe 1960
Darryl Strawberry 1995–96
Gabby Street 1912
Marlin Stuart 1954
Bill Stumpf 1912–13
Tom Sturdivant 1955–59
Johnny Sturm 1941
Bill Sudakis 1974
Steve Sundra 1936, 1938–40
Jeffy Sweeney 1908–15
Ron Swoboda 1971–73

T (42)

Fred Talbot 1966–69
Vito Tamulis 1934–35
Frank Tanana 1993
Jesse Tannehill 1903
Danny Tartabull 1992–95
Wade Taylor 1991
Zack Taylor 1934
Frank Tepedino 1967, 1969–72
Walt Terrell 1989
Ralph Terry 1956–57, 1959–64
Dick Tettelbach 1955
Bob Tewksbury 1986–87
Ira Thomas 1906–07
Lee Thomas 1961
Myles Thomas 1926–29
Stan Thomas 1977
Gary Thomasson 1978
Homer Thompson 1912
Tommy Thompson 1912
Jack Thoney 1904
Hank Thormahlen 1917–20
Marv Throneberry 1955, 1958–59
Luis Tiant 1979–80
Dick Tidrow 1974–79
Bobby Tiefenauer 1965
Eddie Tiemeyer 1909
Ray Tift 1907
Bob Tillman 1967
Thad Tillotson 1967–68
Dan Tipple 1915
Wayne Tolleson 1986–90
Earl Torgeson 1961
Rusty Torres 1971–72
Mike Torrez 1977
Cesar Tovar 1976
Tom Tresh 1961–69
Gus Triandos 1953–64
Steve Trout 1987
Virgil Trucks 1958
Frank Truesdale 1914

Bob Turley 1955–62
Jim Turner 1942–45

U (4)

George Uhle 1933–34
Tom Underwood 1980–81
Bob Unglaub 1904
Cecil Upshaw 1974

V (12)

Elmer Valo 1960
Russ Van Atta 1933–35
Dazzy Vance 1915, 1918
Joe Vance 1937–38
Bobby Vaughn 1909
Hippo Vaughn 1908, 1910–12
Bobby Veach 1925
Randy Velarde 1987–1995
Otto Velez 1973–76
Joe Verbanic 1967–68, 1970
Frank Verdi 1953
Sammy Vick 1917–20

W (76)

Jake Wade 1946
Dick Wakefield 1950
Jim Walewander 1990
Curt Walker 1919
Dixie Walker 1931, 1933–36

Mike Wallace 1974–75
Jimmy Walsh 1914
Joe Walsh 1910–11
Roxy Walters 1915–18
Danny Walton 1971
Paul Waner 1911–45
Jack Wanner 1909
Pee Wee Wanninger 1925
Aaron Ward 1917–26
Gary Ward 1987–89
Joe Ward 1909
Pete Ward 1970
Jack Warhop 1908–15
George Washburn 1941
Claudell Washington 1986–88, 1990
Gary Waslewski 1970–71
Bob Watson 1980–82
Roy Weatherly 1943, 1946
David Weathers 1996
Jim Weaver 1931
Dave Wehrmeister 1981
Lefty Weinert 1931
Ed Wells 1929–32
Butch Wensloff 1943, 1947
Julie Wera 1927, 1929
Bill Werber 1930, 1933
Dennis Werth 1979–81
John Wetteland 1995–96

Stefan Wever 1982
Steve Whitaker 1960–68
Roy White 1965–79
Wally Whitehurst 1996
George Whiteman 1913
Terry Whitfield 1974–76
Ed Whitson 1985–86
Kemp Wicker 1936–38
Al Wickland 1919
Bob Wickman 1992–96
Bob Wiesler 1951, 1954–55
Bill Wight 1946–47
Ted Wilborn 1980
Ed Wilkinson 1911
Bernie Williams 1991–96
Bob Williams 1911–13
Gerald Williams 1992–96
Harry Williams 1913, 1914
Jimmy Williams 1903–07
Stan Williams 1963–64
Walt Williams 1974–75
Archie Wilson 1951–52
Pete Wilson 1908–09
Ted Wilson 1956
Snake Wiltse 1903
Gordie Windhorn 1959
Dave Winfield 1981–90
Mickey Witek 1949
Mike Witt 1990–93

Whitey Witt 1922–25
Bill Wolfe 1903–04
Harry Wolter 1910–13
Harry Wolverton 1912
Dooley Womack 1966–68
Gene Woodling 1949–54
Ron Woods 1969–71
Dick Woodson 1974
Hank Workman 1950
Ken Wright 1974
Yats Wuestling 1930
John Wyatt 1968
Butch Wynegar 1982–86
Jimmy Wynn 1977

Y (4)

Joe Yeager 1905–06
Jim York 1976
Curt Young 1992
Ralph Young 1913

Z (7)

Tom Zachary 1928–30
Jack Zalusky 1903
George Zeber 1977–78
Rollie Zeider 1913
Guy Zinn 1911–12
Bill Zuber 1943–46
Paul Zuvella 1986–87

Gary Cooper was Lou Gehrig in The Pride of the Yankees. *The film was generally acclaimed and received 11 Oscar nominations. But it was cliché-ridden and at times factually incorrect; for instance it shows Gehrig's iron-man streak ending with Lou being replaced during a game. At 41, Cooper was too old to play young Gehrig scenes and was stiff as an athlete. But a clever production trick reversed the film's negative to transform the righthanded Cooper into the lefthanded Gehrig, which meant the NY on his Yankee cap and jersey had to be embroidered backward, and the actor ran the bases clockwise.*

Three generations of Yankee third basemen—(from left) Red Rolfe, Joe Dugan, and Frank "Home Run" Baker—meet the hot-corner custodian of the '50s, Andy Carey.

William Bendix played the title role in the disastrous Babe Ruth Story, *possibly the worst sports movie ever made. "It is an obscenity," said Babe's widow Claire.*

Bendix, a native New Yorker who is said to have been a Yankee bat boy in his youth, agreed, calling it the "worst picture I ever made," and adding, "I remember going to the previews in Los Angeles. In the early part of the picture, when I'm discovered in an orphanage, the scene is full of sixteen- and seventeen-year-old kids. Do I have a kid playing me? No. I have to do it with makeup. And I'm thirty-eight years old at the time. The audience laughed. I would have laughed, too, but I felt too bad."

So did the Babe. Cancer-stricken and heavily medicated, the Bambino left his sickbed to attend the Times Square premiere and stumbled out long before the end. He was whisked back to Manhattan hospital, where he died 21 days later.

POSITION LEADERS YEAR BY YEAR *(Determined by number of games played at that position)*

Year	Pitcher (starts)	Pitcher (games)	Catcher	First Baseman	Second Baseman
1903	Jack Chesbro, 36	Jack Chesbro, 40	Monte Beville, 75	John Ganzel, 129	Jimmy Williams, 132
1904	Jack Chesbro, 51	Jack Chesbro, 55	Deacon McGuire, 97	John Ganzel, 118	Jimmy Williams, 146
1905	Jack Chesbro, 38	Jack Chesbro, 41	Red Kleinow, 83	Hal Chase, 122	Jimmy Williams, 129
1906	Jack Chesbro, 42	Jack Chesbro, 49	Red Kleinow, 95	Hal Chase, 150	Jimmy Williams, 139
1907	Al Orth, 33	Al Orth, 36	Red Kleinow, 86	Hal Chase, 121	Jimmy Williams, 139
1908	Jack Chesbro, 31	Jack Chesbro, 45	Red Kleinow, 89	Hal Chase, 98	Harry Niles, 85
1909	Joe Lake, 26	Jack Warhop, 36	Red Kleinow, 77	Hal Chase, 118	Frank LaPorte, 83
1910	Russ Ford, 33	Jack Warhop, 37	Ed Sweeney, 78	Hal Chase, 130	Frank LaPorte, 79
1911	Russ Ford, 33	Ray Caldwell, 41	Walter Blair, 84	Hal Chase, 124	Earl Gardner, 101
1912	Russ Ford, 35	Jack Warhop, 39	Ed Sweeney, 108	Hal Chase, 121	Hack Simmons, 88
1913	Ray Fisher, 31	Ray Fisher, 43	Ed Sweeney, 112	John Knight, 50	Roy Hartzell, 81
1914	Ray Fisher, 26	Jack Warhop, 37	Ed Sweeney, 78	Charlie Mullen, 93	Luke Boone, 90
1915	Ray Caldwell, 35	Ray Caldwell, 36	Les Nunamaker, 77	Wally Pipp, 134	Luke Boone, 115
1916	Bob Shawkey, 27	Bob Shawkey, 53	Les Nunamaker, 79	Wally Pipp, 148	Joe Gedeon, 122
1917	Ray Caldwell, 29	Slim Love, 33*	Les Nunamaker, 91*	Wally Pipp, 155	Fritz Maisel, 100
1918	Slim Love, 29	George Mogridge, 45*	Truck Hannah, 88*	Wally Pipp, 91	Del Pratt, 126
1919	Jack Quinn, 31	Bob Shawkey, 41	Muddy Ruel, 81	Wally Pipp, 138	Del Pratt, 140
1920	Carl Mays, 37	Carl Mays, 45	Muddy Ruel, 80	Wally Pipp, 153	Del Pratt, 154
1921	Carl Mays, 38	Carl Mays, 49	Wally Schang, 132	Wally Pipp, 153	Aaron Ward, 123
1922	Bob Shawkey, 33	Sam Jones, 45	Wally Schang, 119	Wally Pipp, 152	Aaron Ward, 152
1923	Bob Shawkey, 31	Sam Jones, 39	Wally Schang, 81	Wally Pipp, 144	Aaron Ward, 152
1924	Herb Pennock, 34	Waite Hoyt, 46	Wally Schang, 106	Wally Pipp, 153	Aaron Ward, 120
1925	Herb Pennock, 31 Sam Jones, 31	Herb Pennock, 47	Benny Bengough, 94	Lou Gehrig, 114	Aaron Ward, 113
1926	Urban Shocker, 33 Herb Pennock, 33	Urban Shocker, 41	Pat Collins, 100	Lou Gehrig, 155	Tony Lazzeri, 149
1927	Waite Hoyt, 32	Wilcy Moore, 50*	Pat Collins, 89	Lou Gehrig, 155	Tony Lazzeri, 113
1928	George Pipgras, 38	George Pipgras, 46	Johnny Grabowski, 75	Lou Gehrig, 154	Tony Lazzeri, 110
1929	George Pipgras, 33	Wilcy Moore, 41*	Bill Dickey, 127*	Lou Gehrig, 154	Tony Lazzeri, 147
1930	George Pipgras, 30	George Pipgras, 44 Hank Johnson, 44*	Bill Dickey, 101	Lou Gehrig, 153	Tony Lazzeri, 77
1931	Red Ruffing, 30	Lefty Gomez, 40 Hank Johnson, 40	Bill Dickey, 125	Lou Gehrig, 154	Tony Lazzeri, 90
1932	Lefty Gomez, 31	Lefty Gomez, 37	Bill Dickey, 108	Lou Gehrig, 155	Tony Lazzeri, 133
1933	Lefty Gomez, 30	Lefty Gomez, 35 Red Ruffing, 35 Wilcy Moore, 35*	Bill Dickey, 127	Lou Gehrig, 152	Tony Lazzeri, 138
1934	Lefty Gomez, 33	Johnny Murphy, 40†	Bill Dickey, 104	Lou Gehrig, 153	Tony Lazzeri, 92
1935	Lefty Gomez, 30	Johnny Murphy, 40*	Bill Dickey, 118	Lou Gehrig, 149	Tony Lazzeri, 118
1936	Red Ruffing, 33	Johnny Broaca, 37	Bill Dickey, 107	Lou Gehrig, 155	Tony Lazzeri, 148
1937	Lefty Gomez, 34	Johnny Murphy, 39*	Bill Dickey, 137	Lou Gehrig, 157	Tony Lazzeri, 125
1938	Lefty Gomez, 32	Lefty Gomez, 32 Johnny Murphy, 32*	Bill Dickey, 126	Lou Gehrig, 157	Joe Gordon, 126
1939	Red Ruffing, 28	Johnny Murphy, 38*	Bill Dickey, 126	Babe Dahlgren, 144	Joe Gordon, 151
1940	Red Ruffing, 30	Johnny Murphy, 35*	Bill Dickey, 102	Babe Dahlgren, 155	Joe Gordon, 155
1941	Marius Russo, 27	Johnny Murphy, 35*	Bill Dickey, 104	Johnny Sturm, 124	Joe Gordon, 131
1942	Ernie Bonham, 27	Johnny Murphy, 31*	Bill Dickey, 80	Buddy Hassett, 132	Joe Gordon, 147
1943	Spud Chandler, 30	Johnny Murphy, 37*	Bill Dickey, 71	Nick Etten, 154	Joe Gordon, 152
1944	Hank Borowy, 30	Hank Borowy, 35 Jim Turner, 35*	Mike Garbark, 85	Nick Etten, 154	Snuffy Stirnweiss, 154
1945	Bill Bevens, 25	Jim Turner, 30*	Mike Garbark, 59	Nick Etten, 152	Snuffy Stirnweiss, 152
1946	Spud Chandler, 32	Spud Chandler, 34	Aaron Robinson, 95	Nick Etten, 84	Joe Gordon, 108
1947	Allie Reynolds, 30	Joe Page, 56*	Aaron Robinson, 74	George McQuinn, 142	Snuffy Stirnweiss, 148
1948	Ed Lopat, 31 Vic Raschi, 31 Allie Reynolds, 31	Joe Page, 55*	Gus Niarhos, 82	George McQuinn, 90	Snuffy Stirnweiss, 141
1949	Vic Raschi, 37	Joe Page, 60*	Yogi Berra, 109	Tommy Henrich, 52	Jerry Coleman, 122
1950	Ed Lopat, 32 Vic Raschi, 32	Joe Page, 37*	Yogi Berra, 148	Johnny Mize, 72	Jerry Coleman, 152
1951	Vic Raschi, 34	Allie Reynolds, 40	Yogi Berra, 141	Johnny Mize, 93	Jerry Coleman, 102
1952	Vic Raschi, 31	Allie Reynolds, 35 Johnny Sain, 35*	Yogi Berra, 140	Joe Collins, 119	Billy Martin, 107
1953	Whitey Ford, 30	Allie Reynolds, 41*	Yogi Berra, 133	Joe Collins, 113	Billy Martin, 146
1954	Whitey Ford, 28	Johnny Sain, 45*	Yogi Berra, 149	Joe Collins, 117	Gil McDougald, 92
1955	Bob Turley, 34	Jim Konstanty, 45*	Yogi Berra, 145	Bill Skowron, 74	Gil McDougald, 126
1956	Johnny Kucks, 31	Tom Morgan, 41*	Yogi Berra, 135	Bill Skowron, 120	Billy Martin, 105
1957	Tom Sturdivant, 28	Art Ditmar, 46* Bob Grim, 46*	Yogi Berra, 121	Bill Skowron, 115	Bobby Richardson, 93

Majority or all in relief.
†*Half in starts, half in relief.*

Shortstop	Third Baseman	Outfielder	Outfielder	Outfielder	Designated Hitter
Kid Elberfeld, 90	Wid Conroy, 123	Willie Keeler, 128	Herm McFarland, 103	Lefty Davis, 102	
Kid Elberfeld, 122	Wid Conroy, 110	Willie Keeler, 142	John Anderson, 112	Patsy Dougherty, 106	
Kid Elberfeld, 108	Joe Yeager, 90	Willie Keeler, 139	Dave Fultz, 122	Patsy Dougherty, 108	
Kid Elberfeld, 98	Frank LaPorte, 114	Willie Keeler, 152	Danny Hoffman, 98	Frank Delahanty, 92	
Kid Elberfeld, 118	George Moriarty, 91	Danny Hoffman, 135	Willie Keeler, 107	Wid Conroy, 100	
Neal Ball, 130	Wid Conroy, 119	Charlie Hemphill, 142	Willie Keeler, 88	Jake Stahl, 67	
John Knight, 78	Jimmy Austin, 111	Clyde Engle, 134	Ray Demmitt, 109	Willie Keeler, 95	
John Knight, 79	Jimmy Austin, 133	Birdie Cree, 134	Harry Wolter, 130	Charlie Hemphill, 94	
John Knight, 82	Roy Hartzell, 124	Birdie Cree, 137	Bert Daniels, 120	Harry Wolter, 113	
Jack Martin, 64	Roy Hartzell, 56	Bert Daniels, 131	Guy Zinn, 106	Roy Hartzell, 55	
Roger Peckinpaugh, 93	Ezra Midkiff, 76	Birdie Cree, 144	Harry Wolter, 121	Bert Daniels, 87	
Roger Peckinpaugh, 157	Fritz Maisel, 148	Roy Hartzell, 128	Doc Cook, 126	Birdie Cree, 76	
Roger Peckinpaugh, 142	Fritz Maisel, 134	Doc Cook, 131	Hugh High, 117	Roy Hartzell, 107	
Roger Peckinpaugh, 146	Frank Baker, 96	Lee Magee, 128	Hugh High, 109	Frank Gilhooley, 57	
Roger Peckinpaugh, 148	Frank Baker, 146	Elmer Miller, 112	Tim Hendryx, 107	Hugh High, 100	
Roger Peckinpaugh, 122	Frank Baker, 126	Frank Gilhooley, 111	Ping Bodie, 90	Elmer Miller, 62	
Roger Peckinpaugh, 121	Frank Baker, 141	Duffy Lewis, 141	Ping Bodie, 134	Sammy Vick, 100	
Roger Peckinpaugh, 137	Aaron Ward, 114	Babe Ruth, 139	Ping Bodie, 129	Duffy Lewis, 99	
Roger Peckinpaugh, 149	Frank Baker, 83	Babe Ruth, 152	Bob Meusel, 147	Elmer Miller, 56	
Everett Scott, 154	Frank Baker, 60 / Joe Dugan, 60	Whitey Witt, 138	Rob Meusel, 121	Babe Ruth, 110	
Everett Scott, 152	Joe Dugan, 146	Babe Ruth, 148	Whitey Witt, 144	Bob Meusel, 121	
Everett Scott, 153	Joe Dugan, 148	Babe Ruth, 152	Whitey Witt, 143	Bob Meusel, 143	
Pee Wee Wanninger, 111	Joe Dugan, 96	Earle Combs, 150	Bob Meusel, 131	Babe Ruth, 98	
Mark Koenig, 141	Joe Dugan, 122	Babe Ruth, 149	Earle Combs, 145	Bob Meusel, 107	
Mark Koenig, 122	Joe Dugan, 111	Earle Combs, 152	Babe Ruth, 151	Bob Meusel, 131	
Mark Koenig, 125	Joe Dugan, 91	Babe Ruth, 154	Earle Combs, 149	Bob Meusel, 131	
Leo Durocher, 93	Gene Robertson, 77	Earle Combs, 141	Babe Ruth, 133	Bob Meusel, 96	
Lyn Lary, 113	Ben Chapman, 91	Babe Ruth, 144	Earle Combs, 135	Harry Rice, 87	
Lyn Lary, 155	Joe Sewell, 121	Babe Ruth, 142	Ben Chapman, 137	Earle Combs, 129	
Frank Crosetti, 83	Joe Sewell, 122	Ben Chapman, 149	Earle Combs, 138	Babe Ruth, 127	
Frank Crosetti, 133	Joe Sewell, 131	Ben Chapman, 147	Babe Ruth, 132	Earle Combs, 104	
Frank Crosetti, 119	Jack Saltzgaver, 84	Ben Chapman, 149	Babe Ruth, 111	Myril Hoag, 86	
Frank Crosetti, 87	Red Rolfe, 136	Ben Chapman, 138	George Selkirk, 127	Jesse Hill, 94	
Frank Crosetti, 151	Red Rolfe, 133	Joe DiMaggio, 138	George Selkirk, 135	Jake Powell, 84	
Frank Crosetti, 147	Red Rolfe, 154	Joe DiMaggio, 150	Myril Hoag, 99	Jake Powell, 94	
Frank Crosetti, 157	Red Rolfe, 151	Joe DiMaggio, 145	Tommy Henrich, 130	George Selkirk, 95	
Frank Crosetti, 152	Red Rolfe, 152	George Selkirk, 124	Joe DiMaggio, 117	Charlie Keller, 105	
Frank Crosetti, 145	Red Rolfe, 138	Charlie Keller, 136	Joe DiMaggio, 130	George Selkirk, 111	
Phil Rizzuto, 128	Red Rolfe, 134	Tommy Henrich, 139	Joe DiMaggio, 139	Charlie Keller, 137	
Phil Rizzuto, 144	Frank Crosetti, 62	Joe DiMaggio, 154	Charlie Keller, 152	Tommy Henrich, 119	
Frank Crosetti, 90	Billy Johnson, 155	Charlie Keller, 141	Johnny Lindell, 122	Bud Metheny, 91	
Mike Milosevich, 91	Oscar Grimes, 97	Johnny Lindell, 149	Bud Metheny, 132	Hersh Martin, 80	
Frank Crosetti, 126	Oscar Grimes, 141	Bud Metheny, 128	Hersh Martin, 102	Tuck Stainback, 83	
Phil Rizzuto, 125	Snuffy Stirnweiss, 79	Charlie Keller, 149	Joe DiMaggio, 131	Tommy Henrich, 111	
Phil Rizzuto, 151	Billy Johnson, 132	Joe DiMaggio, 139	Tommy Henrich, 132	Johnny Lindell, 118	
Phil Rizzuto, 128	Billy Johnson, 118	Joe DiMaggio, 152	Tommy Henrich, 102	Johnny Lindell, 79	
Phil Rizzuto, 152	Bobby Brown, 86	Cliff Mapes, 108	Gene Woodling, 98	Hank Bauer, 95	
Phil Rizzuto, 155	Billy Johnson, 100	Joe DiMaggio, 137	Gene Woodling, 118	Hank Bauer, 110	
Phil Rizzuto, 144	Bobby Brown, 90	Gene Woodling, 116	Joe DiMaggio, 113	Hank Bauer, 107	
Phil Rizzuto, 152	Gil McDougald, 117	Mickey Mantle, 141	Hank Bauer, 139	Gene Woodling, 118	
Phil Rizzuto, 133	Gil McDougald, 136	Hank Bauer, 126	Mickey Mantle, 121	Gene Woodling, 119	
Phil Rizzuto, 126	Andy Carey, 120	Mickey Mantle, 144	Irv Noren, 116	Hank Bauer, 108	
Billy Hunter, 98	Andy Carey, 135	Mickey Mantle, 145	Hank Bauer, 133	Irv Noren, 126	
Gil McDougald, 92	Andy Carey, 131	Hank Bauer, 146	Mickey Mantle, 144	Elston Howard, 65	
Gil McDougald, 121	Andy Carey, 81	Mickey Mantle, 139	Hank Bauer, 135	Elston Howard, 71	

POSITION LEADERS YEAR BY YEAR *(Determined by number of games played at that position)*

Year	Pitcher (starts)	Pitcher (games)	Catcher	First Baseman	Second Baseman
1958	Bob Turley, 31	Ryne Duren, 44*	Yogi Berra, 88	Bill Skowron, 118	Gil McDougald, 115
1959	Whitey Ford, 29	Ryne Duren, 41*	Yogi Berra, 116	Bill Skowron, 72	Bobby Richardson, 109
1960	Whitey Ford, 29	Bobby Shantz, 42*	Elston Howard, 91	Bill Skowron, 142	Bobby Richardson, 141
		Ryne Duren, 42*			
1961	Whitey Ford, 39	Luis Arroyo, 65*	Elston Howard, 111	Bill Skowron, 149	Bobby Richardson, 161
1962	Ralph Terry, 39	Marshall Bridges, 52*	Elston Howard, 129	Bill Skowron, 135	Bobby Richardson, 161
1963	Whitey Ford, 37	Hal Reniff, 48*	Elston Howard, 132	Joe Pepitone, 143	Bobby Richardson, 150
	Ralph Terry, 37				
1964	Jim Bouton, 37	Pete Mikkelsen, 50*	Elston Howard, 146	Joe Pepitone, 155	Bobby Richardson, 157
1965	Mel Stottlemyre, 37	Pedro Ramos, 65*	Elston Howard, 95	Joe Pepitone, 115	Bobby Richardson, 158
1966	Mel Stottlemyre, 35	Hal Reniff, 56*	Elston Howard, 100	Joe Pepitone, 119	Bobby Richardson, 147
1967	Mel Stottlemyre, 36	Dooley Womack, 65*	Jake Gibbs, 99	Mickey Mantle, 131	Horace Clarke, 140
1968	Mel Stottlemyre, 36	Dooley Womack, 45*	Jake Gibbs, 121	Mickey Mantle, 131	Horace Clarke, 139
1969	Mel Stottlemyre, 39	Lindy McDaniel, 51*	Jake Gibbs, 66	Joe Pepitone, 132	Horace Clarke, 156
1970	Mel Stottlemyre, 37	Lindy McDaniel, 62*	Thurman Munson, 125	Danny Cater, 131	Horace Clarke, 157
	Fritz Peterson, 37				
1971	Mel Stottlemyre, 35	Lindy McDaniel, 44*	Thurman Munson, 117	Danny Cater, 78	Horace Clarke, 156
	Fritz Peterson, 35				
1972	Mel Stottlemyre, 36	Sparky Lyle, 59*	Thurman Munson, 132	Ron Blomberg, 95	Horace Clarke, 143
				Felipe Alou, 95	
1973	Mel Stottlemyre, 38	Sparky Lyle, 51 *	Thurman Munson, 142	Felipe Alou, 67	Horace Clarke, 147
1974	Pat Dobson, 39	Sparky Lyle, 66*	Thurman Munson, 137	Chris Chambliss, 106	Sandy Alomar, 76
1975	Catfish Hunter, 39	Sparky Lyle, 49*	Thurman Munson, 130	Chris Chambliss, 147	Sandy Alomar, 150
1976	Catfish Hunter, 36	Sparky Lyle, 64*	Thurman Munson, 121	Chris Chambliss, 155	Willie Randolph, 124
1977	Ed Figueroa, 32	Sparky Lyle, 72*	Thurman Munson, 136	Chris Chambliss, 157	Willie Randolph, 147
1978	Ed Figueroa, 35	Rich Gossage, 63*	Thurman Munson, 125	Chris Chambliss, 155	Willie Randolph, 134
	Ron Guidry, 35				
1979	Tommy John, 36	Ron Davis, 44*	Thurman Munson, 88	Chris Chambliss, 134	Willie Randolph, 153
1980	Tommy John, 36	Rich Gossage, 64*	Rick Cerone, 147	Bob Watson, 104	Willie Randolph, 138
1981	Rudy May, 22	Ron Davis, 43*	Rick Cerone, 69	Bob Watson, 50	Willie Randolph, 93
1982	Ron Guidry, 33	George Frazier, 63	Rick Cerone, 89	Bob Watson, 50	Willie Randolph, 143
1983	Shane Rawley, 33	George Frazier, 61	Butch Wynegar, 94	Ken Griffey, Jr., 100	Willie Randolph, 104
1984	Phil Niekro, 31	Dave Righetti, 64	Butch Wynegar, 126	Don Mattingly, 133	Willie Randolph, 142
1985	Ron Guidry, 33	Dave Righetti, 74	Butch Wynegar, 96	Don Mattingly, 159	Willie Randolph, 143
	Phil Niekro, 33				
1986	Dennis Rasmussen, 31	Dave Righetti, 74	Butch Wynegar, 57	Don Mattingly, 160	Willie Randolph, 139
1987	Tommy John, 33	Dave Righetti, 60	Rick Cerone, 111	Don Mattingly, 140	Willie Randolph, 119
1988	Tommy John, 32	Dave Righetti, 60	Don Slaught, 94	Don Mattingly, 143	Willie Randolph, 110
1989	Andy Hawkins, 34	Lee Guetterman, 70	Don Slaught, 105	Don Mattingly, 145	Steve Sax, 158
1990	Tim Leary, 31	Lee Guetterman, 64	Bob Geren, 107	Don Mattingly, 89	Steve Sax, 154
1991	Scott Sanderson, 34	Greg Cadaret, 68	Matt Nokes, 130	Don Mattingly, 127	Steve Sax, 149
1992	Melido Perez, 33	John Habyan, 56	Matt Nokes, 111	Don Mattingly, 143	Pat Kelly, 101
	Scott Sanderson, 33				
1993	Jimmy Key, 34	Steve Howe, 51	Mike Stanley, 122	Don Mattingly, 130	Pat Kelly, 125
1994	Jimmy Key, 25	Bob Wickman, 53	Mike Stanley, 72	Don Mattingly, 97	Pat Kelly, 93
1995	Jack McDowell, 30	Bob Wickman, 63	Mike Stanley, 107	Don Mattingly, 125	Pat Kelly, 87
1996	Andy Pettitte, 34	Jeff Nelson, 73	Joe Girardi, 120	Tino Martinez, 151	Mariano Duncan, 104

Shortstop	Third Baseman	Outfielder	Outfielder	Outfielder	Designated Hitter
Tony Kubek, 134	Andy Carey, 99	Mickey Mantle, 150	Norm Siebern, 133	Hank Bauer, 123	
Tony Kubek, 67	Hector Lopez, 76	Mickey Mantle, 143	Hank Bauer, 111	Norm Siebern, 93	
Tony Kubek, 136	Clete Boyer, 99	Mickey Mantle, 150	Roger Maris, 131	Hector Lopez, 106	
Tony Kubek, 145	Clete Boyer, 141	Roger Maris, 160	Mickey Mantle, 150	Yogi Berra, 87	
Tom Tresh, 111	Clete Boyer, 157	Roger Maris, 154	Mickey Mantle, 117	Hector Lopez, 84	
Tony Kubek, 132	Clete Boyer, 141	Tom Tresh, 144	Hector Lopez, 124	Roger Maris, 86	
Tony Kubek, 99	Clete Boyer, 123	Tom Tresh, 146	Roger Maris, 137	Mickey Mantle, 132	
Tony Kubek, 93	Clete Boyer, 147	Tom Tresh, 154	Mickey Mantle,108	Hector Lopez, 75	
Horace Clarke, 63	Clete Boyer, 85	Mickey Mantle, 97	Roger Maris, 95	Tom Tresh, 84	
Ruben Amaro, 123	Charley Smith, 115	Joe Pepitone, 123	Tom Tresh, 118	Steve Whitaker, 114	
Tom Tresh, 119	Bobby Cox, 132	Roy White, 154	Bill Robinson, 98	Joe Pepitone, 92	
Gene Michael, 118	Jerry Kenney, 83	Roy White, 126	Bobby Murcer, 118	Bill Robinson, 62	
Gene Michael, 123	Jerry Kenney, 135	Roy White, 161	Bobby Murcer, 155	Curt Blefary, 79	
Gene Michael, 136	Jerry Kenney, 109	Roy White, 145	Bobby Murcer, 143	Felipe Alou, 80	
Gene Michael, 121	Celerino Sanchez, 68	Roy White, 155	Bobby Murcer, 151	Johnny Callison, 74	
Gene Michael, 128	Graig Nettles, 157	Roy White, 162	Bobby Murcer, 160	Matty Alou, 94	Jim Hart, 106
Jim Mason, 152	Graig Nettles, 154	Bobby Murcer, 156	Elliott Maddox, 135	Lou Piniella, 130	Ron Blomberg, 58
Jim Mason, 93	Graig Nettles, 157	Roy White, 135	Bobby Bonds, 129	Elliott Maddox, 55	Ed Herrmann, 35
Fred Stanley, 110	Graig Nettles, 158	Roy White, 156	Mickey Rivers, 136	Oscar Gamble, 104	Carlos May, 81
Bucky Dent, 157	Graig Nettles, 156	Mickey Rivers, 136	Roy White, 135	Reggie Jackson, 127	Carlos May, 51
Bucky Dent, 123	Graig Nettles, 159	Mickey Rivers, 138	Reggie Jackson, 104	Lou Piniella, 103	Cliff Johnson, 39
Bucky Dent, 141	Graig Nettles, 144	Reggie Jackson, 125	Lou Piniella, 112	Bobby Murcer, 70	Jim Spencer, 71
Bucky Dent, 141	Graig Nettles, 88	Bobby Brown, 131	Lou Piniella, 104	Reggie Jackson, 94	Eric Soderholm, 51
Bucky Dent, 73	Graig Nettles, 97	Dave Winfield, 102	Jerry Mumphrey, 79	Reggie Jackson, 61	Oscar Gamble, 33
					Reggie Jackson, 33
					Bobby Murcer, 33
Roy Smalley, 93	Graig Nettles, 122	Dave Winfield, 135	Ken Griffey, 125	Jerry Mumphrey, 123	Oscar Gamble, 74
Roy Smalley, 90	Graig Nettles, 129	Dave Winfield, 151	Steve Kamp, 101	Jerry Mumphrey, 83	Don Baylor, 136
Bobby Meacham, 96	Toby Harrah, 74	Dave Winfield, 140	Omar Moreno, 108	Ken Griffey, 82	Don Baylor, 127
Bobby Meacham, 155	Mike Pagliarulo, 134	Dave Winfield, 152	Rickey Henderson, 141	Ken Griffey, 110	Don Baylor, 140
Bobby Meacham, 56 Wayne Tolleson, 56	Mike Pagliarulo, 143	Dave Winfield, 145	Rickey Henderson, 146	Dan Pasqua, 81	Mike Easler, 129
Wayne Tolleson, 118	Mike Pagliarulo, 147	Dave Winfield, 145	Gary Ward, 94	Dan Pasqua, 74	Ron Kittle, 49
Rafael Santana, 148	Mike Pagliarulo, 124	Dave Winfield, 141	Rickey Henderson, 136	Claudell Washington, 117	Jack Clark, 112
Alvaro Espinoza, 146	Mike Pagliarulo, 69	Roberto Kelly, 137	Jesse Barfield, 129	Mel Hall, 75	Steve Balboni, 82
Alvaro Espinoza, 150	Randy Velardi, 74	Roberto Kelly, 160	Jesse Barfield, 151	Oscar Azocar, 57	Steve Balboni, 72
Alvaro Espinoza, 147	Pat Kelly, 80	Roberto Kelly, 125	Mel Hall, 120	Bernie Williams, 85	Kevin Maas, 109
Andy Stankiewicz, 81	Charlie Hayes, 139	Roberto Kelly, 146	Mel Hall, 136	Danny Tartabull, 69	Kevin Maas, 62
Spike Owen, 96	Wade Boggs, 134	Bernie Williams, 139	Paul O'Neill, 138	Dion James, 103	Danny Tartabull, 88
Mike Gallego, 72	Wade Boggs, 93	Bernie Williams, 107	Paul O'Neill, 99	Luis Polonia, 84	Danny Tartabull, 78
Tony Fernandez, 103	Wade Boggs, 117	Bernie Williams, 144	Paul O'Neill, 121	Gerald Williams, 92	Ruben Sierra, 46
Derek Jeter, 157	Wade Boggs, 123	Bernie Williams, 140	Paul O'Neill, 146	Gerald Williams, 92	Ruben Sierra, 61

YEAR BY YEAR

Year	Position	W–L–T	Pct.	World Series Opponent	World Series Record	Manager	Attendance
1903	4th (−17)	72–62–2	.537			Clark Griffith	211,808
1904	2nd (−1½)	92–59–4	.609			Clark Griffith	438,919
1905	6th (−21½)	71–78–3	.477			Clark Griffith	309,100
1906	2nd (−3)	90–61–4	.596			Clark Griffith	434,700
1907	5th (−21)	70–78–4	.473			Clark Griffith	350,020
1908	8th (−39½)	51–103–1	.331			C. Griffith-K. Elberfeld	305,500
1909	5th (−23½)	74–77–2	.490			George Stallings	501,000
1910	2nd (−14½)	88–63–5	.583			G. Stallings-H. Chase	355,857
1911	6th (−25½)	76–76–1	.500			Hal Chase	302,444
1912	8th (−55)	50–102–1	.329			Harry Wolverton	242,194
1913	7th (−38)	57–94–2	.377			Frank Chance	357,551
1914	†6th (−30)	70–84–3	.455			F. Chance-R. Peckinpaugh	359,477
1915	5th (−32½)	69–83–2	.454			Bill Donovan	256,035
1916	4th (−11)	80–74–2	.519			Bill Donovan	469,211
1917	6th (−28½)	71–82–2	.464			Bill Donovan	330,294
1918	4th (−13½)	60–63–3	.488			Miller Huggins	282,047
1919	3rd (−7½)	80–59–2	.576			Miller Huggins	619,154
1920	3rd (−3)	95–59–0	.617			Miller Huggins	1,289,422
1921	1st (+4½)	98–55–0	.641	Giants	3–5	Miller Huggins	1,230,696
1922	1st (+1)	94–60–0	.610	Giants	0–4	Miller Huggins	1,026,134
1923	*1st (+16)	98–54–0	.645	Giants	4–2	Miller Huggins	1,007,066
1924	2nd (−2)	89–63–1	.586			Miller Huggins	1,053,533
1925	7th (−28½)	69–85–2	.448			Miller Huggins	697,267
1926	1st (+3)	91–63–1	.591	Cardinals	3–4	Miller Huggins	1,027,095
1927	*1st (+19)	110–44–1	.714	Pirates	4–0	Miller Huggins	1,164,015
1928	*1st (+2½)	101–53–0	.656	Cardinals	4–0	Miller Huggins	1,072,132
1929	2nd (−18)	88–66–0	.571			M. Huggins-A. Fletcher	960,148
1930	3rd (−16)	86–68–0	.558			Bob Shawkey	1,169,230
1931	2nd (−13½)	94–59–2	.614			Joe McCarthy	912,437
1932	*1st (+13)	107–47–2	.695	Cubs	4–0	Joe McCarthy	962,320
1933	2nd (−7)	91–59–2	.607			Joe McCarthy	728,014
1934	2nd (−7)	94–60–0	.610			Joe McCarthy	854,682
1935	2nd (−3)	89–60–0	.597			Joe McCarthy	657,508
1936	*1st (+19½)	102–51–2	.667	Giants	4–2	Joe McCarthy	976,913
1937	*1st (+13)	102–52–3	.662	Giants	4–1	Joe McCarthy	998,148
1938	*1st (+9½)	99–53–5	.651	Cubs	4–0	Joe McCarthy	970,916
1939	*1st (+17)	106–45–1	.702	Reds	4–0	Joe McCarthy	859,785
1940	3rd (−2)	88–66–1	.571			Joe McCarthy	988,975
1941	*1st (+17)	101–53–2	.656	Dodgers	4–1	Joe McCarthy	964,731
1942	1st (+9)	103–51–0	.669	Cardinals	1–4	Joe McCarthy	988,251
1943	*1st (+13½)	98–56–1	.636	Cardinals	4–1	Joe McCarthy	645,006
1944	3rd (−6)	83–71–0	.539			Joe McCarthy	822,864
1945	4th (−6½)	81–71–0	.533			Joe McCarthy	881,846
1946	3rd (−17)	87–67–0	.565			J. McCarthy-B. Dickey-J. Neun	2,265,512
1947	*1st (+12)	97–57–1	.630	Dodgers	4–3	Bucky Harris	2,178,937
1948	3rd (−2½)	94–60–0	.610			Bucky Harris	2,373,901
1949	*1st (+1)	97–57–1	.630	Dodgers	4–1	Casey Stengel	2,281,676
1950	*1st (+3)	98–56–1	.636	Phillies	4–0	Casey Stengel	2,081,380
1951	*1st (+5)	98–56–0	.636	Giants	4–2	Casey Stengel	1,950,107
1952	*1st (+2)	95–59–0	.617	Dodgers	4–3	Casey Stengel	1,629,665
1953	*1st (+8½)	99–52–0	.656	Dodgers	4–2	Casey Stengel	1,537,811
1954	2nd (−8)	103–51–1	.669			Casey Stengel	1,475,171
1955	1st (+3)	96–58–0	.623	Dodgers	3–4	Casey Stengel	1,490,138
1956	*1st (+9)	97–57–0	.680	Dodgers	4–3	Casey Stengel	1,491,784
1957	1st (+8)	98–56–0	.636	Braves	3–4	Casey Stengel	1,497,134
1958	*1st (+10)	92–62–1	.597	Braves	4–3	Casey Stengel	1,428,428
1959	3rd (−15)	79–75–1	.513			Casey Stengel	1,552,030
1960	1st (+8)	97–57–1	.630	Pirates	3–4	Casey Stengel	1,627,349
1961	*1st (+8)	109–53–1	.673	Reds	4–1	Ralph Houk	1,747,736
1962	*1st (+5)	96–66–0	.593	Giants	4–3	Ralph Houk	1,493,574
1963	1st (+10½)	104–57–10	.646	Dodgers	0–4	Ralph Houk	1,308,920
1964	1st (+1)	99–63–2	.611	Cardinals	3–4	Yogi Berra	1,305,638
1965	6th (−25)	77–85–0	.475			Johnny Keane	1,213,552
1966	10th (−26½)	70–89–1	.440			J. Keane-R. Houk	1,124,648
1967	9th (−20)	72–90–1	.444			Ralph Houk	1,141,714
1968	5th (−20)	83–79–2	.512			Ralph Houk	1,125,124
1969	5th (−28½)	80–81–1	.497			Ralph Houk	1,067,996
1970	2nd (−15)	93–69–1	.574			Ralph Houk	1,136,879
1971	4th (−21)	82–80–0	.506			Ralph Houk	1,070,711
1972	4th (−6½)	79–76–0	.510			Ralph Houk	966,328

YEAR BY YEAR

Year	Position	W–L–T	Pct.	World Series Opponent	World Series Record	Manager	Attendance
1973	4th (−17)	80–82–0	.494			Ralph Houk	1,262,077
1974	2nd (−2)	89–73–0	.549			Bill Virdon	1,273,075
1975	3rd (−12)	83–77–0	.519			B. Virdon–B. Martin	1,288,048
1976	1st (+10½)	97–62–0	.610	Reds	0–4	Billy Martin	2,012,434
1977	*1st (+2½)	100–62–0	.617	Dodgers	4–2	Billy Martin	2,103,092
1978	*1st‡ (+1)	100–63–0	.613	Dodgers	4–2	B. Martin–B. Lemon	2,335,871
1979	4th (−13½)	89–71–0	.556			B. Lemon–B. Martin	2,537,765
1980ᵃ	1st (+3)	103–59–0	.636			Dick Howser	2,627,417
1981ᵇ	1st (+2)	34–22–0	.607	Dodgers	2–4	Gene Michael–B. Lemon	1,614,533ᶜ
	6th (−5)	25–26–0	.490				
1982	5th (−16)	79–83–0	.488			B. Lemon–G. Michael–C. King	2,041,219
1983	3rd (−7)	91–71–0	.562			Billy Martin	2,257,976
1984	3rd (−17)	87–75–0	.537			Yogi Berra	1,821,815
1985	2nd (−2)	97–64–0	.602			Y. Berra–B. Martin	2,214,587
1986	2nd (−5½)	90–72–0	.556			Lou Piniella	2,268,116
1987	4th (−9)	89–73–0	.549			Lou Piniella	2,427,672
1988	5th (−3½)	85–76–0	.528			B. Martin–L. Piniella	2,633,701
1989	5th (−14½)	74–87–0	.460			D. Green–B. Dent	2,170,485
1990	7th (−21)	67–95–0	.414			B. Dent–S. Merrill	2,006,436
1991	5th (−20)	71–91–0	.438			Stump Merrill	1,863,731
1992	†4th (−20)	76–86–0	.469			Buck Showalter	1,748,737
1993	2nd (−7)	88–74–0	.543			Buck Showalter	2,416,942
1994ᵈ	1st (+6½)	70–43–0	.619			Buck Showalter	1,675,557ᵉ
1995ᶠ	2nd (−7)	79–65–0	.549			Buck Showalter	1,705,257ᵍ
1996	1st (+4)	92–70–0	.568	Braves	4–2	Joe Torre	2,250,839

*Won world championship.

†Tied.

‡Won one game playoff at Boston for 1978 AL East title.

ᵃSwept by Kansas City, three games to none, in AL Championship Series.

ᵇWon first half, then swept second-half winner Milwaukee, three games to none, in special playoff series for AL East Championship.

ᶜOnly 51 home games because of players' strike.

ᵈPlayers strike ended season on August 12; no postseason.

ᵉOnly 57 home games because of shortened season.

ᶠWon wild-card entry into playoffs; lost to Seattle, three games to two, in first round.

ᵍOnly 72 home games because of season's delayed start after strike settlement.

World champions: 23

American League champions: 34

American League East champions: 6

Finished first, 36; second, 16; third, 11; fourth, 10; fifth, 9; sixth, 5; seventh, 3; eighth, 2; ninth, 1; tenth, 1.

Highest percentage, .714 in 1927; lowest, .329 in 1912.

Total regular-season record: 8,184–6,312 (.565).

League postseason record: 24–13 (.649).

World Series record: 113–79 (.589).

Yankees have played in the World Series 34 years, winning the world championship 23 times (.676).

In 1957, Phil Rizzuto joined the Yankee broadcasting team of Mel Allen (center) and Red Barber (right), forming a trio now reunited in the Hall of Fame.

GAMES WON, LOST, TIED BY SEASON

Year	Home	Road	Overall
1903	41–26–0	31–36–2	72–62–2
1904	46–29–0	46–30–4	92–59–4
1905	40–35–0	31–43–3	71–78–3
1906	53–23–0	37–38–4	90–61–4
1907*	33–40–2	37–38–2	70–78–4
1908	30–47–0	21–56–1	51–103–1
1909	41–35–1	33–42–1	74–77–2
1910	49–25–3	39–38–2	88–63–5
1911*	36–40–1	40–36–0	76–76–1
1912	31–44–1	19–58–0	50–102–1
1913*	27–47–1	30–47–1	57–94–2
1914	36–40–2	34–44–1	70–84–3
1915	37–43–2	32–40–0	69–83–2
1916	46–31–2	34–43–0	80–74–2
1917*	35–40–0	36–42–2	71–82–2
1918	37–29–1	23–34–2	60–63–3
1919	46–25–2	34–34–0	80–59–2
1920	49–28–0	46–31–0	95–59–0
1921	53–25–0	45–30–0	98–55–0
1922	50–27–0	44–33–0	94–60–0
1923*	46–30–0	52–24–0	98–54–0
1924	45–32–1	44–31–0	89–63–1
1925	42–36–1	27–49–1	69–85–2
1926	50–25–0	41–38–1	91–63–1
1927	57–19–1	53–25–0	110–44–1
1928	52–25–0	49–28–0	101–53–0
1929	49–28–0	39–38–0	88–66–0
1930	47–29–0	39–39–0	86–68–0
1931	51–25–1	43–34–1	94–59–2
1932	62–15–0	45–32–2	107–47–2
1933	51–23–1	40–36–1	91–59–2
1934	53–24–0	41–36–0	94–60–0
1935*	41–33–0	48–27–0	89–60–0
1936	56–21–0	46–30–2	102–51–2
1937	57–20–2	45–32–1	102–52–3
1938	55–22–2	44–31–3	99–53–5
1939*	52–25–0	54–20–1	106–45–1
1940	52–24–0	36–42–1	88–66–1
1941	51–26–1	50–27–1	101–53–2
1942	58–19–0	45–32–0	103–51–0
1943	54–23–0	44–33–1	98–56–1
1944	47–31–0	36–40–0	83–71–0
1945	48–28–0	33–43–0	81–71–0
1946	47–30–0	40–37–0	87–67–0
1947	55–22–0	42–35–1	97–57–1
1948	50–27–0	44–33–0	94–60–0
1949	54–23–1	43–34–0	97–57–1
1950	53–24–0	45–32–1	98–56–1
1951	56–22–0	42–34–0	98–56–0
1952	49–28–0	46–31–0	95–59–0
1953	50–27–0	49–25–0	99–52–0
1954	54–23–1	49–28–0	103–51–1
1955	52–25–0	44–33–0	96–58–0
1956	49–28–0	48–29–0	97–57–0
1957*	48–29–0	50–27–0	98–56–0
1958*	44–33–1	48–29–0	92–62–1
1959	40–37–0	39–38–1	79–75–1
1960	55–22–0	42–35–1	97–57–1
1961	65–16–0	44–37–1	109–53–1
1962	50–30–0	46–36–0	96–66–0
1963	58–22–0	46–35–0	104–57–0
1964	50–31–0	49–32–2	99–63–2
1965	40–43–0	37–42–0	77–85–0
1966	35–46–1	35–43–0	70–89–1
1967	43–38–1	29–52–0	72–90–1
1968*	39–42–1	44–37–1	83–79–2
1969	48–32–0	32–49–1	80–81–1
1970	53–28–0	40–41–1	93–69–1
1971	44–37–0	38–43–0	82–80–0
1972	46–31–0	33–45–0	79–76–0
1973	50–31–0	30–51–0	80–82–0

Year	Home	Road	Overall
1974	47–34–0	42–39–0	89–73–0
1975	43–35–0	40–42–0	83–77–0
1976*	45–35–0	52–27–0	97–62–0
1977	55–26–0	45–36–0	100–62–0
1978	55–26–0	45–37–0	100–63–0
1979	51–30–0	38–41–0	89–71–0
1980	53–28–0	50–31–0	103–59–0
1981†	32–19–0	27–29–0	59–48–0
1982	42–39–0	37–44–0	79–83–0
1983	51–30–0	40–41–0	91–71–0
1984	51–30–0	36–45–0	87–75–0
1985	58–22–0	39–42–0	97–64–0
1986*	41–39–0	49–33–0	90–72–0
1987	51–30–0	38–43–0	89–73–0
1988	46–34–0	39–42–0	85–76–0
1989	41–40–0	33–47–0	74–87–0
1990	37–44–0	30–51–0	67–95–0
1991	39–42–0	32–49–0	71–91–0
1992	41–40–0	35–46–0	76–86–0
1993	50–31–0	38–43–0	88–74–0
1994*†	33–24–0	37–19–0	70–43–0
1995†	46–26–0	33–39–0	79–65–0
1996	49–31–0	43–39–0	92–70–0

* Yankees won more games on road 13 seasons: 1907, 1911, 1913, 1917, 1923, 1935, 1939, 1957, 1958, 1968, 1976, 1986, and 1994.
†Strike-shortened season.

Chuck "Rifleman" Connors wore Yankee pinstripes during 1946 spring training, when he competed against veteran Nick Etten for the first-base position. Connors soon was dealt to his hometown Brooklyn Dodgers. The Seton Hall product played in one game for the 1949 Dodgers and in 66 for the 1951 Chicago Cubs before reaching stardom—as a Hollywood actor. The Boston Celtics' original pivotman, Connors was a two-sport major leaguer.

YANKEE FIRST-PLACE TEAMS

1921 AMERICAN LEAGUE CHAMPIONS

Manager: Miller Huggins.
World Series Roster: Pitchers: Rip Collins, Alex Ferguson, Harry Harper, Waite Hoyt, Carl Mays, Bill Piercy, Jack Quinn, Tom Rogers, Bob Shawkey. *Catchers:* Al DeVormer, Wally Schang. *Infielders:* Frank Baker, Mike McNally, Johnny Mitchell, Roger Peckinpaugh, Wally Pipp, Aaron Ward. *Outfielders:* Chick Fewster, Chicken Hawks, Bob Meusel, Elmer Miller, Braggo Roth, Babe Ruth.

WORLD SERIES

	W	L	Pct.
Giants	5	3	.625
Yankees	3	5	.375

Game 1 (Oct. 5 at Polo Grounds)

| Yankees | 100 | 011 | 000 | — | 3 | 7 | 0 |
| Giants | 000 | 000 | 000 | — | 0 | 5 | 0 |

Yankees: CARL MAYS; Wally Schang.
Giants: PHIL DOUGLAS, Jesse Barnes (9th); Frank Snyder.
Home Runs: None.
Attendance: 30,202.

Game 2 (Oct. 6 at Polo Grounds)

| Giants | 000 | 000 | 000 | — | 0 | 2 | 3 |
| Yankees | 000 | 100 | 02X | — | 3 | 3 | 0 |

Giants: ART NEHF; Earl Smith.
Yankees: WAITE HOYT; Wally Schang.
Home Runs: None
Attendance: 34,939.

Game 3 (Oct. 7 at Polo Grounds)

| Yankees | 004 | 000 | 010 | — | 5 | 8 | 0 |
| Giants | 004 | 000 | 81X | — | 13 | 20 | 0 |

Yankees: Bob Shawkey, JACK QUINN (3rd), Rip Collins (7th), Tom Rogers (7th); Wally Schang, Al DeVormer (8th).
Giants: Fred Toney, JESSE BARNES (3rd): Frank Snyder.
Home Runs: None
Attendance: 36,509.

Game 4 (Oct. 9 at Polo Grounds)

| Giants | 000 | 000 | 031 | — | 4 | 9 | 1 |
| Yankees | 000 | 010 | 001 | — | 2 | 7 | 1 |

Giants: PHIL DOUGLAS; Frank Snyder.
Yankees: CARL MAYS; Wally Schang.
Home Run: Babe Ruth (Yankees).
Attendance: 36,372.

Game 5 (Oct. 10 at Polo Grounds)

| Yankees | 001 | 200 | 000 | — | 3 | 6 | 1 |
| Giants | 100 | 000 | 000 | — | 1 | 10 | 1 |

Yankees: WAITE HOYT; Wally Schang.
Giants: ART NEHF; Earl Smith.
Home Runs: None.
Attendance: 35,758.

Game 6 (Oct. 11 at Polo Grounds)

| Giants | 030 | 401 | 000 | — | 8 | 13 | 0 |
| Yankees | 320 | 000 | 000 | — | 5 | 7 | 2 |

Giants: Fred Toney, JESSE BARNES (1st); Frank Snyder.
Yankees: Harry Harper, BOB SHAWKEY (2nd), Bill Piercy (9th); Wally Schang.
Home Runs: Irish Meusel (Giants), Frank Snyder (Giants), and Chick Fewster (Yankees).
Attendance: 34,283.

NOTE: Capital letters indicate pitcher of decision.

Game 7 (Oct. 12 at Polo Grounds)

| Yankees | 010 | 000 | 000 | — | 1 | 8 | 1 |
| Giants | 000 | 100 | 10X | — | 2 | 6 | 0 |

Yankees: CARL MAYS; Wally Schang.
Giants: PHIL DOUGLAS; Frank Snyder.
Home Runs: None.
Attendance: 36,503.

Game 8 (Oct. 13 at Polo Grounds)

| Giants | 100 | 000 | 000 | — | 1 | 6 | 0 |
| Yankees | 000 | 000 | 000 | — | 0 | 4 | 1 |

Giants: ART NEHF; Frank Snyder.
Yankees: WAITE HOYT; Wally Schang.
Home Runs: None.
Attendance: 25,410

NOTE: Although owned by the Giants, the Polo Grounds was also the Yankees' home field. So the rivals alternated being the "home" team during both the 1921 and 1922 World Series—until Yankee Stadium was opened in 1923.

1922 AMERICAN LEAGUE CHAMPIONS

Manager: Miller Huggins.
World Series Roster: Pitchers: Joe Bush, Waite Hoyt, Sad Sam Jones, Carl Mays, George Murray, Lefty O'Doul, Bob Shawkey. *Catchers:* Al De-Vormer, Fred Hofmann, Wally Schang. *Infielders:* Frank Baker, Joe Dugan, Mike McNally, Wally Pipp, Everett Scott, Aaron Ward. *Outfielders:* Norm McMillan, Bob Meusel, Babe Ruth, Camp Skinner, Elmer Smith, Whitey Witt.

WORLD SERIES

	W	L	T	Pct.
Giants	4	0	1	1.000
Yankees	0	4	1	.000

Game 1 (Oct. 4 at Polo Grounds)

| Yankees | 000 | 001 | 100 | — | 2 | 7 | 0 |
| Giants | 000 | 000 | 03X | — | 3 | 11 | 3 |

Yankees: JOE BUSH, Waite Hoyt (8th); Wally Schang.
Giants: Art Nehf, ROSY RYAN (8th); Frank Snyder.
Home Runs: None.
Attendance: 36,514.

Game 2 (Oct. 5 at Polo Grounds)

| Giants | 300 | 000 | 000 | 0 | — | 3 | 8 | 1 |
| Yankees | 100 | 100 | 010 | 0 | — | 3 | 8 | 0 |

Giants: JESSE BARNES; Frank Snyder.
Yankees: BOB SHAWKEY; Wally Schang.
Home Runs: Irish Meusel (Giants) and Aaron Ward (Yankees).
Attendance: 37,020.

Game 3 (Oct. 6 at Polo Grounds)

| Yankees | 000 | 000 | 000 | — | 0 | 4 | 1 |
| Giants | 002 | 000 | 10X | — | 3 | 12 | 1 |

Yankees: WAITE HOYT, Sad Sam Jones (8th); Wally Schang.
Giants: JACK SCOTT; Earl Smith.
Home Runs: None.
Attendance: 37,620.

Game 4 (Oct. 7 at Polo Grounds)

| Giants | 000 | 040 | 000 | — | 4 | 9 | 1 |
| Yankees | 200 | 000 | 100 | — | 3 | 8 | 0 |

Giants: HUGH McQUILLAN; Frank Snyder.
Yankees: CARL MAYS, Sad Sam Jones (9th); Wally Schang.
Home Run: Aaron Ward (Yankees).
Attendance: 36,242.

Game 5 (Oct. 8 at Polo Grounds)

Yankees	100	010	100	—	3	5	0
Giants	020	000	03X	—	5	10	0

Yankees JOE BUSH; Wally Schang.
Giants: ART NEHF; Frank Snyder.
Home Runs: None.
Attendance: 38,551.

1923 WORLD CHAMPIONS

Manager: Miller Huggins.
World Series Roster: Pitchers: Joe Bush, Waite Hoyt, Sad Sam Jones, Carl Mays, Herb Pennock, George Pipgras, Oscar Roettger, Bob Shawkey. *Catchers:* Benny Bengough, Fred Hofmann, Wally Schang. *Infielders:* Joe Dugan, Mike Gazella, Ernie Johnson, Mike McNally, Wally Pipp, Everett Scott, Aaron Ward. *Outfielders:* Hinkey Haines, Harvey Hendrick, Bob Meusel, Babe Ruth, Elmer Smith, Whitey Witt.

WORLD SERIES

	W	L	Pct.
Yankees	4	2	.667
Giants	2	4	.333

Game 1 (Oct. 10 at Yankee Stadium)

Giants	004	000	001	—	5	8	0
Yankees	120	000	100	—	4	12	1

Giants: Mule Watson, ROSY RYAN (3rd); Frank Snyder.
Yankees: Waite Hoyt, JOE BUSH (3rd); Wally Schang.
Home Run: Casey Stengel (Giants).
Attendance: 55,307.

Game 2 (Oct. 11 at Polo Grounds)

Yankees	010	210	000	—	4	10	0
Giants	010	001	000	—	2	9	2

Yankees: HERB PENNOCK; Wally Schang.
Giants: HUGH McQUILLAN, Jack Bentley (4th); Frank Snyder.
Home Runs: Babe Ruth (Yankees) 2, Aaron Ward (Yankees), and Irish Meusel (Giants).
Attendance: 40,402.

Game 3 (Oct. 12 at Yankee Stadium)

Giants	000	000	100	—	1	4	0
Yankees	000	000	000	—	0	6	1

Giants: ART NEHF; Frank Snyder.
Yankees: SAD SAM JONES, Joe Bush (9th); Wally Schang.
Home Run: Casey Stengel (Giants).
Attendance: 62,430.

Game 4 (Oct. 13 at Polo Grounds)

Yankees	061	100	000	—	8	13	1
Giants	000	000	031	—	4	13	1

Yankees: BOB SHAWKEY, Herb Pennock (8th); Wally Schang.
Giants: JACK SCOTT, Rosy Ryan (2nd), Hugh McQuillan (2nd), Claude Jonnard (8th), Virgil Barnes (9th); Frank Snyder.
Home Run: Ross Youngs (Giants).
Attendance: 46,302.

Game 5 (Oct. 14 at Yankee Stadium)

Giants	010	000	000	—	1	3	2
Yankees	340	100	00X	—	8	14	0

Giants: JACK BENTLEY, Jack Scott (2nd), Virgil Barnes (4th), Claude Jonnard (8th); Hank Gowdy.
Yankees: JOE BUSH; Wally Schang.
Home Run: Joe Dugan (Yankees).
Attendance: 62,817.

Game 6 (Oct. 15 at Polo Grounds)

Yankees	100	000	050	—	6	5	1
Giants	100	111	000	—	4	10	1

Yankees: HERB PENNOCK, Sad Sam Jones (8th); Wally Schang.
Giants: ART NEHF, Rosy Ryan (8th); Frank Snyder.
Home Runs: Babe Ruth (Yankees) and Frank Snyder (Giants).
Attendance: 34,172.

1926 AMERICAN LEAGUE CHAMPIONS

Manager: Miller Huggins.
World Series Roster: Pitchers: Walter Beall, Garland Braxton, Waite Hoyt, Sad Sam Jones, Herb McQuaid, Herb Pennock, Dutch Ruether, Bob Shawkey, Urban Shocker, Myles Thomas. *Catchers:* Benny Bengough, Pat Collins, Hank Severeid. *Infielders:* Spencer Adams, Joe Dugan, Mike Gazella, Lou Gehrig, Mark Koenig, Tony Lazzeri, Aaron Ward. *Outfielders:* Roy Carlyle, Earle Combs, Bob Meusel, Ben Paschal, Babe Ruth.

WORLD SERIES

	W	L	Pct.
Cardinals	4	3	.571
Yankees	3	4	.429

Game 1 (Oct. 2 at Yankee Stadium)

Cardinals	100	000	000	—	1	3	1
Yankees	100	001	00X	—	2	6	0

Cardinals: BILL SHERDEL, Jesse Haines (8th); Bob O'Farrell.
Yankees: HERB PENNOCK; Hank Severeid.
Home Runs: None.
Attendance: 61,658.

Game 2 (Oct. 3 at Yankee Stadium)

Cardinals	002	000	301	—	6	12	1
Yankees	020	000	000	—	2	4	0

Cardinals: GROVER CLEVELAND ALEXANDER; Bob O'Farrell.
Yankees: URBAN SHOCKER, Bob Shawkey (8th), Sad Sam Jones (9th); Hank Severeid, Pat Collins (9th).
Home Runs: Billy Southworth (Cardinals) and Tommy Thevenow (Cardinals).
Attendance: 63,600.

Game 3 (Oct. 5 at St. Louis)

Yankees	000	000	000	—	0	5	1
Cardinals	000	310	00X	—	4	8	0

Yankees: DUTCH RUETHER, Bob Shawkey (5th), Myles Thomas (8th); Hank Severeid.
Cardinals: JESSE HAINES; Bob O'Farrell.
Home Run: Jesse Haines (Cardinals).
Attendance: 37,708.

Game 4 (Oct. 6 at St. Louis)

Yankees	101	142	100	—	10	14	1
Cardinals	100	300	001	—	5	14	0

Yankees: WAITE HOYT; Hank Severeid.
Cardinals: Flint Rhem, ART REINHART (5th), Hi Bell (5th), Wild Bill Hallahan (7th), Vic Keen (9th); Bob O'Farrell.
Home Runs: Babe Ruth (Yankees), 3.
Attendance: 38,825.

Game 5 (Oct. 7 at St. Louis)

Yankees	000	001	001	1	—	3	9	1
Cardinals	000	100	100	0	—	2	7	1

Yankees: HERB PENNOCK; Hank Severeid.
Cardinals: BILL SHERDEL; Bob O'Farrell.
Home Runs: None.
Attendance: 39,552.

Game 6 (Oct. 9 at Yankee Stadium)

Cardinals	300	010	501	—	10	13	2
Yankees	000	100	100	—	2	8	1

Cardinals: GROVER CLEVELAND ALEXANDER; Bob O'Farrell.
Yankees: BOB SHAWKEY, Urban Shocker (7th), Myles Thomas (8th); Hank Severeid, Pat Collins (8th).
Home Run: Les Bell (Cardinals).
Attendance: 48,615.

Game 7 (Oct. 10 at Yankee Stadium)

Cardinals	000	300	000	—	3	8	0
Yankees	001	001	000	—	2	8	3

Cardinals: JESSE HAINES, Grover Cleveland Alexander (7th); Bob O'Farrell.
Yankees: WAITE HOYT, Herb Pennock (7th); Hank Severeid, Pat Collins (7th).
Home Run: Babe Ruth (Yankees).
Attendance: 38,093.

1927 WORLD CHAMPIONS

Manager: Miller Huggins.
World Series Roster: Pitchers: Joe Giard, Waite Hoyt, Wilcy Moore, Herb Pennock, George Pipgras, Dutch Ruether, Bob Shawkey, Urban Shocker, Myles Thomas. *Catchers:* Benny Bengough, Pat Collins, Johnny Grabowski. *Infielders:* Joe Dugan, Mike Gazella, Lou Gehrig, Mark Koenig, Tony Lazzeri, Ray Morehart, Julie Wera. *Outfielders:* Earle Combs, Cedric Durst, Bob Meusel, Ben Paschal, Babe Ruth.

WORLD SERIES

	W	L	Pct.
Yankees	4	0	1.000
Pirates	0	4	.000

Game 1 (Oct. 5 at Pittsburgh)

Yankees	103	010	000	—	5	6	1
Pirates	101	010	010	—	4	9	2

Yankees: WAITE HOYT, Wilcy Moore (8th); Pat Collins.
Pirates: RAY KREMER, Johnny Miljus (6th); Earl Smith.
Home Runs: None.
Attendance: 41,467.

Game 2 (Oct. 6 at Pittsburgh)

Yankees	003	000	030	—	6	11	0
Pirates	100	000	010	—	2	7	2

Yankees: GEORGE PIPGRAS; Benny Bengough.
Pirates: VIC ALDRIDGE, Mike Cvengros (8th), Joe Dawson (9th); Johnny Gooch.
Home Runs: None.
Attendance: 41,634.

Game 3 (Oct. 7 at Yankee Stadium)

Pirates	000	000	010	—	1	3	1
Yankees	200	000	60X	—	8	9	0

Pirates: LEE MEADOWS, Mike Cvengros (7th); Johnny Gooch.
Yankees: HERB PENNOCK; Johnny Grabowski, Benny Bengough (8th).
Home Run: Babe Ruth (Yankees).
Attendance: 60,695.

Game 4 (Oct. 8 at Yankee Stadium)

Pirates	100	000	200	—	3	10	1
Yankees	100	020	001	—	4	12	2

Pirates: Carmen Hill, JOHNNY MILJUS (7th); Earl Smith, Johnny Gooch (7th).
Yankees: WILCY MOORE; Pat Collins.
Home Run: Babe Ruth (Yankees).
Attendance: 57,909.

1928 WORLD CHAMPIONS

Manager: Miller Huggins.
World Series Roster: Pitchers: Fred Heimach, Waite Hoyt, Herb Pennock, George Pipgras, Rosy Ryan, Myles Thomas, Tom Zachary. *Catchers:* Benny Bengough, Pat Collins, Bill Dickey, Johnny Grabowski. *Infielders:* Joe Dugan, Leo Durocher, Mike Gazella, Lou Gehrig, Mark Koenig, Tony Lazzeri, Gene Robertson. *Outfielders:* Earle Combs, Cedric Durst, Bob Meusel, Ben Paschal, Babe Ruth.

WORLD SERIES

	W	L	Pct.
Yankees	4	0	1.000
Cardinals	0	4	.000

Game 1 (Oct. 4 at Yankee Stadium)

Cardinals	000	000	100	—	1	3	1
Yankees	100	200	01X	—	4	7	0

Cardinals: BILL SHERDEL, Syl Johnson (8th); Jimmie Wilson.
Yankees: WAITE HOYT; Benny Bengough.
Home Runs: Bob Meusel (Yankees) and Jim Bottomley (Cardinals).
Attendance: 61,425.

Game 2 (Oct. 5 at Yankee Stadium)

Cardinals	030	000	000	—	3	4	1
Yankees	314	000	10X	—	9	8	2

Cardinals: GROVER CLEVELAND ALEXANDER, Clarence Mitchell (3rd); Jimmie Wilson.
Yankees: GEORGE PIPGRAS; Benny Bengough.
Home Run: Lou Gehrig (Yankees).
Attendance: 60,714.

Game 3 (Oct. 7 at St. Louis)

Yankees	010	203	100	—	7	7	2
Cardinals	200	010	000	—	3	9	3

Yankees: TOM ZACHARY; Benny Bengough.
Cardinals: JESSE HAINES, Syl Johnson (7th), Flint Rhem (8th); Jimmie Wilson.
Home Runs: Lou Gehrig (Yankees) 2.
Attendance: 39,602.

Game 4 (Oct. 9 at St. Louis)

Yankees	000	100	420	—	7	15	2
Cardinals	001	100	001	—	3	11	0

Yankees: WAITE HOYT; Benny Bengough, Pat Collins (7th).
Cardinals: BILL SHERDEL, Grover Cleveland Alexander (7th); Earl Smith.
Home Runs: Babe Ruth (Yankees) 3, Cedric Durst (Yankees), and Lou Gehrig (Yankees).
Attendance: 37,331.

1932 WORLD CHAMPIONS

Manager: Joe McCarthy.
World Series Roster: Pitchers: Johnny Allen, Jumbo Brown, Charlie Devens, Lefty Gomez, Danny MacFayden, Wilcy Moore, Herb Pennock, George Pipgras, Red Ruffing, Ed Wells. *Catchers:* Bill Dickey, Art Jorgens. *Infielders:* Frank Crosetti, Doc Farrell, Lou Gehrig, Lyn Lary, Tony Lazzeri, Joe Sewell. *Outfielders:* Sammy Byrd, Ben Chapman, Earle Combs, Myril Hoag, Babe Ruth.

WORLD SERIES

	W	L	Pct.
Yankees	4	0	1.000
Cubs	0	4	.000

Game 1 (Sept. 28 at Yankee Stadium)

Cubs	200	000	220	—	6	10	1
Yankees	000	305	31X	—	12	8	2

Cubs: GUY BUSH, Burleigh Grimes (6th), Bob Smith (8th); Gabby Hartnett.
Yankees: RED RUFFING; Bill Dickey.
Home Run: Lou Gehrig (Yankees).
Attendance: 41,459.

Game 2 (Sept. 29 at Yankee Stadium)

Cubs	101	000	000	—	2	9	0
Yankees	202	010	00X	—	5	10	1

Cubs: LON WARNEKE; Gabby Hartnett.
Yankees: LEFTY GOMEZ; Bill Dickey.
Home Runs: None.
Attendance: 50,709.

Game 3 (Oct. 1 at Chicago)

Yankees	301	020	001	—	7	8	1
Cubs	102	100	001	—	5	9	4

Yankees: GEORGE PIPGRAS, Herb Pennock (9th); Bill Dickey.
Cubs: CHARLIE ROOT, Pat Malone (5th), Jakie May (8th), Bud Tinning (9th); Gabby Hartnett.
Home Runs: Babe Ruth (Yankees) 2, Lou Gehrig (Yankees) 2, Kiki Cuyler (Cubs), and Gabby Hartnet (Cubs).
Attendance: 49,986.

Game 4 (Oct. 2 at Chicago)

Yankees	102	002	404	—	13	19	4
Cubs	400	001	001	—	6	9	1

Yankees: Johnny Allen, WILCY MOORE (1st), Herb Pennock (7th); Bill Dickey.
Cubs: Guy Bush, Lon Warneke (1st), JAKIE MAY (4th), Bud Tinning (7th), Burleigh Grimes (9th); Gabby Hartnett, Rollie Hemsley (9th).
Home Runs: Tony Lazzeri (Yankees) 2, Frank Demaree (Cubs), and Earle Combs (Yankees).
Attendance: 49,844.

1936 WORLD CHAMPIONS

Manager: Joe McCarthy.
World Series Roster: Pitchers: Johnny Broaca, Jumbo Brown, Lefty Gomez, Bump Hadley, Pat Malone, Johnny Murphy, Monte Pearson, Red Ruffing, Kemp Wicker. *Catchers:* Bill Dickey, Joe Glenn, Art Jorgens. *Infielders:* Frank Crosetti, Lou Gehrig, Don Heffner, Tony Lazzeri, Red Rolfe, Jack Saltzgaver. *Outfielders:* Joe DiMaggio, Roy Johnson, Jake Powell, Bob Seeds, George Selkirk.

WORLD SERIES

	W	L	Pct.
Yankees	4	2	.667
Giants	2	4	.333

Game 1 (Sept. 30 at Polo Grounds)

Yankees	001	000	000	—	1	7	2
Giants	000	011	04X	—	6	9	1

Yankees: RED RUFFING; Bill Dickey.
Giants: CARL HUBBELL; Gus Mancuso.
Home Runs: Dick Bartell (Giants) and George Selkirk (Yankees).
Attendance: 39,419.

Game 2 (Oct. 2 at Polo Grounds)

Yankees	207	001	206	—	18	17	0
Giants	010	300	000	—	4	6	1

Yankees: LEFTY GOMEZ; Bill Dickey.
Giants: HAL SCHUMACHER, Al Smith (3rd), Dick Coffman (3rd), Frank Gabler (5th), Harry Gumbert (9th); Gus Mancuso.
Home Runs: Bill Dickey (Yankees) and Tony Lazzeri (Yankees).
Attendance: 43,543.

Game 3 (Oct. 3 at Yankee Stadium)

Giants	000	010	000	—	1	11	0
Yankees	010	000	01X	—	2	4	0

Giants: FREDDIE FITZSIMMONS; Gus Mancuso.
Yankees: BUMP HADLEY, Pat Malone (9th); Bill Dickey.
Home Runs: Lou Gehrig (Yankees) and Jimmy Ripple (Giants).
Attendance: 64,842.

Game 4 (Oct. 4 at Yankee Stadium)

Giants	000	100	010	—	2	7	1
Yankees	013	000	01X	—	5	10	1

Giants: CARL HUBBELL, Frank Gabler (8th); Gus Mancuso.
Yankees: MONTE PEARSON; Bill Dickey.
Home Run: Lou Gehrig (Yankees).
Attendance: 66,669.

Game 5 (Oct. 5 at Yankee Stadium)

Giants	300	001	000	1	—	5	8	3
Yankees	011	002	000	0	—	4	10	1

Giants: HAL SCHUMACHER; Gus Mancuso.
Yankees: Red Ruffing, PAT MALONE (7th); Bill Dickey.
Home Run: George Selkirk (Yankees).
Attendance: 50,024.

Game 6 (Oct. 6 at Polo Grounds)

Yankees	021	200	017	—	13	17	2
Giants	200	010	100	—	5	9	1

Yankees: LEFTY GOMEZ, Johnny Murphy (7th); Bill Dickey.
Giants: FREDDIE FITZSIMMONS, Slick Castleman (4th), Dick Coffman (9th), Harry Gumbert (9th); Gus Mancuso, Harry Danning (8th).
Home Runs: Jo-Jo Moore (Giants), Mel Ott (Giants), and Jake Powell (Yankees).
Attendance: 38,427.

1937 WORLD CHAMPIONS

Manager: Joe McCarthy.
World Series Roster: Pitchers: Ivy Andrews, Spud Chandler, Lefty Gomez, Bump Hadley, Frank Makosky, Pat Malone, Johnny Murphy, Monte Pearson, Red Ruffing, Kemp Wicker. *Catchers:* Bill Dickey, Joe Glenn, Art Jorgens. *Infielders:* Frank Crosetti, Lou Gehrig, Don Heffner, Tony Lazzeri, Red Rolfe, Jack Saltzgaver. *Outfielders:* Joe DiMaggio, Tommy Henrich, Myril Hoag, Jake Powell, George Selkirk.

WORLD SERIES

	W	L	Pct.
Yankees	4	1	.800
Giants	1	4	.200

Game 1 (Oct. 6 at Yankee Stadium)

Giants	000	010	000	—	1	6	2
Yankees	000	007	01X	—	8	7	0

Giants: CARL HUBBELL, Harry Gumbert (6th), Dick Coffman (6th), Al Smith (8th); Gus Mancuso.
Yankees LEFTY GOMEZ; Bill Dickey.
Home Run: Tony Lazzeri (Yankees).
Attendance: 60,573.

Game 2 (Oct. 7 at Yankee Stadium)

Giants	100	000	000	—	1	7	0
Yankees	000	024	20X	—	8	12	0

Giants: CLIFF MELTON, Harry Gumbert (5th), Dick Coffman (6th); Gus Mancuso.
Yankees: RED RUFFING; Bill Dickey.
Home Runs: None.
Attendance: 57,675.

Game 3 (Oct. 8 at Polo Grounds)

Yankees	012	110	000	—	5	9	0
Giants	000	000	100	—	1	5	4

Yankees: MONTE PEARSON, Johnny Murphy (9th); Bill Dickey.
Giants: HAL SCHUMACHER, Cliff Melton (7th), Don Brennan (9th); Harry Danning.
Home Runs: None.
Attendance: 37,385.

Game 4 (Oct. 9 at Polo Grounds)

Yankees	101	000	001	—	3	6	0
Giants	060	000	10X	—	7	12	3

Yankees: BUMP HADLEY, Ivy Andrews (2nd), Kemp Wicker (8th); Bill Dickey.
Giants: CARL HUBBELL; Harry Danning.
Home Run: Lou Gehrig (Yankees).
Attendance: 44,293.

Game 5 (Oct. 10 at Polo Grounds)

Yankees	011	020	000	—	4	8	0
Giants	002	000	000	—	2	10	0

Yankees: LEFTY GOMEZ; Bill Dickey.
Giants: CLIFF MELTON, Al Smith (6th), Don Brennan (8th); Harry Danning.
Home Runs: Joe DiMaggio (Yankees), Myril Hoag (Yankees), and Mel Ott (Giants).
Attendance: 38,216.

1938 WORLD CHAMPIONS

Manager: Joe McCarthy.
World Series Roster: Pitchers: Ivy Andrews, Spud Chandler, Wes Ferrell, Lefty Gomez, Bump Hadley, Johnny Murphy, Monte Pearson, Red Ruffing, Steve Sundra. *Catchers:* Bill Dickey, Joe Glenn, Art Jorgens. *Infielders:* Frank Crosetti, Babe Dahlgren, Lou Gehrig, Joe Gordon, Bill Knickerbocker, Red Rolfe. *Outfielders:* Joe DiMaggio, Tommy Henrich, Myril Hoag, Jake Powell, George Selkirk.

WORLD SERIES

	W	L	Pct.
Yankees	4	0	1.000
Cubs	0	4	.000

Game 1 (Oct. 5 at Chicago)

Yankees	020	000	100	—	3	12	1
Cubs	001	000	000	—	1	9	1

Yankees: RED RUFFING; Bill Dickey.
Cubs: BILL LEE, Jack Russell (9th); Gabby Hartnett.
Home Runs: None.
Attendance: 43,642.

Game 2 (Oct. 6 at Chicago)

Yankees	020	000	022	—	6	7	2
Cubs	102	000	000	—	3	11	0

Yankees: LEFTY GOMEZ, Johnny Murphy (8th); Bill Dickey.
Cubs: DIZZY DEAN, Larry French (9th); Gabby Hartnett.
Home Runs: Frank Crosetti (Yankees) and Joe DiMaggio (Yankees).
Attendance: 42,108.

Game 3 (Oct. 8 at Yankee Stadium)

Cubs	000	010	010	—	2	5	1
Yankees	000	022	01X	—	5	7	2

Cubs: CLAY BRYANT, Jack Russell (6th), Larry French (7th); Gabby Hartnett.
Yankees: MONTE PEARSON; Bill Dickey.
Home Runs: Bill Dickey (Yankees), Joe Gordon (Yankees), and Joe Marty (Cubs).
Attendance: 55,236.

Game 4 (Oct. 9 at Yankee Stadium)

Cubs	000	100	020	—	3	8	1
Yankees	030	001	04X	—	8	11	1

Cubs: BILL LEE, Charlie Root (4th), Vance Page (7th), Larry French (8th), Tex Carleton (8th), Dizzy Dean (8th); Ken O'Dea.
Yankees: RED RUFFING; Bill Dickey.
Home Runs: Tommy Henrich (Yankees) and Ken O'Dea (Cubs).
Attendance: 59,847.

1939 WORLD CHAMPIONS

Manager: Joe McCarthy.
World Series Roster: Pitchers: Spud Chandler, Atley Donald, Lefty Gomez, Bump Hadley, Oral Hildebrand, Johnny Murphy, Monte Pearson, Red Ruffing, Marius Russo, Steve Sundra. *Catchers:* Bill Dickey, Art Jorgens, Buddy Rosar. *Infielders:* Frank Crosetti, Babe Dahlgren, Lou Gehrig, Joe Gordon, Bill Knickerbocker, Red Rolfe. *Outfielders:* Joe DiMaggio, Tommy Henrich, Charlie Keller, Jake Powell, George Selkirk.

WORLD SERIES

	W	L	Pct.
Yankees	4	0	1.000
Reds	0	4	.000

Game 1 (Oct. 4 at Yankee Stadium)

Reds	000	100	000	—	1	4	0
Yankees	000	010	001	—	2	6	0

Reds: PAUL DERRINGER; Ernie Lombardi.
Yankees: RED RUFFING; Bill Dickey.
Home Runs: None.
Attendance: 58,541.

Game 2 (Oct. 5 at Yankee Stadium)

Reds	000	000	000	—	0	2	0
Yankees	003	100	00X	—	4	9	0

Reds: BUCKY WALTERS; Ernie Lombardi, Willard Hershberger (8th).
Yankees: MONTE PEARSON; Bill Dickey.
Home Run: Babe Dahlgren (Yankees).
Attendance: 59,791.

Game 3 (Oct. 7 at Cincinnati)

Yankees	202	030	000	—	7	5	1
Reds	120	000	000	—	3	10	0

Yankees: Lefty Gomez, BUMP HADLEY (2nd); Bill Dickey.
Reds: JUNIOR THOMPSON, Lee Grissom (5th), Whitey Moore (7th); Ernie Lombardi, Willard Hershberger (8th).
Home Runs: Charlie Keller (Yankees) 2, Joe DiMaggio (Yankees), and Bill Dickey (Yankees).
Attendance: 32,723.

Game 4 (Oct. 8 at Cincinnati)

Yankees	000	000	202	3	—	7	7	1
Reds	000	000	310	0	—	4	11	4

Yankees: Oral Hildebrand, Steve Sundra (5th), JOHNNY MURPHY (7th); Bill Dickey.
Reds: Paul Derringer, BUCKY WALTERS (8th); Ernie Lombardi.
Home Runs: Charlie Keller (Yankees) and Bill Dickey (Yankees).
Attendance: 32,794.

1941 WORLD CHAMPIONS

Manager: Joe McCarthy.
World Series Roster: Pitchers: Ernie Bonham, Norm Branch, Marv Breuer, Spud Chandler, Atley Donald, Lefty Gomez, Johnny Murphy, Steve Peek, Red Ruffing, Marius Russo, Charley Stanceu. *Catchers:* Bill Dickey, Buddy Rosar, Ken Silvestri. *Infielders:* Frank Crosetti, Joe Gordon, Jerry Priddy, Phil Rizzuto, Red Rolfe, Johnny Sturm. *Outfielders:* Frenchy Bordagaray, Joe DiMaggio, Tommy Henrich, Charlie Keller, George Selkirk.

WORLD SERIES

	W	L	Pct.
Yankees	4	1	.800
Dodgers	1	4	.200

Game 1 (Oct. 1 at Yankee Stadium)

| Dodgers | 000 | 010 | 100 | — | 2 | 6 | 0 |
| Yankees | 010 | 101 | 00X | — | 3 | 6 | 1 |

Dodgers: CURT DAVIS, Hugh Casey (6th), Johnny Allen (7th); Mickey Owen, Herman Franks (7th).
Yankees: RED RUFFING; Bill Dickey.
Home Run: Joe Gordon (Yankees).
Attendance: 68,540.

Game 2 (Oct. 2 at Yankee Stadium)

| Dodgers | 000 | 021 | 000 | — | 3 | 6 | 2 |
| Yankees | 011 | 000 | 000 | — | 2 | 9 | 1 |

Dodgers: WHITLOW WYATT; Mickey Owen.
Yankees: SPUD CHANDLER, Johnny Murphy (6th); Bill Dickey, Buddy Rosar (9th).
Home Runs: None.
Attendance: 66,248.

Game 3 (Oct. 4 at Brooklyn)

| Yankees | 000 | 000 | 020 | — | 2 | 8 | 0 |
| Dodgers | 000 | 000 | 010 | — | 1 | 4 | 0 |

Yankees: MARIUS RUSSO; Bill Dickey.
Dodgers: Freddie Fitzsimmons, HUGH CASEY (8th), Larry French (8th), Johnny Allen (9th); Mickey Owen.
Home Runs: None.
Attendance: 33,100.

Game 4 (Oct. 5 at Brooklyn)

| Yankees | 100 | 200 | 004 | — | 7 | 12 | 0 |
| Dodgers | 000 | 220 | 000 | — | 4 | 9 | 1 |

Yankees: Atley Donald, Marv Breuer (5th), JOHNNY MURPHY (8th); Bill Dickey.
Dodgers: Kirby Higbe, Larry French (4th), Johnny Allen (5th), HUGH CASEY (5th); Mickey Owen.
Home Run: Pete Reiser (Dodgers).
Attendance: 33,813.

Game 5 (Oct. 6 at Brooklyn)

| Yankees | 020 | 010 | 000 | — | 3 | 6 | 0 |
| Dodgers | 001 | 000 | 000 | — | 1 | 4 | 1 |

Yankees: ERNIE BONHAM; Bill Dickey.
Dodgers: WHITLOW WYATT; Mickey Owen.
Home Run: Tommy Henrich (Yankees).
Attendance: 34,072.

1942 AMERICAN LEAGUE CHAMPIONS

Manager: Joe McCarthy.
World Series Roster: Pitchers: Ernie Bonham, Hank Borowy, Marv Breuer, Spud Chandler, Atley Donald, Lefty Gomez, Johnny Lindell, Johnny Murphy, Red Ruffing, Marius Russo, Jim Turner. *Catchers:* Bill Dickey, Rollie Hemsley, Buddy Rosar. *Infielders:* Frank Crosetti, Joe Gordon, Buddy Hassett, Jerry Priddy, Phil Rizzuto, Red Rolfe. *Outfielders:* Roy Cullenbine, Joe DiMaggio, Charlie Keller, George Selkirk, Tuck Stainback.

WORLD SERIES

	W	L	Pct.
Cardinals	4	1	.800
Yankees	1	4	.200

Game 1 (Sept. 30 at St. Louis)

| Yankees | 000 | 110 | 032 | — | 7 | 11 | 0 |
| Cardinals | 000 | 000 | 004 | — | 4 | 7 | 4 |

Yankees: RED RUFFING, Spud Chandler (9th); Bill Dickey.
Cardinals: MORT COOPER, Harry Gumbert (8th), Max Lanier (9th); Walker Cooper.
Home Runs: None.
Attendance: 34,769.

Game 2 (Oct. 1 at St. Louis)

| Yankees | 000 | 000 | 030 | — | 3 | 10 | 2 |
| Cardinals | 200 | 000 | 11X | — | 4 | 6 | 0 |

Yankees: ERNIE BONHAM; Bill Dickey.
Cardinals: JOHNNY BEAZLEY; Walker Cooper.
Home Run: Charlie Keller (Yankees).
Attendance: 34,255.

Game 3 (Oct. 3 at Yankee Stadium)

| Cardinals | 001 | 000 | 001 | — | 2 | 5 | 1 |
| Yankees | 000 | 000 | 000 | — | 0 | 6 | 1 |

Cardinals: ERNIE WHITE; Walker Cooper.
Yankees: SPUD CHANDLER, Marv Breuer (9th), Jim Turner (9th); Bill Dickey.
Home Runs: None.
Attendance: 69,123.

Game 4 (Oct. 4 at Yankee Stadium)

| Cardinals | 000 | 600 | 201 | — | 9 | 12 | 1 |
| Yankees | 100 | 005 | 000 | — | 6 | 10 | 1 |

Cardinals: Mort Cooper, Harry Gumbert (6th), Howie Pollet (6th), MAX LANIER (7th); Walker Cooper.
Yankees: Hank Borowy, ATLEY DONALD (4th), Ernie Bonham (7th); Bill Dickey.
Home Run: Charlie Keller (Yankees).
Attendance: 69,902.

Game 5 (Oct. 5 at Yankee Stadium)

| Cardinals | 000 | 101 | 002 | — | 4 | 9 | 4 |
| Yankees | 100 | 100 | 000 | — | 2 | 7 | 1 |

Cardinals: JOHNNY BEAZLEY; Walker Cooper.
Yankees: RED RUFFING; Bill Dickey.
Home Runs: Phil Rizzuto (Yankees), Enos Slaughter (Cardinals), and Whitey Kurowski (Cardinals).
Attendance: 69,052.

1943 WORLD CHAMPIONS

Manager: Joe McCarthy.
World Series Roster: Pitchers: Ernie Bonham, Hank Borowy, Marv Breuer, Tommy Byrne, Spud Chandler, Atley Donald, Johnny Murphy, Marius Russo, Jim Turner, Butch Wensloff, Bill Zuber. *Catchers:* Bill Dickey, Rollie Hemsley, Ken Sears. *Infielders:* Frank Crosetti, Nick Etten, Joe Gordon, Oscar Grimes, Billy Johnson, Snuffy Stirnweiss. *Outfielders:* Charlie Keller, Johnny Lindell, Bud Metheny, Tuck Stainback, Roy Weatherly.

WORLD SERIES

	W	L	Pct.
Yankees	4	1	.800
Cardinals	1	4	.200

Game 1 (Oct. 5 at Yankee Stadium)

| Cardinals | 010 | 010 | 000 | — | 2 | 7 | 2 |
| Yankees | 000 | 202 | 00X | — | 4 | 8 | 2 |

Cardinals: MAX LANIER, Harry Brecheen (8th); Walker Cooper.
Yankees: SPUD CHANDLER; Bill Dickey.
Home Run: Joe Gordon (Yankees).
Attendance: 68,676.

Game 2 (Oct. 6 at Yankee Stadium)

| Cardinals | 001 | 300 | 000 | — | 4 | 7 | 2 |
| Yankees | 000 | 100 | 002 | — | 3 | 6 | 0 |

Cardinals: MORT COOPER; Walker Cooper.
Yankees: ERNIE BONHAM, Johnny Murphy (9th); Bill Dickey.
Home Runs: Marty Marion (Cardinals) and Ray Sanders (Cardinals).
Attendance: 68,578.

Game 3 (Oct. 7 at Yankee Stadium)

Cardinals	000	200	000	—	2	6	4
Yankees	000	001	05X	—	6	8	0

Cardinals: AL BRAZLE, Howie Krist (8th), Harry Brecheen (8th); Walker Cooper.
Yankees: HANK BOROWY, Johnny Murphy (9th); Bill Dickey.
Home Runs: None.
Attendance: 69,990.

Game 4 (Oct. 10 at St. Louis)

Yankees	000	100	010	—	2	6	2
Cardinals	000	000	100	—	1	7	1

Yankees: MARIUS RUSSO; Bill Dickey.
Cardinals: Max Lanier, HARRY BRECHEEN (8th); Walker Cooper.
Home Runs: None.
Attendance: 36,196.

Game 5 (Oct. 11 at St. Louis)

Yankees	000	002	000	—	2	7	1
Cardinals	000	000	000	—	0	10	1

Yankees: SPUD CHANDLER; Bill Dickey.
Cardinals: MORT COOPER, Max Lanier (8th), Murry Dickson; Walker Cooper, Ken O'Dea.
Home Run: Bill Dickey (Yankees).
Attendance: 33,872.

NOTE: Because of wartime travel restrictions, the World Series' first three games were scheduled for New York, as many of the last four as necessary for St. Louis.

1947 WORLD CHAMPIONS

Manager: Bucky Harris.
World Series Roster: Pitchers: Bill Bevens, Spud Chandler, Karl Drews, Randy Gumpert, Don Johnson, Bobo Newsom, Joe Page, Vic Raschi, Allie Reynolds, Spec Shea, Butch Wensloff. *Catchers:* Yogi Berra, Ralph Houk, Sherm Lollar, Aaron Robinson. *Infielders:* Bobby Brown, Lonny Frey, Billy Johnson, George McQuinn, Jack Phillips, Phil Rizzuto, George Stirnweiss. *Outfielders:* Allie Clark, Joe DiMaggio, Tommy Henrich, Charlie Keller, Johnny Lindell.

WORLD SERIES

	W	L	Pct.
Yankees	4	3	.571
Dodgers	3	4	.429

Game 1 (Sept. 30 at Yankee Stadium)

Dodgers	100	001	100	—	3	6	0
Yankees	000	050	00X	—	5	4	0

Dodgers: RALPH BRANCA, Hank Behrman (5th), Hugh Casey (7th); Bruce Edwards.
Yankees: SPEC SHEA, Joe Page (6th); Yogi Berra.
Home Runs: None.
Attendance: 73,365.

Game 2 (Oct. 1 at Yankee Stadium)

Dodgers	001	100	001	—	3	9	2
Yankees	101	121	40X	—	10	15	1

Dodgers: VIC LOMBARDI, Hal Gregg (5th), Hank Behrman (7th), Rex Barney (7th); Bruce Edwards.
Yankees: ALLIE REYNOLDS; Yogi Berra.
Home Runs: Dixie Walker (Dodgers) and Tommy Henrich (Yankees).
Attendance: 69,865.

Game 3 (Oct. 2 at Brooklyn)

Yankees	002	221	100	—	8	13	0
Dodgers	061	200	00X	—	9	13	1

Yankees: BOBO NEWSOM, Vic Raschi (2nd), Karl Drews (3rd), Spud Chandler (4th), Joe Page (6th); Sherm Lollar, Yogi Berra (7th).
Dodgers: Joe Hatten, Ralph Branca (5th), HUGH CASEY (7th); Bruce Edwards.
Home Runs: Joe DiMaggio (Yankees) and Yogi Berra (Yankees).
Attendance: 33,098.

Game 4 (Oct. 3 at Brooklyn)

Yankees	100	100	000	—	2	8	1
Dodgers	000	010	002	—	3	1	3

Yankees: BILL BEVENS; Yogi Berra.
Dodgers: Harry Taylor, Hal Gregg (1st), Hank Behrman (8th), HUGH CASEY (9th); Bruce Edwards.
Home Runs: None.
Attendance: 33,443.

Game 5 (Oct. 4 at Brooklyn)

Yankees	000	110	000	—	2	5	0
Dodgers	000	001	000	—	1	4	1

Yankees: SPEC SHEA; Aaron Robinson.
Dodgers: REX BARNEY, Joe Hatten (5th), Hank Behrman (7th), Hugh Casey (8th); Bruce Edwards.
Home Run: Joe DiMaggio (Yankees).
Attendance: 34,379.

Game 6 (Oct. 5 at Yankee Stadium)

Dodgers	202	004	000	—	8	12	1
Yankees	004	100	001	—	6	15	2

Dodgers: Vic Lombardi, RALPH BRANCA (3rd), Joe Hatten (6th), Hugh Casey (9th); Bruce Edwards.
Yankees: Allie Reynolds, Karl Drews (3rd), JOE PAGE (5th), Bobo Newsom (6th), Vic Raschi (7th), Butch Wensloff (8th); Sherm Lollar, Aaron Robinson (4th).
Home Runs: None.
Attendance: 74,065.

Game 7 (Oct. 6 at Yankee Stadium)

Dodgers	020	000	000	—	2	7	0
Yankees	010	201	10X	—	5	7	0

Dodgers: HAL GREGG, Hank Behrman (4th), Joe Hatten (6th), Rex Barney (6th), Hugh Casey (7th); Bruce Edwards.
Yankees: Spec Shea, Bill Bevens (2nd), JOE PAGE (5th); Aaron Robinson.
Home Runs: None.
Attendance: 71,548.

1949 WORLD CHAMPIONS

Manager: Casey Stengel.
World Series Roster: Pitchers: Ralph Buxton, Tommy Byrne, Ed Lopat, Cuddles Marshall, Joe Page, Duane Pillette, Vic Raschi, Allie Reynolds, Fred Sanford. *Catchers:* Yogi Berra, Gus Niarhos, Charlie Silvera. *Infielders:* Bobby Brown, Jerry Coleman, Tommy Henrich, Billy Johnson, Johnny Mize, Phil Rizzuto, Snuffy Stirnweiss. *Outfielders:* Hank Bauer, Joe DiMaggio, Charlie Keller, Johnny Lindell, Cliff Mapes, Gene Woodling.

WORLD SERIES

	W	L	Pct.
Yankees	4	1	.800
Dodgers	1	4	.200

Game 1 (Oct. 5 at Yankee Stadium)

Dodgers	000	000	000	—	0	2	0
Yankees	000	000	001	—	1	5	1

Dodgers: DON NEWCOMBE; Roy Campanella.
Yankees: ALLIE REYNOLDS; Yogi Berra.
Home Run: Tommy Henrich (Yankees).
Attendance: 66,230.

Game 2 (Oct. 6 at Yankee Stadium)

Dodgers	010	000	000	—	1	7	2
Yankees	000	000	000	—	0	6	1

Dodgers: PREACHER ROE; Roy Campanella.
Yankees: VIC RASCHI, Joe Page (9th); Charlie Silvera, Gus Niarhos (9th).
Home Runs: None.
Attendance: 70,053.

Game 3 (Oct. 7 at Brooklyn)

Yankees	001	000	003	—	4	5	0
Dodgers	000	100	002	—	3	5	0

Yankees: Tommy Byrne, JOE PAGE (4th); Yogi Berra.
Dodgers: RALPH BRANCA, Jack Banta (9th); Roy Campanella.
Home Runs: Pee Wee Reese (Dodgers), Luis Olmo (Dodgers), and Roy Campanella (Dodgers).
Attendance: 32,788.

Game 4 (Oct. 8 at Brooklyn)

Yankees	000	330	000	—	6	10	0
Dodgers	000	004	000	—	4	9	1

Yankees: ED LOPAT, Allie Reynolds (6th); Yogi Berra.
Dodgers: DON NEWCOMBE, Joe Hatten (4th), Carl Erskine (6th), Jack Banta (7th); Roy Campanella.
Home Runs: None.
Attendance: 33,934.

Game 5 (Oct. 9 at Brooklyn)

Yankees	203	113	000	—	10	11	1
Dodgers	001	001	400	—	6	11	2

Yankees: VIC RASCHI, Joe Page (7th); Yogi Berra.
Dodgers: REX BARNEY, Jack Banta (3rd), Carl Erskine (6th), Joe Hatten (6th), Erv Palica (7th), Paul Minner (9th); Roy Campanella.
Home Runs: Joe DiMaggio (Yankees) and Gil Hodges (Dodgers).
Attendance: 33,711.

1950 WORLD CHAMPIONS

Manager: Casey Stengel.
World Series Roster: Pitchers: Tommy Byrne, Tom Ferrick, Whitey Ford, Ed Lopat, Joe Ostrowski, Joe Page, Vic Raschi, Allie Reynolds, Fred Sanford. *Catchers:* Yogi Berra, Ralph Houk, Charlie Silvera. *Infielders:* Bobby Brown, Jerry Coleman, Joe Collins, Johnny Hopp, Billy Johnson, Billy Martin, Johnny Mize, Phil Rizzuto. *Outfielders:* Hank Bauer, Joe DiMaggio, Jackie Jensen, Cliff Mapes, Gene Woodling.

WORLD SERIES

	W	L	Pct.
Yankees	4	0	1.000
Phillies	0	4	.000

Game 1 (Oct. 4 at Philadelphia)

Yankees	000	100	000	—	1	5	0
Phillies	000	000	000	—	0	2	1

Yankees: VIC RASCHI; Yogi Berra.
Phillies: JIM KONSTANTY, Russ Meyer (9th); Andy Seminick.
Home Runs: None.
Attendance: 30,746.

Game 2 (Oct. 5 at Philadelphia)

Yankees	010	000	000	1	—	2	10	0
Phillies	000	010	000	0	—	1	7	0

Yankees: ALLIE REYNOLDS; Yogi Berra.
Phillies: ROBIN ROBERTS; Andy Seminick, Ken Silvestri (8th), Stan Lopata (10th).

Home Run: Joe DiMaggio (Yankees).
Attendance: 32,660.

Game 3 (Oct. 6 at Yankee Stadium)

Phillies	000	001	100	—	2	10	2
Yankees	001	000	011	—	3	7	0

Phillies: Ken Heintzelman, Jim Konstanty (8th), RUSS MEYER (9th); Andy Seminick.
Yankees: Ed Lopat, TOM FERRICK (9th); Yogi Berra.
Home Runs: None.
Attendance: 64,505.

Game 4 (Oct. 7 at Yankee Stadium)

Phillies	000	000	002	—	2	7	1
Yankees	200	003	00X	—	5	8	2

Phillies: BOB MILLER, Jim Konstanty (1st), Robin Roberts (8th); Andy Seminick.
Yankees: WHITEY FORD, Allie Reynolds (9th); Yogi Berra.
Home Run: Yogi Berra (Yankees).
Attendance: 68,098.

1951 WORLD CHAMPIONS

Manager: Casey Stengel.
World Series Roster: Pitchers: Bobby Hogue, Bob Kuzava, Ed Lopat, Tom Morgan, Joe Ostrowski, Stubby Overmire, Vic Raschi, Allie Reynolds, Johnny Sain, Art Schallock, Spec Shea. *Catchers:* Yogi Berra, Ralph Houk, Charlie Silvera. *Infielders:* Bobby Brown, Jerry Coleman, Joe Collins, Johnny Hopp, Billy Martin, Gil McDougald, Johnny Mize, Phil Rizzuto. *Outfielders:* Hank Bauer, Joe DiMaggio, Mickey Mantle, Gene Woodling.

WORLD SERIES

	W	L	Pct.
Yankees	4	2	.667
Giants	2	4	.333

Game 1 (Oct. 4 at Yankee Stadium)

Giants	200	003	000	—	5	10	1
Yankees	010	000	000	—	1	7	1

Giants: DAVE KOSLO; Wes Westrum.
Yankees: ALLIE REYNOLDS, Bobby Hogue (7th), Tom Morgan (8th); Yogi Berra.
Home Run: Al Dark (Giants).
Attendance: 65,673.

Game 2 (Oct. 5 at Yankee Stadium)

Giants	000	000	100	—	1	5	1
Yankees	110	000	01X	—	3	6	0

Giants: LARRY JANSEN, George Spencer (7th); Wes Westrum, Ray Noble (7th).
Yankees: ED LOPAT; Yogi Berra.
Home Run: Joe Collins (Yankees).
Attendance: 66,018.

Game 3 (Oct. 6 at Polo Grounds)

Yankees	000	000	011	—	2	5	2
Giants	010	050	00X	—	6	7	2

Yankees: VIC RASCHI, Bobby Hogue (5th), Joe Ostrowski (7th); Yogi Berra.
Giants: JIM HEARN, Sheldon Jones (8th); Wes Westrum.
Home Runs: Whitey Lockman (Giants) and Gene Woodling (Yankees).
Attendance: 52,035.

Game 4 (Oct. 8 at Polo Grounds)

Yankees	010	120	200	—	6	12	0
Giants	100	000	001	—	2	8	2

Yankees: ALLIE REYNOLDS; Yogi Berra.
Giants: SAL MAGLIE, Sheldon Jones (6th), Monte Kennedy (9th); Wes Westrum.

Home Run: Joe DiMaggio (Yankees).
Attendance: 49,010.

Game 5 (Oct. 9 at Polo Grounds)

Yankees	005	202	400	—	13	12	1
Giants	100	000	000	—	1	5	3

Yankees: ED LOPAT; Yogi Berra.
Giants: LARRY JANSEN, Monte Kennedy (4th), George Spencer (6th), Al Corwin (7th), Alex Konikowski (9th); Wes Westrum.
Home Runs: Gil McDougald (Yankees) and Phil Rizzuto (Yankees).
Attendance: 47,530.

Game 6 (Oct. 10 at Yankee Stadium)

Giants	000	010	002	—	3	11	1
Yankees	100	003	00X	—	4	7	0

Giants: DAVE KOSLO, Jim Hearn (7th), Larry Jansen (8th); Wes Westrum, Ray Noble (8th).
Yankees: VIC RASCHI, Johnny Sain (7th), Bob Kuzava (9th); Yogi Berra.
Home Runs: None.
Attendance: 61,711.

1952 WORLD CHAMPIONS

Manager: Casey Stengel.
World Series Roster: Pitchers: Ewell Blackwell, Tom Gorman, Bob Kuzava, Ed Lopat, Jim McDonald, Bill Miller, Joe Ostrowski, Vic Raschi, Allie Reynolds, Johnny Sain, Ray Scarborough. *Catchers:* Yogi Berra, Ralph Houk, Charlie Silvera. *Infielders:* Loren Babe, Jim Brideweser, Joe Collins, Billy Martin, Gil McDougald, Johnny Mize, Phil Rizzuto. *Outfielders:* Hank Bauer, Mickey Mantle, Irv Noren, Gene Woodling.

WORLD SERIES

	W	L	Pct.
Yankees	4	3	.571
Dodgers	3	4	.429

Game 1 (Oct. 1 at Brooklyn)

Yankees	001	000	010	—	2	6	2
Dodgers	010	002	01X	—	4	6	0

Yankees: ALLIE REYNOLDS, Ray Scarborough (8th); Yogi Berra.
Dodgers: JOE BLACK; Roy Campanella.
Home Runs: Jackie Robinson (Dodgers), Gil McDougald (Yankees), Duke Snider (Dodgers), and Pee Wee Reese (Dodgers).
Attendance: 34,861.

Game 2 (Oct. 2 at Brooklyn)

Yankees	000	115	000	—	7	10	0
Dodgers	001	000	000	—	1	3	1

Yankees: VIC RASCHI; Yogi Berra.
Dodgers: CARL ERSKINE, Billy Loes (6th), Ken Lehman (8th); Roy Campanella.
Home Run: Billy Martin (Yankees).
Attendance: 33,792.

Game 3 (Oct. 3 at Yankee Stadium)

Dodgers	001	010	012	—	5	11	0
Yankees	010	000	011	—	3	6	2

Dodgers: PREACHER ROE; Roy Campanella.
Yankees: ED LOPAT, Tom Gorman (9th); Yogi Berra.
Home Runs: Yogi Berra (Yankees) and Johnny Mize (Yankees).
Attendance: 66,698.

Game 4 (Oct. 4 at Yankee Stadium)

Dodgers	000	000	000	—	0	4	1
Yankees	000	100	01X	—	2	4	1

Dodgers: JOE BLACK, Johnny Rutherford (8th); Roy Campanella.
Yankees: ALLIE REYNOLDS; Yogi Berra.
Home Run: Johnny Mize (Yankees).
Attendance: 71,787.

Game 5 (Oct. 5 at Yankee Stadium)

Dodgers	010	030	100	01	—	6	10	0
Yankees	000	050	000	00	—	5	5	1

Dodgers: CARL ERSKINE; Roy Campanella.
Yankees: Ewell Blackwell. JOHNNY SAIN (6th); Yogi Berra.
Home Runs: Duke Snider (Dodgers) and Johnny Mize (Yankees).
Attendance: 70,536.

Game 6 (Oct. 6 at Brooklyn)

Yankees	000	000	210	—	3	9	10
Dodgers	000	001	010	—	2	8	1

Yankees: VIC RASCHI, Allie Reynolds (8th); Yogi Berra.
Dodgers: BILLY LOES, Preacher Roe (9th); Roy Campanella.
Home Runs: Duke Snider (Dodgers) 2, Yogi Berra (Yankees), and Mickey Mantle (Yankees).
Attendance: 30,037.

Game 7 (Oct. 7 at Brooklyn)

Yankees	000	111	100	—	4	10	4
Dodgers	000	110	000	—	2	8	1

Yankees: Ed Lopat, ALLIE REYNOLDS (4th), Vic Raschi (7th), Bob Kuzava (7th); Yogi Berra.
Dodgers: JOE BLACK, Preacher Roe (6th), Carl Erskine (8th); Roy Campanella.
Home Runs: Gene Woodling (Yankees) and Mickey Mantle (Yankees).
Attendance: 33,195.

1953 WORLD CHAMPIONS

Manager: Casey Stengel.
World Series Roster: Pitchers: Whitey Ford, Tom Gorman, Steve Kraly, Bob Kuzava, Ed Lopat, Jim McDonald, Bill Miller, Vic Raschi, Allie Reynolds, Johnny Sain, Art Schallock. *Catchers:* Yogi Berra, Charlie Silvera, Gus Triandos. *Infielders:* Don Bollweg, Andy Carey, Jerry Coleman, Joe Collins, Billy Martin, Gil McDougald, Willie Miranda, Johnny Mize, Phil Rizzuto. *Outfielders:* Hank Bauer, Mickey Mantle, Irv Noren, Bill Renna, Gene Woodling.

WORLD SERIES

	W	L	Pct.
Yankees	4	2	.667
Dodgers	2	4	.333

Game 1 (Sept. 30 at Yankee Stadium)

Dodgers	000	013	100	—	5	12	2
Yankees	400	010	13X	—	9	12	2

Dodgers: Carl Erskine, Jim Hughes (2nd), CLEM LABINE (6th), Ben Wade (7th); Roy Campanella.
Yankees: Allie Reynolds, JOHNNY SAIN (6th); Yogi Berra.
Home Runs: Jim Gilliam (Dodgers), Yogi Berra (Yankees), Gil Hodges (Dodgers), George Shuba (Dodgers), and Joe Collins (Yankees).
Attendance: 69,374.

Game 2 (Oct. 1 at Yankee Stadium)

Dodgers	000	200	000	—	2	9	1
Yankees	100	000	12X	—	4	5	0

Dodgers: PREACHER ROE; Roy Campanella.
Yankees: ED LOPAT; Yogi Berra.
Home Runs: Billy Martin (Yankees) and Mickey Mantle (Yankees).
Attendance: 66,786.

Game 3 (Oct. 2 at Brooklyn)

Yankees	000	010	010	—	2	6	0
Dodgers	000	011	01X	—	3	9	0

Yankees: VIC RASCHI; Yogi Berra.
Dodgers: CARL ERSKINE; Roy Campanella.
Home Run: Roy Campanella (Dodgers).
Attendance: 35,270.

Game 4 (Oct. 3 at Brooklyn)

Yankees	000	020	001	—	3	9	0
Dodgers	300	102	10X	—	7	12	0

Yankees: WHITEY FORD, Tom Gorman (2nd), Johnny Sain (5th), Art Schallock (7th); Yogi Berra.
Dodgers: BILLY LOES, Clem Labine (9th); Roy Campanella.
Home Runs: Gil McDougald (Yankees) and Duke Snider (Dodgers).
Attendance: 36,775.

Game 5 (Oct. 4 at Brooklyn)

Yankees	105	000	311	—	11	11	1
Dodgers	010	010	041	—	7	14	1

Yankees: JIM McDONALD, Bob Kuzava (8th), Allie Reynolds (9th); Yogi Berra.
Dodgers: JOHNNY PODRES, Russ Meyer (3rd), Ben Wade (8th), Joe Black (9th); Roy Campanella.
Home Runs: Gene Woodling (Yankees), Mickey Mantle (Yankees), Billy Martin (Yankees), Billy Cox (Dodgers), Gil McDougald (Yankees), and Jim Gilliam (Dodgers).
Attendance: 36,775.

Game 6 (Oct. 5 at Yankee Stadium)

Dodgers	000	001	002	—	3	8	3
Yankees	210	000	001	—	4	13	0

Dodgers: Carl Erskine, Bob Milliken (5th), CLEM LABINE (7th); Roy Campanella.
Yankees: Whitey Ford, ALLIE REYNOLDS (8th); Yogi Berra.
Home Run: Carl Furillo (Dodgers).
Attendance: 62,370.

1955 AMERICAN LEAGUE CHAMPIONS

Manager: Casey Stengel.
World Series Roster: Pitchers: Tommy Byrne, Rip Coleman, Whitey Ford, Bob Grim, Johnny Kucks, Don Larsen, Tom Morgan, Tom Sturdivant, Bob Turley, Bob Wiesler. *Catchers:* Yogi Berra, Charlie Silvera. *Infielders:* Andy Carey, Tommy Carroll, Jerry Coleman, Joe Collins, Frank Leja, Billy Martin, Gil McDougald, Phil Rizzuto, Eddie Robinson, Bill Skowron. *Outfielders:* Hank Bauer, Bob Cerv, Elston Howard, Mickey Mantle, Irv Noren.

WORLD SERIES

	W	L	Pct.
Dodgers	4	3	.571
Yankees	3	4	.429

Game 1 (Sept. 28 at Yankee Stadium)

Dodgers	021	000	020	—	5	10	0
Yankees	021	102	00X	—	6	9	1

Dodgers: DON NEWCOMBE, Don Bessent (6th), Clem Labine (8th); Roy Campanella.
Yankees: WHITEY FORD, Bob Grim (9th); Yogi Berra.
Home Runs: Joe Collins (Yankees) 2, Carl Furillo (Dodgers), Elston Howard (Yankees), and Duke Snider (Dodgers).
Attendance: 63,869.

Game 2 (Sept. 29 at Yankee Stadium)

Dodgers	000	110	000	—	2	5	2
Yankees	000	400	00X	—	4	8	0

Dodgers: BILLY LOES, Don Bessent (4th), Karl Spooner (5th), Clem Labine (8th); Roy Campanella.
Yankees: TOMMY BYRNE; Yogi Berra.
Home Runs: None.
Attendance: 64,707.

Game 3 (Sept. 30 at Brooklyn)

Yankees	020	000	100	—	3	7	0
Dodgers	220	200	20X	—	8	11	1

Yankees: BOB TURLEY, Tom Morgan (2nd), Johnny Kucks (5th), Tom Sturdivant (7th); Yogi Berra.
Dodgers: JOHNNY PODRES; Roy Campanella.
Home Runs: Roy Campanella (Dodgers) and Mickey Mantle (Yankees).
Attendance: 34,209.

Game 4 (Oct. 1 at Brooklyn)

Yankees	110	102	000	—	5	9	0
Dodgers	001	330	10X	—	8	14	0

Yankees: DON LARSEN, Johnny Kucks (5th), Rip Coleman (6th), Tom Morgan (7th), Tom Sturdivant (8th); Yogi Berra.
Dodgers: Carl Erskine, Don Bessent (4th), CLEM LABINE (5th); Roy Campanella.
Home Runs: Gil McDougald (Yankees), Roy Campanella (Dodgers), Gil Hodges (Dodgers), and Duke Snider (Dodgers).
Attendance: 36,242.

Game 5 (Oct. 2 at Brooklyn)

Yankees	000	100	110	—	3	6	0
Dodgers	021	010	01X	—	5	9	2

Yankees: BOB GRIM, Bob Turley (7th); Yogi Berra.
Dodgers: ROGER CRAIG, Clem Labine (7th); Roy Campanella.
Home Runs: Duke Snider (Dodgers) 2, Sandy Amoros (Dodgers), Bob Cerv (Yankees), Yogi Berra (Yankees).
Attendance: 36,796.

Game 6 (Oct. 3 at Yankee Stadium)

Dodgers	000	100	000	—	1	4	1
Yankees	500	000	00X	—	5	8	0

Dodgers: KARL SPOONER, Russ Meyer (1st), Ed Roebuck (7th); Roy Campanella.
Yankees: WHITEY FORD; Yogi Berra.
Home Run: Bill Skowron (Yankees).
Attendance: 64,022.

Game 7 (Oct. 4 at Yankee Stadium)

Dodgers	000	101	000	—	2	5	0
Yankees	000	000	000	—	0	8	1

Dodgers: JOHNNY PODRES; Roy Campanella.
Yankees: TOMMY BYRNE, Bob Grim (6th), Bob Turley (8th); Yogi Berra.
Home Runs: None.
Attendance: 62,465.

1956 WORLD CHAMPIONS

Manager: Casey Stengel.
World Series Roster: Pitchers: Tommy Byrne, Rip Coleman, Whitey Ford, Bob Grim, Johnny Kucks, Don Larsen, Mickey McDermott, Tom Morgan, Tom Sturdivant, Bob Turley. *Catchers:* Yogi Berra, Charlie Silvera. *Infielders:* Andy Carey, Tommy Carroll, Jerry Coleman, Joe Collins, Billy Hunter, Billy Martin, Gil McDougald, Bill Skowron. *Outfielders:* Hank Bauer, Bob Cerv, Elston Howard, Mickey Mantle, Norm Siebern, Enos Slaughter, Ted Wilson.

WORLD SERIES

	W	L	Pct.
Yankees	4	3	.571
Dodgers	3	4	.429

Game 1 (Oct. 3 at Brooklyn)

Yankees	200	100	000	—	3	9	1
Dodgers	023	100	00X	—	6	9	0

Yankees: WHITEY FORD, Johnny Kucks (4th), Tom Morgan (6th), Bob Turley (8th); Yogi Berra.
Dodgers: SAL MAGLIE; Roy Campanella.
Home Runs: Mickey Mantle (Yankees), Jackie Robinson (Dodgers), Gil Hodges (Dodgers), and Billy Martin (Yankees)
Attendance: 34,479.

Game 2 (Oct. 5 at Brooklyn)

Yankees	150	100	001	—	8	12	2
Dodgers	061	220	02X	—	13	12	0

Yankees: Don Larsen, Johnny Kucks (2nd), Tommy Byrne (2nd), Tom Sturdivant (3rd), TOM MORGAN (3rd), Bob Turley (5th), Mickey McDermott (6th); Yogi Berra.
Dodgers: Don Newcombe, Ed Roebuck (2nd), DON BESSENT (3rd); Roy Campanella.
Home Runs: Yogi Berra (Yankees) and Duke Snider (Dodgers).
Attendance: 36,217.

Game 3 (Oct. 6 at Yankee Stadium)

Dodgers	010	001	100	—	3	8	1
Yankees	010	003	01X	—	5	8	1

Dodgers: ROGER CRAIG, Clem Labine (7th); Roy Campanella.
Yankees: WHITEY FORD; Yogi Berra.
Home Runs: Billy Martin (Yankees) and Enos Slaughter (Yankees).
Attendance: 73,977.

Game 4 (Oct. 7 at Yankee Stadium)

Dodgers	000	100	001	—	2	6	0
Yankees	100	201	20X	—	6	7	2

Dodgers: CARL ERSKINE, Ed Roebuck (5th), Don Drysdale (7th); Roy Campanella.
Yankees: TOM STURDIVANT; Yogi Berra.
Home Runs: Mickey Mantle (Yankees) and Hank Bauer (Yankees).
Attendance: 69,705.

Game 5 (Oct. 8 at Yankee Stadium)

Dodgers	000	000	000	—	0	0	0
Yankees	000	101	00X	—	2	5	0

Dodgers: SAL MAGLIE; Roy Campanella.
Yankees: DON LARSEN; Yogi Berra.
Home Run: Mickey Mantle (Yankees).
Attendance: 64,519.

Game 6 (Oct. 9 at Brooklyn)

Yankees	000	000	000	0	—	0	7	0
Dodgers	000	000	000	1	—	1	4	0

Yankees: BOB TURLEY; Yogi Berra.
Dodgers: CLEM LABINE; Roy Campanella.
Home Runs: None.
Attendance: 33,224.

Game 7 (Oct. 10 at Brooklyn)

Yankees	202	100	400	—	9	10	0
Dodgers	000	000	000	—	0	3	1

Yankees: JOHNNY KUCKS; Yogi Berra.
Dodgers: DON NEWCOMBE, Don Bessent (4th), Roger Craig (7th), Ed Roebuck (7th), Carl Erskine (9th); Roy Campanella.
Home Runs: Yogi Berra (Yankees) 2, Elston Howard (Yankees), and Bill Skowron (Yankees).
Attendance: 33,782.

1957 AMERICAN LEAGUE CHAMPIONS

Manager: Casey Stengel.
World Series Roster: Pitchers: Tommy Byrne, Al Cicotte, Art Ditmar, Whitey Ford, Bob Grim, Johnny Kucks, Don Larsen, Bobby Shantz, Tom Sturdivant, Rob Turley. *Catchers:* Yogi Berra, Darrell Johnson. *Infielders:* Andy Carey, Jerry Coleman, Joe Collins, Tony Kubek, Jerry Lumpe, Gil McDougald, Bobby Richardson, Bill Skowron. *Outfielders:* Hank Bauer, Elston Howard, Mickey Mantle, Harry Simpson, Enos Slaughter.

WORLD SERIES

	W	L	Pct.
Braves	4	3	.571
Yankees	3	4	.429

Game 1 (Oct. 2 at Yankee Stadium)

Braves	000	000	100	—	1	5	0
Yankees	000	012	00X	—	3	9	1

Braves: WARREN SPAHN, Ernie Johnson (6th), Don McMahon (7th); Del Crandall.
Yankees: WHITEY FORD; Yogi Berra.
Home Runs: None.
Attendance: 69,476.

Game 2 (Oct. 3 at Yankee Stadium)

Braves	011	200	000	—	4	8	0
Yankees	011	000	000	—	2	7	2

Braves: LEW BURDETTE; Del Crandall.
Yankees: BOBBY SHANTZ, Art Ditmar (4th), Bob Grim (8th); Yogi Berra.
Home Runs: Johnny Logan (Braves) and Hank Bauer (Yankees).
Attendance: 65,202.

Game 3 (Oct. 5 at Milwaukee)

Yankees	302	200	500	—	12	9	0
Braves	010	020	000	—	3	8	1

Yankees: Bob Turley, DON LARSEN (2nd); Yogi Berra.
Braves: BOB BUHL, Juan Pizarro (1st), Gene Conley (3rd), Ernie Johnson (5th), Bob Trowbridge (7th), Don McMahon (8th); Del Rice, Del Crandall (9th).
Home Runs: Tony Kubek (Yankees) 2, Mickey Mantle (Yankees), and Hank Aaron (Braves).
Attendance: 45,804.

Game 4 (Oct. 6 at Milwaukee)

Yankees	100	000	003	1	—	5	11	0
Braves	000	400	000	3	—	7	7	0

Yankees: Tom Sturdivant, Bobby Shantz (5th), Johnny Kucks (8th), Tommy Byrne (8th), BOB GRIM (10th); Yogi Berra.
Braves: WARREN SPAHN; Del Crandall.
Home Runs: Hank Aaron (Braves), Frank Torre (Braves), Elston Howard (Yankees), and Eddie Mathews (Braves).
Attendance: 45,804.

Game 5 (Oct. 7 at Milwaukee)

Yankees	000	000	000	—	0	7	0
Braves	000	001	00X	—	1	6	1

Yankees: WHITEY FORD, Bob Turley (8th); Yogi Berra.
Braves: LEW BURDETTE; Del Crandall.
Home Runs: None.
Attendance: 45,811.

Game 6 (Oct. 9 at Yankee Stadium)

Braves	000	010	100	—	2	4	0
Yankees	002	000	10X	—	3	7	0

Braves: Bob Buhl, ERNIE JOHNSON (3rd), Don McMahon (8th); Del Rice.
Yankees: BOB TURLEY; Yogi Berra.
Home Runs: Yogi Berra (Yankees), Frank Torre (Braves), Hank Aaron (Braves), and Hank Bauer (Yankees).
Attendance: 61,408.

Game 7 (Oct. 10 at Yankee Stadium)

Braves	004	000	010	—	5	9	1
Yankees	000	000	000	—	0	7	3

Braves: LEW BURDETTE; Del Crandall.
Yankees: DON LARSEN, Bobby Shantz (3rd), Art Ditmar (4th), Tom Sturdivant (6th), Tommy Byrne (8th); Yogi Berra.
Home Run: Del Crandall (Braves).
Attendance: 61,207.

1958 WORLD CHAMPIONS

Manager: Casey Stengel.
World Series Roster: Pitchers: Murry Dickson, Art Ditmar, Ryne Duren, Whitey Ford, Johnny Kucks, Don Larsen, Duke Maas, Zack Monroe, Bobby Shantz, Tom Sturdivant, Virgil Trucks, Bob Turley. *Catchers:* Yogi Berra, Elston Howard, Darrell Johnson. *Infielders:* Andy Carey, Tony Kubek, Jerry Lumpe, Gil McDougald, Bobby Richardson, Bill Skowron, Marv Throneberry. *Outfielders:* Hank Bauer, Mickey Mantle, Norm Siebern, Enos Slaughter.

WORLD SERIES

	W	L	Pct.
Yankees	4	3	.571
Braves	3	4	.429

Game 1 (Oct. 1 at Milwaukee)

Yankees	000	120	000	0	—	3	8	1
Braves	000	200	010	1	—	4	10	0

Yankees: Whitey Ford, RYNE DUREN (8th); Yogi Berra.
Braves: WARREN SPAHN; Del Crandall.
Home Runs: Bill Skowron (Yankees) and Hank Bauer (Yankees).
Attendance: 46,367.

Game 2 (Oct. 2 at Milwaukee)

Yankees	100	100	003	—	5	7	0
Braves	710	000	23X	—	13	15	1

Yankees: BOB TURLEY, Duke Maas (1st), Johnny Kucks (1st), Murry Dickson (5th), Zack Monroe (8th); Yogi Berra.
Braves: LEW BURDETTE; Del Crandall.
Home Runs: Mickey Mantle (Yankees) 2, Bill Bruton (Braves), Lew Burdette (Braves), and Hank Bauer (Yankees).
Attendance: 46,367.

Game 3 (Oct. 4 at Yankee Stadium)

Braves	000	000	000	—	0	6	0
Yankees	000	020	20X	—	4	4	0

Braves: BOB RUSH, Don McMahon (7th); Del Crandall.
Yankees: DON LARSEN, Ryne Duren (8th); Yogi Berra.
Home Run: Hank Bauer (Yankees).
Attendance: 71,599.

Game 4 (Oct. 5 at Yankee Stadium)

Braves	000	001	110	—	3	9	0
Yankees	000	000	000	—	0	2	1

Braves: WARREN SPAHN; Del Crandall.
Yankees: WHITEY FORD, Johnny Kucks (8th), Murry Dickson (9th); Yogi Berra.
Home Runs: None.
Attendance: 71,563.

Game 5 (Oct. 6 at Yankee Stadium)

Braves	000	000	000	—	0	5	0
Yankees	001	006	00X	—	7	10	0

Braves: LEW BURDETTE, Juan Pizarro (6th), Carlton Willey (8th); Del Crandall.
Yankees: BOB TURLEY; Yogi Berra.
Home Run: Gil McDougald (Yankees).
Attendance: 65,279.

Game 6 (Oct. 8 at Milwaukee)

Yankees	100	001	000	2	—	4	10	1
Braves	110	000	000	1	—	3	10	4

Yankees: Whitey Ford, Art Ditmar (2nd), RYNE DUREN (6th), Bob Turley (10th); Yogi Berra.
Braves: WARREN SPAHN, Don McMahon (10th); Del Crandall.
Home Runs: Hank Bauer (Yankees) and Gil McDougald (Yankees).
Attendance: 46,367.

Game 7 (Oct. 9 at Milwaukee)

Yankees	020	000	040	—	6	8	0
Braves	100	001	000	—	2	5	2

Yankees: Don Larsen, BOB TURLEY (3rd); Yogi Berra.
Braves: LEW BURDETTE, Don McMahon (9th); Del Crandall.
Home Runs: Del Crandall (Braves) and Bill Skowron (Yankees).
Attendance: 46,367.

1960 AMERICAN LEAGUE CHAMPIONS

Manager: Casey Stengel.
World Series Roster: Pitchers: Luis Arroyo, Jim Coates, Art Ditmar, Ryne Duren, Whitey Ford, Eli Grba, Duke Maas, Bobby Shantz, Bill Stafford, Ralph Terry, Bob Turley. *Catchers:* Yogi Berra, Johnny Blanchard, Elston Howard. *Infielders:* Clete Boyer, Joe DeMaestri, Tony Kubek, Dale Long, Gil McDougald, Bobby Richardson, Bill Skowron. *Outfielders:* Bob Cerv, Hector Lopez, Mickey Mantle, Roger Maris.

WORLD SERIES

	W	L	Pct.
Pirates	4	3	.571
Yankees	3	4	.429

Game 1 (Oct. 5 at Pittsburgh)

Yankees	100	100	002	—	4	13	2
Pirates	300	201	00X	—	6	8	0

Yankees: ART DITMAR, Jim Coates (1st), Duke Maas (5th), Ryne Duren (7th); Yogi Berra.
Pirates: VERNON LAW, Elroy Face (8th); Smoky Burgess.
Home Runs: Roger Maris (Yankees), Bill Mazeroski (Pirates), and Elston Howard (Yankees).
Attendance: 36,676.

Game 2 (Oct. 6 at Pittsburgh)

Yankees	002	127	301	—	16	19	1
Pirates	000	100	002	—	3	13	1

Yankees: BOB TURLEY, Bobby Shantz (9th); Elston Howard.
Pirates: BOB FRIEND, Freddie Green (5th), Clem Labine (6th), George Witt (6th), Joe Gibbon (7th), Tom Cheney (9th); Smoky Burgess.
Home Runs: Mickey Mantle (Yankees) 2.
Attendance: 37,308.

Game 3 (Oct. 8 at Yankee Stadium)

Pirates	000	000	000	—	0	4	0
Yankees	600	400	00X	—	10	16	1

Pirates: VINEGAR BEND MIZELL, Clem Labine (1st), Freddie Green (1st), George Witt (4th), Tom Cheney (6th), Joe Gibbon (8th); Hal Smith.
Yankees: WHITEY FORD; Elston Howard.
Home Runs: Bobby Richardson (Yankees) and Mickey Mantle (Yankees).
Attendance: 70,001.

Game 4 (Oct. 9 at Yankee Stadium)

Pirates	000	030	000	—	3	7	0
Yankees	000	100	100	—	2	8	0

Pirates: VERNON LAW, Elroy Face (7th); Smoky Burgess, Bob Oldis (9th).
Yankees: RALPH TERRY, Bobby Shantz (7th), Jim Coates (8th); Yogi Berra.
Home Run: Bill Skowron (Yankees).
Attendance: 67,812.

Game 5 (Oct. 10 at Yankee Stadium)

Pirates	031	000	001	—	5	10	2
Yankees	011	000	000	—	2	5	2

Pirates: HARVEY HADDIX, Elroy Face (7th); Smoky Burgess, Bob Oldis (9th).
Yankees: ART DITMAR, Luis Arroyo (2nd), Bill Stafford (3rd), Ryne Duren (8th); Elston Howard, Yogi Berra (8th).
Home Run: Roger Maris (Yankees).
Attendance: 62,753.

Game 6 (Oct. 12 at Pittsburgh)

Yankees	015	002	220	—	12	17	1
Pirates	000	000	000	—	0	7	1

Yankees: WHITEY FORD; Elston Howard, Johnny Blanchard (2nd).
Pirates: BOB FRIEND, Tom Cheney (3rd), Vinegar Bend Mizell (4th), Freddie Green (6th), Clem Labine (6th), George Witt (9th); Hal Smith.
Home Runs: None.
Attendance: 38,580.

Game 7 (Oct. 13 at Pittsburgh)

Yankees	000	014	022	—	9	13	1
Pirates	220	000	051	—	10	11	0

Yankees: Bob Turley, Bill Stafford (2nd), Bobby Shantz (3rd), Jim Coates (8th), RALPH TERRY (9th); Johnny Blanchard.
Pirates: Vernon Law, Elroy Face (6th), Bob Friend (9th), HARVEY HADDIX (9th); Smoky Burgess, Hal Smith (8th).
Home Runs: Rocky Nelson (Pirates), Bill Skowron (Yankees), Yogi Berra (Yankees), Hal Smith (Pirates), and Bill Mazeroski (Pirates).
Attendance: 36,683.

1961 WORLD CHAMPIONS

Manager: Ralph Houk.
World Series Roster: Pitchers: Luis Arroyo, Tex Clevenger, Jim Coates, Bud Daley, Al Downing, Whitey Ford, Hal Reniff, Rollie Sheldon, Bill Stafford, Ralph Terry, Bob Turley. *Catchers:* Johnny Blanchard, Elston Howard. *Infielders:* Clete Boyer, Joe DeMaestri, Billy Gardner, Bob Hale, Tony Kubek, Bobby Richardson, Bill Skowron. *Outfielders:* Yogi Berra, Hector Lopez, Mickey Mantle, Roger Maris, Jack Reed.

WORLD SERIES

	W	L	Pct.
Yankees	4	1	.800
Reds	1	4	.200

Game 1 (Oct. 4 at Yankee Stadium)

Reds	000	000	000	—	0	2	0
Yankees	000	101	00X	—	2	6	0

Reds: JIM O'TOOLE, Jim Brosnan (8th); Darrell Johnson, Jerry Zimmerman (8th).
Yankees: WHITEY FORD; Elston Howard.
Home Runs: Elston Howard (Yankees) and Bill Skowron (Yankees).
Attendance: 62,397.

Game 2 (Oct. 5 at Yankee Stadium)

Reds	000	211	020	—	6	9	0
Yankees	000	200	000	—	2	4	3

Reds: JOEY JAY; Johnny Edwards.
Yankees: RALPH TERRY, Luis Arroyo (8th); Elston Howard.
Home Runs: Gordy Coleman (Reds) and Yogi Berra (Yankees).
Attendance: 63,083.

Game 3 (Oct. 7 at Cincinnati)

Yankees	000	000	111	—	3	6	1
Reds	001	000	100	—	2	8	0

Yankees: Bill Stafford, Bud Daley (7th), LUIS ARROYO (8th); Elston Howard.
Reds: BOB PURKEY; Johnny Edwards.
Home Runs: Johnny Blanchard (Yankees) and Roger Maris (Yankees).
Attendance: 32,589.

Game 4 (Oct. 8 at Cincinnati)

Yankees	000	112	300	—	7	11	0
Reds	000	000	000	—	0	5	1

Yankees: WHITEY FORD, Jim Coates (6th); Elston Howard.
Reds: JIM O'TOOLE, Jim Brosnan (6th), Bill Henry (9th); Darrell Johnson, Jerry Zimmerman (8th).
Home Runs: None.
Attendance: 32,589.

Game 5 (Oct. 9 at Cincinnati)

Yankees	510	502	000	—	13	15	1
Reds	003	020	000	—	5	11	3

Yankees: Ralph Terry, BUD DALEY (3rd); Elston Howard.
Reds: JOEY JAY, Jim Maloney (1st), Ken Johnson (2nd), Bill Henry (3rd), Sherman Jones (4th), Bob Purkey (5th), Jim Brosnan (7th), Ken Hunt (9th); Johnny Edwards.
Home Runs: Johnny Blanchard (Yankees), Frank Robinson (Reds), Hector Lopez (Yankees), and Wally Post (Reds).
Attendance: 32,589.

1962 WORLD CHAMPIONS

Manager: Ralph Houk.
World Series Roster: Pitchers: Luis Arroyo, Jim Bouton, Marshall Bridges, Tex Clevenger, Jim Coates, Bud Daley, Whitey Ford, Rollie Sheldon, Bill Stafford, Ralph Terry, Bob Turley. *Catchers:* Johnny Blanchard, Elston Howard. *Infielders:* Clete Boyer, Tony Kubek, Phil Linz, Dale Long, Bobby Richardson, Bill Skowron. *Outfielders:* Yogi Berra, Hector Lopez, Mickey Mantle, Roger Maris, Jack Reed, Tom Tresh.

WORLD SERIES

	W	L	Pct.
Yankees	4	3	.571
Giants	3	4	.429

Game 1 (Oct. 4 at San Francisco)

Yankees	200	000	121	—	6	11	0
Giants	011	000	000	—	2	10	0

Yankees: WHITEY FORD; Elston Howard.
Giants: BILLY O'DELL, Don Larsen (8th), Stu Miller (9th); Ed Bailey, John Orsino (9th).
Home Run: Clete Boyer (Yankees).
Attendance: 43,852.

Game 2 (Oct. 5 at San Francisco)

Yankees	000	000	000	—	0	3	1
Giants	100	000	10X	—	2	6	0

Yankees: RALPH TERRY, Bud Daley (8th); Yogi Berra.
Giants: JACK SANFORD; Tom Haller.
Home Run: Willie McCovey (Giants).
Attendance: 43,910.

Game 3 (Oct. 7 at Yankee Stadium)

Giants	000	000	002	—	2	4	3
Yankees	000	000	30X	—	3	5	1

Giants: BILLY PIERCE, Don Larsen (7th), Bob Bolin (8th); Ed Bailey.
Yankees: BILL STAFFORD; Elston Howard.
Home Run: Ed Bailey (Giants).
Attendance: 71,434.

Game 4 (Oct. 8 at Yankee Stadium)

Giants	020	000	401	—	7	9	1
Yankees	000	002	001	—	3	9	1

Giants: Juan Marichal, Bob Bolin (5th), DON LARSEN (6th), Billy O'Dell (7th); Tom Haller.
Yankees: Whitey Ford, JIM COATES (7th), Marshall Bridges (7th); Elston Howard.
Home Runs: Tom Haller (Giants) and Chuck Hiller (Giants).
Attendance: 66,607.

Game 5 (Oct. 10 at Yankee Stadium)

Giants	001	010	001	—	3	8	2
Yankees	000	101	03X	—	5	6	0

Giants: JACK SANFORD, Stu Miller (8th); Tom Haller.
Yankees: RALPH TERRY; Elston Howard.
Home Runs: Jose Pagan (Giants) and Tom Tresh (Yankees).
Attendance: 63,165.

Game 6 (Oct. 15 at San Francisco)

Yankees	000	010	010	—	2	3	2
Giants	000	320	00X	—	5	10	1

Yankees: WHITEY FORD, Jim Coates (5th), Marshall Bridges (8th); Elston Howard.
Giants: BILLY PIERCE; Ed Bailey.
Home Run: Roger Maris (Yankees).
Attendance: 43,948.

Game 7 (Oct. 16 at San Francisco)

Yankees	000	010	000	—	1	7	0
Giants	000	000	000	—	0	4	1

Yankees: RALPH TERRY; Elston Howard.
Giants: JACK SANFORD, Billy O'Dell (8th); Tom Haller.
Home Runs: None.
Attendance: 43,948.

1963 AMERICAN LEAGUE CHAMPIONS

Manager: Ralph Houk.
World Series Roster: Pitchers: Jim Bouton, Marshall Bridges, Al Downing, Whitey Ford, Steve Hamilton, Bill Kunkel, Tom Metcalf, Hal Reniff, Bill Stafford, Ralph Terry, Stan Williams. *Catchers:* Yogi Berra, Elston Howard. *Infielders:* Clete Boyer, Harry Bright, Tony Kubek, Phil Linz, Joe Pepitone, Bobby Richardson. *Outfielders:* Johnny Blanchard, Hector Lopez, Mickey Mantle, Roger Maris, Jack Reed, Tom Tresh.

WORLD SERIES

	W	L	Pct.
Dodgers	4	0	1.000
Yankees	0	4	.000

Game 1 (Oct. 2 at Yankee Stadium)

Dodgers	041	000	000	—	5	9	0
Yankees	000	000	020	—	2	6	0

Dodgers: SANDY KOUFAX; John Roseboro.
Yankees: WHITEY FORD, Stan Williams (6th), Steve Hamilton (9th); Elston Howard.
Home Runs: John Roseboro (Dodgers) and Tom Tresh (Yankees).
Attendance: 69,000.

Game 2 (Oct. 3 at Yankee Stadium)

Dodgers	200	100	010	—	4	10	1
Yankees	000	000	001	—	1	7	0

Dodgers: JOHNNY PODRES, Ron Perranoski (9th); John Roseboro.
Yankees: AL DOWNING, Ralph Terry (6th), Hal Reniff (9th); Elston Howard.
Home Run: Bill Skowron (Dodgers).
Attendance 66,455.

Game 3 (Oct. 5 at Los Angeles)

Yankees	000	000	000	—	0	3	0
Dodgers	100	000	00X	—	1	4	1

Yankees: JIM BOUTON, Hal Reniff (8th); Elston Howard.
Dodgers: DON DRYSDALE; John Roseboro.
Home Runs: None.
Attendance: 55,912.

Game 4 (Oct. 6 at Los Angeles)

Yankees	000	000	100	—	1	6	1
Dodgers	000	010	10X	—	2	2	1

Yankees: WHITEY FORD, Hal Reniff (8th); Elston Howard.
Dodgers: SANDY KOUFAX; John Roseboro.
Home Runs: Frank Howard (Dodgers) and Mickey Mantle (Yankees).
Attendance: 55,912.

1964 AMERICAN LEAGUE CHAMPIONS

Manager: Yogi Berra.
World Series Roster: Pitchers: Jim Bouton, Al Downing, Whitey Ford, Steve Hamilton, Pete Mikkelsen, Hal Reniff, Rollie Sheldon, Bill Stafford, Mel Stottlemyre, Ralph Terry, Stan Williams. *Catchers:* Johnny Blanchard, Elston Howard. *Infielders:* Clete Boyer, Pedro Gonzalez, Mike Hegan, Tony Kubek, Phil Linz, Joe Pepitone, Bobby Richardson. *Outfielders:* Hector Lopez, Mickey Mantle, Roger Maris, Archie Moore, Tom Tresh.

WORLD SERIES

	W	L	Pct.
Cardinals	4	3	.571
Yankees	3	4	.429

Game 1 (Oct. 7 at St. Louis)

Yankees	030	010	010	—	5	12	2
Cardinals	110	004	03X	—	9	12	0

Yankees: WHITEY FORD, Al Downing (6th), Rollie Sheldon (8th), Pete Mikkelsen (8th); Elston Howard.
Cardinals: RAY SADECKI, Barney Schultz (7th); Tim McCarver.
Home Runs: Tom Tresh (Yankees) and Mike Shannon (Cardinals).
Attendance: 30,805.

Game 2 (Oct. 8 at St. Louis)

Yankees	000	101	204	—	8	12	0
Cardinals	001	000	011	—	3	7	0

Yankees: MEL STOTTLEMYRE; Elston Howard.
Cardinals: BOB GIBSON, Barney Schultz (9th), Gordie Richardson (9th), Roger Craig (9th); Tim McCarver.
Home Run: Phil Linz (Yankees).
Attendance: 30,805.

Game 3 (Oct. 10 at Yankee Stadium)

Cardinals	000	010	000	—	1	6	0
Yankees	010	000	001	—	2	5	2

Cardinals: Curt Simmons, BARNEY SCHULTZ (9th); Tim McCarver.
Yankees: JIM BOUTON; Elston Howard.
Home Run: Mickey Mantle (Yankees).
Attendance: 67,101.

Game 4 (Oct. 11 at Yankee Stadium)

Cardinals	000	004	000	—	4	6	1
Yankees	300	000	000	—	3	6	1

Cardinals: Ray Sadecki, ROGER CRAIG (1st), Ron Taylor (6th); Tim McCarver.
Yankees: AL DOWNING, Pete Mikkelsen (7th), Ralph Terry (8th); Elston Howard.
Home Run: Ken Boyer (Cardinals).
Attendance: 66,312.

Game 5 (Oct. 12 at Yankee Stadium)

Cardinals	000	020	000	3	—	5	10	1
Yankees	000	000	002	0	—	2	6	2

Cardinals: BOB GIBSON; Tim McCarver.
Yankees: Mel Stottlemyre, Hal Reniff (8th), PETE MIKKELSEN (8th); Elston Howard.
Home Runs: Tom Tresh (Yankees) and Tim McCarver (Cardinals).
Attendance: 65,633.

Game 6 (Oct. 14 at St. Louis)

Yankees	000	012	050	—	8	10	0
Cardinals	100	000	011	—	3	10	1

Yankees: JIM BOUTON, Steve Hamilton (9th); Elston Howard.
Cardinals: CURT SIMMONS, Ron Taylor (7th), Barney Schultz (8th), Gordie Richardson (8th), Bob Humphreys (9th); Tim McCarver.
Home Runs: Mickey Mantle (Yankees), Roger Maris (Yankees), and Joe Pepitone (Yankees).
Attendance: 30,805.

Game 7 (Oct. 15 at St. Louis)

Yankees	000	003	002	—	5	9	2
Cardinals	000	330	10X	—	7	10	1

Yankees: MEL STOTTLEMYRE, Al Downing (5th), Rollie Sheldon (5th), Steve Hamilton (7th), Pete Mikkelsen (8th); Elston Howard.
Cardinals: BOB GIBSON; Tim McCarver.
Home Runs: Lou Brock (Cardinals), Mickey Mantle (Yankees), Ken Boyer (Cardinals), Clete Boyer (Yankees), and Phil Linz (Yankees).
Attendance: 30,346.

1976 AMERICAN LEAGUE CHAMPIONS

Manager: Billy Martin.
World Series Roster: Pitchers: Doyle Alexander, Dock Ellis, Ed Figueroa, Ron Guidry, Ken Holtzman, Catfish Hunter, Grant Jackson, Sparky Lyle, Dick Tidrow. *Catchers:* Fran Healy, Elrod Hendricks, Thurman Munson. *Infielders:* Sandy Alomar, Chris Chambliss, Jim Mason, Graig Nettles, Willie Randolph, Fred Stanley. *Outfielders:* Oscar Gamble, Elliott Maddox, Carlos May, Lou Piniella, Mickey Rivers, Otto Velez, Roy White.

AL CHAMPIONSHIP SERIES

	W	L	Pct.
Yankees	3	2	.600
Royals	2	3	.400

Game 1 (Oct. 9 at Kansas City)

Yankees	200	000	002	—	4	12	0
Royals	000	000	010	—	1	5	2

Yankees: CATFISH HUNTER; Thurman Munson.
Royals: LARRY GURA, Mark Littell (9th); Buck Martinez, John Wathan (9th).
Home Runs: None.
Attendance: 41,077.

Game 2 (Oct. 10 at Kansas City)

Yankees	012	000	000	—	3	12	5
Royals	200	002	03X	—	7	9	0

Yankees: ED FIGUEROA, Dick Tidrow (6th); Thurman Munson.
Royals: Dennis Leonard, PAUL SPLITTORFF (3rd), Steve Mingori (9th); Buck Martinez.
Home Runs: None.
Attendance: 41,091.

Game 3 (Oct. 12 at Yankee Stadium)

Royals	300	000	000	—	3	6	0
Yankees	000	203	00X	—	5	9	0

Royals: ANDY HASSLER, Marty Pattin (6th), Tom Hall (6th), Steve Mingori (6th), Mark Littell (6th); Buck Martinez, Bob Stinson (8th).
Yankees: DOCK ELLIS, Sparky Lyle (9th); Thurman Munson.
Home Run: Chris Chambliss (Yankees).
Attendance: 56,808.

Game 4 (Oct. 13 at Yankee Stadium)

Royals	030	201	010	—	7	9	1
Yankees	020	000	101	—	4	11	0

Royals: Larry Gura, DOUG BIRD (3rd), Steve Mingori (7th); Buck Martinez.
Yankees: CATFISH HUNTER, Dick Tidrow (4th), Grant Jackson (7th); Thurman Munson.
Home Runs: Graig Nettles (Yankees) 2.
Attendance: 56,355.

Game 5 (Oct. 14 at Yankee Stadium)

Royals	210	000	030	—	6	11	1
Yankees	202	002	001	—	7	11	1

Royals: Dennis Leonard, Paul Splittorff (1st), Marty Pattin (4th), Andy Hassler (5th), MARK LITTELL (7th); Buck Martinez.
Yankees: Ed Figueroa, Grant Jackson (8th), DICK TIDROW (9th); Thurman Munson.
Home Runs: John Mayberry (Royals), George Brett (Royals), and Chris Chambliss (Yankees).
Attendance: 56,821.

WORLD SERIES

	W	L	Pct.
Reds	4	0	1.000
Yankees	0	4	.000

Game 1 (Oct. 16 at Cincinnati)

Yankees	010	000	000	—	1	5	1
Reds	101	001	20X	—	5	10	1

Yankees: DOYLE ALEXANDER, Sparky Lyle (7th); Thurman Munson.
Reds: DON GULLETT, Pedro Borbon (8th); Johnny Bench.
Home Run: Joe Morgan (Reds).
Attendance: 54,826.

Game 2 (Oct. 17 at Cincinnati)

Yankees	000	100	200	—	3	9	1
Reds	030	000	001	—	4	10	0

Yankees: CATFISH HUNTER; Thurman Munson.
Reds: Fred Norman, JACK BILLINGHAM (7th); Johnny Bench.
Home Runs: None.
Attendance: 54,816.

Game 3 (Oct. 19 at Yankee Stadium)

Reds	030	100	020	—	6	13	2
Yankees	000	100	100	—	2	8	0

Reds: PAT ZACHRY, Will McEnaney (7th); Johnny Bench.
Yankees: DOCK ELLIS, Grant Jackson (4th), Dick Tidrow (8th); Thurman Munson.
Home Runs: Dan Driessen (Reds) and Jim Mason (Yankees).
Attendance: 56,667.

Game 4 (Oct. 21 at Yankee Stadium)

Reds	000	300	004	—	7	9	2
Yankees	100	010	000	—	2	8	0

Reds: GARY NOLAN, Will McEnaney (7th); Johnny Bench.
Yankees: ED FIGUEROA, Dick Tidrow (9th), Sparky Lyle (9th); Thurman Munson.
Home Runs Johnny Bench (Reds) 2.
Attendance: 56,700.

1977 WORLD CHAMPIONS

Manager: Billy Martin.
World Series Roster: Pitchers: Ken Clay, Ed Figueroa, Ron Guidry, Don Gullett, Ken Holtzman, Catfish Hunter, Sparky Lyle, Dick Tidrow, Mike Torrez. *Catchers:* Fran Healy, Cliff Johnson, Thurman Munson. *Infielders:* Chris Chambliss, Bucky Dent, Mickey Klutts, Graig Nettles, Willie Randolph, Fred Stanley, George Zeber. *Outfielders:* Paul Blair, Reggie Jackson, Lou Piniella, Mickey Rivers, Roy White.

AL CHAMPIONSHIP SERIES

	W	L	Pct.
Yankees	3	2	.600
Royals	2	3	.400

Game 1 (Oct. 5 at Yankee Stadium)

Royals	222	000	010	—	7	9	0
Yankees	002	000	000	—	2	9	0

Royals: PAUL SPLITTORFF, Doug Bird (9th); Darrell Porter.
Yankees: DON GULLETT, Dick Tidrow (3rd), Sparky Lyle (9th); Thurman Munson.
Home Runs: Hal McRae (Royals), John Mayberry (Royals), Thurman Munson (Yankees), and Al Cowens (Royals).
Attendance: 54,930.

Game 2 (Oct. 6 at Yankee Stadium)

Royals	001	001	000	—	2	3	1
Yankees	000	023	01X	—	6	10	1

Royals: ANDY HASSLER, Mark Littell (6th), Steve Mingori (8th); Darrell Porter, John Wathan (8th).
Yankees: RON GUIDRY; Thurman Munson.
Home Run: Cliff Johnson (Yankees).
Attendance: 56,230.

Game 3 (Oct. 7 at Kansas City)

```
Yankees   000   010   001   —   2   4   1
Royals    011   012   10X   —   6   12   1
```

Yankees: MIKE TORREZ, Sparky Lyle (6th); Thurman Munson.
Royals: DENNIS LEONARD; Darrell Porter.
Home Runs: None.
Attendance: 41,285.

Game 4 (Oct. 8 at Kansas City)

```
Yankees   121   100   001   —   6   13   0
Royals    002   200   000   —   4   8   2
```

Yankees: Ed Figueroa, Dick Tidrow (4th), SPARKY LYLE (4th); Thurman Munson.
Royals: LARRY GURA, Marty Pattin (3rd), Steve Mingori (9th), Doug Bird (9th); Darrell Porter.
Home Runs: None.
Attendance: 41,135.

Game 5 (Oct. 9 at Kansas City)

```
Yankees   001   000   013   —   5   10   0
Royals    201   000   000   —   3   10   1
```

Yankees: Ron Guidry, Mike Torrez (3rd), SPARKY LYLE (8th); Thurman Munson.
Royals: Paul Splittorff, Doug Bird (8th), Steve Mingori (8th), DENNIS LEONARD (9th), Larry Gura (9th), Mark Littell (9th); Darrell Porter.
Home Runs: None.
Attendance: 41,133.

WORLD SERIES

	W	L	Pct.
Yankees	4	2	.667
Dodgers	2	4	.333

Game 1 (Oct. 11 at Yankee Stadium)

```
Dodgers   200   000   001   000   —   3   6   0
Yankees   100   001   010   001   —   4   11   0
```

Dodgers: Don Sutton, Lance Rautzhan (8th), Elias Sosa (8th), Mike Garman (9th), RICK RHODEN (12th); Steve Yeager, Jerry Grote (9th).
Yankees: Don Gullett, SPARKY LYLE (9th); Thurman Munson.
Home Run: Willie Randolph (Yankees).
Attendance: 56,668.

Game 2 (Oct. 12 at Yankee Stadium)

```
Dodgers   212   000   001   —   6   9   0
Yankees   000   100   000   —   1   5   0
```

Dodgers: BURT HOOTON; Steve Yeager.
Yankees: CATFISH HUNTER, Dick Tidrow (3rd), Ken Clay (6th), Sparky Lyle (9th); Thurman Munson.
Home Runs: Ron Cey (Dodgers), Steve Yeager (Dodgers), Reggie Smith (Dodgers), and Steve Garvey (Dodgers).
Attendance: 56,691.

Game 3 (Oct. 14 at Los Angeles)

```
Yankees   300   110   000   —   5   10   0
Dodgers   003   000   000   —   3   7   1
```

Yankees: MIKE TORREZ; Thurman Munson.
Dodgers: TOMMY JOHN, Charlie Hough (7th); Steve Yeager.
Home Run: Dusty Baker (Dodgers).
Attendance: 55,992.

Game 4 (Oct. 15 at Los Angeles)

```
Yankees   030   001   000   —   4   7   0
Dodgers   002   000   000   —   2   4   0
```

Yankees: RON GUIDRY; Thurman Munson.
Dodgers: DOUG RAU, Rick Rhoden (2nd), Mike Garman (9th); Steve Yeager.
Home Runs: Dave Lopes (Dodgers) and Reggie Jackson (Yankees).
Attendance: 55,995.

Game 5 (Oct. 16 at Los Angeles)

```
Yankees   000   000   220   —   4   9   2
Dodgers   100   432   00X   —   10   13   0
```

Yankees: DON GULLETT, Ken Clay (5th), Dick Tidrow (6th), Catfish Hunter (7th); Thurman Munson, Cliff Johnson (8th).
Dodgers: DON SUTTON; Steve Yeager, Johnny Oates (7th).
Home Runs: Steve Yeager (Dodgers), Reggie Smith (Dodgers), Thurman Munson (Yankees), and Reggie Jackson (Yankees).
Attendance: 55,955.

Game 6 (Oct. 18 at Yankee Stadium)

```
Dodgers   201   000   001   —   4   9   0
Yankees   020   320   01X   —   8   8   1
```

Dodgers: BURT HOOTON, Elias Sosa (4th), Doug Rau (5th), Charlie Hough (7th); Steve Yeager.
Yankees: MIKE TORREZ; Thurman Munson.
Home Runs: Reggie Jackson (Yankees) 3, Chris Chambliss (Yankees), and Reggie Smith (Dodgers).
Attendance: 56,407.

1978 WORLD CHAMPIONS

Manager: Bob Lemon.
World Series Roster: Pitchers: Jim Beattie, Ken Clay, Ed Figueroa, Rich Gossage, Ron Guidry, Catfish Hunter, Paul Lindblad, Sparky Lyle, Dick Tidrow. *Catchers:* Mike Heath, Cliff Johnson, Thurman Munson. *Infielders:* Chris Chambliss, Bucky Dent, Brian Doyle, Graig Nettles, Jim Spencer, Fred Stanley. *Outfielders:* Paul Blair, Reggie Jackson, Jay Johnstone, Lou Piniella, Mickey Rivers, Gary Thomasson, Roy White.

Lemon was named manager on July 25, succeeding Billy Martin, who resigned the previous day.

AMERICAN LEAGUE EAST PLAYOFF

(One game to break deadlock after New York and Boston finished schedule tied for first place with matching 99–63 records.)

(Oct. 2 at Boston)

```
Yankees   000   000   410   —   5   8   0
Red Sox   010   001   020   —   4   11   0
```

Yankees: RON GUIDRY, Rich Gossage (7th); Thurman Munson.
Red Sox: MIKE TORREZ, Bob Stanley (7th), Andy Hassler (8th), Dick Drago (9th); Carlton Fisk.
Home Runs: Carl Yastrzemski (Red Sox), Bucky Dent (Yankees), and Reggie Jackson (Yankees).
Attendance: 32,925.

AL CHAMPIONSHIP SERIES

	W	L	Pct.
Yankees	3	1	.750
Royals	1	3	.250

Game 1 (Oct. 3 at Kansas City)

```
Yankees   011   020   030   —   7   16   0
Royals    000   001   000   —   1   2   2
```

Yankees: JIM BEATTIE, Ken Clay (6th); Thurman Munson.
Royals: DENNIS LEONARD, Steve Mingori (5th), Al Hrabosky (8th), Doug Bird (9th); Darrell Porter.
Home Run: Reggie Jackson (Yankees).
Attendance: 41,143.

Game 2 (Oct. 4 at Kansas City)

```
Yankees   000   000   220   —   4   12   1
Royals    140   000   32X   —   10   16   1
```

Yankees: ED FIGUEROA, Dick Tidrow (2nd), Sparky Lyle (7th); Thurman Munson.
Royals: LARRY GURA, Marty Pattin (7th), Al Hrabosky (8th); Darrell Porter.

Home Run: Freddie Patek (Royals).
Attendance: 41,158.

Game 3 (Oct. 6 at Yankee Stadium)

| Royals | 101 | 010 | 020 | — | 5 | 10 | 1 |
| Yankees | 010 | 201 | 02X | — | 6 | 10 | 0 |

Royals: Paul Splittorff, DOUG BIRD (8th), Al Hrabosky (8th); Darrell Porter.
Yankees: Catfish Hunter, RICH GOSSAGE (7th); Thurman Munson.
Home Runs: George Brett (Royals) 3, Reggie Jackson (Yankees), and Thurman Munson (Yankees).
Attendance: 55,535.

Game 4 (Oct. 7 at Yankee Stadium)

| Royals | 100 | 000 | 000 | — | 1 | 7 | 0 |
| Yankees | 010 | 001 | 00X | — | 2 | 4 | 0 |

Royals: DENNIS LEONARD; Darrell Porter.
Yankees: RON GUIDRY, Rich Gossage (9th); Thurman Munson.
Home Runs: Graig Nettles (Yankees) and Roy White (Yankees).
Attendance: 56,356.

WORLD SERIES

	W	L	Pct.
Yankees	4	2	.667
Dodgers	2	4	.333

Game 1 (Oct. 10 at Los Angeles)

| Yankees | 000 | 000 | 320 | — | 5 | 9 | 1 |
| Dodgers | 030 | 310 | 31X | — | 11 | 15 | 2 |

Yankees: ED FIGUEROA, Ken Clay (2nd), Paul Lindblad (5th), Dick Tidrow (7th); Thurman Munson.
Dodgers: TOMMY JOHN, Terry Forster (8th); Steve Yeager.
Home Runs: Dave Lopes (Dodgers) 2, Dusty Baker (Dodgers), and Reggie Jackson (Yankees).
Attendance: 55,997.

Game 2 (Oct. 11 at Los Angeles)

| Yankees | 002 | 000 | 100 | — | 3 | 11 | 0 |
| Dodgers | 000 | 103 | 00X | — | 4 | 7 | 0 |

Yankees: CATFISH HUNTER, Rich Gossage (7th); Thurman Munson.
Dodgers: BURT HOOTON, Terry Forster (7th), Bob Welch (9th); Steve Yeager.
Home Run: Ron Cey (Dodgers).
Attendance: 55,982.

Game 3 (Oct. 13 at Yankee Stadium)

| Dodgers | 001 | 000 | 000 | — | 1 | 8 | 0 |
| Yankees | 110 | 000 | 30X | — | 5 | 10 | 1 |

Dodgers: DON SUTTON, Lance Rautzhan (7th), Charlie Hough (8th); Steve Yeager, Jerry Grote (6th), Joe Ferguson (8th).
Yankees: RON GUIDRY; Thurman Munson.
Home Run: Roy White (Yankees).
Attendance: 56,447.

Game 4 (Oct. 14 at Yankee Stadium)

| Dodgers | 000 | 030 | 000 | 0 | — | 3 | 6 | 1 |
| Yankees | 000 | 002 | 010 | 1 | — | 4 | 9 | 0 |

Dodgers: Tommy John, Terry Forster (8th), BOB WELCH (8th); Steve Yeager, Jerry Grote (9th).
Yankees: Ed Figueroa, Dick Tidrow (6th), RICH GOSSAGE (9th); Thurman Munson.
Home Run: Reggie Smith (Dodgers).
Attendance: 56,445.

Game 5 (Oct. 15 at Yankee Stadium)

| Dodgers | 101 | 000 | 000 | — | 2 | 9 | 3 |
| Yankees | 004 | 300 | 41X | — | 12 | 18 | 0 |

Dodgers: BURT HOOTON, Lance Rautzhan (3rd), Charlie Hough (4th); Steve Yeager, Johnny Oates (7th).
Yankees: JIM BEATTIE; Thurman Munson, Mike Heath (9th).

Home Runs: None.
Attendance: 56,448.

Game 6 (Oct. 17 at Los Angeles)

| Yankees | 030 | 002 | 200 | — | 7 | 11 | 0 |
| Dodgers | 101 | 000 | 000 | — | 2 | 7 | 1 |

Yankees: CATFISH HUNTER, Rich Gossage (8th); Thurman Munson.
Dodgers: DON SUTTON, Bob Welch (6th), Doug Rau (8th); Joe Ferguson.
Home Runs: Dave Lopes (Dodgers) and Reggie Jackson (Yankees).
Attendance: 55,985.

1980 AMERICAN LEAGUE EAST CHAMPIONS

Manager: Dick Howser.
Regular-Season Roster (Minimum 5 games): Pitchers: Doug Bird, Ron Davis, Ed Figueroa, Rich Gossage, Mike Griffin, Ron Guidry, Tommy John, Tim Lollar, Rudy May, Gaylord Perry, Dennis Werth. Catchers: Rick Cerone, Johnny Oates, Dennis Werth. Infielders: Bucky Dent, Brian Doyle, Graig Nettles, Willie Randolph, Aurelio Rodriguez, Eric Soderholm, Jim Spencer, Fred Stanley, Bob Watson. Outfielders: Paul Blair, Bobby Brown, Oscar Gamble, Reggie Jackson, Ruppert Jones, Joe Lefebvre, Bobby Murcer, Lou Piniella, Ted Wilborn.

AL CHAMPIONSHIP SERIES

	W	L	Pct.
Royals	3	0	1.000
Yankees	0	3	.000

Game 1 (Oct. 8 at Kansas City)

| Yankees | 020 | 000 | 000 | — | 2 | 10 | 1 |
| Royals | 022 | 000 | 12X | — | 7 | 10 | 0 |

Yankees: RON GUIDRY, Ron Davis (4th), Tom Underwood (8th); Rick Cerone.
Royals: LARRY GURA; Darrell Porter.
Home Runs: Rick Cerone (Yankees), Lou Piniella (Yankees), and George Brett (Royals).
Attendance: 42,598.

Game 2 (Oct. 9 at Kansas City)

| Yankees | 000 | 020 | 000 | — | 2 | 8 | 0 |
| Royals | 003 | 000 | 00X | — | 3 | 6 | 0 |

Yankees: RUDY MAY; Rick Cerone.
Royals: DENNIS LEONARD, Dan Quisenberry (9th); Darrell Porter.
Home Run: Graig Nettles (Yankees).
Attendance: 42,633.

Game 3 (Oct. 10 at Yankee Stadium)

| Royals | 000 | 010 | 300 | — | 4 | 12 | 1 |
| Yankees | 000 | 002 | 000 | — | 2 | 8 | 0 |

Royals: Paul Splittorff, DAN QUISENBERRY (6th); Darrell Porter.
Yankees: Tommy John, RICH GOSSAGE (7th), Tom Underwood (8th); Rick Cerone.
Home Runs: Frank White (Royals) and George Brett (Royals).
Attendance: 56,588.

1981 AMERICAN LEAGUE CHAMPIONS

Manager: Bob Lemon.
World Series Roster: Pitchers: Ron Davis, George Frazier, Rich Gossage, Ron Guidry, Tommy John, Dave LaRoche, Rudy May, Rick Reuschel, Dave Righetti. Catchers: Rick Cerone, Barry Foote. Infielders: Bucky Dent,† Larry Milbourne, Graig Nettles, Willie Randolph, Dave Revering, Andre Robertson, Aurelio Rodriguez, Bob Watson. Outfielders: Bobby Brown, Oscar Gamble, Reggie Jackson, Jerry Mumphrey, Bobby Murcer, Lou Piniella, Dave Winfield.

*Lemon was named manager on September 6, replacing Gene Michael.
†Dent on the disabled list.

AL EAST PLAYOFFS

(Best-of five series between the division's first- and second-half winners. New York [34–22] won the first half, Milwaukee [31–22] the second half of the schedule interrupted nearly two months at midseason by a players strike.)

	W	L	Pct.
Yankees	3	2	.600
Brewers	2	3	.400

Game 1 (Oct. 7 at Milwaukee)

| Yankees | 000 | 400 | 001 | — | 5 | 13 | 1 |
| Brewers | 011 | 010 | 000 | — | 3 | 8 | 3 |

Yankees: Ron Guidry, RON DAVIS (5th), Rich Gossage (8th); Rick Cerone.
Brewers: MOOSE HAAS, Dwight Bernard (4th), Bob McClure (5th), Jim Slaton (6th), Rollie Fingers (8th); Ted Simmons.
Home Run: Oscar Gamble (Yankees).
Attendance: 35,064.

Game 2 (Oct. 8 at Milwaukee)

| Yankees | 000 | 100 | 002 | — | 3 | 7 | 0 |
| Brewers | 000 | 000 | 000 | — | 0 | 7 | 0 |

Yankees: DAVE RIGHETTI, Ron Davis (7th), Rich Gossage (7th); Rick Cerone.
Brewers: MIKE CALDWELL, Jim Slaton (9th); Ted Simmons.
Home Runs: Lou Piniella (Yankees) and Reggie Jackson (Yankees).
Attendance: 26,395.

Game 3 (Oct. 9 at Yankee Stadium)

| Brewers | 000 | 000 | 320 | — | 5 | 9 | 0 |
| Yankees | 000 | 100 | 200 | — | 3 | 8 | 2 |

Brewers: Randy Lerch, ROLLIE FINGERS (7th); Ted Simmons.
Yankees: TOMMY JOHN, Rudy May (8th); Rick Cerone.
Home Runs: Ted Simmons (Brewers) and Paul Molitor (Brewers).
Attendance: 56,411.

Game 4 (Oct. 10 at Yankee Stadium)

| Brewers | 000 | 200 | 000 | — | 2 | 4 | 2 |
| Yankees | 000 | 001 | 000 | — | 1 | 5 | 0 |

Brewers: PETE VUCKOVICH, Jamie Easterly (6th), Jim Slaton (7th), Bob McClure (8th), Rollie Fingers (9th); Ted Simmons.
Yankees: RICK REUSCHEL, Ron Davis (7th); Rick Cerone.
Home Runs: None.
Attendance: 52,077.

Game 5 (Oct. 11 at Yankee Stadium)

| Brewers | 011 | 000 | 100 | — | 3 | 8 | 0 |
| Yankees | 000 | 400 | 12X | — | 7 | 13 | 0 |

Brewers: MOOSE HAAS, Mike Caldwell (4th), Dwight Bernard (4th), Bob McClure (6th), Jim Slaton (7th), Jamie Easterly (8th), Pete Vuckovich (8th); Ted Simmons.
Yankees: Ron Guidry, DAVE RIGHETTI (5th), Rich Gossage (8th); Rick Cerone.
Home Runs: Gorman Thomas (Brewers), Reggie Jackson (Yankees), Oscar Gamble (Yankees), and Rick Cerone (Yankees).
Attendance: 47,105.

AL CHAMPIONSHIP SERIES

	W	L	Pct.
Yankees	3	0	1.000
A's	0	3	.000

Game 1 (Oct. 13 at Yankee Stadium)

| A's | 000 | 010 | 000 | — | 1 | 6 | 1 |
| Yankees | 300 | 000 | 00X | — | 3 | 7 | 1 |

A's: MIKE NORRIS, Tom Underwood (8th); Jeff Newman.
Yankees: TOMMY JOHN, Ron Davis (7th), Rich Gossage (8th); Rick Cerone.
Home Runs: None.
Attendance: 55,740.

Game 2 (Oct. 14 at Yankee Stadium)

| A's | 001 | 200 | 000 | — | 3 | 11 | 1 |
| Yankees | 100 | 701 | 40X | — | 13 | 19 | 0 |

A's: STEVE McCATTY, Dave Beard (4th), Jeff Jones (5th), Brian Kingman (7th), Bob Owchinko (7th); Mike Heath.
Yankees: Rudy May, GEORGE FRAZIER (4th); Rick Cerone.
Home Runs: Lou Piniella (Yankees) and Graig Nettles (Yankees).
Attendance: 48,497.

Game 3 (Oct. 15 at Oakland)

| Yankees | 000 | 001 | 003 | — | 4 | 10 | 0 |
| A's | 000 | 000 | 000 | — | 0 | 5 | 0 |

Yankees: DAVE RIGHETTI, Ron Davis (7th), Rich Gossage (9th); Rick Cerone.
A's: MATT KEOUGH, Tom Underwood (9th); Jeff Newman.
Home Run: Willie Randolph (Yankees).
Attendance: 47,302.

WORLD SERIES

	W	L	Pct.
Dodgers	4	2	.667
Yankees	2	4	.333

Game 1 (Oct. 20 at Yankee Stadium)

| Dodgers | 000 | 010 | 020 | — | 3 | 5 | 0 |
| Yankees | 301 | 100 | 00X | — | 5 | 6 | 0 |

Dodgers: JERRY REUSS, Bob Castillo (3rd), Dave Goltz (4th), Tom Niedenfuer (5th), Dave Stewart (8th); Steve Yeager.
Yankees: RON GUIDRY, Ron Davis (8th), Rich Gossage (8th); Rick Cerone.
Home Runs: Bob Watson (Yankees) and Steve Yeager (Dodgers).
Attendance: 56,470.

Game 2 (Oct. 21 at Yankee Stadium)

| Dodgers | 000 | 000 | 000 | — | 0 | 4 | 2 |
| Yankees | 000 | 010 | 02X | — | 3 | 6 | 1 |

Dodgers: BURT HOOTON, Terry Forster (7th), Steve Howe (8th), Dave Stewart (8th); Steve Yeager, Mike Scioscia (8th).
Yankees: TOMMY JOHN, Rich Gossage (8th); Rick Cerone.
Home Runs: None.
Attendance: 56,505.

Game 3 (Oct. 23 at Los Angeles)

| Yankees | 022 | 000 | 000 | — | 4 | 9 | 0 |
| Dodgers | 300 | 020 | 00X | — | 5 | 11 | 1 |

Yankees: Dave Righetti, GEORGE FRAZIER (3rd), Rudy May (5th), Ron Davis (8th); Rick Cerone.
Dodgers: FERNANDO VALENZUELA; Steve Yeager, Mike Scioscia (3rd).
Home Runs: Ron Cey (Dodgers), Bob Watson (Yankees), and Rick Cerone (Yankees).
Attendance: 56,236.

Game 4 (Oct. 24 at Los Angeles)

| Yankees | 211 | 002 | 010 | — | 7 | 13 | 1 |
| Dodgers | 002 | 013 | 20X | — | 8 | 14 | 2 |

Yankees: Rick Reuschel, Rudy May (4th), Ron Davis (5th), GEORGE FRAZIER (6th), Tommy John (7th); Rick Cerone.
Dodgers: Bob Welch, Dave Goltz (1st), Terry Forster (4th), Tom Niedenfuer (5th), STEVE HOWE (7th); Mike Scioscia, Steve Yeager (7th).
Home Runs: Willie Randolph (Yankees), Jay Johnstone (Dodgers), and Reggie Jackson (Yankees).
Attendance: 56,242.

Game 5 (Oct. 25 at Los Angeles)

| Yankees | 010 | 000 | 000 | — | 1 | 5 | 0 |
| Dodgers | 000 | 000 | 20X | — | 2 | 4 | 3 |

Yankees: RON GUIDRY, Rich Gossage (8th); Rick Cerone.
Dodgers: JERRY REUSS; Steve Yeager.
Home Runs: Pedro Guerrero (Dodgers) and Steve Yeager (Dodgers).
Attendance: 56,115.

Game 6 (Oct. 28 at Yankee Stadium)

```
Dodgers   000   134   010   —   9   13   1
Yankees   001   001   000   —   2    7   2
```

Dodgers: BURT HOOTON, Steve Howe (6th); Steve Yeager.
Yankees: Tommy John, GEORGE FRAZIER (5th), Ron Davis (6th), Rick Reuschel (6th), Rudy May (7th), Dave LaRoche (9th); Rick Cerone.
Home Runs: Willie Randolph (Yankees) and Pedro Guerrero (Dodgers).
Attendance: 56,513.

1994 AMERICAN LEAGUE EAST LEADERS*

Manager: Buck Showalter.
Regular-Season Roster (Minimum 5 games): Pitchers: Jim Abbott, Joe Ausanio, Paul Gibson, Xavier Hernandez, Sterling Hitchcock, Steve Howe, Scott Kamieniecki, Jimmy Key, Terry Mulholland, Donn Pall, Melido Perez, Jeff Reardon, Bob Wickman. *Catchers:* Jim Leyritz, Bob Melvin, Matt Nokes, Mike Stanley. *Infielders:* Wade Boggs, Kevin Elster, Mike Gallego, Pat Kelly, Don Mattingly, Dave Silvestri, Randy Velarde. *Outfielders:* Daryl Boston, Paul O'Neill, Luis Polonia, Danny Tartabull, Bernie Williams, Gerald Williams.

Closing in on their first playoff berth since 1981, the 1994 Yankees led American League East by 6½ games over second-place Baltimore when members of the Major League Baseball Players Association struck on August 12. And on September 14, team owners canceled the remainder of the schedule and the postseason. The Yankees's 70–43 (.619) was their best record after 113 games since 1963's 73–40 (.646), and their best season-ending winning percentage since 1980's .636.

1995 AMERICAN LEAGUE WILD-CARD WINNERS

Manager: Buck Showalter.
Regular-Season Roster (Minimum 5 games): Pitchers: Joe Ausanio, Scott Bankhead, Brian Boehringer, David Cone, Sterling Hitchcock, Steve Howe, Scott Kamieniecki, Jimmy Key, Bob MacDonald, Josias Manzanillo, Jack McDowell, Melido Perez, Andy Pettitte, Mariano Rivera, John Wetteland, Bob Wickman. *Catchers:* Jim Leyritz, Mike Stanley. *Infielders:* Wade Boggs, Russ Davis, Robert Eenhoorn, Kevin Elster, Tony Fernandez, Derek Jeter, Pat Kelly, Don Mattingly, Randy Velarde, Dave Silvestri. *Outfielders:* Dion James, Paul O'Neill, Luis Polonia, Ruben Rivera, Ruben Sierra, Darryl Strawberry, Danny Tartabull, Bernie Williams, Gerald Williams.

AL DIVISION SERIES

	W	L	Pct.
Mariners	3	2	.600
Yankees	2	3	.400

Game 1 (Oct. 3 at Yankee Stadium)

```
Mariners   000   101   202   —   6    9   0
Yankees    002   002   41X   —   9   13   0
```

Mariners: Chris Bosio, JEFF NELSON (6th), Bobby Ayala (7th), Bill Risley (7th), Bob Wells (8th); Dan Wilson.
Yankees: DAVID CONE, John Wetteland (9th); Mike Stanley.
Home Runs: Ken Griffey, Jr. (Mariners) 2, Wade Boggs (Yankees), and Ruben Sierra (Yankees).
Attendance: 57,178.

Game 2 (Oct. 4 at Yankee Stadium)

```
Mariners   001   001   200   001   000   —   5   16   2
Yankees    000   012   100   001   002   —   7   11   0
```

Mariners: Andy Benes, Bill Risley (6th), Norm Charlton (7th), Jeff Nelson (11th), TIM BELCHER (12th); Dan Wilson, Chris Widger.
Yankees: Andy Pettitte, Bob Wickman (8th), John Wetteland (9th), MARIANO RIVERA (12th); Jim Leyritz.
Home Runs: Paul O'Neill (Yankees), Ruben Sierra (Yankees), Don Mattingly (Yankees), Jim Leyritz (Yankees), Vince Coleman (Mariners), and Ken Griffey, Jr. (Mariners).
Attendance: 57,126.

Game 3 (Oct. 6 at Seattle)

```
Yankees    000   100   120   —   4   6   2
Mariners   000   024   10X   —   7   7   0
```

Yankees: JACK McDOWELL, Steve Howe (6th), Bob Wickman (6th), Sterling Hitchcock (7th), Mariano Rivera (7th); Mike Stanley.
Mariners: RANDY JOHNSON, Bill Risley (8th), Norm Charlton (8th); Dan Wilson.
Home Runs: Tino Martinez (Mariners), Bernie Williams (Yankees) 2, and Mike Stanley (Yankees).
Attendance: 57,944.

Game 4 (Oct. 7 at Seattle)

```
Yankees    302   000   012   —    8   14   1
Mariners   004   011   05X   —   11   16   0
```

Yankees: Scott Kamieniecki, Sterling Hitchcock (6th), Bob Wickman (7th), JOHN WETTELAND (8th), Steve Howe (8th); Mike Stanley.
Mariners: Chris Bosio, Jeff Nelson (3rd), Tim Belcher (7th), NORM CHARLTON (8th), Bobby Ayala (9th), Bill Risley (9th); Dan Wilson.
Home Runs: Paul O'Neill (Yankees), Ken Griffey, Jr. (Mariners), Edgar Martinez (Mariners) 2, and Jay Buhner (Mariners).
Attendance: 57,180.

Game 5 (Oct. 8 at Seattle)

```
Yankees    000   202   000   01   —   5    6   0
Mariners   001   100   020   02   —   6   15   0
```

Yankees: David Cone, Mariano Rivera (8th), JACK McDOWELL (9th); Mike Stanley, Jim Leyritz.
Mariners: Andy Benes, Norm Charlton (7th), RANDY JOHNSON (9th); Dan Wilson, Chris Widger.
Home Runs: Joey Cora (Mariners), Ken Griffey, Jr. (Mariners), and Paul O'Neill (Yankees).
Attendance 57,411.

1996 WORLD CHAMPIONS

Manager: Joe Torre.
World Series Roster: Pitchers: Brian Boehringer, David Cone, Jimmy Key, Graeme Lloyd, Jeff Nelson, Andy Pettitte, Mariano Rivera, Kenny Rogers, Dave Weathers, John Wetteland. *Catchers:* Joe Girardi, Jim Leyritz. *Infielders:* Wade Boggs, Mariano Duncan, Cecil Fielder, Andy Fox, Charlie Hayes, Derek Jeter, Tino Martinez, Luis Soho. *Infielder-outfielder:* Mike Aldrete. *Outfielders:* Paul O'Neill, Tim Raines, Darryl Strawberry, Bernie Williams.

AL DIVISION SERIES

	W	L	Pct.
Yankees	3	1	.750
Rangers	1	3	.250

Game 1 (Oct. 1 at Yankee Stadium)

```
Rangers    000   501   000   —   6    8   0
Yankees    100   100   000   —   2   10   0
```

Rangers: JOHN BURKETT; Ivan Rodriguez.
Yankees: DAVID CONE, Graeme Lloyd (7th), Dave Weathers (8th); Joe Girardi.
Home Runs: Juan Gonzalez (Rangers) and Dean Palmer (Rangers).
Attendance: 57,205 (57,545).

Game 2 (Oct. 2 at Yankee Stadium)

```
Rangers    013   000   000   000   —   4   8   1
Yankees    010   100   110   001   —   5   8   0
```

Rangers: Ken Hill, Dennis Cook (7th), Jeff Russell (8th), MIKE STANTON (10th), Mike Henneman (12th); Ivan Rodriguez.
Yankees: Andy Pettitte, Mariano Rivera (7th), John Wetteland (10th), Graeme Lloyd (12th), Jeff Nelson (12th), Kenny Rogers (12th), BRIAN BOEHRINGER (12th); Jim Leyritz, Joe Girardi (7th).
Home Runs: Cecil Fielder (Yankees) and Juan Gonzalez (Rangers) 2.
Attendance: 57,156 (57,545).

Game 3 (Oct. 4 at Arlington, Texas)

```
Yankees    100  000  002  —   3   7   1
Rangers    000  110  000  —   2   6   1
```

Yankees: Jimmy Key, JEFF NELSON (6th), John Wetteland (9th); Joe Girardi.
Rangers: DARREN OLIVER, Mike Henneman (9th), Mike Stanton (9th); Ivan Rodriguez.
Home Runs: Juan Gonzalez (Rangers) and Bernie Williams (Yankees).
Attendance: 49,178 (50,860).

Game 4 (Oct. 5 at Arlington, Texas)

```
Yankees    000  310  101  —   6  12   1
Rangers    022  000  000  —   4   9   0
```

Yankees: Kenny Rogers, Brian Boehringer (3rd), DAVE WEATHERS (4th), Mariano Rivera (7th), John Wetteland (9th); Joe Girardi.
Rangers: Bobby Witt, Danny Patterson (4th), Dennis Cook (4th), ROGER PAVLIK (5th), Ed Vosberg (7th), Jeff Russell (7th), Mike Stanton (8th), Mike Henneman (9th); Ivan Rodriguez.
Home Runs: Juan Gonzalez (Rangers) and Bernie Williams (Yankees).
Attendance: 49,178 (50,066).

AL CHAMPIONSHIP SERIES

	W	L	Pct.
Yankees	4	1	.800
Orioles	1	4	.200

Game 1 (Oct. 9 at Yankee Stadium)

```
Orioles    011  101  000  00  —   4  11   1
Yankees    110  000  110  01  —   5  11   0
```

Orioles: Scott Erickson, Jesse Orosco (7th), Armando Benitez (7th), Arthur Rhodes (8th), RANDY MYERS (9th); Mark Parent.
Yankees: Andy Pettitte, Jeff Nelson (8th), John Wetteland (9th), MARIANO RIVERA (10th); Jim Leyritz, Joe Girardi (10th).
Home Runs: Brady Anderson (Orioles), Rafael Palmeiro (Orioles), Bernie Williams (Yankees), and Derek Jeter (Yankees).
Attendance: 56,495 (57,545).

Game 2 (Oct. 10 at Yankee Stadium)

```
Orioles    002  000  210  —   5  10   0
Yankees    200  000  100  —   3  11   1
```

Orioles: DAVID WELLS, Alan Mills (7th), Jesse Orosco (7th), Randy Myers (9th), Armando Benitez (9th); Chris Hoiles.
Yankees: David Cone, JEFF NELSON (7th), Graeme Lloyd (8th), Dave Weathers (9th); Joe Girardi.
Home Runs: Todd Zeile (Orioles) and Rafael Palmeiro (Orioles).
Attendance: 56,432 (57,545).

Game 3 (Oct. 11 at Baltimore)

```
Yankees    000  100  040  —   5   8   0
Orioles    200  000  000  —   2   3   2
```

Yankees: JIMMY KEY, John Wetteland (9th); Joe Girardi.
Orioles: MIKE MUSSINA, Jesse Orosco (8th); Terry Mathews (9th) and Chris Hoiles.
Home Runs: Todd Zeile (Orioles) and Cecil Fielder (Yankees).
Attendance: 48,262 (48,635).

Game 4 (Oct. 12 at Baltimore)

```
Yankees    210  200  030  —   8   9   0
Orioles    101  200  000  —   4  11   0
```

Yankees: Kenny Rogers, DAVE WEATHERS (4th), Graeme Lloyd (6th), Mariano Rivera (7th), John Wetteland (9th); Joe Girardi.
Orioles: ROCKY COPPINGER, Arthur Rhodes (6th), Alan Mills (7th), Jesse Orosco (8th), Armando Benitez (8th), Terry Mathews (9th); Chris Hoiles.
Home Runs: Bernie Williams (Yankees), Darryl Strawberry (Yankees) 2, Chris Hoiles (Orioles) and Paul O'Neill (Yankees).
Attendance: 48,262 (48,974).

Game 5 (Oct. 13 at Baltimore)

```
Yankees    006  000  000  —   6  11   0
Orioles    000  001  012  —   4   4   1
```

Yankees: ANDY PETTITTE, John Wetteland (9th); Jim Leyritz.
Orioles: SCOTT ERICKSON, Arthur Rhodes (6th), Alan Mills (7th), Randy Myers (8th); Mark Parent, Chris Hoiles (6th).
Home Runs: Jim Leyritz (Yankees), Cecil Fielder (Yankees), Darryl Strawberry (Yankees), Todd Zeile (Orioles), Eddie Murray (Orioles), and Bobby Bonilla (Orioles).
Attendance: 48,262 (48,718).

WORLD SERIES

	W	L	Pct.
Yankees	4	2	.667
Braves	2	4	.333

Game 1 (Oct. 20 at Yankee Stadium)

```
Braves     026  013  000  —  12  13   0
Yankees    000  010  000  —   1   4   1
```

Braves: JOHN SMOLTZ, Greg McMichael (7th), Denny Neagle (8th), Terrell Wade (9th), Brad Clontz (9th); Javier Lopez, Eduardo Perez (9th).
Yankees: ANDY PETTITTE, Brian Boehringer (3rd), Dave Weathers (6th), Jeff Nelson (8th), John Wetteland (9th); Jim Leyritz.
Home Runs: Andruw Jones (Braves) 2, and Fred McGriff (Braves).
Attendance: 56,365 (57,545).

Game 2 (Oct. 21 at Yankee Stadium)

```
Braves     101  011  000  —   4  10   0
Yankees    000  000  000  —   0   7   1
```

Braves: GREG MADDUX, Mark Wohlers (9th); Javier Lopez.
Yankees: JIMMY KEY, Graeme Lloyd (7th), Jeff Nelson (7th), Mariano Rivera (9th); Joe Girardi.
Home Runs: None.
Attendance: 56,340 (57,545).

Game 3 (Oct. 22 at Atlanta)

```
Yankees    100  100  030  —   5   8   1
Braves     000  001  010  —   2   6   1
```

Yankees: DAVID CONE, Mariano Rivera (7th), Graeme Lloyd (8th), John Wetteland (9th); Joe Girardi.
Braves: TOM GLAVINE, Greg McMichael (8th), Brad Clontz (8th), Mike Bielecki (9th); Javier Lopez.
Home Runs: Bernie Williams (Yankees).
Attendance: 51,843 (52,710).

Game 4 (Oct. 23 at Atlanta)

```
Yankees    000  003  030  2  —   8  12   0
Braves     041  010  000  0  —   6   9   2
```

Yankees: Kenny Rogers, Brian Boehringer (3rd), Dave Weathers (5th), Jeff Nelson (6th), Mariano Rivera (8th), GRAEME LLOYD (9th), John Wetteland (10th); Joe Girardi, Jim Leyritz (6th).
Braves: Denny Neagle, Terrell Wade (6th), Mike Bielecki (6th), Mark Wohlers (8th), STEVE AVERY (10th), Brade Clontz (10th); Javier Lopez, Eduardo Perez (8th).
Home Runs: Fred McGriff (Braves) and Jim Leyritz (Yankees).
Attendance: 51,881 (52,710).

Game 5 (Oct. 24 at Atlanta)

```
Yankees    000  100  000  —   1   4   1
Braves     000  000  000  —   0   5   1
```

Yankees: ANDY PETTITTE, John Wetteland (9th); Jim Leyritz.
Braves: JOHN SMOLTZ, Mark Wohlers (9th); Javier Lopez.
Home Runs: None.
Attendance: 51,881 (52,710).

Game 6 (Oct. 26 at Yankee Stadium)

```
Braves     000  100  001  —   2   8   0
Yankees    003  000  00X  —   3   8   1
```

Braves: GREG MADDUX, Mark Wohlers (8th); Javier Lopez.
Yankees: JIMMY KEY, Dave Weathers (6th), Graeme Lloyd (6th), Mariano Rivera (7th), John Wetteland (9th); Joe Girardi.
Home Runs: None.
Attendance: 56,375 (57,545).

YANKEES' WORLD SERIES SHARES

Year	Share	Opponent	Games	Attendance
1921	$3,510.00 (L)	New York Giants	8	269,976
1922	$2,842.86 (L)	New York Giants	5*	185,947
1923	$6,143.49 (W)	New York Giants	6	301,430
1926	$3,417.75 (L)	St. Louis Cardinals	7	328,051
1927	$5,782.24 (W)	Pittsburgh Pirates	4	201,705
1928	$5,813.20 (W)	St. Louis Cardinals	4	199,072
1932	$5,231.77 (W)	Chicago Cubs	4	191,998
1936	$6,430.55 (W)	New York Giants	6	302,924
1937	$6,471.11 (W)	New York Giants	5	238,142
1938	$5,728.76 (W)	Chicago Cubs	4	200,833
1939	$5,541.89 (W)	Cincinnati Reds	4	183,849
1941	$5,943.31 (W)	Brooklyn Dodgers	5	235,773
1942	$3,351.77 (L)	St. Louis Cardinals	5	277,101
1943	$6,139.46 (W)	St. Louis Cardinals	5	277,312
1947	$5,830.03 (W)	Brooklyn Dodgers	7	389,763
1949	$5,626.74 (W)	Brooklyn Dodgers	5	236,716
1950	$5,737.95 (W)	Philadelphia Phillies	4	196,009
1951	$6,446.09 (W)	New York Giants	6	341,977
1952	$5,982.65 (W)	Brooklyn Dodgers	7	340,706
1953	$8,280.68 (W)	Brooklyn Dodgers	6	307,350
1955	$5,598.58 (L)	Brooklyn Dodgers	7	362,310
1956	$8,714.76 (W)	Brooklyn Dodgers	7	345,903
1957	$5,606.06 (L)	Milwaukee Braves	7	394,712
1958	$8,759.10 (W)	Milwaukee Braves	7	393,909
1960	$5,214.64 (L)	Pittsburgh Pirates	7	349,813
1961	$7,389.13 (W)	Cincinnati Reds	5	223,247
1962	$9,882.74 (W)	San Francisco Giants	7	376,864
1963	$7,874.32 (L)	Los Angeles Dodgers	4	247,279
1964	$5,309.29 (L)	St. Louis Cardinals	7	321,807
1976	†$19,935.48 (L)	Cincinnati Reds	4	223,009
1977	†$27,758.04 (W)	Los Angeles Dodgers	6	337,708
1978	†$31,236.99 (W)	Los Angeles Dodgers	6	337,304
1981	‡$39,609.20 (L)	Los Angeles Dodgers	6	338,081
1996	‡$216,870.08 (W)	Atlanta Braves	6	324,685

*Five games in 1922 World Series included one tie, 3–3 in 10 innings in game two. Proceeds from the 37,020 gate were ordered donated to charity by Commissioner Kenesaw Mountain Landis to ease the controversy when that Polo Grounds game was "called on account of darkness" while the sun was out.
†Total combined share for both league championship series and World Series.
‡Total combined share for division playoffs, league championship series, and World Series.

MAJOR LEAGUE AND AMERICAN LEAGUE RECORDS AND HONORS BY YANKEES

TRIPLE CROWN WINNERS

Year	Player	Pos.	Avg.	HR	RBI
1934	Lou Gehrig*	1B	.363	49	165
1956	Mickey Mantle*	CF	.353	52	130

*Gehrig and Mantle led both major leagues in all three departments.

NOTE: The Triple Crown has been accomplished 16 times in the majors, including nine in the American League.

AMERICAN LEAGUE MOST VALUABLE PLAYER
(Originated in 1922)

Year	Player	Pos.	Avg.	HR	RBI
1923	Babe Ruth	RF	.393	41*	131*
1927	Lou Gehrig	1B	.373	47	175*
1936	Lou Gehrig	1B	.354	49*	152
1939	Joe DiMaggio	CF	.381*	30	126
1941	Joe DiMaggio	CF	.357	30	125*
1942	Joe Gordon	2B	.322	18	103
1943	Spud Chandler	P	20–4	.833*	1.64* ERA
1947	Joe DiMaggio	CF	.315	20	97
1950	Phil Rizzuto	SS	.324	7	66
1951	Yogi Berra	C	.294	27	88
1954	Yogi Berra	C	.307	22	125
1955	Yogi Berra	C	.272	27	108
1956	Mickey Mantle	CF	.353*	52*	130*
1957	Mickey Mantle	CF	.365	34	94
1960	Roger Maris	RF	.283	39	112†
1961	Roger Maris	RF	.269	61*	142‡
1962	Mickey Mantle	CF	.321	30	89
1963	Elston Howard	C	.287	28	85
1976	Thurman Munson	C	.302	17	105
1985	Don Mattingly	1B	.324	35	145*

*Led major leagues.
†Led American League.
‡Tied for major-league lead.

NOTE: When the "League Award" originated in 1922, a winner was prohibited from repeating—until 1931, when the Baseball Writers Association of America took over selection of the award annually.

AMERICAN LEAGUE CY YOUNG AWARD (Originated in 1956)

Year	Player	W–L	Saves	Pct.	ERA	IP	K	BB
1958†	Bob Turley	21–7	1	.750*	2.97	245⅓	168	128
1961†	Whitey Ford	25–4	0	.862*	3.21	283*	209	92
1977	Sparky Lyle	13–5	26	.722	2.17	137	68	33
1978	Ron Guidry	25–3	0	.893*	1.74*	274	248	72

*Led major leagues.
†Combined choice for both major leagues. Only one Cy Young Award was voted through 1966. Beginning in 1967, two awards were made, one for each league.

NOTE: The 25 victories achieved by Ford in 1961 and Guidry in 1978 topped the major leagues those seasons. Turley's 21 wins in 1958 led the American League, as did Lyle's 72 appearances in 1977.

AMERICAN LEAGUE ROOKIE OF THE YEAR (Originated in 1947)

Year	Player	Pos.	Avg.	HR	RBI
1951	Gil McDougald	3B–2B	.306	14	63
1954	Bob Grim	P	20–6	.769	3.26 ERA
1957	Tony Kubek	IF–OF	.297	3	39
1962	Tom Tresh	SS–OF	.286	20	93
1968	Stan Bahnsen	P	17–12	.586	2.05 ERA
1970	Thurman Munson	C	.302	6	53
1981	Dave Righetti	P	8–4	.667	2.06 ERA
1996	Derek Jeter	SS	.314	10	78

BABE RUTH AWARD (World Series MVP) (Originated in 1949)

Year	Player	Position
1949	Joe Page	P
1950	Jerry Coleman	2B
1951	Phil Rizzuto	SS
1952	Johnny Mize	PH-1B
1953	Billy Martin	2B
1956	Don Larsen	P
1958	Elston Howard	LF-PH
1961	Whitey Ford	P
1962	Ralph Terry	P
1977	Reggie Jackson	RF
1978	Bucky Dent	SS
1996	John Wetteland	P

SPORT MAGAZINE'S WORLD SERIES MVP AWARD
(Originated in 1955)

Year	Player	Pos.
1956	Don Larsen	P
1958	Bob Turley	P
1960	Bobby Richardson	2B
1961	Whitey Ford	P
1962	Ralph Terry	P
1977	Reggie Jackson	RF
1978	Bucky Dent	SS

AMERICAN LEAGUE CHAMPIONSHIP SERIES MVP

Year	Player	Position
1996	Bernie Williams	CF

DAWSON AWARD (Outstanding Yankee rookie in spring training)

Year	Player	Pos.
1956	Norm Siebern	OF
1957	Tony Kubek	SS
1958	Johnny Blanchard	C
1959	Gordie Windhorn	OF
1960	Johnny James	P
1961	Rollie Sheldon	P
1962	Tom Tresh	SS
1963	Pedro Gonzalez	2B
1964	Pete Mikkelsen	P
1965	Art Lopez	OF
1966	Roy White	OF
1967	Bill Robinson	OF
1968	Mike Ferraro	3B
1969	Jerry Kenney	OF
	Bill Burbach	P
1970	John Ellis	C–1B
1971	(none selected)	
1972	Rusty Torres	OF
1973	Otto Velez	OF
1974	Tom Buskey	P
1975	Tippy Martinez	P
1976	Willie Randolph	2B
1977	George Zeber	IF
1978	Jim Beattie	P
1979	Paul Mirabella	P
1980	Mike Griffin	P
1981	Gene Nelson	P
1982	Andre Robertson	SS
1983	Don Mattingly	1B–OF
1984	Jose Rijo	P
1985	Scott Bradley	C
1986	Bob Tewksbury	P
1987	Keith Hughes	OF
1988	Al Leiter	P
1989	(none selected)	
1990	Alan Mills	P
1991	Hensley Meulens	OF
1992	Gerald Williams	OF
1993	Mike Humphreys	OF
1994	Sterling Hitchcock	P
1995	(none selected)	
1996	Mark Hutton	P

SPORTING NEWS AWARDS

MAJOR LEAGUE EXECUTIVE OF THE YEAR (Originated in 1936)

1937	Ed Barrow	1952	George Weiss
1941	Ed Barrow	1960	George Weiss
1950	George Weiss	1961	Dan Topping
1951	George Weiss	1974	Gabe Paul

MAJOR LEAGUE MANAGER OF THE YEAR (Originated in 1936)

1936	Joe McCarthy	1953	Casey Stengel
1938	Joe McCarthy	1958	Casey Stengel
1943	Joe McCarthy	1961	Ralph Houk
1947	Bucky Harris	1974	Bill Virdon
1949	Casey Stengel		

SPORTSMAN OF THE YEAR

1978	Ron Guidry
1996	Joe Torre

AMERICAN LEAGUE MANAGER OF THE YEAR (Originated in 1986)

1994	Buck Showalter
1996	Joe Torre*

Shared with Johnny Oates of Texas Rangers.

MAJOR LEAGUE PLAYER OF THE YEAR (Originated in 1936)

1939	Joe DiMaggio	1958	Bob Turley
1943	Spud Chandler	1961	Roger Maris
1950	Phil Rizzuto	1978	Ron Guidry
1956	Mickey Mantle	1985	Don Mattingly

AMERICAN LEAGUE MOST VALUABLE PLAYER (1929–45)

1931	Lou Gehrig	1941	Joe DiMaggio
1934	Lou Gehrig	1942	Joe Gordon
1936	Lou Gehrig	1943	Spud Chandler
1939	Joe DiMaggio		

AMERICAN LEAGUE PLAYER OF THE YEAR (Originated in 1948)

1950	Phil Rizzuto	1976	Thurman Munson
1956	Mickey Mantle	1984	Don Mattingly
1960	Roger Maris	1985	Don Mattingly
1961	Roger Maris	1986	Don Mattingly
1962	Mickey Mantle		

AMERICAN LEAGUE PITCHER OF THE YEAR (Originated in 1948)

1955	Whitey Ford	1963	Whitey Ford
1958	Bob Turley	1978	Ron Guidry
1961	Whitey Ford		

AMERICAN LEAGUE FIREMAN OF THE YEAR (Originated in 1960)

1961	Luis Arroyo	1986	Dave Righetti
1972	Sparky Lyle	1987	Dave Righetti
1978	Rich Gossage	1996	John Wetteland

AMERICAN LEAGUE ROOKIE OF THE YEAR (Originated in 1946)

Year	Player		Year	Player
1950	Whitey Ford*		1962	Tom Tresh
1954	Bob Grim		1968	Stan Bahnsen (pitcher)
1957	Tony Kubek		1981	Dave Righetti (pitcher)
1958	Ryne Duren (pitcher)		1996	Derek Jeter

Ford was a combined choice for both major leagues.

NOTE: Two rookies—one pitcher, one nonpitcher—have been chosen most years since 1958.

SPORTING NEWS ALL-STAR SELECTIONS (Originated in 1926)

Year	Player	Pos.	Year	Player	Pos.
1926	Herb Pennock	P		Allie Reynolds	P
	Babe Ruth	OF		Phil Rizzuto	SS
1927	Lou Gehrig	1B	1954	Yogi Berra	C
	Babe Ruth	OF	1955	Whitey Ford	P
1928	Lou Gehrig	1B	1956	Yogi Berra	C
	Waite Hoyt	P		Whitey Ford	P
	Babe Ruth	OF		Mickey Mantle	OF
1929	Babe Ruth	OF	1957	Yogi Berra	C
1930	Babe Ruth	OF		Mickey Mantle	OF
1931	Lou Gehrig	1B		Gil McDougald	SS
	Babe Ruth	OF	1958	Bob Turley	P
1932	Bill Dickey	C	1960	Roger Maris	OF
	Tony Lazzeri	2B		Bill Skowron	1B
1933	Bill Dickey	C	1961	Whitey Ford	P
1934	Lou Gehrig	1B		Elston Howard	C
	Lefty Gomez	P		Tony Kubek	SS
1936	Bill Dickey	C		Mickey Mantle	OF
	Lou Gehrig	1B		Roger Maris	OF
1937	Joe DiMaggio	OF		Bobby Richardson	2B
	Lou Gehrig	1B	1962	Mickey Mantle	OF
	Red Rolfe	3B		Bobby Richardson	2B
	Red Ruffing	P		Ralph Terry	P
1938	Bill Dickey	C		Tom Tresh	SS
	Joe DiMaggio	OF	1963	Whitey Ford	P
	Lefty Gomez	P		Elston Howard	C
	Red Rolfe	3B		Joe Pepitone	1B
	Red Ruffing	P		Bobby Richardson	2B
1939	Bill Dickey	C	1964	Elston Howard	C
	Joe DiMaggio	OF		Mickey Mantle	OF
	Joe Gordon	2B		Bobby Richardson	2B
	Red Rolfe	3B	1965	Bobby Richardson	2B
	Red Ruffing	P		Mel Stottlemyre	P
1940	Joe DiMaggio	OF	1966	Bobby Richardson	2B
	Joe Gordon	2B	1971	Bobby Murcer	OF
1941	Bill Dickey	C	1972	Bobby Murcer	OF
	Joe DiMaggio	OF	1973	Thurman Munson	C
	Joe Gordon	2B		Bobby Murcer	OF
1942	Ernie Bonham	P	1974	Thurman Munson	C
	Joe DiMaggio	OF	1975	Thurman Munson	C
	Joe Gordon	2B		Graig Nettles	3B
1943	Spud Chandler	P	1976	Chris Chambliss	1B
	Billy Johnson	3B		Thurman Munson	C
1945	Snuffy Stirnweiss	2B		Mickey Rivers	OF
1946	Aaron Robinson	C	1977	Graig Nettles	3B
1947	Joe DiMaggio	OF		Willie Randolph	2B
1948	Joe DiMaggio	OF	1978	Ron Guidry	P
1949	Tommy Henrich	OF–1B		Graig Nettles	3B
	Joe Page	P	1980	Rick Cerone	C
	Phil Rizzuto	SS		Reggie Jackson	OF–DH
1950	Yogi Berra	C		Tommy John	P
	Vic Raschi	P		Willie Randolph	2B
	Phil Rizzuto	SS	1981	Ron Guidry	P
1951	Allie Reynolds	P	1982	Dave Winfield	OF
	Phil Rizzuto	SS	1983	Ron Guidry	P
1952	Yogi Berra	C		Dave Winfield	OF
	Mickey Mantle	OF	1984	Don Mattingly	1B

Year	Player	Pos.	Year	Player	Pos.
	Dave Righetti	P	1987	Don Mattingly	1B
1985	Don Baylor	DH		Willie Randolph	2B
	Ron Guidry	P	1993	Jimmy Key	P
	Rickey Henderson	OF		Mike Stanley	C
	Don Mattingly	1B	1994	Wade Boggs	3B
1986	Don Mattingly	1B		Jimmy Key	P
	Dave Righetti	P	1996	Andy Pettitte	P

NOTE: The *Sporting News'* All-Star selections are made at season's end.

HALL OF FAMERS

Hall of Famer/Yankee Years/Capacity	Elected
Babe Ruth (1920–34 player)	1936
Lou Gehrig (1923–39 player)	1939
Willie Keeler (1903–09 player)	1939
Clark Griffith (1903–07 player–manager)	1945
Frank Chance (1913–14 player–manager)	1946
Jack Chesbro (1903–09 player)	1946
Herb Pennock (1923–33 player)	1948
Ed Barrow (1920–45 executive)	1953
Bill Dickey (*1928–43 player, 1946 player, manager)	1954
Frank Baker (1916–19, 1921–22 player)	1955
Joe DiMaggio (*1936–42, 1946–51 player)	1955
Joe McCarthy (1931–46 manager)	1957
Bill McKechnie (1913 player)	1962
Miller Huggins (1918–29 manager)	1964
Casey Stengel (1949–60 manager)	1966
Branch Rickey (1907 player)	1967
Red Ruffing (*1930–42, 1945–46 player)	1967
Waite Hoyt (1921–30 player)	1969
Earle Combs (1924–35 player)	1970
George Weiss (1932–60 executive)	1970
Yogi Berra (1946–63 player, 1964 manager)	1971
Lefty Gomez (1930–42 player)	1972
Whitey Ford (*1950, 1953–67 player)	1974
Mickey Mantle (1951–68 player)	1974
Bucky Harris (1947–48 manager)	1975
Bob Lemon (1978–79, 1981 manager)	1976
Joe Sewell (1931–33 player)	1977
Larry MacPhail (1945–47 executive)	1978
Johnny Mize (1949–53 player)	1981
Enos Slaughter (1954–59 player)	1985
Catfish Hunter (1975–79 player)	1987
Gaylord Perry (1980 player)	1991
Tony Lazzeri (1926–37 player)	1991
Reggie Jackson (1977–81 player)	1993
Phil Rizzuto (*1941–42, 1946–56 player)	1994
Phil Niekro (1984–85 player)	1997

Yankee career interrupted by military service.

NOTES

A number of Hall of Famers listed here also served as Yankee coaches. However, time served in that capacity is not included under "Yankee Years" column.

Four other Hall of Famers wore Yankee uniforms briefly, a dozen or fewer games. Dazzy Vance pitched in eight games (0–3) for the Yankees in 1915 and in two games (0–0) in 1918 before resurfacing in the majors four years later with the Brooklyn Dodgers and blossoming as a star pitcher at age 31. And Stan Coveleski, Burleigh Grimes, and Paul Waner concluded their careers in pinstripes. Coveleski had a 5–1 record while pitching in 12 games for the 1928 Yankees; Grimes was 1–2 in 10 games in 1934; and Waner batted .143 in nine games in 1944 and was walked as a pinch hitter in his only 1945 appearance before retiring.

Longtime Yankee broadcasters Mel Allen (1939–64) and Red Barber (1954–66) also have special niches at Cooperstown.

RETIRED NUMBERS

No.	Player	Year
1	Billy Martin	1986
3	Babe Ruth	1948
4	Lou Gehrig	1939
5	Joe DiMaggio	1952
7	Mickey Mantle	1969
8	Bill Dickey and Yogi Berra	1972 (both)
9	Roger Maris	1984
10	Phil Rizzuto	1985
15	Thurman Munson	1979
16	Whitey Ford	1974
23	Don Mattingly	1997
32	Elston Howard	1984
37	Casey Stengel	1970
44	Reggie Jackson	1993

NOTES

DiMaggio, Mantle, and Berra wore different numbers as rookies—DiMaggio 9, Mantle 6, and Berra 35.

After Babe Ruth, number 3 was worn by George Selkirk, Allie Clark, Joe Medwick (during spring training), Bud Metheny, and Cliff Mapes until the number was retired in 1948, shortly before Ruth's death.

Mapes had the distinction of wearing two now-retired numbers during his less than four full seasons as a Yankee. Labeled the "next Babe Ruth," the big outfielder was presented Ruth's number 3 as a rookie in 1948—only to have it taken away and retired during that season. Mapes then wore number 7 until July 31, 1951, when he was traded to the St. Louis Browns. Mantle, meanwhile, wore number 6 for a few months that 1951 season before being sent back to the minors. When he was recalled after 40 games at Triple-A Kansas City, Mapes was gone and Mantle was issued number 7—the last Yankee ever to wear that number.

ALL-STAR GAME SELECTIONS (All-Star Game originated in 1933)

YANKEE ALL-STARS

1933 (6)—*Ben Chapman*, outfield; *Bill Dickey, catcher; *Lou Gehrig*, first base; *Lefty Gomez*, pitcher; *Tony Lazzeri, second base; *Babe Ruth*, outfield.

1934 (6)—Ben Chapman, outfield; *Bill Dickey*, catcher; *Lou Gehrig*, first base; *Lefty Gomez*, pitcher; Red Ruffing, pitcher; *Babe Ruth*, outfield.

1935 (3)—Ben Chapman, outfield; *Lou Gehrig*, first base; *Lefty Gomez*, pitcher.

1936 (7)—Frank Crosetti, shortstop; Bill Dickey, catcher; *Joe DiMaggio*, outfield; *Lou Gehrig*, first base; *Lefty Gomez*, pitcher; *Monte Pearson, pitcher; George Selkirk, outfield.

1937 (6)—Bill Dickey, catcher; *Joe DiMaggio*, outfield; Lou Gehrig, first base; *Lefty Gomez*, pitcher; *Johnny Murphy, pitcher; *Red Rolfe*, third base.

1938 (6)—Bill Dickey, catcher; *Joe DiMaggio*, outfield; Lou Gehrig, first base; *Lefty Gomez*, pitcher; *Red Rolfe, third base; *Red Ruffing, pitcher.

1939 (9)—*Frank Crosetti, shortstop; Bill Dickey, catcher; *Joe DiMaggio*, outfield; *Lefty Gomez*, pitcher; Joe Gordon, second base; *Johnny Murphy, pitcher; Red Rolfe, third base; Red Ruffing, pitcher; George Selkirk, outfield.

1940 (7)—Bill Dickey, catcher; *Joe DiMaggio*, outfield; Joe Gordon, second base; Charlie Keller, outfield; *Monte Pearson, pitcher; *Red Rolfe, third base; Red Ruffing, pitcher.

1941 (6)—Bill Dickey, catcher; *Joe DiMaggio*, outfield; Joe Gordon, second base; Charlie Keller, outfield; *Red Ruffing, pitcher; *Marius Russo, pitcher.

1942 (9)—*Ernie Bonham, pitcher; *Spud Chandler*, pitcher; *Bill Dickey, catcher; *Joe DiMaggio*, outfield; *Joe Gordon*, second base; *Tommy Henrich*, outfield; *Phil Rizzuto, shortstop; *Buddy Rosar, catcher; *Red Ruffing, pitcher.

1943† (6)—*Ernie Bonham, pitcher; *Spud Chandler, pitcher; *Bill Dickey, catcher; *Joe Gordon, second base; *Charlie Keller, outfield; *Johnny Lindell, outfield.

1944 (3)—*Hank Borowy*, pitcher; *Rollie Hemsley*, catcher; *Joe Page, pitcher.

1945—No game.

1946 (6)—*Spud Chandler, pitcher; Bill Dickey, catcher; *Joe DiMaggio*, outfield; Joe Gordon, second base; *Charlie Keller*, outfield; Snuffy Stirnweiss, third base.

1947 (9)—*Spud Chandler, pitcher; *Joe DiMaggio*, outfield; *Tommy Henrich*, outfield; Billy Johnson, third base; *Charlie Keller, outfield; *George McQuinn*, first base; Joe Page, pitcher; *Aaron Robinson, catcher; Spec Shea, pitcher.

1948 (6)—*Yogi Berra, catcher; Joe DiMaggio, outfield; *Tommy Henrich*, outfield; *George McQuinn*, first base; *Joe Page, pitcher; Vic Raschi, pitcher.

1949 (5)—Yogi Berra, catcher; *Joe DiMaggio*, outfield; *Tommy Henrich*, outfield; Vic Raschi, pitcher; *Allie Reynolds, pitcher.

1950 (8)—*Yogi Berra*, catcher; *Tommy Byrne, pitcher; Jerry Coleman, second base; Joe DiMaggio, outfield; Tommy Henrich, first base; *Vic Raschi*, pitcher; Allie Reynolds, pitcher; *Phil Rizzuto*, shortstop.

1951 (4)—Yogi Berra, catcher; *Joe DiMaggio*, outfield; Ed Lopat, pitcher; Phil Rizzuto, shortstop.

1952 (7)—*Hank Bauer*, outfield; Yogi Berra, catcher; *Mickey Mantle*, outfield; *Vic Raschi*, pitcher; *Allie Reynolds, pitcher; *Phil Rizzuto*, shortstop; Gil McDougald, second base.

1953 (7)—*Hank Bauer*, outfield; Yogi Berra, catcher; *Mickey Mantle*, outfield; Johnny Mize, first base; Allie Reynolds, pitcher; Phil Rizzuto, shortstop; *Johnny Sain, pitcher.

1954—*Hank Bauer*, outfield; Yogi Berra, catcher; *Whitey Ford*, pitcher; Mickey Mantle, outfield; Irv Noren, outfield; *Allie Reynolds, pitcher.

1955 (4)—*Yogi Berra*, catcher; Whitey Ford, pitcher; *Mickey Mantle*, outfield; *Bob Turley, pitcher.

1956 (6)—*Yogi Berra*, catcher; Whitey Ford, pitcher; *Johnny Kucks, pitcher; *Mickey Mantle*, outfield; Billy Martin, second base; *Gil McDougald, shortstop.

1957 (8)—*Yogi Berra*, catcher; Bob Grim, pitcher; *Elston Howard, catcher; *Mickey Mantle*, outfield; Gil McDougald, shortstop; *Bobby Richardson, second base; *Bobby Shantz, pitcher; Bill Skowron, first base.

1958 (9)—Yogi Berra, catcher; *Ryne Duren, pitcher; *Whitey Ford, pitcher; *Elston Howard, catcher; *Tony Kubek, shortstop; *Mickey Mantle*, outfield; Gil McDougald, shortstop; *Bill Skowron*, first base; *Bob Turley*, pitcher.

1959‡ (9)—*Yogi Berra*, catcher; Ryne Duren, pitcher; Whitey Ford, pitcher; *Elston Howard, catcher; Tony Kubek, shortstop, outfield; *Mickey Mantle*, outfield; Gil McDougald, shortstop; *Bobby Richardson, second base; *Bill Skowron*, first base. (Skowron started first game, Berra and Mantle second game.)

1960‡ (7)—*Yogi Berra*, catcher; Jim Coates, pitcher; *Whitey Ford*, pitcher; Elston Howard, catcher; *Mickey Mantle*, outfield; *Roger Maris*, outfield; *Bill Skowron*, first base. (Berra, Mantle, Maris, and Skowron started both games, Ford second game.)

1961‡ (8)—*Luis Arroyo, pitcher; Yogi Berra, catcher; *Whitey Ford*, pitcher; Elston Howard, catcher; *Tony Kubek, shortstop; *Mickey Mantle*, outfield; *Roger Maris*, outfield; *Bill Skowron, first base. (Mantle started both games, Ford, Kubek, and Maris first game.)

1962‡ (7)—Yogi Berra, catcher; Elston Howard, catcher; *Mickey Mantle*, outfield; *Roger Maris*, outfield; Bobby Richardson, second base; *Ralph Terry*, pitcher; Tom Tresh, shortstop. (Maris started both games, Mantle first game.)

1963 (6)—Jim Bouton, pitcher; *Elston Howard*, catcher; *Mickey Mantle*, outfield; *Joe Pepitone*, first base; Bobby Richardson, second base; Tom Tresh, outfield.

1964 (5)—*Whitey Ford, pitcher; *Elston Howard*, catcher; *Mickey Mantle*, outfield; Joe Pepitone, first base; *Bobby Richardson*, second base.

1965 (5)—*Elston Howard, catcher; *Mickey Mantle*, outfield; Joe Pepitone, first base; Bobby Richardson, second base; *Mel Stottlemyre, pitcher.

1966 (2)—Bobby Richardson, second base; Mel Stottlemyre, pitcher.

1967 (2)—Al Downing, pitcher; Mickey Mantle, first base.

1968 (2)—Mickey Mantle, first base; Mel Stottlemyre, pitcher.

1969 (2)—*Mel Stottlemyre*, pitcher; Roy White, outfield.

1970 (3)—Fritz Peterson, pitcher; Mel Stottlemyre, pitcher; *Roy White, outfield.

1971 (2)—*Bobby Murcer*, outfield; Thurman Munson, catcher.

1972 (1)—*Bobby Murcer*, outfield.

1973 (3)—Sparky Lyle, pitcher; *Bobby Murcer*, outfield; Thurman Munson, catcher.

1974 (2)—*Bobby Murcer*, outfield; *Thurman Munson*, catcher.

1975 (4)—*Bobby Bonds*, outfield; Catfish Hunter, pitcher; *Thurman Munson*, catcher; *Graig Nettles*, third base.

1976 (6)—Chris Chambliss, first base; Catfish Hunter, pitcher; *Sparky Lyle, pitcher; *Thurman Munson*, catcher; *Willie Randolph, second base; Mickey Rivers, outfield.

1977 (5)—*Reggie Jackson*, outfield; Sparky Lyle, pitcher; Thurman Munson, catcher; Graig Nettles, third base; *Willie Randolph*, second base.

1978 (3)—Rich Gossage, pitcher; Ron Guidry, pitcher; *Reggie Jackson, outfield; Graig Nettles, third base.

1979 (4)—Ron Guidry, pitcher; Reggie Jackson, outfield; *Tommy John, pitcher; Graig Nettles, third base.

1980 (6)—*Bucky Dent*, shortstop; Rich Gossage, pitcher; *Reggie Jackson*, outfield; Tommy John, pitcher; *Graig Nettles*, third base; *Willie Randolph*, second base.

1981 (6)—Ron Davis, pitcher; *Bucky Dent*, shortstop; *Rich Gossage, pitcher; *Reggie Jackson*, outfield; *Willie Randolph*, second base; *Dave Winfield*, outfield.

1982 (3)—*Rich Gossage, pitcher; *Ron Guidry, pitcher; *Dave Winfield*, outfield.

1983 (2)—*Ron Guidry, pitcher; *Dave Winfield*, outfield.

1984 (3)—*Phil Niekro, pitcher; Don Mattingly, first base; *Dave Winfield*, outfield.

1985 (3)—*Rickey Henderson*, outfield; Don Mattingly, first base; *Dave Winfield*, outfield.

1986 (4)—*Rickey Henderson*, outfield; Don Mattingly, first base; Dave Righetti, pitcher; *Dave Winfield*, outfield.

1987 (5)—*Rickey Henderson*, outfield; *Don Mattingly*, first base; *Willie Randolph*, second base; Dave Righetti, pitcher; *Dave Winfield*, outfield.

1988 (3)—*Rickey Henderson*, outfield; Don Mattingly, first base; *Dave Winfield*, outfield.

1989 (2)—Don Mattingly, first base; Steve Sax, second base.

1990 (1)—*Steve Sax*, second base.

†1991 (1)—*Scott Sanderson, pitcher.

1992 (1)—*Roberto Kelly*, outfield.

1993 (2)—*Wade Boggs*, third base; Jimmy Key, pitcher.

1994 (3)—*Wade Boggs*, third base; *Jimmy Key*, pitcher; Paul O'Neill, outfield.

1995 (3)—*Wade Boggs*, third base; Paul O'Neill, outfield; Mike Stanley, catcher.

1996 (3)—Wade Boggs, third base; *Andy Pettitte, pitcher; *John Wetteland, pitcher.

Italics indicate starters.
*Did not play.
†1991 and 1943 were the only years in which a Yankee didn't play in the All-Star Game—the latter despite (1) six being chosen and (2) Joe McCarthy being the American League manager. McCarthy was responding to criticism of his using too many Yankees in past All-Star Games.
‡Two All-Star Games were played 1959–62.

YANKEE ALL-STAR GAME MANAGERS

Year	Manager	Winner	Score
1936	Joe McCarthy	NL	4–3
1937	Joe McCarthy	AL	8–3
1938	Joe McCarthy	NL	4–1
1939	Joe McCarthy	AL	3–1
1942	Joe McCarthy	AL	3–1
1943	Joe McCarthy	AL	5–3
1944	Joe McCarthy	NL	7–1
1948	Bucky Harris	AL	5–2
1950	Casey Stengel	NL	4–3
1951	Casey Stengel	NL	8–3
1952	Casey Stengel	NL	3–2
1953	Casey Stengel	NL	5–1
1954	Casey Stengel	AL	11–9
1956	Casey Stengel	NL	7–3
1957	Casey Stengel	AL	6–5
1958	Casey Stengel	AL	4–3
1959	Casey Stengel	NL	5–4 (1st)
		AL	5–3 (2nd)
1962	Ralph Houk	NL	3–1 (1st)
		AL	9–4 (2nd)
1963	Ralph Houk	NL	5–3
1977	Billy Martin	NL	7–5
1978	Billy Martin	NL	7–3
1979	Bob Lemon	NL	7–6
1995	Buck Showalter	NL	3–2

MANAGERS' ALL-STAR GAME RECORDS

Manager	G	W	L	Pct.
Casey Stengel	10	4	6	.400
Joe McCarthy	7	4	3	.571
Ralph Houk	3	1	2	.333
Billy Martin	2	0	2	.000
Bucky Harris	1	1	0	1.000
Bob Lemon	1	0	1	.000
Buck Showalter	1	0	1	.000

ALL-STAR GAME HOME RUNS

1933—Babe Ruth (one on; AL 4–2), at Comiskey Park, Chicago.
1936—Lou Gehrig (none on; NL 4–3), at Braves Field, Boston.
1937—Lou Gehrig (one on; AL 8–3), at Griffith Stadium, Washington.
1939—Joe DiMaggio (none on; AL 3–1), at Yankee Stadium, New York.
1946—Charlie Keller (one on; AL 12–0), at Fenway Park, Boston.
1955—Mickey Mantle (two on; NL 6–5), at County Stadium, Milwaukee.
1956—Mickey Mantle (none on; NL 7–3), at Griffith Stadium, Washington.
1959—Yogi Berra (one on; AL 5–3), at the Coliseum, Los Angeles.*

*Second of two games that season.

Catcher Bill Dickey played in eight All-Star Games.

ALL-STAR GAME BATTING

	Year	G	AB	R	H	2B	3B	HR	RBI	Avg.
Hank Bauer, OF	1952–54	3	7	0	2	0	0	0	0	.286
Yogi Berra, C-PH	1949–62	15	41	5	8	0	0	1	3	.195
Wade Boggs, 3B	1993–96	4	9	1	2	0	0	0	0	.222
Bobby Bonds, OF	1975	1	3	0	0	0	0	0	0	.000
Hank Borowy, P	1944	1	1	0	1	0	0	0	1	1.000
Chris Chambliss, PH	1976	1	1	0	0	0	0	0	0	.000
Spud Chandler, P	1942	1	1	0	0	0	0	0	0	.000
Ben Chapman, OF	1933–35	3	7	0	2	0	1	0	0	.286
Jerry Coleman, 2B	1950	1	2	0	0	0	0	0	0	.000
Frank Crosetti, PH	1936	1	1	0	0	0	0	0	0	.000
Bucky Dent, SS	1980–81	2	4	0	3	1	0	0	0	.750
Bill Dickey, C-PH	1934, 1936–41, 1946	8	19	3	5	2	0	0	1	.263
Joe DiMaggio, OF-PH	1936–42, 1947–50	11	40	7	9	2	0	1	6	.225
Ryne Duren, P	1959	1	1	0	0	0	0	0	0	.000
Whitey Ford, P	1954–56, 1959–61	3*	3	0	0	0	0	0	0	.000
Lou Gehrig, 1B	1933–38	6	18	4	4	1	0	2	5	.222
Joe Gordon, 2B	1939–42, 1946	5	14	1	2	1	0	0	2	.143
Lefty Gomez, P	1933–35, 1937–38	5	6	0	1	0	0	0	1	.167
Rollie Hemsley, C	1944	1	2	0	0	0	0	0	0	.000
Rickey Henderson, OF	1985–88	4	11	1	3	0	0	0	0	.273
Tommy Henrich, OF-PH	1942, 1947–48, 1950	4	9	1	1	1	0	0	0	.111
Elston Howard, C	1960–64	6	9	1	0	0	0	0	0	.000
Reggie Jackson, OF	1977, 1979–81	4	6	0	2	0	0	0	0	.333
Tommy John, P	1980	1	1	0	0	0	0	0	0	.000
Billy Johnson, 3B	1947	1	0	0	0	0	0	0	0	.000
Charlie Keller, OF	1940–41, 1946	3	7	2	1	0	0	1	2	.143
Roberto Kelly, OF	1992	1	2	0	1	1	0	0	2	.500
Tony Kubek, PH-SS	1959, 1961	2	5	1	0	0	0	0	0	.000
Mickey Mantle, OF-PH	1953–62, 1964, 1967–68	16	43	5	10	0	0	2	4	.233
Roger Maris, OF-PH	1960–62	6	17	2	2	1	0	0	2	.118
Billy Martin, PH	1956	1	1	0	0	0	0	0	0	.000
Don Mattingly, LB-PH	1984–95	6	8	0	1	1	0	0	0	.125
Gil McDougald, PH-SS-PR	1952, 1957–59	4	4	1	1	0	0	0	1	.250
George McQuinn, 1B	1947–48	2	8	1	2	0	0	0	0	.250
Johnny Mize, PH	1953	1	1	0	1	0	0	0	0	1.000
Thurman Munson, PH-C	1971, 1973–77	6	10	1	2	1	0	0	0	.200
Bobby Murcer, OF	1971–74	4	11	0	1	0	0	0	0	.091
Graig Nettles, 3B	1975, 1977–80	5	9	0	2	0	0	0	0	.222
Irv Noren, OF	1954	1	0	0	0	0	0	0	0	.000
Paul O'Neill, PH-OF	1994–95	2	2	0	0	0	0	0	0	.000
Joe Pepitone, 1B-PR-PH	1963–65	3	5	0	0	0	0	0	0	.000
Willie Randolph, 2B	1977, 1980–81, 1987	4	13	0	4	0	0	0	0	.308
Vic Raschi, P	1948, 1950, 1952	1	1	0	1	0	0	0	2	1.000
Allie Reynolds, P	1950, 1953	1*	1	0	0	0	0	0	0	.000
Bobby Richardson, 2B-PR-PH	1959, 1962–66	6	11	1	1	0	0	0	0	.091
Mickey Rivers, PH-OF	1976	1	2	0	1	0	0	0	0	.500
Phil Rizzuto, SS	1950–53	4	9	0	2	0	0	0	0	.222
Red Rolfe, 3B	1937, 1939	3	8	2	3	0	1	0	2	.375
Red Ruffing, P	1934, 1939–40	2*	2	0	1	0	0	0	2	.500
Babe Ruth, OF	1933–34	2	6	2	2	0	0	1	2	.333
Steve Sax, PH-OF	1989–90	2	2	0	0	0	0	0	0	.000
George Selkirk, OF-PH	1936, 1939	2	2	0	1	0	0	0	1	.500
Spec Shea, P	1947	1	1	0	0	0	0	0	0	.000
Bill Skowron, 1B	1957–60	5	14	1	6	1	0	0	0	.429
Mike Stanley, C	1995	1	1	0	0	0	0	0	0	.000
Snuffy Stirnweiss, 2B	1946	1	3	1	1	0	0	0	0	.333
Tom Tresh, OF	1962–63	2	2	0	1	1	0	0	1	.500
Roy White, PH	1969	1	1	0	0	0	0	0	0	.000
Dave Winfield, OF-PH	1981–88	8	25	4	9	5	0	0	1	.360

*Did not bat in every game he pitched.

PITCHERS WHO DIDN'T BAT IN AN ALL-STAR GAME

Jim Bouton, 1963
Jim Coates, 1960
Ron Davis, 1981
Al Downing, 1967
Goose Gossage, 1978, 1980
Bob Grim, 1957
Ron Guidry, 1978–79
Catfish Hunter, 1975, 1979
Ed Lopat, 1951
Sparky Lyle, 1973, 1977
Joe Page, 1947
Fritz Peterson, 1970
Dave Righetti, 1986–87
Mel Stottlemyre, 1966, 1968, 1969, 1970
Bob Turley, 1958

ALL-STAR GAME PITCHING

	Year	IP	H	R	SO	BB	W–L	Pct.
Hank Borowy	1944	3	3	0	0	1	0–0	.000
Jim Bouton	1963	1	0	0	0	0	0–0	.000
Spud Chandler	1942	4	2	0	2	0	1–0	1.000
Jim Coates	1960	2	2	0	0	0	0–0	.000
Ron Davis	1981	1	1	1	1	0	0–0	.000
Al Downing	1967	2	2	0	2	0	0–0	.000
Ryne Duren	1959	3	1	0	4	1	0–0	.000
Whitey Ford	1954–56, 1959–61	12	19	13	5	3	0–2	.000
Lefty Gomez	1933–35, 1937–38	18	11	6	9	3	3–1	.750
Rich Gossage	1978, 1980	2	5	4	1	1	0–1	.000
Bob Grim	1957	⅓	0	0	0	0	0–0	.000
Ron Guidry	1978–79	⅔	1	0	0	1	0–0	.000
Catfish Hunter	1975–76	4	7	4	5	0	0–1	.000
Tommy John	1980	2⅓	4	3	1	0	0–1	.000
Jimmy Key	1993–94	3	3	2	2	0	0–0	.000
Ed Lopat	1951	1	3	3	0	0	0–1	.000
Sparky Lyle	1973, 1977	3	4	2	2	0	0–0	.000
Joe Page	1947	1⅓	1	0	0	1	0–0	.000
Fritz Peterson	1970	0*	1	0	0	0	0–0	.000
Vic Raschi	1948–50, 1952	11	7	3	8	4	1–0	1.000
Allie Reynolds	1950, 1953	5	3	2	2	2	0–1	.000
Dave Righetti	1986–87	1	3	0	0	0	0–0	.000
Red Ruffing	1934, 1939–40	7	13	7	6	2	0–1	.000
Spec Shea	1947	3	3	1	2	2	1–0	1.000
Mel Stottlemyre	1966, 1968–70	6	5	3	4	1	0–1	.000
Bob Turley	1958	1⅔	3	3	0	2	0–0	.000

*Peterson pitched to one batter in ninth inning, allowing RBI single to Willie McCovey during National League's three-run game-tying rally en route to its 5–4 victory in 15 innings.

ALL-STAR GAME STARTING PITCHERS (17)

Lefty Gomez, 1933–35, 1937–38
Red Ruffing, 1939–40
Spud Chandler, 1942
Hank Borowy, 1944
Vic Raschi, 1950, 1952
Whitey Ford, 1954, 1960 (2nd game), 1961 (1st game)
Bob Turley, 1958
Mel Stottlemyre, 1969
Jimmy Key, 1994

ALL-STAR GAME WINNING PITCHERS (6)

1933—Lefty Gomez (AL 4–2), at Comiskey Park, Chicago.
1935—Lefty Gomez (AL 4–1), at Municipal Stadium, Cleveland.
1937—Lefty Gomez (AL 8–3), at Griffith Stadium, Washington.
1942—Spud Chandler (AL 3–1), at the Polo Grounds, New York.
1947—Spec Shea (AL 2–1), at Wrigley Field, Chicago.
1948—Vic Raschi (AL 5–2), at Sportsman's Park, St. Louis.

ALL-STAR GAME LOSING PITCHERS (10)

1938—Lefty Gomez (NL 4–1), at Crosley Field, Cincinnati.
1940—Red Ruffing (NL 4–0), at Sportsman's Park, St. Louis.
1951—Ed Lopat (NL 8–3), at Briggs Stadium, Detroit.
1953—Allie Reynolds (NL 5–1), at Crosley Field, Cincinnati.
1959—Whitey Ford (NL 5–4), at Forbes Field, Pittsburgh.*
1960—Whitey Ford (NL 6–0), at Yankee Stadium, New York.†
1969—Mel Stottlemyre (NL 9–3), at RFK Stadium, Washington.
1975—Catfish Hunter (NL 6–3), at County Stadium, Milwaukee.
1978—Rich Gossage (NL 4–3), at San Diego Stadium.
1980—Tommy John (NL 4–2), at Dodger Stadium, Los Angeles.

*First of two games that season.
†Second of two games that season.

ALL-STAR GAMES AT YANKEE STADIUM

July 11, 1939

National League	001	000	000	—	1 7 1
American League	000	210	00X	—	3 6 1

NL: Paul Derringer (Reds), BILL LEE (Cubs) (4th), Lou Fette (Braves) (7th); Ernie Lombardi (Reds).
AL: Red Ruffing (Yankees), TOMMY BRIDGES (Tigers) (4th), Bob Feller (Indians) (6th); Bill Dickey (Yankees).
Home Run: Joe DiMaggio (Yankees).
Managers: Joe McCarthy (Yankees), Gabby Hartnett (Cubs).
Attendance: 62,892.

July 13, 1960

(Second All-Star Game that year)

National League	021	000	102	—	6 10 0
American League	000	000	000	—	0 8 0

NL: VERN LAW (Pirates), Johnny Podres (Dodgers) (3rd), Stan Williams (Dodgers) (5th), Larry Jackson (Cardinals) (7th), Bill Henry (Reds) (8th), Lindy McDaniel (Cardinals) (9th); Del Crandall (Braves), Ed Bailey (Reds), Smoky Burgess (Pirates).
AL: WHITEY FORD (Yankees), Early Wynn (White Sox) (4th), Gerry Staley (White Sox) (6th), Frank Lary (Tigers) (8th), Gary Bell (Indians) (9th); Yogi Berra (Yankees), Sherm Lollar (White Sox).
Home Runs: Eddie Mathews (Braves), Willie Mays (Giants), Stan Musial (Cardinals), and Ken Boyer (Cardinals).
Managers: Al Lopez (White Sox), Walter Alston (Dodgers).
Attendance: 38,362.

July 19, 1977

National League	401	000	020	—	7 9 1
American League	000	002	102	—	5 8 0

NL: DON SUTTON (Dodgers), Gary Lavelle (Giants) (4th), Tom Seaver (Reds) (6th), Rick Reuschel (Cubs) (8th), Rich Gossage (Pirates) (9th); Johnny Bench (Reds), Ted Simmons (Cardinals), John Stearns (Mets).
AL: JIM PALMER (Orioles), Jim Kern (Indians) (3rd), Dennis Eckersley (Indians) (4th), Dave LaRoche (Angels) (6th), Bill Campbell (Red Sox) (7th), Sparky Lyle (Yankees) (8th); Carlton Fisk (Red Sox), Butch Wynegar (Twins).
Home Runs: Joe Morgan (Reds), Greg Luzinski (Phillies), Steve Garvey (Dodgers), and George Scott (Red Sox).
Managers: Billy Martin (Yankees), Sparky Anderson (Reds).
Attendance: 56,683.

NOTE: Capital letters indicate pitchers of decision.

YANKEE AMERICAN LEAGUE LEADERS

HITTING CHAMPIONS

Batting

Year	Player	Pos.	Avg.
1924	Babe Ruth	OF	.378
1934	Lou Gehrig	1B	.363*
1939	Joe DiMaggio	CF	.381*
1940	Joe DiMaggio	CF	.352
1945	Snuffy Stirnweiss	2B	.309
1956	Mickey Mantle	CF	.353*
1984	Don Mattingly	1B	.343
1994	Paul O'Neill	RF	.359

Home Runs

Year	Player	Pos.	Homers
1916	Wally Pipp	1B	12†
1917	Wally Pipp	1B	9
1920	Babe Ruth	OF	54*
1921	Babe Ruth	OF	59*
1923	Babe Ruth	OF	41†
1924	Babe Ruth	OF	46*
1925	Bob Meusel	OF	33
1926	Babe Ruth	OF	47*
1927	Babe Ruth	OF	60*
1928	Babe Ruth	OF	54*
1929	Babe Ruth	OF	46*
1930	Babe Ruth	OF	49
1931	Lou Gehrig	1B	46†
	Babe Ruth	OF	46†
1934	Lou Gehrig	1B	49*
1936	Lou Gehrig	1B	49*
1937	Joe DiMaggio	CF	46*

In 1984, Don Mattingly (number 23) and Dave Winfield dueled for the batting crown until their final at-bats. Mattingly prevailed, .343 to .340. In his first full season as a regular, the 24-year-old Mattingly also led the majors in doubles (44), the league in hits (207), and the Yankees in RBIs (110). The 32-year-old Winfield added a third straight 100-RBI season, and manager Yogi Berra observed: "Winfield was my most valuable player."

Year	Player	Pos.	Homers
1944	Nick Etten	1B	22
1948	Joe DiMaggio	CF	39
1955	Mickey Mantle	CF	37
1956	Mickey Mantle	CF	52*
1958	Mickey Mantle	CF	42
1960	Mickey Mantle	CF	40
1961	Roger Maris	RF	61*
1976	Graig Nettles	3B	32
1980	Reggie Jackson	RF–DH	41‡

Slugging

Year	Player	Pos.	Avg.
1920	Babe Ruth	OF	.847*
1921	Babe Ruth	OF	.846*
1922	Babe Ruth	OF	.672
1923	Babe Ruth	OF	.764*
1924	Babe Ruth	OF	.739*
1926	Babe Ruth	OF	.737*
1927	Babe Ruth	OF	.772*
1928	Babe Ruth	OF	.709*
1929	Babe Ruth	OF	.697*
1930	Babe Ruth	OF	.732*
1931	Babe Ruth	OF	.700*
1934	Lou Gehrig	1B	.706*
1936	Lou Gehrig	1B	.696*
1937	Joe DiMaggio	CF	.673*
1945	Snuffy Stirnweiss	2B	.476
1950	Joe DiMaggio	CF	.585
1955	Mickey Mantle	CF	.611
1956	Mickey Mantle	CF	.705*
1960	Roger Maris	RF	.581
1961	Mickey Mantle	CF	.687*
1962	Mickey Mantle	CF	.605
1986	Don Mattingly	1B	.573*

Runs Batted In

Year	Player	Pos.	RBIs
1920	Babe Ruth	OF	137*
1921	Babe Ruth	OF	171*
1923	Babe Ruth	OF	131*
1925	Bob Meusel	OF	138
1926	Babe Ruth	OF	145*
1927	Lou Gehrig	1B	175*
1928	Lou Gehrig	1B	142†
	Babe Ruth	OF	142†
1930	Lou Gehrig	1B	174
1931	Lou Gehrig	1B	184*
1934	Lou Gehrig	1B	165*
1941	Joe DiMaggio	CF	125*
1945	Nick Etten	1B	111
1948	Joe DiMaggio	CF	155*
1956	Mickey Mantle	CF	130*
1960	Roger Maris	RF	112
1961	Roger Maris	RF	142†
1985	Don Mattingly	1B	145*

Runs

Year	Player	Pos.	Runs
1920	Babe Ruth	OF	158*
1921	Babe Ruth	OF	177*
1923	Babe Ruth	OF	151*
1924	Babe Ruth	OF	143*
1926	Babe Ruth	OF	139*
1927	Babe Ruth	OF	158*
1928	Babe Ruth	OF	163*
1931	Lou Gehrig	1B	163*
1933	Lou Gehrig	1B	138*
1935	Lou Gehrig	1B	125
1936	Lou Gehrig	1B	167*
1937	Joe DiMaggio	CF	151*
1939	Red Rolfe	3B	139*
1944	Snuffy Stirnweiss	2B	125*
1945	Snuffy Stirnweiss	2B	107
1948	Tommy Henrich	OF–1B	138*

Runs (Continued)

Year	Player	Pos.	RBIs
1954	Mickey Mantle	CF	129*
1956	Mickey Mantle	CF	132*
1957	Mickey Mantle	CF	121*
1958	Mickey Mantle	CF	127*
1960	Mickey Mantle	CF	119*
1961	Mickey Mantle	CF	132†
	Roger Maris	RF	132†
1972	Bobby Murcer	CF	102
1976	Roy White	OF	104
1985	Rickey Henderson	OF	146*
1986	Rickey Henderson	OF	130*

NOTE: Henderson also led the majors with 113 runs scored in 1989 while splitting the season between Yankees (65 games) and A's (85 games). Outfielder Patsy Dougherty also led the majors with 113 runs scored in 1904 while splitting the AL season between Boston (49 games) and New York (106 games).

Hits

Year	Player	Pos.	Hits
1927	Earle Combs	CF	231
1931	Lou Gehrig	1B	211
1939	Red Rolfe	3B	213*
1944	Snuffy Stirnweiss	2B	205*
1945	Snuffy Stirnweiss	2B	195
1962	Bobby Richardson	2B	209
1984	Don Mattingly	1B	207
1986	Don Mattingly	1B	238*

Singles

Year	Player	Pos.	Hits
1904	Willie Keeler	OF	164*
1905	Willie Keeler	OF	147
1906	Willie Keeler	OF	166*
1927	Earle Combs	CF	166
1929	Earle Combs	CF	151
1944	Snuffy Stirnweiss	2B	146*
1950	Phil Rizzuto	SS	150*
1961	Bobby Richardson	2B	148
1962	Bobby Richardson	2B	158
1964	Bobby Richardson	2B	148
1967	Horace Clarke	2B	140
1969	Horace Clarke	2B	146
1975	Thurman Munson	C	151
1989	Steve Sax	2B	171*

Doubles

Year	Player	Pos.	Doubles
1927	Lou Gehrig	1B	52*
1928	Lou Gehrig	1B	47‡
1939	Red Rolfe	3B	46
1984	Don Mattingly	1B	44*
1985	Don Mattingly	1B	48*
1986	Don Mattingly	1B	53*

Triples

Year	Player	Pos.	Triples
1924	Wally Pipp	1B	19
1926	Lou Gehrig	1B	20
1927	Earle Combs	CF	23*
1928	Earle Combs	CF	21*
1930	Earle Combs	CF	22
1934	Ben Chapman	CF	13
1936	Joe DiMaggio	CF	15†
	Red Rolfe	3B	15†
1943	Johnny Lindell	OF	12‡
1944	Johnny Lindell	OF	16
	Snuffy Stirnweiss	2B	16

1945	Snuffy Stirnweiss	2B	22*
1947	Tommy Henrich	OF–1B	13
1948	Tommy Henrich	OF–1B	14
1955	Andy Carey	3B	11
	Mickey Mantle	CF	11
1957	Hank Bauer	OF	9
	Gil McDougald	IF	9

NOTE: Outfielder–first baseman Harry Simpson shared the league lead with 9 triples in 1957 while splitting the season between A's (50 games) and Yankees (75 games).

Total Bases

Year	Player	Pos.	Bases
1921	Babe Ruth	OF	457*
1923	Babe Ruth	OF	399*
1924	Babe Ruth	OF	391*
1926	Babe Ruth	OF	365*
1927	Lou Gehrig	1B	447*
1928	Babe Ruth	OF	380*
1930	Lou Gehrig	1B	419
1931	Lou Gehrig	1B	410*
1934	Lou Gehrig	1B	409*
1937	Joe DiMaggio	CF	418*
1941	Joe DiMaggio	CF	348*
1944	Johnny Lindell	OF	297
1945	Snuffy Stirnweiss	2B	301
1948	Joe DiMaggio	CF	355
1956	Mickey Mantle	CF	376*
1958	Mickey Mantle	CF	307
1960	Mickey Mantle	CF	294
1961	Roger Maris	RF	366*
1972	Bobby Murcer	CF	314
1985	Don Mattingly	1B	370*
1986	Don Mattingly	1B	388*

Stolen Bases

Year	Player	Pos.	Stolen Bases
1914	Fritz Maisel	3B	74*
1931	Ben Chapman	OF–IF	61*
1932	Ben Chapman	OF	38*
1933	Ben Chapman	OF	27*
1938	Frank Crosetti	SS	27*
1944	Snuffy Stirnweiss	2B	55*
1945	Snuffy Stirnweiss	2B	33*
1985	Rickey Henderson	OF	80
1986	Rickey Henderson	OF	87
1988	Rickey Henderson	OF	93*

NOTE: Henderson also led the majors with 77 stolen bases in 1989 while splitting the season between Yankees (65 games) and A's (85 games).

Walks

Year	Player	Pos.	Walks
1920	Babe Ruth	OF	148*
1921	Babe Ruth	OF	144*
1922	Whitey Witt	OF	89*
1923	Babe Ruth	OF	170*
1924	Babe Ruth	OF	142*
1926	Babe Ruth	OF	144*
1927	Babe Ruth	OF	138*
1928	Babe Ruth	OF	135*
1930	Babe Ruth	OF	136*
1931	Babe Ruth	OF	128*
1932	Babe Ruth	OF	130*
1933	Babe Ruth	OF	114*
1935	Lou Gehrig	1B	132*
1936	Lou Gehrig	1B	130*
1937	Lou Gehrig	1B	127*
1940	Charlie Keller	OF	106
1943	Charlie Keller	OF	106
1944	Nick Etten	1B	97
1955	Mickey Mantle	CF	113*

Walks (Continued)

Year	Player	Pos.	Walks
1957	Mickey Mantle	CF	146*
1958	Mickey Mantle	CF	129*
1961	Mickey Mantle	CF	126*
1962	Mickey Mantle	CF	122*
1972	Roy White	OF	99†
1980	Willie Randolph	2B	119*

NOTE: Outfielder Rickey Henderson led the league with 126 walks in 1989 while splitting the season between Yankees (65 games) and A's (85 games).

Struck Out

(Strikeouts not included in American League batting records until 1913.)

Year	Player	Pos.	Strikeouts
1916	Wally Pipp	1B	82
1920	Aaron Ward	3B	84
1921	Bob Meusel	OF	88*
1923	Babe Ruth	OF	93*
1924	Babe Ruth	OF	81*
1926	Tony Lazzeri	2B	96*
1927	Babe Ruth	OF	89*
1928	Babe Ruth	OF	87
1937	Frank Crosetti	SS	105
1938	Frank Crosetti	SS	97
1942	Joe Gordon	2B	95*
1946	Charlie Keller	OF	101‡
1952	Mickey Mantle	CF	111‡
1954	Mickey Mantle	CF	107*
1958	Mickey Mantle	CF	120†
1959	Mickey Mantle	CF	126*
1960	Mickey Mantle	CF	125

*Led major leagues.
†Shared major league lead.
‡Shared league lead.

PITCHING TRIPLE CROWN WINNERS

		Wins	ERA	Strikeouts
1934	Lefty Gomez	26–5	2.33	158
1937	Lefty Gomez	21–11	2.33*	194*

*Led Majors.

NOTE: Pitching Triple Crown has been accomplished 29 times in the majors, including 10 in the AL. Detroit's Hal Newhouser was the last to do it, in 1945. Dwight Gooden, as a Met in 1985, was the last to achieve it in the majors.

Gomez is among six pitchers to do it more than once, joining fellow Hall of Famers Christy Mathewson, Grover Cleveland Alexander, Walter Johnson, Lefty Grove, and Sandy Koufax.

PITCHING LEADERS

Games

Year	Player	Games
1904	Jack Chesbro	55*
1906	Jack Chesbro	49*
1918	George Mogridge	45†
1921	Carl Mays	49*
1935	Russ Van Atta	58*
1948	Joe Page	55
1949	Joe Page	60*
1961	Luis Arroyo	65†
1977	Sparky Lyle	72
1994	Bob Wickman	53

NOTE: Russ Van Atta led the majors with 58 appearances in 1935 while dividing the season between Yankees (5 games) and St. Louis Browns (53 games).

Innings

Year	Player	Innings
1904	Jack Chesbro	455*
1906	Al Orth	339
1921	Carl Mays	337*
1925	Herb Pennock	277
1928	George Pipgras	301
1934	Lefty Gomez	282
1961	Whitey Ford	283*
1962	Ralph Terry	299
1963	Whitey Ford	269
1965	Mel Stottlemyre	291
1975	Catfish Hunter	328*

Victories

Year	Player	Record
1904	Jack Chesbro	41–12*
1906	Al Orth	27–17†
1921	Carl Mays	27–9†
1927	Waite Hoyt	22–7‡
1928	George Pipgras	24–13‡
1934	Lefty Gomez	26–5
1937	Lefty Gomez	21–11
1938	Red Ruffing	21–7
1943	Spud Chandler	20–4‡
1955	Whitey Ford	18–7‡
1958	Bob Turley	21–7
1961	Whitey Ford	25–4*
1962	Ralph Terry	23–12
1963	Whitey Ford	24–7
1975	Catfish Hunter	23–14†
1978	Ron Guidry	25–3*
1985	Ron Guidry	22–6
1994	Jimmy Key	17–4*
1996	Andy Pettitte	21–8

Winning Percentage

Year	Player	Percentage	
1904	Jack Chesbro	.774	(41–12)
1921	Carl Mays	.750*	(27–9)
1922	Joe Bush	.788*	(26–7)
1923	Herb Pennock	.760	(19–6)
1927	Waite Hoyt	.759*	(22–7)
1932	Johnny Allen	.810*	(17–4)
1934	Lefty Gomez	.839*	(26–5)
1936	Monte Pearson	.731	(19–7)
1938	Red Ruffing	.750*	(21–7)
1941	Lefty Gomez	.750	(15–5)
1942	Ernie Bonham	.808*	(21–5)
1943	Spud Chandler	.833*	(20–4)
1947	Allie Reynolds	.704	(19–8)
1950	Vic Raschi	.724	(21–8)
1953	Ed Lopat	.800*	(16–4)
1955	Tommy Byrne	.762	(16–5)
1956	Whitey Ford	.760	(19–6)
1957	Tom Sturdivant	.727†	(16–6)
1958	Bob Turley	.750*	(21–7)
1961	Whitey Ford	.862*	(25–4)
1963	Whitey Ford	.774	(24–7)
1978	Ron Guidry	.893*	(25–3)
1985	Ron Guidry	.786	(22–6)
1993	Jimmy Key	.750	(18–6)

Strikeouts

Year	Player	Strikeouts
1932	Red Ruffing	190
1933	Lefty Gomez	163
1934	Lefty Gomez	158
1937	Lefty Gomez	194*
1951	Vic Raschi	164†
1952	Allie Reynolds	160
1964	Al Downing	217

Earned Run Average

Year	Player	ERA
1920	Bob Shawkey	2.45
1927	Wilcy Moore	2.28*
1934	Lefty Gomez	2.33
1937	Lefty Gomez	2.33*
1943	Spud Chandler	1.64*
1947	Spud Chandler	2.46
1952	Allie Reynolds	2.06*
1953	Ed Lopat	2.42
1956	Whitey Ford	2.47*
1957	Bobby Shantz	2.45*
1958	Whitey Ford	2.01*
1978	Ron Guidry	1.74*
1979	Ron Guidry	2.78
1980	Rudy May	2.47

Saves

Year	Player	Saves
1916	Bob Shawkey	9*
1918	George Mogridge	7*
1921	Carl Mays	7†
1922	Sam Jones	8*
1927	Wilcy Moore	13†
1928	Waite Hoyt	8*
1936	Pat Malone	9
1938	Johnny Murphy	11
1939	Johnny Murphy	19*
1941	Johnny Murphy	15*
1942	Johnny Murphy	11
1945	Jim Turner	10
1947	Joe Page	17‡
1949	Joe Page	27*
1954	Johnny Sain	22
1957	Bob Grim	19*
1958	Ryne Duren	20†
1961	Luis Arroyo	29*
1972	Sparky Lyle	35
1976	Sparky Lyle	23
1978	Rich Gossage	27
1980	Rich Gossage	33†
1986	Dave Righetti	46
1996	John Wetteland	43

NOTE: Allen Russell led the majors with 5 saves in 1919 while dividing the season between the Yankees (23 games) and Red Sox (21 games).

Shutouts

Year	Player	No.
1920	Carl Mays	6
1928	Herb Pennock	5*
1930	George Pipgras	3‡
1934	Lefty Gomez	6†
1937	Lefty Gomez	6*
1938	Lefty Gomez	4
	Red Ruffing	4
1939	Red Ruffing	5
1942	Ernie Bonham	6
1943	Spud Chandler	5‡
1951	Allie Reynolds	7†
1952	Allie Reynolds	6
1958	Whitey Ford	7*
1960	Whitey Ford	4‡
1978	Ron Guidry	9*
1980	Tommy John	6†

Complete Games

Year	Player	No.
1904	Jack Chesbro	48*
1906	Al Orth	36
1934	Lefty Gomez	25*
1942	Ernie Bonham	22‡
1943	Spud Chandler	20‡

1955	Whitey Ford	18
1958	Bob Turley	19‡
1963	Ralph Terry	18‡
1965	Mel Stottlemyre	18
1969	Mel Stottlemyre	24
1975	Catfish Hunter	30*
1983	Ron Guidry	21*
1995	Jack McDowell	8

*Led major leagues.
†Shared major league lead.
‡Shared league lead.

YANKEE CLUB RECORDS

BATTING

Most years with Yankees	Yogi Berra	18	(1946–63)
	Mickey Mantle	18	(1951–68)
Most games, season	Bobby Richardson	162	(1961)
	Roy White	162	(1970)
	Chris Chambliss	162	(1978)
	Don Mattingly	162	(1986)
	Roberto Kelly	162	(1990)
Most at bats, season	Bobby Richardson	692	(1952)†
Most runs, season	Babe Ruth	177	(1921)*
Most hits, season	Don Mattingly	238	(1986)
Most singles, season	Steve Sax	171	(1989)
Most doubles, season	Don Mattingly	53	(1986)
Most triples, season	Earle Combs	23	(1927)*
Most home runs, right-hander, season	Joe DiMaggio	46	(1937)
Most home runs, left-hander, season	Roger Maris	61	(1961)*
	Babe Ruth	60	(1927)*
Most home runs, rookie, season	Joe DiMaggio	29	(1936)
Most grand-slam home runs, season	Don Mattingly	6	(1987)*
Most grand-slam home runs, career	Lou Gehrig	23*	
Most home runs, season, at home	Babe Ruth	32	(1921) (PG)
	Lou Gehrig	30	(1934) (YS)
	Roger Maris	30	(1961) (YS)
Most home runs, season, on the road	Babe Ruth	32	(1927)*
Most home runs, one month, right-hander	Joe DiMaggio	15	(7/37)
Most home runs, one month, left-hander	Babe Ruth	17	(9/27)*
Most consecutive games scoring a run	Red Rolfe	18	(1939)*
Most total bases, season	Babe Ruth	457	(1921)*
Most sacrifice hits, season	Willie Keeler	42	(1905)
Most sacrifice flies, season	Roy White	17	(1971)†
Most stolen bases, season	Rickey Henderson	93	(1988)
Most caught stealing, season	Ben Chapman	23	(1931)
Most walks, season	Babe Ruth	170	(1923)*
Most strikeouts, season	Danny Tartabull	156	(1993)
Fewest strikeouts, season	Joe Sewell	3	(1932)
Most hit by pitch, season	Don Baylor	24	(1985)
Most runs batted in, season	Lou Gehrig	184	(1931)†
Most consecutive games with a home run	Don Mattingly	8	(1987)*

BATTING (*Continued*)

Most consecutive games with an RBI	Babe Ruth	11	(1931)
Highest batting average, season	Babe Ruth	.393	(1923)
Highest slugging average, season	Babe Ruth	.847	(1920)*
Longest hitting streak	Joe DiMaggio	56	(1941)*
Most grounded into double plays, season	Dave Winfield	30	(1983)
Fewest grounded into double plays, season	Mickey Mantle	2	(1961)
	Mickey Rivers	2	(1977)

Most earned runs allowed, season	Sam Jones	127	(1925)
Most hits allowed, season	Jack Chesbro	337	(1904)
Most hit batsmen, season	Jack Warhop	26	(1909)
Most wild pitches, season	Tim Leary	23	(1990)
Most home runs allowed, season	Ralph Terry	40	(1962)
Lowest ERA, right-hander, season	Spud Chandler	1.64	(1943)
Lowest ERA, left-hander, season	Ron Guidry	1.74	(1978)

*Major league record.
†American League record.
(PG) Polo Grounds; (YS) Yankee Stadium.

PITCHING

Most years with Yankees	Whitey Ford	16	(1950, 1953–67)
Most games, right-hander, season	John Habyan	66	(1991)
Most games, left-hander, season	Dave Righetti	74	(1985)
	Dave Righetti	74	(1986)
Most games started, season	Jack Chesbro	51	(1904)
Most complete games, season	Jack Chesbro	48	(1904)
Most games finished, right-hander, season	Rich Gossage	58	(1980)
Most games finished, left-hander, season	Dave Righetti	68	(1986)
Most innings pitched, season	Jack Chesbro	454	(1904)
Most victories, right-hander, season	Jack Chesbro	41	(1904)*
Most victories, left-hander, season	Lefty Gomez	26	(1934)
Most 20-victory seasons	Bob Shawkey	4	
	Lefty Gomez	4	
	Red Ruffing	4	
Most losses, season	Al Orth	21	(1907)
	Joe Lake	21	(1908)
	Russ Ford	21	(1912)
	Sam Jones	21	(1925)
Highest winning percentage, season	Ron Guidry (25–3)	.893	(1978)
Most consecutive victories, season	Jack Chesbro	14	(1904)
	Whitey Ford	14	(1961)
Most consecutive losses, season	Bill Hogg	9	(1908)
	Thad Tillotson	9	(1967)
Most saves, left-hander, season	Dave Righetti	46	(1986)*
Most saves, right-hander, season	John Wetteland	43	(1996)
Most walks, left-hander, season	Tommy Byrne	179	(1949)
Most walks, right-hander, season	Bob Turley	177	(1955)
Most strikeouts, season	Ron Guidry	248	(1978)
Most strikeouts, 9-inning game	Ron Guidry	18	(6/17/78)
Most strikeouts, extra-inning game	Whitey Ford	15	(4/22/59)
Most shutouts, season	Ron Guidry	9	(1978)
Most 1–0 shutouts won, career	Bob Shawkey	7	
Most shutouts lost, season	Bill Zuber	7	(1945)
Most runs allowed, season	Russ Ford	165	(1912)

ALL-TIME TEAM RECORDS

Most players: 49 in 1989
Fewest players: 25 in 1923, 1927
Most games: 164 in 1964, 1968
Most at bats: 5,705 in 1964
Most runs: 1,067 in 1931
Fewest runs: 459 in 1908
Most opponents runs: 898 in 1930
Most hits: 1,683 in 1930
Fewest hits: 1,137 in 1968
Most singles: 1,237 in 1988
Most doubles: 315 in 1936
Most triples: 110 in 1930
Most homers: 240 in 1961
Most home runs by pinch hitters: 10 in 1961
Most home runs with bases filled: 10 in 1987
Most total bases: 2,703 in 1936
Most sacrifices (sacrifice hits and flies): 218 in 1922, 1926
Most sacrifice hits: 178 in 1906
Most sacrifice flies: 72 in 1974
Most stolen bases: 289 in 1910
Most caught stealing: 82 in 1920
Most bases on balls: 766 in 1932
Most strikeouts: 1,043 in 1967
Fewest strikeouts: 420 in 1924
Most hit by pitch: 53 in 1990
Fewest hit by pitch: 14 in 1969
Most runs batted in: 995 in 1936
Highest batting average: .309 in 1930
Lowest batting average: .214 in 1968
Highest slugging average: .489 in 1927
Lowest slugging average: .287 in 1914
Most grounded into double play: 152 in 1982
Fewest grounded into double play: 91 in 1963
Most left on bases: 1,247 in 1993
Fewest left on bases: 1,010 in 1920
Most .300 hitters: 9 in 1930
Most putouts: 4,520 in 1964
Fewest putouts: 3,993 in 1935
Most assists: 2,086 in 1904
Fewest assists: 1,493 in 1948
Most chances accepted: 6,383 in 1980
Fewest chances accepted: 5,551 in 1935
Most errors: 386 in 1912
Fewest errors: 102 in 1987
Most errorless games: 91 in 1964
Most consecutive errorless games: 10 in 1977, 1993, 1995
Most double plays: 214 in 1956
Fewest double plays: 81 in 1912
Most consecutive games, one or more double plays: 19 (27 double plays) in 1992

ALL-TIME RECORDS (*Continued*)

Most passed balls: 32 in 1913
Fewest passed balls: 0 in 1931
Highest fielding average: .983 in 1964, 1987, 1993
Lowest fielding average: .939 in 1912
Most games won: 110 in 1927
Most home games won: 65 in 1961
Most road games won: 54 in 1939
Most games lost: 103 in 1908
Most home games lost: 47 in 1908, 1913
Most road games lost: 58 in 1912
Highest percentage games won: .714 in 1927
Lowest percentage games won: .329 in 1912
Most shutouts won, season: 24 in 1951
Most shutouts lost, season: 27 in 1914
Most 1–0 games won: 6 in 1908, 1968
Most 1–0 games lost: 9 in 1914
Most consecutive games won, season: 19 in 1947
Most consecutive games lost, season: 13 in 1913
Most consecutive extra-inning games: 4 in 1992
Most runs, game: New York, 25, Philadelphia 2, May 24, 1936
Most runs, game, by opponent, on road: Cleveland 24, New York 6, July 29, 1928
Most runs, game, by opponent, at home: Detroit 19, New York 1, June 17, 1925; Toronto 19, New York 3, Sept. 10, 1977
Most runs, shutout game: New York 21, Philadelphia 0, Aug. 13, 1939, 2nd game, 8 innings
Most runs, shutout game, by opponent: Chicago 15, New York 0, July 15, 1907; Chicago 15, New York 0, May 4, 1950
Most runs, double header shutout: 24, New York vs. Philadelphia, Sept. 4, 1944
Longest 1–0 game won: 15 innings, New York 1, Philadelphia 0, July 4, 1925, first game
Longest 1–0 game lost: 14 innings, Boston 1, New York 0, September 24, 1969
Most runs, inning: 14, New York vs. Washington, July 6, 1920, fifth inning
Most hits, game: 30, New York vs. Boston, Sept. 28, 1923
Most doubles, game: 10, New York at Toronto, April 12, 1988
Most home runs, game: 8, New York vs. Philadelphia, June 28, 1939, first game
Most consecutive games, one or more home runs: 25 (40 homers), 1941
Most home runs in consecutive games in which home runs were made: 40 (25 games), 1941
Most total bases, game: 53, New York vs. Philadelphia, June 28, 1939, first game
Most grand slams, game: 2, New York vs. Philadelphia, May 24, 1936
New York at Toronto, June 29, 1987

YANKEES' LONGEST WINNING STREAKS

19—1947	15—1906, 1960
18—1953	14—1941
16—1926	13—1954, 1961

YANKEES' LONGEST LOSING STREAKS

13 (one tie)—1913	11—1911
12—1908	9—1912 (twice), 1916, 1945, 1953, 1982

What's this—Whitey Ford wearing a Yankee cap and a Red Sox jacket after reporting to the team in July 1950 at Boston? If the baby-faced 21-year-old looks bewildered, even shellshocked in this snapshot, it may be because he was hammered in his big-league debut at not-so-friendly Fenway.

"I took the night train to Boston and pitched my first day in a Yankee uniform," Ford recalled. "The Red Sox had a fearsome lineup: Ted Williams, Bobby Doerr, Vern Stephens, Walt Dropo, Dom DiMaggio, Johnny Pesky, Billy Goodman.

"We were losing something like 11–2, so Casey wasn't taking too much of a chance bringing me in to relieve Tommy Byrne. Stephens was on third base, Dropo on first, and Doerr was the batter.

"He singled for a run, and that was just the start. I gave them something like seven hits, six walks, and five runs—even a wild pitch—in four or five innings. There were a couple of shots off the left-field wall, and I think Stephens may have put one over it. It looked like batting practice, and we lost 17–4 or so.

"So I wasn't so hot that day, and part of the reason was that I was tipping my pitches. Their first-base coach [ex-Yankee great Earle Combs] kept hollering to each batter, and [first baseman] Tommy Henrich came over and said, 'Hey, Eddie, that guy is calling every pitch you throw.'

"The next day [coach] Jim Turner put me under the microscope out in the bullpen to find out how I was tipping off my pitches. He discovered I was twisting my elbow whenever I threw a curve.

"Well, I can't say my debut wasn't memorable. What a baptism!"

PITCHING LEADERS YEAR BY YEAR

Year	Pitcher (W–L #1)	Pitcher (W–L #2)	Pitcher (W–L #3)	Saves
1903	Jack Chesbro, 21–15	Jesse Tannehill, 15–15	Clark Griffith, 14–10	Doc Adkins, 1
				Snake Wiltse, 1
1904	Jack Chesbro, 41–12*	Jack Powell, 23–19	Al Orth, 11–3	Clark Griffith, 1
1905	Jack Chesbro, 20–15	Al Orth, 18–18	Bill Hogg, 9–12	Clark Griffith, 3
1906	Al Orth, 27–17	Jack Chesbro, 24–16	Bill Hogg, 14–13	Clark Griffith, 2
1907	Al Orth, 14–21	Bill Hogg, 11–8	Joe Doyle, 11–11	Bob Keefe, 2
1908	Jack Chesbro, 14–20	Rube Manning, 13–16	Joe Lake, 9–22	Jack Chesbro, 3
1909	Joe Lake, 14–11	Jack Warhop, 13–15	Lew Brockett, 10–8	Jack Warhop, 4
1910	Russ Ford, 26–6	Jack Quinn, 18–12	Jack Warhop, 14–14	Ray Caldwell, 2
				Hippo Vaughn, 2
				Jack Warhop, 2
1911	Russ Ford, 22–11	Ray Caldwell, 14–14	Jack Warhop, 12–13	Ray Caldwell, 3
				Jack Quinn, 3
1912	Russ Ford, 13–21	Jack Warhop, 10–19	George McConnell, 8–12	Jack Warhop, 3
1913	Ray Fisher, 11–17	Russ Ford, 11–18	Ray Caldwell, 9–8	Russ Ford, 3
1914	Ray Caldwell, 17–9	King Cole, 11–9	Ray Fisher, 10–12	Ray Caldwell, 2
				Marty McHale, 2
1915	Ray Caldwell, 19–16	Ray Fisher, 18–11	Jack Warhop, 7–9	King Cole, 1
				Cy Pieh, 1
1916	Bob Shawkey, 24–14	Nick Cullop, 13–6	Ray Fisher, 10–8	Bob Shawkey, 9*
1917	Bob Shawkey, 13–15	Ray Caldwell, 13–16	George Mogridge, 9–11	Allen Russell, 2
1918	George Mogridge, 16–13	Slim Love, 13–12	Ray Caldwell, 9–8	George Mogridge, 5
1919	Bob Shawkey, 20–11	Jack Quinn, 15–15	Hank Thormahlen, 13–9	Bob Shawkey, 4
1920	Carl Mays, 26–11	Bob Shawkey, 20–13	Jack Quinn, 18–10	Jack Quinn, 3
1921	Carl Mays, 27–9†	Waite Hoyt, 19–13	Bob Shawkey, 18–12	Carl Mays, 7†
1922	Joe Bush, 26–7	Bob Shawkey, 20–12	Waite Hoyt, 19–12	Sam Jones, 8*
1923	Sam Jones, 21–8	Herb Pennock, 19–6	Joe Bush, 19–15	Sam Jones, 4
1924	Herb Pennock, 21–9	Waite Hoyt, 18–13	Joe Bush, 17–16	Waite Hoyt, 4
1925	Herb Pennock, 16–17	Sam Jones, 15–21	Urban Shocker, 12–12	Waite Hoyt, 6
1926	Herb Pennock, 23–11	Urban Shocker, 19–11	Waite Hoyt, 16–12	Sam Jones, 5
1927	Waite Hoyt, 22–7†	Wilcy Moore, 19–7	Herb Pennock, 19–8	Wilcy Moore, 13†
1928	George Pipgras, 24–13†	Waite Hoyt, 23–7	Herb Pennock, 17–6	Waite Hoyt, 8*
1929	George Pipgras, 18–12	Ed Wells, 13–9	Tom Zachary, 12–0	Wilcy Moore, 8
1930	Red Ruffing, 15–5	George Pipgras, 15–15	Hank Johnson, 14–11	George Pipgras, 4
				Roy Sherid, 4
1931	Lefty Gomez, 21–9	Red Ruffing, 16–14	Hank Johnson, 13–8	Hank Johnson, 4
1932	Lefty Gomez, 24–7	Red Ruffing, 18–7	Johnny Allen, 17–4	Johnny Allen, 4
				Wilcy Moore, 4
1933	Lefty Gomez, 16–10	Johnny Allen, 15–7	Russ Van Atta, 12–4	Wilcy Moore, 8
1934	Lefty Gomez, 26–5*	Red Ruffing, 19–11	Johnny Murphy, 14–10	Johnny Murphy, 4
1935	Red Ruffing, 16–11	Johnny Broaca, 15–7	Johnny Allen, 13–6	Johnny Murphy, 5
1936	Red Ruffing, 20–12	Monte Pearson, 19–7	Bump Hadley, 14–4	Pat Malone, 9*
1937	Lefty Gomez, 21–11*	Red Ruffing, 20–7	Johnny Murphy, 13–4	Johnny Murphy, 10
1938	Red Ruffing, 21–7*	Lefty Gomez, 18–12	Monte Pearson, 16–7	Johnny Murphy, 11*
1939	Red Ruffing, 21–7	Atley Donald, 13–3	Monte Pearson, 12–5	Johnny Murphy, 19*
1940	Red Ruffing, 15–12	Marius Russo, 14–8	Ernie Bonham, 9–3	Johnny Murphy, 9
1941	Lefty Gomez, 15–5	Red Ruffing, 15–6	Marius Russo, 14–10	Johnny Murphy, 15*
1942	Ernie Bonham, 21–5	Spud Chandler, 16–5	Hank Borowy, 15–4	Johnny Murphy, 11*
1943	Spud Chandler, 20–4†	Ernie Bonham, 15–8	Hank Borowy, 14–9	Johnny Murphy, 8
1944	Hank Borowy, 17–12	Atley Donald, 13–10	Monk Dubiel, 13–13	Jim Turner, 7
1945	Bill Bevens, 13–9	Hank Borowy, 10–5	Monk Dubiel, 10–9	Jim Turner, 10*
1946	Spud Chandler, 20–8	Bill Bevens, 16–13	Randy Gumpert, 11–3	Johnny Murphy, 7

Earned Run Average	Innings	Strikeouts
Clark Griffith, 2.70	Jack Chesbro, 325	Jack Chesbro, 147
Jack Chesbro, 1.82	Jack Chesbro, 455*	Jack Chesbro, 239
Jack Chesbro, 2.20	Al Orth, 305	Jack Chesbro, 156
Walter Clarkson, 2.32	Al Orth, 339*	Jack Chesbro, 152
Jack Chesbro, 2.53	Al Orth, 249	Joe Doyle, 94
Jack Chesbro, 2.93	Jack Chesbro, 289	Jack Chesbro, 124
Joe Lake, 1.88	Jack Warhop, 243	Joe Lake, 117
Russ Ford, 1.65	Russ Ford, 300	Russ Ford, 209
Russ Ford, 2.28	Russ Ford, 281	Russ Ford, 158
George McConnell, 2.75	Russ Ford, 292	Russ Ford, 112
Ray Caldwell, 2.43	Ray Fisher, 246	Ray Fisher, 92
Ray Caldwell, 1.94	Jack Warhop, 217	Ray Keating, 109
Ray Fisher, 2.11	Ray Caldwell, 305	Ray Caldwell, 130
Nick Cullop, 2.05	Bob Shawkey, 277	Bob Shawkey, 122
Ray Fisher, 2.19	Bob Shawkey, 236	Ray Caldwell, 102
George Mogridge, 2.27	George Mogridge, 230	Slim Love, 95
George Mogridge, 2.50	Jack Quinn, 264	Bob Shawkey, 122
Bob Shawkey, 2.45*	Carl Mays, 312	Bob Shawkey, 126
Carl Mays, 3.04	Carl Mays, 337*	Bob Shawkey, 126
Bob Shawkey, 2.91	Bob Shawkey, 300	Bob Shawkey, 130
Waite Hoyt, 3.01	Joe Bush, 276	Joe Bush, 125
		Bob Shawkey, 125
Herb Pennock, 2.83	Herb Pennock, 286	Bob Shawkey, 114
Herb Pennock, 2.96	Herb Pennock, 277*	Sam Jones, 92
Urban Shocker, 3.38	Herb Pennock, 266	Waite Hoyt, 79
Wilcy Moore, 2.28*	Waite Hoyt, 256	Waite Hoyt, 86
Herb Pennock, 2.56	George Pipgras, 301	George Pipgras, 139
Tom Zachary, 2.47	George Pipgras, 225	George Pipgras, 125
George Pipgras, 4.11	George Pipgras, 221	Red Ruffing, 117
Lefty Gomez, 2.63	Lefty Gomez, 243	Lefty Gomez, 150
Red Ruffing, 3.09	Lefty Gomez, 265	Red Ruffing, 190*
Lefty Gomez, 3.18	Lefty Gomez, 235	Lefty Gomez, 163*
	Red Ruffing, 235	
Lefty Gomez, 2.33*	Lefty Gomez, 282*	Lefty Gomez, 158*
Red Ruffing, 3.12	Lefty Gomez, 246	Lefty Gomez, 138
Monte Pearson, 3.71	Red Ruffing, 271	Monte Pearson, 118
Lefty Gomez, 2.33*	Lefty Gomez, 278	Lefty Gomez, 194*
Red Ruffing, 3.32	Red Ruffing, 247	Lefty Gomez, 129
Red Ruffing, 2.94	Red Ruffing, 233	Lefty Gomez, 102
Marius Russo, 3.29	Red Ruffing, 226	Red Ruffing, 97
Marius Russo, 3.09	Marius Russo, 210	Marius Russo, 105
Ernie Bonham, 2.27	Spud Chandler, 201	Hank Borowy, 85
Spud Chandler, 1.64*	Spud Chandler, 253	Spud Chandler, 134
Hank Borowy, 2.63	Hank Borowy, 253	Hank Borowy, 107
Ernie Bonham, 3.28	Bill Bevens, 184	Bill Bevens, 76
Spud Chandler, 2.10	Spud Chandler, 257	Spud Chandler, 138

Catcher Joe Girardi has a word with ace reliever John Wetteland as the Braves rally in the ninth inning of game six of the '96 World Series, pulling within one run before the Series MVP slammed the door for a clinching 3–2 victory—"so amped up I didn't know where the ball was going."

PITCHING LEADERS YEAR BY YEAR

Year	Pitcher (W–L #1)	Pitcher (W–L #2)	Pitcher (W–L #3)	Saves
1947	Allie Reynolds, 19–8	Spec Shea, 14–5	Joe Page, 14–8	Joe Page, 17†
1948	Vic Raschi, 19–8	Ed Lopat, 17–11	Allie Reynolds, 16–7	Joe Page, 16
1949	Vic Raschi, 21–10	Allie Reynolds, 17–6	Tommy Byrne, 15–7	Joe Page, 27*
1950	Vic Raschi, 21–8	Ed Lopat, 18–8	Allie Reynolds, 16–12	Joe Page, 13
1951	Ed Lopat, 21–9	Vic Raschi, 21–10	Allie Reynolds, 17–8	Allie Reynolds, 7
1952	Allie Reynolds, 20–8	Vic Raschi, 16–6	Johnny Sain, 11–6	Johnny Sain, 7
1953	Whitey Ford, 18–6	Ed Lopat, 16–4	Johnny Sain, 14–7	Allie Reynolds, 13
1954	Bob Grim, 20–6	Whitey Ford, 16–8	Allie Reynolds, 13–4	Johnny Sain, 22*
1955	Whitey Ford, 18–7	Bob Turley, 17–13	Tommy Byrne, 16–5	Jim Konstanty, 11
1956	Whitey Ford, 19–6	Johnny Kucks, 18–9	Tom Sturdivant, 16–8	Tom Morgan, 11
1957	Tom Sturdivant, 16–6	Bob Turley, 13–6	Bob Grim, 12–8	Bob Grim, 19*
1958	Bob Turley, 21–7*	Whitey Ford, 14–7	Don Larsen, 9–6	Ryne Duren, 20*
1959	Whitey Ford, 16–10	Duke Maas, 14–8	Art Ditmar, 13–9	Ryne Duren, 14
1960	Art Ditmar, 15–9	Jim Coates, 13–3	Whitey Ford, 12–9	Bobby Shantz, 11
1961	Whitey Ford, 25–4*	Ralph Terry, 16–3	Luis Arroyo, 15–5	Luis Arroyo, 29*
1962	Ralph Terry, 23–12*	Whitey Ford, 17–8	Bill Stafford, 14–9	Marshall Bridges, 18
1963	Whitey Ford, 24–7	Jim Bouton, 21–7	Ralph Terry, 17–15	Hal Reniff, 18
1964	Jim Bouton, 18–13	Whitey Ford, 17–6	Al Downing, 13–8	Pete Mikkelsen, 12
1965	Mel Stottlemyre, 20–9	Whitey Ford, 16–13	Al Downing, 12–14	Pedro Ramos, 19
1966	Fritz Peterson, 12–11	Mel Stottlemyre, 12–20	Al Downing, 10–11	Pedro Ramos, 13
1967	Mel Stottlemyre, 15–15	Al Downing, 14–10	Fritz Peterson, 8–14	Dooley Womack, 18
1968	Mel Stottlemyre, 21–12	Stan Bahnsen, 17–12	Fritz Peterson, 12–11	Steve Hamilton, 11
1969	Mel Stottlemyre, 20–14	Fritz Peterson, 17–16	Stan Bahnsen, 9–16	Jack Aker, 11
1970	Fritz Peterson, 20–11	Mel Stottlemyre, 15–13	Stan Bahnsen, 14–11	Lindy McDaniel, 29
1971	Mel Stottlemyre, 16–12	Fritz Peterson, 15–13	Stan Bahnsen, 14–12	Jack Aker, 4
				Lindy McDaniel, 4
1972	Fritz Peterson, 17–15	Steve Kline, 16–9	Mel Stottlemyre, 14–18	Sparky Lyle, 35*
1973	Mel Stottlemyre, 16–16	Doc Medich, 14–9	Lindy McDaniel, 12–6	Sparky Lyle, 27
1974	Pat Dobson, 19–15	Doc Medich, 19–15	Dick Tidrow, 11–9	Sparky Lyle, 15
1975	Catfish Hunter, 23–14	Doc Medich, 16–16	Rudy May, 14–12	Tippy Martinez, 8
1976	Ed Figueroa, 19–10	Dock Ellis, 17–8	Catfish Hunter, 17–15	Sparky Lyle, 23
1977	Ron Guidry, 16–7	Ed Figueroa, 16–11	Don Gullett, 14–4	Sparky Lyle, 26
1978	Ron Guidry, 25–3*	Ed Figueroa, 20–9	Catfish Hunter, 12–6	Rich Gossage, 27*
1979	Tommy John, 21–9	Ron Guidry, 18–8	Ron Davis, 14–2	Rich Gossage, 18
1980	Tommy John, 22–9	Ron Guidry, 17–10	Rudy May, 15–5	Rich Gossage, 33*
1981	Ron Guidry, 11–5	Tommy John, 9–8	Dave Righetti, 8–4	Rich Gossage, 20
1982	Ron Guidry, 14–8	Shane Rawley, 11–10	Dave Righetti, 11–10	Rich Gossage, 30
1983	Ron Guidry, 21–9	Dave Righetti, 14–8	Shane Rawley, 14–14	Rich Gossage, 22
1984	Phil Niekro, 16–8	Ron Guidry, 10–11	Joe Cowley, 9–2	Dave Righetti, 31
1985	Ron Guidry, 22–6*	Phil Niekro, 16–12	Joe Cowley, 12–6	Dave Righetti, 29
1986	Dennis Rasmussen, 18–6	Brian Fisher, 9–5	Bob Tewksbury, 9–5	Dave Righetti, 46*
1987	Rick Rhoden, 16–10	Tommy John, 13–6	Charles Hudson, 11–7	Dave Righetti, 31
1988	John Candelaria, 13–7	Richard Dotson, 12–9	Rick Rhoden, 12–12	Dave Righetti, 25
1989	Andy Hawkins, 15–15	Eric Plunk, 7–5	Walt Terrell, 6–5	Dave Righetti, 25
1990	Lee Guetterman, 11–7	Tim Leary, 9–19	Dave LaPoint, 7–10	Dave Righetti, 36
1991	Scott Sanderson, 16–10	Greg Cadaret, 8–6	Wade Taylor, 7–12	Steve Farr, 23
1992	Melido Perez, 13–16	Scott Sanderson, 12–11	Rich Monteleone, 7–3	Steve Farr, 30
1993	Jimmy Key, 18–6	Bob Wickman, 14–4	Jim Abbott, 11–14	Steve Farr, 25
1994	Jimmy Key, 17–4*	Melido Perez, 9–4	Jim Abbott, 9–8	Steve Howe, 15
1995‡	Jack McDowell, 15–10	Andy Pettitte, 12–9	Sterling Hitchcock, 11–10	John Wetteland, 31
1996	Andy Pettitte, 21–8	Kenny Rogers, 12–8	Jimmy Key, 12–11	John Wetteland, 4–3

*Led league.

†Tied for league lead.

‡David Cone was 18–8 in 1995—9–6 for Toronto before being traded to New York on July 28 and going 9–2 for the Yankees.

Earned Run Average	Innings	Strikeouts
Spud Chandler, 2.46*	Allie Reynolds, 242	Allie Reynolds, 129
Spec Shea, 3.41	Allie Reynolds, 236	Vic Raschi, 124
Ed Lopat, 3.27	Vic Raschi, 275	Tommy Byrne, 129
Ed Lopat, 3.47	Vic Raschi, 257	Allie Reynolds, 160
Ed Lopat, 2.91	Vic Raschi, 258	Vic Raschi, 164*
Allie Reynolds, 2.07*	Allie Reynolds, 244	Allie Reynolds, 160*
Ed Lopat, 2.43	Whitey Ford, 207	Whitey Ford, 110
Whitey Ford, 2.82	Whitey Ford, 211	Whitey Ford, 125
Whitey Ford, 2.62	Whitey Ford, 254	Bob Turley, 210
Whitey Ford, 2.47*	Whitey Ford, 226	Whitey Ford, 141
Bobby Shantz, 2.45	Tom Sturdivant, 202	Bob Turley, 152
Whitey Ford, 2.01*	Bob Turley, 245	Bob Turley, 168
Art Ditmar, 2.90	Whitey Ford, 204	Whitey Ford, 114
Art Ditmar, 3.06	Art Ditmar, 200	Ralph Terry, 92
Bill Stafford, 2.68	Whitey Ford, 283*	Whitey Ford, 209
Whitey Ford, 2.90	Ralph Terry, 299*	Ralph Terry, 176
Jim Bouton, 2.53	Whitey Ford, 269	Whitey Ford, 189
Whitey Ford, 2.13	Jim Bouton, 271	Al Downing, 217*
Mel Stottlemyre, 2.63	Mel Stottlemyre, 291	Al Downing, 179
Fritz Peterson, 3.31	Mel Stottlemyre, 251	Al Downing, 152
Al Downing, 2.63	Mel Stottlemyre, 255	Al Downing, 171
Stan Bahnsen, 2.06	Mel Stottlemyre, 279	Stan Bahnsen, 162
Fritz Peterson, 2.55	Mel Stottlemyre, 303	Fritz Peterson, 150
Fritz Peterson, 2.91	Mel Stottlemyre, 271	Fritz Peterson, 127
Mel Stottlemyre, 2.87	Fritz Peterson, 274	Fritz Peterson, 139
Steve Kline, 2.40	Mel Stottlemyre, 260	Mel Stottlemyre, 110
Doc Medich, 2.95	Mel Stottlemyre, 273	Doc Medich, 145
Pat Dobson, 3.07	Pat Dobson, 281	Pat Dobson, 157
Catfish Hunter, 2.58	Catfish Hunter, 328*	Catfish Hunter, 177
Ed Figueroa, 3.02	Catfish Hunter, 299	Catfish Hunter, 173
Ron Guidry, 2.82	Ed Figueroa, 239	Ron Guidry, 176
Ron Guidry, 1.74*	Ron Guidry, 274	Ron Guidry, 248
Ron Guidry, 1.78*	Tommy John, 276	Ron Guidry, 201
Rudy May, 2.47*	Tommy John, 265	Ron Guidry, 166
Tommy John, 2.64	Rudy May, 148	Ron Guidry, 104
Tommy John, 3.66	Ron Guidry, 222	Dave Righetti, 163
Ron Guidry, 3.42	Ron Guidry, 250	Dave Righetti, 169
Phil Niekro, 3.09	Phil Niekro, 216	Phil Niekro, 136
Ron Guidry, 3.27	Ron Guidry, 259	Phil Niekro, 149
Dennis Rasmussen, 3.88	Dennis Rasmussen, 202	Ron Guidry, 140
Rick Rhoden, 3.86	Tommy John, 188	Rick Rhoden, 107
John Candelaria, 3.38	Rick Rhoden, 197	John Candelaria, 121
Lee Guetterman, 2.45	Andy Hawkins, 208	Andy Hawkins, 98
Lee Guetterman, 3.39	Tim Leary, 208	Tim Leary, 138
Greg Cadaret, 3.62	Scott Sanderson, 208	Scott Sanderson, 130
Melido Perez, 2.87	Melido Perez, 248	Melido Perez, 218
Jimmy Key, 3.00	Jimmy Key, 237	Jimmy Key, 173
Jimmy Key, 3.27	Jimmy Key, 168	Melido Perez, 109
Jack McDowell, 3.93	Jack McDowell, 218	Jack McDowell, 157
Mariano Rivera, 2.09	Andy Pettitte, 221	Andy Pettitte, 162

The Yankees once had a mascot—briefly. "Dandy"—as in Yankee Doodle—was soon put on waivers and evicted from the Stadium.

ALL-TIME PITCHING LEADERS

Games

1. Righetti	522
2. W. Ford	498
3. Ruffing	426
4. Lyle	420
5. Shawkey	415
6. Murphy	383
7. Guidry	368
8. Gomez	367
9. Hoyt	365
10. Stottlemyre	360
11. Pennock	346
12. Hamilton	311
13. Gossage	319
14. Reynolds	295
15. Peterson	288
16. Page	278
17. Chesbro	269
18. Caldwell	248
19. Pipgras	247
20. Reniff	247

Innings

W. Ford	3,171
Ruffing	3,169
Stottlemyre	2,662
Gomez	2,498
Shawkey	2,489
Guidry	2,392
Hoyt	2,273
Pennock	2,190
Chesbro	1,953
Peterson	1,856
Caldwell	1,718
Reynolds	1,700
Raschi	1,537
Lopat	1,497
Chandler	1,485
Warhop	1,423
Fisher	1,380
John	1,366
Pipgras	1,352
Quinn	1,279

Complete Games

1. Ruffing	261
2. Gomez	173
3. Chesbro	169
4. Pennock	165
5. Shawkey	161
6. W. Ford	156
7. Hoyt	156
8. Stottlemyre	152
9. Caldwell	151
10. Chandler	109
11. Warhop	105
12. R. Ford	103
13. Orth	102
14. Raschi	99
15. Reynolds	96
16. Guidry	95
17. Bonham	91
18. Lopat	91
19. Pipgras	84
20. Quinn	82

ERA (800 innings)

R. Ford	2.54
Chesbro	2.58
Orth	2.72
Bonham	2.73
W. Ford	2.74
Chandler	2.84
Fisher	2.91
Stottlemyre	2.97
Caldwell	2.99
Warhop	3.09
Peterson	3.10
Shawkey	3.10
Bahnsen	3.10
Righetti	3.11
Quinn	3.12
Lopat	3.25
Downing	3.25
Mays	3.25
Guidry	3.29
Reynolds	3.30

Victories

1. W. Ford	236
2. Ruffing	231
3. Gomez	189
4. Guidry	170
5. Shawkey	168
6. Stottlemyre	164
7. Pennock	162
8. Hoyt	157
9. Reynolds	131
10. Chesbro	128
11. Raschi	120
12. Lopat	113
13. Peterson	109
14. Chandler	109
15. Caldwell	96
16. Murphy	93
17. Pipgras	93
18. John	91
19. Turley	82
20. Mays, Bonham	79

Percentage (100 decisions)

Chandler	.717
Raschi	.706
W. Ford	.690
Reynolds	.686
Mays	.670
Lopat	.657
Gomez	.652
Guidry	.651
Ruffing	.651
Pennock	.643
Byrne	.643
Murphy	.637
Hoyt	.616
Bonham	.612
Turley	.612
John	.603
Pipgras	.595
Chesbro	.577
Terry	.569
Shawkey	.562

Saves

1. Righetti	224
2. Gossage	151
3. Lyle	141
4. Murphy	104
5. Farr	78
6. Page	76
7. Wetteland	73
8. McDaniel	58
9. Arroyo	43
Duren	43
11. Reniff	41
Reynolds	41
13. Sain	39
14. Hamilton	36
15. Aker	31
Howe	31
17. Grim	28
Hoyt	28
19. Morgan	26
Shawkey	26

Strikeouts

1. W. Ford	1,956
2. Guidry	1,778
3. Ruffing	1,526
4. Gomez	1,468
5. Stottlemyre	1,257
6. Shawkey	1,163
7. Downing	1,028
8. Reynolds	967
9. Righetti	940
10. Chesbro	913
11. Turley	909
12. Peterson	893
13. Raschi	832
14. Caldwell	803
15. Hoyt	713
16. Pennock	656
17. Pipgras	652
18. Terry	615
19. Chandler	614
20. Byrne	592

Shutouts

W. Ford	45
Ruffing	40
Stottlemyre	40
Gomez	28
Reynolds	27
Shawkey	26
Chandler	26
Guidry	26
Raschi	24
Turley	21
Lopat	20
Pennock	19
Peterson	18
Bonham	17
Chesbro	16
Terry	16
Hoyt	15
Pipgras	13
Caldwell	13
Downing, John	12

Mickey Mantle and Ty Cobb, 1960.

LEADING RELIEF PITCHERS (since 1943)

		W	S	Pts.
1943	Murphy	12	8	20
1944	Turner	4	7	11
1345	Turner	3	10	13
1946	Murphy	4	7	11
1947	Page	14	17*	31
1948	Page	7	16	23
1949	Page	13	27*	40*
1950	Ferrick	8	9	17
1951	Kuzava	5	5	10
1952	Sain	3	7	10
1953	Reynolds	7	13	20
1954	Sain	6	22*	28
1955	Konstanty	7	11	18
1956	Morgan	6	11	17
1957	Grim	12	19*	31*
1958	Duren	6	20*	26
1959	Duren	3	14	17
1960	Shantz	5	11	16
1961	Arroyo	15	29*	44*
1962	Bridges	8	18	26
1963	Reniff	4	18	22
1964	Mikkelson	7	12	19
	Ramos	5	19	24
1966	Ramos	3	13	16
1967	Womack	5	18	23
1968	McDaniel	4	10	14
1969	Aker	8	11	19
1970	McDaniel	9	29	38
1971	McDaniel	5	4	9
1972	Lyle	9	35*	44*
1973	Lyle	5	27	32
1974	Lyle	9	15	24
1975	Tidrow	6	5	11
	Lyle	5	6	11
1976	Lyle	7	23	30
1977	Lyle	13	26	39
1978	Gossage	10	27*	37*
1979	Davis	14	9	23
	Gossage	5	18	23
1980	Gossage	6	33*	39
1981	Gossage	3	20	23
1982	Gossage	4	30	34
1983	Gossage	13	22	35
1984	Righetti	5	31	36
1985	Righetti	12	29	41
1986	Righetti	8	46*	54
1987	Righetti	8	31	39
1988	Righetti	5	25	30
1989	Righetti	2	25	27
1990	Righetti	1	36	37
1991	Farr	5	23	28
1992	Farr	2	30	32
1993	Farr	2	25	27
1994	Howe	3	15	18
1995	Wetteland	1	31	32
1996	Wetteland	2	43	45

Led league.

20-GAME WINNERS (Final standing of team in parentheses after pitcher's name.)

Year	Pitcher	W	L	Year	Pitcher	W	L
1903	Jack Chesbro (4)	21	15	1939	Red Ruffing (1)	21	7
1904	Jack Chesbro (2)	41	12	1942	Ernie Bonham (1)	21	5
	Jack Powell (2)	23	19	1943	Spud Chandler (1)	20	4
1906	Al Orth (2)	27	17	1946	Spud Chandler (3)	20	8
	Jack Chesbro (2)	24	16	1949	Vic Raschi (1)	21	10
1910	Russ Ford (2)	26	6	1950	Vic Raschi (1)	21	8
1911	Russ Ford (6)	22	11	1951	Eddie Lopat (1)	21	9
1916	Bob Shawkey (4)	24	14		Vic Raschi (1)	21	10
1919	Bob Shawkey (3)	20	11	1952	Allie Reynolds (1)	20	8
1920	Carl Mays (3)	26	11	1954	Bob Grim (2)	20	6
	Bob Shawkey (3)	20	13	1958	Bob Turley (1)	21	7
1921	Carl Mays (1)	27	9	1961	Whitey Ford (1)	25	4
1922	Joe Bush (1)	26	7	1962	Ralph Terry (1)	23	12
	Bob Shawkey (1)	20	12	1963	Whitey Ford (1)	24	7
1923	Sam Jones (1)	21	8		Jim Bouton (1)	21	7
1924	Herb Pennock (2)	21	9	1965	Mel Stottlemyre (6)	20	9
1926	Herb Pennock (1)	23	11	1968	Mel Stottlemyre (5)	21	12
1927	Waite Hoyt (1)	22	7	1969	Mel Stottlemyre (5)	20	14
1928	George Pipgras (1)	24	13	1970	Fritz Peterson (2)	20	11
	Waite Hoyt (1)	23	7	1975	Catfish Hunter (3)	23	14
1931	Lefty Gomez (2)	21	9	1978	Ron Guidry (1)	25	3
1932	Lefty Gomez (1)	24	7		Ed Figueroa (1)	20	9
1934	Lefty Gomez (2)	26	5	1979	Tommy John (4)	21	9
1936	Red Ruffing (1)	20	12	1980	Tommy John (1)	22	9
1937	Lefty Gomez (1)	21	11	1983	Ron Guidry (3)	21	9
	Red Ruffing (1)	20	7	1985	Ron Guidry (2)	22	6
1938	Red Ruffing (1)	21	7	1996	Andy Pettitte (1)	21	8

Curt Gowdy got his big-time broadcasting break as number-two announcer behind Mel Allen at the Yankee microphone in 1949. He succeeded Russ Hodges, who had moved across the Harlem River to the Polo Grounds to be number one on Giant baseball broadcasts.

NO-HIT GAMES BY YANKEES

		Site	N.Y.	Foe
1910	Tom Hughes vs. Cleveland, Aug. 30 (nine hitless innings before allowing a hit in the 10th inning and seven more in the 11th to lose, 5–0)	H	0	5
1917	George Mogridge vs. Boston, April 24	A	2	1
1923	Sam Jones vs. Philadelphia, Sept. 4	A	2	0
1938	Monte Pearson vs. Cleveland, Aug. 27 (2nd game)	H	13	0
*1951	Allie Reynolds vs. Cleveland, July 12	A	1	0
	Allie Reynolds vs. Boston, Sept. 28 (1st game)	H	8	0
1956	Don Larsen vs. Brooklyn, Oct. 8† (Game 5 of World Series)	H	2	0
1983	Dave Righetti vs. Boston, July 4	H	4	0
1990	Andy Hawkins vs. Chicago, July 1 (eight hitless innings as Yankee errors in eighth paved way for four Chicago runs, so home-team White Sox did not bat in ninth inning)	A	0	4
1996	Dwight Gooden vs. Seattle, May 14	H	2	0
1993	Jim Abbott vs. Cleveland, Sept. 4	H	4	0

*Reynolds is among only four major leaguers to pitch two no-hitters in one season—along with Cincinnati's Johnny Vander Meer in 1938, Detroit's Virgil Trucks in 1952, and California's Nolan Ryan in 1973.
†Only perfect game in World Series history.

NO-HIT GAMES AGAINST YANKEES

		Site	N.Y.	Foe
1908	Cy Young of Boston, June 30	H	0	8
1916	George Foster of Boston, June 21	A	0	2
1919	Ray Caldwell of Cleveland, Sept. 10 (1st game)	H	0	3
1946	Bob Feller of Cleveland, April 30	H	0	1
1952	Virgil Trucks of Detroit, Aug. 25	H	0	1
1958	Hoyt Wilhelm of Baltimore, Sept. 20	A	0	1

BATTING LEADERS YEAR BY YEAR

Year	Batting Average	Hits	Doubles	Triples	Home Runs
1903	Keeler, .318	Keeler, 164	Williams, 30	Williams, Conroy, 12	McFarland, 5
1904	Keeler, .343	Keeler, 185	Williams, 31	Anderson, Conroy, 12	Ganzel, 6
1905	Keeler, .302	Keeler, 169	Williams, 20	Conroy, 11	Williams, 6
1906	Chase, .323	Chase, 193	Williams, 25	Chase, Conroy, 10	Conroy, 4
1907	Chase, .287	Chase, 143	Chase, 23	Conroy, LaPorte, Williams, 11	Hoffman, 4
1908	Hemphill, .297	Hemphill, 150	Conroy, 22	Hemphill, 9	Niles, 4
1909	LaPorte, .298	Engle, 137	Engle, 20	Demmitt, 12	Chase, Demmitt, 4
1910	Knight, .312	Chase, 152	Knight, 25	Cree, 16	Wolter, Cree, 4
1911	Cree, .348	Cree, 181	Chase, 32	Cree, 22	Wolter, Cree, 4
1912	Paddock, .288	Chase, 143	Daniels, 25	Hartzell, Daniels, 11	Zinn, 6
1913	Cree, .272	Cree, 145	Cree, 25	Peckinpaugh, 7	Wolter, Sweeney, 2
1914	Cree, .309	Cook, 133	Maisel, 23	Maisel, Hartzell, 9	Peckinpaugh, 3
1915	Maisel, .281	Maisel, 149	Pipp, 20	Pipp, 13	Peckinpaugh, 5
1916	Pipp, .262	Pipp, 143	Baker, 23	Pipp, 14	Pipp, 12*
1917	Baker, .282	Baker, 156	Pipp, 29	Pipp, 12	Pipp, 9*
1918	Baker, .306	Baker, 154	Baker, 24	Pipp, 9	Baker, 6
1919	Peckinpaugh, .305	Baker, 166	Pratt, Bodie, 27	Pipp, 10	Baker, 10
1920	Ruth, .376	Pratt, 180	Meusel, 40	Pipp, 14	Ruth, 54*
1921	Ruth, .378	Ruth, 204	Ruth, 44	Ruth, Meusel, 16	Ruth, 59*
1922	Pipp, .329	Pipp, 190	Pipp, 32	Meusel, 11	Ruth, 35
1923	Ruth, .393	Ruth, 205	Ruth, 45	Ruth, 13	Ruth, 41*
1924	Ruth, .378*	Ruth, 200	Meusel, 40	Pipp, 19*	Ruth, 46*
1925	Combs, .343	Combs, 203	Combs, 36	Combs, 13	Meusel, 33*
1926	Ruth, .372	Ruth, 184	Gehrig, 47	Gehrig, 20*	Ruth, 47*
1927	Gehrig, .373	Combs, 231*	Gehrig, 52*	Combs, 23*	Ruth, 60*
1928	Gehrig, .374	Gehrig, 210	Gehrig, 47*	Combs, 21*	Ruth, 54*
1929	Lazzeri, .354	Combs, 202	Lazzeri, 37	Combs, 15	Ruth, 46*
1930	Gehrig, .379	Gehrig, 220	Gehrig, 42	Combs, 22*	Ruth, 49*
1931	Ruth, .373	Gehrig, 211*	Lary, 35	Gehrig, 15	Ruth, Gehrig, 46*
1932	Gehrig, .349	Gehrig, 208	Gehrig, 42	Lazzeri, 16	Ruth, 41
1933	Gehrig, .334	Gehrig, 198	Gehrig, 41	Combs, 16	Ruth, 34
1934	Gehrig, .363*	Gehrig, 210	Gehrig, 40	Chapman, 13*	Gehrig, 49*
1935	Gehrig, .329	Rolfe, 192	Chapman, 38	Selkirk, 12	Gehrig, 30
1936	Dickey, .362	DiMaggio, 206	DiMaggio, 44	DiMaggio, Rolfe, 15*	Gehrig, 49*
1937	Gehrig, .351	DiMaggio, 215	Gehrig, 37	DiMaggio, 15	DiMaggio, 46*
1938	DiMaggio, .324	Rolfe, 196	Rolfe, 36*	DiMaggio, 13	DiMaggio, 32
1939	DiMaggio, .381*	Rolfe, 213*	Rolfe, 46*	Rolfe, 10	DiMaggio, 30
1940	DiMaggio, .352*	DiMaggio, 179	Gordon, 32	Keller, 15	DiMaggio, 31

PITCHERS WITH TOP WINNING PCT. AGAINST YANKEES

Pitcher	W	L	Pct.	Pitcher	W	L	Pct.
Kevin Brown	12	3	.800	Vida Blue	16	9	.640
Dickie Kerr	14	4	.778	Dick Hall	12	7	.632
Babe Ruth	17	5	.773	John Hiller	12	7	.632
Teddy Higuera	13	4	.765	Schoolboy Rowe	20	12	.625
Bob McClure	10	4	.714	Denny McLain	15	9	.625
Jimmy Key	12	5	.706	Mike Cuellar	18	11	.621
Bill Lee	12	5	.706	Mike Caldwell	13	8	.619
Bernie Boland	16	7	.696	Nolan Ryan	13	8	.619
Frank Lary	28	13	.683	Ellis Kinder	14	9	.609
Firpo Marberry	22	11	.667	Steve Barber	17	11	.607
Jim Palmer	30	15	.667	Dean Chance	15	10	.600
Dave Boswell	10	5	.667	*Luis Tiant	22	15	.595
Roger Clemens	15	8	.652	Jack Morris	17	12	.586
Larry Gura	11	6	.647	Sam McDowell	14	10	.583

*Tiant is the only pitcher to defeat the Yankees five times in a season since expansion in 1961. He was 5–1 for the Red Sox against his future teammates in 1974.

PITCHERS WITH 30 VICTORIES AGAINST YANKEES

Pitcher	Wins	Pitcher	Wins
*Walter Johnson	60	Stan Coveleski	32
Eddie Cicotte	35	Chief Bender	30
Lefty Grove	35	Hooks Dauss	30
Hal Newhouser	33	Bob Feller	30
Early Wynn	33	George Mullin	30
Red Faber	32	Jim Palmer	30

*Johnson and Mel Parnell share the distinction of shutting out the Yankees most times in a season—four. Johnson did it for Washington in 1908, Parnell for Boston in 1953.

RBIs	Runs	Stolen Bases
Williams, 82	Keeler, 98	Conroy, 33
Anderson, 82	Dougherty, 80†	Conroy, 30
Williams, 60	Keeler, 81	Fultz, 44
Williams, 77	Keeler, 96	Hoffman, 33
Chase, 68	Hoffman, 81	Conroy, 41
Hemphill, 44	Hemphill, 62	Hemphill, 42
Engle, 71	Demmitt, 68	Austin, 30
Chase, 73	Daniels, 68	Daniels, 41
Hartzell, 91	Cree, 90	Cree, 48
Chase, 58	Daniels, 72	Daniels, 37
Cree, 63	Hartzell, 60	Daniels, 27
Peckinpaugh, 51	Maisel, 78	Maisel 74*
Pipp, 58	Maisel, 77	Maisel 51
Pipp, 99*	Pipp, 70	Magee, 29
Pipp, 72	Pipp, 82	Maisel, 29
Baker, 68	Baker, Pratt, 65	Bodie, 16
Baker, 78	Peckinpaugh, 89	Pratt, 22
Ruth, 137*	Ruth, 158*	Ruth, 14
Ruth, 171*	Ruth, 177*	Meusel, Pipp, Ruth, 17
Ruth, 96	Witt, 98	Meusel, 13
Ruth, 131*	Ruth, 151*	Ruth, 17
Ruth, 121*	Ruth, 143*	Meusel, 26
Meusel, 138*	Combs, 117	Paschal, 14
Ruth, 145*	Ruth, 139*	Meusel 16
Gehrig, 175*	Ruth, 158*	Meusel, 24
Gehrig, Ruth, 142*	Ruth, 163*	Lazzeri, 15
Ruth, 154	Gehrig, 127	Combs, Lazzeri, 11
Gehrig, 174*	Ruth, 150	Combs, 16
Gehrig, 184*	Gehrig, 163*	Chapman, 61*
Gehrig, 151	Combs, 143	Chapman, 38*
Gehrig, 139	Gehrig, 138*	Chapman, 27*
Gehrig, 165*	Gehrig, 128	Chapman, 26
Gehrig, 119	Gehrig, 125	Chapman, 17
Gehrig, 152	Gehrig, 167*	Crosetti, 18
DiMaggio, 167	DiMaggio, 151*	Crosetti, 13
DiMaggio, 140	Rolfe, 132	Crosetti, 27*
DiMaggio, 126	Rolfe, 139*	Selkirk, 12
DiMaggio, 133	Gordon, 112	Gordon, 18

*Led league.

Mickey Mantle, sick and weak after missing the first two games of the 1961 World Series, insisted on playing when the Series moved to Cincinnati. The deep hip wound that had hospitalized him was heavily bandaged. Mantle played in obvious pain, and after banging out a key hit in game four, he was finished for the Series. With blood from the abscess oozing through his pants, Mick was replaced by a runner.

BATTING LEADERS YEAR BY YEAR

Year	Batting Average	Hits	Doubles	Triples	Home Runs
1941	DiMaggio, .357	DiMaggio, 193	DiMaggio, 43	DiMaggio, 11	Keller, 33
1942	Gordon, .322	DiMaggio, 186	Henrich, 30	DiMaggio, 13	Keller, 26
1943	Johnson, .280	Johnson, 166*	Etten, 35	Lindell, 12*	Keller, 31
1944	Stirnweiss, .319	Stirnweiss, 205*	Stirnweiss, 35	Lindell, Stirnweiss, 16*	Etten, 22*
1945	Stirnweiss, .309*	Stirnweiss, 195*	Stirnweiss, 32	Stirnweiss, 22*	Etten, 18
1946	DiMaggio, .290	Keller, 148	Keller, 29	Keller, 10	Keller, 30
1947	DiMaggio, .315	DiMaggio, 168	Henrich, 35	Henrich, 13*	DiMaggio, 20
1948	DiMaggio, .320	DiMaggio, 190	Henrich, 42	Henrich, 14*	DiMaggio, 39*
1949	Henrich, .287	Rizzuto, 169	Rizzuto, 22	Rizzuto, Woodling, 7	Henrich, 24
1950	Rizzuto, .324	Rizzuto, 200	Rizzuto, 36	Woodling, DiMaggio, 10	DiMaggio, 32
1951	McDougald, .306	Berra, 161	McDougald, 23	Woodling, 8	Berra, 27
1952	Mantle, .311	Mantle, 171	Mantle, 37	Rizzuto, 10	Berra, 30
1953	Bauer, .304	McDougald, 154	McDougald, 27	McDougald, 7	Berra, 27
1954	Noren, .319	Berra, 179	Berra, 28	Mantle, 12	Mantle, 27
1955	Mantle, .306	Mantle, 158	Mantle, 25	Mantle, Carey, 11*	Mantle, 37*
1956	Mantle, .353*	Mantle, 188	Berra, 29	Bauer, 7	Mantle, 52*
1957	Mantle, .365	Mantle, 173	Mantle, 28	Bauer, McDougald, 9*	Mantle, 34
1958	Mantle, .304	Mantle, 158	Bauer, Skowron, 22	Bauer, 6	Mantle, 42*
1959	Richardson, .301	Mantle, 154	Berra, Kubek, 25	McDougald, 8	Mantle, 31
1960	Skowron, .309	Skowron, 166	Skowron, 34	Maris, 7	Mantle, 40*
1961	Howard, .348	Richardson, 173	Kubek, 38	Mantle, Kubek, 6	Maris, 61*
1962	Mantle, .321	Richardson, 209*	Richardson, 38	Skowron, 6	Maris, 33
1963	Howard, 287	Richardson, 167	Tresh, 28	Howard, Richardson, 6	Howard, 28
1964	Howard, .318	Richardson, 181	Howard, 27	Tresh, Boyer, 5	Mantle, 35
1965	Tresh, .279	Tresh, 168	Tresh, 29	Tresh, Boyer, 6	Tresh, 26
1966	Mantle, .288	Richardson, 153	Boyer, 22	Boyer, Clarke, Tresh, Pepitone, 4	Pepitone, 31
1967	Clarke, .272	Clarke, 160	Tresh, 23	Pepitone, Smith, Tresh, Whitaker, 3	Mantle, 22
1968	White, .267	White, 154	White, 20	White, Robinson, 7	Mantle, 18
1969	White, .290	Clarke, 183	White, 30	Clarke, 7	Pepitone, 27
1970	Munson, .302	White, 180	White, 30	Kenney, 7	Murcer, 23
1971	Murcer, .331	Murcer, 175	Murcer, 25	Clarke, White, 7	Murcer, 25
1972	Murcer, .292	Murcer, 171	Murcer, 30	Murcer, 7	Murcer, 33
1973	Murcer, .304	Murcer, 187	Murcer, Munson, 29	Munson, 4	Murcer, Nettles, 22
1974	Piniella, .305	Murcer, 166	Maddox, Piniella, 26	White, 8	Nettles, 22
1975	Munson, .318	Munson, 190	Chambliss, 38	White, 5	Bonds, 32
1976	Rivers, .312	Chambliss, 188	Chambliss, 32	Rivers, 8	Nettles, 32*
1977	Rivers, .326	Rivers, 184	Jackson, 39	Randolph, 11	Nettles, 37
1978	Piniella, .314	Munson, 183	Piniella, 34	Rivers, 8	Jackson, Nettles, 27
1979	Piniella, Jackson, .297	Randolph, Chambliss, 155	Chambliss, 27	Randolph, 13	Jackson, 29
1980	Watson, .307	Jackson, 154	Cerone, 30	Randolph, 7	Jackson, 41*
1981	Mumphrey, .307	Winfield, 114	Winfield, 25	Mumphrey, 5	Jackson, Nettles, 15
1982	Mumphrey, .300	Randolph, 155	Mumphrey, Winfield, 24	Mumphrey, 10	Winfield, 37
1983	Baylor, .303	Winfield, 169	Baylor, 33	Winfield, 8	Winfield, 32
1984	Mattingly, .343*	Mattingly, 207*	Mattingly, 44*	Moreno, 6	Baylor, 27
1985	Mattingly, .324	Mattingly, 211	Mattingly, 48*	Winfield, 6	Mattingly, 35
1986	Mattingly, .352	Mattingly, 238*	Mattingly, 53*	Henderson, Winfield, 5	Mattingly, 31
1987	Mattingly, .327	Mattingly, 186	Mattingly, 38	Henderson, Pagliarulo, 3	Pagliarulo, 32
1988	Winfield, .322	Mattingly, 186	Winfield, 37	Washington, 3	Clark, 27
1989	Sax, .315	Sax, 205	Mattingly, 37	R. Kelly, Sax, Slaught, 3	Mattingly, 23
1990	R. Kelly, .285	R. Kelly, 183	R. Kelly, 32	R. Kelly, 4	Barfield, 25
1991	Sax, .304	Sax, 198	Sax, 38	P. Kelly, B. Williams, 4	Nokes, 24
1992	Mattingly, .288	Mattingly, 184	Mattingly, 40	Hall, 3	Tartabull, 25
1993	O'Neill, .311	Boggs, 169	O'Neill, 34	B. Williams, 4	Tartabull, 31
1994	O'Neill, .359*	O'Neill, 132	B. Williams, 29	Polonia, 6	O'Neill, 21
1995	Boggs, .324	B. Williams, 173	Mattingly, 32	B. Williams, 9	O'Neill, 22
1996	Duncan, .340	Jeter, 183	O'Neill, 35	B. Williams, 7	B. Williams, 29

†Dougherty's 80 runs led Yankees in 1904, and his overall 113 runs that year topped the majors as he divided the season between the Red Sox (49 games) and Yankees (106 games).

BATTING AVERAGE (500 or more games)

1. Ruth	.349	11. Piniella	.295
2. Gehrig	.340	12. Skowron	.294
3. Combs	.325	13. Keeler	.294
4. DiMaggio	.325	14. Lazzeri	.293
5. Dickey	.313	15. Cree	.292
6. Meusel	.311	16. Munson	.292
7. Mattingly	.307	17. Selkirk	.290
8. Chapman	.305	18. Winfield	.290
9. Mantle	.298	19. Rolfe	.289
10. Schang	.297	20. Keller	.286

RBIs	**Runs**	**Stolen Bases**
DiMaggio, 125*	DiMaggio, 122	Rizzuto, 14
DiMaggio, 114	DiMaggio, 123	Rizzuto, 22
Etten, 107	Keller, 97	Stirnweiss, 11
Lindell, 103	Stirnweiss, 125*	Stirnweiss, 55*
Etten, 111*	Stirnweiss, 107*	Stirnweiss, 33*
Keller, 101	Keller, 98	Stirnweiss, 18
Henrich, 98	Henrich, 109	Rizzuto, 11
DiMaggio, 155*	Henrich, 138*	Rizzuto, 6
Berra, 91	Rizzuto, 110	Rizzuto, 18
Berra, 124	Rizzuto, 125	Rizzuto, 12
Berra, 88	Berra, 92	Rizzuto, 18
Berra, 98	Berra, 97	Rizzuto, 17
Berra, 108	Mantle, 105	Mantle, 8
Berra, 125	Mantle, 129*	Mantle, Carey, 5
Berra, 108	Mantle, 121	Hunter, 9
Mantle, 130*	Mantle, 132*	Mantle, 10
Mantle, 94	Mantle, 121*	Mantle, 16
Mantle, 97	Mantle, 127*	Mantle, 18
Lopez, 93	Mantle, 104	Mantle, 21
Maris, 112*	Mantle, 119*	Mantle, 14
Maris, 142*	Mantle, Maris, 132*	Mantle, 12
Maris, 100	Richardson, 99	Richardson, 11
Pepitone, 89	Tresh, 91	Richardson, 15
Mantle, 111	Mantle, 92	Tresh, 13
Tresh, 74	Tresh, 94	Richardson, 7
Pepitone, 83	Pepitone, 85	White, 14
Pepitone, 64	Clarke, 74	Clarke, 21
White, 62	White, 89	Clarke, White, 20
Murcer, 82	Clarke, Murcer, 82	Clarke, 33
White, 94	White, 109	White, 24
Murcer, 94	Murcer, 94	Clarke, 17
Murcer, 96	Murcer, 102*	White, 23
Murcer, 95	White, 88	White, 16
Murcer, 88	Maddox, 75	White, 15
Munson, 102	Bonds, 93	Bonds, 30
Munson, 105	White, 104*	Rivers, 43
Jackson, 110	Nettles, 99	Rivers, 22
Jackson, 97	Randolph, 87	Randolph, 36
Jackson, 89	Randolph, 98	Randolph, 32
Jackson, 111	Randolph, 99	Randolph, 30
Winfield, 68	Randolph, 59	Randolph, 14
Winfield, 106	Randolph, 85	Randolph, 16
Winfield, 116	Winfield, 99	Baylor, 17
Mattingly, 110	Winfield, 106	Moreno, 20
Mattingly, 145*	Henderson, 146*	Henderson, 80*
Mattingly, 113	Henderson, 130*	Henderson, 87*
Mattingly, 115	Randolph, 96	Henderson, 41
Winfield, 107	Henderson, 118	Henderson, 93*
Mattingly, 113	Sax, 88	Sax, 43
Barfield, 78	R. Kelly, 85	Sax, 43
Hall, 80	Sax, 85	R. Kelly, 32
Mattingly, 86	Mattingly, 86	R. Kelly, 28
Tartabull, 102	Tartabull, 87	P. Kelly, 14
O'Neill, 83	B. Williams, 80	Polonia, 20
O'Neill, 96	B. Williams, 93	Polinia, 10
Martinez, 117	B. Williams, 108	B. Williams, 17

Ace Whitey Ford, in an unaccustomed role, dons the "tools of ignorance."

ALL-TIME BATTING LEADERS

Games		At Bats		Runs		RBIs	
1. Mantle	2,401	Mantle	8,102	Ruth	1,959	Gehrig	1,991
2. Gehrig	2,164	Gehrig	8,001	Gehrig	1,888	Ruth	1,970
3. Berra	2,116	Berra	7,546	Mantle	1,677	DiMaggio	1,537
4. Ruth	2,084	Ruth	7,217	DiMaggio	1,390	Mantle	1,509
5. White	1,881	Mattingly	7,003	Combs	1,186	Berra	1,430
6. Dickey	1,789	DiMaggio	6,821	Berra	1,174	Dickey	1,209
7. Mattingly	1,785	White	6,650	Randolph	1,027	Lazzeri	1,154
8. DiMaggio	1,736	Randolph	6,303	Mattingly	1,007	Mattingly	1,099
9. Randolph	1,694	Dickey	6,300	Crosetti	1,006	Meusel	1,005
10. Crosetti	1,682	Crosetti	6,277	White	964	Nettles	834
11. Rizzuto	1,661	Lazzeri	6,094	Lazzeri	952	Pipp	825
12. Lazzeri	1,659	Rizzuto	5,816	Rolfe	942	Winfield	818
13. Nettles	1,535	Combs	5,748	Dickey	930	Henrich	795
14. Howard	1,492	Pipp	5,594	Henrich	901	White	758
15. Pipp	1,488	Nettles	5,519	Rizzuto	877	Howard	732
16. Combs	1,455	Richardson	5,386	Pipp	820	Keller	723
17. Munson	1,423	Munson	5,344	Bauer	792	Munson	701
18. Richardson	1,412	Howard	5,044	Meusel	764	Murcer	687
19. Bauer	1,406	Meusel	5,032	Nettles	750	Skowron	672
20. McDougald	1,336	Rolfe	4,827	Winfield	722	Bauer	654

Hits		Doubles		Triples		Home Runs	
1. Gehrig	2,721	Gehrig	535	Gehrig	162	Ruth	659
2. Ruth	2,518	Mattingly	442	Combs	154	Mantle	536
3. Mantle	2,415	Ruth	424	DiMaggio	131	Gehrig	493
4. DiMaggio	2,214	DiMaggio	389	Pipp	121	DiMaggio	361
5. Mattingly	2,153	Mantle	344	Lazzeri	115	Berra	358
6. Berra	2,148	Dickey	343	Ruth	106	Nettles	250
7. Dickey	1,969	Meusel	338	Meusel	87	Mattingly	222
8. Combs	1,866	Lazzeri	327	Henrich	73	Winfield	205
9. White	1,803	Berra	321	Dickey	72	Maris	203
10. Lazzeri	1,784	Combs	309	Mantle	72	Dickey	202
11. Randolph	1,731	White	300	Keller	69	Keller	184
12. Rizzuto	1,588	Henrich	269	Rolfe	67	Henrich	183
13. Pipp	1,577	Crosetti	260	Stirnweiss	66	Murcer	175
14. Meusel	1,565	Pipp	259	Crosetti	65	Lazzeri	169
15. Munson	1,558	Randolph	259	Chapman	64	Pepitone	166
16. Crosetti	1,541	Rolfe	257	Rizzuto	62	Skowron	165
17. Richardson	1,432	Rizzuto	239	Cree	62	Howard	161
18. Howard	1,405	Winfield	236	Conroy	59	White	160
19. Nettles	1,396	Munson	229	Randolph	58	Bauer	158
20. Rolfe	1,394	Howard	211	Bauer	56	Gordon	153
Bauer	211						

SINGLE-SEASON LEADERS BY POSITION

	Home Runs			RBIs			Average		
1st Base	49	Gehrig	1934	184	Gehrig	1931	.379	Gehrig	1930
2nd Base	30	Gordon	1940	114	Lazzeri	1926	.354	Lazzeri	1929
3rd Base	37	Nettles	1977	107	Nettles	1977	.342	Boggs	1994
Shortstop	16	Smalley	1982	107	Lary	1931	.324	Rizzuto	1950
Outfield	61	Maris	1961	170	Ruth	1921	.393	Ruth	1923
Catcher	30	Berra	1952, 1956	133	Dickey	1937	.362	Dickey	1936
Pitcher	5	Ruffing	1936	22	Ruffing	1936, 1941	.339	Ruffing	1935

TOP TEN, SINGLE SEASON

At Bats			Batting Average			Hits			Doubles		
Richardson	692	1962	Ruth	.393	1923	Mattingly	238	1986	Mattingly	53	1986
Clarke	686	1970	DiMaggio	.381	1939	Combs	231	1927	Gehrig	52	1927
Richardson	679	1964	Gehrig	.379	1930	Gehrig	220	1930	Mattingly	48	1985
Mattingly	677	1986	Ruth	.378	1921	Gehrig	218	1927	Gehrig	47	1926
Richardson	664	1965	Ruth	.378	1924	DiMaggio	215	1937	Meusel	47	1927
Richardson	662	1961	Ruth	.376	1920	Rolfe	213	1939	Gehrig	47	1928
Crosetti	656	1939	Gehrig	.374	1928	Gehrig	211	1931	Rolfe	46	1939
Mattingly	652	1985	Gehrig	.373	1927	Mattingly	211	1985	Ruth	45	1923
Sax	652	1991	Ruth	.373	1931	Gehrig	210	1928	Meusel	45	1928
Sax	651	1989	Ruth	.372	1925	Gehrig	210	1934	Ruth	44	1921
									DiMaggio	44	1936
									Mattingly	44	1984

Triples

Combs	23	1927
Combs	22	1930
Stirnweiss	22	1945
Cree	22	1911
Combs	21	1928
Gehrig	20	1926
Pipp	19	1924
Gehrig	18	1927
Gehrig	17	1930
Four tied	16	

Home Runs

Maris	61	1961
Ruth	60	1927
Ruth	59	1921
Ruth	54	1920
Ruth	54	1928
Mantle	54	1961
Mantle	52	1956
Ruth	49	1930
Gehrig	49	1934
Gehrig	49	1936

Games Pitched

Righetti	74	1985
Righetti	74	1986
Nelson	73	1996
Lyle	72	1977
Guetterman	70	1989
Cadaret	68	1991
Lyle	66	1974
Habyan	66	1991
Arroyo	65	1961
Ramos	65	1965
Womack	65	1967

Complete Games

Chesbro	48	1904
Powell	38	1904
Orth	36	1906
Chesbro	33	1903
R. Ford	32	1912
Mays	30	1921
Hunter	30	1975
R. Ford	29	1910
Orth	26	1905
Mays	26	1920

Total Bases

Ruth	457	1921
Gehrig	447	1927
Gehrig	419	1931
DiMaggio	418	1937
Ruth	417	1927
Gehrig	410	1931
Gehrig	409	1934
Gehrig	403	1936
Ruth	399	1923
Ruth	391	1924

Runs

Ruth	177	1921
Gehrig	167	1936
Ruth	163	1928
Gehrig	163	1931
Ruth	158	1920
Ruth	158	1927
Ruth	151	1923
DiMaggio	151	1937
Ruth	150	1930
Gehrig	149	1927
Ruth	149	1931

Victories

Chesbro	41	1904
Orth	27	1906
Mays	27	1921
R. Ford	26	1910
Mays	26	1920
Bush	26	1922
Gomez	26	1934
Guidry	25	1978
W. Ford	25	1961
Chesbro	24	1906
Shawkey	24	1916
Pipgras	24	1928
W. Ford	24	1963

Saves

Righetti	46	1986
Wetteland	43	1996
Righetti	36	1990
Lyle	35	1972
Gossage	33	1980
Righetti	31	1984
Righetti	31	1987
Wetteland	31	1995
Gossage	30	1982
Farr	30	1992
Arroyo	29	1961
McDaniel	29	1970
Righetti	29	1985

RBIs

Gehrig	184	1931
Gehrig	175	1927
Gehrig	174	1930
Ruth	170	1921
DiMaggio	167	1937
Gehrig	165	1934
Ruth	164	1927
Ruth	163	1931
Gehrig	159	1937
Ruth	155	1926
DiMaggio	155	1948

Walks

Ruth	170	1923
Ruth	148	1920
Mantle	146	1957
Ruth	144	1921
Ruth	144	1926
Ruth	142	1924
Ruth	138	1927
Ruth	136	1930
Ruth	135	1928
Gehrig	132	1935

Shutouts

Guidry	9	1978
R. Ford	8	1910
W. Ford	8	1964
Reynolds	7	1951
W. Ford	7	1958
Stottlemyre	7	1971
Stottlemyre	7	1972
Hunter	7	1975
Thirteen tied	6	

Strikeouts (Pitcher)

Guidry	248	1978
Chesbro	239	1904
Perez	218	1992
Downing	217	1964
Turley	210	1955
R. Ford	209	1910
W. Ford	209	1961
Powell	202	1904
Guidry	201	1979
Ruffing	194	1937

Strikeouts (Batter)

Tartabull	156	1993
Barfield	150	1990
R. Kelly	148	1990
Clark	141	1988
Bonds	137	1975
Jackson	133	1978
Jackson	129	1977
Maas	128	1991
Mantle	126	1959
Mantle	125	1960

Stolen Bases

Henderson	93	1988
Henderson	87	1986
Henderson	80	1985
Maisel	74	1914
Chapman	61	1931
Stirnweiss	55	1944
Maisel	51	1915
Cree	48	1911
Fultz	44	1905
Rivers	43	1976
Sax	43	1989
Sax	43	1990

Earned Run Average

Chandler	1.64	1943
R. Ford	1.65	1910
Guidry	1.74	1978
Chesbro	1.82	1904
Vaughn	1.83	1910
Lake	1.88	1909
Caldwell	1.94	1914
W. Ford	2.01	1958
Cullop	2.05	1916
Bahnsen	2.06	1968

Hitting Streaks

DiMaggio	56	1941
Chase	33	1907
Peckinpaugh	29	1919
Combs	29	1931
Gordon	29	1942
Ruth	26	1921
Mattingly	24	1986
DiMaggio	23	1940
DiMaggio	22	1937
Pipp	21	1923
B. Williams	21	1993

ALL-TIME STOLEN-BASE LEADERS

Henderson	326		Rizzuto	149
Randolph	251		Lazzeri	147
Chase	248		Daniels	145
White	233		Peckinpaugh	143
Conroy	184		Cree	132
Chapman	184		Meusel	131
Maisel	183		Stirnweiss	130
Mantle	153		Keeler	118
Clarke	151		Sax	117
R. Kelly	151		Pipp	114

HOME RUNS

60 Home Runs in a Season
61   Roger Maris, 1961*
60   Babe Ruth, 1927*

50 Home Runs in a Season
59   Babe Ruth, 1921*
54   Babe Ruth, 1920*
      Babe Ruth, 1928*
      Mickey Mantle, 1961
52   Mickey Mantle, 1956*

40 Home Runs in a Season
49   Babe Ruth, 1930†
      Lou Gehrig, 1934*
      Lou Gehrig, 1936*
47   Babe Ruth, 1926*
      Lou Gehrig, 1927
46   Babe Ruth, 1924*
      Babe Ruth, 1929*
      Babe Ruth, 1931**
      Lou Gehrig, 1931 **
      Joe DiMaggio, 1937*
42   Mickey Mantle, 1958†
41   Babe Ruth, 1923*
      Lou Gehrig, 1930
      Babe Ruth, 1932
      Reggie Jackson 1980‡
40   Mickey Mantle, 1960†

30 Home Runs in a Season
39   Joe DiMaggio, 1948†
      Roger Maris, 1960
37   Lou Gehrig, 1937
      Mickey Mantle, 1955†
      Graig Nettles, 1977
      Dave Winfield, 1982
35   Babe Ruth, 1922
      Lou Gehrig, 1929
      Mickey Mantle, 1964
      Don Mattingly, 1985
34   Lou Gehrig, 1932
      Babe Ruth, 1933
      Mickey Mantle, 1957
33   Bob Meusel, 1925†
      Charlie Keller, 1941
      Roger Maris, 1962
      Bobby Murcer, 1972
32   Lou Gehrig, 1933
      Joe DiMaggio, 1938
      Joe DiMaggio, 1950
      Graig Nettles, 1976†
      Reggie Jackson, 1977
      Dave Winfield, 1983
      Mike Pagliarulo, 1987
31   Joe DiMaggio, 1940
      Tommy Henrich, 1941
      Charlie Keller, 1943
      Mickey Mantle, 1959
      Joe Pepitone, 1966
      Don Mattingly, 1986
      Danny Tartabull, 1993
30   Lou Gehrig, 1935
      Joe DiMaggio, 1939
      Joe Gordon, 1940
      Joe DiMaggio, 1941
      Charlie Keller, 1946
      Mickey Mantle, 1962
      Don Mattingly, 1987

20 Home Runs in a Season
29   Bill Dickey, 1937
      Lou Gehrig, 1938
      Reggie Jackson, 1979
      Bernie Williams, 1996

28   Joe Gordon, 1939
      Yogi Berra, 1950
      Bill Skowron, 1961
      Elston Howard, 1963
      Joe Pepitone, 1964
      Rickey Henderson, 1986
      Mike Pagliarulo, 1986
27   Lou Gehrig, 1928
      Bill Dickey, 1938
      Yogi Berra, 1951
      Yogi Berra, 1953
      Mickey Mantle, 1954
      Yogi Berra, 1955
      Reggie Jackson, 1978
      Graig Nettles, 1978
      Don Baylor, 1984
      Jack Clark, 1988
      Dave Winfield, 1987
26   Charlie Keller, 1942
      Hank Bauer, 1956
      Bill Skowron, 1960
      Roger Maris, 1964
      Tom Tresh, 1965
      Bobby Murcer, 1969
      Dave Winfield, 1985
25   Babe Ruth, 1925
      Joe Gordon, 1938
      Joe DiMaggio, 1946
      Tommy Henrich, 1948
      Johnny Mize, 1950
      Tom Tresh, 1963
      Bobby Murcer, 1971
      Dave Winfield, 1988
      Jesse Barfield, 1990
      Danny Tartabull, 1992
      Tino Martinez, 1996
24   Bob Meusel, 1921
      Bill Dickey, 1939
      Joe Gordon, 1941
      Tommy Henrich, 1949
      Yogi Berra, 1957
      Rickey Henderson, 1985
      Dave Winfield, 1986
      Matt Nokes, 1991
23   Mickey Mantle, 1952
      Bill Skowron, 1956
      Bill Skowron, 1962
      Roger Maris, 1963
      Mickey Mantle, 1966
      Bobby Murcer, 1970
      Jim Spencer, 1979
      Don Mattingly, 1984
      Don Baylor, 1985
      Don Mattingly, 1989
22   Babe Ruth, 1934
      Tommy Henrich, 1938
      Nick Etten, 1944†
      Yogi Berra, 1954
      Yogi Berra, 1958
      Yogi Berra, 1961
      Mickey Mantle, 1967
      Roy White, 1970
      Graig Nettles, 1973
      Bobby Murcer, 1973
      Graig Nettles, 1974
      Paul O'Neill, 1995
21   George Selkirk, 1939
      Charlie Keller, 1940
      Joe DiMaggio, 1942
      Mickey Mantle, 1953
      Elston Howard, 1961
      Johnny Blanchard, 1961
      Don Baylor, 1983
      Paul O'Neill, 1994
20   Graig Nettles, 1975
      Lou Gehrig, 1925
      Joe DiMaggio, 1947
      Yogi Berra, 1949
      Hank Bauer, 1955
      Tom Tresh, 1962
      Thurman Munson, 1973
      Graig Nettles, 1979
      Roy Smalley, 1982
      Graig Nettles, 1983

*Led major leagues.
**Shared majors' lead.
†Led American League.
‡Shared league lead.

4 Home Runs in a Game
Lou Gehrig, June 3, 1932*

*Consecutive.
(Gehrig was the first player in modern major league history to hit four homers in a game.)

4 Consecutive Home Runs
Lou Gehrig, 1932
Johnny Blanchard, 1961
Mickey Mantle, 1963
Bobby Murcer, 1970†
Reggie Jackson, 1977 (WS)‡

(WS) World Series.

3 Home Runs in a Game
Babe Ruth, 1926 (WS)   Joe DiMaggio, 1948*
Tony Lazzeri, 1927   Joe DiMaggio, 1948
Lou Gehrig, 1927   Johnny Mize, 1950*
Babe Ruth, 1928 (WS)*   Mickey Mantle, 1955
Lou Gehrig, 1929   Tom Tresh, 1965*
Babe Ruth, 1930   Bobby Murcer, 1970*†
Lou Gehrig, 1930   Bobby Mucer, 1973
Ben Chapman, 1932   Cliff Johnson, 1977
Tony Lazzeri, 1936   Reggie Jackson, 1977 (WS)*‡
Joe DiMaggio, 1937   Mike Stanley, 1995
Bill Dickey, 1939   Paul O'Neill, 1995
Charlie Keller, 1940   Darryl Strawberry, 1996

*Consecutive.
†Murcer's three home runs in the second game of a Yankee Stadium doubleheader against the Indians followed a homer in his last at bat in the opener, tying him for the major league record of hitting home runs in four consecutive official times at bat.
‡Jackson's three home runs against the Dodgers, prefaced by a walk, at Yankee Stadium in game six of the World Series, followed a homer in his final at bat in game five at Los Angeles. So Jackson hit a Series record four home runs in four successive official trips.
(WS) World Series.

2 Home Runs in a Game (Career)
Babe Ruth, 72 times*   Lou Gehrig, 43 times
Mickey Mantle, 46 times   Joe DiMaggio, 35 times

*All-time major league leader.

Switch-Hitting Home Runs in a Game
Mickey Mantle   10 times*   Bernie Williams   3 times
Roy White   5 times   Roy Smalley   once
Tom Tresh   3 times

*Major league record.

2 Home Runs in One Inning
Joe DiMaggio   1936
Joe Pepitone   1962
Cliff Johnson   1977

Pinch Home Runs (Career)
Yogi Berra   9   Johnny Blanchard   6*
Bob Cerv   8   Johnny Mize   5
Mickey Mantle   7   Bill Skowron   5
Bobby Murcer   7

*Includes 4 during 1961 season.

2 Consecutive Pinch Home Runs

Ray Caldwell	1915
Charlie Keller	1948
Johnny Blanchard	1961
Ray Barker	1965

Most Home Runs in a Month

Babe Ruth, 17 (September 1927)
Mickey Mantle, 16 (May 1956)

(Ruth hit 15 homers in a month three other times, Joe DiMaggio once, and Roger Maris once.)

Most Career Grand-Slam Home Runs

Lou Gehrig*	23
Joe DiMaggio	13
Babe Ruth	12
Mickey Mantle	9
Tony Lazzeri	8
Bill Dickey	8
Yogi Berra	8
Charlie Keller	7
Don Mattingly	6†
Mike Stanley	6

*All-time major league leader.
†All in one season.
NOTES
Babe Ruth twice hit grand slams on consecutive days.
Four Yankee pitchers have hit grand slams: Red Ruffing (1933), Spud Chandler (1940), Don Larsen (1956), and Mel Stottlemyre (1965).

Home Run in First Major League At Bat

John Miller, 1966

Home Runs in First Two Major League Games

Joe Lefebvre, 1980

Home Runs into Center-Field Bleachers in New Yankee Stadium

Ken Singleton, Orioles,	1977
Reggie Jackson, Yankees	1977*
Reggie Jackson, Yankees	1981
Mike Greenwell, Red Sox	1987
Jay Buhner, Mariners	1988
Candy Maldonado, Blue Jays	1992
Danny Tartabull, Yankees	1993
Dion James, Yankees	1993
Bernie Williams, Yankees	1994
Danny Tartabull, Yankees (twice)	1994
Tino Martinez, Mariners	1995

*World Series.

MISCELLANEOUS CLUB RECORDS

BATTING

Hitting for the Cycle

Bob Meusel	5/7/21, 7/3/22, 7/26/28
Lou Gehrig	6/25/34, 8/1/37
Joe DiMaggio	7/9/37, 5/20/48
Bert Daniels	7/25/12
Tony Lazzeri	6/3/32
Buddy Rosar	7/19/40
Joe Gordon	9/8/40
Mickey Mantle	7/23/57
Bobby Murcer	8/29/72

200 Hits in Rookie Season

Earle Combs, 203	1925
Joe DiMaggio, 206	1936

Most At Bats in a Game

Bobby Richardson, 11 1962 (22 innings)

Most Hits in a Game
Myril Hoag, 6 1934

Most Singles in a Game
Myril Hoag, 6 1934

Most Doubles in a Game
Johnny Lindell, 4 1944
Jim Mason, 4 1974

Most Triples in a Game
Hal Chase, 3 1906
Earle Combs, 3 1927
Joe DiMaggio, 3 1938

Most Homers in a Game
Lou Gehrig, 4 1932

Most Grand Slams in a Game
Tony Lazzeri, 2 1936

Most Total Bases in a Game
Lou Gehrig, 16 1932

Most RBIs in a Game
Tony Lazzeri, 11 1936

Most Runs in a Game
Don Mattingly, most recent (1988) of 12 times a Yankee has scored 5 runs in a game.

Most Sacrifice Flies in a Game
Bob Meusel, 3 1926
Don Mattingly, 3 1986

Most Stolen Bases in a Game
Luis Polonia, most recent (1994) of 15 times a Yankee has stolen 4 bases in a game.

Most Times Caught Stealing in a Game
Fritz Maisel, 3 1916
Lee Mager, 3 1916

Most Times Walked in a Game
Harry Hemphill, 5 1911
Roger Peckinpaugh, 5 1919
Whitey Witt, 5 1924
Lou Gehrig, 5 1935
Ben Chapman, 5 1936
Hersh Martin, 5 1945

Most Times Struck Out in a Game
Johnny Broaca, 5 1934
Bernie Williams, 5 1991

Most Times Grounded into DP in a Game
Eddie Robinson, 3 1955
Jim Leyritz, 3 1990
Matt Nokes, 3 1992

PITCHING

Most Strikeouts in a Game
Ron Guidry, 18 1978

Most Consecutive Strikeouts in a Game
Ron Davis, 8 1981

Most Walks in a Game
Boardwalk Brown, 15 1914

Most Balks in a Game
Vic Raschi, 4 1950

BABE RUTH'S RECORD 60 HOME RUNS IN 1927 (Yankees played a 154-game schedule plus a tie game on April 14)

Home Run	Yankee Game	Ruth's Game	Date	Inning	Opponent	Pitcher
1	4	4	April 15	1	Philadelphia	Ehmke
2	11	11	April 23	1	at Philadelphia	Walberg (L)
3	12	12	April 24	6	at Washington	Thurston
4	14	14	April 29	5	at Boston	Harriss
5	16	16	May 1	1	Philadelphia	Quinn
6	16	16	May 1	8	Philadelphia	Walberg (L)
7	24	24	May 10	1	at St. Louis	Gaston
8	25	25	May 11	1	at St. Louis	Nevers
9	29	29	May 17	8	at Detroit	Collins
10	33	33	May 22	6	at Cleveland	Karr
11	34	34	May 23	1	at Washington	Thurston
12	37	37	May 28	7	Washington	Thurston
13	39	39	May 29	8	Boston	MacFayden
14	41	41	May 30	11	at Philadelphia	Walberg (L)
15	42	42	May 31	1	at Philadelphia	Quinn
16	43	43	May 31	5	at Philadelphia	Ehmke
17	47	47	June 5	6	Detroit	Whitehill (L)
18	48	48	June 7	4	Chicago	Thomas
19	52	52	June 11	3	Cleveland	Buckeye (L)
20	52	52	June 11	5	Cleveland	Buckeye (L)
21	53	53	June 12	7	Cleveland	Uhle
22	55	55	June 16	1	St. Louis	Zachary (L)
23	60	60	June 22	5	at Boston	Wiltse (L)
24	60	60	June 22	7	at Boston	Wiltse (L)
25	70	66	June 30	4	Boston	Harriss
26	73	69	July 3	1	at Washington	Lisenbee
27	78	74	July 8	2	at Detroit	Hankins
28	79	75	July 9	1	at Detroit	Holloway
29	79	75	July 9	4	at Detroit	Holloway
30	83	79	July 12	9	at Cleveland	Shaute (L)
31	94	90	July 24	3	at Chicago	Thomas
32	95	91	July 26	1	St. Louis	Gaston
33	95	91	July 26	6	St. Louis	Gaston
34	98	94	July 28	8	St. Louis	Stewart (L)
35	106	102	August 5	8	Detroit	Smith
36	110	106	August 10	3	at Washington	Zachary (L)
37	114	110	August 16	5	at Chicago	Thomas
38	115	111	August 17	11	at Chicago	Connally
39	118	114	August 20	1	at Cleveland	Miller (L)
40	120	116	August 22	6	at Cleveland	Shaute (L)
41	124	120	August 27	8	at St. Louis	Nevers
42	125	121	August 28	1	at St. Louis	Wingard (L)
43	127	123	August 31	8	Boston	Welzer
44	128	124	September 2	1	at Philadelphia	Walberg (L)
45	132	128	September 6	6	at Boston	Welzer
46	132	128	September 6	7	at Boston	Welzer
47	133	129	September 6	9	at Boston	Russell
48	134	130	September 7	1	at Boston	MacFayden
49	134	130	September 7	8	at Boston	Harriss
50	138	134	September 11	4	St. Louis	Gaston
51	139	135	September 13	7	Cleveland	Hudlin
52	140	136	September 13	4	Cleveland	Shaute (L)
53	143	139	September 16	3	Chicago	Blankenship
54	147	143	September 18	5	Chicago	Lyons
55	148	144	September 21	9	Detroit	Gibson
56	149	145	September 22	9	Detroit	Holloway
57	152	148	September 27	6	Philadelphia	Grove (L)
58	153	149	September 29	1	Washington	Lisenbee
59	153	149	September 29	5	Washington	Hopkins
60	154	150	September 30	8	Washington	Zachary (L)

(L) Indicates left-handed pitcher.

NOTES

Ruth's 60th home run came on the second-last game of the Yankees' regular-season schedule. In the final game, on Oct. 1, Ruth went hitless in three at bats.

A left-handed batter, Ruth hit 41 of his homers off right-handed pitchers, 19 off left-handers.

Ruth hit 28 of his home runs at Yankee Stadium, 32 on the road: 8 in Boston, 5 in Philadelphia, 4 each in Cleveland, Detroit, St. Louis, and Washington, and 3 in Chicago.

Ruth's homers by month: 4 in April, 12 in May, 9 each in June, July, and August, and 17 in September.

Ruth had eight two-homer games.

All 60 of Ruth's home runs were hit in day games, there being no night baseball in the majors in 1927.

ROGER MARIS'S RECORD 61 HOME RUNS IN 1962 (Yankees played a 162-game schedule plus a tie game on April 22)

Home Run	Yankee Game	Maris's Game	Date	Inning	Opponent	Pitcher
1	11	11	April 26	5	at Detroit	Foytack
2	17	17	May 3	7	at Minnesota	Ramos
3	20	20	May 6 (N)	5	at Los Angeles	Grba
4	29	29	May 17	8	Washington	Burnside (L)
5	30	30	May 19 (N)	1	at Cleveland	Perry
6	31	31	May 20	3	at Cleveland	Bell
7	32	32	May 21	1	Baltimore	Estrada
8	35	35	May 24	4	Boston	Conley
9	38	38	May 28	2	Chicago	McLish
10	40	40	May 30	6	at Boston	Conley
11	40	40	May 30	8	at Boston	Fornieles
12	41	41	May 31 (N)	3	at Boston	Muffett
13	43	43	June 2 (N)	3	at Chicago	McLish
14	44	44	June 3	8	at Chicago	Shaw
15	45	45	June 4	3	at Chicago	Kemmerer
16	48	48	June 6 (N)	6	Minnesota	Palmquist
17	49	49	June 7	3	Minnesota	Ramos
18	52	52	June 9 (N)	7	Kansas City	Herbert
19	55	55	June 11	3	Los Angeles	Grba
20	55	55	June 11	7	Los Angeles	James
21	57	57	June 13 (N)	6	at Cleveland	Perry
22	58	58	June 14 (N)	4	at Cleveland	Bell
23	61	61	June 17 (N)	4	at Detroit	Mossi (L)
24	62	62	June 18	8	at Detroit	Casale
25	63	63	June 19 (N)	9	at Kansas City	Archer (L)
26	64	64	June 20 (N)	1	at Kansas City	Nuxhall (L)
27	66	66	June 22 (N)	2	at Kansas City	Bass
28	74	74	July 1	9	Washington	Sisler
29	75	75	July 2	3	Washington	Burnside (L)
30	75	75	July 2	7	Washington	Klippstein
31	77	77	July 4	8	Detroit	Lary
32	78	78	July 5	7	Cleveland	Funk
33	82	82	July 9	7	Boston	Monbouquette
34	84	84	July 13 (N)	1	at Chicago	Wynn
35	86	86	July 15	3	at Chicago	Herbert
36	92	92	July 21 (N)	1	at Boston	Monbouquette
37	95	95	July 25(N)	4	Chicago	Baumann (L)
38	95	95	July 25 (N)	8	Chicago	Larsen
39	96	96	July 25 (N)	4	Chicago	Kemmerer
40	96	96	July 25 (N)	6	Chicago	Hacker
41	106	105	August 4 (N)	1	Minnesota	Pascual
42	114	113	August 11 (N)	5	at Washington	Burnside (L)
43	115	114	August 12	4	at Washington	Donovan
44	116	115	August 13	4	at Washington	Daniels
45	117	116	August 13	1	at Washington	Kutyna
46	118	117	August 15 (N)	4	Chicago	Pizarro (L)
47	119	118	August 16	1	Chicago	Pierce (L)
48	119	118	August 16	3	Chicago	Pierce (L)
49	123	122	August 20	3	at Cleveland	Perry
50	125	124	August 22 (N)	6	at Los Angeles	McBride
51	129	128	August 26	6	at Kansas City	Walker
52	135	134	September 2	6	Detroit	Lary
53	135	134	September 2	8	Detroit	Aguirre (L)
54	140	139	September 6	4	Washington	Cheney
55	141	140	September 7 (N)	3	Cleveland	Stigman (L)
56	143	142	September 9	7	Cleveland	Grant
57	151	150	September 16	3	at Detroit	Lary
58	152	151	September 17	12	at Detroit	Fox
59	155	154	September 20 (N)	3	at Baltimore	Pappas
60	159	158	September 26 (N)	3	Baltimore	Fisher
61	163	161	October 1	4	Boston	Stallard

(L) Indicates left-handed pitcher. (N) Indicates night game.

NOTES

Maris's 61st home run came on the final game of the Yankees' regular-season schedule.

A left-handed batter, Maris hit 49 of his homers off right-handed pitchers, 12 off left-handers.

Maris hit 30 of his home runs at Yankee Stadium, 31 on the road: 5 each in Chicago, Cleveland, and Detroit, 4 each in Boston, Kansas City, and Washington, 2 in Los Angeles, and 1 each in Baltimore and Bloomington, Minnesota.

Maris's homers by month: one in April, 11 in May, 15 in June, 13 in July, 11 in August, 9 in September, and one in October.

Maris had seven two-homer games.

Thirty-six of Maris's home runs were hit during day games, 25 during night games.

JOE DiMAGGIO'S RECORD BATTING STREAK (56 Consecutive Games, May 15–July 16, 1941)

Date	Opposing Team and Pitcher	AB	R	H	2B	3B	HR	RBI
May 15	Chicago—Smith (L)	4	0	1	0	0	0	1
May 16	Chicago—Lee (L)	4	2	2	0	1	1	1
May 17	Chicago—Rigney	3	1	1	0	0	0	0
May 18	St. Louis—Harris (2), Niggeling (1)	3	3	3	1	0	0	1
May 19	St. Louis—Galehouse	3	0	1	1	0	0	0
May 20	St. Louis—Auker	5	1	1	0	0	0	1
May 21	Detroit—Rowe (1), Benton (1)	5	0	2	0	0	0	1
May 22	Detroit—McKain (L)	4	0	1	0	0	0	1
May 23	Boston—Newsome	5	0	1	0	0	0	2
May 24	Boston—Johnson (L)	4	2	1	0	0	0	2
May 25	Boston—Grove (L)	4	0	1	0	0	0	0
May 27	at Washington—Chase (L) (1), Anderson (2), Carrasquel (1)	5	3	4	0	0	1	3
May 28	at Washington—Hudson (night)	4	1	1	0	1	0	0
May 29	at Washington—Sundra	3	1	1	0	0	0	0
May 30	at Boston—Johnson (L)	2	1	1	0	0	0	0
May 30	at Boston—Harris (L)	3	0	1	1	0	0	0
June 1	at Cleveland—Milnar (L)	4	1	1	0	0	0	0
June 1	at Cleveland—Harder	4	0	1	0	0	0	0
June 2	at Cleveland—Feller	4	2	2	1	0	0	0
June 3	at Detroit—Trout	4	1	1	0	0	1	1
June 5	at Detroit—Newhouser (L)	5	1	1	0	1	0	1
June 7	at St. Louis—Muncrief (1), Allen (1), Caster (1)	5	2	3	0	0	0	1
June 8	at St. Louis—Auker	4	3	2	0	0	2	4
June 8	at St. Louis—Caster (1), Kramer (1)	4	1	2	1	0	1	3
June 10	at Chicago—Rigney	5	1	1	0	0	0	0
June 12	at Chicago—Lee (L) (night)	4	1	2	0	0	1	1
June 14	Cleveland—Feller	2	0	1	1	0	0	1
June 15	Cleveland—Bagby	3	1	1	0	0	1	1
June 16	Cleveland—Milnar (L)	5	0	1	1	0	0	0
June 17	Chicago—Rigney	4	1	1	0	0	0	0
June 18	Chicago—Lee (L)	3	0	1	0	0	0	0
June 19	Chicago—Smith (L) (1), Ross (2)	3	2	3	0	0	1	2
June 20	Detroit—Newsom (2), McKain (L) (2)	5	3	4	1	0	0	1
June 21	Detroit—Trout	4	0	1	0	0	0	1
June 22	Detroit—Newhouser (L) (1), Newsom (1)	5	1	2	1	0	1	2
June 24	St. Louis—Muncrief	4	1	1	0	0	0	0
June 25	St. Louis—Galehouse	4	1	1	0	0	1	3
June 26	St. Louis—Auker	4	0	1	1	0	0	1
June 27	at Philadelphia—Dean (L)	3	1	2	0	0	1	2

It was all in the family when the DiMaggio brothers got together. Joe meets with younger brother Dom, an 11-season Red Soxer (left), and with older brother Vince, a 10-year National Leaguer. The DiMaggios—all center fielders—hit 573 home runs all together, a total for brothers second only to Hank and Tommie Aaron's 768. The DiMaggios rank number one in RBIs with 2,739 to the Aarons' 2,391.

JOE DiMAGGIO'S RECORD BATTING STREAK (56 Consecutive Games, May 15–July 16, 1941) (Continued)

Date	Opposing Team and Pitcher	AB	R	H	2B	3B	HR	RBI
June 28	at Philadelphia—Babich (1), Harris (1)	5	1	2	1	0	0	0
June 29	at Washington—Leonard	4	1	1	1	0	0	0
June 29	at Washington—Anderson	5	1	1	0	0	0	1
July 1	Boston—Harris (L) (1), Ryba (1)	4	0	2	0	0	0	1
July 1	Boston—Wilson	3	1	1	0	0	0	1
July 2	Boston—Newsome	5	1	1	0	0	1	3
July 5	Philadelphia—Marchildon	4	2	1	0	0	1	2
July 6	Philadelphia—Babich (1), Hadley (3)	5	2	4	1	0	0	2
July 6	Philadelphia—Knott	4	0	2	0	1	0	2
July 10	at St. Louis—Niggeling (night)	2	0	1	0	0	0	0
July 11	at St. Louis—Harris (3), Kramer (1)	5	1	4	0	0	1	2
July 12	at St. Louis—Auker (1), Muncrief (1)	5	1	2	1	0	0	1
July 13	at Chicago—Lyons (2), Hallet (1)	4	2	3	0	0	0	0
July 13	at Chicago—Lee (L)	4	0	1	0	0	0	0
July 14	at Chicago—Rigney	3	0	1	0	0	0	0
July 15	at Chicago—Smith (L)	4	1	2	1	0	0	2
July 16	at Cleveland—Milnar (L) (2), Krakauskas (L) (1)	4	3	3	1	0	0	0
	Totals (Batting Avg.: .408 Pct.)	223	56	91	16	4	15	55

(L) Indicates left-handed pitcher.

NOTES

DiMaggio's streak was halted on July 17 at Cleveland in a night game won by the Yankees, 4–3. He hit the ball hard on the ground all three official at bats and was walked once.

DiMaggio was thrown out in the first and seventh innings on sparkling plays by third baseman Ken Keltner on balls drilled off left-hander Al Smith, who walked him in the fourth. And batting against right-hander Jim Bagby, Jr., in the eighth inning, DiMaggio ripped one of the hardest grounders of his career, he would reflect years later; but shortstop Lou Boudreau turned it into a double play despite a last-instant bad hop.

A right-handed batter, DiMaggio hit safely against 63 right-handed pitchers and 28 left-handers while totaling 91 hits in the 56 games.

Of the 56 games, 53 were during the day and 3 at night.

DiMaggio hit safely in 29 games in Yankee Stadium, 27 on the road.

DiMaggio did not attempt to bunt his way on base during his streak and struck out only seven times in 223 official at bats—246 trips to the plate including being struck by pitches twice and walked 21 times.

During the streak the Yankees won 41, tied 2, and lost 13—a .759 clip that promoted them from fourth place, 5½ games behind Cleveland, to first place, 6 games ahead of the Indians.

The day after DiMaggio's streak ended, he began another that lasted 16 games before being stopped by St. Louis Browns knuckleballer Johnny Niggeling. It was the first time in 84 games since May 2 that DiMaggio had failed to reach base and only the second time in 74 games that he failed to hit safely.

DiMaggio went on to hit .357 for the season, second only to his .381 of 1939 during his 13-year Yankee career.

DON LARSEN'S PERFECT GAME FIVE OF 1956 WORLD SERIES

MONDAY, OCTOBER 8, AT YANKEE STADIUM

Dodgers	AB	R	H	O	A	E		Yankees	AB	R	H	O	A	E
Gilliam, 2b	3	0	0	2	0	0		Bauer, rf	4	0	1	4	0	0
Reese, ss	3	0	0	4	2	0		Collins, 1b	4	0	1	7	0	0
Snider, cf	3	0	0	1	0	0		Mantle, cf	3	1	1	4	0	0
Robinson, 3b	3	0	0	2	4	0		Berra, c	3	0	0	7	0	0
Hodges, 1b	3	0	0	5	1	0		Slaughter, lf	2	0	0	1	0	0
Amoros, lf	3	0	0	3	0	0		Martin, 2b	3	0	1	3	4	0
Furillo, rf	3	0	0	0	0	0		McDougald, ss	2	0	0	0	2	0
Campanella, c	3	0	0	7	2	0		Carey, 3b	3	1	1	1	1	0
Maglie, p	2	0	0	0	1	0		Larsen, p	2	0	0	0	1	0
ªMitchell	1	0	0	0	0	0		Totals	26	2	5	27	8	0
Totals	27	0	0	24	10	0								

Dodgers	000	000	000	0
Yankees	000	101	00X	2

ªCalled out on strikes for Maglie in ninth. Runs batted in—Mantle, Bauer. Home run—Mantle. Sacrifice hit—Larsen. Double plays—Reese and Hodges; Hodges, Campanella, Robinson; Campanella and Robinson. Left on bases—Brooklyn 0, New York 3. Earned runs—New York 2, Brooklyn 0. Bases on balls—Off Maglie 2. Struck out—By Larsen 7; by Maglie 5. Winning pitcher—Larsen. Losing pitcher—Maglie. Umpires—Pinelli (NL), Soar (AL), Boggess (NL), Napp (AL), Gorman (NL), Runge (AL). Time—2:06. Attendance—64,519.

NOTE: The game stands not only as the lone perfect game in World Series history, but also as the only no-hitter.

BILL BEVENS' NEAR NO-HITTER IN GAME FOUR OF 1947 WORLD SERIES

FRIDAY, OCTOBER 3, AT EBBETS FIELD, BROOKLYN

Yankees	AB	R	H	PO	A	E
Stirnweiss, 2b	4	1	2	2	1	0
Henrich, rf	5	0	1	2	0	0
Berra, c	4	0	0	6	1	1
DiMaggio, cf	2	0	0	2	0	0
McQuinn, 1b	4	0	1	7	0	0
Johnson, 3b	4	1	1	3	2	0
Lindell, lf	3	0	2	3	0	0
Rizzuto, ss	4	0	1	1	2	0
Bevens, p	3	0	0	0	1	0
Totals	33	2	8	26	7	1

Dodgers	AB	R	H	PO	A	E
Stanky, 2b	1	0	0	2	3	0
ᵉLavagetto	1	0	1	0	0	0
Reese, ss	4	0	0	3	5	1
Robinson, 1b	4	0	0	11	1	0
Walker, rf	2	0	0	0	1	0
Hermanski, lf	4	0	0	2	0	0
Edwards, c	4	0	0	7	1	1
Furillo, cf	3	0	0	2	0	0
ᵇGionfriddo	0	1	0	0	0	0
Jorgensen, 3b	2	1	0	0	1	1
Taylor, p	0	0	0	0	0	0
Gregg, p	1	0	0	0	1	0
ᵃVaughan	0	0	0	0	0	0
Berhman, p	0	0	0	0	1	0
Casey, p	0	0	0	0	1	0
ᶜReiser	0	0	0	0	0	0
ᵈMiksis	0	1	0	0	0	0
Totals	26	3	1	27	15	3

```
Yankees    100   100   000    2
Dodgers    000   010   002    3
```

ᵃ*Walked for Gregg in seventh.* ᵇ*Ran for Furillo in ninth.* ᶜ*Walked for Casey in ninth.* ᵈ*Ran for Reiser in ninth.* ᵉ*Doubled for Stanky in ninth. Runs batted in—DiMaggio, Lindell, Reese, Lavagetto 2. Two-base hits—Lindell, Lavagetto. Three-base hit—Johnson. Sacrifice hits—Stanky, Bevens. Stolen bases—Rizzuto, Reese, Gionfriddo. Double plays—Reese, Stanky, and Robinson; Gregg, Reese, and Robinson; Casey, Edwards, and Robinson. Bases on balls—Off Taylor 1; off Gregg 3; off Bevens 10. Struck out—By Gregg 5; by Bevens 5. Pitching record—Off Taylor 2 hits, 1 run in 0 inning (pitched to four batters); off Gregg 4 hits, 1 run in 7 innings; off Berman 2 hits, 0 runs in 11/3 innings; off Casey 0 hits, 0 runs in ⅔ inning. Wild pitch—Bevens. Earned runs—Brooklyn 3, New York 1. Left on base—New York 9, Brooklyn 8. Winning pitcher—Casey. Losing pitcher—Bevens. Umpires—Goetz (NL), McGowan (AL), Pinelli (NL), Rommel (AL), Boyer (AL), Magerkurth (NL). Time—2:20. Attendance—33,433.*

NOTE: Bevens' no-hit bid was ruined by pinch hitter Cookie Lavagetto's double with two out in the ninth inning which drove home the tying and winning runs, the two runners aboard via walks.

In one of the most electrifying moments in baseball history, pinch-hitter Cookie Lavagetto's two-run double off the right-field wall at Ebbets Field spoiled Yankee Bill Bevens' no-hit bid with two out in the ninth inning and gave the Dodgers a 3–2 victory that evened the 1947 Series at two games apiece. It was Bevens' last start ever. After a relief appearance in game seven, he was through as a major leaguer at age 30.

ALL-TIME POSITION LEADERS

MOST GAMES (At that position as a Yankee)

Pos.	Player		Games
1B	Lou Gehrig (1923–39)		2,136
2B	Tony Lazzeri (1926–37)		1,446
SS	Phil Rizzuto (1941–42, 1946–56)*		1,647 (a)
3B	Graig Nettles (1973–83)		1,509
OF	Babe Ruth (1920–34)		2,042 (b)
OF	Mickey Mantle (1951–68)		2,019
OF	Joe DiMaggio (1936–42, 1946–51)*		1,721 (c)
C	Bill Dickey (1928–43, 1946)*		1,712 (d)
DH	Don Baylor (1983–85)		403
LHP	Whitey Ford (1950, 1953–67)*	(games)	498
RHP	Red Ruffing (1930–42, 1945–46)*	(games)	426
LHP	Whitey Ford (1950, 1953–67)*	(starts)	438
RHP	Red Ruffing (1930–42, 1945–46)*	(starts)	390

(a) Frank Crosetti played in 21 more games for the Yankees than Rizzuto, 1,682–1,661; but Rizzuto played 132 more games at shortstop, 1,647–1,515.

(b) Mickey Mantle played in 317 more games for the Yankees than Ruth, 2,401–2,084; but Ruth played 23 more games in the outfield, 2,042–2,019.

(c) Roy White played in 145 more games for the Yankees than DiMaggio, 1,881–1,736; but DiMaggio played more games in the outfield.

(d) Yogi Berra played in 327 more games for the Yankees than Dickey, 2,116–1,789; but Dickey caught 18 more games, 1,712–1,694.

* Career interrupted by military service.

ALL-TIME YANKEE TEAMS

Chosen in 1953 Poll of 48 Media Members and Baseball Officials on Yankees' 50th Anniversary

Selected	Pos.	Runner-up
Lou Gehrig (46)	1B	Hal Chase (2)
Tony Lazzeri (36)	2B	Joe Gordon (12)
Phil Rizzuto (42)	SS	Frank Crosetti (3)
Red Rolfe (38)	3B	Joe Dugan (10)
Frank Crosetti (23)	Util. IF	Joe Gordon (11)
Babe Ruth (unanimous)	OF	—
Joe DiMaggio (unanimous)	OF	—
Bob Meusel (24)	OF	Earle Combs (14)
Bill Dickey (unanimous)	C	—
Red Ruffing (28)	RHP	Waite Hoyt (11)
Lefty Gomez (24) } (tie) Herb Pennock (24)	LHP	—
Johnny Murphy (25)	Relief	Wilcy Moore (11)

Chosen by Fans in 1969

First Team	Pos.	Second Team
Lou Gehrig	1B	Joe Pepitone
Tony Lazzeri	2B	Bobby Richardson
Phil Rizzuto	SS	Frank Crosetti
Red Rolfe	3B	Clete Boyer
Mickey Mantle	LF	Charlie Keller
Joe DiMaggio	CF	Mickey Mantle
Babe Ruth	RF	Mickey Mantle
Bill Dickey	C	Yogi Berra
Red Ruffing	RHP	Allie Reynolds
Whitey Ford	LHP	Lefty Gomez

MOST HOME RUNS (As a Yankee)

Pos.	Player		Homers
1B	Lou Gehrig (1923–39)		493
2B	Joe Gordon (1938–43, 1946)		153
SS	Frank Crosetti (1932–48)		98
3B	Graig Nettles (1973–83)		250
OF	Babe Ruth (1920–34)		659
OF	Mickey Mantle (1951–68)		536
OF	Joe DiMaggio (1936–42, 146–51)		361
C	Yogi Berra (1946–63)		358
P	Red Ruffing (1930–42, 1945–46)		31

NOTE: Some home runs may have come while playing another position—such as Berra while in the lineup as an outfielder or pinch hitter, Mantle as a first baseman, etc.

SINGLE-SEASON LEADERS BY POSITION

Batting Average			***Home Runs***	
1B	Lou Gehrig, .379 (1930)		1B	Lou Gehrig, 49 (1934)
2B	Tony Lazzeri, .354 (1929)		2B	Joe Gordon, 30 (1940)
SS	Phil Rizzuto, .324 (1950)		SS	Roy Smalley, 16 (1982)
3B	Wade Boggs, .342 (1994)		3B	Graig Nettles, 37 (1977)
OF	*Babe Ruth, .393 (1923)		OF	Roger Maris, 61 (1961)
OF	Joe DiMaggio, .381 (1939)		OF	†Babe Ruth, 60 (1927)
OF	Mickey Mantle, .365 (1957)		OF	Mickey Mantle, 54 (1961)
C	Bill Dickey, .362 (1936)		C	Yogi Berra, 30 (1952, 1956)
P	Red Ruffing, .339 (1935)‡		P	Red Ruffing, 5 (1936)

RBIs			***Fielding***	
1B	Lou Gehrig, 184 (1931)		1B	Don Mattingly, .998 (1993)
2B	Tony Lazzeri, 114 (1926)		2B	Snuffy Stirnweiss, .993 (1948)
SS	Lyn Lary, 107 (1931)		SS	Fred Stanley, .983 (1976)
3B	Graig Nettles, 107 (1977)		3B	Graig Nettles, .975 (1978)
OF	**Babe Ruth, 170 (1921)		OF	Roy White, 1.000 (1971)
OF	Joe DiMaggio, 167 (1937)		C	Elston Howard, .998 (1964)
OF	Roger Maris, 142 (1961)			Thurman Munson, .998 (1971)
C	Bill Dickey, 133 (1937)			
P	Red Ruffing, 22 (1936, 1941)			

* Ruth had six of the top seven batting averages ever compiled by a Yankee outfielder. Besides his .393 in 1923, he batted .378 in both 1921 and 1924, .376 in 1920, .373 in 1931, and .372 in 1926.

†Ruth also hit 59 homers in 1921 and 54 in 1920 and 1928.

‡Ruffing's .339 was best by a pitcher during a full Yankee season. But Red batted .364 overall in 1930, the season he was traded to New York in May—hitting .374 in 52 games for the Yankees following his .273 in six games for the Red Sox. Meanwhile, Ruffing was hurling 15 victories that season, going 15-5 for New York after a 0-3 start for Boston.

** Ruth had seven of the top eight RBI totals ever compiled by a Yankee outfielder. Besides driving in 170 runs in 1921, he had 164 in 1927, 163 in 1931, 155 in 1926, 154 in 1929, 153 in 1930, and 142 in 1928.

YANKEES' LEAGUE FIELDING LEADERS

First Base

John Ganzel (.988), 1903	Don Mattingly (.996), 1984
Wally Pipp (.992), 1915	Don Mattingly (.995), 1985
Wally Pipp (.994), 1924	Don Mattingly (.996), 1986
Bill Skowron (.993), 1958	Don Mattingly (.996), 1987
Joe Pepitone (.997), 1965	Don Mattingly (.997), 1992
Joe Pepitone (.995), 1966	Don Mattingly (.998), 1993
Joe Pepitone (.995), 1969	Don Mattingly (.998), 1994
Chris Chambliss (.997), 1978	Tino Martinez (.996), 1996

Second Base

Aaron Ward (.980), 1923	Gil McDougald (.985), 1955
Snuffy Stirnweiss (.982), 1944	Horace Clarke (.990), 1967
Snuffy Stirnweiss (.993), 1948	Sandy Alomar (.985), 1975
Jerry Coleman (.981), 1949	Steve Sax (9.87), 1989

Shortstop

Everett Scott (.964), 1922	Phil Rizzuto (.982), 1950
Everett Scott (.961), 1923	Fred Stanley (.983), 1976
Frank Crosetti (.968), 1939	Bucky Dent (.982), 1980
Phil Rizzuto (.971), 1949	

Third Base

Frank Baker (.972), 1918	Red Rolfe (.964), 1935
Joe Dugan (.974), 1923	Red Rolfe (.957), 1936
Joe Dugan (.970), 1925	Wade Boggs (.970), 1993

Outfield

Birdie Cree (.988), 1913	Gene Woodling (.996), 1953
Whitey Witt (.979), 1923	Mickey Mantle (.995), 1955
Sammy Byrd (.988), 1934	Mickey Mantle (.995), 1959
George Selkirk (.989), 1939	Tom Tresh (.996), 1964
Joe DiMaggio (.997), 1947	Roy White (1.000), 1971
Gene Woodling (.996), 1952	Paul O'Neill (1.000), 1996

Catcher

Benny Bengough (.993), 1925	Yogi Berra (.997), 1959
Bill Dickey (.996), 1931	Elston Howard (.995), 1962
Bill Dickey (.995), 1935	Elston Howard (.998), 1964
Bill Dickey (.989), 1939	Thurman Munson (.998), 1971
Bill Dickey (.994), 1941	Rick Cerone (.998), 1987
Yogi Berra (1.000), 1958	Mike Stanley (.996), 1993

GOLD GLOVE WINNERS

1957	Bobby Shantz	P	1977	Graig Nettles	3B
1958	Bobby Shantz	P	1978	Chris Chambliss	1B
	Norm Siebern	OF		Graig Nettles	3B
1959	Bobby Shantz	P	1982	Ron Guidry	P
1960	Roger Maris	OF		Dave Winfield	OF
	Bobby Shantz	P	1983	Ron Guidry	P
1961	Bobby Richardson	2B		Dave Winfield	OF
1962	Mickey Mantle	OF	1985	Ron Guidry	P
	Bobby Richardson	2B		Don Mattingly	1B
1963	Elston Howard	C		Dave Winfield	OF
	Bobby Richardson	2B	1986	Ron Guidry	P
1964	Elston Howard	C		Don Mattingly	1B
	Bobby Richardson	2B	1987	Don Mattingly	1B
1965	Joe Pepitone	1B		Dave Winfield	OF
	Bobby Richardson	2B	1988	Don Mattingly	1B
	Tom Tresh	OF	1989	Don Mattingly	1B
1966	Joe Pepitone	1B	1991	Don Mattingly	1B
1969	Joe Pepitone	1B	1992	Don Mattingly	1B
1972	Bobby Murcer	OF	1993	Don Mattingly	1B
1973	Thurman Munson	C	1994	Wade Boggs	3B
1974	Thurman Munson	C		Don Mattingly	1B
1975	Thurman Munson	C	1995	Wade Boggs	3B

NOTE: The Yankees have had Gold Glove winners at every position except shortstop since the award was born in the mid-1950s.

YANKEE ADMINISTRATION AND LEADERSHIP

TEAM OWNERS

1903–14	Frank Farrell and William Devery
1915–22	Jacob Ruppert and Tillinghast L'Hommedieu Huston
1922–39	Jacob Ruppert
1939–45	Ruppert Estate (through Ed Barrow)
1945–47	Larry MacPhail, Dan Topping, and Del Webb
1947–64	Dan Topping and Del Webb
1964–73	Columbia Broadcasting System (CBS)
1973–96	Group headed by George Steinbrenner

TEAM PRESIDENTS

1903–06	Joseph Gordon	1966–73	Mike Burke
1907–14	Frank Farrell	1973–77	Gabe Paul
1915–39	Jacob Ruppert	1978–79	Al Rosen
1939–45	Ed Barrow	1979–80	George Steinbrenner
1945–47	Larry MacPhail	1981–82	Lou Saban
1948–53	Dan Topping	1983–86	Gene McHale
1954–64	Dan Topping & Del Webb	1987–96	None
1964–66	Dan Topping		

Hall of Famers Phil Rizzuto, Mickey Mantle, and Joe DiMaggio all tried sportscasting after retiring as players. Only Scooter has stayed with it decade after decade.

A clown invades the pregame lineups exchange at home plate. Yankee manager Ralph Houk seems to be amused, and Twins manager Billy Martin apparently is not, by Max Patkin, the "clown prince of baseball."

MANAGERS' RECORDS

	G	W	L	T	Pct.	AL/WC*	Years
Yogi Berra†	342	192	148	2	.565	1/0	1964, 1984–85
Frank Chance‡	290	117	168	5	.411	0/0	1913–14
Hal Chase***	167	86	80	1	.518	0/0	1910–11
Bucky Dent†	89	36	53	0	.404	0/0	1989–90
Bill Dickey†‡	105	57	48	0	.543	0/0	1946
Bill Donovan‡	465	220	239	6	.479	0/0	1915–17
Kid Elberfeld**	98	27	71	0	.276	0/0	1908
Art Fletcher	11	6	5	0	.545	0/0	1929
Dallas Green	121	56	65	0	.463	0/0	1989
Clark Griffith‡	807	419	370	18	.531	0/0	1903–08
Bucky Harris	308	191	117	0	.620	1/1	1947–48
Ralph Houk†	1,757	944	806	7	.539	3/2	1961–63, 1966–73
Dick Howser†	163	103	60	0	.632	††/0	1978[a], 1980
Miller Huggins	1,796	1,067	719	10	.597	6/3	1918–29
Johnny Keane	182	81	101	0	.445	0/0	1965–66
Clyde King	62	29	33	0	.468	0/0	1982
Bob Lemon	172	99	73	0	.576	2/1	1978–79, 1981–82
Billy Martin†	941	556	385	0	.591	2/1	1975–78, 1979, 1983, 1985, 1988
Joe McCarthy	2,348	1,460	867	21[b]	.627	8/7	1931–46
Stump Merrill	275	120	155	0	.436	0/0	1990–91
Gene Michael†	168	92	76	0	.548	0/0	1981, 1982
Johnny Neun	14	8	6	0	.571	0/0	1946
Roger Peckinpaugh**	20	10	10	0	.500	0/0	1914
Lou Piniella†	417	224	193	0	.537	0/0	1986–87, 1988
Bob Shawkey†	154	86	68	0	.558	0/0	1930
Buck Showalter	581	313	268	0	.539	0/0[c]	1992–95
George Stallings	295	152	136	7	.528	0/0	1909–10
Casey Stengel	1,851	1,149	696	6	.623	10/7	1949–60
Joe Torre	162	92	70	0	.568	1/1	1996
Bill Virdon	266	142	124	0	.534	0/0	1974–75
Harry Wolverton‡	153	50	102	1	.329	0/0	1912
Totals	14,580	8,184	6,312	84	.565	34/23	1903–96

*AL/WC: American League winner/world champion.
†Played for Yankees previously.
‡Played for Yankees while manager.
**Played for Yankees before, during, and after tenure as manager.
††Yankees won AL East, but lost league championship series to Royals.
[a]While a Yankee coach, Howser managed one game, a loss, in 1978 in an interim role during Martin-Lemon managerial transition.
[b]McCarthy's 21 "ties" include 3 "no-decision" games.
[c]Showalter managed Yankees to first-place finish in strike-shortened 1994 season and to wild-card berth in 1995 playoffs.

YANKEE CAPTAINS

Hal Chase*	–1912	Thurman Munson	1976–79
Roger Peckinpaugh	1914–21	Graig Nettles	1982–84
Babe Ruth	1922†	Ron Guidry‡	1986–89
Everett Scott	1922–25	Willie Randolph‡	1986–89
Lou Gehrig	1935–41	Don Mattingly	1991–95

*Unknown when Chase began his captaincy.
†Ruth captained the Yankees less than a week, May 20–25, 1922. He was named captain upon rejoining the team from a suspension decreed by the commissioner for barnstorming following the 1921 season against the commissioner's orders. Five days after his return, Ruth was stripped of the captaincy and fined for climbing into the stands in pursuit of an insulting customer.
‡Cocaptains until Guidry's retirement in July 1989, when Randolph became sole captain.

NOTE: Gehrig and Munson each was captain until his death, even though Gehrig did not suit up in 1940 or 1941.

Ace Andy Pettitte was 21–8 in 1996.

YANKEE FREE-AGENT SIGNINGS

Player	Pos.	Date
Catfish Hunter	P	Dec. 31, 1974
Don Gullett	P	Nov. 18, 1976
Reggie Jackson	OF	Nov. 29, 1976
Rich Gossage	P	Nov. 22, 1977
Rawly Eastwick	P	Dec. 9, 1977
Luis Tiant	P	Nov. 13, 1978
Tommy John	P	Nov. 22, 1978
Rudy May	P	Nov. 8, 1979
Bob Watson	1B	Nov. 8, 1979
Dave Winfield	OF	Dec. 15, 1980
Bill Castro	P	Feb. 15, 1981
Ron Guidry	P	Dec. 15, 1981
Dave Collins	OF/1B	Dec. 23, 1981
Don Baylor	DH	Dec. 1, 1982
Steve Kemp	OF	Dec. 9. 1982
Bob Shirley	P	Dec. 15, 1982
Dale Murray	P	Nov. 21, 1983
Phil Niekro	P	Jan. 6, 1984
Ed Whitson	P	Dec. 27, 1984
Joe Niekro	P	Jan. 8, 1986
Phil Niekro	P	Jan. 8, 1986
Butch Wynegar	C	Jan. 8, 1986
Al Holland	P	Feb. 6, 1986
Tommy John	P	May 2, 1986
Rod Scurry	P	Dec. 5, 1986
Claudell Washington	OF	Dec. 11, 1986
Len Sakata	IF	Dec. 16, 1986
Gary Ward	OF	Dec. 24, 1986
Tommy John	P	Jan. 8, 1987
Wayne Tolleson	IF	Jan. 8, 1987
Willie Randolph	2B	Jan. 8, 1987
Bob Shirley	P	Jan. 28, 1987
Rick Cerone	C	Feb. 13, 1987
Ron Guidry	P	May 1, 1987
Dave Righetti	P	Dec. 23, 1987
Jack Clark	1B	Jan. 6, 1988
John Candelaria	P	Jan. 18, 1988
Jose Cruz	OF	Feb. 25, 1988
Steve Sax	2B	Nov. 23, 1988
Dave LaPoint	P	Dec. 3, 1988
Andy Hawkins	P	Dec. 8, 1988
Jamie Quirk	C	Dec. 20, 1988
Ron Guidry	P	Feb. 3, 1989
Tommy John	P	Feb. 13, 1989
Pascual Perez	P	Nov. 21, 1989
Mel Hall	OF	Nov. 30, 1989
Rick Cerone	C	Dec. 22, 1989
Damaso Garcia	2B	Dec. 22, 1989
Tim Leary	P	Nov. 19, 1990
Steve Farr	P	Nov. 26, 1990
Danny Tartabull	OF	Jan. 6, 1992
Mike Gallego	IF	Jan. 7, 1992
Spike Owen	SS	Dec. 4, 1992
Steve Howe	P	Dec. 8, 1992
Jimmy Key	P	Dec. 10, 1992
Wade Boggs	3B	Dec. 15, 1992
Luis Polonia	OF	Dec. 20, 1993
Donn Pall	P	Jan. 18, 1994
Scott Bankhead	P	Nov. 1, 1994
Tony Fernandez	IF	Dec. 14, 1994
Wade Boggs	3B	Dec. 5, 1995
Mariano Duncan	IF/OF	Dec. 11, 1995
David Cone	P	Dec. 21, 1995
Pat Kelly	2B	Dec. 27, 1995
Kenny Rogers	P	Jan. 4, 1996
Mike Stanton	P	Dec. 11, 1996
Mark Whiten	OF	Dec. 19, 1996
David Wells	P	Jan. 9, 1997

TOP YANKEE CHOICES IN JUNE AMATEUR DRAFT

Year	Player/Round	Pos.
1965	Bill Burbach (1)	RHP
1966	Jim Lyttle (1)	OF
1967	Ron Blomberg (1)*	1B/OF
1968	Thurman Munson (1)	C
1969	Charlie Spikes (1)	OF
1970	Dave Cheadle (1)	LHP
1971	Terry Whitfield (1)	OF
1972	Scott McGregor (1)	LHP
1973	Doug Heinold (1)	P
1974	Dennis Sherrill (1)	SS
1975	Jim McDonald (1)	1B
1976	Pat Tabler (1)	OF
1977	Steve Taylor (1)	P
1978	Rex Hudler (1)	SS
1979	Todd Demeter (2)	IF
1980	Billy Cannon (3)	SS
1981	John Elway (2)	OF
1982	Tim Birtsas (2)	LHP
1983	Mitch Lyden (4)	C
1984	Jeff Pries (1)	RHP
1985	Rich Balabon (1)	RHP
1986	Rich Scheid (2)	LHP
1987	Bill DaCosta (3)	RHP
1988	Todd Malone (4)	LHP
1989	Andy Fox (2)	3B
1990	Carl Everett (1)	OF
1991	Brien Taylor (1)*	LHP
1992	Derek Jeter (1)	SS
1993	Matt Drews (1)	RHP
1994	Brian Buchanan (1)	OF
1995	Shea Morenz (1)	OF
1996	Eric Milton (1)	LHP

*Number-one pick in draft.

SPRING TRAINING SITES

1903–04	Atlanta, Georgia
1905	Montgomery, Alabama
1906	Birmingham, Alabama
1907–08	Atlanta, Georgia
1909	Macon, Georgia
1910–11	Athens, Georgia
1912	Atlanta, Georgia
1913	Hamilton, Bermuda
1914	Houston, Texas
1915	Savannah, Georgia
1916–18	Macon, Georgia
1919–20	Jacksonville, Florida
1921	Shreveport, Louisiana
1922–24	New Orleans, Louisiana
1925–42	St. Petersburg, Florida
1943*	Asbury Park, New Jersey
1944–45*	Atlantic City, New Jersey
1946–50	St. Petersburg, Florida
1951	Phoenix, Arizona
1952–61	St. Petersburg, Florida
1962–95	Fort Lauderdale, Florida
1996–97	Tampa, Florida

*Trained nearby because of World War II travel restrictions.

YANKEES AND METS

The Yankees and Mets have played 103 times, with the Yanks winning 59, losing 43, and tying one in spring training and mayor's competitions—all exhibition games before interleague play began in 1997.

Sixty men have played for both teams:

Player	with Yankees	with Mets
Jack Aker	1969–72	1974
Neil Allen	1985, 1987–88	1979–83
Sandy Alomar, Sr.	1974–76	1967
Tucker Ashford	1981	1983
Yogi Berra	1946–63	1965
Daryl Boston	1994	1990–92
Tim Burke	1992	1991–92
Ray Burris	1979	1979–80
John Candelaria	1988–89	1987
Duke Carmel	1965	1963
Rick Cerone	1980–84, 1987, 1990	1991
David Cone	1995–96	1987–92
Billy Cowan	1969	1965
Dock Ellis	1976–77	1979
Kevin Elster	1994–95	1986–92
Tony Fernandez	1995	1993
Tim Foli	1984	1970–71, 1978–79
Bob Friend	1966	1966
Rob Gardner	1970–72	1965–66
Paul Gibson	1993–94	1992–93
Dwight Gooden	1996	1984–94
Jesse Gonder	1960–61	1963–65
Lee Guetterman	1988–92	1992
Greg Harris	1994	1981
Keith Hughes	1987	1990
Stan Jefferson	1989	1986
Dave Kingman	1977	1975–77, 1981–83
Tim Leary	1990–92	1981, 1983–84
Phil Linz	1962–65	1967–68
Phil Lombardi	1986–87	1989
Elliott Maddox	1974–76	1978–80
Josias Manzanillo	1995	1993–95
Lee Mazzilli	1982	1976–81, 1986–89
Doc Medich	1972–75	1977
Dale Murray	1983–84	1978–79
Bob Ojeda	1994	1986–90
John Pacella	1982	1977, 1979–80
Lenny Randle	1979	1977–78
Willie Randolph	1976–88	1992
Jeff Reardon	1994	1979–81
Hal Reniff	1961–67	1967
Rafael Santana	1988–89	1984–87
Don Schulze	1989	1987
Bill Short	1960	1968
Charlie Smith	1967–68	1964–65
Roy Staiger	1979	1975–77
Darryl Strawberry	1995–96	1983–90
Tom Sturdivant	1995–59	1964
Bill Sudakis	1974	1972
Ron Swoboda	1971–73	1965–70
Frank Tanana	1993	1993
Walt Terrell	1989	1982–84
Ralph Terry	1956–57, 1959–64	1966–67
Marv Throneberry	1955–59	1962–63
Dick Tidrow	1974–79	1984
Mike Torrez	1977	1983–84
Claudell Washington	1986–88, 1990	1980
Wally Whitehurst	1996	1989
Gene Woodling	1949–54	1962

Nine played for both teams during the same season: Burke (1992), Burris (1979), Friend (1966), Gibson (1993), Guetterman (1992), Kingman (1977), Manzanillo (1995), Reniff (1967), and Tanana (1993).

Strawberry is the only one to play for both current New York teams and two relocated New York teams, the Dodgers and Giants.

Four have managed the Yankees and Mets (Yankees seasons listed first; Mets seasons second): Casey Stengel (1949–60/1962–65), Yogi Berra (1964, 1984–85/1972–75), Dallas Green (1989/1993–96), and Joe Torre (1996/1977–81). Only Berra has managed both teams in the World Series—the 1964 Yankees and 1973 Mets, both teams losing the Series in seven games.

Four have coached the Yankees and Mets: Berra (1963, 1976–83/1965–71), Frank Howard (1989, 1991–92/1982–83, 1984, 1994–96), Bill Monbouquette (1985/1982–83), and Mel Stottlemyre (1996/1984–93).

Two longtime Yankees later served as Met general manager. George Weiss, 1948–60 Yankee GM, became the Mets' first GM/president, 1962–66. And Johnny Murphy, the Yankees' ace relief pitcher of the '30s and '40s, was the Mets' 1968–69 GM before dying in January 1970, soon after the Miracle Mets won the 1969 World Series.

SELECTED YANKEE DATES

March 12, 1903	Approved as members of the American League after Orioles franchise is purchased for $18,000 and moved from Baltimore to New York, where it is renamed the Highlanders.
April 22, 1903	First game: Lose 3–1, at Washington.
April 30, 1903	First home game: Defeat Washington, 6–2, at Hilltop Park, 168th Street at Broadway.
April 1913	Team changes its name from Highlanders to Yankees and moves into the Polo Grounds as tenant of the National League's New York Giants.
April 22, 1915	Pinstripes first appear on Yankee uniforms.
June 17, 1917	First Sunday game at home: Lose, 2–1, to St. Louis Browns.
May 11, 1919	First legalized Sunday game at home—a scoreless 12-inning tie with Washington.
January 3, 1920	Babe Ruth, not yet 25, purchased from Boston Red Sox for a reported $139,000, by far the most ever paid for an athlete—plus a $350,000 mortgage on Boston's Fenway Park.
September 1921	Clinch first pennant.
October 5, 1921	Play in World Series for the first time. Shut out New York Giants, 3–0, behind Carl Mays' five-hitter, before 30,202 at the Polo Grounds.
April 18, 1923	Open Yankee Stadium. Defeat Boston Red Sox, 4–1, as Babe Ruth fittingly christens "The House That Ruth Built" with its first home run. (The Stadium's left-field stands would be enlarged in 1928, its right-field stands in 1937.)
October 15, 1923	Win first world championship, eliminating New York Giants, 4 games to 2.
June 1, 1925	Lou Gehrig pinch hits during 5–3 loss to Washington at Yankee Stadium, launching his record for 2,130 consecutive games played, a mark that would stand for 56 years until broken by Baltimore's Cal Ripkin, Jr., in 1995.
September 30, 1927	Babe Ruth's record 60th home run climaxes season-long barrage by Yankees' "Murderer's Row" lineup.
April 16, 1929	Yankees appear with numbers on their uniforms, the first major league team to do so on a permanent basis.
September 29, 1934	Babe Ruth strikes his 659th and final Yankee home run (708th overall) in 9–6 victory at Washington—the day before he goes 0-for-3 in his last Yankee game there. The following February 26, the Yankees release the 40-year-old icon to allow him to join the Boston Braves as player, assistant manager, and vice president.
November 21, 1934	Joe DiMaggio, just before his 20th birthday, purchased from San Francisco Seals of Pacific Coast League for a reported $25,000 and five journeyman players—for 1936 delivery to Yankees.
May 30, 1938	Record crowd of 81,841 jams Yankee Stadium to overflowing (6,000 are turned away and another 511, unable to find standing room, get refunds) for a holiday doubleheader with the Red Sox. The throng is treated to a Yankee sweep—and a brawl featuring Boston shortstop-manager Joe Cronin, a future American League president.

May 2, 1939	Lou Gehrig's playing streak of 2,130 consecutive games ends, the dying "iron man" never to play again.
June 26, 1939	Yankees play in night game for first time, a 3–2 loss to Athletics in Philadelphia.
July 4, 1939	First Yankee number retired: number 4 at Lou Gehrig Day, when the slugging first baseman delivers his stirring "luckiest man" speech.
June 2, 1941	Lou Gehrig dies at age 37.
July 17, 1941	Joe DiMaggio's 56-game hitting streak ends in Cleveland.
May 28, 1946	First night game at Yankee Stadium: Lose to Washington, 2–1.
April 27, 1947	Babe Ruth Day at Yankee Stadium.
June 13, 1948	Dying Babe Ruth's uniform number 3 is retired in Yankee Stadium farewell. He dies August 16, his body lying in state at the Stadium.
October 12, 1948	Casey Stengel named manager.
April 17, 1951	Mickey Mantle hits a run-scoring single in four at bats in his debut, a 5–0 victory over the Red Sox at Yankee Stadium on opening day. The 19-year-old right fielder makes his first putout on a Ted Williams sky-out.
December 12, 1951	Joe DiMaggio retires.
April 17, 1953	Mickey Mantle wallops 565-foot home run at Washington.
October 5, 1953	Yankees eliminate Brooklyn Dodgers, 4 games to 2, to win record fifth consecutive world championship.
October 8, 1956	Don Larsen pitches the only perfect game in World Series history.
April 1959	Baseball's first message scoreboard installed at Yankee Stadium.
October 1, 1961	Roger Maris's 61st homer of the season (this one off Boston's Tracy Stallard) eclipses Babe Ruth's single-season record.
June 24, 1962	Longest game in Yankee history. Jack Reed's 2-run homer, the only home run of his career, decides the 22-inning, 7-hour marathon at Detroit. Jim Bouton is the winning pitcher, Phil Regan the loser in the 9–7 Yankee victory.
May 22, 1963	Mickey Mantle nearly slams a fair ball out of Yankee Stadium when his game-winning homer against A's strikes facade atop right-field stands, 108 feet, 1 inch above playing field. The ball was still on rise,

	and it was estimated the ball would have traveled at least 620 feet had it cleared the facade and been the only fair ball ever hit out of the Stadium. "It was the hardest ball I ever hit," Mantle would recall.
June 8, 1969	No. 7 is retired during Mickey Mantle Day at Yankee Stadium.
July 3, 1973	A limited partnership headed by George Steinbrenner purchases Yankees for CBS.
April 6, 1974	The club begins its first of two seasons at Shea Stadium while Yankee Stadium is reconstructed.
December 31, 1974	Catfish Hunter signs a record five-year contract.
April 15, 1976	Rebuilt Yankee Stadium opens.
November 18, 1976	Don Gullett becomes first free agent signed by Yankees in baseball's first reentry draft.
November 29, 1976	Reggie Jackson joins the Yankees after signing a five-year contract as a free agent.
October 18, 1977	Reggie Jackson hits three home runs on as many pitches during game six of World Series against the Los Angeles Dodgers.
October 2, 1978	Defeat Red Sox, 5–4, at Boston in only the second playoff game in American League history—climaxing a Yankee comeback from 14 games out.
August 2, 1979	Thurman Munson dies at age 32 in the crash of a jet plane he was piloting in Ohio during an open date.
September 1980	Yankees punctuate season as AL East champions with a league-record attendance of 2,627,417.
December 15, 1980	Dave Winfield becomes a Yankee after signing a record long-term contract as a free agent.
July 24, 1983	Infamous "Pine Tar" game. George Brett's home run is disallowed—temporarily. League president Lee McPhail overrules umpire and restores the homer, and the game is concluded on August 18, Kansas City winning, 5–4.
July 18, 1987	Don Mattingly homers in eighth consecutive game, tying Dale Long's major-league record.
September 29, 1987	Don Mattingly smashes his sixth grand slam of the season, a major league record.
June 23, 1988	Billy Martin is replaced as Yankee manager for the fifth and last time.
July 1, 1990	Andy Hawkins pitches a no-hitter at Chicago—and loses, 4–0.

At spring training in 1935, Babe Ruth faced his old Yankee teammates, including Lou Gehrig, in an unfamiliar uniform. He was serving as player, assistant manager, and vice president of the National League Boston Braves. Babe would last only 28 games and hit just six home runs that season before quitting the game forever.

Reading List

Allen, Maury. *Where Have You Gone, Joe DiMaggio?* New York: E. P. Dutton, 1971.

Anderson, Dave, and Milton Lancelot. *Upset.* Garden City, NY: Doubleday, 1967.

Anderson, Dave, Murray Chass, Robert Creamer, and Harold Rosenthal. *The Yankees.* New York: Random House, 1981.

Angell, Roger. *Five Seasons.* New York: Simon & Schuster, 1977.

Angell, Roger. *The Summer Game.* New York: Viking, 1971.

Barber, Red. *The Broadcasters.* New York: Dial, 1970.

Barrow, Edward Grant (with James M. Kahn). *My Fifty Years in Baseball.* New York: Coward-McCann, 1951.

Berkow, Ira. *Beyond the Dream.* New York: Atheneum, 1975.

Berra, Yogi (with Tom Horton). *Yogi: It Ain't Over* . . . New York: Harper Paperbacks, 1997.

Bouton, Jim. *Ball Four.* New York: World, 1970.

Bouton, Jim (with Neil Offen). *I Managed Good, But Boy Did They Play Bad.* Chicago: Playboy Press, 1973.

Broeg, Bob. *Super Stars of Baseball.* St. Louis: The Sporting News, 1971.

Brown, Gene and Arleen Keylin. *Sports as Reported by the New York Times.* New York: Arno Press, 1976.

Buchanan, Lamont. *The World Series and Highlights of Baseball.* New York: E. P. Dutton, 1951.

Carmichael, John P. *My Greatest Day in Baseball.* New York: Grosset and Dunlap, 1963.

Creamer, Robert W. *Babe.* New York: Simon & Schuster, 1974.

Creamer, Robert W. *Stengel: His Life and Times.* New York: Simon & Schuster, 1984.

Devaney, John, and Burt Goldblatt. *The World Series, a Complete Pictorial History.* Chicago: Rand McNally, 1972.

Dickey, Glenn. *The History of American League Baseball.* New York: Stein and Day, 1980.

Dickson, Paul. *Baseball's Greatest Quotations.* New York: HarperCollins, 1991.

DiMaggio, Joe. *Lucky to Be a Yankee.* New York: Rudolph Field, 1946.

Durant, John. *The Yankees.* New York: Hastings House, 1949.

Durso, Joseph. *Casey.* Englewood Cliffs, NJ: Prentice-Hall, 1967.

Durso, Joseph. *Yankee Stadium.* Boston: Houghton Mifflin, 1972.

Einstein, Charles (ed.). *The Fireside Book of Baseball.* New York: Simon & Schuster, 1956.

Einstein, Charles (ed.). *The Second Fireside Book of Baseball.* New York: Simon & Schuster, 1958.

Einstein, Charles (ed.). *The Third Fireside Book of Baseball.* New York: Simon & Schuster, 1968.

Fischler, Stan, and Richard Friedman. *The Comeback Yankees.* New York: Grosset and Dunlap, 1979.

Ford, Whitey, Mickey Mantle, and Joseph Durso. *Whitey and Mickey.* New York: Viking, 1977.

Forker, Dom. *The Men of Autumn.* Dallas: Taylor, 1989.

Gallagher, Mark. *Day by Day in New York Yankees History.* New York: Leisure Press, 1983.

Gallagher, Mark. *The Yankee Encyclopedia.* New York: Leisure Press, 1982; Champaign, IL.: Sagamore, 1996.

Goldstein, Richard. Spartan Seasons. New York: Macmillan, 1980.

Golenbock, Peter. *Dynasty.* Englewood Cliffs, NJ: Prentice-Hall, 1975.

Golenbock, Peter. *Wild, High and Tight: The Life and Death of Billy Martin.* New York: St. Martin's, 1994.

Graham Frank. *Great Pennant Races of the Major Leagues.* New York: Random House, 1967.

Graham, Frank. *Lou Gehrig: A Quiet Hero.* New York: G. P. Putnam's Sons, 1942.

Graham, Frank. *The New York Yankees.* New York: G. P. Putnam's Sons, 1943.

Greenspan, Bud. *Play It Again, Bud!* New York: Peter H. Wyden, Inc., 1973.

Heyn, Ernest V. *Twelve Sport Immortals.* New York: Bartholomew House, 1949.

Holmes, A. Lawrance. *More Than a Game.* New York: Macmillan, 1967.

Honig, Donald. *The American League: An Illustrated History.* New York: Crown, 1983, 1987.

Honig, Donald. *Baseball: An Illustrated History of America's Game.* New York: Crown, 1981, 1987, 1990.

Honig, Donald. *Baseball Between the Lines*. New York: Coward, McCann and Geoghegan, 1976.

Honig, Donald. *Baseball When the Grass Was Real*. New York: Coward, McCann and Geoghegan, 1975.

Honig, Donald. *The Man in the Dugout*. Chicago: Follett, 1977.

Honig, Donald. *The New York Yankees*. New York: Crown, 1981, 1987.

Honig, Donald. *The October Heroes*. New York: Simon & Schuster, 1979.

Honig, Donald. *The World Series: An Illustrated History*. New York: Crown, 1986.

Houk, Ralph (with Charles Dexter). *Ballplayers Are Human, Too*. New York: G. P. Putnam's Sons, 1962.

Houk, Ralph, and Robert W. Creamer. *Seasons of Glory*. New York: G. P. Putnam's Sons, 1988.

Izenberg, Jerry. *At Large*. New York: Simon & Flynn, 1968.

Izenberg, Jerry. *The Rivals*. New York: Holt, Rinehart and Winston, 1968.

Jackson, Reggie (with Mike Lupica). *Reggie*. New York: Villard, 1984.

Jacobson, Steve. *The Best Team Money Could Buy*. New York: Atheneum, 1978.

Jennison, Christopher. *Wait 'Til Next Year*. New York: W. W. Norton, 1974.

Johnson, Dick, and Glenn Stout. *DiMaggio: An Illustrated Life*. New York: Walker, 1995.

Kahn, Roger. *The Boys of Summer*. New York: Harper & Row, 1971.

Koufax, Sandy (with Ed Linn). *Koufax*. New York: Viking, 1966.

Lieb, Frederick G. *The Boston Red Sox*. New York: G. P. Putnam's Sons, 1947.

Lieb, Frederick G. *The Story of the World Series*. New York: G. P. Putnam's Sons, 1965.

Lyle, Sparky, and Peter Golenbock. *The Bronx Zoo*. New York: Crown, 1979.

Madden, Bill, and Moss Klein. *Damned Yankees*. New York: Warner Books, 1990.

Mantle, Mickey (with Mickey Herskowitz). *All My Octobers*. New York: HarperCollins, 1994.

Mantle, Mickey. *The Education of a Baseball Player*. New York: Simon & Schuster, 1967.

Mantle, Mickey (with Herb Gluck). *The Mick*. Garden City, NY: Doubleday, 1985.

Mantle, Mickey, and Phil Pepe. *My Favorite Summer: 1956*. New York: Doubleday, 1991.

Marsh, Irving T., and Edward Ehre. *Best Sports Stories*, 1949 edition. New York: E. P. Dutton, 1950.

Marsh, Irving T., and Edward Ehre. *Best Sports Stories*, 1957 edition. New York: E. P. Dutton, 1958.

Marsh, Irving T., and Edward Ehre. *Best Sports Stories*, 1958 edition. New York: E. P. Dutton, 1959.

Marsh, Irving T., and Edward Ehre. *Best Sports Stories*, 1962 edition. New York: E. P. Dutton, 1963.

Marsh, Irving T., and Edward Ehre. *Best Sports Stories*, 1978 edition. New York: E. P. Dutton, 1979.

Martin, Billy, and Peter Golenbock. *Number 1*. New York: Delacorte Press, 1980.

Meany, Tom. *The Yankee Story*. New York: E. P. Dutton, 1962.

Metz, Robert. *CBS: Reflections in a Bloodshot Eye*. Chicago: Playboy Press, 1975.

Miers, Earl Schenk. *Baseball*. New York: Grosset and Dunlap, 1970.

Moreland, George L. *Balldom*. New York: Balldom Publishing, 1914.

Munson, Thurman (with Martin Appel). *Thurman Munson*. New York: Coward, McCann and Geoghegan, 1979.

Neft, David S., and Richard M. Cohen. *The World Series* (4th edition). New York: St. Martin's, 1990.

Nettles, Graig, and Peter Golenbock. *Balls*. New York: G. P. Putnam's Sons, 1984.

Osborne, Charles (ed.). *Yesterday in Sport*. New York: Time-Life Books, 1968.

Pepe, Phil. *The Wit and Wisdom of Yogi Berra*. New York: Hawthorn Books, 1974.

Piniella, Lou, and Maury Allen. *Sweet Lou*. New York: G. P. Putnam's Sons, 1986.

Reichler, Joe (ed.). *The Game and the Glory*. Englewood Cliffs, NJ: Prentice-Hall, 1976.

Reichler, Joseph L. (ed.). *The World Series*. New York: Simon & Schuster, 1978.

Ritter, Lawrence S. *The Glory of Their Times*. New York: Macmillan, 1966.

Rizzuto, Phil (with Tom Horton). *The October Twelve*. New York: Forge, 1994.

Robinson, Ray. *The Iron Horse*. New York: W. W. Norton, 1990.

Rosenbaum, Art, and Bob Stevens. *The Giants of San Francisco*. New York: Coward, McCann and Geoghegan, 1963.

Rosenthal, Harold. *The Yankees*. New York: Random House, 1981.

Sahadi, Lou. *Year of the Yankees*. Chicago: Contemporary Books, 1979.

Salant, Nathan. *This Date in New York Yankees History*. Briar Cliff Manor, NY: Stein and Day, 1979, 1983.

Schaap, Dick. *Sport*. New York: Arbor House, 1975.

Silverman, Al. *Joe DiMaggio: The Golden Year 1941*. Englewood Cliffs, NJ: Prentice-Hall, 1969.

Smith, Ken. *Baseball's Hall of Fame*. New York: Grosset and Dunlap, 1974.

Smith, Robert. *The Illustrated History of Baseball*. New York: Grosset and Dunlap, 1973.

Stengel, Casey (with Harry T. Paxton). *Casey at the Bat*. New York: Random House, 1962.

Sullivan, George. *The Picture History of the Boston Red Sox*. New York: Bobbs-Merrill, 1979.

Thorn, John, and Pete Palmer (eds.), with Michael Gershman. *Total Baseball* (4th edition). New York: Viking, 1995.

Tuite, James (ed.). *Sports of the Times: The Arthur Daley Years*. New York: Quadrangle, 1975.

Winfield, Dave (with Tom Parker). *Winfield*. New York: W. W. Norton, 1988.

Wolff, Rick (editorial director). *The Baseball Encyclopdia* (9th edition). New York: Macmillan, 1993.

Vecsey, George (ed.). *The Way It Was*. New York: McGraw-Hill, 1974.

Veeck, Bill (with Ed Linn). *Veeck—as in Wreck*. New York: G. P. Putnam's Sons, 1962.

The Sporting News' annual *Baseball Guide* and *Official Baseball Register* are recommended reading each year, as is the *Yankees Information Guide*.